Solutions Manual

to accompany

Managerial Accounting
Creating Value in a Dynamic Business Environment

Fifth Edition

Ronald W. Hilton
Cornell University

McGraw-Hill
Irwin

Boston   Burr Ridge, IL   Dubuque, IA   Madison, WI   New York   San Francisco   St. Louis
Bangkok   Bogotá   Caracas   Kuala Lumpur   Lisbon   London   Madrid   Mexico City
Milan   Montreal   New Delhi   Santiago   Seoul   Singapore   Sydney   Taipei   Toronto

McGraw-Hill Higher Education

*A Division of The **McGraw-Hill** Companies*

Solutions Manual to accompany
MANAGERIAL ACCOUNTING: CREATING VALUE IN A DYNAMIC BUSINESS ENVIRONMENT
Ronald W. Hilton

Published by McGraw-Hill/Irwin, an imprint of the McGraw-Hill Companies, Inc., 1221 Avenue of
the Americas, New York, NY 10020. Copyright © 2002, 1999, 1997, 1994, 1991 by the McGraw-Hill
Companies, Inc. All rights reserved.

Material from the Uniform CPA Examination, Questions and Unofficial Answers, Copyright 1978, 1979, 1980,
1981, 1982, 1983, 1984, 1987, 1988, 1989, 1990, 1991 by the American Institute of Certified Public
Accountants, Inc. is adapted with permission.

Material from the Certificate in Management Accounting Examinations, Copyright 1977, 1978, 1979, 1980,
1981, 1982, 1983, 1984, 1986, 1987, 1989, 1990, 1991, 1992, 1993, 1994, 1995, 1996, 1997 by the Institute of
Management Accountants is adapted with permission.

3 4 5 6 7 8 9 0 BKM/BKM 0 9 8 7 6 5 4 3

ISBN 0-07-239469-2

www.mhhe.com

Contents

Preface

The best way for most students to learn managerial accounting is to read the text and then solve a representative sample of the review questions, exercises, problems and cases at the end of each chapter. These end-of-chapter materials span a wide range of topics, types of organizations, and levels of difficulty. The topic of each exercise, problem, and case is indicated in the text. The estimated amount of time required is shown in the solutions manual. In addition to these assignment items, the text also includes Current Issues in Managerial Accounting at the end of each chapter's assignment material. The discussion of these current articles can range widely, depending on the perspective of the reader. The Solutions Manual includes a cursory summary of each current issue and alludes to the main points that may be raised in a discussion of the issue. Also available to instructors is the *Instructor's Resource Manual*, which contains a variety of helpful materials for designing and teaching a managerial accounting course. Included in the *Instructor's Resource Manual* is a table indicating the corresponding learning objectives to each exercise, problem, and case. Also included in the manual are sample assignments, demonstration problems, tips for new teachers, a chapter conversion chart, a listing of the transparency masters, learning objectives, corresponding video segments, mini-quizzes, chapter overviews, and a discussion of key lecture concepts for each chapter.

Ronald W. Hilton

McGraw-Hill/Irwin

We hope this Solutions Manual to accompany MANAGERIAL ACCOUNTING 5/e and the text are error free. If, however, you discover errors we would like to know of them as soon as possible to correct them in reprints and to notify others by way of errata listed under Updates on our web site. Please help us by using this postage-paid tear-out form to report any that you find. Thank you.

Additional forms can be found at the back of this manual.

Attention: G. Korosa

Name_____ School_____

Please fold and seal so that our address is visible, and mail.

BUSINESS REPLY MAIL
FIRST-CLASS MAIL   PERMIT NO.204   OAKBROOK, IL

POSTAGE WILL BE PAID BY ADDRESSEE

ATTENTION: G. Korosa

THE McGRAW-HILL COMPANIES
1333 BURR RIDGE PKY.
BURR RIDGE, IL 60521-0085

NO POSTAGE
NECESSARY
IF MAILED
IN THE
UNITED STATES

(fold)

(fold)

CHAPTER 1
The Changing Role of Managerial Accounting in a Dynamic Business Environment

ANSWERS TO REVIEW QUESTIONS

1-1   The explosion in e-commerce will affect managerial accounting in significant ways. One effect will be a drastic reduction in paper work. Millions of transactions between businesses will be conducted electronically with no hard-copy documentation. Along with this method of communicating for business transactions comes the very significant issue of information security. Businesses need to find ways to protect confidential information in their own computers, while at the same time sharing the information necessary to complete transactions. Another effect of e-commerce is the dramatically increased speed with which business transactions can be conducted. In addition to these business-to-business transactional issues, there will be dramatic changes in the way managerial accounting procedures are carried out, one example being e-budgeting, which is the enterprise-wide and electronic completion of a company's budgeting process.

1-2   Plausible goals for the organizations listed are as follows:

(a) Amazon.com: (1) To achieve and maintain profitability, and (2) to grow on-line sales of books, music, and other goods.

(b) American Red Cross: (1) To raise funds from the general public sufficient to have resources available to meet any disaster that may occur, and (2) to provide assistance to people who are victims of a disaster anywhere in the country on short notice.

(c) General Motors: (1) To earn income sufficient to provide a good return on the investment of the company's stockholders, and (2) to provide the highest-quality product possible.

(d) J. C. Penney: (1) To penetrate the retail market in virtually every location in the United States, and (2) to grow over time in terms of number of retail locations, total assets, and earnings.

(e) City of Pittsburgh: (1) To maintain an urban environment as free of pollution as possible, and (2) to provide public safety, police, and fire protection to the city's citizens.

(f) Hertz: (1) To be a recognizable household name associated with rental car services, and (2) to provide reliable and economical transportation services to the company's customers.

1-3 The four basic management activities are listed and defined as follows:

(a) Decision making: Choosing among the available alternatives.

(b) Planning: Developing a detailed financial and operational description of anticipated operations.

(c) Directing operations: Running the organization on a day-to-day basis.

(d) Controlling: Ensuring that the organization operates in the intended manner and achieves its goals.

1-4 Examples of the four primary management activities in the context of a national fast-food chain, such as McDonald's or Pizza Hut, are as follows:

(a) Decision making: Choosing among several possible locations for a new fast-food outlet.

(b) Planning: Developing a cost budget for the food and paper products to be used during the next quarter in a particular fast-food restaurant.

(c) Directing operations: Developing detailed schedules for personnel for the next month to provide counter service in a particular fast-food restaurant.

(d) Controlling: Comparing the actual cost of paper products used during a particular month in a restaurant with the anticipated cost of paper products for that same time period.

1-5 Examples of the objectives of managerial-accounting activity in an airline company are described below:

(a) Providing information for decision making and planning and proactively participating as part of the management team in the decision making and planning processes: Managerial accountants provide estimates of the cost of adding a flight on the route from New York to Miami and actively participate in making the decision about adding the flight.

(b) Assisting managers in directing and controlling operations: Managerial accountants provide information about the actual costs of flying the routes in the airline's northeastern geographical sector during a particular month.

(c) Motivating managers and other employees toward the organization's goals: A budget is provided for the cost of handling baggage at O'Hare Airport in Chicago. The budget is given to the airline's baggage handling manager, who is expected to strive to achieve the budget.

(d) Measuring the performance of activities, subunits, managers, and other employees within the organization: Quarterly income statements are prepared for each of the airline's major geographical sectors, and these income reports are used to evaluate the earnings performance of each sector during the relevant time period.

(e) Assessing the organization's competitive position and working with other managers to ensure the organization's long-run competitiveness in its industry: Information about industry-wide performance standards is obtained and compared with the airline's own performance. For example, how does the airline stack up against its competitors in ticket prices, on-time departures, mishandled baggage, customer complaints, and safety?

1-6   Four important differences between managerial accounting and financial accounting are listed below:

(a) Managerial-accounting information is provided to managers within the organization, whereas financial-accounting information is provided to interested parties outside the organization.

(b) Managerial-accounting reports are not required and are unregulated, whereas financial-accounting reports are required and must conform to generally accepted accounting principles.

(c) The primary source of data for managerial-accounting information is the organization's basic accounting system, plus various other sources. These sources include such data as rates of defective products manufactured, physical quantities of material and labor used in production, occupancy rates in hotels and hospitals, and average takeoff delays in airlines. The primary source of data for financial-accounting information is almost exclusively the organization's basic accounting system, which accumulates financial information.

(d) Managerial-accounting reports often focus on subunits within the organization, such as departments, divisions, geographical regions, or product lines. These reports are based on a combination of historical data, estimates, and projections of future events. Financial-accounting reports focus on the enterprise in its entirety. These reports are based almost exclusively on historical transaction data.

1-7   The cost-accounting system is one part of an organization's overall accounting system, the purpose of which is to accumulate cost information. Cost information accumulated by the cost-accounting system is used for both managerial-accounting and financial-accounting purposes. Managerial accounting is the broad task of preparing information for making decisions about planning, directing, and controlling an organization's operations.

1-8   Managers in line positions are directly involved in the provision of services or the production of goods in an organization. Managers in staff positions support the organization's overall objectives, but they are indirectly involved in operations. Examples of line positions in a university are the president, who is the university's chief executive officer, and the provost, who is the university's chief academic officer. Examples of staff positions in a university are the university counsel, who is the university's chief lawyer, and the director of maintenance, who is charged with maintaining the university's facilities.

1-9   An organization's controller (or comptroller) is the chief managerial and financial accountant. The controller usually is responsible for supervising the personnel in the accounting department and for preparing the information and reports used in both managerial and financial accounting. The treasurer typically is responsible for raising capital and safeguarding the organization's assets. Among the treasurer's responsibilities is the management of an organization's investments, credit policy, and insurance coverage.

1-10   A college or university could use the balanced scorecard as a management tool just like any other business. There is one important difference, however, between a profit-seeking enterprise and a nonprofit organization like a university. A profit-seeking enterprise generally has long-term profitability as its foremost goal, and the other points on the balanced scorecard are oriented toward helping the entries achieve that goal of profitability. Universities, on the other hand, usually have multiple goals, which are sometimes in competition with each other. For example, a land-grant university may have teaching, research and public service as its three primary goals. Nevertheless, it is possible for a college or university to develop performance measures for each of the areas in the balanced scorecard. Some examples follow:

- *Financial:* Amount of the unrestricted endowment supporting the university's activities, and the extent to which the university operates with a balanced budget.

- *Internal operations:* Tenure rates for faculty, and the extent to which the university's facilities are up to date and well maintained.

- *Customer:* Class evaluations by students, and job placement rates for students.

- *Innovation and learning:* Dollars of research grants obtained, and publication of journal articles and books by faculty.

1-11 This quote from a managerial accountant at Caterpillar suggests that managerial accountants are *physically located* throughout an organization where the day-to-day work is being done, rather than being sequestered off by themselves as was the tendency some years ago. Managerial accountants are increasingly *deployed* as key members of management teams.

1-12 Managerial-accounting information often brings to the attention of managers important issues that need their managerial experience and skills. In many cases, managerial-accounting information will not answer the question or solve the problem, but rather make management aware that the issue or problem exists. In this sense, managerial accounting sometimes is said to serve an attention-directing role.

1-13 Both manufacturing and service industry firms are engaged in production. The primary difference between these types of companies is that manufacturing firms produce inventoriable goods, whereas the services produced by service industry firms are not inventoriable. Services, such as air transportation or hotel service, are consumed as they are produced.

1-14 (a) In a just-in-time (or JIT) production environment, raw materials and components are purchased or produced just in time to be used at each stage in the production process.

(b) A computer-integrated manufacturing (CIM) system is the most advanced form of automated manufacturing system, with computers controlling the entire production process.

(c) A cost management system is a management planning and control system with the following objectives: to measure the cost of the resources consumed in performing the organization's significant activities; to identify and eliminate non-value-added costs; to determine the efficiency and effectiveness of all major activities; and to identify and evaluate new activities that can improve the future performance of the organization.

(d) Empowerment is the concept of encouraging and authorizing workers to take their own initiative to improve operations, reduce costs, and improve product quality and customer service.

(e) Total quality management (or TQM) is the broad set of management and control processes designed to focus the entire organization and all of its employees on providing products or services that do the best possible job of satisfying the customer.

1-15 E-commerce is defined as buying and selling over digital media. E-business is a broader concept, which not only encompasses e-commerce, but also includes the electronic business processes that form the engine of modern business.

1-16 CMA stands for Certified Management Accountant. This title is the professional certification for managerial accountants administered by the Institute of Management Accountants. The requirements for becoming a CMA include fulfilling specified educational requirements and successfully passing the CMA examination.

1-17 (a) Competence: Ongoing development of knowledge and skills, performance of duties in accordance with relevant laws, adherence to regulations and technical standards, and preparation of complete and clear reports for management.

(b) Confidentiality: Refrainment from disclosing, using, or appearing to use confidential information acquired in the course of the managerial accountant's work.

(c) Integrity: Avoidance of conflicts of interest in activities that would prejudice the managerial accountant's ability to carry out his or her duties ethically, and refrainment from other activities that would discredit the profession.

(d) Objectivity: Communication of information fairly, objectively, and fully.

1-18 Non-value-added costs are the costs of activities that can be eliminated with no deterioration of product quality, performance, or perceived value.

1-19 Managers rely on many information systems in addition to managerial-accounting information. Examples of other information systems include economic analysis and forecasting, marketing research, legal research and analysis, and technical information provided by engineers and production specialists.

1-20 Managerial accounting is just as important in nonprofit organizations as it is in profit-seeking enterprises. Managers in nonprofit organizations also need managerial-accounting information for decision making, planning, directing, and controlling operations.

1-21 Becoming the low-cost producer in an industry requires a clear understanding by management of the costs incurred in its production process. Reports and analysis of these costs are a primary function of managerial accounting.

1-22 A professional is a person engaged in a specified occupation that requires advanced training, skill, and a well-defined body of knowledge. According to this definition from Webster, a managerial accountant is a professional.

1-23 Some activities in the value chain of a manufacturer of cotton shirts are as follows:

(a) Growing and harvesting cotton

(b) Transporting raw materials

(c) Designing shirts

(d) Weaving cotton material

(e) Manufacturing shirts

(f) Transporting shirts to retailers

(g) Advertising cotton shirts

Some activities in the value chain of an airline are as follows:

(a) Making reservations and ticketing

(b) Designing the route network

(c) Scheduling

(d) Purchasing aircraft

(e) Maintaining aircraft

(f) Running airport operations, including handling baggage

(g) Serving food and beverages in flight

(h) Flying passengers and cargo

1-24 Strategic cost management is the process of understanding and managing, to the organization's advantage, the cost relationships among the activities in an organization's value chain.

SOLUTIONS TO EXERCISES

EXERCISE 1-25 (20 MINUTES)

1. Estimates of any operating costs associated with the proposed luxury cars would be relevant. For example, estimates of the cost of gasoline, routine maintenance, and insurance on the new vehicles would be useful.

2. Data about the cost of maintaining the machine weekly or biweekly would be relevant. In addition, the production manager should consider information about the likely rates of defective products under each maintenance alternative.

3. Estimates of the cost of lost merchandise due to shoplifting and the cost of employing security personnel would be relevant to this decision.

4. Estimates of building costs for the library addition as well as estimates of benefits to the population from having the addition would be useful. Estimating the benefits may require value judgments about the benefits to the public from having additional library space and more books.

EXERCISE 1-26 (25 MINUTES)

1. Developing a bonus reward system for managerial personnel is an example of motivating managers and other employees toward the organization's goals. To be effective, the bonus system must provide incentives for managers to work toward achieving those goals.

2. Comparing actual and planned costs is consistent with two objectives of managerial accounting activity: (1) assisting managers in controlling operations, and (2) measuring the performance of activities, subunits, managers, and other employees within the organization.

3. Determining manufacturing costs is related to all of the objectives of managerial accounting. It is especially closely related to the objective of providing information for decision making and planning.

4. Measuring inventory costs is most closely associated with the first two objectives of managerial accounting activity: (1) providing information for decision making and planning, and (2) assisting managers in directing and controlling operational activities. Since inventory costs are used in external financial reports, they are also relevant to measuring the performance of managers and subunits within the organization.

EXERCISE 1-26 (CONTINUED)

5. Estimating costs is particularly relevant to the objective of providing information for decision making and planning.

6. Measuring operating costs is relevant to all of the objectives of managerial accounting activity.

7. Comparing operating statistics such as those mentioned for a hotel is particularly relevant to the following objective of managerial accounting: Assessing the organization's competitive position and working with other managers to ensure the organization's long-run competitiveness in its industry.

EXERCISE 1-27 (30 MINUTES)

Answers will vary widely for this exercise, depending on the company chosen by each student. Companies' financial goals often include profitability, earnings per share, growth in the stock price, sales growth, and so forth. Managerial accounting can make an important contribution to all of these goals.

SOLUTIONS TO PROBLEMS

PROBLEM 1-28 (25 MINUTES)

1. Managerial accounting can be of significant benefit when it comes to solving the company's problems. Managerial accounting is defined as the process of identifying, measuring, analyzing, interpreting, and communicating information in pursuit of an organization's goals. Several of the problems lie in this area and may be attributed to a lack of formal planning, controlling, directing, and decision-making expertise.

    For example, bulging inventories and the fact that growth "...has occurred in spite of what we've done" may indicate the absence of a formal planning system— one that involves developing a detailed financial and operational description of anticipated activities. Dangerously low cash balances and the need for short-term loans may be eliminated by the use of a cash budget, which depicts cash inflows and outflows over a period of time. The addition of ski equipment may or may not have been the proper decision. Did Nelson correctly identify all possible alternatives and then make the proper selection?

    The canoe-building activities and white-water rafting trips may be losing money. Are costs skyrocketing hopelessly out of control? It is difficult to tell because the income statement does not provide adequate information—it is a summary of past transactions for the entire business. A performance report that identifies the company's major areas of activity would be of assistance, especially if the report measured budgeted vs. actual costs and highlighted (directed attention toward) significant deviations for management attention. If such a report were prepared, managers could better direct operational activities and ensure that the company achieves its goals (i.e., the control function).

2. Yes, a cross-functional team would be useful in this situation. Several of the company's problems affect multiple functional areas within the firm. For example, bulging inventories, which impact profitability and cash balances, may be the result of poor ordering practices and/or ineffective marketing programs. Issues related to the operation of a seasonal business may be overcome with the selection of different "off-season" product lines and aggressive marketing campaigns. These problems, coupled with the fact that a number of the key executives manage in "silos" and lack the "big-picture" outlook for the firm, seem to indicate the desirability of teams that have different employee backgrounds and interests (such as marketing, operations, and finance) represented.

3. Nelson's business is operating in a sparsely populated state and suffers from the ability to draw from more heavily populated areas such as those in Florida, California, Texas, and New York. In addition, the firm is getting hammered by mail-

PROBLEM 1-28 (CONTINUED)

order businesses and businesses that operate via toll-free telephone numbers. These issues, combined with Nelson's Internet background, seem to make his firm a likely candidate for e-commerce.

Consumer-to-business channels (sometimes called c-to-b) allow consumers to order goods on line from businesses. In contrast, businesses order goods from other firms via business-to-business (b-to-b) channels. Consumer-to-business channels would be a natural in dealing with the firm's population and competitive problems. However, keeping in mind that there are some difficulties related to suppliers (e.g., quality, reliability, and prices), b-to-b channels may be of assistance as well.

PROBLEM 1-29 (25 MINUTES)

1. The balanced scorecard is a business model that helps to assess a firm's competitive position and ensures that the firm is progressing toward long-term survival. Although balanced scorecards differ from one firm to the next, most have a combination of financial measures, customer-satisfaction measures, internal operating measures, and measures of innovation and learning.

2. Functional areas for the airline include marketing, finance, operations (e.g., maintenance, reservations, customer service, and scheduling), human resources, purchasing, accounting, planning, and information systems/technology.

3. Financial measures:
   - Net income
   - Earnings per share
   - Passenger revenue per seat mile
   - Operating expenses per seat mile
   - Cost per meal served
   - Revenue growth

   Customer-satisfaction measures:
   - Load factors
   - Number of passenger complaints
   - Average wait time when calling reservations center
   - Number of bags lost
   - Market share
   - Response time for resolving customer problems

   Internal operating measures:
   - Percentage of on-time arrivals
   - Percentage of on-time departures
   - Average trip length (in miles)
   - Percentage of tickets sold through travel agents, reservation agents, and the Internet
   - Number of cities/new cities served
   - Number of aircraft in fleet
   - Average age of aircraft in fleet
   - Aircraft turnaround time between flights

PROBLEM 1-29 (CONTINUED)

Innovation/learning measures:

Enhancements to product line (new class of service)	Employee turnover
	Employee satisfaction scores
New unique features of frequent-flier club	Employee training programs

4. Yes. By focusing on only one factor, other important facets of the business are ignored, which could lead to long-run problems. For example, paying too much attention to load factors may result in a decrease in profitability (e.g., the sale of too many inexpensive seats). A significant focus on profitability could result in the airline providing marginal service to its customers (poor meals; long wait times when calling reservations centers; a large number of lost bags by a small, poorly-trained crew, and so forth).

PROBLEM 1-30 (45 MINUTES)

1. Allen's considerations are determined largely by her position as an accountant, with responsibilities to AccuSound Corporation, others in the company, and herself. Allen's job involves collecting, analyzing, and reporting operating information. Although not responsible for product quality, Allen should exercise initiative and good judgment in providing management with information having potentially adverse economic impact.

   Allen should determine whether the controller's request violates her professional or personal standards or the company's code of ethics, should the company have such a code. As Allen decides how to proceed, she should protect proprietary information and should not violate the chain of command by discussing this matter with the controller's superiors.

2. a. The controller has reporting responsibilities and should protect the overall company interests by encouraging further study of the problem by those in his or her department, by informing superiors in this matter, and by working with others in the company to find solutions.

   b. The quality control engineer has responsibilities for product quality and should protect overall company interests by continuing to study the quality of reworked rejects, by informing the plant manager and his staff in this matter, and by working with others in the company to find solutions.

PROBLEM 1-30 (CONTINUED)

c. The plant manager and his or her staff have responsibilities for product quality and cost and should protect overall company interests by exercising the stewardship expected of them. Plant management should be sure that products meet quality standards. Absentee owners need information from management, and the plant management staff have a responsibility to inform the board of directors elected by the owners of any problems that could affect the well-being of the firm.

3. Allen needs to protect the interests of the company, others in the company, and herself. Allen is vulnerable if she conceals the problem and it eventually surfaces. Allen must take some action to reduce her vulnerability. One possible action would be to obey the controller and prepare the advance material for the board without mentioning or highlighting the probable failure of reworks. Because this approach differs from the long-standing practice of highlighting information with potentially adverse economic impact, Allen should write a report to the controller detailing the probable failure of reworks, the analysis made by her and the quality control engineer, and the controller's instructions in this matter.

PROBLEM 1-31 (30 MINUTES)

1. Line activities are primary to the purpose of the organization. They are the activities that create and distribute the goods and services of the organization. Line reporting refers to the reporting relationship between different hierarchical management levels in line activities (e.g., the reporting relationship between the general supervisor and the plant manager).

    Staff activities are services provided by departments in the organization in support of its line activities. The role of the division controller in the division is an example of a staff activity. The reporting relationship between the division controller and the division manager is an example of a staff reporting relationship.

2. a. The division controller is responsible to both the corporate controller and the division manager. The corporate controller assigns the division controller to the division and has final responsibility for promotion and salary. Thus, the division controller is an employee of the controller's department and reports to the corporate controller. At the same time, the division controller serves as a staff resource to the division manager. The division controller is required to file an independent commentary on the division's financial results, which could well differ from the division manager's commentary.

The division manager evaluates the division controller's performance and makes salary and promotion recommendations to the corporate controller.

b. The motivation of the division controller would be affected by this dual reporting relationship. The division controller is being evaluated by two people whose responsibilities are not always congruent. What may be considered good performance by one person may be considered unsatisfactory by the other. Thus, the division controller will have difficulty knowing what factors influence his or her progress in the company. The circumstances described in the problem do not provide positive motivation for the division controller.

SOLUTION TO CASE

CASE 1-32 (40 minutes)

1. Andrea Nolan's ethical responsibilities require that she not tell her friend, Rob Borman, about Progressive's cash flow problems. Nolan, as a management accountant, must comply with the following standards for ethical conduct:

   Confidentiality. Nolan must refrain from disclosing confidential information acquired in the course of her work except when authorized, unless legally obligated to do so. In this situation, Nolan is neither authorized nor legally obligated to do so.

   Integrity. Under this standard for ethical conduct, Nolan has the responsibility to:

   - Refrain from engaging in any activity that would prejudice her ability to carry out her duties ethically.

   - Refrain from either actively or passively subverting the attainment of the organization's legitimate and ethical objectives.

2. Nolan has an ethical responsibility to inform Progressive that Borman has decided to postpone the paper order. As a management accountant, Nolan must comply with the following standards of ethical conduct:

   Confidentiality. Nolan should refrain from appearing to use confidential information acquired in the course of her work for unethical advantage, either personally or through third parties.

   Integrity. Under this standard for ethical conduct, Nolan has the responsibility to:

   - Refrain from either actively or passively subverting the attainment of the organization's legitimate and ethical objectives.

   - Communicate unfavorable, as well as favorable, information and professional judgments or opinions.

3. Nolan should resolve this matter by discussing the situation with her immediate superior. Nolan should tell her superior of her long-time friendship with Borman. However, she should make it clear that she has not and will not disclose confidential company information to Borman or any other outside party except when authorized or legally obligated to do so. If a satisfactory resolution to the problem is not achieved, Nolan should submit the matter to the next-higher managerial level. However, she should inform her immediate superior that she is going to take this step.

CURRENT ISSUES IN MANAGERIAL ACCOUNTING

ISSUE 1-33

"DISNEY'S MAGIC TRANSFORMATIONS? COMPANY EYES BIGGER SHARE OF RETAILING WITH REVAMP OF STORES, NEW PRODUCTS," *THE WALL STREET JOURNAL*, OCTOBER 4, 2000, BRUCE ORWALL.

1. All of the objectives of managerial accounting activity, which are listed below, would be relevant in Disney's major decision to expand its retail operation.

   (a) Providing information for decision making and planning and proactively participating as part of the management team in the decision making and planning processes: Managerial accountants would provide estimates of the costs and benefits of adding stores or product lines to Disney's retail operations.

   (c) Assisting managers in directing and controlling operations: Managerial accountants would provide information about the actual costs of operating new stores and market segments.

   (c) Motivating managers and other employees toward the organization's goals: A budget is provided for the cost of operating new stores and market segments, and managers are expected to strive to meet budgetary targets.

   (d) Measuring the performance of activities, subunits, managers, and other employees within the organization: Quarterly income statements would be prepared for each of the company's major geographical sectors, and these income reports are used to evaluate the earnings performance of each sector during the relevant time period.

   (e) Assessing the organization's competitive position and working with other managers to ensure the organization's long-run competitiveness in its industry: Information about industry-wide performance standards would be obtained and compared with Disney's own retail performance.

2. Research and development, design of products, services, or processes, production, marketing, distribution, and customer service are important elements of the value chain for Disney. The revamped stores and design changes will move beyond Disney character-based goods. Adult-oriented merchandise will focus more on parenting rather than general goods. The new store design will include a new multimedia sales pitch featuring computer terminals. Each store will slim it offerings to about 1,800, down from 3,400. Disney will cut the number of licensees it uses from 4,200 to 2,200. Disney also plans a retail pricing drop of about 30 percent.

ISSUE 1-34

"SONY ROLLS OUT PLAYSTATION ADS DESPITE SHORTAGE," *THE WALL STREET JOURNAL*, OCTOBER 6, 2000, JOSEPH PEREIRA.

1. The article primarily deals with Sony's marketing and customer service when bringing out its new PlayStation 2. Its dilemmas include the shortage of the product before Christmas, marketing to hard-core video gamers, and broadening the PS2's appeal to a wider audience.

2. Although the article does not mention e-business, it does stand to reason that Sony's web site will carry relevant information concerning the PS2. A web site could help with marketing and customer service issues the company is trying to address.

ISSUE 1-35

"PURSUE E-BUSINESS OR DIE," *STRATEGIC FINANCE*, MARCH 2000, ROBERT THAMES.

Leveraging knowledge, relationships, and information with a well-defined business model focused on core competencies allows a business to respond quickly within the e-business environment. Creating an enterprise resource planning system, eliminating waste from the value chain, knowing your customers, and receiving accurate profit information are cornerstones of this approach.

A real-time information system provides controls and status information that allow forward decision-making. Integrated technology architecture is necessary for an ERP system to be valuable, but realistically this takes years to achieve. Waiting for the newest hardware or software means never achieving a system because it is never implemented. However, the system has to be up to date enough to provide just-in-time information.

Removal of waste from the entire value chain is effectively achieved by implementing technology as well as through building strong alliances and partnerships. Lowering manufacturing costs and streamlining distribution are also key components.

The ERP, as well as online selling, places a business in the position to gather information about customers' spending habits and preferences. This information combined with clear and accurate information about the company's activities and costs, allow a company to quickly modify itself to take advantage of opportunities. A self-assessment of business processes carried out with the cooperation of employees can provide an in-depth aspect to this information. Continuous testing of this information against best business practices can identify which redundant business processes to eliminate.

Moving purchases of goods and services to electronic procurement and following these cornerstones will allow a business to serve customers and markets that track to the core competencies of the business.

ISSUE 1-36

"SAP ACTS TO HEAD OFF MORE SYSTEM PROBLEMS," *THE WALL STREET JOURNAL,* NOVEMBER 4, 1999, NEAL E. BOUDETTE.

1. SAP develops and sells ERP software which offers the benefits of implementing an enterprise resource planning system to handle an array of business functions in an organization, ranging from supply ordering to filling customer orders, to keeping payroll and personnel records, to product costing

2. Managerial accounting information could help the management team assess the costs and benefits of installing an ERP system. For example, what new costs would be incurred, and what current costs could be avoided.

ISSUE 1-37

"WHY THINGS GO BETTER AT COKE," *JOURNAL OF BUSINESS STRATEGY,* JANUARY/FEBRUARY 1999, RICK WISE.

The elements of coke's story are not unique. Customer selection, value capture, strategic control, scope and organizational systems are the five dimensions upon which coke focused when revitalizing and reinventing itself. These dimensions include becoming customer-centric, becoming expansive and dynamic in its view of the marketplace, and placing an emphasis on the strategic dimensions that drive shareholder value growth.

Coke determined which sets of customers held the greatest potential for long-term growth and focused on them. The company moved from capturing value through product sales and service fees to financing, adopting and creating ancillary products, providing business solutions, and licensing. It focused on activities that were customer-relevant in order to generate higher profits. Coke's management then reorganized it business systems to focus on these elements.

In the past twenty years, Coke has moved from syrup distribution to a highly-aligned and efficient manufacturer-bottler-distribution system. Coke has become the world's strongest brand, has become more cost-effective in advertising, and has created a large number of solid positions in international markets.

ISSUE 1-38

"COUNTING MORE, COUNTING LESS: TRANSFORMATION IN THE MANAGEMENT ACCOUNTING PROFESSION, " *THE WALL STREET JOURNAL*, SEPTEMBER 1999, KEITH A. RUSSELL, GARY H. SIEGEL, AND C.S. "BUD" KULESZA.

Management accountants will use several methods to broaden their role to that of strategic partners. Already many (45 percent in the larger companies) have physically located themselves in the operating departments they service. About 56 percent are working on cross-functional teams and are actively involved in the decision making process.

Management accountants are redefining themselves. Only 33 percent use the term accounting to describe their function. About two thirds use finance or some other descriptive term when defining their activities.

These activities and methods to move toward strategic partnership have improved the image of management accountants to the extent that 70 percent of those outside the finance function believe that management accountants bring more value to their company.

Activities are shifting from traditional accounting work to the more value-added activities of internal consulting, long-term strategic planning, computer systems and operations, managing the accounting/finance function, process improvement, and performing financial and economic analysis.

These changes in the role of the finance function are resulting in accountants becoming business partners and consultants in management decisions. As finance is more involved with other aspects of business, accountants are becoming involved in more planning and strategic decisions. Computerized technology, team decision-making and evaluating company efficiency are other areas affecting accountants and the business roles within which they are involved.

Changes expected over the next three years include less reporting of information and more planning and analysis; more computerized technology and software; more partnering and consulting in management decisions; more involvement with operations; and more analysis of profitability and performance evaluation.

ISSUE 1-39

"A MILE WIDE AND A MILE DEEP," *CFO*, FEBRUARY 1999, JOHN J. XENAKIS.

High-end software vendors have moved from the vanilla applications of the early 1990s to a business model more reminiscent of the 1980s. They are targeting vertical industries, market niches and bundling broad-based value-added applications such as analytics. Analytics, a category of software, enables managers to gain meaningful information from the billions of transactions stored in accounting software databases. These trends have resulted in a spree of buyouts and mergers in order to gain new software. Strategic positioning has resulted in nearly all software now being web-based and e-commerce based.

ISSUE 1-40

"INDUSTRY OUTLOOK: FOOD DISTRIBUTION," *BUSINESS WEEK,* JANUARY 8, 2001, JULIE FORSTER.

1. Through the managerial accounting process, executives at General Mills knew the company was wasting money on empty truck miles.

2. Empty truck miles occur when drivers empty their loads at a location and have to drive to another location with empty trucks to pick up their next load. Empty truck miles also occur when drivers transport less than a full load to a location.

3. The cost of these empty truck miles has been substantially reduced and often eliminated through the establishment of an e-commerce site accessible by industry competitors. By making available route information regarding loads, capacities, and timetables, competing companies can piggyback on each other's trucks and deliver goods at a lower cost by loading trucks to capacity.

ISSUE 1-41

"DESIGNED FOR INTERACTION," *FORTUNE,* JANUARY 22, 2001, JESSICA SUNG.

1. The new approach to form management teams at SEI Investments depends on the close physical proximity of team participants. SEI formation of management teams depends on moveable furniture and employees being able to connect into ceiling level communications ports. This allows them the flexibility to create teams 'on the fly'. Their no walls structure allows the moving of people and furniture into close proximity so everyone is visible and accessible to one another, even the CEO. The

environment allows more than closer communication, it allows people to live together.

2. Since this type of team building is predicated on the physical closeness of the participants, it would be successful only where the physical requirements make it feasible.

CHAPTER 2
Basic Cost Management Concepts and Accounting for Mass Customization Operations

ANSWERS TO REVIEW QUESTIONS

2-1   Product costs are costs that are associated with manufactured goods until the time period during which the products are sold, when the product costs become expenses. Period costs are expensed during the time period in which they are incurred.

2-2   The most important difference between a manufacturing firm and a service industry firm, with regard to the classification of costs, is that the goods produced by a manufacturing firm are inventoried, whereas the services produced by a service industry firm are consumed as they are produced. Thus, the costs incurred in manufacturing products are treated as product costs until the period during which the goods are sold. Most of the costs incurred in a service industry firm to produce services are operating expenses that are treated as period costs.

2-3   Product costs are also called inventoriable costs because they are assigned to manufactured goods that are inventoried until a later period, when the products are sold. The product costs remain in the Finished-Goods Inventory account until the time period when the goods are sold.

2-4   The five types of production processes are as follows:

   ▪ Job shop: Low production volume; little standardization; one-of-a-kind products. Examples include custom home construction, feature film production, and ship building.

   ▪ Batch: Multiple products; low volume. Examples include construction equipment, tractor trailers, and yachts.

   ▪ Assembly line: A few major products; higher volume. Examples include kitchen appliances and automobile assembly.

   ▪ Mass customization: High production volume; many standardized components; customized combination of components. An example is the computer industry.

- Continuous flow: High production volume; highly standardized commodity products. Examples include food processing, textiles, lumber, and chemicals.

2-5   The term mass customization is used to describe an industry such as the computer industry, where large numbers of identical components are mass produced, and then these are components are combined in a customized way to customer specifications. For example, when a customer places an order for a Dell computer on line, the company assembles just the components requested by the customer, loads the requested software, and ships the customized computer system. Viewed in this light, the term mass customization is not internally inconsistent.

2-6   The cost of idle time is treated as manufacturing overhead because it is a normal cost of the manufacturing operation that should be spread out among all of the manufactured products. The alternative to this treatment would be to charge the cost of idle time to a particular job that happens to be in process when the idle time occurs. Idle time often results from a random event, such as a power outage. Charging the cost of the idle time resulting from such a random event to only the job that happened to be in process at the time would overstate the cost of that job.

2-7   Overtime premium is included in manufacturing overhead in order to spread the extra cost of the overtime over all of the products produced, since overtime often is a normal cost of the manufacturing operation. The alternative would be to charge the overtime premium to the particular job in process during overtime. In most cases, such treatment would overstate the cost of that job, since it is only coincidental that a particular job happened to be done on overtime. The need for overtime to complete a particular job results from the fact that other jobs were completed during regular hours.

2-8   The phrase "different costs for different purposes" refers to the fact that the word "cost" can have different meanings depending on the context in which it is used. Cost data that are classified and recorded in a particular way for one purpose may be inappropriate for another use.

2-9   The city of Tampa would use cost information for planning when it developed a budget for its operations during the next year. Included in that budget would be projected costs for police and fire protection, street maintenance, and city administration. At the end of the year this budget would be used for cost control. The actual costs incurred would be compared to projected costs in the budget. City administrators would also use cost data in making decisions, such as where to locate a new fire station.

2-10   Fixed costs remain constant in total across changes in activity, whereas variable costs change in proportion to the level of activity.

2-11   The fixed cost per unit declines as the level of activity (or cost driver) increases. The cost per unit is reduced because the total fixed cost, which does not change as activity changes, is spread over a larger number of activity units.

2-12   The variable cost per unit remains constant as the level of activity (or cost driver) changes. Total variable costs change in proportion to activity, and the additional variable cost when one unit of activity is added is the variable cost per unit.

2-13   A volume-based cost driver, such as the number of passengers, causes costs to be incurred because of the quantity of service offered by the airline. An operations-based cost driver, such as hub domination, affects costs because of the basic way in which the airline conducts its operations. Greater control over a hub airport's facilities and services gives an airline greater ability to control its operating costs.

2-14   a. Number of students: volume-based cost driver. This characteristic of the college relates to the quantity of services provided.

       b. Number of disciplines offered for study: operations-based cost driver. The greater the diversity in a college's course offerings, the greater will be the costs incurred, regardless of the overall size of the student body.

       c. Urban versus rural location: operations-based cost driver. A college's location will affect the type of housing and food facilities required, the cost of obtaining services, and the cost of transportation for college employees acting on behalf of the college.

2-15   Examples of direct costs of the food and beverage department in a hotel include the money spent on the food and beverages served, the wages of table service personnel, and the costs of entertainment in the dining room and lounge. Examples of indirect costs of the food and beverage department include allocations of the costs of advertising for the entire hotel, of the costs of the grounds and maintenance department, and of the hotel general manager's salary.

2-16   Costs that are likely to be controllable by a city's airport manager include the wages of personnel hired by the airport manager, the cost of heat and light in the airport manager's administrative offices, and the cost of some materials consumed in the process of operating the airport, such as cleaning, painting, and maintenance materials. Costs that are likely to be uncontrollable by the city's airport manager include depreciation of the airport facilities, fees paid by the airport to the federal government for air traffic control services, and insurance for the airport employees and patrons.

2-17 a. Uncontrollable cost

b. Controllable cost

c. Uncontrollable cost

2-18 Out-of-pocket costs are paid in cash at or near the time they are incurred. An opportunity cost is the potential benefit given up when the choice of one action precludes the selection of a different action.

2-19 A sunk cost is a cost that was incurred in the past and cannot be altered by any current or future decision. A differential cost is the difference in a cost item under two decision alternatives.

2-20 A marginal cost is the extra cost incurred in producing one additional unit of output. The average cost is the total cost of producing a particular quantity of product or service, divided by the number of units of product or service produced.

2-21 The process of registering for classes varies widely among colleges and universities, and the responses to this question will vary as well. Examples of information that might be useful include the credit requirements and course requirements to obtain a particular degree, and a list of the prerequisites for each of the elective courses in a particular major. Such information could help the student plan an academic program over several semesters or quarters. An example of information that might create information overload is a comprehensive listing of every course offered by the college in the past five years.

2-22 The purchase cost of the old bar code scanners is a sunk cost, since it occurred in the past and cannot be changed by any future course of action. The manager is exhibiting a common behavioral tendency to pay too much attention to sunk costs.

2-23 a. Direct cost

b. Direct cost

c. Indirect cost

d. Indirect cost

SOLUTIONS TO EXERCISES

EXERCISE 2-24 (10 MINUTES)

The general formula for solving all three cases is as follows:

Beginning inventory of finished goods	+	Cost of goods manufactured during period	–	Ending inventory of finished goods	=	Cost-of-goods sold expense

Using this formula, we can find the missing amounts as follows:

	Case		
	I	II	III
Beginning inventory of finished goods	$ 84,000*	$12,000	$ 7,000
Add: Cost of goods manufactured	419,000	95,000	318,000*
Subtract: Ending inventory of finished goods	98,000	8,000	21,000
Cost of goods sold	$405,000	$99,000*	$304,000

*Amount missing in exercise.

EXERCISE 2-25 (10 MINUTES)

1.

Hours worked	40
Wage rate	× $ 18
Total compensation	$720

2. Classification:

Direct labor (36 hours × $18)	$648
Overhead (idle time: 4 hours × $18)	72
Total compensation	$720

EXERCISE 2-26 (10 MINUTES)

1.

Regular wages (40 hours × $16)	$ 640
Overtime wages (5 hours × $20)	100
Total compensation	$ 740

2.

Overtime hours	5 hrs.
Overtime premium per hour ($20 − $16)	× $ 4
Total overtime premium	$ 20

EXERCISE 2-26 (CONTINUED)

3.   Classification:

Direct labor (45 hours × $16)	$ 720
Overhead (overtime premium: 5 hours × $4)..	20
Total compensation..	$ 740

EXERCISE 2-27 (30 MINUTES)

Mass customization is well suited to Dell Computer's operations because of the company's direct-selling approach, in which customers order customized computer systems, often on line. Then Dell orders just the components necessary to assemble the computer systems that have been ordered, and delivery is made in a relatively short period of time.

EXERCISE 2-28 (20 MINUTES)

1.   Tire costs: Product cost, variable, direct material

2.   Sales commissions: Period cost, variable

3.   Wood glue: Product cost, variable, either direct material or manufacturing overhead (i.e., indirect material) depending on how significant the cost is

4.   Wages of security guards: Product cost, variable, manufacturing overhead

5.   Salary of financial vice-president: Period cost, fixed

6.   Advertising costs: Period cost, fixed

7.   Straight-line depreciation: Product cost, fixed, manufacturing overhead

8.   Wages of assembly-line personnel: Product cost, variable, direct labor

9.   Delivery costs on customer shipments: Period cost, variable

10.   Newsprint consumed: Product cost, variable, direct material

11.   Plant insurance: Product cost, fixed, manufacturing overhead

12.   Glass costs: Product cost, variable, direct material

EXERCISE 2-29 (25 MINUTES)

1.

ALEXANDRIA ALUMINUM COMPANY
SCHEDULE OF COST OF GOODS MANUFACTURED
FOR THE YEAR ENDED DECEMBER 31, 20x1

Direct material:		
Raw-material inventory, January 1	$ 60,000	
Add: Purchases of raw material	250,000	
Raw material available for use	$310,000	
Deduct: Raw-material inventory, December 31	70,000	
Raw material used		$240,000
Direct labor		400,000
Manufacturing overhead:		
Indirect material	$ 10,000	
Indirect labor	25,000	
Depreciation on plant and equipment	100,000	
Utilities	25,000	
Other	30,000	
Total manufacturing overhead		190,000
Total manufacturing costs		$830,000
Add: Work-in-process inventory, January 1		120,000
Subtotal		$950,000
Deduct: Work-in-process inventory, December 31		115,000
Cost of goods manufactured		$835,000

2.

ALEXANDRIA ALUMINUM COMPANY
SCHEDULE OF COST OF GOODS SOLD
FOR THE YEAR ENDED DECEMBER 31, 20x1

Finished-goods inventory, January 1	$150,000
Add: Cost of goods manufactured	835,000
Cost of goods available for sale	$985,000
Deduct: Finished-goods inventory, December 31	165,000
Cost of goods sold	$820,000

EXERCISE 2-29 (CONTINUED)

3.

ALEXANDRIA ALUMINUM COMPANY
INCOME STATEMENT
FOR THE YEAR ENDED DECEMBER 31, 20X1

Sales revenue	$1,105,000
Less: Cost of goods sold	820,000
Gross margin	$ 285,000
Selling and administrative expenses	110,000
Income before taxes	$ 175,000
Income tax expense	70,000
Net income	$ 105,000

EXERCISE 2-30 (15 MINUTES)

	Number of Muffler Replacements		
	500	600	700
Total costs:			
Fixed costs	(a) $42,000	$42,000	(b) $42,000
Variable costs	(c) 25,000	30,000	(d) 35,000
Total costs	(e) $67,000	$72,000	(f) $77,000
Cost per muffler replacement:			
Fixed cost	(g) $ 84	(h) $ 70	(i) $ 60
Variable cost	(j) 50	(k) 50	(l) 50
Total cost per muffler replacement	(m) $134	(n) $120	(o) $110

Explanatory Notes:

(a) Total fixed costs do not vary with activity.

(c) Variable cost per replacement = $30,000/600 = $50

Total variable cost for 500 replacements = $50 × 500 = $25,000

(g) Fixed cost per replacement = $42,000/500 = $84

(j) Variable cost per replacement = $25,000/500 = $50

EXERCISE 2-31 (15 MINUTES)

1. Phone bill, January: $100 + ($.25 × 6,000).. $1,600
   Phone bill, February: $100 + ($.25 × 5,000) $1,350

2. Cost per call, January: $1,600/6,000 .... $ .267 (rounded)
   Cost per call, February: $1,350/5,000... $ .27

3. Fixed component, January .... $ 100
   Variable component, January: $.25 × 6,000 1,500
   Total... $1,600

4. Since each phone call costs $.25, the marginal cost of making the 6,001st call is $.25.

5. The average cost of a phone call in January (rounded) is $.267 ($1,600/6,000).

EXERCISE 2-32 (5 MINUTES)

Martin Shrood's expenditure is a *sunk* cost. It is irrelevant to any future decision Martin may make about the land.

EXERCISE 2-33 (5 MINUTES)

Annual cost using European component: $8,900 × 10... $89,000
Annual cost using Part A200: ($5,100 + $500) × 10.. 56,000
Annual differential cost $33,000

EXERCISE 2-34 (5 MINUTES)

1. The $14,000 is the *opportunity cost* associated with using the computer in the Department of Education for work in the governor's office.

2. The $14,000 leasing cost should be assigned to the governor's office. It was incurred as a result of activity in that office.

EXERCISE 2-35 (10 MINUTES)

1. Your decision to see the game really cost you $100, the amount forgone when you refused to sell the ticket. A convenient way to think about this is as follows: You could have sold the ticket for $100, thereby resulting in a profit on the deal of $40 ($100 sales proceeds minus $60 out-of-pocket purchase cost). Instead, you went to the game, which left you relieved of your $60 out-of-pocket cost. The difference between the $60 *reduction* in your wealth and the $40 *profit* you could have had is $100. Thus, $100 is the true cost of going to the game.

2. The $100 is an *opportunity cost.* At the time you made the decision to attend the game, the $60 you actually had paid for the ticket is a *sunk cost.* It is not relevant to any future decision.

EXERCISE 2-36 (15 MINUTES)

1. The marginal cost would include any food and beverages consumed by the passenger and perhaps an imperceptible increase in fuel costs.

2. In most cases, only the cost of the food and beverage consumed by the customer would be a marginal cost. It is unlikely that the restaurant would need to employ additional service personnel, dishwashers, and so on.

3. The marginal cost of a flight would include the aircraft fuel, wages of the flight crew and airport maintenance personnel, and the food and beverages consumed by the passengers and crew.

4. The marginal cost would include the additional wages or commissions earned by the agency employees and the additional electricity used for light, heat, and computer equipment.

5. The marginal cost of the skis would include the direct material. It is unlikely that labor and other costs would change with the addition of only one more product unit.

SOLUTIONS TO PROBLEMS

PROBLEM 2-37 (20 MINUTES)

1.
   1.   Income statement
   2.   Balance sheet
   3.   Income statement
   4.   Income statement
   5.   Cost-of-goods-manufactured schedule
   6.   Income statement
   7.   Cost-of-goods-manufactured schedule
   8.   Cost of-goods-manufactured schedule
   9.   Balance sheet, cost-of-goods-manufactured schedule
  10.   Income statement
  11.   Income statement

2.   The asset that differs among these businesses is inventory. Service businesses typically carry no (or very little) inventory. Retailers and wholesalers normally stock considerable inventory. Manufacturers also carry significant inventories, typically subdivided into three categories: raw material, work in process, and finished goods.

3.   The income statements of service business normally have separate sections for operating revenues, operating expenses, and other income (expenses). In contrast, those of retailers, wholesalers, and manufacturers disclose sales revenue, followed immediately by cost of goods sold and gross margin. Operating expenses are listed next followed by other income (expenses).

4.   The basic difference falls in the area of inventory. Traditional manufacturers produce finished goods, which are then placed in warehouses awaiting sale. In contrast, with a direct-sales, mass-customization firm, the receipt of a sales order triggers the manufacturing process as well as the purchasing system, the latter to acquire needed raw materials. Finished-goods and raw-material inventories (along with work in process) of mass-customizers are, therefore, much lower than the inventories carried by traditional firms.

PROBLEM 2-38 (30 MINUTES)

1.   Manufacturing overhead:

Indirect labor..	$109,000
Building depreciation ($80,000 x 75%)..	60,000
Other factory costs.............................	344,000
Total...	$513,000

2.   Cost of goods manufactured:
        Direct material:

Raw-material inventory, Jan. 1..................	$ 15,800	
Add: Purchases of raw material.................	175,000	
Raw material available for use..................	$190,800	
Deduct: Raw-material inventory, Dec. 31....	18,200	
Raw material used...................................		$172,600
Direct labor..		254,000
Manufacturing overhead............................		513,000
Total manufacturing costs..........................		$939,600
Add: Work-in-process inventory, Jan. 1.........		35,700
Subtotal..		$975,300
Deduct: Work-in-process inventory, Dec. 31....		62,100
Cost of goods manufactured........................		$913,200

3.   Cost of goods sold:

Finished-goods inventory, Jan. 1..................	$ 111,100
Add: Cost of goods manufactured...............	913,200
Cost of goods available for sale..................	$1,024,300
Deduct: Finished-goods inventory, Dec. 31...	97,900
Cost of goods sold....................................	$ 926,400

4.   Net income:

Sales revenue...		$1,495,000
Less: Cost of goods sold...........................		926,400
Gross margin..		$ 568,600
Selling and administrative expenses:		
Salaries..	$133,000	
Building depreciation ($80,000 x 25%)......	20,000	
Other..	195,000	348,000
Income before taxes.................................		$ 220,600
Income tax expense ($220,600 x 30%)..........		66,180
Net income...		$ 154,420

5.   Pine Tree sold 11,500 units during the year ($1,495,000 ÷ $130). Since 160 of the units came from finished-goods inventory (1,350 – 1,190), the company would have manufactured 11,340 units (11,500 – 160).

PROBLEM 2-39 (25 MINUTES)

Since gross margin equals 30% of sales, cost of goods sold equals 70% of sales, or $231,000 ($330,000 x 70%). Thus, the finished goods destroyed by the fire cost $44,000, computed as follows:

Finished-goods inventory, Jan. 1 (given)..................	$ 37,000
Add: Cost of goods manufactured*.........................	238,000
Cost of goods available for sale (given)...................	$275,000
Deduct: Finished-goods inventory, Apr. 12*.............	44,000
Cost of goods sold (calculated above)....................	$231,000

*Fill in these blanks, given the other numbers in this table.

Direct material used:

Direct material averages 25% of prime costs (i.e., direct material + direct labor).

Thus: Let X = direct material used

$$X = (X + \$120,000) \times 25\%$$
$$0.75X = \$30,000$$
$$X = \$40,000$$

Manufacturing overhead:

Manufacturing overhead equals 50% of Chung's total production costs.

Thus: Let Y = manufacturing overhead

$$Y = (\text{direct material used} + \text{direct labor} + \text{manufacturing overhead}) \times 50\%$$
$$Y = (\$40,000 + \$120,000 + Y) \times 50\%$$
$$0.50Y = \$80,000$$
$$Y = \$160,000$$

The work in process destroyed by the fire cost $103,000, computed as follows:

Direct material...	$ 40,000
Direct labor (given)...	120,000
Manufacturing overhead....................................	160,000
Total manufacturing costs................................	$320,000
Add: Work-in-process inventory, Jan. 1 (given)...	21,000
Subtotal..	$341,000
Deduct: Work-in-process inventory, Apr. 12*.......	103,000
Cost of goods manufactured (from above)..........	$238,000

*$103,000 = $341,000 – $238,000

PROBLEM 2-40 (25 MINUTES)

1.   Fixed manufacturing overhead per unit:
   $600,000 ÷ 24,000 units produced = $25

    Average unit manufacturing cost:

Direct material.............................	$ 20
Direct labor.................................	37
Variable manufacturing overhead..	48
Fixed manufacturing overhead......	25
Average unit cost....................	$130

Production..................................	24,000 units
Sales..	20,000 units
Ending finished-goods inventory...	4,000 units

    Cost of December 31finished-goods inventory:
   4,000 units x $130 = $520,000

2.   Net income:

Sales revenue (20,000 units x $185)............	$3,700,000
Cost of goods sold (20,000 units x $130).....	2,600,000
Gross margin...	$1,100,000
Selling and administrative expenses...........	860,000
Income before taxes................................	$ 240,000
Income tax expense ($240,000 x 30%).........	72,000
Net income...	$ 168,000

3.   (a)   No change. Direct labor is a variable cost, and the cost per unit will remain constant.

       (b)   No change. Despite the decrease in the number of units produced, this is a fixed cost, which remains the same in total.

       (c)   No change. Selling and administrative costs move more closely with changes in sales than with units produced. Additionally, this is a fixed cost.

       (d)   Increase. The average unit cost of production will change because of the per-unit fixed manufacturing overhead. A reduced production volume will be divided into the fixed dollar amount, which increases the cost per unit.

PROBLEM 2-41 (40 MINUTES)

	Case A	Case B	Case C
Beginning inventory, raw material	$60,000*	$ 20,000	$ 15,000
Ending inventory, raw material	90,000	10,000*	30,000
Purchases of raw material	100,000	85,000	70,000*
Direct material used	70,000	95,000	55,000*
Direct labor	200,000*	100,000	125,000
Manufacturing overhead	250,000	150,000*	160,000
Total manufacturing costs	520,000	345,000	340,000
Beginning inventory, work in process	35,000	20,000	15,000*
Ending inventory, work in process	30,000*	35,000	5,000
Cost of goods manufactured	525,000	330,000*	350,000
Beginning inventory, finished goods	50,000	40,000	20,000*
Cost of goods available for sale	575,000*	370,000*	370,000
Ending inventory, finished goods	30,000*	40,000*	25,000
Cost of goods sold	545,000	330,000	345,000*
Sales	800,000*	500,000*	480,000
Gross margin	255,000	170,000	135,000*
Selling and administrative expenses	105,000*	75,000	45,000*
Income before taxes	150,000	95,000*	90,000
Income tax expense	40,000	45,000	35,000*
Net income	110,000*	50,000*	55,000

*Amount missing in problem.

PROBLEM 2-42 (25 MINUTES)

1.   a.   Total prime costs:

Direct material	$ 2,100,000
Direct labor:	
Wages	485,000
Fringe benefits	95,000
Total prime costs	$ 2,680,000

PROBLEM 2-42 (CONTINUED)

b.   Total manufacturing overhead:

Depreciation on factory building	$ 115,000
Indirect labor: wages	140,000
Production supervisor's salary	45,000
Service department costs	100,000
Indirect labor: fringe benefits	30,000
Fringe benefits for production supervisor	9,000
Total overtime premiums paid	55,000
Cost of idle time: production employees	40,000
Total manufacturing overhead	$ 534,000

c.   Total conversion costs:

Direct labor ($485,000 + $95,000)	$ 580,000
Manufacturing overhead	534,000
Total conversion costs	$1,114,000

d.   Total product costs:

Direct material	$2,100,000
Direct labor	580,000
Manufacturing overhead	534,000
Total product costs	$3,214,000

e.   Total period costs:

Advertising expense	$ 99,000
Administrative costs	150,000
Rental of office space for sales personnel	15,000
Sales commissions	5,000
Product promotion costs	10,000
Total period costs	$ 279,000

2.   The $15,000 in rental cost for sales office space rental is an opportunity cost. It measures the opportunity cost of using the former sales office space for raw-material storage.

3.   The cost of the finished-goods inventory on hand at year end, $115,000, is a sunk cost. It has already been incurred and is not relevant to any future decision.

PROBLEM 2-43 (35 MINUTES)

1.

SAN FERNANDO FASHIONS COMPANY
SCHEDULE OF COST OF GOODS MANUFACTURED
FOR THE YEAR ENDED DECEMBER 31, 20X2

Direct material:		
Raw-material inventory, January 1	$ 40,000	
Add: Purchases of raw material..	180,000	
Raw material available for use	$220,000	
Deduct: Raw-material inventory, December 31......................	25,000	
Raw material used..		$195,000
Direct labor		200,000
Manufacturing overhead:		
Indirect material...	$ 10,000	
Indirect labor..	15,000	
Utilities: plant...	40,000	
Depreciation: plant and equipment.......................................	60,000	
Other..	80,000	
Total manufacturing overhead		205,000
Total manufacturing costs...		$600,000
Add: Work-in-process inventory, January 1		40,000
Subtotal..		$640,000
Deduct: Work-in-process inventory, December 31.................		30,000
Cost of goods manufactured...		$610,000

2.

SAN FERNANDO FASHIONS COMPANY
SCHEDULE OF COST OF GOODS SOLD
FOR THE YEAR ENDED DECEMBER 31, 20X2

Finished goods inventory, January 1	$ 20,000
Add: Cost of goods manufactured...	610,000
Cost of goods available for sale	$630,000
Deduct: Finished-goods inventory, December 31	50,000
Cost of goods sold..	$580,000

PROBLEM 2-43 (CONTINUED)

3.
SAN FERNANDO FASHIONS COMPANY
INCOME STATEMENT
FOR THE YEAR ENDED DECEMBER 31, 20x2

Sales revenue	$950,000
Less: Cost of goods sold	580,000
Gross margin	$370,000
Selling and administrative expenses	150,000
Income before taxes	$220,000
Income tax expense	90,000
Net income	$130,000

PROBLEM 2-44 (15 MINUTES)

1.	Regular hours: $40 \times \$12$	$480
	Overtime hours: $8 \times \$16$	128
	Total cost of wages	$608

2.	a. Direct labor: $38 \times \$12$	$456
	b. Manufacturing overhead (idle time): $1 \times \$12$	12
	c. Manufacturing overhead (overtime premium): $8 \times (\$16 - \$12)$	32
	d. Manufacturing overhead (indirect labor): $9 \times \$12$	108
	Total cost of wages	$608

PROBLEM 2-45 (20 MINUTES)

1. a, d, g, i

2. a, d, g, j

3. b, f

4. b, d, g, k

5. a, d, g, k

6. a, d, g, j

PROBLEM 2-45 (CONTINUED)

7.   b, c, f

8.   b, d, g, k

9.   b, c and d*, e and f and g*, k*

      *The building is used for several purposes.

10.   b, c, f

11.   b, c, h

12.   b, c, f

13.   b, c, e

14.   b, c and d†, e and f and g†, k†

      †The building that the furnace heats is used for several purposes.

15.   b, d, g, k

PROBLEM 2-46 (20 MINUTES)

1.   3 hours × ($12 + $3) = $45

      Notice that the overtime premium on the flight is not a direct cost of the flight.

2.   3 hours × $12 × .5 = $18

      This is the overtime premium, which is part of Gaines' overall compensation.

3.   The overtime premium should be included in overhead and allocated across all of the company's flights.

4.   The $82 is an opportunity cost of using Gaines on the flight departing from Topeka on August 11. The cost should be assigned to the August 11 flight departing from Topeka.

PROBLEM 2-47 (15 MINUTES)

1.   Graph of raw-material cost:

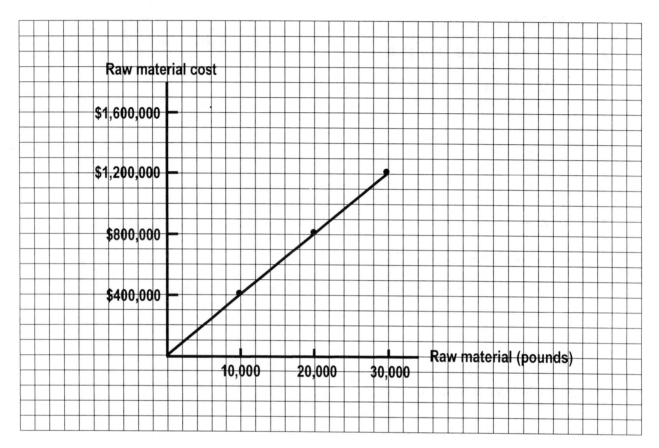

2.

Production Level in Pounds	Unit Cost	Total Cost
1	$40 per pound	$40
10	$40 per pound	$400
1,000	$40 per pound	$40,000

PROBLEM 2-48 (25 MINUTES)

1. Graph of fixed production cost:

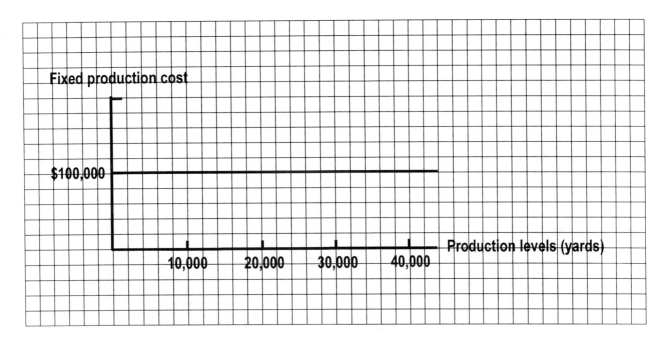

2.	Production Level in Yards	Unit Fixed Cost	Total Fixed Cost
	1	$100,000 per yard	$100,000
	10	$10,000 per yard	$100,000
	10,000	$10 per yard	$100,000
	40,000	$2.50 per yard	$100,000

PROBLEM 2-48 (CONTINUED)

3.   Graph of unit fixed production cost:

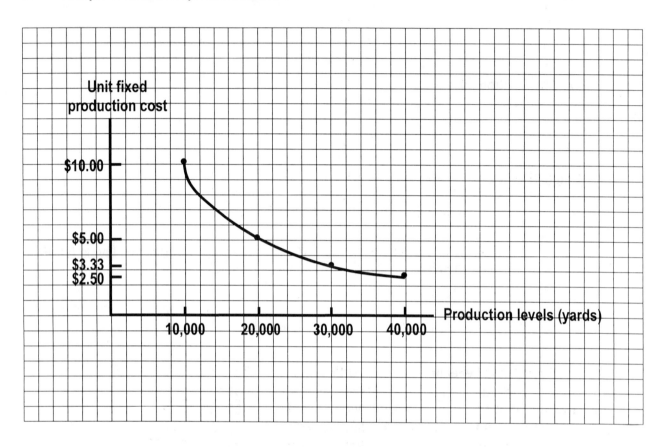

PROBLEM 2-49 (10 MINUTES)

Cost Item Number	Direct or Indirect	Partially Controllable by Department Supervisor
1.	indirect	no
2.	indirect	no
3.	direct	yes
4.	direct	no
5.	direct	yes

PROBLEM 2-50 (10 MINUTES)

Cost Item Number	Product Cost or Period Cost
1.	period*
2.	product
3.	product
4.	product
5.	product
6.	period*
7.	product
8.	period*
9.	product

*Service industry firms typically treat all costs as operating expenses which are period expenses. Such firms do not inventory costs.

PROBLEM 2-51 (15 MINUTES)

	Variable or Fixed	20x2 Forecast	Explanation
Direct material..	V	$3,600,000	$3,000,000 $\times$ 1.20
Direct labor..	V	2,640,000	$2,200,000 $\times$ 1.20
Manufacturing overhead			
Utilities (primarily electricity)................	V	168,000	$140,000 $\times$ 1.20
Depreciation on plant and equipment...	F	230,000	same
Insurance..	F	160,000	same
Supervisory salaries............................	F	300,000	same
Property taxes......................................	F	210,000	same
Selling costs			
Advertising..	F	195,000	same
Sales commissions	V	108,000	$90,000 $\times$ 1.20
Administrative costs			
Salaries of top management and staff..	F	372,000	same
Office supplies.....................................	F	40,000	same
Depreciation on building and equipment.....................................	F	80,000	same

PROBLEM 2-52 (15 MINUTES)

1. f, average cost

2. e, marginal cost

3. c, sunk cost

4. a, opportunity cost

5. d, differential cost

6. b, out-of-pocket cost

7. e, marginal cost

PROBLEM 2-53 (20 MINUTES)

1. b, d, e, k

2. a, c, e, k

3. h

4. a, d, e*, j

   *The hotel general manager may have some control over the total space allocated to the kitchen.

5. d, e, i

6. i

7. d, e, i

8. a, d, e, k

9. a, d, e, k

10. j

11. g (The $300 cost savings is a differential cost.)

12. a, c, e

PROBLEM 2-53 (CONTINUED)

13.   d, e, k

14.   e, k

15.   b, d*, e, k

*Unless the dishwasher has been used improperly.

PROBLEM 2-54 (40 MINUTES)

1.   Caterpillar is a manufacturing firm. Its income statement highlights the firm's cost-of-goods-sold expense, which is the cost of all of the processed food products sold during the year. Cost of goods sold is subtracted from net sales to arrive at the gross profit. The company's other operating expenses then are subtracted from the gross profit.

       Wal-Mart Stores, Inc. is a retail firm. Its income statement also shows the firm's cost of sales, which is another name for cost of goods sold. The cost of sales includes all of the costs of acquiring merchandise for resale. The company's other operating expenses are identified separately from cost of sales.

       Southwest Airlines Company is an airline, which is a service industry firm. The company does not sell an inventoriable product, but rather provides air transportation service. Therefore, the company's income statement does not list any cost-of-goods-sold expense. All of its expenses are operating expenses.

2.   Cost-accounting data are used to measure all of the costs on all three companies' income statements. For example, the cost-accounting system at Caterpillar measures the cost of direct labor, direct material, and manufacturing overhead incurred in the manufacturing process. Wal-Mart Stores' cost-accounting system measures the cost of acquiring merchandise for resale. Southwest Airlines' cost-accounting system measures the cost of aviation fuel consumed.

3.   The ticket agents' salaries would be included in salaries, wages, and benefits. Depreciation of the airline's computer equipment would be included in depreciation.

4.   Wal-Mart Stores' cost of newspaper advertising would be included in selling expenses. The cost of merchandise sold would be included in cost of sales (same as cost of goods sold).

PROBLEM 2-54 (CONTINUED)

5. The salary for a Caterpillar brand manager would be included in selling expenses. Production employees' salaries are product costs, so they are part of the cost of goods sold. Similarly, raw-material costs are product costs, and they are included in cost of goods sold.

PROBLEM 2-55 (10 MINUTES)

1. $400   ($850 − $450)
2. $330   ($1,540 − $1,210)
3. $310   ($1,850 − $1,540)
4. $425   ($850/2)
5. $385   ($1,540/4)
6. $370   ($1,850/5)

PROBLEM 2-56 (25 MINUTES)

1. b, c, g, h, j, m

2. a, c, i, j, l

3. b, d, i, j, m

4. a, d, i, j, l

5. a, c, i, j, l

6. e

7. a, c, i, j, l

8. f

9. b, d, k, m

10. a, c, i, j, m

11. b, c, i, j, l

PROBLEM 2-56 (CONTINUED)

12. a, c, i, j, l

13. b, c, g, j, l

14. b, d, i, j, l

15. b, c, i, j, l

PROBLEM 2-57 (25 MINUTES)

1.

Output (.75 liter bottles)	Calculation	Unit Cost
10,000	$177,000/10,000	$17.70
15,000	$195,500/15,000	$13.03 (rounded)
20,000	$214,000/20,000	$10.70

The unit cost is minimized at a sales volume of 20,000 bottles.

2.

Output (.75 liter bottles)	Sales Revenue	Total Costs	Profit
10,000	$180,000	$177,000	$ 3,000
15,000	225,000	195,500	29,500
20,000	240,000	214,000	26,000

Profit is maximized at a production level of 15,000 bottles of wine.

3. The 15,000-bottle level is best for the company, since it maximizes profit.

4. The unit cost decreases as output increases, because the fixed cost per unit declines as production and sales increase.

   A lower price is required to motivate consumers to purchase a larger amount of wine.

PROBLEM 2-58 (15 MINUTES)

1.　If the company buys 30,000 units of Part MR24, at a price of $X per unit, its total cost will be:

$$(30,000 \times \$X) + \$60,000$$

If the company manufactures the parts, its total cost will be:

$$(30,000 \times \$11) + \$150,000$$

By equating these two expressions for total cost, we can solve for the price, X, at which the total cost is the same under the two alternatives:

$$30,000\,X + 60,000 = (30,000)(11) + 150,000$$
$$30,000X = 420,000$$
$$X = 14$$

Thus the firm will realize a net benefit by purchasing Part MR24 if the outside supplier charges a price less than $14.

2.　If the firm buys Y units of Part MR24 at a price of $12.875 per unit, the total cost will be:

$$(\$12.875 \times Y) + \$60,000$$

If the company manufactures Y units of Part MR24, the total cost will be:

$$(\$11 \times Y) + \$150,000$$

If we equate these expressions, we can solve for the number of parts, Y, at which the firm will be indifferent between making and buying Part MR24.

$$12.875\,Y + 60,000 = 11Y + 150,000$$
$$1.875Y = 90,000$$
$$Y = 48,000$$

Thus, the company will be indifferent between the two alternatives if it requires 48,000 units of Part MR24 each month.

SOLUTIONS TO CASES

CASE 2-59 (30 MINUTES)

1.

MEMORANDUM

Date: Today

To: James Cassanitti

From: I. M. Student

Subject: Costs related to Printer Case Department

The $29,500 building rental cost allocated to the Printer Case Department is part of larger rental costs for the entire building. Even if the Printer Case Department is closed down, Pinnelas Printer Company still will occupy the entire building. Therefore, the entire rental cost, including the $29,500 portion allocated to the Printer Case Department, will be incurred whether or not the department closes.

The real cost of the space occupied by the Printer Case Department is the $39,000 the company is paying to rent warehouse space. This cost would be avoided if the Printer Case Department were closed, since the storage operation could be moved into the company's main building. The $39,000 rental cost is the *opportunity cost* of using space in the main building for the Printer Case Department.

The supervisor of the Printer Case Department will be retained by the company regardless of the decision about the Printer Case Department. However, if the Printer Case Department is kept in operation the company will have to hire a new supervisor for the Assembly Department. The salary of that new supervisor is a relevant cost of continuing to operate the Printer Case Department.

Another way of looking at the situation is to realize that with the Printer Case Department in operation, the company will need two supervisors: the current Printer Case Department supervisor and a new supervisor for the Assembly Department. Alternatively, if the Printer Case Department is closed, only the current Printer Case Department supervisor will be needed. He or she will move to the Assembly Department. The difference, then, between the two alternatives is the cost of compensation for the new Assembly Department supervisor if the Printer Case Department is not closed.

CASE 2-59 (CONTINUED)

2. The controller has an ethical obligation to state accurately the projected cost savings from closing the Printer Case Department. The production manager and other decision makers have a right to know the financial implications of closing the department. Several of the ethical standards for management accountants (listed in Chapter 1) apply, including the following:

Competence:

- Prepare complete and clear reports and recommendations after appropriate analyses of relevant and reliable information.

Objectivity:

- Communicate information fairly and objectively.

- Disclose fully all relevant information that could reasonably be expected to influence an intended user's understanding of the reports, comments, and recommendations presented.

CASE 2-60 (50 MINUTES)

1. a. FastQ Company would be indifferent to acquiring either the small-volume copier, 1024S, or the medium-volume copier, 1024M, at the point where the costs for 1024S and 1024M are equal. This point may be calculated using the following formula, where X equals the number of copies:

$$(\text{Variable costs}_S \times X_S) + \text{fixed costs}_S = (\text{variable cost}_M \times X_M) + \text{fixed cost}_M$$

$$
\begin{array}{cc}
\text{1024S} & \text{1024M} \\
\$.14X + \$8,000 & = \$.09X + \$11,000 \\
\$.05X & = \$3,000 \\
X & = 60,000 \text{ copies}
\end{array}
$$

The conclusion is that FastQ Company would be indifferent to acquiring either the 1024S or 1024M machine at an annual volume of 60,000 copies.

b. A decision rule for selecting the most profitable copier, when the volume can be estimated, would establish the points where FastQ Company is indifferent to each machine. The volume where the costs are equal between alternatives can be calculated using the following formula, where X equals the number of copies:

$$(\text{Variable costs}_S \times X_S) + \text{fixed costs}_S = (\text{variable cost}_M \times X_M) + \text{fixed cost}_M$$

For the 1024S machine compared to the 1024M machine:

$$\begin{array}{cc} \text{1024S} & \text{1024M} \end{array}$$

$$\$.14X + \$8{,}000 = \$.09X + \$11{,}000$$

$$\$.05X = \$3{,}000$$

$$X = 60{,}000 \text{ copies}$$

For the 1024M machine compared to the 1024G machine:

$$\begin{array}{cc} \text{1024M} & \text{1024G} \end{array}$$

$$\$.09X + \$11{,}000 = \$.05X + \$20{,}000$$

$$\$.04X = \$9{,}000$$

$$X = 225{,}000 \text{ copies}$$

The decision rule is to select the alternative as shown in the following chart.

Anticipated Annual Volume	Optimal Model Choice
0–60,000	1024S
60,000–225,000	1024M
225,000 and higher	1024G

CASE 2-60 (CONTINUED)

2. a. The previous purchase price of the endor on hand, $5.00 per gallon, and the average cost of the endor inventory, $4.75 per gallon, are sunk costs. These costs were incurred in the past and will have no impact on future costs. They cannot be changed by any future action and are irrelevant to any future decision. Although the current price of endor is $5.50 per gallon, no endor will be purchased at this price. Thus, it too is irrelevant to the current special order. If the order is accepted, the required 800 gallons of endor will be replaced at a cost of $5.75 per gallon. Therefore, the real cost of endor for the special order is $4,600 (800 × $5.75).

    b. The $20,000 paid by Alderon for its stock of tatooine is a sunk cost. It was incurred in the past and is irrelevant to any future decision. The current market price of $11 per kilogram is irrelevant, since no more tatooine will be purchased. If the special order is accepted, Alderon will use 1,500 kilograms of its tatooine stock, thereby losing the opportunity to sell its entire 2,000-kilogram stock for $14,000. Thus, the $14,000 is an opportunity cost of using the tatooine in production instead of selling it to Solo Industries. Moreover, if Alderon uses 1,500 kilograms of tatooine in production, it will have to pay $1,000 for its remaining 500 kilograms to be disposed of at a hazardous waste facility. This $1,000 disposal cost is an out-of-pocket cost.

    The real cost of using the tatooine in the special order is $15,000 ($14,000 opportunity cost + $1,000 out-of-pocket cost).

3. The projected donations from the wildlife show amount to $100,000 (10 percent of the TV audience at $10,000 per 1 percent of the viewership). The projected donations from the manufacturing series amount to $75,000 (15 percent of the TV audience at $5,000 per 1 percent of the viewership). Therefore, the differential revenue is $25,000, with the advantage going to the wildlife show. However, if the manufacturing show is aired, the station will be able to sell the wildlife show to network TV. Therefore, airing the wildlife show will result in the incurrence of a $25,000 opportunity cost.

    The conclusion, then, is that the station's management should be indifferent between the two shows, since each would generate revenue of $100,000.

Wildlife show (10 × $10,000)	$100,000	donation
Manufacturing show (15 × $5,000)	$ 75,000	donation
Manufacturing show (sell wildlife show)	25,000	sales proceeds
	$100,000	total revenue

CURRENT ISSUES IN MANAGERIAL ACCOUNTING

ISSUE 2-61

"R. J. REYNOLDS POSTS A NARROWER LOSS BUT A 12.6% DECREASE IN SALES VOLUME," *THE WALL STREET JOURNAL*, JANUARY 28, 2000, GORDON FAIRCLOUGH.

1. Fixed costs remain constant in total within the relevant range. Common examples of fixed costs include supervisory salaries, property taxes and depreciation.

2. Since variable costs rise with increased production and sales, and fixed costs remain the same, a company would be better off with higher variable costs during a decline in production. Total costs would decrease as sales decreased. The exception to this would be when fixed costs are nearly negligible, such as in the case of RJR.

ISSUE 2-62

"GETTING RID OF GUESSWORK," *BUSINESS WEEK*, AUGUST 28, 2000, ADRIAN J. SLYWOTZKY.

1. A choiceboard involves mass customization by manufacturers, allowing customers to design their own products built to their specifications. The article sites Dell Computer Corporation, Cisco Systems, Inc., and Mattel Inc. as innovators in using choiceboards in their manufacturing and marketing activities.

2. Industries currently developing choiceboard systems include:

   - Computer manufacturers

   - Toy manufacturers

   - Furniture manufacturers

   - Door manufacturers

   - Auto manufacturers

ISSUE 2-63

"PEPSICO'S NEW FORMULA," *BUSINESS WEEK*, APRIL 10, 2000, JOHN A. BYRNE.

Enrico's *Power of One* strategy leverages the synergies of soft drinks and snacks. It has been 35 years since Don Kendall and Herman W. Lay sketched out the merger of Pepsi-Cola and Frito-Lay. At the time Pepsi earned 2.5 times the net profits of Frito-Lay. Today, that situation is reversed.

For the first time in decades, Enrico has focused the company on just two things, packaged foods and drinks. This focus has concentrated on the three areas of Frito-Lay snacks, Pepsi-Cola beverages, and Tropicana juices.

Instead of going head to head in the U.S. markets that Coke has controlled for twenty years, Enrico has focused on new and emerging overseas markets where gaining share is more viable. In the U.S. market, Enrico has focused on placing Pepsi and Frito-Lay products together on supermarket shelves. This *Power of One* strategy is attractive to supermarkets since Pepsi's products provide an average 9 percent operating margin compared with a 2 percent average for other products on supermarket shelves.

ISSUE 2-64

"GM-FIAT DEAL DOESN'T EASE OVERCAPACITY IN EUROPE," *THE WALL STREET JOURNAL*, MARCH 14, 2000, SCOTT MILLER.

1. Excess capacity is the ability of a company to produce its product beyond that which is needed to meet sales expectations. Capacity to produce a product entails fixed costs, such as equipment maintenance, lighting and heating. These costs are incurred even if production capacity is not being fully utilized.

2. Excess capacity, production ability not being used, results in higher fixed costs relative to profitability.

ISSUE 2-65

"U.S. SUES AMERICAN AIR IN ANTITRUST CASE -- NO. 2 CARRIER FACES CHARGES OF FORCING SMALL RIVALS OUT OF ITS HUB IN DALLAS," *THE WALL STREET JOURNAL*, MAY 14, 1999, ANNA WILDE MATHEWS AND SCOTT MCCARTNEY.

1. Variable costs are costs that vary in total as production levels change. Variable costs remain constant per unit. Common examples of variable costs include direct material and electricity.

2. In the long-run, a company must cover both its variable and fixed costs to be profitable.

3. Ethical issues mentioned in the article include a company selling a product or service below its variable costs in the short-run in order to drive the competition out of business.

ISSUE 2-66

"YEAR OF THE OUTSOURCER," *BUSINESS WEEK*, JANUARY 8, 2001, PETE ENGARDIO AND PETER BURROWS.

1. Outsourcing, with the increased diversity of product offerings, should provide a cushion and result in continued growth, albeit for different reasons than recent history suggests.

2. Although forecasts for consumer electronics point downward, electronics-sector companies like Solectron, Flextronics, and Celestrics still expect to do well. Even though overall demand may slow, financial pressure will force companies like Hewlett-Packard, Lucent, and Motorola to cut costs through outsourcing production while shedding their own factories.

CHAPTER 3
Product Costing and Cost Accumulation in a Batch Production Environment

ANSWERS TO REVIEW QUESTIONS

3-1   (a) Use in financial accounting: In financial accounting, product costs are needed to determine the value of inventory on the balance sheet and to compute the cost-of-goods-sold expense on the income statement.

      (b) Use in managerial accounting: In managerial accounting, product costs are needed for planning, for cost control, and for decision making.

      (c) Use in cost management: In order to manage, control, or reduce the costs of manufacturing products or providing services, management needs a clear idea of what those costs are.

      (d) Use in reporting to interested organizations: Product cost information is used in reporting on relationships between firms and various outside organizations. For example, public utilities such as electric and gas companies record product costs to justify rate increases that must be approved by state regulatory agencies.

3-2   In a job-order costing system, costs are assigned to batches or job orders of production. Job-order costing systems are used by firms that produce relatively small numbers of dissimilar products. In a process-costing system, production costs are averaged over a large number of product units. Process-costing systems are used by firms that produce large numbers of nearly identical products.

3-3   Concepts of product costing are applied in service industry firms to inform management of the costs of producing services. For example, banks record the costs of producing financial services for the purposes of planning, cost control, and decision making.

3-4   a. Material requisition form: A document upon which the production department supervisor requests the release of raw materials for production.

      b. Labor time record: A document upon which employees record the time they spend working on each production job or batch.

c. Job-cost record: A document on which the costs of direct material, direct labor, and manufacturing overhead are recorded for a particular production job or batch. The job-cost sheet is a subsidiary ledger account for the Work-in-Process Inventory account in the general ledger.

3-5   Although manufacturing-overhead costs are not directly traceable to products, manufacturing operations cannot take place without incurring overhead costs. Consequently, overhead costs are applied to products for the purpose of making pricing decisions, in order to ensure that product prices cover all of the costs of production.

3-6   The primary benefit of using a predetermined overhead rate instead of an actual overhead rate is to provide timely information for decision making, planning, and control.

3-7   An advantage of prorating overapplied or underapplied overhead is that it results in the adjustment of all the accounts affected by misestimating the overhead rate. These accounts include the Work-in-Process Inventory account, the Finished-Goods Inventory account, and the Cost of Goods Sold account. The resulting balances in these accounts are more accurate when proration is used than when overapplied or underapplied overhead is closed directly into Cost of Goods Sold. The primary disadvantage of prorating overapplied or underapplied overhead is that it is more complicated and time-consuming than the simpler alternative of closing overapplied or underapplied overhead directly into Cost of Goods Sold.

3-8   An important cost-benefit issue involving accuracy versus timeliness in accounting for overhead involves the use of a predetermined overhead rate or an actual overhead rate. Since an actual overhead rate is computed after costs have been incurred and activity has been recorded, it is more accurate than a predetermined rate. However, a predetermined overhead rate is more timely than an actual rate, since the predetermined rate is computed earlier and in time to be used for making decisions, planning, and controlling operations.

3-9   The difference between actual and normal costing systems involves the procedure for applying manufacturing overhead to Work-in-Process Inventory. Under actual costing, applied overhead is the product of the actual overhead rate (computed at the end of the period) and the actual amount of the cost driver used. Under normal costing, applied overhead is the product of the predetermined overhead rate (computed at the beginning of the period) and the actual amount of the cost driver used.

3-10 When a single volume-based cost driver is used to apply manufacturing overhead, the managerial accountant's primary objective is to select a cost driver that varies in a pattern similar to the pattern in which manufacturing overhead varies. Moreover, if a single cost driver is used, it should be some productive input that is common to all of the firm's products.

3-11 The benefit of using multiple overhead rates is that the resulting product-costing information is more accurate and more useful for decision making than is the information that results from using a single overhead rate. However, the use of multiple cost drivers and overhead rates is more complicated and more costly.

3-12 The development of departmental overhead rates involves a two-stage process. In stage one, overhead costs are assigned to the firm's production departments. First, overhead costs are distributed to all departments, including both service and production departments. Second, costs are allocated from the service departments to the production departments. At the end of stage one, all overhead costs have been assigned to the production departments.

In stage two, the costs that have been accumulated in the production departments are applied to the production jobs that pass through the departments.

3-13 a. Overhead cost distribution: Assignment of all manufacturing-overhead costs to department overhead centers.

b. Service department cost allocation: Allocation of service department costs to production departments on the basis of the relative proportion of each service department's output that is used by the various production departments.

c. Overhead application (or overhead absorption): The assignment of all manufacturing overhead costs accumulated in a production department to the jobs that the department has worked on.

These three processes are used in developing departmental overhead rates.

3-14 Activity-based costing (ABC) is a two-stage process in which overhead costs first are assigned to cost pools associated with significant production-related activities. In the second stage, the costs of each activity are assigned to production jobs in proportion to the consumption of each activity by each job.

3-15 Job-order costing concepts are used in professional service firms. However, rather than referring to production "jobs," such organizations use terminology that reflects their operations. For example, hospitals and law firms assign costs to "cases," and governmental agencies often refer to "programs" or "missions." It is important in such organizations to accumulate the costs of providing the services associated with a case, project, contract, or program. Such cost information is used for planning, cost control, and pricing, among other purposes.

3-16 A cost driver is a characteristic of an event or activity that results in the incurrence of costs by that event or activity. A volume-based cost driver is one that is closely associated with production activity, such as the number of units produced, direct-labor hours, or machine hours.

3-17 When direct material, direct labor, and manufacturing-overhead costs are incurred, they are applied to Work-in-Process Inventory by debiting the account. When goods are finished, the costs are removed from that account with a credit, and they are transferred to Finished-Goods Inventory by debiting that account. Subsequently, when the goods are sold, Finished-Goods Inventory is credited, and the costs are added to Cost of Goods Sold with a debit.

3-18 Hospitals use job-order costing concepts to accumulate the costs associated with each case treated in the hospital. For example, the costs of treating a heart patient would be assigned to that patient's case. These costs would include the hospital room, food and beverages, medications, and specialized services such as diagnostic testing and X rays.

3-19 Some manufacturing firms are switching from direct-labor hours to machine hours or throughput time as the basis for overhead application as a result of increased automation in their factories. With increased automation comes a reduction in the amount of direct labor used in the production process. In such cases, direct labor may cease to be a cost driver that varies in a pattern similar to the way in which manufacturing-overhead costs are incurred.

3-20 Overapplied or underapplied overhead is caused by errors in estimating the predetermined overhead rate. These errors can occur in the numerator (budgeted manufacturing overhead), or in the denominator (budgeted level of the cost driver).

3-21 Overapplied or underapplied overhead can be closed directly into Cost of Goods Sold, or it can be prorated among Work-in-Process Inventory, Finished-Goods Inventory, and Cost of Goods Sold.

3-22 A large retailer could use EDI to exchange such documents as purchase orders, shipping and receiving notices, and invoices electronically with its suppliers. Electronic data interchange (EDI) is the direct exchange of data via a computer-to-computer interface.

3-23 An engineer could use bar code technology to record how she spends her time. Bar codes would be assigned to her and to each of her activities. Each time she arrived at work, left work, or changed activity at work, the engineer would scan her personal bar code and the bar code of the appropriate action or activity. Examples of activities are designing, redesigning, or testing a product; change orders; visiting the factory floor; constructing a prototype; and being trained.

SOLUTIONS TO EXERCISES

EXERCISE 3-24 (10 MINUTES)

1. Process

2. Job-order

3. Job-order (contracts or projects)

4. Process

5. Process

6. Job-order

7. Process

8. Job-order (contracts or projects)

9. Process

10. Job-order

EXERCISE 3-25 (15 MINUTES)

1. $\text{Predetermined overhead rate} = \dfrac{\text{budgeted overhead}}{\text{budgeted production volume}}$

    (a) At 200,000 chicken volume:

    $$\text{Overhead rate} = \frac{\$100,000 + (\$.10)(200,000)}{200,000} = \$.60 \text{ per chicken}$$

    (b) At 300,000 chicken volume:

    $$\text{Overhead rate} = \frac{\$100,000 + (\$.10)(300,000)}{300,000} = \$.43 \text{ per chicken (rounded)}$$

    (c) At 400,000 chicken volume:

    $$\text{Overhead rate} = \frac{\$100,000 + (\$.10)(400,000)}{400,000} = \$.35 \text{ per chicken}$$

EXERCISE 3-25 (CONTINUED)

2. The predetermined overhead rate does not change in proportion to the change in production volume. As production volume increases, the $100,000 of fixed overhead is allocated across a larger activity base. When volume rises by 50%, from 200,000 to 300,000 chickens, the decline in the overhead rate is 28.33% [(.60 − .43)/.60]. When volume rises by 33.33%, from 300,000 to 400,000 chickens, the decline in the overhead rate is 18.6% [(.43 − .35)/.43].

EXERCISE 3-26 (5 MINUTES)

Work-in-Process Inventory...	5,480	
Raw-Material Inventory..		4,600
Wages Payable...		680
Manufacturing Overhead..		200
Finished-Goods Inventory..	5,480	
Work-in-Process Inventory		5,480

EXERCISE 3-27 (30 MINUTES)

Job-order costing is the appropriate product-costing system for feature film production, because a film is a unique production. The production process for each film would use labor, material and support activities (i.e., overhead) in different ways. This would be true of or any type of film (e.g., filming on location, filming in the studio, or using animation).

EXERCISE 3-28 (20 MINUTES)

1.	Raw-material inventory, January 1..	$134,000
	Add: Raw-material purchases	191,000
	Raw material available for use...	$325,000
	Deduct: Raw-material inventory, January 31	124,000
	Raw material used in January	$201,000
	Direct labor	300,000
	Total prime costs incurred in January..	$501,000
2.	Total prime cost incurred in January..	$501,000
	Applied manufacturing overhead (60% × $300,000)......................	180,000
	Total manufacturing cost for January	$681,000

EXERCISE 3-28 (CONTINUED)

3.
Total manufacturing cost for January	$681,000
Add: Work-in-process inventory, January 1	235,000
Subtotal	$916,000
Deduct: Work-in-process inventory, January 31	251,000
Cost of goods manufactured	$665,000

4.
Finished-goods inventory, January 1	$125,000
Add: Cost of goods manufactured	665,000
Cost of goods available for sale	$790,000
Deduct: Finished-goods inventory, January 31	117,000
Cost of goods sold	$673,000

Since the company accumulates overapplied or underapplied overhead until the end of the year, no adjustment is made to cost of goods sold until December 31.

5.
Applied manufacturing overhead for January	$180,000
Actual manufacturing overhead incurred in January	175,000
Overapplied overhead as of January 31	$ 5,000

The balance in the Manufacturing Overhead account on January 31 is a $5,000 credit balance.

EXERCISE 3-29 (15 MINUTES)

1.
$$\text{Applied manufacturing overhead} = \text{total manufacturing costs} \times 30\%$$
$$= \$2,500,000 \times 30\%$$
$$= \$750,000$$

$$\text{Applied manufacturing overhead} = \text{direct-labor cost} \times 80\%$$

$$\text{Direct-labor cost} = \text{applied manufacturing overhead} \div 80\%$$
$$= \$750,000 \div .8$$
$$= \$937,500$$

2.
$$\begin{aligned}
\text{Direct-material cost} &= \text{total manufacturing cost} \\
&\quad - \text{direct labor cost} \\
&\quad - \text{applied manufacturing overhead} \\
&= \$2,500,000 - \$937,500 - \$750,000 \\
&= \$812,500
\end{aligned}$$

3. Let X denote work-in-process inventory on December 31.

Total manufacturing cost	+	work-in-process inventory, Jan.1	–	work-in-process inventory, Dec. 31	=	cost of goods manufactured
$2,500,000	+	.75X	–	X	=	$2,425,000
				.25X	=	$2,500,000 – $2,425,000
				X	=	$300,000

Work-in-process inventory on December 31 amounted to $300,000.

EXERCISE 3-30 (25 MINUTES)

JOB-COST RECORD

Job Number	TB78	Description	teddy bears
Date Started	4/1	Date Completed	4/15

Number of Units Completed   1,000

Direct Material

Date	Requisition Number	Quantity	Unit Price	Cost
4/1	101	400	$.80	$320
4/5	108	500	.30	150

Direct Labor

Date	Time Card Number	Hours	Rate	Cost
4/15	72	500	$12	$6,000

Manufacturing Overhead

Date	Activity Base	Quantity	Application Rate	Cost
4/15	direct-labor hours	500	$2	$1,000

Cost Summary

Cost Item	Amount
Total Direct Material	$ 470
Total Direct Labor	6,000
Total Manufacturing Overhead	1,000
Total Cost	$7,470
Unit Cost	$ 7.47

Shipping Summary

Date	Units Shipped	Units Remaining In Inventory	Cost Balance
4/30	700	300	$2,241*

*300 units remaining in inventory × $7.47 = $2,241

EXERCISE 3-31 (30 MINUTES)

1.

CRUNCHEM CEREAL COMPANY
SCHEDULE OF COST OF GOODS MANUFACTURED
FOR THE YEAR ENDED DECEMBER 31, 20x1

Direct material:

Raw-material inventory, January 1	$ 30,000	
Add: Purchases of raw material	278,000	
Raw material available for use	$308,000	
Deduct: Raw-material inventory, December 31	33,000	
Raw material used		$275,000
Direct labor		120,000
Manufacturing overhead		252,000*
Total manufacturing costs		$647,000
Add: Work-in-process inventory, January 1		39,000
Subtotal		$686,000
Deduct: Work-in-process inventory, December 31		42,900
Cost of goods manufactured		$643,100

*Applied manufacturing overhead is $252,000 ($120,000 × 210%). Actual manufacturing overhead is also $252,000, so there is no overapplied or underapplied overhead.

2.

Finished-goods inventory, January 1	$ 42,000
Add: Cost of goods manufactured	643,100
Cost of goods available for sale	$685,100
Deduct: Finished-goods inventory, December 31	46,200
Cost of goods sold	$638,900

EXERCISE 3-32 (20 MINUTES)

1.

Raw-Material Inventory	
227,000	
	174,000
53,000	

Work-in-Process Inventory	
18,000	
174,000	
324,000	
180,000	
	120,000
576,000	

Wages Payable	
	324,000

Manufacturing Overhead	
180,000	

Finished-Goods Inventory	
30,000	
120,000	
	132,000
18,000	

Sales Revenue	
	195,000

Accounts Receivable	
195,000	

Cost of Goods Sold	
132,000	

2.

REIMEL FURNITURE COMPANY, INC.
PARTIAL BALANCE SHEET
AS OF DECEMBER 31, 20X2

Current assets
Cash.. XXX
Accounts receivable... XXX
Inventory
    Raw material .... $ 53,000
    Work in process.. 576,000
    Finished goods 18,000

REIMEL FURNITURE COMPANY, INC.
PARTIAL INCOME STATEMENT
FOR THE YEAR ENDED DECEMBER 31, 20X2

Sales revenue $195,000
Less: Cost of goods sold.. 132,000
Gross margin .... $ 63,000

EXERCISE 3-33 (20 MINUTES)

1. Raw material:

Beginning inventory...	$ 71,000
Add: Purchases	?
Deduct: Raw material used	326,000
Ending inventory	$ 81,000
Therefore, purchases for the year were.................................	$336,000

2. Direct labor:

Total manufacturing cost..	$686,000
Deduct: Direct material	326,000
Direct labor and manufacturing overhead	360,000

Direct labor + manufacturing overhead	=	$360,000
Direct labor + (60%) (direct labor)	=	$360,000
(160%) (direct labor)	=	$360,000
Direct labor	=	$\dfrac{\$360,000}{1.6}$
Direct labor	=	$225,000

3. Cost of goods manufactured:

Work in process, beginning inventory	$ 80,000
Add: Total manufacturing costs	686,000
Deduct: Cost of goods manufactured.......................................	?
Work in process, ending inventory	$ 30,000
Therefore, cost of goods manufactured was...........................	$736,000

EXERCISE 3-33 (CONTINUED)

4. Cost of goods sold:

Finished goods, beginning inventory	$ 90,000
Add: Cost of goods manufactured	736,000
Deduct: Cost of goods sold	?
Finished goods, ending inventory	$110,000
Therefore, cost of goods sold was	$716,000

EXERCISE 3-34 (20 MINUTES)

Calculation of proration amounts:

Account	Amount	Percentage	Calculation of Percentage
Work in Process...........................	$ 35,250	25%	35,250 ÷ $141,000
Finished Goods............................	49,350	35%	49,350 ÷ $141,000
Cost of Goods Sold	56,400	40%	56,400 ÷ $141,000
Total..	$141,000	100%	

Account	Underapplied Overhead	x	Percentage	Amount Added to Account
Work in Process...........................	$16,000*	x	25%	$4,000
Finished Goods............................	16,000	x	35%	5,600
Cost of Goods Sold	16,000	x	40%	6,400

*Underapplied overhead = actual overhead – applied overhead
        $16,000 = $157,000 – $141,000

Journal entry:

Work-in-Process Inventory...	4,000	
Finished-Goods Inventory..	5,600	
Cost of Goods Sold...	6,400	
Manufacturing Overhead		16,000

© *2002 The McGraw-Hill Companies, Inc.*
Solutions Manual

EXERCISE 3-35 (15 MINUTES)

1. Predetermined overhead rate $= \dfrac{\$997,500}{75,000 \text{ hours}} = \$13.30$ per hour

2. To compute actual manufacturing overhead:

Depreciation		$ 231,000
Property taxes		21,000
Indirect labor		82,000
Supervisory salaries		200,000
Utilities		59,000
Insurance		30,000
Rental of space		300,000
Indirect material:		
Beginning inventory, January 1	$ 48,000	
Add: Purchases	94,000	
Indirect material available for use	$142,000	
Deduct: Ending inventory, December 31	63,000	
Indirect material used		79,000
Actual manufacturing overhead		$1,002,000

$$\begin{matrix} \text{Overapplied} \\ \text{overhead} \end{matrix} = \begin{matrix} \text{actual} \\ \text{manufacturing} \\ \text{overhead} \end{matrix} - \begin{matrix} \text{applied} \\ \text{manufacturing} \\ \text{overhead} \end{matrix}$$

$$= \$1,002,000 - (\$13.30 \times 80,000^*) = \$62,000$$

*Actual direct-labor hours.

3.

Manufacturing Overhead	62,000	
Cost of Goods Sold		62,000

EXERCISE 3-36 (20 MINUTES)

1. Predetermined overhead rate $= \dfrac{\text{budgeted manufacturing overhead}}{\text{budgeted level of cost driver}}$

   (a) $\dfrac{\$364,000}{10,000 \text{ machine hours}}$ = $36.40 per machine hour

   (b) $\dfrac{\$364,000}{20,000 \text{ direct-labor hours}}$ = $18.20 per direct-labor hour

   (c) $\dfrac{\$364,000}{\$280,000^*}$ = $1.30 per direct-labor dollar or 130% of direct-labor cost

*Budgeted direct-labor cost = 20,000 × $14

2. | Actual manufacturing overhead | – | applied manufacturing overhead | = | overapplied or underapplied overhead |

   (a) $340,000 – (11,000)($36.40) = $60,400 overapplied overhead

   (b) $340,000 – (18,000)($18.20) = $12,400 underapplied overhead

   (c) $340,000 – ($270,000[†])(130%) = $11,000 overapplied overhead

[†]Actual direct-labor cost = 18,000 × $15

EXERCISE 3-37 (5 MINUTES)

1. Work-in-Process Inventory.. 340,000
      Manufacturing Overhead...   340,000

2. Work-in-Process Inventory.. 400,400
      Manufacturing Overhead...   400,400

EXERCISE 3-38 (10 MINUTES)

Budgeted overhead rate = budgeted overhead / budgeted direct professional labor

$$160\% = 400{,}000DM / 250{,}000DM$$

Contract to redecorate mayor's offices:

Direct material	3,500DM
Direct professional labor	6,000DM
Overhead (160% × $6,000)	9,600DM
Total contract cost	19,100DM

EXERCISE 3-39 (15 MINUTES)

1.   Memorandum

Date: Today

To: President

From: I.M. Student

Subject: Cost driver for overhead application

I recommend direct-labor hours as the best volume-based cost driver upon which to base the application of manufacturing overhead. Since our products are made by hand, direct labor is a very significant production input. Moreover, the incurrence of manufacturing overhead cost appears to be related to the use of direct labor.

EXERCISE 3-39 (CONTINUED)

2.

Memorandum

Date: Today

To: President

From: I.M. Student

Subject: Cost driver for overhead application

I recommend either machine hours or units of production as the most appropriate cost driver for the application of manufacturing overhead. Since our production process is highly automated, machine hours are the most significant production input. Also, our chips are nearly identical, so the amount of overhead incurred in their production does not vary much across product lines. The incurrence of manufacturing overhead cost appears to be related closely both to machine time and units of production.

EXERCISE 3-40 (15 MINUTES)

Work-in-Process Inventory: Tanning Department............................	6,000[a]	
Manufacturing Overhead		6,000

    [a] $6,000 = 100$ sq. ft. per set $\times$ 20 sets $\times$ \$3 per sq. ft.

Work-in-Process Inventory: Assembly Department.........................	540[b]	
Manufacturing Overhead		540

    [b] $540 = 3$ machine hours $\times$ 20 sets $\times$ \$9 per machine hour.

Work-in-Process Inventory: Saddle Department	3,200[c]	
Manufacturing Overhead		3,200

    [c] $3,200 = 40$ direct-labor hours $\times$ 20 sets $\times$ \$4 per direct-labor hour.

EXERCISE 3-41 (10 MINUTES)

Overhead distribution: Allocation of the hospital's building maintenance and custodial costs to all of the hospital's departments.

Service-department cost allocation: Allocation of the hospital's Personnel Department costs to the direct-patient-care departments in the hospital.

Overhead application: Assignment of the overhead costs in the maternity ward to each patient-day of care provided to new mothers.

EXERCISE 3-42 (20 MINUTES)

There are many key activities that can be suggested for each business. Some possibilities are listed below. After each activity, a suggested cost driver is given in parentheses.

(1) airline:
- (a) reservations (reservations booked)
- (b) baggage handling (pieces of baggage handled)
- (c) flight crew operations (air miles flown)
- (d) aircraft operations (air miles flown)
- (e) in-flight service (number of passengers)

(2) restaurant
- (a) purchasing (pounds or cost of food purchased)
- (b) kitchen operations (meals prepared)
- (c) table service (meals served)
- (d) table clearing (meals served)
- (e) dish washing (dishes washed)

(3) fitness club:
- (a) front desk operations (number of patrons)
- (b) membership records (number of records)
- (c) personnel (number of employees)
- (d) equipment maintenance (maintenance hours)
- (e) fitness consultation (hours of service)

(4) bank:
- (a) teller window operations (number of customers)
- (b) loan processing (loan applications)
- (c) check processing (checks processed)
- (d) personnel (number of employees)
- (e) security (number of customers)

(5) hotel: (a) front desk operations (number of guests)
                     (b) bell service (pieces of luggage handled)
                     (c) housekeeping service (number of guest-days)
                     (d) room service (meals delivered)
                     (e) telephone service (phone calls made)

(6) hospital: (a) admissions (patients admitted)
                     (b) diagnostic lab (tests performed)
                     (c) nursing (nursing hours)
                     (d) surgery (hours in operating room)
                     (e) general patient care (patient-days of care)

SOLUTIONS TO PROBLEMS

PROBLEM 3-43 (45 MINUTES)

1.

TWISTO PRETZEL COMPANY
SCHEDULE OF COST OF GOODS MANUFACTURED
FOR THE YEAR ENDED DECEMBER 31, 20x1

Direct material:		
Raw-material inventory, 12/31/x0	$10,100	
Add: Purchases of raw material	39,000	
Raw material available for use..	$49,100	
Deduct: Raw-material inventory, 12/31/x1........................	11,000	
Raw material used..		$38,100
Direct labor		79,000
Manufacturing overhead:		
Indirect material	$ 4,900	
Indirect labor	29,000	
Depreciation on factory building....................................	3,800	
Depreciation on factory equipment................................	2,100	
Utilities	6,000	
Property taxes	2,400	
Insurance	3,600	
Rental of warehouse space..	3,100	
Total actual manufacturing overhead	$54,900	
Add: Overapplied overhead*	3,100	
Overhead applied to work in process		58,000
Total manufacturing costs		$175,100
Add: Work-in-process inventory, 12/31/x0		8,100
Subtotal...		$183,200
Deduct: Work-in-process inventory, 12/31/x1		8,300
Cost of goods manufactured		$174,900

*The Schedule of Cost of Goods Manufactured lists the manufacturing costs applied to work in process. Therefore, the overapplied overhead, $3,100, must be added to total actual overhead to arrive at the amount of overhead applied to work in process. If there had been underapplied overhead, the balance would have been deducted from total actual manufacturing overhead. The amount of overapplied overhead is found by subtracting actual overhead, $54,900 (as computed above), from applied overhead, $58,000 (given).

PROBLEM 3-43 (CONTINUED)

2.

TWISTO PRETZEL COMPANY
SCHEDULE OF COST OF GOODS SOLD
FOR THE YEAR ENDED DECEMBER 31, 20X1

Finished-goods inventory, 12/31/x0	$ 14,000
Add: Cost of goods manufactured*	174,900
Cost of goods available for sale..	$188,900
Deduct: Finished-goods inventory, 12/31/x1......................................	15,400
Cost of goods sold..	$173,500
Deduct: Overapplied overhead†	3,100
Cost of goods sold (adjusted for overapplied overhead)	$170,400

*The cost of goods manufactured is obtained from the Schedule of Cost of Goods Manufactured.

†The company closes underapplied or overapplied overhead into cost of goods sold. Hence, the balance in overapplied overhead is deducted from cost of goods sold for the month.

3.

TWISTO PRETZEL COMPANY
INCOME STATEMENT
FOR THE YEAR ENDED DECEMBER 31, 20X1

Sales revenue		$205,800
Less: Cost of goods sold		170,400
Gross margin..		$ 35,400
Selling and administrative expenses:		
Salaries..	$13,800	
Utilities	2,500	
Depreciation	1,200	
Rental of office space.............................	1,700	
Other expenses	4,000	
Total...		23,200
Income before taxes		$12,200
Income tax expense..		5,100
Net income..		$ 7,100

PROBLEM 3-44 (20 MINUTES)

1. $$\text{Predetermined overhead rate} = \frac{\text{budgeted manufacturing overhead}}{\text{budgeted direct-labor hours}}$$

$$= \frac{\$240,000}{(2,000)(10)} = \$12 \text{ per hour}$$

2. Journal entries:

(a)	Raw-Material Inventory	33,000	
	Accounts Payable..		33,000
(b)	Work-in-Process Inventory	460	
	Raw-Material Inventory		460
(c)	Manufacturing Overhead	100	
	Manufacturing-Supplies Inventory		100
(d)	Manufacturing Overhead	8,000	
	Accumulated Depreciation: Building		8,000
(e)	Manufacturing Overhead	400	
	Cash..		400
(f)	Work-in-Process Inventory	34,000	
	Wages Payable		34,000

To record direct-labor cost.

Work-in-Process Inventory	20,400	
Manufacturing Overhead.................................		20,400

To apply manufacturing overhead to work in process ($20,400 = 1,700 × $12 per hour).

(g)	Manufacturing Overhead	910	
	Property Taxes Payable....................................		910
(h)	Manufacturing Overhead	2,500	
	Wages Payable		2,500
(i)	Finished-Goods Inventory	14,400	
	Work-in-Process Inventory...............................		14,400

PROBLEM 3-44 (CONTINUED)

(j) Accounts Receivable...   13,500

         Sales Revenue   13,500

    Cost of Goods Sold 10,800*

         Finished-Goods Inventory.................................   10,800

*$10,800 = (9/12)($14,400)

PROBLEM 3-45 (25 MINUTES)

The completed T-accounts are shown below.

Raw-Material Inventory

Bal. 1/1	21,000	
	135,000	120,000
Bal. 12/31	36,000	

Accounts Payable

		2,500 Bal. 1/1
136,500	135,000	
	1,000 Bal. 12/31	

Work-in-Process Inventory

Bal. 1/1	17,000	
Direct material	120,000	
Direct labor	150,000	718,000
Mfg. overhead	450,000	
Bal. 12/31	19,000	

Finished-Goods Inventory

Bal. 1/1	12,000	
	718,000	710,000
Bal. 12/31	20,000	

Manufacturing Overhead

452,500	450,000

Cost of Goods Sold

710,000	

Wages Payable

	2,000 Bal. 1/1
147,000	150,000
	5,000 Bal. 12/31

Sales Revenue

	810,000

Accounts Receivable

Bal. 1/1	11,000	
	810,000	806,000
Bal. 12/31	15,000	

PROBLEM 3-46 (35 MINUTES)

1. Predetermined overhead rate = budgeted overhead ÷ budgeted machine hours
   = $840,000 ÷ 16,000 = $52.50 per machine hour

2. (a)

Work-in-Process Inventory..	80,000*	
Raw-Material Inventory		80,000
Work-in-Process Inventory..	130,800**	
Wages Payable		130,800

* $21,000 + $44,000 + $15,000 = $80,000
** $35,000 + $22,000 + $65,000 + $8,800 = $130,800

(b)

Manufacturing Overhead	238,500	
Accumulated Depreciation..		34,000
Wages Payable		60,000
Manufacturing Supplies Inventory ..		5,000
Miscellaneous Accounts		139,500

(c)

Work-in-Process Inventory..	231,000*	
Manufacturing Overhead		231,000

* (1,200 + 700 + 2,000 + 500) x $52.50 = $231,000

(d)

Finished-Goods Inventory...	315,250*	
Work-in-Process Inventory..		315,250

* Job 64: $84,000 + $21,000 + $35,000 + (1,200 x $52.50) = $203,000
  Job 65: $53,500 + $22,000 + (700 x $52.50) = $112,250
  $315,250 = $203,000 + $112,250

(e)

Accounts Receivable	146,950*	
Sales Revenue		146,950

* $112,250 + $34,700 = $146,950

Cost of Goods Sold..	112,250	
Finished-Goods Inventory...		112,250

3. Job no. 66 and no. 67 are in production as of March 31:

Job 66: $44,000 + $65,000 + (2,000 x $52.50)	$214,000
Job 67: $15,000 + $8,800 + (500 x $52.50)	50,050
Total	$264,050

PROBLEM 3-46 (CONTINUED)

4. Finished-goods inventory increased by $203,000 ($315,250 - $112,250).

5. The company's actual overhead amounted to $238,500, whereas applied overhead totaled $231,000. Thus, overhead was underapplied by $7,500.

PROBLEM 3-47 (35 MINUTES)

1. Predetermined overhead rate = budgeted overhead ÷ budgeted direct-labor cost
    = $5,460,000 ÷ $4,200,000 = 130% of direct labor cost

2. Additions (debits) total $15,605,000 [$5,600,000 + $4,350,000 + ($4,350,000 x 130%)].

3. The finished-goods inventory consisted of job no. 2143, which cost $351,500 [$156,000 + $85,000 + ($85,000 x 130%)].

4. Since there is no work in process at year-end, all amounts in the Work-in-Process account must be transferred to Finished-Goods Inventory. Thus:

    Finished-Goods Inventory 15,761,800*
        Work-in-Process Inventory...........................   15,761,800

    *Beginning balance in Work-in-Process Inventory + additions to the account:
    $156,800 + $15,605,000 = $15,761,800

5. Connelly's applied overhead totals 130% of direct-labor cost, or $5,655,000 ($4,350,000 x 130%). Actual overhead was $5,554,000, itemized as follows, resulting in overapplied overhead of $101,000.

Indirect materials used...	$ 65,000
Indirect labor..	2,860,000
Factory depreciation	1,740,000
Factory insurance...	59,000
Factory utilities	830,000
Total	$5,554,000

    Manufacturing Overhead 101,000
        Cost of Goods Sold......................................   101,000

PROBLEM 3-47 (CONTINUED)

6. The company's cost of goods sold totals $15,309,300:

Finished-goods inventory, Jan. 1................	$	0
Add: Cost of goods manufactured.............		15,761,800
Cost of goods available for sale.................		$15,761,800
Less: Finished-goods inventory, Dec. 31.....		351,500
Unadjusted cost of goods sold..................		$15,410,300
Less: Overapplied overhead......................		101,000
Cost of goods sold..................................		$15,309,300

7. No, selling and administrative expenses are operating expenses of the firm and are treated as period costs rather than product costs. Such costs are unrelated to manufacturing overhead and cost of goods sold.

PROBLEM 3-48 (30 MINUTES)

1. Traceable costs total $2,500,000, computed as follows:

	Total Cost	Percent Traceable	Traceable Cost
Professional staff salaries.........	$2,500,000	80%	$2,000,000
Administrative support staff......	300,000	60	180,000
Travel.....................................	250,000	90	225,000
Photocopying...........................	50,000	90	45,000
Other operating costs...............	100,000	50	50,000
Total.................................	$3,200,000		$2,500,000

HDK's overhead (i.e., the nontraceable costs) total $700,000 ($3,200,000 - $2,500,000).

2. Predetermined overhead rate = budgeted overhead ÷ traceable costs
    = $700,000 ÷ $2,500,000 = 28% of traceable costs

3. Target profit percentage = target profit ÷ total cost
    = $640,000 ÷ $3,200,000 = 20% of cost

PROBLEM 3-48 (CONTINUED)

4. The total cost of the Martin Manufacturing project is $64,000, and the billing is $76,800, as follows:

Professional staff salaries................	$41,000
Administrative support staff.........	2,600
Travel...................................	4,500
Photocopying............................	500
Other operating costs...................	1,400
Subtotal.............................	$50,000
Overhead ($50,000 x 28%).............	14,000
Total cost.............................	$64,000
Markup ($64,000 x 20%)................	12,800
Billing to Martin........................	$76,800

5. Possible nontraceable costs include utilities, rent, depreciation, advertising, top management salaries, and insurance.

6. Professional staff members are compensated for attending training sessions and firm-wide planning meetings, paid vacations, and completion of general, non-client-related paperwork and reports. These activities benefit multiple clients, the consultant, and/or the overall firm, making traceability to specific clients difficult if not impossible.

PROBLEM 3-49 (30 MINUTES)

1. Machining Dept. overhead rate = budgeted overhead ÷ budgeted machine hours
= $4,000,000 ÷ 400,000 = $10 per machine hour

Assembly Dept. overhead rate = budgeted overhead ÷ budgeted direct-labor cost
= $3,080,000 ÷ $5,600,000 = 55% of direct-labor cost

PROBLEM 3-49 (CONTINUED)

2. The ending work-in-process inventory is carried at a cost of $153,530, computed as follows:

Machining Department:			
	Direct material..	$24,500	
	Direct labor...	27,900	
	Manufacturing overhead (360 x $10)............	3,600	$ 56,000
Assembly Department:			
	Direct material..	$ 6,700	
	Direct labor...	58,600	
	Manufacturing overhead ($58,600 x 55%).....	32,230	97,530
	Total cost..		$153,530

3. Actual overhead in the Machining Department amounted to $4,260,000, whereas applied overhead totaled $4,250,000 (425,000 hours x $10). Thus, overhead was underapplied by $10,000 during the year.

4. Actual overhead in the Assembly Department amounted to $3,050,000, whereas applied overhead totaled $3,179,000 ($5,780,000 x 55%). Thus, overhead was overapplied by $129,000.

5. The company's manufacturing overhead was overapplied by $119,000 ($129,000 - $10,000). As a result, excessive overhead flowed from Work-in-Process Inventory, to Finished-Goods Inventory, to Cost of Goods Sold, meaning that the Cost of Goods Sold account must be decreased at year-end.

6. The Work-in-Process account is charged with applied overhead, or $7,429,000 ($4,250,000 + $3,179,000).

7. The firm's selection of cost drivers (or application bases) seems appropriate. There should be a strong correlation between the cost driver and the amount of overhead incurred. In the Machining Department, much of the overhead is probably related to the operation of machines. Similarly, in the Assembly Department, a considerable portion of the overhead incurred is related to manual assembly (i.e., labor) operations.

PROBLEM 3-50 (25 MINUTES)

1. Predetermined overhead rate $= \dfrac{\text{budgeted manufacturing overhead}}{\text{budgeted machine hours}}$

    $= \dfrac{\$1,464,000}{73,200} = \$20 \text{ per machine hour}$

2. Journal entries:

(a)	Raw-Material Inventory.....................................	7,850	
	Accounts Payable.....................................		7,850
(b)	Work-in-Process Inventory.............................	180	
	Raw-Material Inventory.............................		180
(c)	Manufacturing Overhead...............................	30	
	Manufacturing-Supplies Inventory..........		30
(d)	Manufacturing Overhead...............................	800	
	Cash...		800
(e)	Work-in-Process Inventory.............................	75,000	
	Wages Payable...		75,000
(f)	Selling and Administrative Expense	1,800	
	Prepaid Insurance.....................................		1,800
(g)	Raw-Material Inventory.....................................	3,000	
	Accounts Payable.....................................		3,000
(h)	Accounts Payable	1,700	
	Cash...		1,700
(i)	Manufacturing Overhead...............................	21,000	
	Wages Payable...		21,000
(j)	Manufacturing Overhead...............................	7,000	
	Accumulated Depreciation: Equipment..		7,000
(k)	Finished-Goods Inventory	1,100	
	Work-in-Process Inventory.....................		1,100

PROBLEM 3-50 (CONTINUED)

(l)	Work-in-Process Inventory	140,000*	
	Manufacturing Overhead		140,000

*Applied manufacturing overhead = 7,000 machine hours × $20 per hour.

(m)	Accounts Receivable..	176,000	
	Sales Revenue		176,000
	Cost of Goods Sold	139,000	
	Finished-Goods Inventory		139,000

PROBLEM 3-51 (45 MINUTES)

1.
HURON CORPORATION
SCHEDULE OF COST OF GOODS MANUFACTURED
FOR THE YEAR ENDED DECEMBER 31, 20X2

Direct material:

Raw material inventory, 12/31/x1.........................	$ 89,000	
Add: Purchases of raw material	731,000	
Raw material available for use............................	$820,000	
Deduct: Raw-material inventory, 12/31/x2	59,000	
Raw material used..		$761,000
Direct labor		474,000
Manufacturing overhead:		
Indirect material	$ 45,000	
Indirect labor	150,000	
Depreciation on factory building..........................	125,000	
Depreciation on factory equipment......................	60,000	
Utilities	70,000	
Property taxes	90,000	
Insurance	40,000	
Total actual manufacturing overhead............	$580,000	
Deduct: Underapplied overhead*...................	2,500	
Overhead applied to work in process..................		577,500
Total manufacturing costs		$1,812,500
Add: Work-in-process inventory, 12/31/x1		-0-
Subtotal..		$1,812,500
Deduct: Work-in-process inventory, 12/31/x2		40,000
Cost of goods manufactured		$1,772,500

*The Schedule of Cost of Goods Manufactured lists the manufacturing costs applied to work in process. Therefore, the underapplied overhead, $2,500, must be deducted from total actual overhead to arrive at the amount of overhead applied to work in process. If there had been overapplied overhead, the balance would have been added to total manufacturing overhead.

The amount of underapplied overhead is found by subtracting the applied manufacturing overhead, $577,500, from the total actual manufacturing overhead, $580,000.

PROBLEM 3-51 (CONTINUED)

2.
HURON CORPORATION
SCHEDULE OF COST OF GOODS SOLD
FOR THE YEAR ENDED DECEMBER 31, 20X2

Finished-goods inventory, 12/31/x1	$ 35,000
Add: cost of goods manufactured..	1,772,500
Cost of goods available for sale...	$1,807,500
Deduct: Finished-goods inventory, 12/31/x2...	40,000
Cost of goods sold..	$1,767,500
Add: Underapplied overhead*...	2,500
Cost of goods sold (adjusted for underapplied overhead)......................	$1,770,000

*The company closes underapplied or overapplied overhead into cost of goods sold. Hence the $2,500 balance in underapplied overhead is added to cost of goods sold for the month.

3.
HURON CORPORATION
INCOME STATEMENT
FOR THE YEAR ENDED DECEMBER 31, 20X2

Sales revenue	$2,105,000
Less: Cost of goods sold..	1,770,000
Gross margin	$ 335,000
Selling and administrative expenses	269,000
Income before taxes...	$ 66,000
Income tax expense	25,000
Net income	$ 41,000

PROBLEM 3-52 (15 MINUTES)

1. $40,000. Since there was no work-in-process inventory at the beginning of 20x2, all of the costs in the year-end work-in-process inventory were incurred during 20x2.

2. The direct-material cost would have been larger, probably by roughly 20 percent, because direct material is a variable cost.

3. Depreciation is a fixed cost, so it would not have been any larger if the firm's volume had increased.

PROBLEM 3-52 (CONTINUED)

4.   Only the $30,000 of equipment depreciation would have been included in manufacturing overhead on the Schedule of Cost of Goods Manufactured. The $30,000 of depreciation related to selling and administrative equipment would have been treated as a period cost and expensed during 20x2.

PROBLEM 3-53 (30 MINUTES)

1.

MARCO POLO MAP COMPANY
SCHEDULE OF COST OF GOODS MANUFACTURED
FOR THE MONTH OF MARCH

Direct material:		
Raw-material inventory, March 1	$ 17,000	
Add: March purchases of raw material	113,000	
Raw material available for use	$130,000	
Deduct: Raw-material inventory, March 31	26,000	
Raw materials used		$104,000
Direct labor		160,000*
Manufacturing overhead applied (50% of direct labor)		80,000
Total manufacturing costs		$344,000
Add: Work-in-process inventory, March 1		40,000
Subtotal		$384,000
Deduct: Work-in-process inventory,		
March 31 (90% × $40,000)		36,000
Cost of goods manufactured		$348,000†

*Work upward from the bottom of the statement, using the information available. Direct labor + manufacturing overhead = total manufacturing costs – direct material cost = $344,000
– $104,000 = $240,000. Since manufacturing overhead = 50% of direct labor, then manufacturing overhead = $80,000 and direct labor = $160,000.

†Cost of goods manufactured = cost of goods sold + increase in finished-goods inventory = $345,000 + $3,000 = $348,000.

PROBLEM 3-53 (CONTINUED)

2.

MARCO POLO MAP COMPANY
SCHEDULE OF PRIME COSTS
FOR THE MONTH OF MARCH

Raw material:
Beginning inventory	$ 17,000
Add: Purchases	113,000
Raw material available for use	$130,000
Deduct: Ending inventory	26,000
Raw material used	$104,000
Direct labor	160,000
Total prime costs	$264,000

3.

MARCO POLO MAP COMPANY
SCHEDULE OF CONVERSION COSTS
FOR THE MONTH OF MARCH

Direct labor	$160,000
Manufacturing overhead applied (50% of direct labor)	80,000
Total conversion cost	$240,000

PROBLEM 3-54 (30 MINUTES)

1. $$\text{Predetermined overhead rate} = \frac{\text{budgeted manufacturing overhead}}{\text{budgeted machine hours}}$$

$$= \frac{\$235,000}{47,000} = \$5 \text{ per machine hour}$$

2. Calculation of applied manufacturing overhead:

Applied manufacturing overhead = machine hrs. used x predetermined overhead rate
$20,000 = 4,000 hrs. x $5 per hr.

3.

Underapplied overhead	=	actual overhead – applied overhead
$6,000	=	$26,000 – $20,000

4.
Cost of Goods Sold	6,000	
Manufacturing Overhead		6,000

PROBLEM 3-54 (CONTINUED)

5. (a) Calculation of proration amounts:

Account	Explanation	Amount*	Percentage	Calculation of Percentage
Work in Process	Job P82 only	$ 2,500	12.5%	2,500 ÷ 20,000
Finished Goods	Job N08 only	12,500	62.5%	12,500 ÷ 20,000
Cost of Goods Sold	Job A79 only	5,000	25.0%	5,000 ÷ 20,000
Total		$20,000	100.0%	

*Machine hours used on job × predetermined overhead rate.

Account	Underapplied Overhead	×	Percentage	Amount Added to Account
Work in Process	$6,000	×	12.5%	$ 750
Finished Goods	6,000	×	62.5%	3,750
Cost of Goods Sold	6,000	×	25.0%	1,500
Total				$6,000

(b) Journal entry:

Work-in-Process Inventory	750	
Finished-Goods Inventory..	3,750	
Cost of Goods Sold..	1,500	
Manufacturing Overhead		6,000

PROBLEM 3-55 (40 MINUTES)

1. In accordance with the Standards of Ethical Conduct for Management Accountants, the appropriateness of Marc Jackson's three alternative courses of action is described as follows:

- *Follow Brown's directive and do nothing further.* This action is inappropriate as Jackson has ethical responsibilities to take further action in accordance with the following standards of ethical conduct.

Competence. Management accountants have a responsibility to perform their professional duties in accordance with relevant laws, regulations, and technical standards.

Integrity. Management accountants should (1) refrain from either actively or passively subverting the attainment of the organization's legitimate and ethical objectives, (2) communicate favorable as well as unfavorable information, and (3) refrain from engaging in or supporting any activity that would discredit the profession.

Objectivity. Management accountants have a responsibility to communicate information fairly and objectively, and to disclose fully all relevant information that could reasonably be expected to influence an intended user's understanding of the reports presented.

- *Attempt to convince Brown to make the proper adjustments and to advise the external auditors of her actions.* This action is appropriate as Jackson has taken the ethical conflict to his immediate superior for resolution. Unless Jackson suspects that his superior is involved, this alternative is the first step for the resolution of an ethical conflict.

- *Tell the Audit Committee of the Board of Directors about the problem and give them the appropriate accounting data.* This action is not appropriate as a first step since the resolution of ethical conflicts requires Jackson to first discuss the matter with his immediate superior.

2. The next step that Jackson should take in resolving this conflict is to inform Brown that he is planning to discuss the conflict with the next higher managerial level. Jackson should pursue discussions with successively higher levels of management, including the Audit Committee and the Board of Directors, until the matter is satisfactorily resolved. At the same time, Jackson should "clarify relevant concepts by confidential discussion with an objective advisor to obtain an understanding of possible courses of action." If the ethical conflict still exists after exhausting all levels of internal review, Jackson may have no course other than to resign from the organization.

PROBLEM 3-56 (25 MINUTES)

1.

Quarter	Predetermined Overhead Rate	Calculations
1st	$4 per hour	$100,000/25,000
2nd	5 per hour	$80,000/16,000
3rd	4 per hour	$50,000/12,500
4th	5 per hour	$70,000/14,000

2.

	January	April
Direct material	$100	$100
Direct labor	300	300
Manufacturing overhead:		
20 hrs × $4 per hr	80	
20 hrs × $5 per hr		100
Total cost	$480	$500

3.

	January	April
Total cost	$480	$500
Markup (10%)	48	50
Price	$528	$550

4. Predetermined rate $= \dfrac{\text{annual budgeted manufacturing overhead}}{\text{annual budgeted direct-labor hours}}$

$= \dfrac{\$300,000}{67,500} = \$4.44$ per hour (rounded)

5.

	January	April
Direct material	$100.00	$100.00
Direct labor	300.00	300.00
Manufacturing overhead (20 hrs × $4.44)	88.80	88.80
Total cost	$488.80	$488.80

PROBLEM 3-56 (CONTINUED)

6.

Total cost...	$488.80
Markup (10%)	48.88
Price...	$537.68

Notice that with quarterly overhead rates, the firm may underprice its product in January and overprice it in April.

PROBLEM 3-57 (45 MINUTES)

1. Predetermined overhead rate:

$$\frac{\text{Budgeted manufacturing overhead}}{\text{Budgeted direct-labor hours}} = \frac{\$606,000^*}{120,000}$$

$$= \$5.05 \text{ per direct-labor hour}$$

*$606,000 = $390,000 + $216,000

2. Cost of job 77:

Cost in beginning work-in-process inventory	$ 54,000
Direct material..	45,000
Direct labor (3,500 hours × $6.00 per hour)*	21,000
Applied manufacturing overhead	
(3,500 hours × $5.05 per hour)	17,675
Total cost..	$137,675

$$\text{*Direct-labor rate} = \frac{\text{direct-labor wages}}{\text{direct-labor hours}} = \frac{\$51,000}{8,500} = \$6.00 \text{ per hour}$$

3. Manufacturing overhead applied to job 79:

Direct-labor hours × predetermined overhead rate = 2,000 hours × $5.05 per hour

= $10,100

PROBLEM 3-57 (CONTINUED)

4.   Total manufacturing overhead applied during November:

     Total direct-labor hours × predetermined overhead rate = 8,500 hours × $5.05

                                                            = $42,925

5.   Actual manufacturing overhead incurred during November:

Indirect material (supplies)	$12,000
Indirect-labor wages	15,000
Supervisory salaries	6,000
Building occupancy costs, factory facilities	6,400
Production equipment costs...	8,100
Total..	$47,500

6.   Underapplied overhead for November:

     Actual manufacturing overhead – applied manufacturing overhead

        = $47,500 – $42,925

        = $4,575 underapplied

PROBLEM 3-58 (45 MINUTES)

1.   Former product-costing system: traditional system based on a single, volume-related cost driver.

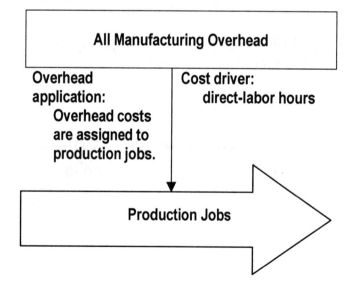

PROBLEM 3-58 (CONTINUED)

2.   Current product-costing system: departmental overhead rates based on different cost drivers.

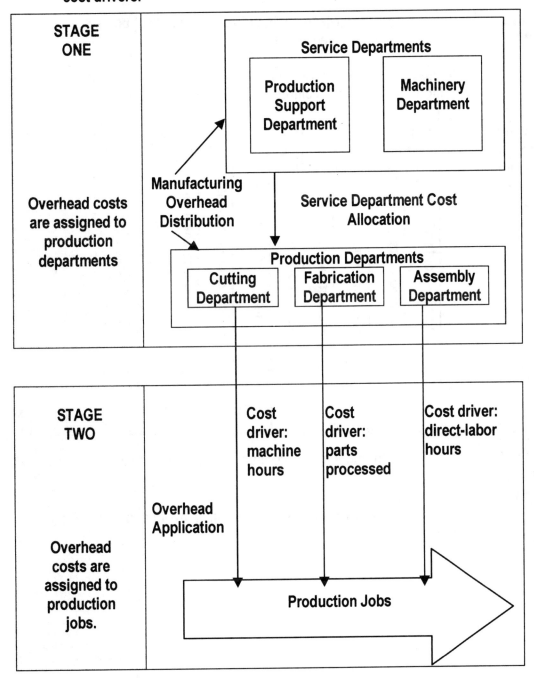

PROBLEM 3-58 (CONTINUED)

3.   Contemplated product-costing system: activity-based costing.

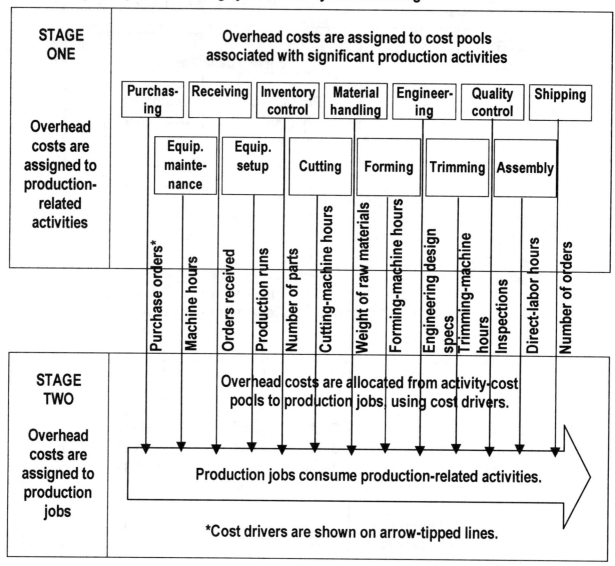

PROBLEM 3-59 (75 MINUTES)

1. Predetermined overhead rate $= \dfrac{\text{budgeted manufacturing overhead}}{\text{budgeted direct - labor hours}}$

    $= \dfrac{\$426,300}{20,300} = \$21$ per direct - labor hour

2. Journal entries:

    (a) Raw-Material Inventory 5,000
               Accounts Payable 5,000

    (b) Raw-Material Inventory 4,000
               Accounts Payable 4,000

    (c) Work-in-Process Inventory 11,250*
               Raw-Material Inventory 11,250

    *(250 sq. ft. $\times$ \$5 per sq. ft.) + (1,000 lbs. $\times$ \$10 per lb.)

         Manufacturing Overhead** 100
               Manufacturing-Supplies Inventory 100

    **Valve lubricant is an indirect material, so it is considered an overhead cost.

    (d) Work-in-Process Inventory 34,000
         Manufacturing Overhead 13,000
               Wages Payable 47,000

         Work-in-Process Inventory 35,700*
               Manufacturing Overhead 35,700

    *Applied manufacturing overhead = 1,700 direct-labor hours $\times$ \$21 per hour.

    (e) Manufacturing Overhead 12,000
               Accumulated Depreciation: Building and
                  Equipment 12,000

    (f) Manufacturing Overhead 1,200
               Cash 1,200

PROBLEM 3-59 (CONTINUED)

(g)	Manufacturing Overhead.............................	2,100	
	Accounts Payable.............................		2,100
(h)	Manufacturing Overhead.............................	2,400	
	Cash..		2,400
(i)	Manufacturing Overhead.............................	3,100	
	Prepaid Insurance.............................		3,100
(j)	Selling and Administrative Expenses..............	8,000	
	Cash..		8,000
(k)	Selling and Administrative Expenses..............	4,000	
	Accumulated Depreciation: Buildings and Equipment		4,000
(l)	Selling and Administrative Expenses..............	1,000	
	Cash..		1,000
(m)	Finished-Goods Inventory..............................	34,050*	
	Work-in-Process Inventory		34,050

*Cost of Job T81:

Direct material (250 × $5)	$ 1,250
Direct labor (800 × $20)	16,000
Manufacturing overhead (800 × $21) ..	16,800
Total cost	$34,050

(n)	Accounts Receivable.....................................	26,600*	
	Sales Revenue..		26,600

*(76 ÷ 2) × $700 per trombone

	Cost of Goods Sold...	17,025**	
	Finished-Goods Inventory.......................		17,025

**17,025 = $34,050 ÷ 2.

PROBLEM 3-59 (CONTINUED)

3. T-accounts and posting of journal entries:

Cash			
Bal	10,000		
		1,200	(f)
		2,400	(h)
		8,000	(j)
		1,000	(l)

Accounts Payable			
		13,000	Bal
		5,000	(a)
		4,000	(b)
		2,100	(g)

Accounts Receivable		
Bal.	21,000	
(n)	26,600	

Wages Payable		
	8,000	Bal.
	47,000	(d)

Prepaid Insurance			
Bal.	5,000		
		3,100	(i)

Accumulated Depreciation: Buildings and Equipment

	102,000	Bal.
	12,000	(e)
	4,000	(k)

Manufacturing-Supplies Inventory			
Bal.	500		
		100	(c)

Manufacturing Overhead				
(c)	100	35,700	(d)
(d)	13,000		
(e)	12,000		
(f)	1,200		
(g)	2,100		
(h)	2,400		
(i)	3,100		

Raw-Material Inventory				
Bal.	149,000			
(a)	5,000	11,250	(c)
(b)	4,000		

Cost of Goods Sold		
(n)	17,025	

Selling and Administrative Expenses

(j)	8,000	
(k)	4,000	
(l)	1,000	

Work-in-Process Inventory				
Bal.	91,000			
(c)	11,250	34,050	(m)
(d)	34,000		
(d)	35,700		

	Finished-Goods Inventory					Sales Revenue		
Bal.	220,000						26,600	(n)
(m)	34,050	17,025	(n)					

4. (a) Calculation of actual overhead:

Indirect material (valve lubricant)..	$ 100
Indirect labor..	13,000
Depreciation: factory building and equipment......................	12,000
Rent: warehouse...	1,200
Utilities..	2,100
Property taxes...	2,400
Insurance...	3,100
Total actual overhead...	$33,900

(b) $$\text{Overapplied overhead} = \left(\begin{array}{c}\text{actual manufacturing}\\ \text{overhead}\end{array}\right) - \left(\begin{array}{c}\text{applied manufacturing}\\ \text{overhead}\end{array}\right)$$

$$= \$33,900 - \$35,700^*$$

$$= \$1,800 \text{ overapplied}$$

*$35,700 = 1,700 direct-labor hours × $21 per hour.

(c)

Manufacturing Overhead	1,800	
Cost of Goods Sold		1,800

5.

SCHOLASTIC BRASS CORPORATION
SCHEDULE OF COST OF GOODS MANUFACTURED
FOR THE MONTH OF MARCH

Direct material:		
Raw-material inventory, March 1	$149,000	
Add: March purchases of raw material	9,000	
Raw material available for use	$158,000	
Deduct: Raw-material inventory, March 31	146,750	
Raw material used		$ 11,250
Direct labor		34,000
Manufacturing overhead:		
Indirect material	$ 100	
Indirect labor	13,000	
Depreciation on factory building and equipment	12,000	
Rent: Warehouse	1,200	
Utilities	2,100	
Property taxes	2,400	
Insurance	3,100	
Total actual manufacturing overhead	$33,900	
Add: overapplied overhead	1,800*	
Overhead applied to work in process		35,700
Total manufacturing costs		$ 80,950
Add: Work-in-process inventory, March 1		91,000
Subtotal		$171,950
Deduct: Work-in-process inventory, March 31		137,900
Cost of goods manufactured		$ 34,050†

*The Schedule of Cost of Goods Manufactured lists the manufacturing costs *applied* to work in process. Therefore, the overapplied overhead, $1,800, must be added to actual overhead to arrive at the amount of overhead *applied* to work in process during March.

†Cost of Job T81, which was completed during March.

6.

SCHOLASTIC BRASS CORPORATION
SCHEDULE OF COST OF GOODS SOLD
FOR THE MONTH OF MARCH

Finished-goods inventory, March 1...	$220,000
Add: Cost of goods manufactured	34,050
Cost of goods available for sale	$254,050
Deduct: Finished-goods inventory, March 31	237,025
Cost of goods sold...	$ 17,025
Deduct: Overapplied overhead*...	1,800
Cost of goods sold (adjusted for overapplied overhead)	$ 15,225

*The company closes underapplied or overapplied overhead into cost of goods sold. Hence the balance in overapplied overhead is deducted from cost of goods sold for the month.

7.

SCHOLASTIC BRASS CORPORATION
INCOME STATEMENT
FOR THE MONTH OF MARCH

Sales revenue	$26,600
Less: Cost of goods sold	15,225
Gross margin...	$11,375
Selling and administrative expenses	13,000
Income (loss)	$(1,625)

PROBLEM 3-60 (20 MINUTES)

JOB-COST RECORD

Job Number	T81	**Description**	Trombones
Date Started	March 5	**Date Completed**	March 20
		Number of Units Completed	76

Direct Material

Date	Requisition Number	Quantity	Unit Price	Cost
3/5	112	250	$5.00	$1,250

Direct Labor

Date	Time Card Number	Hours	Rate	Cost
3/8 to 3/12	308-312	800	$20	$16,000

Manufacturing Overhead

Date	Activity Base	Quantity	Application Rate	Cost
3/8 to 3/12	Direct-labor hours	800	$21	$16,800

Cost Summary

Cost Item	Amount
Total direct material	$ 1,250
Total direct labor	16,000
Total manufacturing overhead	16,800
Total cost	$34,050
Unit cost	$448.03*

Shipping Summary

Date	Units Shipped	Units Remaining In Inventory	Cost Balance
March	38	38	$17,025†

*Rounded

†$17,025 = $34,050 ÷ 2

PROBLEM 3-61 (55 MINUTES)

The answers to the questions are as follows:

1.	$216,000		6.	$60,000
2.	$19,000		7.	$150,000
3.	$70,000		8.	$40,000
4.	$38,000		9.	$15,000
5.	$80,000		10.	Zero

The completed T accounts, along with supporting calculations, follow.

Raw-Material Inventory

Bal. 10/31	15,000		
	70,000	40,000	
Bal. 11/30	45,000		

Accounts Payable

		12,000	Bal. 10/31
	81,000	70,000	
		1,000	Bal. 11/30

Work-in-Process Inventory

Bal. 10/31	8,000		
Direct		150,000	
material	40,000		
Direct			
labor	80,000		
Overhead	60,000		
Bal. 11/30	38,000		

Finished-Goods Inventory

Bal. 10/31	35,000		
	150,000	180,000	
Bal. 11/30	5,000		

Cost of Goods Sold

180,000	

Manufacturing Overhead

60,000	60,000

Sales Revenue

	216,000

Wages Payable

	1,000	Bal. 10/31	
79,500	80,000		
	1,500	Bal. 11/30	

Accounts Receivable

Bal. 10/31	8,000		
	216,000	205,000	
Bal. 11/30	19,000		

Supporting Calculations:

1.   Sales revenue

$$= \text{cost of goods sold} \times 120\%$$
$$= \$180,000 \times 120\%$$
$$= \$216,000$$

PROBLEM 3-61 (CONTINUED)

2. Ending balance in accounts receivable = beginning balance + sales revenue – collections

$$= \$8,000 + \$216,000 - \$205,000$$

$$= \$19,000$$

3. Purchases of raw material = addition to accounts payable

Addition to accounts payable = ending balance + payments – beginning balance

$$= \$1,000 + \$81,000 - \$12,000$$

$$= \$70,000$$

4. November 30 balance in work-in-process inventory = direct material + direct labor + manufacturing overhead

$$= \$20,500 + (500)(\$20) + (500)(\$15^*)$$

$$= \$38,000$$

$$^*\text{Predetermined overhead rate} = \frac{\text{budgeted overhead}}{\text{budgeted direct-labor hours}^\dagger}$$

$$= \frac{\$720,000}{48,000}$$

$$= \$15 \text{ per direct-labor hour}$$

$$^\dagger\text{Budgeted direct-labor hours} = \frac{\text{budgeted direct-labor cost}}{\text{direct-labor rate}} = \frac{\$960,000}{\$20} = 48,000$$

5. Addition to work in process for direct labor = November credit to wages payable

November credit to wages payable = ending balance + payments – beginning balance

$$= \$1,500 + \$79,500 - \$1,000 = \$80,000$$

6. November applied overhead = direct labor hours × predetermined overhead rate

   = 4,000* × $15

   = $60,000

   Direct labor hours = $\dfrac{\text{addition to work in process for direct labor}}{\text{direct-labor rate}}$

   = $\dfrac{\$80,000}{\$20} = 4,000 \text{ hours}$

7. Cost of goods completed during November = beginning balance in work in process + additions during November − ending balance in work in process

   = $8,000 + ($40,000 + $80,000 + $60,000) − $38,000

   = $150,000

8. Raw material used in November = November credit to raw-material inventory = $40,000 (given)

9. October 31 balance in raw-material inventory = November 30 balance in raw-material inventory + direct material used − purchases

   = $45,000 + $40,000 − $70,000

   = $15,000

10. Overapplied or underapplied overhead = actual overhead − applied overhead

    = $60,000 − $60,000 = 0

PROBLEM 3-62 (50 MINUTES)

1. Schedule of budgeted overhead costs:

	Department A	Department B
Variable overhead		
A 20,000 × $16...	$320,000	
B 20,000 × $ 4...		$ 80,000
Fixed overhead...	200,000	200,000
Total overhead..	$520,000	$280,000
Grand total of budgeted overhead (A + B):	$800,000	

$$\text{Predetermined overhead rate} = \frac{\text{total budgeted overhead rate}}{\text{total budgeted direct-labor hours}}$$

$$= \frac{\$800,000}{40,000} = \$20 \text{ per hour}$$

2. Product prices:

	Basic System	Advanced System
Total cost	$1,100	$1,500
Markup, 10% of cost	110	150
Price..	$1,210	$1,650

3. Departmental overhead rates:

	Department A	Department B
Budgeted overhead		
(from requirement 1)	$520,000	$280,000
Budgeted direct-labor hours...........................	20,000	20,000
Predetermined overhead rates	$520,000	$280,000
	20,000	20,000
	$26 per direct-labor hour	$14 per direct-labor hour

PROBLEM 3-62 (CONTINUED)

4. New product costs:

	Basic System	Advanced System
Direct material	$ 400	$ 800
Direct labor	300	300
Manufacturing overhead:		
Department A:		
Basic system 5 × $26..........................	130	
Advanced system 15 × $26...........................		390
Department B:		
Basic system 15 × $14.....................................	210	
Advanced system 5 × $14.............................		70
Total	$1,040	$1,560

5. New product prices:

	Basic System	Advanced System
Total cost	$1,040	$1,560
Markup, 10% of cost	104	156
Price	$1,144	$1,716

PROBLEM 3-62 (CONTINUED)

6.   TELETECH CORPORATION

                                            Memorandum

Date: Today

To: President, TeleTech Corporation

From: I. M. Student

Subject: Departmental overhead rates

Until now the company has used a single, plantwide overhead rate in computing product costs. This approach resulted in a product cost of $1,100 for the basic system and a cost of $1,500 for the advanced system. Under the company's pricing policy of adding a 10 percent markup, this yielded prices of $1,210 for the basic system and $1,650 for the advanced system.

When departmental overhead rates are computed, it is apparent that the two production departments have very different cost structures. Department A is a relatively expensive department to operate, while Department B is less costly. It is important to recognize the different rates of cost incurrence in the two departments, because our two products require different amounts of time in the two departments. The basic system spends most of its time in Department B, the inexpensive department. The advanced system spends most of its time in Department A, the more expensive department. Thus, using departmental overhead rates shows that the basic system costs less than we had previously realized; the advanced system costs more. The revised product costs are $1,040 and $1,560 for the basic and advanced systems, respectively. With a 10 percent markup, these revised product costs yield prices of $1,144 for the basic system and $1,716 for the advanced system. We have been overpricing the basic system and underpricing the advanced system.

I recommend that the company switch to a product costing system that incorporates departmental overhead rates.

PROBLEM 3-63 (30 MINUTES)

1. Cost rates per unit of each cost driver.

(a) Activity	(b) Activity Cost Pool	(c) Quantity of Cost Driver		(b) ÷ (c) Cost Rate per Unit of Cost Driver	
Machine setup.........	$100,000	200	setups	$500	per setup
Material					
receiving	60,000	80,000	lbs.	$.75	per lb.
Inspection	80,000	1,600	inspections	$50	per inspection
Machinery-related ...	420,000	60,000	machine hrs.	$7	per machine hr.
Engineering	140,000	7,000	engineering hrs.	$20	per engineering hr
Total overhead	$800,000				

2. Overhead assigned to each product line:

Activity	Overhead Assigned to Basic System Line		Overhead Assigned to Advanced System Line	
Machine setup..........	$ 25,000	(50 setups × $500)	$ 75,000	(150 setups × $500)
Material receiving.....	22,500	(30,000 lbs × $.75)	37,500	(50,000 lbs × $.75)
Inspection	35,000	(700 inspections × $50)	45,000	(900 inspections × $50)
Machinery-related	140,000	(20,000 machine hrs. × $7)	280,000	(40,000 machine hrs. × $7)
Engineering	60,000	(3,000 eng. hrs. × $20)	80,000	(4,000 eng hrs. × $20)
Total overhead	$282,500		$517,500	

3. Overhead assigned per unit of each type of fax machine:

Basic system .... $282.50 ($282,500 ÷ 1,000 units)
Advanced system.. $517.50 ($517,500 ÷ 1,000 units)

PROBLEM 3-63 (CONTINUED)

4. Comparison of total product cost assigned to each type of fax machine under three alternative product costing systems:

	Basic System	Advanced System
Plantwide overhead rate*..	$1,100.00	$1,500.00
Departmental overhead rate**	1,040.00	1,560.00
Activity-based costing†...	982.50	1,617.50

*From the data given in the preceding problem.

**From the solution to the preceding problem.

†The assigned overhead as calculated in requirement (3) above, plus the direct material and direct-labor costs given in the data for the preceding problem:

Basic system... $982.50 = $700.00 + $282.50
Advanced system .... $1,617.50 = $1,100.00 + $517.50

SOLUTIONS TO CASES

CASE 3-64 (45 MINUTES)

1. A job-order costing system is appropriate in any environment where costs can be readily identified with specific products, batches, contracts, or projects. This situation typically occurs in a manufacturing setting when relatively small numbers of heterogeneous products are produced.

2. The only job remaining in CompuFurn's work-in-process inventory on December 31 is job PS812. The cost of job PS812 can be calculated as follows:

Job PS812 balance, 11/30		$250,000
December additions:		
Direct material	$124,000	
Purchased parts	87,000	
Direct labor	200,500	
Manufacturing overhead (19,500 machine hrs × $5*)	97,500	509,000
Work-in-process inventory, 12/31		$759,000

$$* \text{Manufacturing overhead rate} = \frac{\$4,500,000}{900,000 \text{ hours}} = \$5 \text{ per machine hour}$$

3. The cost of the chairs remaining in CompuFurn's finished-goods inventory on December 31 is $455,600, calculated as follows:

- Units of chairs in finished-goods inventory on December 31:

	Chair Units
Finished-goods inventory, 11/30..	19,400
Add: Units completed in December...	15,000
Units available...	34,400
Deduct: Units shipped in December..	21,000
Finished-goods inventory, 12/31...	13,400

CASE 3-64 (CONTINUED)

Since CompuFurn uses the first-in, first-out (FIFO) inventory method, all units remaining in finished- goods inventory were completed in December.

- Unit cost of chairs completed in December:

Work in process inventory, 11/30............................		$431,000
December additions:		
Direct material...	$ 3,000	
Purchased parts	10,800	
Direct labor...	43,200	
Manufacturing overhead (4,400 machine hrs × $5)	22,000	79,000
Total cost..		$510,000

$$\text{Unit cost} = \frac{\text{total cost}}{\text{units completed}} = \frac{\$510,000}{15,000} = \$34 \text{ per unit}$$

- Cost of finished-goods inventory   = unit cost × quantity
    = $34 × 13,400
    = $455,600

4. Overapplied overhead is $7,500, calculated as follows:

Machine hours used:

January - November	830,000
December..	49,900
Total	879,900

Applied manufacturing overhead = 879,900 machine hours × $5 = $4,399,500

Actual manufacturing overhead:

January - November	$4,140,000
December..	252,000
Total	$4,392,000

Overapplied overhead   = applied overhead – actual overhead
    = $4,399,500 – $4,392,000
    = $7,500

CASE 3-64 (CONTINUED)

5.   If the amount of overapplied or underapplied overhead is not significant, the amount is generally treated as a period cost and closed to Cost of Goods Sold. If the amount is significant, the amount is sometimes prorated over the relevant accounts, i.e., Work-in-Process Inventory, Finished-Goods Inventory, and Cost of Goods Sold.

CASE 3-65 (50 MINUTES)

1.   Manufacturers use predetermined overhead rates to allocate to production jobs the production costs that are not directly traceable to specific jobs. As a result, management will have timely, accurate job-cost information. Predetermined overhead rates are easy to apply and avoid fluctuations in job costs caused by changes in production volume or overhead costs throughout the year.

2.   The manufacturing overhead applied through November 30 is calculated as follows:

Machine hours $\times$ predetermined overhead rate   =   overhead applied

73,000 $\times$ $15   = $1,095,000

3.   The manufacturing overhead applied in December is calculated as follows:

Machine hours $\times$ predetermined overhead rate   =   overhead applied

6,000 $\times$ $15   = $90,000

4.   Underapplied manufacturing overhead through December 31 is calculated as follows:

Actual overhead ($1,100,000 + $96,000)	$1,196,000
Applied overhead ($1,095,000 + $90,000)	(1,185,000)
Underapplied overhead	$ 11,000

CASE 3-65 (CONTINUED)

5. The balance the Finished-Goods Inventory account on December 31 is comprised only of Job No. N11-013 and is calculated as follows:

November 30 balance for Job No. N11-013..	$55,000
December direct material..	4,000
December direct labor...	12,000
December overhead (1,000 × $15)...	15,000
Total finished-goods inventory..	$86,000

6. FiberCom's Schedule of Cost of Goods Manufactured for the year just completed is constructed as follows:

FIBERCOM COMPANY
SCHEDULE OF COST OF GOODS MANUFACTURED
FOR THE YEAR ENDED DECEMBER 31

Direct material:		
Raw-material inventory, 1/1..		$ 105,000
Raw-material purchases ($965,000 + $98,000)		1,063,000
Raw material available for use......................................		$1,168,000
Deduct: Indirect material used ($125,000 + $9,000)....	$134,000	
Raw-material inventory 12/31	85,000	219,000
Raw material used...		$ 949,000
Direct labor ($845,000 + $80,000).....................................		925,000
Manufacturing overhead:		
Indirect material ($125,000 + $9,000)...........................	$134,000	
Indirect labor ($345,000 + $30,000)..............................	375,000	
Utilities ($245,000 + $22,000)......................................	267,000	
Depreciation ($385,000 + $35,000)...............................	420,000	
Total actual manufacturing overhead		1,196,000
Deduct: Underapplied overhead...................................		11,000
Overhead applied to work in process		$1,185,000
Total manufacturing costs		$3,059,000
Add: Work-in-process inventory, 1/1		60,000
Subtotal...		$3,119,000
Deduct: Work-in-process inventory, 12/31*......................		150,200
Cost of goods manufactured		$2,968,800

*Supporting calculations follow.

CASE 3-65 (CONTINUED)

*Supporting calculations for work in process 12/31:

	D12-002	D12-003	Total
Direct material	$37,900	$26,000	$ 63,900
Direct labor	20,000	16,800	36,800
Applied overhead:			
2,500 hrs. × $15	37,500		37,500
800 hrs. × $15		$12,000	12,000
Total	$95,400	$54,800	$150,200

CURRENT ISSUES IN MANAGERIAL ACCOUNTING

ISSUE 3-66

" 'BUSINESS-METHOD' PATENTS, KEY TO PRICELINE, DRAW GROWING PROTEST," *THE WALL STREET JOURNAL*, OCTOBER 3, 2000, JULIA ANGWIN.

1. Although the initial application of upselling is based upon separating customers from their spare change, in effect what sells the customers is obtaining a very good deal for very little cost. Upselling could be effective on this basis, but the cash aspect would not exist.

2. Only products in which a profit could be made would be sold using upselling. The overall profit margin for a product would be reduced as the number of units sold under this method increased. This would have to be figured into the cost management formula.

3. Database software would be useful in tying a company's product-costing database together with its sales operations.

4. There are arguments for and against patenting business methods. The question is designed to generate student discussion.

ISSUE 3-67

"IT WORKED FOR TOYOTA. CAN IT WORK FOR TOYS?," *FORTUNE*, JANUARY 11, 1999, ALEX TAYLOR III.

1. The Alexander Doll Company produced boxes of costume material and vinyl doll parts. In fact, parts for more than 90,000 dolls were stored and nothing was built to order. When an order came for 300 dolls only 117 could be produced from the parts stored for the 90,000 incomplete dolls. This was Alexander's form of batch processing.

2. TBM organized the workers into seven or eight person teams, each of which is responsible for completing about 300 doll or wardrobe assemblies a day. The amount of work in progress has been cut by 96% and orders can now be filled in one or two weeks instead of two months.

ISSUE 3-68

"PRICELINE FOUNDER CLOSES ONLINE BIDDING SITE FOR GAS AND GROCERIES," *THE WALL STREET JOURNAL*, OCTOBER 96, 2000, JULIA ANGWIN.

1. When deciding how low a price to accept on its Chicago-to-LA flight, United Airlines' management would ask questions such as:

   - Will it be profitable?

   - Does it build brand loyalty?

   - Will it undermine brand loyalty?

   - Will it promote repeat business?

2. Cost information is relevant to the decision making process in regards to how well the ticket price competes in the market and if the invested capital makes more of a profit in this venture than another venture in which it could be used.

ISSUE 3-69

"THERE'S A NEW ECONOMY OUT THERE, AND IT LOOKS NOTHING LIKE THE OLD ONE," *THE WALL STREET JOURNAL*, DECEMBER 31, 1999, THOMAS PETZINGER, JR.

1. Managerial accounting information would serve the same five objectives described in Chapter 1 in the new business world discussed in the article. There would, however, be less integration across those functions if companies are broken up into smaller, more independent businesses.

2. Managerial accounting information would be just as valuable to companies under the suggested future for the structure of business.

3. Job-order costing systems would serve the same role in product costing, but would concentrate more on the outsourcing and supply chain management functions.

ISSUE 3-70

"GUSTY WIND FORCES ANOTHER LAUNCH DELAY FOR DISCOVERY," *THE ASSOCIATED PRESS*, OCTOBER 10, 2000, MARCIA DUNN.

1. Firms employing the services of the shuttle would use job costing, just as NASA uses job costing. Each launch's costs are computed independently with substantial costs incurred before each launch. Therefore, a canceled launch increases the costs of firms employing the shuttle's services.

2. It would be important to determine a cost figure for a delay as mentioned above.

3. Determining a cost for delays is critical so the project can be properly and fully costed.

ISSUE 3-71

"AUDITING MANUFACTURING COSTS, "*INTERNAL AUDITOR*, JUNE 2000, TERESA KILPATRICK.

Most manufacturing systems contain numerous reports that may be designed for production and material requirements planning. Once the auditor has identified report sources, information can be imported for analysis. IDEA utilizes open database connectivity drivers that convert a wide range of common spreadsheet and text formats.

Using IDEA's file-extraction summarization techniques, auditors can perform several tests to verify the integrity of the data itself, as well as the calculation extensions and totals in each report.

Auditors can use IDEA to import files that contain cost calculation fields such as quantity of raw material components, raw material prices, labor hours per piece, and machine rates. The equation editor can perform an independent calculation of cost. IDEA can then automate the process of comparing this item cost file with the system item cost through its file comparison feature.

Proper data analysis can provide an objective view of the collection and allocation of overhead costs to products. For example, auditors can analyze prices paid for raw material by importing the accounts payable file into IDEA and then using the equation editor. Using data analysis, auditors can also perform a simple test to compare a file of work-in-process valued items with finished goods items.

ISSUE 3-72

"DON'T GET TRAPPED, " *STRATEGIC FINANCE*, NOVEMBER 1999, DAPHNE MAIN AND
CAROLYN L. LOUSTEAU.

1. Entrapment is the inability to eliminate an albatross project. There are four
    psychological reasons that can lead to entrapment. They are: over-optimism/illusion
    of control, self-justification, framing, and sunk costs. Over-optimism occurs when
    managers feel the need to sell their project. As a result, the projections are almost
    always rosy, which lead to inflated expectations for a project. Research has shown
    that people consistently overestimate revenues and under estimate costs. People
    also think they can control what happens to their decisions once they are in place.
    External factors, such as weather or changes in economic conditions, are beyond
    the control of project managers. Managers tend to commit more resources to a
    losing project in order to justify their initial investment. They tend to search for
    evidence that suggests the project should be continued but disregard evidence to
    the contrary. This self-justification leads to entrapment. How a decision is perceived
    can lead to entrapment. When thinking in terms of saving jobs, managers tend to be
    more conservative in decision making; on the other hand, if a decision is perceived
    in terms of losing jobs, managers tend to be more likely to make risky decisions.
    When justifying the decision to continue a project, managers tend to argue that they
    should not waste money already sunk into a project. In fact, money already spent on
    a project should not influence decisions if entrapment is to be avoided.

2. The four psychological reasons leading to entrapment should be avoided when
    making sound business decisions concerning project continuance. Not doing so
    will lead to unsound business practices. Managerial accounting information can
    help managers avoid entrapment by clarifying the costs in involved in a situation and
    by clearly identifying any sunk costs.

ISSUE 3-73

"BOEING WEIGHS GIVING JAPAN 747X WING JOB," *THE WALL STREET JOURNAL*,
JANUARY 2, 2001, JEFF COLE.

1. Outsourcing and supply chain management are important management tools in
    acquiring the raw materials and components needed to manufacture products.
    The costs of outsourced components are included as a product cost along with
    raw material in a job-order costing system.

Solutions Manual

2. Mitsubishi would incur close to $900 million of the four billion dollars in development costs, Boeing's startup costs of the 747 would in effect be transferred to direct material costs on a job-order production basis. Although Boeing would allow Mitsubishi to share in this high value market for its initial startup investment, the advantage to Boeing would be to delay significant costs to the time the market for the aircraft matures.

CHAPTER 4
Process Costing and Hybrid Product-Costing Systems

ANSWERS TO REVIEW QUESTIONS

4-1   In a job-order costing system, costs are assigned to batches or job orders of production. Job-order costing is used by firms that produce relatively small numbers of dissimilar products. In a process-costing system, costs are averaged over a large number of product units. Process costing is used by firms that produce large numbers of nearly identical products.

4-2   Process costing would be an appropriate product-costing system in the following industries: petroleum, food processing, lumber, chemicals, textiles, and electronics. Each of these industries is involved in the production of very large numbers of highly similar products.

4-3   Process costing could be used in the following nonmanufacturing enterprises: processing of tests in a medical diagnostic laboratory, processing of tax returns by the Internal Revenue Service, and processing of loan applications in a bank.

4-4   Product-costing systems are used for the following purposes:

(a) In financial accounting: Product costs are needed to value inventory on the balance sheet and to compute the cost-of-goods-sold expense on the income statement.

(b) In managerial accounting: Product costs are needed for planning, for cost control, and to provide managers with data for decision making.

(c) In reporting to interested organizations: Product cost information is used to report on relationships between firms and various outside organizations. For example, hospitals keep track of the costs of medical procedures that are reimbursed by insurance companies or by the federal government under the Medicare program.

4-5   An equivalent unit is a measure of the amount of productive effort applied in the production process. In process costing, costs are assigned to equivalent units rather than to physical units.

4-6 The following four steps are used in process costing:

(a) Analysis of physical flow of units: All of the units in the beginning and ending inventories, those started during the period, and those transferred out to finished goods are accounted for.

(b) Calculation of equivalent units: The equivalent units of activity are computed for direct material and for conversion.

(c) Computation of unit costs: The costs per equivalent unit for direct material and conversion are computed.

(d) Analysis of total costs: The cost of the goods completed and transferred out and the cost of the ending work-in-process inventory are determined.

4-7 (a) Journal entry to enter direct-material costs into Work-in-Process Inventory account:

Work-in-Process Inventory: Department A XXX
    Raw-Material Inventory... XXX

(b) Journal entry to record transfer of goods from the first to the second department in the production sequence:

Work-in-Process Inventory: Department B XXX
    Work-in-Process Inventory: Department A XXX

4-8 Transferred-in costs are the costs assigned to partially completed products that have been transferred from one production department into the next department.

4-9 The $175,000 of transferred-in costs were incurred prior to January 1 and in the mixing department. The costs must have been incurred prior to January 1, because they are included in the cost of the beginning work-in-process inventory on that date. Moreover, these costs must have been incurred in the mixing department, because they have been transferred into the cooking department.

4-10 The name "weighted-average method" comes from the fact that the cost per equivalent unit computed under this method is a weighted average of costs incurred during the current period and costs incurred during prior periods.

4-11 The difference between normal and actual costing lies in the calculation of the manufacturing-overhead cost of the current period. Under actual costing, the manufacturing-overhead cost of the current period is the actual overhead cost incurred during the period. Under normal costing, the current-period manufacturing overhead is computed as the product of the predetermined overhead rate and the actual level of the cost driver used to apply manufacturing overhead.

4-12 If manufacturing overhead were applied according to some activity base (or cost driver) other than direct labor, then direct-labor costs and manufacturing-overhead costs would be accounted for separately instead of being combined into one account called "conversion costs." Thus, instead of two columns for direct-material and conversion costs, there would be three columns: direct material, direct labor, and manufacturing overhead.

4-13 Operation costing is a hybrid product-costing system that is used when conversion activities are very similar across product lines, but the direct materials differ significantly. This is often the case in batch manufacturing operations. Conversion costs are accumulated by department, and process-costing methods are used to assign these costs to products. In contrast, direct-material costs are accumulated by job order or by batch, and job-order costing is used to assign direct-material costs to products.

4-14 The departmental production report is the key document in a process-costing system rather than the job-cost sheet used in job-order costing. The departmental production report shows the analysis of the physical flow of units, the calculation of equivalent units, the computation of the cost per equivalent unit, and the analysis of the total costs incurred in the production department. The report shows the cost of the ending work-in-process inventory as well as the cost of the goods completed and transferred out of the department.

4-15 There is no direct material in the March 1 work in process for the stitching department because direct material (rawhide lacing) is added at the end of the process in that department.

SOLUTIONS TO EXERCISES

EXERCISE 4-16 (10 MINUTES)

The general formula for all three cases is the following:

Work-in-process, beginning	+	Units started during month	–	Units completed during month	=	Work-in-process, ending

Using this formula, the missing amounts are:

1.   12,000 units

2.   5,300 kilograms

3.   750,000 gallons

EXERCISE 4-17 (30 MINUTES)

All three of these companies manufacture large numbers of relatively homogeneous products (i.e., lumber and paper). Therefore, process costing is an appropriate product-costing system.

EXERCISE 4-18 (15 MINUTES)

1. 6,000 equivalent units (refer to (a) in the following table)

2. 4,400 equivalent units (refer to (b) in the following table)

CALCULATION OF EQUIVALENT UNITS: RAINBOW GLASS COMPANY
Weighted-Average Method

	Physical Units	Percentage of Completion with Respect to Conversion	Equivalent Units	
			Direct Material	Conversion
Work in process, October 1	1,000	60%		
Units started during October ..	5,000			
Total units to account for........	6,000			
Units completed and transferred out during October...........	4,000	100%	4,000	4,000
Work in process, October 31 ..	2,000	20%	2,000	400
Total units accounted for	6,000			
Total equivalent units			(a) 6,000	(b) 4,400

EXERCISE 4-19 (15 MINUTES)

CALCULATION OF EQUIVALENT UNITS: TERRA ENERGY COMPANY - LODI PLANT
Weighted-Average Method

	Physical Units	Percentage of Completion with Respect to Conversion	Equivalent Units	
			Direct Material	Conversion
Work in process, November 1.................	2,000,000	25%		
Units started during November	950,000			
Total units to account for......................	2,950,000			
Units completed and transferred out during November........................	2,710,000	100%	2,710,000	2,710,000
Work in process, November 30..............	240,000	80%	240,000	192,000
Total units accounted for	2,950,000			
Total equivalent units			2,950,000	2,902,000

EXERCISE 4-20 (20 MINUTES)

CALCULATION OF EQUIVALENT UNITS: FIT-FOR-LIFE FOODS CORPORATION
Weighted-Average Method

	Physical Units	Percentage of Completion with Respect to Direct Material	Percentage of Completion with Respect to Conversion	Equivalent Units Direct Material	Equivalent Units Conversion
Work in process, January 1	20,000	80%	60%		
Units started during the year ..	120,000				
Total units to account for........	140,000				
Unit completed and transferred out during the year	125,000	100%	100%	125,000	125,000
Work in process, December 31	15,000	70%	30%	10,500	4,500
Total units accounted for	140,000				
Total equivalent units				135,500	129,500

EXERCISE 4-21 (15 MINUTES)

CALCULATION OF COST PER EQUIVALENT UNIT: IDAHO LUMBER COMPANY
Weighted-Average Method

	Direct Material	Conversion	Total
Work in process, November 1...................	$ 65,000	$180,000	$ 245,000
Costs incurred during November	425,000	690,000	1,115,000
Total costs to account for	$490,000	$870,000	$1,360,000
Equivalent units	7,000	1,740	
Costs per equivalent unit	$70*	$500†	$570

*$70 = $490,000 ÷ 7,000
†$500 = $870,000 ÷ 1,740

EXERCISE 4-22 (15 MINUTES)

CALCULATION OF COST PER EQUIVALENT UNIT: OTSEGO GLASS COMPANY
Weighted-Average Method

	Direct Material	Conversion	Total
Work in process, June 1.........................	$ 37,000	$ 36,750	$ 73,750
Costs incurred during June	150,000	230,000	380,000
Total costs to account for	$187,000	$266,750	$453,750
Equivalent units	17,000	48,500	
Costs per equivalent unit	$11.00*	$5.50†	$16.50

*$11.00 = $187,000 ÷ 17,000

†$5.50 = $266,750 ÷ 48,500

EXERCISE 4-23 (25 MINUTES)

SAVANNAH TEXTILES COMPANY
Weighted-Average Method

	Direct Material	Conversion	Total
Work in process, September 1..................	$ 94,000	$ 44,400	$138,400
Costs incurred during September............	164,000	272,800	436,800
Total costs to account for........................	$258,000	$317,200	$575,200
Equivalent units...................................	60,000	52,000	
Costs per equivalent unit.........................	$4.30	$6.10	$10.40

1. Cost of goods completed and
   transferred out during September:

$$\begin{pmatrix} \text{number of units} \\ \text{transferred out} \end{pmatrix} \times \begin{pmatrix} \text{total cost per} \\ \text{equivalent unit} \end{pmatrix}$$ .... 50,000 × $10.40 $520,000

2. Cost remaining in September 30
   work in process:

Direct material (10,000* × $4.30)	$43,000	
Conversion (2,000* × $6.10)	12,200	
Total		55,200
Total costs accounted for...............		$575,200

*Equivalent units in September 30 work in process:

	Direct Material	Conversion
Total equivalent units (weighted average)........................	60,000	52,000
Units completed and transferred out	(50,000)	(50,000)
Equivalent units in ending work in process	10,000	2,000

EXERCISE 4-24 (25 MINUTES)

TULSA PAPERBOARD COMPANY
Weighted-Average Method

	Direct Material	Conversion	Total
Work in process, February 1....................	$ 5,500	$ 17,000	$ 22,500
Costs incurred during February	110,000	171,600	281,600
Total costs to account for	$115,500	$188,600	$304,100
Equivalent units	110,000	92,000	
Costs per equivalent unit	$ 1.05	$ 2.05	$ 3.10

1. Cost of goods completed and
   transferred out during February:

   $$\left(\begin{array}{c}\text{number of units}\\\text{transferred out}\end{array}\right) \times \left(\begin{array}{c}\text{total cost per}\\\text{equivalent unit}\end{array}\right)$$ ....   90,000 × $3.10 $279,000

2. Cost remaining in February 28 work
   in process:

Direct material (20,000* × $1.05).	$ 21,000	
Conversion (2,000* × $2.05)........	4,100	
Total		25,100
Total costs accounted for		$304,100

*Equivalent units in February 28 work in process:

	Direct Material	Conversion
Total equivalent units (weighted average).......................	110,000	92,000
Units completed and transferred out	(90,000)	(90,000)
Equivalent units in ending work in process	20,000	2,000

EXERCISE 4-25 (45 MINUTES)

1. Diagram of production process:

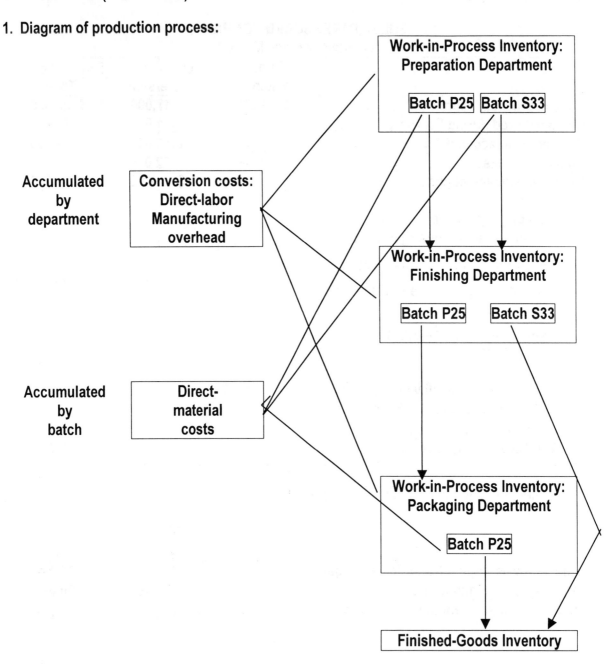

EXERCISE 4-25 (CONTINUED)

2. The product cost for each basketball is computed as follows:

	Professional	Scholastic
Direct material:..		
Batch P25 ($42,000 ÷ 2,000)..	$21.00	-0-
Batch S33 ($45,000 ÷ 4,000)..	-0-	$11.25
Conversion: Preparation Department............................	7.50	7.50
Conversion: Finishing Department................................	6.00	6.00
*Conversion: Packaging Department..............................	.50	-0-
Total product cost	$35.00	$24.75

*The two production departments each worked on a total of 6,000 balls, but the Packaging Department handled only the 2,000 professional balls.

3. Journal entries:

Work-in-Process Inventory: Preparation Department..........	39,500*	
Raw-Material Inventory		39,500

    *$39,500 = $42,000 of direct material
    for batch P25 – $2,500 of packaging material

Work-in-Process Inventory: Preparation Department..........	45,000*	
Raw-Material Inventory		45,000

    *Direct-material cost for batch S33.

Work-in-Process Inventory: Preparation Department..........	45,000*	
Applied Conversion Costs...		45,000

    *$45,000 = 6,000 units × $7.50 per unit

Work-in-Process Inventory: Finishing Department..............	129,500*	
Work-in-Process Inventory: Preparation Department		129,500

    *$129,500 = $39,500 + $45,000 + $45,000

EXERCISE 4-25 (CONTINUED)

Work-in-Process Inventory: Finishing Department..............	36,000*	
Applied Conversion Costs...		36,000

*$36,000 = 6,000 units × $6.00 per unit

Work-in-Process Inventory: Packaging Department............	66,500*	
Finished-Goods Inventory...	99,000†	
Work-in-Process Inventory: Finishing Department		165,500

*$66,500 = $39,500 + (2,000 × $7.50) + (2,000 × $6.00).
These are the costs accumulated for batch P25 only.

†$99,000 = $45,000 + (4,000 × $7.50) + (4,000 × $6.00).
These are the costs accumulated for batch S33 only.

Work-in-Process Inventory: Packaging Department............	3,500	
Raw-Material Inventory		2,500*
Applied Conversion Costs...		1,000†

*Cost of packaging material for batch P25.

†$1,000 = 2,000 units × $.50 per unit

Finished-Goods Inventory...	70,000*	
Work-in-Process Inventory: Packaging Department ..		70,000

*$70,000 = $66,500 + $3,500

EXERCISE 4-26 (10 MINUTES)

1.   Work-in-Process Inventory: Pouring Department   1,090,000

      Raw-Material Inventory   70,000

      Wages Payable   340,000

      Manufacturing Overhead   680,000

2.   Work-in-Process Inventory: Finishing Department   900,000

      Work-in-Process Inventory: Pouring Department   900,000

3.   Work-in-Process Inventory: Finishing Department   725,000

      Raw-Material Inventory   25,000

      Wages Payable   280,000

      Manufacturing Overhead   420,000

4.   Finished-Goods Inventory   400,000

      Work-in-Process Inventory: Finishing Department ...   400,000

SOLUTIONS TO PROBLEMS

PROBLEM 4-27 (50 MINUTES)

1. Physical flow of units:

	Physical Units
Work in process, 1/1/x1	200,000
Units started during 20x1	1,000,000
Total units to account for	1,200,000
Units completed and transferred out during 20x1	900,000
Work in process, 12/31/x1	300,000
Total units accounted for	1,200,000

2. Equivalent units:

	Physical Units	Percentage of Completion with Respect to Conversion	Equivalent Units Direct Material	Equivalent Units Conversion
Work in process, 1/1/x1	200,000	80%		
Units started during 20x1	1,000,000			
Total units to account for	1,200,000			
Units completed and transferred out during 20x1	900,000	100%	900,000	900,000
Work in process, 12/31/x1	300,000	50%	300,000	150,000
Total units accounted for	1,200,000			
Total equivalent units			1,200,000	1,050,000

PROBLEM 4-27 (CONTINUED)

3. Costs per equivalent unit:

	Direct Material	Conversion	Total
Work in process, 1/1/x1..................................	$ 200,000	$ 504,000[a]	$ 704,000
Costs incurred during 20x1	1,300,000	3,192,000[b]	4,492,000
Total costs to account for............................	$1,500,000	$3,696,000	$5,196,000
Equivalent units..	1,200,000	1,050,000	
Costs per equivalent unit..............................	$1.25[c]	$3.52[d]	$4.77[e]

[a]Conversion cost = direct labor + overhead
= direct labor + (60% × direct labor)
= 160% × direct labor
= 160% × $315,000
= $504,000

[b]Conversion cost = 160% × direct labor
= 160% × $1,995,000
= $3,192,000

[c]$1.25 = $1,500,000 ÷ 1,200,000

[d]$3.52 = $3,696,000 ÷ 1,050,000

[e]$4.77 = $1.25 + $3.52

PROBLEM 4-27 (CONTINUED)

4.   Cost of ending inventories:

Cost of goods completed and transferred out:

$$\begin{pmatrix} \text{number of units} \\ \text{transferred out} \end{pmatrix} \times \begin{pmatrix} \text{total cost per} \\ \text{equivalent unit} \end{pmatrix}$$ .... $900,000 \times \$4.77$ $\underline{\$4,293,000}$

Cost remaining in 12/31/x1 work-in-process inventory:

Direct material:

$$\begin{pmatrix} \text{number of} \\ \text{equivalent} \\ \text{units of} \\ \text{direct material} \end{pmatrix} \times \begin{pmatrix} \text{cost per} \\ \text{equivalent} \\ \text{unit of} \\ \text{direct material} \end{pmatrix}$$ .... $300,000 \times \$1.25$ $\$375,000$

Conversion:

$$\begin{pmatrix} \text{number of} \\ \text{equivalent} \\ \text{units of} \\ \text{conversion} \end{pmatrix} \times \begin{pmatrix} \text{cost per} \\ \text{equivalent} \\ \text{unit of} \\ \text{conversion} \end{pmatrix}$$ .... $150,000 \times \$3.52$ $\underline{528,000}$

Total cost of 12/31/x1 work in process .... $\underline{\$903,000}$

Check: Cost of goods completed and transferred out .... $\$4,293,000$
           Cost of 12/31/x1 work-in-process inventory .... $\underline{903,000}$
           Total costs accounted for... $\underline{\$5,196,000}$

The cost of the ending work-in-process inventory is $903,000

Ending finished-goods inventory: Of the 900,000 units completed during 20x1, 200,000 units remain in finished-goods inventory on December 31, 20x1. Therefore:

$$\$4,293,000 \times (200,000 \div 900,000) = \$954,000*$$

The cost of the ending finished-goods inventory is $954,000.

*Also, $954,000 = 200,000 \times \$4.77$ per unit

PROBLEM 4-28 (45 MINUTES)

1.

	Physical Units
Work in process, June 1	50,000
Units started during June	200,000
Total units to account for...	250,000
Units completed and transferred out during June.............................	190,000
Work in process, June 30	60,000
Total units accounted for...	250,000

2.

	Physical Units	Percentage of Completion with Respect to Conversion	Equivalent Units Direct Material	Conversion
Work in process, June 1	50,000	40%		
Units started during June	200,000			
Total units to account for.........	250,000			
Units completed and transferred out during June..................	190,000	100%	190,000	190,000
Work in process, June 30	60,000	60%	60,000	36,000
Total units accounted for.........	250,000			
Total equivalent units..............			250,000	226,000

3.

	Direct Material	Conversion	Total
Work in process, June 1................	$120,000	$ 34,400	$154,400
Costs incurred during June	492,500	349,800	842,300
Total costs to account for	$612,500	$384,200	$996,700
Equivalent units	250,000	226,000	
Costs per equivalent unit	$2.45	$1.70	$4.15

PROBLEM 4-28 (CONTINUED)

4. Cost of goods completed and transferred out during June:

$$\begin{pmatrix} \text{number of units} \\ \text{transferred out} \end{pmatrix} \times \begin{pmatrix} \text{total cost per} \\ \text{equivalent unit} \end{pmatrix} \dots\dots\dots\dots \qquad 190{,}000 \times \$4.15 \qquad \underline{\$788{,}500}$$

Cost remaining in June 30 work-in-process inventory:

Direct material:

$$\begin{pmatrix} \text{number of} \\ \text{equivalent} \\ \text{units of} \\ \text{direct material} \end{pmatrix} \times \begin{pmatrix} \text{cost per} \\ \text{equivalent} \\ \text{unit of} \\ \text{direct material} \end{pmatrix} \dots\dots\dots\dots \qquad 60{,}000 \times \$2.45 \qquad \$147{,}000$$

Conversion:

$$\begin{pmatrix} \text{number of} \\ \text{equivalent} \\ \text{units of} \\ \text{conversion} \end{pmatrix} \times \begin{pmatrix} \text{cost per} \\ \text{equivalent} \\ \text{unit of} \\ \text{conversion} \end{pmatrix} \dots\dots\dots\dots \qquad 36{,}000 \times \$1.70 \qquad \underline{\quad 61{,}200}$$

Total cost of June 30 work in process .... $\underline{\$208{,}200}$

Check: Cost of goods completed and transferred out............................ $\$788{,}500$
         Cost of June 30 work-in-process inventory .... $\underline{\quad 208{,}200}$
         Total costs accounted for.. $\underline{\$996{,}700}$

PROBLEM 4-29 (50 MINUTES)

The missing amounts are shown below. A completed production report follows.

Units started during July..	45,000
Units completed and transferred out during July	50,000
Total equivalent units: conversion..	56,000
Work in process, July 1: conversion..	$ 79,800
Costs incurred during July: direct material...	371,850
Cost per equivalent unit: conversion...	13.20
Cost of goods completed and transferred out during July	1,072,500
Cost remaining in ending work-in-process inventory: direct material..............	123,750

PRODUCTION REPORT: VESUVIUS TILE COMPANY
Weighted-Average Method

	Physical Units	Percentage of Completion with Respect to Conversion	Equivalent Units Direct Material	Equivalent Units Conversion
Work in process, July 1...................	20,000	30%		
Units started during July................	45,000			
Total units to account for...............	65,000			
Units completed and transferred out during July..........................	50,000	100%	50,000	50,000
Work in process, July 31................	15,000	40%	15,000	6,000
Total units accounted for...............	65,000			
Total equivalent units....................			65,000	56,000

PROBLEM 4-29 (CONTINUED)

	Direct Material	Conversion	Total
Work in process, July 1	$164,400	$ 79,800	$ 244,200
Costs incurred during July	371,850	659,400	1,031,250
Total costs to account for	$536,250	$739,200	$1,275,450
Equivalent units	65,000	56,000	
Costs per equivalent unit	$8.25*	$13.20†	$21.45**

*$8.25 = $536,250 ÷ 65,000
†$13.20 = $739,200 ÷ 56,000
**$21.45 = $8.25 + $13.20

Cost of goods completed and transferred out during July:

$$\begin{pmatrix} \text{number of units} \\ \text{transferred out} \end{pmatrix} \times \begin{pmatrix} \text{total cost per} \\ \text{equivalent unit} \end{pmatrix}$$ .... 50,000 × $21.45 $1,072,500

Cost remaining in July 31 work-in-process inventory:

Direct material:

$$\begin{pmatrix} \text{number of} \\ \text{equivalent} \\ \text{units of} \\ \text{direct material} \end{pmatrix} \times \begin{pmatrix} \text{cost per} \\ \text{equivalent} \\ \text{unit of} \\ \text{direct material} \end{pmatrix}$$ .... 15,000 × $8.25 $ 123,750

Conversion:

$$\begin{pmatrix} \text{number of} \\ \text{equivalent} \\ \text{units of} \\ \text{conversion} \end{pmatrix} \times \begin{pmatrix} \text{cost per} \\ \text{equivalent} \\ \text{unit of} \\ \text{conversion} \end{pmatrix}$$ .... 6,000 × $13.20   79,200

Total cost of July 31 work in process $202,950

Check: Cost of goods completed and transferred out .. $1,072,500
         Cost of July 31 work-in-process inventory   202,950
         Total costs accounted for $1,275,450

PROBLEM 4-30 (40 MINUTES)

1.   a.

	Physical Units	Percentage of Completion with Respect to Conversion	Equivalent Units	
			Direct Material	Conversion
Work in process, May 1	25,000	40%		
Units started during May	30,000			
Total units to account for	55,000			
Units completed and				
transferred out during May	35,000	100%	35,000	35,000
Work in process, May 31	20,000	80%	20,000	16,000
Total units accounted for	55,000			
Total equivalent units			55,000	51,000

b.

	Direct Material	Conversion	Total
Total costs to account for	$308,000	$2,483,700	
Equivalent units	55,000	51,000	
Costs per equivalent unit	$5.60	$48.70	$54.30*

*$54.30 = $5.60 + $48.70

PROBLEM 4-30 (CONTINUED)

c. Cost of goods completed and transferred out during May:

$$\begin{pmatrix} \text{number of units} \\ \text{transferred out} \end{pmatrix} \times \begin{pmatrix} \text{total cost per} \\ \text{equivalent unit} \end{pmatrix} \qquad 35{,}000 \times \$54.30 \qquad \underline{\$1{,}900{,}500}$$

Cost remaining in May 31 work-in-process inventory:

Direct material:

$$\begin{pmatrix} \text{number of} \\ \text{equivalent} \\ \text{units of} \\ \text{direct material} \end{pmatrix} \times \begin{pmatrix} \text{cost per} \\ \text{equivalent} \\ \text{unit of} \\ \text{direct material} \end{pmatrix} \quad \dots\dots\dots\dots\dots 20{,}000 \times \$5.60 \qquad \$112{,}000$$

Conversion:

$$\begin{pmatrix} \text{number of} \\ \text{equivalent} \\ \text{units of} \\ \text{conversion} \end{pmatrix} \times \begin{pmatrix} \text{cost per} \\ \text{equivalent} \\ \text{unit of} \\ \text{conversion} \end{pmatrix} \quad \dots\dots\dots\dots\dots 16{,}000 \times \$48.70 \qquad \underline{779{,}200}$$

Total cost of May 31 work in process... $\underline{\$891{,}200}$

Check:		
Cost of goods completed and transferred out..........................		$1,900,500
Cost of May 31 work-in-process inventroy		891,200
Total costs accounted for...		$2,791,700

2. Journal entry:

Finished-Goods Inventory...	1,900,500	
Work-in-Process Inventory		1,900,500

PROBLEM 4-31 (45 MINUTES)

1.

	Physical Units
Work in process, April 1	10,000
Units started during April	100,000
Total units to account for	110,000
Units completed and transferred out during April	80,000
Work in process, April 30	30,000
Total units accounted for	110,000

2.

	Physical Units	Percentage of Completion with Respect to Conversion	Equivalent Units	
			Direct Material	Conversion
Work in process, April 1	10,000	20%		
Units started during April	100,000			
Total units to account for	110,000			
Units completed and transferred out during April	80,000	100%	80,000	80,000
Work in process, April 30	30,000	33 1/3%	30,000	10,000
Total units accounted for	110,000			
Total equivalent units			110,000	90,000

3.

	Direct Material	Conversion	Total
Work in process, April 1	$ 22,000	$ 4,500	$ 26,500
Costs incurred during April	198,000	158,400	356,400
Total costs to account for	$220,000	$162,900	$382,900
Equivalent units	110,000	90,000	
Costs per equivalent unit	$2.00	$1.81	$3.81

4. Cost of goods completed and transferred out during April:

$$\left(\begin{array}{c}\text{number of units}\\\text{transferred out}\end{array}\right) \times \left(\begin{array}{c}\text{total cost per}\\\text{equivalent unit}\end{array}\right)$$ .... 80,000 × $3.81   <u>$304,800</u>

Cost remaining in April 30 work-in-process inventory:

Direct material:

$$\left(\begin{array}{c}\text{number of}\\\text{equivalent}\\\text{units of}\\\text{direct material}\end{array}\right) \times \left(\begin{array}{c}\text{cost per}\\\text{equivalent}\\\text{unit of}\\\text{direct material}\end{array}\right)$$ .... 30,000 × $2.00 $60,000

Conversion:

$$\left(\begin{array}{c}\text{number of}\\\text{equivalent}\\\text{units of}\\\text{conversion}\end{array}\right) \times \left(\begin{array}{c}\text{cost per}\\\text{equivalent}\\\text{unit of}\\\text{conversion}\end{array}\right)$$ .... 10,000 × $1.81   <u>18,100</u>

Total cost of April 30 work-in-process...   <u>$78,100</u>

Check: Cost of goods completed and transferred out....................... $304,800
Cost of April 30 work-in-process inventory..........................   <u>78,100</u>
Total costs accounted for ....   <u>$382,900</u>

PROBLEM 4-32 (40 MINUTES)

1.

	Physical Units	Percentage of Completion with Respect to Conversion	Equivalent Units	
			Direct Material	Conversion
Work in process, August 1	40,000	80%		
Units started during August	80,000			
Total units to account for..............	120,000			
Units completed and transferred out during August	100,000	100%	100,000	100,000
Work in process, August 31	20,000	30%	20,000	6,000
Total units accounted for..............	120,000			
Total equivalent units...................			120,000	106,000

2.

	Direct Material	Conversion	Total
Total costs to account for	$138,000	$1,089,680	
Equivalent units	120,000	106,000	
Costs per equivalent unit	$1.15	$10.28	$11.43*

*$11.43 = $1.15 + $10.28

3. Cost of goods completed and transferred out during August:

$$\begin{pmatrix} \text{number of units} \\ \text{transferred out} \end{pmatrix} \times \begin{pmatrix} \text{total cost per} \\ \text{equivalent unit} \end{pmatrix} \text{ ....} \quad 100,000 \times \$11.43 \quad \underline{\$1,143,000}$$

PROBLEM 4-32 (CONTINUED)

4.   Cost remaining in August 31 work-in-process inventory:

Direct material:

$$\begin{pmatrix} \text{number of} \\ \text{equivalent} \\ \text{units of} \\ \text{direct material} \end{pmatrix} \times \begin{pmatrix} \text{cost per} \\ \text{equivalent} \\ \text{unit of} \\ \text{direct material} \end{pmatrix} \text{.....................} \quad 20{,}000 \times \$1.15 \qquad \$23{,}000$$

Conversion:

$$\begin{pmatrix} \text{number of} \\ \text{equivalent} \\ \text{units of} \\ \text{conversion} \end{pmatrix} \times \begin{pmatrix} \text{cost per} \\ \text{equivalent} \\ \text{unit of} \\ \text{conversion} \end{pmatrix} \text{.....................} \quad 6{,}000 \times \$10.28 \qquad \underline{61{,}680}$$

Total cost of August 31 work in process... $\underline{\$\ 84{,}680}$

Check: Cost of goods completed and transferred out............................. $\$1{,}143{,}000$
    Cost of August 31 work-in-process inventory .... $\underline{84{,}680}$
    Total costs accounted for:... $\underline{\$1{,}227{,}680}$

5.   Journal entry:

Finished-Goods Inventory	1,143,000	
Work-in-Process Inventory......................................		1,143,000

PROBLEM 4-33 (35 MINUTES)

1. Direct material cost was $1,404,000:

    XY634............ $ 267,000
    AA788.......... 689,000
    GU321.......... 448,000
    Total....... $1,404,000

    Goodson's total direct-labor payroll amounted to $126,500 for 6,325 hours of work ($126,500 ÷ $20 per hour). Thus, conversion cost was $506,000:

    Direct labor.. $126,500
    Overhead applied (6,325 hours x $60)........ 379,500
    Total... $506,000

2. Goods completed during April cost $1,872,000 (24,000 units x $78) as the following calculations show:

	Physical Units	Percentage Of Completion With Respect to Conversion	Equivalent Units Direct Material	Conversion
Work in process, April 1..................	4,000	75%		
Units started during April................	25,000			
Total units to account for................	29,000			
Units completed and transferred out during April.........................	24,000	100%	24,000	24,000
Work in process, April 30................	5,000	40%	5,000	2,000
Total units accounted for................	29,000			
Total equivalent units.....................			29,000	26,000

	Direct Material	Conversion	Total
Work in process, April 1.........................	$ 220,000	$ 66,000	$ 286,000
Costs incurred during April....................	1,404,000	506,000	1,910,000
Total costs to account for......................	$1,624,000	$572,000	$2,196,000
Equivalent units...................................	29,000	26,000	
Cost per equivalent unit........................	$56[a]	$22[b]	$78[c]

[a]$1,624,000 ÷ 29,000 = $56
[b]$572,000 ÷ 26,000 = $22
[c]$56 + $22 = $78

3. The cost of the ending work-in-process inventory is $324,000:

Direct material (5,000 x $56)........	$280,000
Conversion cost (2,000 x $22).....	44,000
Total.................................	$324,000

4. (a)   No material would be added during May. All material is introduced at the start of Goodson's manufacturing process, and these units were begun in April.

(b)   Since the work-in-process inventory is 40% complete at the end of April, 60% of the conversion would be done in May.

5. Given that the ending work-in-process inventory is at the 40% stage of completion, these units would not have reached the 70% point in April where HH887 is added. Therefore, there would be zero equivalent units with respect to part HH887 in the ending work-in-process inventory.

PROBLEM 4-34 (30 MINUTES)

1. The ending work-in-process inventory consisted of 500 units (300 + 900 – 700).

2. The cost of goods completed during June totaled $57,400 (700 units x $82):

	Physical Units	Percentage Of Completion With Respect to Conversion	Equivalent Units Direct Material	Conversion
Work in process, June 1.....................	300	30%		
Units started during June.................	900			
Total units to account for..................	1,200			
Units completed and transferred during June..............................	700	100%	700	700
Work in process, June 30..................	500	60%	500	300
Total units accounted for..................	1,200			
Total equivalent units.......................			1,200	1,000

	Direct Material	Conversion	Total
Work in process, June 1........................	$15,000	$ 6,300	$21,300
Costs incurred during June....................	45,000	25,700	70,700
Total costs to account for.....................	$60,000	$32,000	$92,000
Equivalent units...................................	1,200	1,000	
Cost per equivalent unit........................	$50[a]	$32[b]	$82[c]

[a]$60,000 ÷ 1,200 = $50
[b]$32,000 ÷ 1,000 = $32
[c]$50 + $32 = $82

Finished-Goods Inventory.................................	57,400	
Work-in-Process Inventory.....................		57,400

3. The cost of the June 30 work-in-process inventory is $34,600:

Direct materials (500 x $50).........	$25,000
Conversion cost (300 x $32)........	9,600
Total....................................	$34,600

4.   Equivalent units measure the amount of manufacturing activity (i.e., for direct material or conversion) that has been applied to a batch of physical units. If, for example, a company has 600 physical units in process that are 40% complete as to conversion, the firm has done the equivalent amount of conversion activity as would be required to do *all* of the conversion work for 240 units (600 x 40%).

Equivalent units are needed to state manufacturing activity on a common measurement scale. One cannot add completed units to units in process. Such a combination is like adding apples and oranges, as some units are complete and some are incomplete. Instead, these units are first converted to equivalent units, and the latter are then used in unit-cost calculations.

PROBLEM 4-35 (50 MINUTES)

The missing amounts are shown below. A completed production report follows.

Work in process, May 1 (in units)...	15,000
Units completed and transferred out during May	65,000
Total equivalent units: conversion..	71,000
Work in process, May 1: conversion..	$ 37,500
Costs incurred during May: direct material	570,000
Cost per equivalent unit: conversion	12.25
Cost of goods completed and transferred out during May	1,407,250
Cost remaining in ending work-in-process inventory: direct material	94,000

PRODUCTION REPORT: HERCULES TIRE AND RUBBER COMPANY
Weighted-Average Method

	Physical Units	Percentage of Completion with Respect to Conversion	Equivalent Units Direct Material	Conversion
Work in process, May 1	15,000	20%		
Units started during May...............	60,000			
Total units to account for..............	75,000			
Units completed and transferred out during May....................	65,000	100%	65,000	65,000
Work in process, May 31	10,000	60%	10,000	6,000
Total units accounted for..............	75,000			
Total equivalent units....................			75,000	71,000

PROBLEM 4-35 (CONTINUED)

	Direct Material	Conversion	Total
Work in process, May 1................	$135,000	$ 37,500	$ 172,500
Costs incurred during May...........	570,000	832,250	1,402,250
Total costs to account for............	$705,000	$869,750	$1,574,750
Equivalent units..........................	75,000	71,000	
Costs per equivalent unit.............	$9.40*	$12.25†	$21.65**

*$9.40 = $705,000 ÷ 75,000
†$12.25 = $869,750 ÷ 71,000
**$21.65 = $9.40 + $12.25

PROBLEM 4-35 (CONTINUED)

Cost of goods completed and transferred out during May:

$$\left(\begin{array}{l}\text{number of units}\\\text{transferred out}\end{array}\right) \times \left(\begin{array}{l}\text{total cost per}\\\text{equivalent unit}\end{array}\right)$$ .... 65,000 × $21.65 $\underline{\$1,407,250}$

Cost remaining in May 31 work-in-process inventory:

Direct material:

$$\left(\begin{array}{l}\text{number of}\\\text{equivalent}\\\text{units of}\\\text{direct material}\end{array}\right) \times \left(\begin{array}{l}\text{cost per}\\\text{equivalent}\\\text{unit of}\\\text{direct material}\end{array}\right)$$ .... 10,000 × $9.40 $94,000

Conversion:

$$\left(\begin{array}{l}\text{number of}\\\text{equivalent}\\\text{units of}\\\text{conversion}\end{array}\right) \times \left(\begin{array}{l}\text{cost per}\\\text{equivalent}\\\text{unit of}\\\text{conversion}\end{array}\right)$$ .... 6,000 × $12.25 $\underline{73,500}$

Total cost of May 31 work-in-process .... $\underline{\$167,500}$

Check: Cost of goods completed and transferred out....... $1,407,250
        Cost of May 31 work-in-process inventory............ $\underline{167,500}$
        Total costs accounted for....................................... $\underline{\$1,574,750}$

PROBLEM 4-36 (30 MINUTES)

1. **a.**

	Tax Returns (physical units)	Percentage of Completion with Respect to Conversion (labor and overhead)	Equivalent Units	
			Labor	Overhead
Returns in process, February 1....	200	25%		
Returns started in February..........	825			
Total returns to account for..........	1,025			
Returns completed during February.......................	900	100%	900	900
Returns in process, February 28..	125	80%	100	100
Total returns accounted for..........	1,025			
Total equivalent units of activity..			1,000	1,000

b.

	Labor	Overhead	Total
Returns in process, February 1..................	£ 6,000	£ 2,500	£ 8,500
Costs incurred during February..................	89,000	45,000	134,000
Total costs to account for............................	£95,000	£47,500	£142,500
Equivalent units..	1,000	1,000	
Costs per equivalent unit............................	£95.00	£47.50	£142.50

2. Cost of returns in process on February 28:

Labor: equivalent units × cost per equivalent unit

100 × £95.00.. £ 9,500

Overhead: equivalent units × cost per equivalent unit

100 × £47.50.. 4,750

Total cost of returns in process on February 28 .... £14,250

PROBLEM 4-37 (45 MINUTES)

1.
PRODUCTION REPORT: MIXING DEPARTMENT
(Weighted-Average Method)

	Physical Units	Percentage of Completion with Respect to Conversion	Equivalent Units Direct Material	Conversion
Work in process, November 1.......	4,000	75%		
Units started during November	16,000			
Total units to account for..............	20,000			
Units completed and transferred out during November..........	15,000	100%	15,000	15,000
Work in process, November 30	5,000	20%	5,000	1,000
Total units accounted for	20,000			
Total equivalent units....................			20,000	16,000

	Direct Material	Conversion	Total
Work in process, November 1.......	$ 22,800	$ 46,510	$ 69,310
Costs incurred during November.	81,600*	196,690†	278,290
Total costs to account for	$104,400	$ 243,200	$347,600
Equivalent units	20,000	16,000	
Costs per equivalent unit..............	$5.22	$15.20	$20.42

*$81,600 = $10,000 + $51,000 + (4,000 ÷ 10,000)($51,500)
†$196,690 = $103,350 + (.40)($103,350) + $52,000

PROBLEM 4-37 (CONTINUED)

Cost of goods completed and transferred out during November:

$$\begin{pmatrix} \text{number of units} \\ \text{transferred out} \end{pmatrix} \times \begin{pmatrix} \text{total cost per} \\ \text{equivalent unit} \end{pmatrix} \dots\dots\dots\dots\dots\dots \; 15{,}000 \times \$20.42 \qquad \underline{\$306{,}300}$$

Cost remaining in November 30 work-in-process inventory

Direct material:

$$\begin{pmatrix} \text{number of} \\ \text{equivalent} \\ \text{units of} \\ \text{direct material} \end{pmatrix} \times \begin{pmatrix} \text{cost per} \\ \text{equivalent} \\ \text{unit of} \\ \text{direct material} \end{pmatrix} \dots\dots\dots\dots\dots \; 5{,}000 \times \$5.22 \qquad \$26{,}100$$

Conversion

$$\begin{pmatrix} \text{number of} \\ \text{equivalent} \\ \text{units of} \\ \text{conversion} \end{pmatrix} \times \begin{pmatrix} \text{cost per} \\ \text{equivalent} \\ \text{unit of} \\ \text{conversion} \end{pmatrix} \dots\dots\dots\dots\dots \; 1{,}000 \times \$15.20 \qquad \underline{15{,}200}$$

Total cost of November 30 work in process .... $\underline{\$41{,}300}$

Check: Cost of goods completed and transferred out........	$306,300	
Cost of November 30 work-in-process inventory...	41,300	
Total costs accounted for	$347,600	

2. a. Work-in-Process Inventory: Mixing Department 81,600
        Raw-Material Inventory... 81,600

    b. Work-in-Process Inventory: Mixing Department 103,350
        Wages Payable... 103,350

    c. Work-in-Process Inventory: Mixing Department 93,340*
        Manufacturing Overhead....................................... 93,340

    *$93,340 = (.40)($103,350) + ($52,000)

    d. Work-in-Process Inventory: Finishing Department........ 306,300
        Work-in-Process Inventory: Mixing Department .. 306,300

PROBLEM 4-38 (40 MINUTES)

1. The unit costs and total costs for each of the products manufactured by Plasto Corporation during the month of May are calculated as follows:

	Extrusion	Form	Trim	Finish
Units produced......................	16,000	11,000	5,000	2,000
Material costs	$192,000	$ 44,000	$15,000	$12,000
Unit material cost	12.00	4.00	3.00	6.00
Conversion costs*................	392,000	132,000	69,000	42,000
Unit conversion cost.....	24.50	12.00	13.80	21.00

*Direct labor and manufacturing overhead.

Unit Costs	Plastic Sheets	Standard Model	Deluxe Model	Executive Model
Material costs:				
Extrusion..........................	$12.00	$12.00	$12.00	$12.00
Form...............................		4.00	4.00	4.00
Trim................................			3.00	3.00
Finish.............................				6.00
Conversion costs:				
Extrusion..........................	24.50	24.50	24.50	24.50
Form...............................		12.00	12.00	12.00
Trim................................			13.80	13.80
Finish.............................				21.00
Total unit cost......................	$36.50	$52.50	$69.30	$96.30
Units produced....................	× 5,000	× 6,000	× 3,000	× 2,000
Total product cost*..............	$182,500	$315,000	$207,900	$192,600

*Total costs accounted for:

Product	Total Product Costs
Plastic sheets	$182,500
Standard model	315,000
Deluxe model	207,900
Executive model	192,600
Total	$898,000

2. Journal entries:

Work-in-Process Inventory: Extrusion	584,000	
Raw-Material Inventory..		192,000
Applied Conversion Costs		392,000
Finished-Goods Inventory..	182,500	
Work-in-Process Inventory: Extrusion..................		182,500
Work-in-Process Inventory: Forming	577,500	
Work-in-Process Inventory: Extrusion..................		401,500
Raw-Material Inventory..		44,000
Applied Conversion Costs		132,000

Finished-Goods Inventory..	315,000	
Work-in-Process Inventory: Forming		315,000
Work-in-Process Inventory: Trimming	346,500	
Work-in-Process Inventory: Forming		262,500
Raw-Material Inventory..		15,000
Applied Conversion Costs		69,000
Finished-Goods Inventory..	207,900	
Work-in-Process Inventory: Trimming		207,900
Work-in-Process Inventory: Finishing...........................	192,600	
Work-in-Process Inventory: Trimming		138,600
Raw-Material Inventory..		12,000
Applied Conversion Costs		42,000
Finished-Goods Inventory..	192,600	
Work-in-Process Inventory: Finishing		192,600

PROBLEM 4-39 (35 MINUTES)

1. Conversion cost per unit in department I:

$$= \frac{\text{direct labor} + \text{manufacturing overhead}}{\text{units produced*}}$$

$$= \frac{\$38,000 + \$230,000}{11,000 + 4,000 + 5,000}$$

$$= \$13.40 \text{ per unit}$$

*Note that all of the products sold after processing in departments I, II, or III were produced orginally in department I.

2. Conversion cost per unit in department II:

$$= \frac{\text{direct labor} + \text{manufacturing overhead}}{\text{units produced*}}$$

$$= \frac{\$22,000 + \$68,000}{4,000 + 5,000}$$

$$= \$10.00 \text{ per unit}$$

*Note that all of the products sold after processing in departments II and III were colored in department II.

3. Cost of a clear glass sheet:

$$= \frac{\text{direct material per}}{\text{unit in department I}} + \frac{\text{conversion cost per}}{\text{unit in department I}}$$

$$= \frac{\$450,000}{20,000} + \$13.40$$

$$= \$35.90 \text{ per sheet}$$

PROBLEM 4-39 (CONTINUED)

4. Cost of an unetched, colored glass sheet:

$$= \begin{array}{c} \text{cost per clear} \\ \text{glass sheet} \end{array} + \begin{array}{c} \text{direct material} \\ \text{per unit in department II} \end{array} + \begin{array}{c} \text{conversion cost per} \\ \text{unit in department II} \end{array}$$

$$= \$35.90 + \frac{\$72,000}{9,000} + \$10.00$$

$$= \$53.90 \text{ per sheet}$$

5. Cost of an etched, colored glass sheet:

$$= \begin{array}{c} \text{cost per unetched} \\ \text{colored glass sheet} \end{array} + \begin{array}{c} \text{conversion cost per} \\ \text{unit in department III} \end{array}$$

$$= \$53.90 + \frac{\$38,000 + \$73,750}{5,000}$$

$$= \$76.25 \text{ per sheet}$$

PROBLEM 4-40 (45 MINUTES)

1. Conversion costs:

	Rolling	Molding	Punching	Dipping
Direct labor	$300,000	$112,000	$128,000	$ 45,000
Manufacturing overhead..............	450,000	168,000	192,000	67,500
Total conversion cost...................	$750,000	$280,000	$320,000	$112,500
Total units produced:				
Rolling only...........................	20,000			
Rolling, molding, punching		8,000	8,000	
Rolling, molding, punching,				
dipping				3,000
Conversion cost per unit	$37.50	$35.00	$40.00	$37.50

2.   Product costs:

	Ceralam Sheets Sold after Rolling	Nonreflective Ceralam Housings	Reflective Ceralam Housings	Total Costs
Direct material:				
Ceralam sheets.....................	$480,000	$200,000	$120,000	$ 800,000
Chemical dip........................			30,000	30,000
Conversion costs:				
Rolling................................	450,000[a]	187,500[a]	112,500[a]	750,000
Molding		175,000[b]	105,000[b]	280,000
Punching............................		200,000[c]	120,000[c]	320,000
Dipping..............................			112,500[d]	112,500
Total cost	$930,000	$762,500	$600,000	$2,292,500
Units manufactured..................	12,000	5,000	3,000	
Unit cost.............................	$77.50	$152.50	$200.00	

[a]Number of units × rolling cost per unit ($37.50)
[b]Number of units × molding cost per unit ($35.00)
[c]Number of units × punching cost per unit ($40.00)
[d]Number of units × dipping cost per unit ($37.50)

3.   Journal entries:

Work-in-Process Inventory: Rolling	1,550,000	
Raw-Material Inventory...		800,000*
Applied Conversion Costs		750,000†

*$800,000 = direct-material cost for ceralam sheets
†$750,000 = conversion cost in rolling operation

Finished-Goods Inventory..	930,000*	
Work-in-Process Inventory: Rolling.........................		930,000

*$930,000 = 12,000 ceralam sheets sold after
                  rolling × $77.50 per unit

Cost of Goods Sold..	930,000*	
Finished-Goods Inventory..		930,000

*$930,000 = cost of ceralam sheets sold after
                  rolling

Work-in-Process Inventory: Molding..................................	620,000*	
Work-in-Process Inventory: Rolling.........................		620,000

*$620,000 = cost remaining in Work-in-Process
                  Inventory: Rolling
           = $1,550,000 – $930,000

Work-in-Process Inventory: Molding..................................	280,000*	
Applied Conversion Costs		280,000

*$280,000 = conversion cost in molding operation

Work-in-Process Inventory: Punching	900,000*	
Work-in-Process Inventory: Molding.........................		900,000

*$900,000 = cost remaining in Work-in-Process
                  Inventory: Molding
           = $620,000 + $280,000

Work-in-Process Inventory: Punching	320,000*	
Applied Conversion Costs		320,000

*$320,000 = conversion cost in punching operation

PROBLEM 4-40 (CONTINUED)

Finished-Goods Inventory..	762,500*	
Work-in-Process Inventory: Punching......................		762,500

*$762,500 = 5,000 nonreflective ceralam housings
sold after punching × $152.50 per unit

Cost of Goods Sold..	762,500*	
Finished-Goods Inventory..		762,500

*$762,500 = cost of nonreflective ceralam
housings sold after punching

Work-in-Process Inventory: Dipping	457,500*	
Work-in-Process Inventory: Punching......................		457,500

*$457,500 = cost remaining in Work-in-Process
Inventory: Punching
= $900,000 + $320,000 – $762,500

Work-in-Process Inventory: Dipping	142,500	
Raw-Material Inventory...		30,000*
Applied Conversion Costs		112,500†

*$30,000   = direct-material cost for chemical dip
†$112,500 = conversion cost in dipping operation

Finished-Goods Inventory..	600,000*	
Work-in-Process Inventory: Dipping........................		600,000

*$600,000 = 3,000 reflective ceralam housings
sold after dipping × $200.00 per unit

Cost of Goods Sold..	600,000	
Finished-Goods Inventory..		600,000

PROBLEM 4-41 (30 MINUTES)

1. a. Cost of units completed and transferred to finished-goods inventory during May:

Units completed and transferred out..	11,900
Total cost per equivalent unit	× $9.00
Cost of units completed and transferred out...............................	$107,100

b. To compute the cost of the Finishing Department's work-in-process inventory on May 31, first determine the number of units in ending work-in-process inventory, as follows:

Work-in-process inventory, May 1 (in units).................................	1,400
Add: Units transferred in..	14,000
Units to account for	15,400
Less: Units transferred to finished goods	11,900
Work-in-process inventory, May 31 (in units)...............................	3,500

Then compute the transferred-in, direct-material, and conversion costs in the May 31 work-in-process inventory:

Input	Equivalent Units		Cost per Equivalent Unit	Cost
Transferred-in.........................	3,500	×	$5.00	$17,500
Direct material........................	3,500	×	$1.00	3,500
Conversion	3,500 × 40%	×	$3.00	4,200
Total cost of May 31 work-in-process inventory				$25,200

2.

Equivalent units of transferred-in costs...	15,400
Transferred-in cost per equivalent unit..	× $5.00
Total transferred-in cost...	$77,000
Deduct: Transferred-in cost in May 1 work-in-process inventory..........	6,750
Total cost transferred in from the Assembly Department	$70,250

Journal entry to record transfer:

Work-in-Process Inventory: Finishing Department.............	70,250	
Work-in-Process Inventory: Assembly Department.....		70,250

SOLUTIONS TO CASES

CASE 4-42 (45 MINUTES)

1. Equivalent units of material 8,000
    Equivalent units of conversion 7,500

2. Cost per equivalent unit of material $3.30
    Cost per equivalent unit of conversion $2.80

3. October 31 work-in-process inventory... $4,700
    Cost of goods completed and transferred out...................................... $42,700

4. Weighted-average unit cost of completed leather belts $6.10

These answers are supported by the following process-costing schedules. The firm's cost per belt used for planning and control, $5.35, is substantially lower than the actual cost per belt incurred in October, $6.10. Management should investigate this situation to determine whether production costs can be reduced. If not, then the cost used for planning and control purposes should be changed to reflect the firm's actual experience.

CALCULATION OF EQUIVALENT UNITS: LAREDO LEATHER CO. - DALLAS PLANT
Weighted-Average Method

	Physical Units	Percentage of Completion with Respect to Conversion	Equivalent Units Direct Material	Equivalent Units Conversion
Work in process, October 1	400	25%		
Units started during October	7,600			
Total units to account for	8,000			
Units completed and transferred out during October	7,000	100%	7,000	7,000
Work in process, October 31	1,000	50%	1,000	500
Total units accounted for	8,000			
Total equivalent units			8,000	7,500

CASE 4-42 (CONTINUED)

CALCULATION OF COSTS PER EQUIVALENT UNIT: DALLAS PLANT
Weighted-Average Method

	Direct Material	Conversion	Total
Work in process, October 1	$ 1,250	$ 300	$ 1,550
Costs incurred during October.........................	25,150	20,700	45,850
Total costs to account for	$26,400	$21,000	$47,400
Equivalent units	8,000	7,500	
Costs per equivalent unit	$3.30	$2.80	$6.10

ANALYSIS OF TOTAL COSTS: DALLAS PLANT
Weighted-Average Method

Cost of goods completed and transferred out during October:

$$\left(\begin{array}{c}\text{number of units}\\\text{transferred out}\end{array}\right) \times \left(\begin{array}{c}\text{total cost per}\\\text{equivalent unit}\end{array}\right) \text{.........................}$$ $7{,}000 \times \$6.10$ $\underline{\$42{,}700}$

Cost remaining in October 31 work-in-process inventory:

Direct material:

$$\left(\begin{array}{c}\text{number of}\\\text{equivalent}\\\text{units of}\\\text{direct material}\end{array}\right) \times \left(\begin{array}{c}\text{cost per}\\\text{equivalent}\\\text{unit of}\\\text{direct material}\end{array}\right) \text{..........................}$$ $1{,}000 \times \$3.30$ $\$3{,}300$

Conversion:

$$\left(\begin{array}{c}\text{number of}\\\text{equivalent}\\\text{units of}\\\text{conversion}\end{array}\right) \times \left(\begin{array}{c}\text{cost per}\\\text{equivalent}\\\text{unit of}\\\text{conversion}\end{array}\right) \text{......................................}$$ $500 \times \$2.80$ $\underline{1{,}400}$

Total cost of October 31 work in process.. $\underline{\$4{,}700}$

CASE 4-42 (CONTINUED)

Check: Cost of goods completed and transferred out...	$42,700
Cost of October 31 work-in-process inventory..	4,700
Total costs accounted for.....................................	$47,400

5. If the units were 60 percent complete as of October 31, there would be 7,600 equivalent units with respect to conversion. (To see this, just change the 500 in the right-hand column of the table in the solution to requirement (4) to 600. This changes the last number in the right-hand column from 7,500 to 7,600.)

Now the unit cost of conversion drops from $2.80, as currently computed, to $2.76 (rounded, $21,000 ÷ 7,600). Thus, the unit cost drops from $6.10 to $6.06 (rounded).

As controller, Jeff Daley has an ethical obligation to refuse his friend's request to alter the estimate of the percentage of completion. What Daley can do is to help Murray think of some legitimate ways to bring about real cost reductions. Several ethical standards for management accountants (listed in Chapter 1) apply in this situation. Among the relevant standards are the following:

Competence:

*   Prepare complete and clear reports and recommendations after appropriate analyses of relevant and reliable information.

Objectivity:

*   Communicate information fairly and objectively.

*   Disclose fully all relevant information that could reasonably be expected to influence an intended user's understanding of the reports, comments, and recommendations presented.

CASE 4-43 (60 MINUTES)

PRODUCTION REPORT: HOME GARDEN COMPANY - GRADING DEPARTMENT
Weighted-Average Method

	Physical Units	Percentage of Completion with Respect to Conversion	Equivalent Units	
			Direct Material	Conversion
Work in process, November 1.........	-0-	—		
Units started during November.......	36,000			
Total units to account for................	36,000			
Units completed and transferred out during November..................	36,000	100%	36,000	36,000
Work in process, November 30.......	-0-	—	-0-	-0-
Total units accounted for................	36,000			
Total equivalent units......................			36,000	36,000

	Direct Material	Conversion	Total
Work in process, November 1............................	-0-	-0-	-0-
Costs incurred during November.......................	$265,680	$86,400	$352,080
Total costs to account for.................................	$265,680	$86,400	$352,080
Equivalent units..	36,000	36,000	
Costs per equivalent unit..................................	$7.38	$2.40	$9.78

Cost of goods completed and transferred out of the Grading Department during November:

$$\begin{pmatrix} \text{number of units} \\ \text{transferred out} \end{pmatrix} \times \begin{pmatrix} \text{total cost per} \\ \text{equivalent unit} \end{pmatrix} \text{.........................} \quad 36{,}000 \times \$9.78 \qquad \underline{\$352{,}080}$$

Cost remaining in November 30 work-in-process inventory in the
   Grading Department ....   -0-

Check: Cost of goods completed and transferred out............. $352,080
     Cost of November 30 work-in-process inventory........   -0-
     Total costs accounted for... $352,080

CASE 4-43 (CONTINUED)

PRODUCTION REPORT: HOME GARDEN COMPANY - SATURATING DEPARTMENT
Weighted-Average Method

	Physical Units	Percentage of Completion with Respect to Conversion	Equivalent Units Transferred in	Conversion
Work in process, November 1.........	1,600	50%		
Units transferred in during November	36,000			
Total units to account for................	37,600			
Units completed and transferred out during November..................	35,600	100%	35,600	35,600
Work in process, November 30.......	2,000	50%	2,000	1,000
Total units accounted for................	37,600			
Total equivalent units......................			37,600	36,600

	Transferred In	Conversion	Total
Work in process, November 1..........................	$ 13,850	$ 3,750	$ 17,600
Costs incurred during November.....................	352,080*	85,920	438,000
Total costs to account for...............................	$365,930	$89,670	$455,600
Equivalent units..	37,600	36,600	
Costs per equivalent unit................................	$9.7322	$2.45	$12.1822

*Cost of goods completed and transferred out of Grading Department during November, under the weighted-average method.

CASE 4-43 (CONTINUED)

Cost of goods completed and transferred out of the Saturating Department during November:

$$\begin{pmatrix} \text{number of units} \\ \text{transferred out} \end{pmatrix} \times \begin{pmatrix} \text{total cost per} \\ \text{equivalent unit} \end{pmatrix} \dots\dots\dots\dots \quad 35{,}600 \times \$12.1822 \qquad \underline{\$433{,}686^{\dagger}}$$

Cost remaining in November 30 work-in-process inventory in the Saturating Department:

Transferred-in costs:

$$\begin{pmatrix} \text{number of} \\ \text{equivalent} \\ \text{units of} \\ \text{transferred-in cost} \end{pmatrix} \times \begin{pmatrix} \text{transferred-in} \\ \text{cost per} \\ \text{equivalent} \\ \text{unit} \end{pmatrix} \dots\dots\dots \quad 2{,}000 \times \$9.7322 \qquad \$19{,}464^{\dagger}$$

Direct material:

None

Conversion:

$$\begin{pmatrix} \text{number of} \\ \text{equivalent} \\ \text{units of} \\ \text{conversion} \end{pmatrix} \times \begin{pmatrix} \text{conversion} \\ \text{cost per} \\ \text{equivalent} \\ \text{unit} \end{pmatrix} \dots\dots\dots\dots \quad 1{,}000 \times \$2.45 \qquad \underline{2{,}450}$$

Total cost of November 30 work in process	$\underline{\$21{,}914}$

Check:		
Cost of goods completed and transferred out..............	$433{,}686	
Cost of November 30 work-in-process inventory.........	$\underline{21{,}914}$	
Total costs accounted for...	$\underline{\$455{,}600}$	

†Rounded

CURRENT ISSUES IN MANAGERIAL ACCOUNTING

ISSUE 4-44

"BOTTLED UP: PROFITS AREN'T FLOWING LIKE THEY USED TO AT PACKAGED-GOODS COMPANIES. GREEN KETCHUP AND TUNA IN A POUCH SAVE HEINZ?, " *FORTUNE*, SEPTEMBER 18, 2000, JULIE CRESWELL.

1. Heinz is a food processor and manufactures large quantities of relatively homogeneous products. Thus, process costing would be an appropriate product costing system for Heintz.

2. Heinz has recently begun to compete for more noticeable and attractive shelve space, and, after years of neglect, the company has begun to market and package to reflect the growing demographic changes in America. By bringing on the StarKist Tuna in a Pouch it has recognized that eating habits have changed in America. The green ketchup in an EZ Squirt bottle is an attempt to gain a young audience because eating habits begin early. Fruit and Vegetable Wash is a new product offering.

ISSUE 4-45

"INTERNATIONAL PAPER SHUTTING PLANTS TO CUT SUPPLY," *THE WALL STREET JOURNAL*, OCTOBER 19, 2000, ALLANNA SULLIVAN.

1. International paper would use process costing since they produce large quantities of relatively homogeneous products.

2. Paper supply costs and total production costs should be reduced. The fixed costs of the closed plants would be eliminated while the fixed costs of the remaining plants would remain stable. Production of the remaining plants would increase.

ISSUE 4-46

"U.S. IS UNLIKELY TO RELEASE MORE OIL SOON," *THE WALL STREET JOURNAL*, OCTOBER 19, 2000, JOHN J. FLAKA. ALSO SEE "NO SURGE IN CRUDE DELIEVERIES EXPECTED," *THE WALL STREET JOURNAL*, OCTOBER 16, 2000, BHUSHAN BAHREE.

1. The government's release of 30 million gallons of crude oil is only about one day's supply of oil for the United States, so I would have a negligible effect on the oil companies.

2. Oil companies would use process costing since they produce large quantities of relatively homogeneous products.

ISSUE 4-47

"GEORGIA-PACIFIC PROFIT DECLINES BY 43 PERCENT: SLUGGISH BUILDING PRODUCTS SECTOR CITED," *THE WALL STREET JOURNAL*, OCTOBER 19, 2000, BETSY MCKAY.

1. Georgia-Pacific would use process costing since the company produces large quantities of relatively homogeneous products.

2. Lower prices for building materials would not *directly* affect the company's product costs, but lower prices would pressure management to attempt to reduce product costs in order to remain price competitive in a weakening market.

CHAPTER 5
Activity-Based Costing and Cost Management Systems

ANSWERS TO REVIEW QUESTIONS

5-1   In a traditional, volume-based product-costing system, only a single predetermined overhead rate is used. All manufacturing-overhead costs are combined into one cost pool, and they are applied to products on the basis of a single cost driver that is closely related to production volume. The most frequently used cost drivers in traditional product-costing systems are direct-labor hours, direct-labor dollars, machine hours, and units of production.

5-2   Aerotech Corporation's management was being misled by the traditional product-costing system, because the high-volume product lines were being overcosted and the low-volume product line was being undercosted. The high-volume products essentially were subsidizing the low-volume line. The traditional product-costing system failed to show that the low-volume products were driving more than their share of overhead costs. As a result of these misleading costs, the company's management was mispricing its products.

5-3   An activity-based costing system is a two-stage process of assigning costs to products. In stage one, activity-cost pools are established. In stage two a cost driver is identified for each activity-cost pool. Then the costs in each pool are assigned to each product line in proportion to the amount of the cost driver consumed by each product line.

5-4   A cost driver is a characteristic of an event or activity that results in the incurrence of costs by that event or activity. In activity-based costing systems, the most significant cost drivers are identified. Then a database is created that shows how these cost drivers are distributed across products. This database is used to assign costs to the various products depending on the extent to which they use each cost driver.

5-5   The four broad categories of activities identified in an activity-based costing system are as follows:

   (a)   Unit-level activities: Must be done for each unit of production.

   (b)   Batch-level activities: Must be performed for each batch of products.

   (c)   Product-sustaining activities: Needed to support an entire product line.

(d) Facility-level (or general-operations-level) activities: Required for the entire production process to occur.

5-6 An activity-based costing system alleviated the problems Aerotech Corporation was having under its traditional, volume-based product-costing system by more accurately assigning costs to products. Products were assigned costs based on the extent to which they used various cost drivers that were determined to be closely related to the incurrence of a variety of overhead costs.

5-7 Product-costing systems based on a single, volume-based cost driver tend to overcost high-volume products, because all overhead costs are combined into one pool and distributed across all products on the basis of only one cost driver. This simple averaging process fails to recognize the fact that a disproportionate amount of costs often is associated with low-volume or complex products. The result is that low-volume products are assigned less than their share of manufacturing costs, and high-volume products are assigned more than their share of the costs.

5-8 In traditional, volume-based costing systems, only direct material and direct labor are considered direct costs. In contrast, under an activity-based costing system, an effort is made to account for as many costs as possible as direct costs of production. Any cost that can possibly be traced to a particular product line is treated as a direct cost of that product.

5-9 A cost management system (CMS) has the following objectives:

(a) To measure the cost of the resources consumed in performing the organization's significant activities.

(b) To identify and eliminate non-value-added costs. These are costs of activities that can be eliminated with no deterioration of product quality, performance, or perceived value.

(c) To determine the efficiency and effectiveness of all major activities performed in the enterprise.

(d) To identify and evaluate new activities that can improve the future performance of the organization.

5-10 Non-value-added costs are the costs of activities that can be eliminated with no deterioration of product quality, performance, or perceived value. Some examples of potential non-value-added costs are as follows: time spent unnecessarily moving raw materials, work in process, or finished goods between operations; unnecessary time spent by raw materials or work in process waiting for the next operation; storage of unnecessary inventories of raw materials, parts, or partially completed products; costs incurred in repairing defective units when the defects could be eliminated with better quality control systems.

5-11 Time is spent in a manufacturing process in the following five ways: process time, inspection time, move time, waiting time, and storage time. There is the potential for non-value-added costs in any of these five areas. Inefficient or unnecessary steps in the production process may result in non-value-added costs. Other potential non-value-added activities include unnecessary inspections, unnecessary movement of materials and goods between operations, unnecessary time spent waiting by materials or partially completed goods, and excessive inventory in storage.

5-12 Two factors that tend to result in product cost distortion under traditional, volume-based product-costing systems are as follows:

(a) Non-unit level overhead costs: Many overhead costs vary with cost drivers that are not unit-level activities. Use of a unit-level cost driver to assign such costs tends to result in cost distortion.

(b) Product diversity: When a manufacturer produces a diverse set of products, which exhibit different consumption ratios for overhead activities, use of a single cost driver to assign costs results in cost distortion.

5-13 Activity-based management means the use of an activity-based costing system to improve the operations of an organization.

5-14 Three important factors in selecting cost drivers for an ABC system are as follows:

(a) *Degree of correlation* between consumption of an activity and consumption of the cost driver.

(b) *Cost of measurement* of the cost driver.

(c) *Behavioral effects*, that is, how the cost driver selected will affect the behavior of the individuals involved in the activity related to the cost driver.

5-15 A homogeneous cost pool is a grouping of overhead costs in which each cost component is consumed in roughly the same proportion by each cost object (e.g., product line).

5-16 An activity dictionary lists all of the activities identified and used in an activity-based costing analysis. The activity dictionary provides for consistency in the terminology and level of complexity in the ABC analysis in the organization's various subunits.

5-17 Designing and implementing an ABC system requires a large amount of data from all facets of an organization's operations. A multidisciplinary team will be more effective in obtaining access to this data, and the result will be a better ABC system. Moreover, a multidisciplinary team typically helps in gaining acceptance of the new product-costing system.

5-18 Tipoffs that a new product-costing system may be needed include the following (eight required):

(a) Line managers do not believe the product costs reported by the accounting department.

(b) Marketing personnel are unwilling to use reported product costs in making pricing decisions.

(c) Complex products that are difficult to manufacture are reported to be very profitable although they are not priced at a premium.

(d) Product-line profit margins are difficult to explain.

(e) Sales are increasing, but profits are declining.

(f) Line managers suggest that apparently profitable products be dropped.

(g) Marketing or production managers are using "bootleg costing systems," which are informal systems they designed, often on a personal computer.

(h) Some products that have reported high profit margins are not sold by competitors.

(i) The firm seems to have captured a highly profitable product niche all for itself.

(j) Overhead rates are very high, and increasing over time.

(k) Product lines are diverse.

(l) Direct labor is a small percentage of total costs.

(m) The results of bids are difficult to explain.

(n) Competitors' high-volume products seem to be priced unrealistically low.

(o) The accounting department spends significant amounts of time on special costing projects to support bids or pricing decisions.

5-19   Line mangers are close to the production process and may realize that a complex product, which is difficult to manufacture, is undercosted by a traditional, volume-based costing system. Because of the cost distortion that is common in such systems, the undercosted product may appear to be profitable when it is really losing money. Line mangers may have a "gut feeling" for this situation, even if the cost-accounting system suggests otherwise.

5-20   Diverse products typically consume support activities (such as purchasing, material handling, engineering, and inspection) in differing degrees. When there are significant differences among product lines in the ways that they consume support services (and thereby cause overhead costs), a traditional, volume-based costing system may distort product costs. Some products are overcosted; others are undercosted. An ABC system can eliminate (or at least alleviate) such cost distortion.

5-21   Activity-based costing is just as appropriate in the service industry as in the manufacturing industry. Just as in manufacturing firms, diverse services typically consume support activities in varying degrees. ABC systems are more accurate in tracking the usage of these support activities to the services (products) that are produced than are traditional, volume-based costing systems.

5-22   At Braintree Hospital, an activity-based costing system has enabled management to measure and track the cost of providing nursing care to each individual patient. The wide variety of patient ailments requires a wide variation in the amount and type of nursing care provided to patients. This variation in ailments is analogous to the product-line diversity in a manufacturing firm.

5-23   As indicated in the chapter, Pennsylvania Blue Shield, like many manufacturers, classifies activities as unit level, batch level, product-sustaining level, or facility level. Maintenance of the medical-services provider network (i.e., the physicians and hospitals that provide medical care to claimants) is a product-sustaining-level activity because it benefits an entire product line (service line, in this case) of personal health insurance policies.

SOLUTIONS TO EXERCISES

EXERCISE 5-24 (15 MINUTES)

1. Material-handling cost per lens:

$$\frac{\$50,000}{[(25)(200) + (25)(200)]^*} \times 200 = \$1,000$$

*The total number of direct-labor hours.

An alternative calculation, since both types of product use the same amount of the cost driver, is the following:

$$\frac{\$50,000}{50^*} = \$1,000$$

*The total number of units (of both types) produced.

2. Material-handling cost per mirror = $1,000. The analysis is identical to that given for requirement (1).

3. Material-handling cost per lens:

$$\frac{\dfrac{\$50,000}{(5+15)^*} \times 5^\dagger}{25} = \$500$$

*The total number of material moves.
†The number of material moves for the lens product line.

4. Material-handling cost per mirror:

$$\frac{\dfrac{\$50,000}{(5+15)} \times 15^*}{25} = \$1,500$$

*The number of material moves for the mirror product line.

EXERCISE 5-25 (15 MINUTES)

1. a. Quality-control costs assigned to the Satin Sheen line under the traditional system:

Quality-control costs $= 14.5\% \times$ direct-labor cost

Quality-control
costs assigned to
Satin Sheen line $= 14.5\% \times \$27,500$

$= \$3,988$ (rounded)

b. Quality-control costs assigned to the Satin Sheen line under activity-based costing:

Activity	Pool Rate	Quantity for Satin Sheen	Assigned Cost
Incoming material inspection.......	$11.50 per type.....	12 types........	$ 138
In-process inspection....................	.14 per unit......	17,500 units..	2,450
Product certification......................	77.00 per order....	25 orders	1,925
Total quality-control costs assigned			$4,513

2. The traditional product-costing system undercosts the Satin Sheen product line, with respect to quality-control costs, by $525 ($4,513 – $3,988).

EXERCISE 5-26 (20 MINUTES)

There is no single correct answer to this exercise. There are many reasonable solutions.

Cost pool 1:

Raw materials and components	2,950,000 *yen*
Inspection	30,000 *yen*
Total...	2,980,000 *yen*

Cost driver: raw-material cost

EXERCISE 5-26 (CONTINUED)

Cost pool 2:

Depreciation, machinery	1,400,000 *yen*
Electricity, machinery	120,000 *yen*
Equipment maintenance, wages	150,000 *yen*
Equipment maintenance, parts	30,000 *yen*
Total	1,700,000 *yen*

Cost driver: number of units produced.

Cost pool 3:

Setup wages	40,000 *yen*
Total	40,000 *yen*

Cost driver: number of production runs.

Cost pool 4:

Engineering design	610,000 *yen*
Total	610,000 *yen*

Cost driver: number of parts in a product.

Cost pool 5:

Depreciation, plant	700,000 *yen*
Insurance, plant	600,000 *yen*
Electricity, light	60,000 *yen*
Custodial wages, plant	40,000 *yen*
Property taxes	120,000 *yen*
Natural gas, heating	30,000 *yen*
Total	1,550,000 *yen*

Cost driver: for costs allocated to support departments, square footage; for costs assigned to products, number of units produced.

EXERCISE 5-27 (5 MINUTES)

Cost pool 1: unit-level
Cost pool 2: unit-level
Cost pool 3: batch-level
Cost pool 4: product-sustaining-level
Cost pool 5: facility-level

EXERCISE 5-28 (30 MINUTES)

Answers will vary widely, depending on the web site chosen. In general, though, activity-based costing could be a useful tool in helping any governmental unit understand what its cost drivers are for the various activities in which it engages.

EXERCISE 5-29 (25 MINUTES)

1. Use of a single predetermined overhead rate averages all manufacturing-overhead costs together. Every production job is assigned the same amount of overhead cost per unit of the single, volume-based cost driver.

   Dividing overhead into cost pools enables Hewlett-Packard Company to assign overhead costs to products more accurately. The production manufacturing-overhead cost pool is assigned to products on the basis of direct labor. Products that require large amounts of direct labor will be assigned relatively larger amounts of the overhead costs in this pool, such as production supervision and indirect labor. The procurement manufacturing-overhead cost pool is assigned to products on the basis of direct-material cost. Products that require larger amounts of direct material will be assigned relatively larger amounts of such overhead costs as purchasing and raw-material inspection.

2. The benefits of using multiple cost drivers stem from the increased accuracy in product costs. This improved accuracy helps management to make better decisions about pricing, bidding, product mix, and adding or dropping product lines.

3. The costs of using multiple cost drivers include the time spent dividing overhead costs into pools, selecting cost drivers, and measuring the amount of each cost driver used by each product line; and increased data management requirements.

EXERCISE 5-30 (20 MINUTES)

Wheelco's product-costing system probably is providing misleading cost information to management. A common problem in a traditional, volume-based costing system is that high-volume products are overcosted and low-volume products are undercosted. There is evidence of this in the exercise, since Wheelco's competitors are selling the high-volume A22 wheel at a price lower than Wheelco's reported manufacturing cost. In contrast, Wheelco is selling its specialty D52 wheel at a huge markup above the product's reported cost. An activity-based costing system probably would report a lower product cost for wheel A22 and a substantially higher cost for wheel D52.

The president's strategy of pushing the firm's specialty products probably will aggravate Wheelco's problem even further. These products probably are not as profitable as the firm's traditional product-costing system makes them appear.

Recommendation: Install an activity-based costing system. If the new reported product costs shift as suggested in the preceding comments, then lower the price on the high-volume products, such as wheel A22. The prices of the specialty wheels probably will need to be raised. It is possible that Wheelco should discontinue low-volume products.

EXERCISE 5-31 (15 MINUTES)

1. Key features of an activity-based costing system:

    (a) Two-stage procedure for cost assignment.

    (b) Stage one: Establish activity cost pools.

    (c) Stage two: Select cost drivers for each activity-cost pool. Then assign the costs in each cost pool to the company's product lines in proportion to the amount of the related cost driver used by each product line.

2. As described in the answer to the preceding exercise, the new system probably will reveal distortion in the firm's reported product costs. In all likelihood, the high-volume products are overcosted and the low-volume specialty products are undercosted.

EXERCISE 5-31 (CONTINUED)

3. Strategic options:

(a) Lower the prices on the firm's high-volume products to compete more effectively.

(b) Increase the prices on low-volume specialty products.

(c) Consider eliminating the specialty product lines. This option may not be desirable if there is a marketing need to produce a full product line. Also, the specialty wheels may give Wheelco prestige.

EXERCISE 5-32 (20 MINUTES)

The activity of the Finger Lakes Winery may be classified as follows:

U: Unit-level

B: Batch-level

P: Product-sustaining-level

F: Facility-level

Activity	Classification	Activity	Classification
(1)	P	(11)	B
(2)	P	(12)	B
(3)	P	(13)	U
(4)	P	(14)	U
(5)	P	(15)	U
(6)	P	(16)	U
(7)	P	(17)	B
(8)	B	(18)	F
(9)	B	(19)	F
(10)	B		

EXERCISE 5-33 (20 MINUTES)

The definitions used by Carrier Corporation for each of the activity levels are as follows:*

- Unit: This activity or cost occurs every time a unit is produced. An example is the utility cost for production equipment. This level of activity usually relates directly to production volume.

- Batch: This activity is performed for each batch produced or acquired. Examples include moving raw material between the stock room and production line or setting up a machine for a run.

- Product-sustaining: This activity is performed to maintain product designs, processes, models, and parts. Examples include expediting parts, maintaining the bill of materials, or issuing orders for product changes. Sustaining activities are required for supporting a key manufacturing capability or process.

- Facility: These activities are performed to enable production. They are fundamental to supporting the business entity at the most basic level. Examples are managing or cleaning the building.

These definitions are consistent with those given in the chapter. An argument for the ABC project team's classification would be that the activity or account in question was characterized by the definition of the activity-level classification given above. An argument against the team's classification would be that the particular activity or account did not satisfy the definition.

For example, moving materials is a batch-level activity because a raw material must be moved to the product area when a production run or batch is started. Depreciation is a facility-level account because depreciation on plant and equipment represents the cost of providing production facilities in which manufacturing can take place.

———————————

*Robert Adams and Ray Carter, "United Technologies' Activity-Based Accounting Is a Catalyst for Success" *As Easy as ABC*, 18, p.4. United Technologies uses the term *structural*-level activity, instead of *facility*-level activity as we have done.

EXERCISE 5-34 (30 MINUTES)

1.

REDWOOD COMPANY
COMPUTATION OF SELLING COSTS
BY ORDER SIZE AND PER SKEIN WITHIN EACH ORDER SIZE

	Order Size			
	Small	Medium	Large	Total
Sales commissions[a] (Unit cost: $675,000/225,000 = $3.00 per box.........................	$ 6,000	$135,000	$534,000	$ 675,000
Catalogs[b] (Unit cost: $295,400/590,800 = $.50 per catalog	127,150	105,650	62,600	295,400
Costs of catalog sales[c] (Unit cost: $105,000/175,000 = $.60 per skein.......................	47,400	31,200	26,400	105,000
Credit and collection[d] (Unit cost: $60,000/6,000 = $10.00 per order...................	4,850	24,150	31,000	60,000
Total cost per order size	$185,400	$296,000	$654,000	$1,135,400
Units (skeins) sold[e]........................	103,000	592,000	2,180,000	
Unit cost per order size[f]	$1.80	$.50	$.30	

[a]Retail sales in boxes × unit cost:
    Small, 2,000 × $3
    Medium, 45,000 × $3
    Large, 178,000 × $3
[b]Catalogs distributed × unit cost
[c]Catalog sales × unit cost
[d]Number of retail orders × unit cost
[e]Small: (2,000 × 12) + 79,000 = 103,000
 Medium: (45,000 × 12) + 52,000 = 592,000
 Large: (178,000 × 12) + 44,000 = 2,180,000
[f]Total cost per order size ÷ units sold

2. The analysis of selling costs shows that small orders cost more than large orders. This fact could persuade management to market large orders more aggressively and/or offer discounts for them.

SOLUTIONS TO PROBLEMS

PROBLEM 5-35 (25 MINUTES)

1. a. Manufacturing overhead costs include all indirect manufacturing costs (all production costs except direct material and direct labor). Typical overhead costs include:

    - Indirect labor (e.g., a lift-truck driver, maintenance and inspection labor, engineering labor, and supervisors).

    - Indirect material.

    - Other indirect manufacturing costs (e.g., building maintenance, machine and tool maintenance, property taxes, insurance, depreciation on plant and equipment, rent, and utilities).

    b. Companies develop overhead rates before production to facilitate the costing of products as they are completed and shipped, rather than waiting until actual costs are accumulated for the period of production.

2. The increase in the overhead rate should not have a negative impact on the company, because the increase in indirect costs was offset by a decrease in direct labor.

3. Rather than using a plantwide overhead rate, Oceana Manufacturing could implement separate activity cost pools. Examples are as follows:

    - Separate costs into departmental overhead accounts (or other relevant pools), with one account for each production and service department. Each department would allocate its overhead to products on the basis that best reflects the use of these overhead services.

    - Treat individual machines as separate cost centers, with the machine costs collected and charged to the products using machine hours.

4. An activity-based costing system might benefit Oceana Manufacturing because it assigns costs to products according to their usage of activities in the production process. More accurate product costs are the result.

PROBLEM 5-36 (30 MINUTES)

1. Predetermined overhead rate = budgeted overhead ÷ budgeted direct-labor hours
   = $800,000 ÷ 25,000* = $32 per direct labor hour

   *25,000 budgeted direct-labor hours = (3,000 units of Standard)(3 hrs./unit) +
   (4,000 units of Enhanced)(4 hrs./unit)

	Standard	Enhanced
Direct material.................	$ 25	$ 40
Direct labor:		
3 hours x $12............	36	
4 hours x $12............		48
Manufacturing overhead:		
3 hours x $32............	96	
4 hours x $32............		128
Total cost......................	$157	$216

2. Activity-based overhead application rates:

Activity	Cost		Activity Cost Driver		Application Rate
Order processing	$150,000	÷	500 orders processed (OP)	=	$300 per OP
Machine processing	560,000	÷	40,000 machine hrs. (MH)	=	$14 per MH
Product inspection	90,000	÷	10,000 inspection hrs. (IH)	=	$9 per IH

Order processing, machine processing, and product inspection costs of a Standard unit and an Enhanced unit:

Activity	Standard	Enhanced
Order processing:		
300 OP x $300....................	$ 90,000	
200 OP x $300....................		$ 60,000
Machine processing:		
18,000 MH x $14................	252,000	
22,000 MH x $14................		308,000
Product inspection:		
2,000 IH x $9.....................	18,000	
8,000 IH x $9.....................		72,000
Total	$360,000	$440,000
Production volume (units)	3,000	4,000
Cost per unit	$120*	$110**

* $360,000 ÷ 3,000 units = $120
** $440,000 ÷ 4,000 units = $110

The manufactured cost of a Standard unit is $181, and the manufactured cost of an Enhanced unit is $198:

	Standard	Enhanced
Direct material.......................................	$ 25	$ 40
Direct labor:		
3 hours x $12.................................	36	
4 hours x $12.................................		48
Order processing, machine processing, and product inspection....................	120	110
Total cost...	$181	$198

3. a. The Enhanced product is overcosted by the traditional product-costing system. The labor-hour application base resulted in a $216 unit cost; in contrast, the more accurate ABC approach yielded a lower unit cost of $198. The opposite situation occurs with the Standard product, which is undercosted by the traditional approach ($157 vs. $181 under ABC).

PROBLEM 5-36 (CONTINUED)

b. Yes, especially since Peterson's selling prices are based heavily on cost. An overcosted product will result in an inflated selling price, which could prove detrimental in a highly competitive marketplace. Customers will be turned off and will go elsewhere, which hurts profitability. With undercosted products, selling prices may be too low to adequately cover a product's more accurate (higher) cost. This situation is also troublesome and will result in a lower income being reported for the company.

PROBLEM 5-37 (30 MINUTES)

1. Type A manufacturing overhead cost:
   16,000 machine hours x $80 = $1,280,000
   $1,280,000 ÷ 8,000 units = $160 per unit

   Type B manufacturing overhead cost:
   22,500 machine hours x $80 = $1,800,000
   $1,800,000 ÷ 15,000 units = $120 per unit

	Type A	Type B
Direct material...................	$ 35	$ 60
Direct labor.......................	20	20
Manufacturing overhead....	160	120
Unit cost....................	$215	$200

2. Activity-based application rates:

Activity	Cost		Activity Driver		Application Rate
Manufacturing setups	$ 672,000	÷	80 setups (SU)	=	$8,400 per SU
Machine processing	1,848,000	÷	38,500 machine hours (MH)	=	$48 per MH
Product shipping	560,000	÷	175 outgoing shipments (OS)	=	$3,200 per OS

Manufacturing setup, machine processing, and product shipping costs of a Type A unit and a Type B unit:

Activity	Type A	Type B
Manufacturing setups:		
50 SU x $8,400................	$ 420,000	
30 SU x $8,400................		$ 252,000
Machine processing:		
16,000 MH x $48..............	768,000	
22,500 MH x $48..............		1,080,000
Product shipping:		
100 OS x $3,200..............	320,000	
75 OS x $3,200................		240,000
Total	$1,508,000	$1,572,000
Production volume (units)....	8,000	15,000
Cost per unit.......................	$188.50*	$104.80**

* $1,508,000 ÷ 8,000 units = $188.50
** $1,572,000 ÷ 15,000 units = $104.80

The manufactured cost of a Type A cabinet is $243.50, and the manufactured cost of a Type B cabinet is $184.80. The calculations follow:

	Type A	Type B
Direct material..	$ 35.00	$ 60.00
Direct labor..	20.00	20.00
Manufacturing setup, machine		
processing, and outgoing shipments..	188.50	104.80
Total cost...	$243.50	$184.80

3. Yes, the Type A storage cabinet is undercosted. The use of machine hours produced a unit cost of $215; in contrast, the more accurate activity-based-costing approach shows a unit cost of $243.50. The difference between these two amounts is $28.50.

PROBLEM 5-37 (CONTINUED)

4.   No, the discount is not advisable. The regular selling price of $260, when compared against the more accurate ABC cost figure, shows that each sale provides a profit to the firm of $16.50 ($260.00 - $243.50). However, a $30 discount will actually produce a loss of $13.50 ($243.50 - $230.00), and the more units that are sold, the larger the loss.   Notice that with the less-accurate, machine-hour-based figure ($215), the marketing manager will be misled, believing that each discounted unit sold would boost income by $15 ($230 - $215).

PROBLEM 5-38 (35 MINUTES)

1.   Activity-based costing results in improved costing accuracy for two reasons. First, companies that use ABC are not limited to a single driver when allocating costs to products and activities. Not all costs vary with units, and ABC allows users to select a host of nonunit-level cost drivers. Second, consumption ratios often differ greatly among activities. No single cost driver will accurately assign costs for all activities in this situation.

2.   Allocation of administrative cost based on billable hours:
      Information systems: 3,100 ÷ 5,000 = 62%; $342,000 x 62% = $212,040
      E-commerce consulting: 1,900 ÷ 5,000 = 38%; $342,000 x 38% = $129,960

	Information Systems Services	E-Commerce Consulting
Billings:		
3,100 hours x $125............	$387,500	
1,900 hours x $125............		$237,500
Less: Administrative cost.......	212,040	129,960
Income.................................	$175,460	$107,540
Income ÷ billings..................	45.28%	45.28%

PROBLEM 5-38 (CONTINUED)

3. Activity-based application rates:

Activity	Cost		Activity Driver		Application Rate
Staff support	$180,000	÷	250 clients	=	$720 per client
In-house computing	136,400	÷	4,400 computer hours (CH)	=	$31 per CH
Miscellaneous office charges	25,600	÷	1,000 client transactions (CT)	=	$25.60 per CT

Staff support, in-house computing, and miscellaneous office charges of information systems services and e-commerce consulting:

Activity	Information Systems Services	E-Commerce Consulting
Staff support:		
200 clients x $720................	$144,000	
50 clients x $720................		$ 36,000
In-house computing:		
2,600 CH x $31....................	80,600	
1,800 CH x $31....................		55,800
Miscellaneous office charges:		
400 CT x $25.60...................	10,240	
600 CT x $25.60...................		15,360
Total	$234,840	$107,160

PROBLEM 5-38 (CONTINUED)

Profitability of information systems services and e-commerce consulting:

	Information Systems Services	E-Commerce Consulting
Billings:		
3,100 hours x $125...........	$387,500	
1,900 hours x $125...........		$237,500
Less: Administrative cost......	234,840	107,160
Income................................	$152,660	$130,340
Income ÷ billings..................	39.40%	54.88%

4. Yes, his attitude should change. Even though both services are needed and professionals are paid the same rate, the income percentages show that e-commerce consulting provides a higher return per sales dollar than information systems services (54.88% vs. 39.40%). Thus, all other things being equal, professionals should spend more time with e-commerce.

5. Probably not. Although both services produce an attractive return for Simon and Sloan, the firm is experiencing a very tight labor market and will likely have trouble finding qualified help. In addition, the professional staff is currently overworked, which would probably limit the services available to new clients.

PROBLEM 5-39 (30 MINUTES)

1. Detroit Metal Works (DMW) is currently using a plantwide overhead rate that is applied on the basis of direct-labor dollars. In general, a plantwide manufacturing-overhead rate is acceptable only if a similar relationship between overhead and direct labor exists in all departments or the company manufactures products that receive the same proportional services from each department

   In most cases, departmental overhead rates are preferable to plantwide overhead rates because plantwide overhead rates do not provide the following:

   • A framework for reviewing overhead costs on a departmental basis, identifying departmental cost overruns, or taking corrective action to improve departmental cost control.

PROBLEM 5-39 (CONTINUED)

- Sufficient information about product profitability, thus increasing the difficulties associated with management decision making.

2. Because the company uses a plantwide overhead rate applied on the basis of direct-labor dollars, the elimination of direct labor in the Drilling Department through the introduction of robots may appear to reduce the overhead cost of the Drilling Department to zero. However, this change will not reduce fixed manufacturing costs such as depreciation and plant supervision. In reality, the use of robots is likely to increase fixed costs because of increased depreciation. Under the current method of allocating overhead costs, these costs merely will be absorbed by the remaining departments.

3. a. In order to improve the allocation of overhead costs in the Cutting and Grinding departments, management should move toward an activity-based costing system. The firm should:

   - Establish activity-cost pools for each significant activity.

   - Select a cost driver for each activity that best reflects the relationship of the activity to the overhead costs incurred.

   b. In order to accommodate the automation of the Drilling Department in its overhead accounting system, the company should:

   - Establish a separate overhead pool and rate for the Drilling Department.

   - Identify fixed and variable overhead costs and establish fixed and variable overhead rates.

   - Apply overhead costs to the Drilling Department on the basis of robot or machine hours.

ROBLEM 5-40 (40 MINUTES)

1. Overhead to be assigned to film development chemical order:

Activity Cost Pool	Pool Rate		Level of Cost Driver	Assigned Overhead Cost
Machine setups	$2,000 per setup	×	5 setups	$10,000
Material handling	$2 per pound	×	10,000 pounds	20,000
Hazardous waste control	$5 per pound	×	2,000 pounds	10,000
Quality control	$75 per inspection	×	10 inspections	750
Other overhead costs	$10 per machine hour	×	500 machine hours	5,000
Total				$45,750

2. Overhead cost per box of chemicals $= \dfrac{45,750}{1,000 \text{ boxes}} = \$45.75 \text{ per box}$

3. Predetermined overhead rate $= \dfrac{\text{total budgeted overhead cost}}{\text{total budgeted machine hours}} = \dfrac{\$625,000}{20,000}$

    $= \$31.25 \text{ per machine hr.}$

4. Overhead to be assigned to film development chemical order, given a single predetermined overhead rate:

    a. Total overhead assigned $= \$31.25 \text{ per machine hr.} \times 500 \text{ machine hr.}$

    $= \$15,625$

    b. Overhead cost per box of chemicals $= \dfrac{\$15,625}{1,000 \text{ boxes}} = \$15.625 \text{ per box}$

5. The film development chemicals entail a relatively large number of machine setups, a large amount of hazardous materials, and several inspections. Thus, they are quite costly in terms of driving overhead costs. Use of a single predetermined overhead rate obscures this characteristic of the production job. Underestimating the overhead cost per box could have adverse consequences for Knoxville Photographic Supply Company. For example, it could lead to poor decisions about product pricing. The activity-based costing system will serve management much better than the system based on a single, predetermined overhead rate.

PROBLEM 5-41 (20 MINUTES)

(a)   Overhead assigned to photographic plates:

Activity Cost Pool	Pool Rate		Level of Cost Driver	Assigned Overhead Cost
Machine setups	$2,000 per setup	×	3 setups	$6,000
Material handling	$2 per pound	×	900 pounds	1,800
Hazardous waste control	$5 per pound	×	300 pounds	1,500
Quality control	$75 per inspection	×	3 inspections	225
Other overhead costs	$10 per machine hour	×	50 machine hours	500
Total				$10,025

$$\text{Overhead cost per unit} = \frac{\$10,025}{100 \text{ plates}} = \$100.25$$

(b)   Unit cost per plate:

Direct material...............................	$120.00
Direct labor.....................................	40.00
Manufacturing overhead...............	100.25
Total cost per plate........................	$260.25

PROBLEM 5-42 (45 MINUTES)

1.   Quebec Electronics should not continue with its plans to emphasize the Royal model and phase out the Nova model. As shown in the following activity-based costing analysis, the Royal model has a contribution margin of less than 3 percent, while the Nova model generates a contribution margin of nearly 43 percent.

Cost per event for each cost driver:

Soldering....................	$	942,000	÷	1,570,000	=	$ .60	per solder joint
Shipments..................		860,000	÷	20,000	=	43.00	per shipment
Quality control...........		1,240,000	÷	77,500	=	16.00	per inspection
Purchase orders........		950,400	÷	190,080	=	5.00	per order
Machine power...........		57,600	÷	192,000	=	.30	per hour
Machine setups..........		750,000	÷	30,000	=	25.00	per setup

PROBLEM 5-42 (CONTINUED)

Costs per model:

	Royal	Nova
Direct costs:		
Material[a]	$2,336,000	$ 4,576,000
Direct labor[b]	168,000	396,000
Machine hours[c]	288,000	3,168,000
Total direct costs	$2,792,000	$ 8,140,000
Assigned costs:		
Soldering[d]	$ 231,000	$ 711,000
Shipments[e]	163,400	696,600
Quality control[f]	340,800	899,200
Purchase orders[g]	549,900	400,500
Machine power[h]	4,800	52,800
Machine setups[i]	350,000	400,000
Total assigned costs	$1,639,900	$ 3,160,100
Total cost	$4,431,900	$11,300,100

Calculations:

	Royal	Nova
[a]Material	4,000 × $584	22,000 × $208
[b]Direct labor	4,000 × $42	22,000 × $18
[c]Machine hours	4,000 × $72	22,000 × $144
[d]Soldering	385,000 × $.60	1,185,000 × $.60
[e]Shipments	3,800 × $43	16,200 × $43
[f]Quality control	21,300 × $16	56,200 × $16
[g]Purchase orders	109,980 × $5	80,100 × $5
[h]Machine power	16,000 × $.30	176,000 × $.30
[i]Machine setups	14,000 × $25	16,000 × $25

PROBLEM 5-42 (CONTINUED)

Profitability analysis:

	Royal	Nova	Total
Sales	$4,560,000	$19,800,000	$24,360,000
Less: Cost of goods sold	4,431,900	11,300,100	15,732,000
Gross margin	$ 128,100	$ 8,499,900	$ 8,628,000
Units sold	4,000	22,000	
Per-unit calculations:			
Selling price	$1,140.00	$900.00	
Less: Cost of goods sold	1,107.98	513.64	
Contribution margin	$ 32.02	$386.36	
Contribution margin percentage	2.8%[a]	42.9%[b]	

[a]$32.02/$1,140.00 = 2.8%
[b]$386.36/$900.00 = 42.9%

2. Activity-based management (ABM) is the use of information obtained from activity-based costing to improve operations in the firm. For example, a firm could revise product prices on the basis of revised cost information. For the long term, activity-based costing can assist management in making decisions regarding the viability of product lines, distribution channels, marketing strategies, and so on. ABM highlights possible improvements, including reducing or eliminating non-value-added activities, selecting lower cost activities, sharing activities with other products, and eliminating waste. ABM is an integrated approach that focuses management's attention on activities with the ultimate aim of continuous improvement. As a whole-company philosophy, ABM focuses on strategic as well as tactical and operational activities of the company.

PROBLEM 5-43 (60 MINUTES)

1. General advantages associated with activity-based costing include the following:

    - Provides management with a more thorough understanding of complex product costs and product profitability for improved resource management and pricing decisions.

    - Allows management to focus on value-added and non-value-added activities, so that non-value-added activities can be controlled or eliminated, thus streamlining production processes.

    - Highlights the relationship between activities and identifies opportunities to reduce costs (i.e., designing products with fewer parts in order to reduce the cost of the manufacturing process).

    - Provides a more appropriate means of charging overhead costs to products.

PROBLEM 5-43 (CONTINUED)

2. Using Manchester Technology's unit cost data, the total contribution margin expected from the PC board is $2,360,000, calculated as follows:

	Per Unit	Total for 40,000 Units
Revenue	$300	$12,000,000
Direct material	$140	$ 5,600,000
Material-handling charge (10% of material).......................	14	560,000
Direct labor ($14 per hr. × 4 hr.)	56	2,240,000
Variable overhead ($4 per hr. × 4 hr.)*...........................	16	640,000
Machine time ($10 per hr. × 1.5 hr.)	15	600,000
Total cost	$241	$ 9,640,000
Unit contribution margin	$ 59	
Total contribution margin (40,000 × $59)		$ 2,360,000

*Variable overhead rate: $1,120,000 ÷ 280,000 hr. = $4 per hr.

The total contribution margin expected from the TV board is $1,950,000, calculated as follows:

	Per Unit	Total for 65,000 Units
Revenue	$150	$9,750,000
Direct material	$ 80	$5,200,000
Material-handling charge (10% of material).......................	8	520,000
Direct labor ($14 per hr. × 1.5 hr.)	21	1,365,000
Variable overhead ($4 per hr. × 1.5 hr.)*........................	6	390,000
Machine time ($10 per hr. × .5 hr.)...............................	5	325,000
Total cost	$120	$7,800,000
Unit contribution margin	$ 30	
Total contribution margin (65,000 × $30)		$1,950,000

*Variable-overhead rate: $1,120,000 ÷ 280,000 hr. = $4 per hr.

PROBLEM 5-43 (CONTINUED)

3. The pool rates, which apply to both the PC board and the TV board, are calculated as follows:

Procurement............................	$400,000/4,000,000	=	$.10 per part
Production scheduling...........	$220,000/110,000	=	$2.00 per board
Packaging and shipping.........	$440,000/110,000	=	$4.00 per board
Machine setup........................	$446,000/278,750	=	$1.60 per setup
Hazardous waste disposal.....	$48,000/16,000	=	$3.00 per lb.
Quality control........................	$560,000/160,000	=	$3.50 per inspection
General supplies.....................	$66,000/110,000	=	$.60 per board
Machine insertion...................	$1,200,000/3,000,000	=	$.40 per part
Manual insertion.....................	$4,000,000/1,000,000	=	$4.00 per part
Wave soldering.......................	$132,000/110,000	=	$1.20 per board

Using activity-based costing, the total contribution margin expected from the PC board is $1,594,000, calculated as follows:

	Per Unit	Total for 40,000 Units
Revenue	$300.00	$12,000,000
Direct material	$140.00	$ 5,600,000
Procurement ($.10 per part × 55 parts)...............................	5.50	220,000
Production scheduling	2.00	80,000
Packaging and shipping...	4.00	160,000
Machine setup ($1.60 per setup × 3 setups)	4.80	192,000
Hazardous waste disposal ($3 per lb. × .35 lb.)	1.05	42,000
Quality control		
($3.50 per inspection × 2 inspections)	7.00	280,000
General supplies	.60	24,000
Machine insertion ($.40 per part × 35 parts)	14.00	560,000
Manual insertion ($4 per part × 20 parts)	80.00	3,200,000
Wave soldering..	1.20	48,000
Total cost	$ 260.15	$10,406,000
Unit contribution margin	$ 39.85	
Total contribution margin		$ 1,594,000

© 2002 The McGraw-Hill Companies, Inc.
Solutions Manual

Using activity-based costing, the total contribution margin expected from the TV board is $2,557,100, calculated as follows:

	Per Unit	Total for 65,000 Units
Revenue	$ 150.00	$9,750,000
Direct material	$ 80.00	$5,200,000
Procurement ($.10 per part × 25 parts)............................	2.50	162,500
Production scheduling	2.00	130,000
Packaging and shipping...	4.00	260,000
Machine setups ($1.60 per setup × 2 setups)	3.20	208,000
Hazardous waste disposal ($3 per lb. × .02 lb.)	.06	3,900
Quality control..	3.50	227,500
General supplies	.60	39,000
Machine insertion ($.40 per part × 24 parts)	9.60	624,000
Manual insertion...	4.00	260,000
Wave soldering..	1.20	78,000
Total cost...	$ 110.66	$7,192,900
Unit contribution margin	$ 39.34	
Total contribution margin...		$2,557,100

4. The analysis using the previously reported costs shows that the unit contribution of the PC board is almost double that of the TV board. On this basis, management is likely to accept the suggestion of the production manager and concentrate promotional efforts on expanding the market for the PC boards.

However, the analysis using activity-based costing does not support this decision. This analysis shows that the unit dollar contribution from each of the boards is almost equal, and the total contribution from the TV board exceeds that of the PC board by almost $1,000,000. As a percentage of selling price, the contribution from the TV board is double that of the PC board (26 percent versus 13 percent).

PROBLEM 5-44 (45 MINUTES)

1. a. WGCC's predetermined overhead rate, using direct-labor cost as the single cost driver, is $5 per direct labor dollar, calculated as follows:

$$\text{Overhead rate} = \frac{\text{total manufacturing-overhead cost}}{\text{budgeted direct-labor cost}}$$

$$= \$3,000,000/\$600,000$$

$$= \$5 \text{ per direct-labor dollar}$$

b. The full product costs and selling prices of one pound of Kona and one pound of Malaysian coffee are calculated as follows:

	Kona	Malaysian
Direct material...	$3.20	$4.20
Direct labor..	.30	.30
Overhead (.30 × $5).....................................	1.50	1.50
Full product cost	$5.00	$6.00
Markup (30%)	1.50	1.80
Selling price	$6.50	$7.80

2. A new product cost, under an activity-based costing approach, is $7.46 per pound of Kona and $4.82 per pound of Malaysian coffee, calculated as follows:

Activity	Cost Driver	Budgeted Activity	Budgeted Cost	Unit Cost
Purchasing	Purchase orders	1,158	$579,000	$500
Material handling	Setups	1,800	720,000	400
Quality control	Batches	720	144,000	200
Roasting	Roasting hours	96,100	961,000	10
Blending	Blending hours	33,600	336,000	10
Packaging	Packaging hours	26,000	260,000	10

Kona Coffee

Standard cost per pound:

Direct material..	$3.20
Direct labor..	.30
Purchasing (4 orders × $500/2,000 lb.).......................................	1.00
Material handling (12 setups × $400/2,000 lb.)	2.40
Quality control (4 batches × $200/2,000 lb.)...............................	.40
Roasting (20 hours × $10/2,000 lb.)	.10
Blending (10 hours × $10/2,000 lb.)	.05
Packaging (2 hours × $10/2,000 lb.)..	.01
Total cost..	$7.46

Malaysian Coffee

Standard cost per pound:

Direct material..	$4.20
Direct labor..	.30
Purchasing (4* orders × $500/100,000 lb.).................................	.02
Material handling (30 setups × $400/100,000 lb.)	.12
Quality control (10 batches × $200/100,000 lb.).........................	.02
Roasting (1,000 hours × $10/100,000 lb.)	.10
Blending (500 hours × $10/100,000 lb.)	.05
Packaging (100 hours × $10/100,000 lb.)....................................	.01
Total cost..	$4.82

*Budgeted sales ÷ purchase order size
   100,000 lbs. ÷ 25,000 lbs. = 4 orders

PROBLEM 5-44 (CONTINUED)

a. The ABC analysis indicates that several activities other than direct labor drive overhead. The cost computations show that the current system significantly undercosted Kona coffee, the low-volume product, and overcosted the high-volume product, Malaysian coffee.

b. The implication of the ABC analysis is that the low-volume products are using resources but are not covering their share of the cost of those resources. The Kona blend is currently priced at $6.50 [see requirement 1(b)], which is significantly below its activity-based cost of $7.46. The company should set long-run prices above cost. If there is excess capacity and many of the costs are fixed, it may be acceptable to price some products below full activity-based cost temporarily in order to build demand for the product. Otherwise, the high-volume, high-margin products are subsidizing the low-volume, low-margin products.

PROBLEM 5-45 (50 MINUTES)

1.

Activity Cost Pool	Type of Activity
I: Machine-related costs	Unit-level
II: Setup and inspection	Batch-level
III: Engineering	Product-sustaining-level
IV: Plant-related costs	Facility-level

PROBLEM 5-45 (CONTINUED)

2. Calculation of pool rates:

    I: Machine-related costs:

$$\frac{\$450,000}{9,000 \text{ machine hrs.}} = \$50 \text{ per machine hr.}$$

    II. Setup and inspection:

$$\frac{\$180,000}{40 \text{ runs}} = \$4,500 \text{ per run}$$

    III. Engineering:

$$\frac{\$90,000}{100 \text{ change orders}} = \$900 \text{ per change order}$$

    IV. Plant-related costs:

$$\frac{\$96,000}{1,920 \text{ sq. ft.}} = \$50 \text{ per sq. ft.}$$

3. Unit costs for odds and ends:

    I: Machine-related costs:

        Odds: \$50 per machine hr. $\times$ 4 machine hr. per unit   = \$200 per unit

        Ends: \$50 per machine hr. $\times$ 1 machine hr. per unit   = \$50 per unit

    II: Setup and inspection:

        Odds: \$4,500 per run $\div$ 50 units per run   = \$90 per unit

        Ends: \$4,500 per run $\div$ 250 units per run   = \$18 per unit

PROBLEM 5-45 (CONTINUED)

III: Engineering:

Odds: $$\frac{\$900 \text{ per change order} \times 100 \text{ change orders} \times 75\%}{1,000 \text{ units}}$$

$$= \frac{\$67,500}{1,000 \text{ units}} = \$67.50 \text{ per unit}$$

Ends: $$\frac{\$900 \text{ per change order} \times 100 \text{ change orders} \times 25\%}{5,000 \text{ units}}$$

$$= \frac{\$22,500}{5,000 \text{ units}} = \$4.50 \text{ per unit}$$

IV. Plant-related costs:

Odds: $$\frac{\$50 \text{ per sq. ft.} \times 1,920 \text{ sq. ft.} \times 80\%}{1,000 \text{ units}}$$

$$= \frac{\$76,800}{1,000 \text{ units}} = \$76.80 \text{ per unit}$$

Ends: $$\frac{\$50 \text{ per sq. ft.} \times 1,920 \text{ sq. ft.} \times 20\%}{5,000 \text{ units}}$$

$$= \frac{\$19,200}{5,000 \text{ units}} = \$3.84 \text{ per unit}$$

PROBLEM 5-45 (CONTINUED)

4. New product cost per unit using the ABC system:

	Odds	Ends
Direct material	$ 40.00	$ 60.00
Direct labor	30.00	45.00
Manufacturing overhead:		
Machine-related..	200.00	50.00
Setup and inspection.............................	90.00	18.00
Engineering	67.50	4.50
Plant-related	76.80	3.84
Total cost per unit..	$504.30	$181.34

5. New target prices:

	Odds	Ends	
New product cost (ABC)................................	$504.30	$181.34	
Pricing policy...	× 120%	× 120%	
New target price	$605.16	$217.61	(rounded)

6. Full assignment of overhead costs:

	Odds	Ends
Manufacturing overhead costs:		
Machine-related..	$200.00	$50.00
Setup and inspection.............................	90.00	18.00
Engineering	67.50	4.50
Plant-related	76.80	3.84
Total overhead cost per unit..........................	$434.30	$76.34
× Production volume	× 1,000	× 5,000
Total overhead assigned................................	$434,300	$381,700
	Total = $816,000	

PROBLEM 5-45 (CONTINUED)

7.   Cost distortion:

	Odds	Ends
Traditional volume-based costing system:		
reported product cost..	$ 166.00	$249.00
Activity-based costing system:		
reported product cost..	504.30	181.34
Amount of cost distortion per unit...................................	$(338.30)	$ 67.66

	Traditional system undercosts odds by $338.30 per unit	Traditional system overcosts ends by $67.66 per unit
Production volume..	× 1,000	× 5,000
Total amount of cost distortion for entire		
product line...	$(338,300)	$338,300

Sum of these two
amounts is zero.

PROBLEM 5-46 (60 MINUTES)

1. Kara Lindley's predecessor at Northwest Aircraft Industries (NAI) would have used a 10 percent material-handling rate, calculated as follows:

Payroll	$180,000
Employee benefits	36,000
Telephone	38,000
Other utilities	22,000
Materials and supplies...	6,000
Depreciation	6,000
Total Material-Handling Department costs	$288,000

$$\text{Material-handling rate} \quad = \quad \frac{\text{total Material-Handling Department costs}}{\text{total direct-material costs}}$$

$$= \quad \frac{\$288,000}{\$2,006,000 + \$874,000}$$

$$= \quad 10\%$$

2. a. The revised material-handling costs to be allocated on a per-purchase-order basis is $1.00, calculated as follows:

Total Material-Handling Department costs		$288,000
Deduct: Direct costs:		
Direct government payroll	$36,000	
Fringe benefits (20% × $36,000)	7,200	
Direct phone line...	2,800	46,000
Material-handling costs applicable to purchase orders....................		$242,000
÷ Total number of purchase orders		÷242,000
Material-handling cost per purchase order		$ 1.00

b. Purchase orders might be a more reliable cost driver than is the dollar amount of direct material, because resources are consumed in processing a purchase order. The size of the order does not necessarily have an impact on the consumption of resources.

3. There is a $74,600 reduction in material-handling costs allocated to government contracts by NAI as a result of the new allocation method, calculated as follows:

Previous method:

Government material	$ 2,006,000
× Material-handling rate	× 10%
Total (previous method)	$ 200,600

New method:

Directly traceable material-handling costs [$36,000 + (20% × $36,000) + $2,800]	$ 46,000
Purchase orders (80,000 × $1.00)	80,000
Total (new method)	$ 126,000
Net reduction	$ 74,600

PROBLEM 5-46 (CONTINUED)

4. A forecast of the cumulative dollar impact over a three-year period from 20x1 through 20x3 of Kara Lindley's recommended change for allocating Material-Handling Department costs to the Government Contracts Unit is $234,346, calculated as follows:

	20x2	20x3

Calculation of forecasted variable material-handling costs:

Direct-material cost:		
20x2 ($2,880,000 × 1.025)	$2,952,000	
20x3 ($2,952,000 × 1.025)		$ 3,025,800
Material-handling rate (10%)	$ 295,200	$ 302,580
Deduct: Direct traceable costs	46,000[a]	46,000[a]
Variable material-handling costs..........................	$ 249,200	$ 256,580

Calculation of forecasted purchase orders:

	20x2	20x3	
20x2 (242,000 × 1.05)	254,100		
20x3 (254,100 × 1.05)		266,805	
Government purchase orders (33% of total)............	83,853	88,046	(rounded)

Calculation of material-handling costs allocated to government contracts:

	20x2	20x3
Variable material-handling costs.............................	$ 249,200	$ 256,580
Purchase orders..	÷ 254,100	÷ 266,805
Variable material-handling costs per purchase order (rounded)	$ .98	$ .96
Government purchase orders....................................	× 83,853	× 88,046
Projected variable material-handling costs (rounded)	$ 82,176	$ 84,524
Fixed material-handling costs	46,000[a]	46,000[a]
Total material-handling costs allocated to government contracts	$ 128,176	$ 130,524

[a]$36,000 + (20% × $36,000) + $2,800 = $46,000

PROBLEM 5-46 (CONTINUED)

Calculation of cumulative dollar impact:

Government material at 70%..	$2,066,400[b]	$2,118,060[c]
Material-handling at 10% (previous method)	$ 206,640[d]	$ 211,806[e]
Deduct: Material-handling costs allocated to government contracts (new method)......................	128,176	130,524
Net reduction in government contract material-handling costs..	$ 78,464	$ 81,282

[b]70% × $2,952,000 = $2,066,400
[c]70% × $3,025,800 = $2,118,060
[d]10% × $2,066,400 = $206,640
[e]10% × $2,118,060 = $211,806

In summary, the cumulative dollar impact of the recommended change in allocating Material-Handling Department costs is $234,346, calculated as follows:

20x1 [from requirement (3)]	$ 74,600
20x2	78,464
20x3	81,282
Total..	$234,346

5.   a.   Referring to the standards of ethical conduct for management accountants, Kara Lindley faces the following ethical issues:

Competence:

- Prepare complete and clear reports and recommendations after appropriate analysis of relevant and reliable information. Lindley has an obligation to prepare the most relevant and reliable report.

Integrity:

- Refrain from engaging in any activity that would prejudice Lindley's ability to carry out her duties ethically.

- Communicate unfavorable as well as favorable information and professional judgments and opinions.

- Refrain from engaging in or supporting any activity that would discredit Lindley's profession.

Objectivity:

- Disclose fully all relevant information that could reasonably be expected to influence an intended user's understanding of reports and recommendations presented. Lindley has information that Jay Preston should see if he is going to make a reliable judgment about the results of the Government Contracts Unit.

b. The steps Kara Lindley could take to resolve this ethical conflict are as follows:

- Lindley should first follow the established policies at NAI.

- If this approach does not resolve the conflict or if such policies do not exist, she should discuss the problem with her immediate superior, except when it appears that the superior is involved. If the Government Contracts Unit manager, Paul Anderson, is her superior, then she obviously cannot discuss the problem with him. In this case she should go to the next-higher managerial level and continue, up to the audit committee of the board of directors, until the conflict is resolved.

- She should also discuss the situation with an objective advisor to clarify the issues involved and obtain an understanding of possible courses of action.

- If the ethical conflict still exists after exhausting all levels of internal review, then she may have no other course of action than to resign from the company and submit an informative memorandum to an appropriate representative of the company.

PROBLEM 5-47 (50 MINUTES)

1. a. The calculation of total budgeted costs for the Manufacturing Department at Marconi Manufacturing is as follows:

Direct material:

Tuff Stuff ($5.00 per unit × 20,000 units)..............	$100,000	
Ruff Stuff ($3.00 per unit × 20,000 units)	60,000	
Total direct material		$ 160,000
Direct labor..		800,000
Overhead:		
Indirect labor..	$ 24,000	
Fringe benefits...	5,000	
Indirect material...	31,000	
Power..	180,000	
Setup...	75,000	
Quality assurance...	10,000	
Other utilities	10,000	
Depreciation...	15,000	
Total overhead...		350,000
Total Manufacturing Department budgeted cost		$1,310,000

b. The unit costs of Tuff Stuff and Ruff Stuff, with overhead assigned on the basis of direct-labor hours, are calculated as follows:

Tuff Stuff:

Direct material...	$ 5.00
Direct labor ($8.00 per hour × 2 hours)*	16.00
Overhead ($3.50 per hour × 2 hours)*...................	7.00
Tuff Stuff unit cost	$28.00

*Budgeted direct labor hours:

Tuff Stuff (20,000 units × 2 hours)	40,000
Ruff Stuff (20,000 units × 3 hours)............................	60,000
Total budgeted direct-labor hours............................	100,000

Direct-labor rate: $800,000 per 100,000 hours = $8.00 per hour
Overhead rate: $350,000 per 100,000 hours = $3.50 per hour

Ruff Stuff:

Direct material...	$ 3.00
Direct labor ($8.00 per hour × 3 hours)*..............	24.00
Overhead ($3.50 per hour × 3 hours)*..................	10.50
Ruff Stuff unit cost...	$37.50

*Budgeted direct labor hours

Tuff Stuff (20,000 units × 2 hours)..........................	40,000
Ruff Stuff (20,000 units × 3 hours)..........................	60,000
Total budgeted direct-labor hours...........................	100,000

Direct-labor rate: $800,000 per 100,000 hours   = $8.00 per hour
Overhead rate: $350,000 per 100,000 hours   = $3.50 per hour

2.   The total budgeted cost of the Fabricating and Assembly Departments, after separation of overhead into the activity cost pools, is calculated as follows:

	Total	Fabricating		Assembly	
		Percent	Dollars	Percent	Dollars
Direct material..........	$ 160,000	100%	$160,000		
Direct labor...............	800,000	75%	600,000	25%	$200,000
Overhead:					
Indirect labor	$ 24,000	75%	$ 18,000	25%	$ 6,000
Fringe benefits	5,000	80%	4,000	20%	1,000
Indirect material	31,000		20,000		11,000
Power	180,000		160,000		20,000
Setup	75,000		5,000		70,000
Quality assurance	10,000	80%	8,000	20%	2,000
Other utilities	10,000	50%	5,000	50%	5,000
Depreciation	15,000	80%	12,000	20%	3,000
Total overhead	$ 350,000		$232,000		$118,000
Total cost	$1,310,000		$992,000		$318,000

PROBLEM 5-47 (CONTINUED)

3. The unit costs of the products using activity-based costing are calculated as follows:

Fabricating:

Total cost	$992,000
Less: Direct material...	160,000
Less: Direct labor...	600,000
Pool overhead cost..	$232,000

Hours:			
	Tuff Stuff (4.4 hours × 20,000 units)	88,000	hours
	Ruff Stuff (6.0 hours × 20,000 units).....................	120,000	hours
	Total machine hours...............................	208,000	hours
Pool rate per machine hour ($232,000/208,000)	$1.12 per hour (rounded)		

Fabrication cost per unit:	Tuff Stuff ($1.12 × 4.4 hours).....	$4.93 per unit (rounded)
	Ruff Stuff ($1.12 × 6.0 hours)	$6.72 per unit (rounded)

Assembly:

Total cost	$318,000
Less: Direct labor...	200,000
Pool overhead cost..	$118,000

Setups:		
	Tuff Stuff...	1,000
	Ruff Stuff	272
	Total setups	1,272
Pool rate per setup ($118,000/1,272).....................................		$92.77 per setup (rounded)

Setup cost per unit:

Tuff Stuff ($92.77 per setup × 1,000 set-ups/20,000 units) ...	$4.64 per unit (rounded)
Ruff Stuff ($92.77 per setup × 272 set-ups/20,000 units)......	$1.26 per unit (rounded)

Tuff Stuff unit cost:

Direct material	$ 5.00
Direct labor (2 hours × $8 per hour).................................	16.00
Fabrication overhead..	4.93
Assembly overhead	4.64
Tuff Stuff unit cost...	$30.57

PROBLEM 5-47 (CONTINUED)

Ruff Stuff unit cost:

Direct material	$ 3.00
Direct labor (3 hours × $8 per hour).......................................	24.00
Fabrication overhead..	6.72
Assembly overhead	1.26
Ruff Stuff unit cost	$34.98

4. Ruff Stuff unit costs:

Cost with overhead assigned on direct-labor hours	$37.50
Cost using activity-based costing..	$34.98

The activity-based costing unit costs may lead the company to decide to lower its price for Ruff Stuff in order to be more competitive in the market and continue production of the product. It now appears that Ruff Stuff has lower unit costs and can afford lower prices. Using ABC for assigning overhead costs generally leads to a more accurate estimate of the costs incurred to produce a product. Management should be able to make better informed decisions regarding pricing and production of the company's products.

PROBLEM 5-48 (60 MINUTES)

1.

	Standard Model	Deluxe Model	Heavy-Duty Model
Product costs based on traditional, volume-based costing system................................	$105.00	$215.00	$232.00
Markup percentage	× 110%	× 110%	× 110%
Target price..	$115.50	$236.50	$255.20

PROBLEM 5-48 (CONTINUED)

2. Product costs based on activity-based costing system:

	Standard Model	Deluxe Model	Heavy-Duty Model
Direct material	$10.00	$ 25.00	$ 42.00
Direct labor	10.00	20.00	20.00
Machinery depreciation and maintenance[a]	32.00	208.00	75.20
Engineering, inspection and repair of defects[b]	17.04	43.50	34.08
Purchasing, receiving, shipping, and material handling[c]	15.28	52.00	29.25
Factory depreciation, taxes, insurance, and miscellaneous overhead costs[d]	12.50	89.25	25.59
Total	$96.82	$437.75	$226.12

[a]Pool I:

Depreciation, machinery		$1,480,000
Maintenance, machinery		120,000
Total		$1,600,000

Standard:	($1,600,000 × 40%)	÷	20,000	=	$32.00
Deluxe:	($1,600,000 × 13%)	÷	1,000	=	$208.00
Heavy-Duty:	($1,600,000 × 47%)	÷	10,000	=	$75.20

[b]Pool II:

Engineering		$350,000
Inspection and repair of defects		375,000
Total		$725,000

Standard:	($725,000 × 47%)	÷	20,000	=	$17.04
Deluxe:	($725,000 × 6%)	÷	1,000	=	$43.50
Heavy-Duty:	($725,000 × 47%)	÷	10,000	=	$34.08

[c]Pool III:

Purchasing, receiving, and shipping		$250,000
Material handling		400,000
Total		$650,000

Standard:	($650,000 × 47%)	÷	20,000	=	$15.28
Deluxe:	($650,000 × 8%)	÷	1,000	=	$52.00
Heavy-Duty:	($650,000 × 45%)	÷	10,000	=	$29.25

dPool IV:

Depreciation, taxes, and insurance for factory..........................	$300,000
Miscellaneous manufacturing overhead...................................	295,000
Total...	$595,000

Standard:	($595,000 × 42%)	÷	20,000	=	$12.50
Deluxe:	($595,000 × 15%)	÷	1,000	=	$89.25
Heavy-Duty:	($595,000 × 43%)	÷	10,000	=	$25.59

3.

	Standard Model	Deluxe Model	Heavy Duty Model
Product costs based on activity-based costing system...	$ 96.82	$437.75	$226.12
Markup percentage	× 110%	× 110%	× 110%
New target price..	$106.50	$481.53	$248.73

The new target price of the standard model, $106.50, is lower than the current actual selling price, $110.

PROBLEM 5-48 (CONTINUED)

4.

MEMORANDUM

Date: Today

To: President Minnesota Electric Motor Corporation

From: I.M. Student

Subject: Product costing

Based on the cost data from our traditional, volume-based product-costing system, our standard model is not very profitable. Its reported actual contribution margin is only $5 ($110 – $105). However, the validity of this conclusion depends on the accuracy of the product costs reported by our product-costing system. Our competitors are selling motors like our standard model for $106. This price suggests that their product cost is substantially below our previously reported cost of $105.

Our new, activity-based costing system reveals serious product cost distortions stemming from our old costing system. The new costing system shows that the standard model costs only $96.82, which implies a target price of $106.50. This price is lower than our current actual selling price and consistent with the price our competitors are charging.

In contrast, our new product-costing system reveals that the deluxe model's product cost is $437.75 instead of the previously reported cost of $215. The new product cost suggests a target price of $481.53 for the deluxe model, rather than $236.50, which was our previous target price for the deluxe model.

PROBLEM 5-48 (CONTINUED)

5.   The company should adopt and maintain the activity-based costing system. The price of the standard model should be lowered to the $106. Lowering the price should enable the firm to regain its competitive position in the market for the standard model. Further price cuts should be considered if marketing studies indicate such a move will increase demand.

The price of the deluxe model should be set near the target price of $481.53. If the deluxe model does not sell at this price, management should consider discontinuing the product line. Input from the marketing staff should be sought before such an action is taken. An important consideration is the extent to which sales in the standard model and heavy-duty model markets depend on the firm's offering a complete product line.

A slight price reduction should be considered for the heavy-duty model (from $255.20 down to $248.73). However, the product cost distortion from the old costing system did not affect this model as seriously as it did the other two.

PROBLEM 5-49 (30 MINUTES)

	Standard Model	Deluxe Model	Heavy-Duty Model
Traditional, volume-based costing system:			
reported product cost	$105.00	$215.00	$232.00
Activity-based costing system:			
reported product cost	96.82	437.75	226.12
Amount of cost distortion per unit.........................	$ 8.18	$(222.75)	$ 5.88
	Traditional system overcosts standard model by $8.18 per unit	Traditonal system undercosts deluxe model by $222.75 per unit	Traditional system overcosts heavy-duty model by $5.88 per unit
Product volume...	× 20,000	× 1,000	× 10,000
Total amount of cost distortion for entire product line...	$163,600	$(222,750)	$58,800

Sum of these three
amounts is $(350). It
would be zero except for
the slight rounding errors
in the calculation of the
new product costs to the
nearest cent.

PROBLEM 5-50 (20 MINUTES)

1. The controller, Erin Jackson, has acted ethically up to this point. She correctly pointed out to the president that the firm's traditional, volume-based product-costing system was distorting the reported product cost for the company's three products. She designed an activity-based costing system to provide more accurate product-costing data.

2. The production manager, Alan Tyler, is not acting ethically. Although we can sympathize with his plight, we cannot condone his pressuring the controller to suppress or alter the new product-costing data she has compiled.

    What can Tyler do that is ethical and has the potential for positive results? First, he could take a hard look at the deluxe model's production process. Are there non-value-added activities that could be reduced or eliminated? Second, he could argue to the president that the company should carry a full product line, if he has reason to believe that is the firm's best strategy.

3. Jackson has an ethical obligation to the president, to the company, to her profession, and to herself to report accurate product-costing data to the president. There is nothing wrong with her offer to her friend to go over her analysis again to verify its accuracy. However, she must report what she finds with no suppression or alteration of the data. Several of the ethical standards for managerial accounting apply in this case. (See Chapter 1 for a listing of these standards.) The standards that are most clearly relevant include the following:

Integrity:

*   Communicate unfavorable as well as favorable information and professional judgments or opinions.

Objectivity:

*   Communicate information fairly and objectively.

*   Disclose fully all relevant information that could reasonably be expected to influence an intended user's understanding of the reports, comments, and recommendations presented.

Jackson is in a tough spot. Her professional obligation to report accurate product costs is clear. She cannot ethically avoid this responsibility. Yet her friend Tyler is in a tenuous position. What can Jackson ethically do for him? First, she can be compassionate and understanding of his concern, yet remain firm in meeting her professional obligations. Second, she can assist the production manager in finding ways to manufacture the deluxe model electric motor more efficiently and at a lower cost. For example, she can share her ABC analysis with Tyler to help him identify non-value-added activities and costs.

SOLUTIONS TO CASES

CASE 5-51 (60 MINUTES)

1. Based on the cost data from Gigabyte's traditional, volume-based product-costing system, product G is the firm's least profitable product. Its reported actual gross margin is only $22.00, as compared with $84.75 and $104.50 for products T and W, respectively. However, the validity of this conclusion depends on the accuracy of the product costs reported by Gigabyte's product-costing system.

2. Again, based on the product costs reported by the firm's traditional, volume-based product-costing system, product W appears to be very profitable. As in requirement (1), however, the validity of this assessment depends on the accuracy of the reported product costs.

3. Gigabyte's competitors have moved aggressively into the market for gismos (product G), but they have abandoned the whatchamacallit (product W) market to Gigabyte.

    These competing firms apparently believe they can sell gismos at a much lower price than Gigabyte's management feels is feasible. This evidence suggests that Gigabyte's competitors may believe their product cost for gismos is below Gigabyte's reported product cost. In contrast, Gigabyte's competitors apparently believe that they cannot afford to sell whatchamacallits at Gigabyte's current price of $200. Perhaps the competing firms' reported production costs for product W are higher than the cost reported by Gigabyte's product-costing system.

    The danger to Gigabyte is that the company will be forced out of the market for its second largest selling product. This could be disastrous to Gigabyte, Inc.

4. Percentages for raw-material costs:

Product	Raw-Material Cost per Unit	Annual Volume	Annual Raw-Material Cost	Percentage of Total Raw-Material Cost*
G	$35.00	8,000	$ 280,000	25%
T	52.50	15,000	787,500	69%
W	17.50	4,000	70,000	6%
Total			$1,137,500	100%

*Percentages rounded to nearest whole percent.

CASE 5-51 (CONTINUED)

5. Product costs based on an activity-based costing system:

	Product G	Product T	Product W
Direct material...	$ 35.00	$ 52.50	$ 17.50
Direct labor...	16.00	12.00	8.00
Machine setup[a]	.13	.11	.66
Machinery[b]	38.28	40.83	76.56
Inspection[c]	9.84	15.75	52.50
Material handling[d]..	27.34	40.25	13.13
Engineering[e]	15.08	2.30	47.40
Total..	$141.67	$163.74	$215.75

[a]Machine setup:

Product G:	($5,250 × 20%)	÷	8,000 units	=	$ .13
Product T:	($5,250 × 30%)	÷	15,000 units	=	$ .11
Product W:	($5,250 × 50%)	÷	4,000 units	=	$ .66

[b]Machinery:

Product G:	($1,225,000 × 25%)	÷	8,000 units	=	$38.28
Product T:	($1,225,000 × 50%)	÷	15,000 units	=	$40.83
Product W:	($1,225,000 × 25%)	÷	4,000 units	=	$76.56

[c]Inspection:

Product G:	($525,000 × 15%)	÷	8,000 units	=	$ 9.84
Product T:	($525,000 × 45%)	÷	15,000 units	=	$15.75
Product W:	($525,000 × 40%)	÷	4,000 units	=	$52.50

[d]Material handling:

Product G:	($875,000 × 25%)	÷	8,000 units	=	$27.34
Product T:	($875,000 × 69%)	÷	15,000 units	=	$40.25
Product W:	($875,000 × 6%)	÷	4,000 units	=	$13.13

[e]Engineering:

Product G:	($344,750 × 35%)	÷	8,000 units	=	$15.08
Product T:	($344,750 × 10%)	÷	15,000 units	=	$ 2.30
Product W:	($344,750 × 55%)	÷	4,000 units	=	$47.40

CASE 5-51 (CONTINUED)

6. Comparison of reported product costs, new target prices, and actual selling prices:

	Product G	Product T	Product W
Reported product costs:			
Traditional, volume-based costing system	$191.00	$169.50	$ 95.50
Activity-based costing system	141.67	163.74	215.75
Target price based on new product costs			
(150% × new product cost)	212.51	245.61	323.63
Current actual selling price	213.00	254.25	200.00

CASE 5-52 (15 MINUTES)

MEMORANDUM

Date: Today

To: President, Gigabyte, Inc.

From: I.M. Student

Subject: Gigabyte's competitive position

Gigabyte's product-costing system has been providing misleading product cost information. Our traditional, volume-based costing system overcosted gismos and thingamajigs, but it substantially undercosted whatchamacallits. As a result Gigabyte has been overpricing gismos and underpricing whatchamacallits. The company has been losing money on every sale in the product W market. Our competitors have taken advantage of our mispricing by moving aggressively into the gismo market and abandoning the whatchamacallit market to Gigabyte. As a result, our profitability has suffered.

I recommend the following courses of action:

1. Implement the new activity-based costing system and revise its database frequently.

2. Lower the target price of gismos to $213, the current actual selling price. This price yields our usual 50 percent markup over product cost.

3. Consider lowering the price of thingamajigs to $246 in order to increase demand. The lower price still yields Gigabyte a 50 percent markup over product cost.

4. Raise the price of whatchamacallits to $324. If the product does not sell at that price, consider discontinuing the product line.

CASE 5-53 (30 MINUTES)

	Product G	Product T	Product W
Traditional, volume-based costing system:			
reported product cost	$191.00	$169.50	$ 95.50
Activity-based costing system:			
reported product cost	141.67	163.74	215.75
Amount of cost distortion per unit........................	$ 49.33	$ 5.76	$(120.25)
	Traditional system overcosts product G by $49.33 per unit	Traditonal system overcosts product T by $5.76 per unit	Traditional system undercosts product W by $120.25 per unit
Product volume...	× 8,000	× 15,000	× 4,000
Total amount of cost distortion for entire product line	$394,640	$ 86,400	$(481,000)

Sum of these three
amounts is $40. It
would be zero except for
the slight rounding errors
in the calculation of the
new product costs to the
nearest cent.

CASE 5-54 (45 MINUTES)

1. Activity-based costing (ABC) differs from traditional costing in that it focuses on activities that consume resources as the fundamental cost drivers. ABC is a two-stage cost assignment process focused on causality and the determination of cost drivers. It usually uses several different activities to assign costs to products or services. Therefore, it is more detailed and more accurate than traditional costing. It also helps managers distinguish between value added and non-value added activities.

2. Calculations of total activity cost pools and pool rates:

Machining.................
($424,528 × 1.06) ÷ (15,000 hours + 30,000 hours)
= $450,000* ÷ 45,000 hours = $10 per machine hour

*Rounded

Assembly ....
($216,981 × 1.06) ÷ (6,000 hours + 5,500 hours)
= $230,000* ÷ 11,500 hours = $20 per assembly hour

*Rounded

Material handling......
($56,604 × 1.06) ÷ [(5 parts × 5,000 units) + (10 parts × 5,000 units)]
= $60,000* ÷ (25,000 parts + 50,000 parts)
= $60,000 ÷ 75,000 parts = $.80 per part

*Rounded

Inspection ....
($117,925 × 1.06) ÷ (5,000 hours + 7,500 hours)
= $125,000* ÷ 12,500 hours = $10 per inspection hour

*Rounded

CASE 5-54 (CONTINUED)

3.

	JR-14		RM-13	
	20x1 Cost Data	Estimated 20x2 Product Cost	20x1 Cost Data	Estimated 20x2 Product Cost
Direct material:				
No cost increase..................		$1,000,000		$1,750,000
Direct labor:				
Direct labor	$185,185		$92,593	
× 1.08 cost increase...........		200,000 (rounded)		100,000 (rounded)
Machining:				
Machining activity in hours	15,000		30,000	
× $10 per hour		150,000		300,000
Assembly:				
Assembly activity in hours	6,000		5,500	
× $20 per hour		120,000		110,000
Material handling:				
Number of parts	5		10	
× sales in units	× 5,000		× 5,000	
	25,000		50,000	
× $.80 per unit....................		20,000		40,000
Inspection:				
Inspection hours	5,000		7,500	
× $10 per hour		50,000		75,000
Total cost.............................		$1,540,000		$2,375,000

CASE 5-54 (CONTINUED)

4.

WHITESTONE COMPANY
BUDGETED STATEMENT OF OPERATING MARGIN FOR 20X2

	JR-14	RM-13	Total
Sales revenue	$1,810,500	$2,229,500	$4,040,000
Cost of goods manufactured and sold:			
Beginning finished-goods inventory.............	$ 240,000	$ 300,000	$ 540,000
Add: Direct material	1,000,000	1,750,000	2,750,000
Direct labor	200,000	100,000	300,000
Machining..	150,000	300,000	450,000
Assembly	120,000	110,000	230,000
Material handling.................................	20,000	40,000	60,000
Inspection	50,000	75,000	125,000
Cost of goods available for sale....................	$1,780,000	$2,675,000	$4,455,000
Less: Ending finished-goods inventory* ...	215,600	332,500	548,100
Cost of goods sold..	$1,564,400	$2,342,500	$3,906,900
Operating margin	$ 246,100	$ (113,000)	$ 133,100

*Ending finished-goods inventory = (total product cost ÷ units produced) × ending inventory in units:

JR-14: ($1,540,000 ÷ 5,000 units) × 700 units = $215,600

RM-13: ($2,375,000 ÷ 5,000 units) × 700 units = $332,500

CURRENT ISSUES IN MANAGERIAL ACCOUNTING

ISSUE 5-55

"ACTIVITY-BASED COSTING FOR A HOSPICE," *STRATEGIC FINANCE*, MARCH 2000, SIDNEY J. BAXENDALE AND VICTORIA DORNBUSCH.

Hospice of Central Kentucky found it could provide accurate cost information through ABC and used this data to negotiate with insurance companies. Negotiations were enhanced with the knowledge that patient days drive accounting/finance, management, and information systems activities, and costs per patient day increase with accuracy. HCK increased its revenue by determining that insurance carriers could select a payment type at admission but could not change the type once the choice was made.

ISSUE 5-56

"LEARNING TO LOVE ABC," *JOURNAL OF ACCOUNTANCY*, AUGUST 1999, GARY COKINS.

As the power of personal computers have grown and their prices have fallen, the information for ABC systems has become more available and cost effective to obtain and use. Moreover, several companies have found that simpler designs of ABC generally produce higher levels of accuracy. Most important of all, those who have successfully implemented ABC say that when gathering data for ABC, close enough is not only good enough, it's often the key to its success. Therefore, simpler is better.

ISSUE 5-57

"MANUFACTURING MASTERS ITS ABCS," *BUSINESS WEEK*, AUGUST 7, 2000, HUGH FILMAN.

Alcoa employed ABC to capture indirect costs such as machine setups, quality control, packing and shipping. Managers can now determine if they want to produce a particular product line or sell off certain assets. Smarter production decisions are being made, and a new pricing structure has resulted.

ISSUE 5-58

"YES, ABC IS FOR SMALL BUSINESS, TOO," *JOURNAL OF ACCOUNTANCY*, AUGUST 1999, DOUGLAS T. HICKS.

Smaller organizations are beginning to see that ABC can work as effectively for them as it does for large companies. The concept of activity-based costing is actually very simple. An organization has to perform certain activities to provide the products and services it sells, and those activities cost money. The cost of each of the activities is measured and assigned only to those products and services requiring the activity, using appropriate cost drivers. It is then possible to get an accurate picture of the real cost of producing each product or providing each service. Non-activity costs such as direct material or outsourced services do not need to be included because they are already traceable to specific products or services. This process can work as effectively for smaller organizations as it does for large companies.

ISSUE 5-59

"SUCCEEDING WITH 80/20," *MANAGEMENT ACCOUNTING*, FEBRUARY 1999, LAKSHMI U. TATIKONDA, DAN O'BRIEN, AND RAO J. TATIKONDA.

After two years of study and $200,000 the committee found that low-volume products caused more overhead than high-volume products. Just as the preliminary stages of the ABC project were completed, the company was acquired by ITW. The management of ITW implemented the 80/20 rule, which states that 80 percent of the profit is derived from 20 percent of the products sold. ITW reduced the complexity of processes and systems and modified the layout of its plant to accommodate just-in-time production. Equipment was arranged in empowered decision-making production cells according to product lines, which flattened the organizational structure and saved millions of dollars. The stockroom, purchase orders, receiving reports, pick orders, and material handling were eliminated. Costs related to purchasing, inspection, setup, overtime, idle time, inventory control, engineering change notices, and the mainframe computer were reduced.

CHAPTER 6
Activity-Based Management and Today's Advanced Manufacturing Environment

ANSWERS TO REVIEW QUESTIONS

6-1   The philosophy of a just-in-time (JIT) inventory and production management system is that no materials are purchased and no products are manufactured until they are needed. The essence of the JIT philosophy is to reduce all inventories to their absolute minimum.

6-2   The key features of a just-in-time inventory and production management system are as follows: a smooth production rate; a pull method of coordinating steps in the production process; purchase of materials and manufacture of subassemblies and products in small lot sizes; quick and inexpensive setups of production machinery; high-quality levels of raw material and finished products; effective preventive maintenance of equipment; an atmosphere of teamwork to improve the production system; and multiskilled workers and flexible facilities.

6-3   "TQC" stands for total quality control. Since no parts are purchased or manufactured until they are needed for production in a JIT system, it is crucial that they be just right for their intended purpose.

6-4   In a just-in-time (JIT) production system, raw materials and parts are purchased or produced just in time to be used at each stage of the production process. This approach to inventory and production management brings considerable cost savings from reduced inventory levels.

   The key to the JIT system is the "pull" approach to controlling manufacturing. The diagram on the next page displays a simple multistage production process. The flow of manufacturing activity is depicted by the solid arrows running down the diagram from one stage of production to the next. However, the signal that triggers more production activity in each stage comes from the *next* stage of production. These signals, depicted by the dashed-line arrows, run up the diagram. We begin with sales at the bottom of the exhibit. When sales activity warrants more production of finished goods, the goods are "pulled" from production stage III by a signal that more goods are needed. Similarly, when production employees in stage III need more inputs, they send a signal back to stage II. This signal triggers production activity in stage II. Working our way back up to the beginning of the process, purchases of raw materials and parts are triggered by a signal that they are needed in stage I.

The "Pull" Method in a JIT System

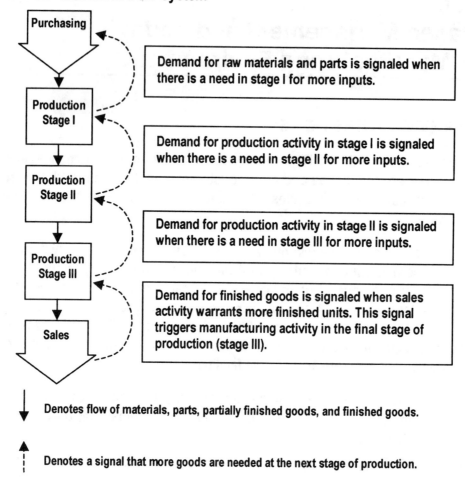

Purchasing	Demand for raw materials and parts is signaled when there is a need in stage I for more inputs.
Production Stage I	Demand for production activity in stage I is signaled when there is a need in stage II for more inputs.
Production Stage II	Demand for production activity in stage II is signaled when there is a need in stage III for more inputs.
Production Stage III	
Sales	Demand for finished goods is signaled when sales activity warrants more finished units. This signal triggers manufacturing activity in the final stage of production (stage III).

↓ Denotes flow of materials, parts, partially finished goods, and finished goods.

↑ Denotes a signal that more goods are needed at the next stage of production.

This pull system of production management, which characterizes the JIT approach, results in a smooth flow of production and significantly reduced inventory levels.

6-5   Five key features of JIT purchasing are as follows: only a few suppliers; long-term contracts with suppliers; materials and parts delivered in small lot sizes immediately before they are needed; only minimal inspection of delivered parts and materials; and grouped payments to each vendor.

6-6　(a) CMS stands for cost management system.

(b) JIT stands for just-in-time.

(c) CNC stands for computer-numerically controlled.

(d) CAM stands for computer-aided manufacturing.

(e) CAD stands for computer-aided design.

(f) AMHS stands for automated material-handling system.

(g) FMS stands for flexible manufacturing system.

(h) CIM stands for computer-integrated manufacturing.

6-7　The key differences in the plant layouts used by Aerotech's Phoenix and Bakersfield facilities are as follows:

(a) The Bakersfield plant uses a flexible manufacturing system.

(b) The Bakersfield plant uses an automated material-handling system.

(c) The Bakersfield plant uses a computer-aided design approach.

(d) The Bakersfield plant has substantially less space devoted to storage of raw materials, work in process, and finished goods.

6-8　The installation of a flexible manufacturing system (FMS) usually results in a shift in the cost structure from variable costs to fixed costs.

6-9　*Off-line quality control* consists of the activities during the product design and engineering phases that improve the manufacturability of the product, reduce production costs, and ensure high quality.

Cellular manufacturing is the organization of a production facility into FMS cells, which are groupings of machines and personnel designed to manufacture a particular set of products.

Activity-based management (ABM) is the use of activity-based costing information to improve operations and eliminate non-value-added costs.

6-10　The two-dimensional activity-based costing model provides one way of picturing the relationship between ABC and ABM. The vertical dimension of the model depicts the cost assignment view of an ABC system. From the *cost assignment viewpoint,* the ABC system uses two-stage cost allocation to *assign* the costs of resources to the firm's cost objects. These cost objects could be products manufactured, services produced, or customers served.

Depicted in the horizontal dimension of the model that follows is the *process view* of an ABC system. The emphasis now is on the activities themselves, the processes by which work is accomplished in the organization. The left-hand side of the model depicts activity analysis, which is the detailed identification and description of the activities conducted in the enterprise. Activity analysis entails the identification not only of the activities, but also of their *root causes,* the events that *trigger* activities, and the *linkages* among activities. The right-hand side of the model depicts the evaluation of activities through performance measures. These processes of *activity analysis and evaluation* constitute activity-based management.

Two-Dimensional ABC Model

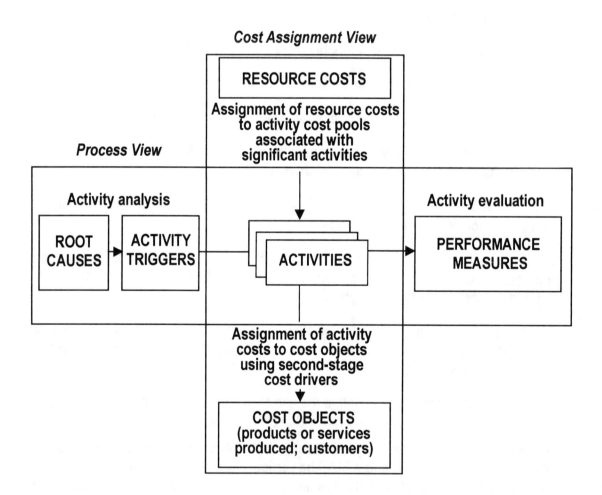

6-11 Activity analysis is the detailed identification and description of the activities conducted in an enterprise. Activity analysis entails the identification not only of activities, but also of their root causes, of the events that trigger them, and of the linkages among them. Three criteria for determining whether an activity adds value are as follows:

(a) Is the activity necessary?

(b) Is the activity efficiently performed?

(c) Is the activity sometimes value-added and sometimes non-value-added?

6-12 An activity's trigger is the preceding event that indicates that the activity should be performed. The activity's root cause is the event or activity that, if it had not occurred, would have prevented the activity in question from happening. For example, the event that triggers the activity of rework is the identification of a defective part during inspection. However, the inspection is *not* the root cause of the rework activity. The root cause of the defective part, and hence the need for rework, could lie in erroneous part specifications, in an unreliable vendor, or in faulty production.

6-13 Four techniques for reducing or eliminating non-value-added costs that result from non-value-added activities are as follows:

(a) Activity reduction

(b) Activity elimination

(c) Activity selection

(d) Activity sharing

6-14 Examples of activity sharing include the use of common parts in several related products, and the use of a common service facility (e.g., a photocopying center) by several departments.

6-15 Customer profitability analysis refers to using the concepts of activity-based costing to determine how serving particular customers causes activities to be performed and costs to be incurred. Examples of activities that can be differentially demanded by customers include order frequency, order size, special packaging or handling, customized parts or engineering, and special machine setups. Such activities can make some customers more profitable than others.

6-16   Activity-based costing is used to analyze customer-related costs and determine the cost drivers for these costs. This ABC data then forms the basis for the customer profitability analysis by assigning the appropriate amount of customer-related costs to each customer.

6-17   A customer profitability profile, usually expressed in graphical form, shows the company's cumulative operating income as a percentage of total operating income. The customers included in the profile generally are ranked either by operating income or by sales revenue.

6-18   In some cases, companies do eliminate unprofitable customers. However, it is important for companies to not to be too quick in doing so. Companies often develop customer relationships over long time horizons by offering low prices and a high level of service up front. As the relationship develops, however, the customer may not require the same level of service and might be willing to pay a premium for the service. Customer profitability analysis helps management see the overall financial picture for each customer, and how management can use this information to help establish a strategic plan for the coming months, quarters, or years. Management may decide that it is worth keeping an unprofitable customer now to maintain the potential for future profitability.

6-19   A trend analysis tracks customer-related costs over time to determine whether they are increasing, decreasing, remaining relatively stable or behaving in any particularly unusual manner. Trend analysis can help management decide which customer-related costs need their attention most urgently, and which customers need the most attention. Perhaps even better than comparing the customer-related costs to the company's norms, would be to compare them to industry-wide norms, or the norms for the industry's best performers. Such information can sometimes be generated from benchmarking studies, which focus on the best practices of organizations both within the industry and beyond.

6-20   *Continuous improvement* may be defined as the constant effort to eliminate waste, reduce response time, simplify the design of both products and processes, and improve product quality and customer service.

The *price down/cost down* concept is the tendency of prices to fall over the life cycle of a newly introduced product. Moreover, if prices are to fall over time, manufacturers must continually reduce costs.

Target costing is the process of designing a product, and the processes used to produce it, in order to achieve a manufacturing cost that will enable the firm to make a profit when the product is sold at an estimated market-driven price. This estimated price is called the *target price,* the desired profit margin is called the *target profit,* and the cost at which the product must be manufactured is called the *target cost.*

Value engineering (or value analysis) is a cost-reduction and process-improvement technique that utilizes information collected about a product's design and production processes and then examines attributes of the design and processes to identify candidates for improvement. The attributes examined include such characteristics as part diversity and process complexity.

Kaizen costing is the process of cost reduction during the manufacturing phase of an existing product. The Japanese word *kaizen* refers to continual and gradual improvement through small betterment activities, rather than large or radical improvement made through innovation or large investments in technology.

6-21   Kaizen costing is most consistent with the old saying "slow and steady wins the race." Kaizen costing is the process of cost reduction during the manufacturing phase of an existing product. The Japanese word *kaizen* refers to continual and gradual improvement through small betterment activities, rather than large or radical improvement made through innovation or large investments in technology.

6-22   *Employee empowerment* is the concept that workers are encouraged to take their own initiative to improve operations, reduce costs, and improve product quality and customer service.

Benchmarking is the continual search for the most effective method of accomplishing a task, by comparing existing methods and performance levels with those of other organizations, or with other subunits within the same organization. An example of benchmarking is an airline's determining how many of its competitors' flights are delayed and comparing the data with its own flight-delay record.

The most effective methods of accomplishing various tasks in a particular industry, often discovered through benchmarking, are referred to as *best practices*.

Reengineering is the complete redesign of a process, with an emphasis on finding creative new ways to accomplish an objective. Reengineering has sometimes been described as taking a blank piece of paper and starting from scratch to redesign a business process. Rather than searching continually for minute improvements, re-engineering involves a radical shift in thinking about how an objective should be met.

Organizational culture is the mind-set of employees, including their shared beliefs, values and goals.

A *change champion* is an individual who recognizes the need for change and, through his or her own efforts, seeks to bring it about. A successful change champion is usually at a high level in the organizational hierarchy, has strong entrepreneurial skills, demonstrates political savvy within the organization, and has the ability to persuade and motivate others.

6-23   The *theory of constraints* (TOC) is a management approach that seeks to maximize long-term profit through proper management of organization bottlenecks or constrained resources. The key idea in TOC is to identify the constraints in a system that are preventing the organization from achieving a higher level of success. Then the goal is to relieve or relax those constraints. TOC recommends subordinating all other management goals to the objective of solving the constraint problem. For example, if limited capacity in a particular machining operation is increasing cycle time, reducing throughput, and reducing profits, then management would concentrate much of its efforts on expanding the capacity of that bottleneck operation. If efforts are continually made to relax constraints, *continuous improvement* in organizational performance is a likely result.

6-24   The elimination of production bottleneck activities is an example of the theory of constraints. (See the preceding answer.)

6-25   Five keys to the successful implementation of ABC, ABM, or other cost management approaches are the following:

   (a) Strong functional organizational culture

   (b) Top management support and commitment

   (c) Change champion

   (d) Change process

   (e) Continuing education

6-26   It is human nature to resist change. Moving from a traditional, volume-based product-costing system to an activity-based costing system is a radical change in the managerial-accounting system. People may be uneasy about such a change because they fear they will not understand the new system, will not be able to effectively use the information that the new system provides, or may be evaluated in a different way, one that may prove unfavorable toward them.

   The same comments can be applied to the implementation of any of the management concepts discussed in the chapter (e.g., continuous improvement, ABM, Kaizen costing, re-engineering).

SOLUTIONS TO EXERCISES

EXERCISE 6-27 (15 MINUTES)

	Traditional Factory*	JIT/FMS Factory*
Raw materials	D	D
Electricity, machines	I	D
Electricity, lighting, and air-conditioning	I	I
Engineering salaries	I	D
Custodial wages	I	I
Depreciation, plant	I	I
Depreciation, equipment	I	D
Insurance	I	I
Machine repair, wages	I	D
Machine repair, parts	I	D
Direct labor	D	D
Supervisory salaries	I	I
Property taxes	I	I
Factory supplies	I	D
Inspection	I	D

*D denotes direct; I denotes indirect

EXERCISE 6-28 (25 MINUTES)

1. Airline:

   (a) "Deadheading," the practice of flying a nonworking flight-crew member to another city to work on a flight departing from that location. The crew member sometimes displaces a paying customer.

   (b) Preparing excess food for a flight, which is not consumed, because the flight occupancy was misforecast.

   (c) Returning, repairing, or replacing lost or mishandled luggage.

   (d) Canceling a flight because of an aircraft maintenance problem that should have been prevented by routine maintenance.

EXERCISE 6-28 (CONTINUED)

2.   Bank:

   (a)   Correcting customer account errors due to keypunch errors in the bank.

   (b)   Following up on checks or deposit slips lost by the bank.

   (c)   Performing banking procedures manually when the computer is down.

   (d)   Defaulted loans made to risky borrowers as a result of inadequate credit checks.

   (e)   Losses due to employee embezzlement and petty theft.

3.   Hotel:

   (a)   Breakage of dishes and glassware; loss of or damage to linens and towels.

   (b)   Loss of room keys.

   (c)   Overstaffing the front desk during nonpeak hours.

   (d)   Preparing excess food.

EXERCISE 6-29 (30 MINUTES)

The sky's the limit on responding to this problem. A good model for the response is contained in Chapters 5 and 6 for Aerotech Corporation.

(1)   The major steps in Aerotech's traditional production process are described at the beginning of Chapter 5.

(2)   Aerotech's Bakersfield plant layout, which uses advanced manufacturing technology, is shown in Exhibit 6-1.

(3)   An explanation of how Aerotech's Bakersfield facility eliminated or reduced non-value-added costs is given in Chapter 6. See the pages around Exhibit 6-1. For example, the Bakersfield facility eliminated the holding areas between production departments, thus eliminating the non-value-added cost of waiting time. Aerotech also installed an automated material-handling system in the Bakersfield facility that resulted in substantial reductions in the non-value-added costs of move time.

EXERCISE 6-30 (40 MINUTES, PLUS TIME AT RESTAURANT)

Several restaurant activities are listed in the following table, along with the required characteristics for each activity. Many other possibilities could be listed, depending on the level of detail.

Activity Description	Value-Added or Non-Value-Added	Activity Trigger	Root Cause
Taking reservations	VA	Customer calls on phone	Customer desires reservation
Customers waiting for a table	NVA	Customer arrives, but no table is ready	An error was made in reservation; service is slow; customers are slow; customers arrive without reservations
Seating customers	VA	Table becomes available	Customer's reservation (or turn in line) comes up; table becomes ready
Taking orders	VA	Customers indicate readiness to order	Kitchen staff needs to know what to prepare
Serving meals to customers	VA	Meals are ready	Meals are ready; customers are hungry
Returning meal to kitchen for revised preparation	NVA	Customer complains about meal	An error was made in explaining the menu; there is an error in the printed menu description; meal was prepared wrong; customer is picky

EXERCISE 6-30 (CONTINUED)

Customers eating meal	VA	Meals are served and are satisfactory	Customers are hungry
Clearing the table	VA	Customers are finished	Customers are finished
Delivering check to table	VA	Customers are finished ordering and eating	Customers need to know amount of bill
Collecting payment	VA	Customers have produced cash or credit card	Restaurant needs to collect payment for services rendered

EXERCISE 6-31 (30 MINUTES)

1. Description of course registration process:

   (a) Receive list of courses in mail, along with "bubble sheet" for filling in desired courses and sections.

   (b) During allotted week, select courses and fill in bubble sheet.

   (c) Return bubble sheet to bursar's office. Often must stand in line for more than an hour to turn in sheet. Required, since sheet and student ID must be checked by bursar's personnel.

   (d) One month later, receive preliminary schedule. If acceptable, no further action necessary. Just pay tuition. Automatically enrolled. Final schedule received shortly, before next semester starts. If didn't pay tuition, schedule is dropped.

EXERCISE 6-31 (CONTINUED)

(e) If schedule is unacceptable, attend "Drop/Add" with 15,000 other students in the basketball arena. This is a madhouse and a guaranteed headache. Posted around the entrance are lists of open classes, but the list is often out of date within an hour or so. Using carbon-copy drop/add forms, select new class(es).

(f) Stand in line corresponding to last four digits of social security number so that bursar's personnel can check course availability. Often in line for 30 minutes or more, depending on time of day.

(g) If course available and requirements for course met, enrolled on the spot. If not, must initiate process all over again, or could be placed on a wait list. Schedule resulting from drop/add process received shortly before classes start.

(h) If schedule unacceptable or if did/didn't get off waiting list once school begins, fill out drop/add form, get approval by the relevant professor, and submit to the bursar. Long lines once again.

2. Activity analysis:

(a) Activity analysis looks at activity linkages, activity triggers, and root causes. It should also consider the goals of the parties involved. Starting with the goals, students want a faster, easier registration method that does not require standing in line for hours to obtain information or approvals. They want to be able to prioritize their class selections, get relatively fast feedback on whether or not they are in a class, and know where they stand on the waiting list. The college wants a faster, easier registration method that does not require so much paperwork and direct labor, is less costly, provides timely information on class availability, is accurate, and enrolls only paid students.

(b) Activity linkages:

Described in requirement (1).

EXERCISE 6-31 (CONTINUED)

(c) Activity triggers:

The time of year triggers the registration process. The approval requirement triggers time delays. A high volume of students turning in sheets at same time triggers delays. Class availability and preferences trigger the need for Drop/Add. The mad-house at Drop/Add is triggered by a lack of up-to-date information, a high volume of students, and approval requirements. The waiting list procedure and the late delivery of schedules trigger more registration frustration, approval time, and time at the bursar's office the first week of classes.

(d) Root causes:

The information system cannot automatically approve students' credentials or confirm that registration has been done correctly. The time during which students must submit schedules is very compressed, and all must flow through the bursar, which has only four lines, essentially on the same day, thus creating a bottleneck. Students are not able to list classes in order of preference, so Drop/Add is required for most of the student body. The drop/add process is highly inefficient and information is not timely. The information system does not provide timely information, so problems with registration must be fixed in a rush during the busiest time of the semester.

3. Reengineering:

Based on the root causes, activity triggers, linkages, and goals, the college could benefit from a computerized information network that is accessible to students at all computer labs around campus and by modem. This system would enable many more students to register for classes at the same time, at their leisure, and allow them to note preferences via a point-weighting system. The system would automatically check credentials (i.e., student ID, social security number, tuition status) against existing records, thus eliminating the bursar bottleneck, and it would lead students through the process to ensure accuracy. The process would enable the bursar to quickly run a class-fill program on the submitted data to produce schedules. The absence of drop/add forms would reduce bursar paperwork and cost significantly. A drop/add time period could be established for students to quickly confirm class availability without dealing with the drop/add madhouse. The system would reveal placement and progress on the waiting list, and would produce final schedules that could be delivered via mail or an e-mail system, a week or so after Drop/Add. Then any problems could be remedied before classes begin. (This solution is courtesy of Amy Murchison, a managerial-accounting student.)

© *2002 The McGraw-Hill Companies, Inc.*

Solutions Manual

EXERCISE 6-32 (15 MINUTES)

Several activities performed (or at least supported) by an airline's ground employees, along with possible performance measures, are as follows:

Activity	Performance Measure
Making reservations over the phone	Reservations booked per hour Percentage of reservations with errors Number of customer complaints
Tagging luggage	Bags tagged per hour Percentage of bags incorrectly tagged
Handling luggage	Bags handled per hour, per employee Number of bags damaged Percentage of bags sent to wrong destination
Maintaining aircraft	Maintenance procedures per shift, per employee (both routine and repair) Number of repair incidents per month Number of flight delays due to maintenance problems
Enplaning passengers	Number of passengers enplaned Number of customer complaints Average time required at gate to enplane passengers
Preparing aircraft for departure	Number of aircraft departures per month Percentage of flights with delays Average delay per flight delayed

EXERCISE 6-33 (30 MINUTES)

Memorandum

Date: Today

To: President, Big Apple Design Company

From: I. M. Student, Controller, Big Apple Design Company

Subject: Customer-Profitability Analysis

The customer-profitability analysis ranks customers on the basis of operating income. As the graph shows, customers 5 and 6 are not profitable for Big Apple Design Company. There are several possible courses of action, including the following four:

- Drop customers 5 and 6.

- Raise the prices for customers 5 and 6.

- Cut the costs of serving customers 5 and 6 by cutting back on services.

- Try to increase higher-priced services to customers 5 and 6 in order to make these customer relationships profitable.

EXERCISE 6-34 (25 MINUTES)

1. Customers ranked by sales revenue:

(1)	108	(11)	113
(2)	114	(12)	135
(3)	112	(13)	133
(4)	116	(14)	106
(5)	110	(15)	111
(6)	124	(16)	107
(7)	121	(17)	134
(8)	127	(18)	119
(9)	125	(19)	136
(10)	128	(20)	137

EXERCISE 6-34 (CONTINUED)

Yes, the ranking by sales revenue is different from that based on operating income.

2.   No, Aerotech's least profitable customers are not the ones with the lowest sales revenue. The least profitable customers are numbers 119 and 134.

3.   Yes, the profile would be different, because the ordering of the customers along the horizontal axis would match the order in requirement (1) instead of the ordering in Exhibit 6-11.

4.   A customer characterized by high sales revenue would not necessarily be the most profitable, because the customer may demand costly services such as special handling or packaging, frequent small shipments, or unique design features.

EXERCISE 6-35 (15 MINUTES)

1.   Trend analysis (percentages rounded):

Customer-Related Cost Item	Year 1	Year 2	Year 3	Year 4	Year 5
Cost of engineering changes......................	1.1%	1.9%	1.1%	1.1%	12.0%
Special packaging.....................................	11.0%	11.5%	13.0%	12.0%	12.0%

2.   Conclusions:

The cost of engineering changes for customer number 614, which remained consistently low for four tears, spiked to a very high level in year 5. Something unusual must have occurred in year 5, and this should be investigated by management.

Special packaging costs, although consistent across the five-year period, are quite high. This may be necessary, due to the special needs of customer number 614, but this consistently high cost should be investigated by management. There may be a way to cut this cost, possibly with the cooperation of the customer.

EXERCISE 6-36 (30 MINUTES)

FedEx could use customer profitability analysis to analyze which customers (particularly commercial customers) are more expensive to serve and, thus, less profitable. See the Management Accounting Practice (M.A.P.) inset on page 243 of the text.

EXERCISE 6-37 (25 MINUTES)

1. Process time: steps 3, 5, 6, 7, 8, 10, 11

   Inspection time: steps 1, 9

   Move time: steps 2, 5, 6, 7, 10, 11

   Waiting time: steps 4, 5, 7

   Storage time: steps 1, 11

2. Candidates for non-value-added activities:

   (a) Step 2: Carrying ingredients on hand carts.

   (b) Step 4: Storing dough until bagel machine is free. (Could move toward a JIT system for dough mixing.)

   (c) Step 5: Keeping cut-out bagels until boiling vat is free. (Could move toward JIT system.)

   (d) Step 7: Carrying bagels to oven room.

   (e) Step 7: Continual opening and closing of oven door.

   (f) Step 9: Consumption of misshapen bagels by the staff. (Could these faulty products be sold at a reduced price?)

   (g) Step 10: Carrying wire baskets to the packaging room.

   (h) Step 11: Driving forklift to freezer.

EXERCISE 6-38 (40 MINUTES)

(1)   Redesigned bagel production process:

(a)   Ingredients, such as flour and raisins, are received and inspected in the morning or afternoon they are to be used. Then they are placed on a conveyor belt that transports the ingredients to the mixing room next door.

(b)   Dough is mixed in 40-pound batches in four heavy-duty mixers. The dough is placed on large boards, which are set on the conveyor. The conveyor transports the boards of dough into the bagel room next door.

(c)   The board is tipped automatically and the dough slides into the hopper of a bagel machine. This machine pulls off a piece of dough, rolls it into a cylindrical shape, and then squeezes it into a doughnut shape. The bagel machines can be adjusted in a setup procedure to accommodate different sizes and styles of bagels. Workers remove the uncooked bagels and place them on a tray. The trays are set on the conveyor, which carries the uncooked bagels into an adjoining room.

(d)   This room houses three 50-gallon vats of boiling water. The bagels are boiled for approximately one minute.

(e)   Bagels are removed from the vats with a long-handled strainer and placed on a wooden board. The boards full of bagels are placed on the conveyor, which transports them to the oven room.

(f)   The two ovens contain eight racks that rotate but remain upright, much like the seats on a Ferris wheel. A rack full of bagels is finished baking after one complete revolution in the oven. When a rack full of bagels is removed from the oven, a fresh rack replaces it. The oven door automatically opens and closes as each rack completes a revolution in the oven.

(g)   After the bagels are removed from the oven, they are placed in baskets for cooling.

(h)   While the bagels are cooling, they are inspected. Misshapen bagels are removed and set aside for sale at a reduced price.

EXERCISE 6-38 (CONTINUED)

(i)   After the bagels are cool, the wire baskets are placed on the conveyor and transported to the packaging room next door.

(j)   Here the bagels are dumped automatically into the hopper on a bagging machine. This machine packages a half dozen bagels in each bag and seals the bag with a twist tie.

(k)   Then the packaged bagels are placed in cardboard boxes, each holding 24 bags.

(l)   The boxes are placed in the freezer, where the bagels are frozen and stored for shipment. The freezer has a door in the packaging room, and another door in the shipping/receiving room.

(2)   Key features of a JIT system:

The new production process of Better Bagels, Inc. has a *smooth, uniform production rate* with each part of the process being initiated by the subsequent operation. Thus, the bagelry uses a *pull method* of *coordinating production steps.* The *ingredients are purchased as needed in small lot sizes,* delivered twice daily, and sent immediately to the mixing room. The bagel machine is designed for *quick setups* for different bagel sizes and consistency. Only *high-quality ingredients* are used in order to eliminate down time and to follow a *total quality control* philosophy. *The machinery is carefully maintained.* The bagelry's *employees are encouraged to suggest improvements* in the product or production process. Employees whose suggestions are adopted receive cash awards or peer recognition. All of the bagelry's employees are trained in each phase of the production process. Thus, Better Bagel's *multiskilled work force* enables the firm to operate with fewer employees.

(3)   New equipment:

Better Bagels, Inc. would need to purchase a new conveyor system that would transport partially completed bagels between production steps. The conveyor would tip the bagels automatically into appropriate production machines at various points in the process. Also needed would be an efficient oven that would open and close automatically (and quickly) to minimize heat loss.

EXERCISE 6-39 (25 MINUTES)

1. Target cost = $125 – $25 = $100

2. Target profit = $25

3. Target price = $125

4. Target costing involves designing a product, as well as the process used to manufacture it, so that ultimately the product can be manufactured at a cost that will enable the firm to make a profit when the product is sold at an estimated market-driven price. In the case of the photon gismo, the design engineering team needs to redesign the gismo and/or the production process so that the gismo can be manufactured for $100.

5. Value engineering is a cost-reduction and process-improvement technique that utilizes information collected about a product's design and production process, and then examines this information to identify candidates for improvement. An example, in the context of the photon gismo, is using a machine to assemble several parts, instead of assembling them manually.

6. The activity phase of a two-dimensional ABC system could help solve the problem with the photon gismo. This phase would identify activities in the gismo's production process, as well as the linkages, triggers, and root causes of those activities. For example, suppose that part of the photon gismo's cost includes the inspection of a particular component that is sometimes damaged in the assembly operation. Furthermore, suppose that the root cause of that damage is subsequently determined to be excessive tightening of a bolt on the mounting chassis for the photon gismo's parts. Eliminating the problem of excessive tightening would potentially also eliminate the need for inspecting the component.

EXERCISE 6-40 (25 MINUTES)

A wide range of answers is possible for this exercise.

1.   All colleges and universities have admissions departments, course registration procedures, and teaching operations. All aspects of these operations could be benchmarked against similar institutions of higher education. For example, how does an undergraduate school of business administration with an enrollment of 1,000 students compare with five other similar business schools on the following dimensions:

   a.   Average grade point average (GPA) of students admitted to the business school.

   b.   Number of course offerings.

   c.   Number of corporate recruiters visiting the campus.

   d.   Average number of employment offers received per student.

   e.   Percentage of graduates who try for professional certification and are successful in doing so. (For example, of the school's graduates who take the CPA or CMA examination, what is the percentage of students who pass the exam?)

2.   A college or university could also benefit from benchmarking "outside the box." All colleges and universities have grounds and maintenance departments, food service operations, and housing operations. So do hospitals and hotels. These types of college operations could be benchmarked against similar operations in hospitals or hotels.

   Colleges have course scheduling procedures. Scheduling is also an important activity in airlines, bus lines, railroads, hospitals, and landscaping firms, to name a few.

   Public service is an important component of the mission of many colleges and universities. Effectiveness in this area could be benchmarked against a service organization such as the American Red Cross.

   Academic advising and counseling for students in a college or university could be benchmarked against similar operations in employment search firms and human resources departments in for-profit businesses.

   In short, the sky's the limit on the kinds of organizations against which a college or university might effectively benchmark its operations.

SOLUTIONS TO PROBLEMS

PROBLEM 6-41 (45 MINUTES)

1. Andromeda Corporation: Traditional plant layout.

Shipping/ Receiving/ Inspection	Finished-Goods Storage		Maintenance And Custodial
	1. Cutting Machines	9. Packaging	Quality Control
Raw-Materials Storage	Work-in-Process Storage	Work-in-Process Storage	
	2. Heading Machines	8. Inspection And Testing	Tool and Die Department
	Work-in-Process Storage		
	3. Oil Filtration System	Work-in-Process Storage	
Purchasing And Inventory Control	4. Slotting Machines	7. Salt Bath (Heat Treatment)	Industrial Engineering
	Work-in-Process Storage		
Production Scheduling	5. Threading Machines	Work-in-Process Storage	Electronic Data Processing
	Work-in-Process Storage	6. Bolt Washers	
Sales and Marketing	Plant Manager And Staff	Personnel	Accounting

PROBLEM 6-41 (CONTINUED)

2. (a) Andromeda Corporation: Advanced manufacturing system and plant layout.

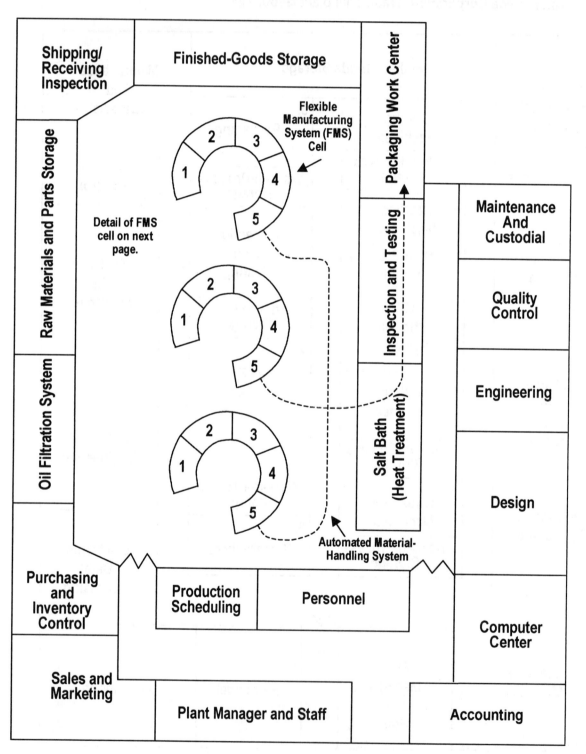

PROBLEM 6-41 (CONTINUED)

(b)   Andromeda Corporation: FMS cell.

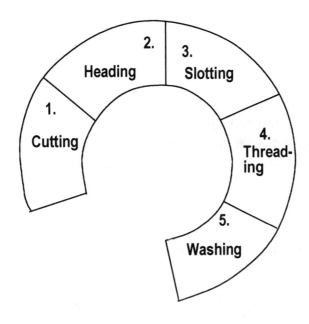

PROBLEM 6-42 (30 MINUTES)

Memorandum

Date: Today

To: President, Andromeda Corporation

From: I.M. Student

Subject: Non-value-added costs

I have identified several activities in the company's production process that may be non-value-added activities, that is, activities that are not essential and do not add value to the product. As a result, I believe the firm is incurring substantial non-value-added costs. Several of these costs are listed below.

1.   Storage time

(a)   Raw materials are ordered too far in advance of their use. They remain stored in inventory.

(b)   Finished goods often are produced before they are needed for sale. They remain stored in inventory.

2.   Waiting time

Partially completed bolts are produced before the next production operation is ready for them. The work in process sits waiting in various holding areas.

3.   Move time

Too much time is spent moving raw material, work in process, and finished goods from process to process.

PROBLEM 6-42 (CONTINUED)

4. **Labor force**

Our work force is larger than it needs to be. If we purchased a flexible manufacturing system, more of the work could be done by automated equipment. Each production employee would be able to handle several operations in an FMS cell.

I believe the firm can eliminate most of the non-value-added costs by installing a flexible manufacturing system and an automated material-handling system. In conjunction with these changes in manufacturing technology, the company should adopt a just-in-time production and inventory management system. This system would reduce inventories of all types and save the non-value-added costs of unnecessary investment in raw materials, work in process, and finished goods.

PROBLEM 6-43 (30 MINUTES)

1. If Kelifo Electric Vehicle Company (KEVCO) implements a "demand pull" production philosophy, both its planning and operating processes could experience the following effects.

Planning

- Production planning will change from a centralized batch function process to a more decentralized activity. In some cases, production teams will be responsible for the entire production process of a product.

- The method and timing of how the company prepares its production schedule (including capacity requirements) will change to parallel the "demand pull" approach as opposed to the "production push" approach.

- The Purchasing Department will need to plan to have high-quality, reliable, and flexible suppliers who can quickly deliver orders of varying sizes as needed.

Operations

- Change-over time (set-up time) will reduce lead times significantly.

- A kanban-like system will have to be implemented. A triggering device such as a kanban card is necessary so that the department or cell knows when to begin production.

- Greater employee participation will result from cell production team arrangements.

2. Five benefits to KEVCO in changing to a "demand pull" production operating philosophy are as follows:

- Less rework and fewer defective units because of cell-level accountability and control and product problem solving at the cell level.

- A lower cash investment in inventory and plant space. Handling, storage, insurance, breakage, and obsolescence all will be lower.

- More satisfied customers should result because of shorter lead times and higher quality.

- Improved labor productivity as a result of rearranging the production process and the creation of manufacturing cell teams.

- A reduction of the number of suppliers, leading to improved relationships and communication.

3. Some of the behavioral effects of the proposed change at KEVCO on team participation in planning and production include the following:

- Higher team morale and motivation, since each cell team is responsible for all cell production and will, therefore, have more control over their work and an increased sense of ownership.

- Higher individual satisfaction, development, and motivation, as management will encourage participation, training, and input on how to improve the product and production process.

- A possible resistance to change by those employees who may feel insecure or threatened by the change.

- A sense of partnership with management in achieving the goals and objectives of the organization.

PROBLEM 6-44 (25 MINUTES)

1. Annual financial impact:

Return on released funds	
[($3,600,000 - $600,000) x 12%].......................	$360,000
Savings in insurance and property taxes...............	27,000
Lease revenue (30,000 square feet x 75% x $2).......	45,000
Depreciation on remodeled facilities	
($600,000 ÷ 10 years).....................................	(60,000)
Savings in warranty and repair costs...................	25,000
Salary savings*...	30,000
Added stockout costs......................................	(70,000)
Savings from JIT system...............................	$357,000

> * Note: The cost of the two transferred employees is excluded because Alliance will continue to have these individuals on the payroll.

2. With a just-in-time purchasing system, companies avoid costly build-ups of raw-material inventories because materials and parts are ordered only when needed. The suppliers under such a system are highly reliable and deliver quality goods on time. Thus, despite the absence of inventories that firms can rely on if needed, the likelihood of excessive stockouts is fairly low.

3. Long-term contracts under a JIT purchasing system set tight standards with respect to the quality of materials purchased. The quality is high, which reduces the need for incoming inspections.

4. Under a traditional purchasing system, goods are purchased (frequently in large lots) and then placed in inventory until used. In contrast, with JIT, costly inventories are avoided by having the materials arrive "just-in-time" to be issued to production. Materials are therefore purchased only when needed, which often translates into numerous small acquisitions throughout the period.

PROBLEM 6-45 (30 MINUTES)

1. Activity-based management refers to the use of activity-based costing to improve operations and eliminate non-value-added costs. These costs arise from non-value-added activities—operations that are either (a) unnecessary and dispensable or (b) necessary but inefficient and improvable. Put simply, such activities can be eliminated without harming overall quality, performance, or perceived value.

PROBLEM 6-45 (CONTINUED)

2. Cost of non-value-added activities:

      Incoming receipts: $300,000 ÷ 2,000 purchase orders = $150 per purchase order

      Warehousing: $360,000 ÷ 9,000 inventory moves = $40 per move

      Outgoing shipments: $225,000 ÷ 15,000 shipments = $15 per shipment

Warehousing: 550 moves x $40	$22,000
Outgoing shipments: 250 shipments x $15	3,750
Total	$25,750

3. Extra inventory moves in the warehouse may be caused by books being shelved (i.e., stocked) incorrectly, poor planning for the arrival and subsequent placement/stocking of new titles, and other similar situations. Extra shipments would likely be the result of errors in order entry and order filling, goods lost in transit, or damaged merchandise being sent to customers.

4. As the following figures show, the elimination of non-value-added activities allows BookNet.Com to achieve the target-cost percentage for software only.

Activity	Cost-Driver Quantity	% Books	% Software	Cost-Driver Quantity: Books	Cost-Driver Quantity: Software
Incoming receipts.......	2,000	70%	30%	1,400	600
Warehousing....	9,000	80%	20%	6,650*	1,800
Outgoing shipments...	15,000	25%	75%	3,750	11,000**

* (9,000 moves x 80%) – 550

** (15,000 shipments x 75%) – 250

PROBLEM 6-45 (CONTINUED)

	Books	Software
Incoming receipts:		
1,400 purchase orders x $150...........	$210,000	
600 purchase orders x $150.............		$ 90,000
Warehousing:		
6,650 moves x $40..........................	266,000	
1,800 moves x $40..........................		72,000
Outgoing shipments:		
3,750 shipments x $15.....................	56,250	
11,000 shipments x $15...................		165,000
Total cost..	$532,250	$327,000
Cost as a percentage of sales:		
$532,250 ÷ $3,900,000.....................	13.65%	
$327,000 ÷ $2,600,000.....................		12.58%

5. Additional cost cutting of $25,250 is needed for books to achieve the 13% target of $507,000 ($3,900,000 x 13%). Tools that the company might use include customer-profitability analysis, target costing, value engineering, kaizen costing, benchmarking, and reengineering.

PROBLEM 6-46 (50 MINUTES, PLUS TIME SPENT AT GROCERY STORE AND BANK)

This is a chance to think carefully about how detailed and precise an activity analysis can be. It's also an opportunity to invoke your sense of humor and air your pet peeves about a couple of errands we all have to do routinely.

There is clearly no single correct answer. Reasonable answers will vary widely.

1.   Activity sequences and linkages:

Grocery Store	Bank
(1) Strategically choose time of day, keeping in mind (a) how urgent need is, (b) likely crowding, and (c) how well stocked the shelves will be	(1) Strategically choose time of day and branch location
(2) Drive or walk to store	(2) Choose among inside teller window, drive-up lane, or ATM
(3) Park car	(3) Park car
(4) Walk to front door	(4) Walk to front door
(5) Get cart; search parking lot if necessary	(5) Prepare banking documents
(6) Walk aisles to find items	(6) Wait in line
(7) Read product labels	(7) Explain banking needs to teller (or operate ATM)
(8) Compare prices	(8) Wait while transaction is completed
(9) Select items	(9) Check teller's (or ATM's) work
(10) Strategically choose checkout line (Express line? Cash only? Which one is shortest? Which one is fastest? Which clerk is fastest? etc.)	(10) Leave bank

(11) Wait in line; jockey for position if new checkout lane opens

(11) Leave parking lot

(12) Unpack cart

(13) Items are checked out

(14) Items are bagged (paper or plastic?)

(15) Carry out bags (or have bags carried out)

(16) Load car

(17) Leave parking lot

2. Specifying whether an activity is value-added or non-value added often depends on how well the business is organized for the activity. For example, some grocery stores make it easier to park close to the entrance than do others. Thus, getting from your car to the front door could be value-added or non-value-added, depending on how convenient the store's parking lot is. The designations of VA or NVA will vary widely, depending on individual experiences.

Grocery Store		Bank	
Activity	VA or NVA	Activity	VA or NVA
(1)	VA	(1)	VA
(2)	VA	(2)	VA
(3)[a]	VA, NVA	(3)[a]	VA, NVA
(4)[a]	VA, NVA	(4)[a]	VA, NVA
(5)[b]	VA, NVA	(5)[i]	VA, NVA
(6)[c]	VA, NVA	(6)[j]	NVA
(7)[d]	VA, NVA	(7)[k]	VA, NVA
(8)[d]	VA, NVA	(8)[l]	NVA
(9)	VA	(9)[m]	NVA
(10)[e]	NVA	(10)	VA
(11)[e]	NVA	(11)[h]	VA, NVA
(12)	VA		
(13)	VA		
(14)[f]	NVA		
(15)[g]	NVA		
(16)[g]	NVA		
(17)[h]	VA, NVA		

[a]Depends on the configuration of the parking lot in relation to the design of the building and the location of the front door.

[b]Getting a cart in the store or by the front door, VA; searching the parking lot, NVA.

[c]Depends on the store layout. The author is inclined to say NVA, since it would be an improvement if grocery stores would adopt a standard layout (e.g., the soda always in aisle 4, or the dairy-case pizza always In aisle 6 on the end near the registers).

[d]Depends on how convenient the store makes these tasks. Interestingly, this is one area where the law has helped the consumer. Stores now must display unit pricing information, and food companies must include nutritional information on the labels of many items.

PROBLEM 6-46 (CONTINUED)

[e]This part of grocery shopping drives the author up the wall. Why not have all non-express-lane customers wait in *one* line and then feed into the next available checkout lane? This configuration is typical of banks, but the author has seen it done in only one grocery store.

[f]Bagging can be simultaneous with checking out, especially if bar code scanners are in use.

[g]The store could adopt the technology of an automated material-handling system (AMHS) here. Bags of groceries would be placed in bins with the customer's number indicated. Then the bins would be transported by conveyor to a location by the front door. When the customer drove up, a store employee would load the groceries into the car. The author has seen this system in operation, but rarely.

[h]Depends on the configuration of the parking lot.

[i]Depends on how user-friendly the documents are.

[j]NVA, but a lot better than in a typical grocery store. See note (e) above.

[k]Depends on the bank's operating procedures and level of teller training.

[l]Electronic operating systems process transactions much faster than do manual systems.

[m]NVA, because we wouldn't have to check if errors were extremely rare or nonexistent.

3. Two striking examples of successful reengineering are the widespread introduction of bar code scanners by grocery stores (and other retailers) and ATMs (automatic teller machines) by banks. The introduction of electronic banking (from the home) is another emerging example of reengineering in the banking industry. Similarly, the introduction of shopping services and telephone ordering by grocery stores continues the re-engineering process in this industry. Also, many retail companies are dramatically reengineering their sales and billing procedures due to the ever-increasing use of buying via the internet.

PROBLEM 6-47 (30 MINUTES)

1. Contribution margin of lost sales (20,000) units:

Revenue		$12.00*
Variable costs:		
Costs of goods sold		$ 4.50*
Selling and administrative		1.00*
Total variable costs		$ 5.50
Unit contribution margin		$ 6.50
Volume of lost sales		× 20,000
Total contribution margin of lost sales		$(130,000)
Overtime premiums		(40,000)†
Rental savings...		60,000
Rental income from owned warehouse		
(12,000 sq. ft. × .75 × $1.50).......................................		13,500
Elimination of insurance		14,000
Opportunity cost of funds released from inventory		
investment:		
Investment in inventory	$600,000	
Interest before taxes	× .20	120,000
Estimated before-tax dollar savings		$ 37,500

*Total amount on the income statement ÷ 900,000 units

†The cost of overtime premiums, $40,000, is less than the additional forgone contribution margin if the overtime is not used (15,000 units × $6.50 = $97,500). Therefore, the overtime should be used.

2. Conditions that should exist in order for a company to install just-in-time inventory methods successfully include the following:

- Top management must be committed and provide the necessary leadership support in order to ensure a companywide coordinated effort.

- A detailed system for integrating the sequential operations of the manufacturing process needs to be developed and implemented. Raw materials must arrive when needed for each subassembly so that the production process functions smoothly.

- Accurate sales forecasts are needed for effective finished-goods planning and production scheduling.

- Products should be designed to use standardized parts to reduce manufacturing time and decrease costs.

- Reliable vendors who can deliver quality raw materials on time with minimum lead time must be identified.

PROBLEM 6-48 (45 MINUTES)

1. Two dimensional ABC:

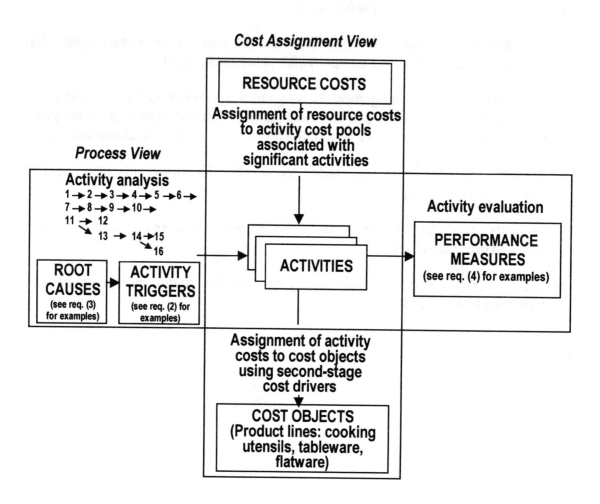

PROBLEM 6-48 (CONTINUED)

2. Triggers for selected activities:

Activity Number	Trigger
(2)	Realization by purchasing personnel that they do not fully understand the part specifications
(9)	Realization by purchasing personnel that the ordered part will be (or may be) late in arriving
(11)	Receipt of order
(12)	Discovery during inspection that parts do not meet specifications
(13)	Discovery that parts do not satisfy intended purpose

3. Possible root causes:

Activity Number	Possible Root Causes*
(2)	Unclear specifications Incomplete specifications Clear, but apparently wrong, specifications Undertrained purchasing personnel
(9)	Vendor delay Delay in placing order Failure by purchasing personnel to make deadline clear
(11)	Use of vendor that has not been fully certified as a reliable supplier Critical importance of parts
(12)	Misspecification of parts Error by purchasing personnel in placing order Vendor error Inspector error
(13)	Misspecification of parts Incomplete specifications Poor product design Error by purchasing personnel in placing order Vendor error

*This list is not necessarily complete. Other root causes may exist.

4.   Suggested performance measures:

Activity Number	Performance Measures
(5)	Average price paid
(6)	Number of vendors Number of vendors that are precertified as dependable
(10)	Percentage of orders received on time Average delay for delinquent orders
(12)	Number of orders returned Percentage of orders returned
(16)	Average dollar value tied up in parts inventory

PROBLEM 6-49 (40 MINUTES)

1. The net cash savings realized by AgriCo's Service Division as a result of the just-in-time inventory program is $43,000, computed as follows:

		Cash Savings (loss)
Funds released from inventory investment	$400,000	
Interest	× .15	$60,000
Insurance savings ($80,000 × .60)......................................		48,000
Warehouse rental revenue		
[(8,000 sq. ft. × .75) × $2.50 per sq. ft.]............................		15,000
Warehouse rental cost: no effect		—
Transferred employees: no effect		—
Contribution of lost sales (3,800 units at $10.00)*		(38,000)
Overtime premium (7,500 units at $5.60)†........................		(42,000)
Net cash savings...		$43,000

*Calculation of unit contribution margin:		
Revenue ($6,160,000 ÷ 280,000 units)		$22.00
Less variable costs:		
Cost of goods sold ($2,660,000 ÷ 280,000 units)....................	$9.50	
Selling and administrative expenses ($700,000 ÷ 280,000 units)	2.50	12.00
Contribution margin		$10.00

†The incremental cost of $5.60 per unit for overtime is less than the additional $10.00 per unit contribution for the 7,500 units that would have been lost sales. Therefore, the overtime hours should be used.

PROBLEM 6-49 CONTINUED)

2.   Factors, other than financial, that should be considered before a company implements a JIT inventory program include:

- Customer dissatisfaction: Stockouts of finished goods or spare parts could result in customers' downtime, which may be costly.

- Distributor relations: Stockouts of spare parts or finished goods can impair the manufacturer's image with its distributors, who represent the direct contacts with the ultimate customers.

- Supplier dissatisfactions: Placement of smaller and more frequent orders can result in higher material and delivery costs from suppliers. Additionally, with changes in their production and procurement processes, suppliers may choose to discontinue supplying to a just-in-time customer.

- Competition: The marketplace will determine the impact of service degradation due to stockouts. Brand loyalty can deteriorate when service standards are lowered. Therefore, it is crucial that before adopting JIT, management think through all the implications. It is important to maintain the company's prior service standards and if possible to improve on them.

PROBLEM 6-50 (50 MINUTES)

1. Predetermined overhead rate = $\dfrac{\text{budgeted manufacturing overhead}}{\text{budgeted direct-labor hours}}$

    = $\dfrac{\$1,496,000}{20,000 \text{ hr}}$

    = $74.80 per hr.

2. There is no single correct response to this requirement. One reasonable response is shown in the following table. Overhead costs are categorized into nine cost pools designated (a) through (i). Cost drivers are identified as follows:

    (a) Production (in units)

    (b) Raw-material cost

    (c) Factory space

    (d) Machine hours

    (e) Production runs

    (f) Shipments of finished goods

    (g) Shipments of raw materials

    (h) Number of different raw materials and parts used in a product

    (i) Engineering specifications and change orders

3. See the following table.

4. See the following table.

PROBLEM 6-50 (CONTINUED)

Overhead Item	Req. (2) Cost Pool and Cost Driver	Req. (3) Production Activity	Req. (4) Candidate for Elimination	Req. (6) Direct Costs of an FMS Cell
Supervision	h	process		
Machine maintenance—labor	d	process		X
Machine maintenance—materials	d	process		X
Electrical power	d	process		X
Natural gas (for heating)	c	process		
Factory supplies	a	process		X
Setup labor	e	process		X
Lubricants	d	process		X
Property taxes	c	process		
Insurance	c	process		
Depreciation on manufacturing equipment	d	process		X
Depreciation on trucks and forklifts	b	move	X	X
Depreciation on material conveyors	b	move		X
Building depreciation	c	process		
Grinding wheels	a	process		X
Drill bits	a	process		X
Purchasing	b	process		X
Waste collection	a	process	X	X
Custodial labor	c	process		
Telephone service	h	process		X
Engineering design	i	process		X
Inspection of raw materials	g	inspection		X
Receiving	g	process		X
Inspection of finished goods	a	inspection		X
Packaging	a	process		X
Shipping	f	move		X
Wages of parts clerks (find parts for production departments)	h	storage	X	X
Wages of material handlers	b	move	X	X
Fuel for trucks and forklifts	b	move	X	X
Depreciation on raw-material warehouse	b	storage	X	
Depreciation on finished-goods warehouse	a	storage	X	

PROBLEM 6-50 (CONTINUED)

5. Activity accounting identifies the costs and other performance measures that pertain to significant activities in the firm. Identification of activities and their costs helps management to identify and examine non-value-added costs. For example, management may be able to eliminate (or significantly reduce) the cost of fuel and depreciation for the trucks and forklifts and the wages of material handlers by installing an automated material-handling system. Similarly, adoption of a JIT approach to production could enable management to eliminate or reduce the wages of parts clerks and the depreciation on the two warehouses.

6. See the preceding table (right-hand column).

7. Almost all of the costs that are not traceable to an FMS cell are general facility costs, such as factory depreciation, property taxes, and insurance. These costs could be allocated to departments and FMS cells on the basis of factory space usage. Then the costs would be reallocated from these work centers to products in a two-stage allocation process.

8. Computation of pool rate:

Receiving	$20,000
Inspection of raw material	20,000
Total	$40,000

$$\text{Pool rate} = \frac{\text{budgeted cost}}{\text{budgeted level of cost driver}} = \frac{\$40,000}{400}$$

$$= \$100 \text{ per shipment}$$

PROBLEM 6-51 (40 MINUTES)

1. Customer-profitability analysis:

	Trace Telecom	Caltex Computer
Sales revenue	$190,000	$123,800
Cost of goods sold	80,000	62,000
Gross margin	$110,000	$ 61,800
Selling and administrative costs:		
General selling costs	$ 24,000	$ 18,000
General administrative costs	19,000	16,000
Customer-related costs:		
Sales activity	8,000	6,000
Order taking	3,000	4,000
Special handling	40,000	30,000
Special shipping	9,000	10,000
Total selling and administrative costs	$103,000	$ 84,000
Operating income	$ 7,000	$ (22,200)

PROBLEM 6-51 (CONTINUED)

2.   Customer-profitability graph:

Customer Operating Income (in dollars)

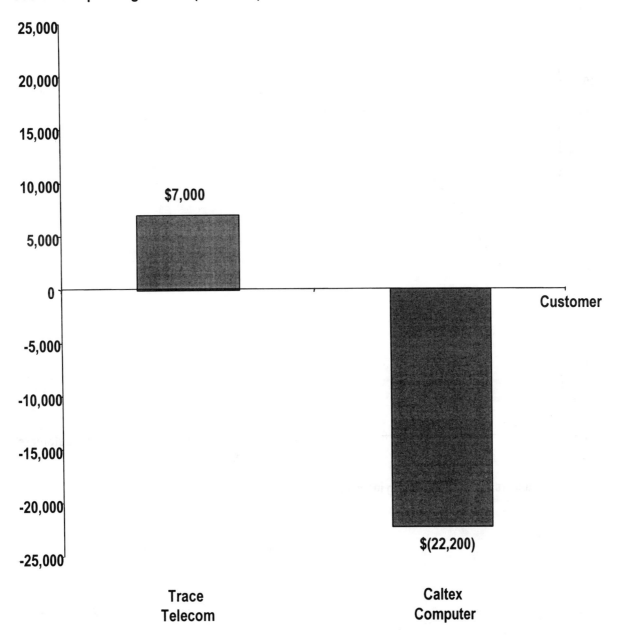

PROBLEM 6-52 (45 MINUTES)

1.   Customer-profitability profile (supporting details in the table following the profile):

Cumulative Operating Income as a
Percentage of Total Operating Income

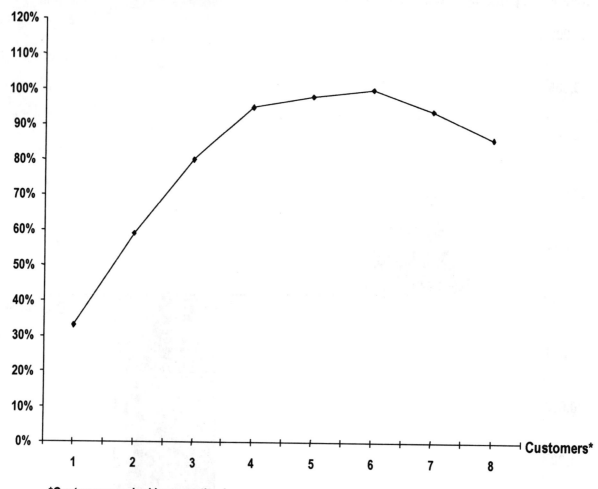

*Customers ranked by operating income.

PROBLEM 6-52 (CONTINUED)

Supporting details for customer-profitability profile:

Customer Number[a]	Customer	Operating Profit	Cumulative Operating Profit	Cumulative Operating Profit as a Percentage of Operating Income
(1)	Network-All, Inc.	$93,000	$ 93,000	33%
(2)	Golden Gate Service Associates	71,000	164,000	59%
(3)	Graydon Computer Company	60,000	224,000	80%
(4)	Mid-State Computing Company	42,000	266,000	95%
(5)	Trace Telecom[b]	7,000	273,000	98%
(6)	The California Group	6,000	279,000	100%
(7)	Tele-Install, Inc.	(18,000)	261,000	94%
(8)	Caltex Computer[c]	(22,200)	238,800	86%

[a]Customer numbers are ranked by operating income.
[b]From solution to preceding problem.
[c]From solution to preceding problem.

2.   Memorandum

Date: Today

To: I. Sellit, Vice President for Marketing

From: I. M. Student

Subject: Customer-profitability profile

The attached customer-profitability profile shows that two of our customer relationships are unprofitable (Tele-Install, Inc. and Caltex Computer). As the profile shows, over half of our operating income is generated by our two most profitable customer relationships, and 95 percent of our operating profit is generated by just half of our customers.

An activity-based costing analysis of customer-related costs provided the data for the customer-profitability analysis portrayed in the profile.

PROBLEM 6-53 (40 MINUTES)

1. Referring to the specific ethical standards for management accountants of competence, confidentiality, integrity, and objectivity, Marie Waters violated the following standards of ethical conduct when she asked Andrew Fulton to suppress pertinent information.

    Competence. Marie Waters, controller, has a responsibility to:

    *   Prepare complete and clear reports and recommendations after appropriate analyses of relevant and reliable information.

    *   Perform professional duties in accordance with relevant laws, regulations, and technical standards.

    In this instance, Waters' request to Fulton, the assistant controller, to suppress information about the component failures is unethical. This action keeps both Waters and Fulton from performing their duties in accordance with technical standards and has a favorable impact on earnings as requested by Jack March, vice president of manufacturing. The reported financial information, with the omission, lacks relevance and reliability for decision making. Management does not have a clear solution to overcome the component failure problem.

    Confidentiality. Does not apply.

    Integrity. Waters has a responsibility to:

    *   Refrain from either actively or passively subverting the attainment of the organization's legitimate and ethical objectives.

    *   Communicate unfavorable as well as favorable information and professional judgments or opinions.

    Waters' request is unethical since she has responsibilities to report all information of use to decision makers in the company. She should protect the overall interests and goal attainment of Resolute Electronics Corporation by encouraging further study of the problem by her staff, informing her superiors of this matter, and working with others to find solutions.

Objectivity. Waters has a responsibility to:

- Disclose fully all relevant information that could reasonably be expected to influence intended users' understanding of the reports, comments, and recommendations presented.

Waters' request is unethical because it would suppress information that could influence an understanding of the results of operations. Waters is also not communicating information objectively by withholding information about the contingent liability.

2. The steps that Andrew Fulton, assistant controller, could follow to resolve this situation are as follows:

- Follow the established policy on ethical conduct at REC, if a policy exists.

- Fulton has discussed the matter with Waters. If a satisfactory solution is not found and losses continue to mount, Fulton should discuss it again with Waters and may write a report detailing the probable economic effects of the situation and mentioning Waters' request to suppress the component failures.

- Fulton should advise Waters that he intends to take the matter further and discuss the issue with her superior. If the matter is not resolved satisfactorily, Fulton should continue up through higher levels in the organization (eventually to the board of directors) until the matter is resolved.

- Fulton should clarify the relevant concepts with a confidential and objective advisor to obtain an understanding of possible courses of action.

- If, after exhausting all internal review levels, the ethical conflict still exists, Fulton may have no recourse but to resign and write an informative memorandum to the appropriate organizational representative.

- Except where legally prescribed, communication of such problems to authorities or individuals not employed or engaged by the organization is not considered appropriate.

PROBLEM 6-54 (45 MINUTES)

1. See the graph on the following page.

2. See the graph on the following page.

3. See the graph on the following page.

4. See the graph on the following page.

5. See the graph on the following page.

6. Kaizen costing seeks to lower costs during the manufacturing phase through continuous improvement in the production process. Costs are lowered through constant small betterment activities, which every employee in the company is trying to achieve.

   By lowering its costs and improving quality through continuous improvement efforts, the company will be in a better position to compete in the global market on both price and quality.

PROBLEM 6-54 (CONTINUED)

Cost per TV set

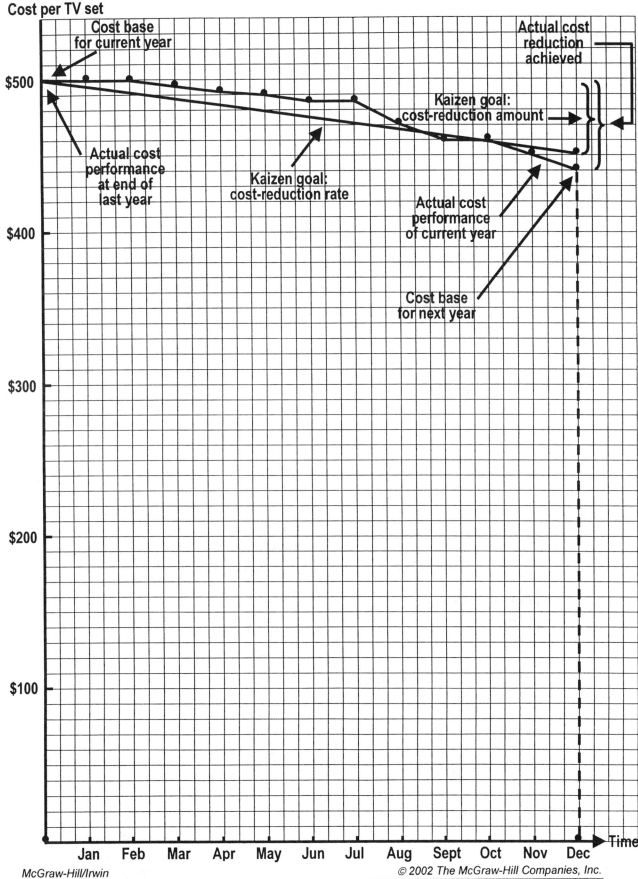

PROBLEM 6-55 (60 MINUTES)

1. Pickwick Paper Company: Current production process.

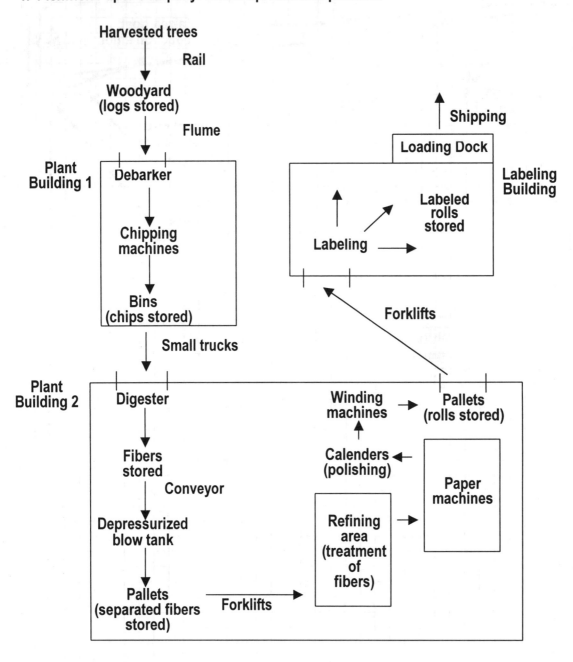

PROBLEM 6-55 (CONTINUED)

2.   Candidates for non-value-added costs:

   (a)   Storage time. Logs in the woodyard and finished rolls of paperboard in the labeling building are stored for a long time.

   (b)   Move time: A lot of effort and employee time is devoted to moving work in process. Logs are unloaded from the railroad cars and subsequently reloaded into the flume. Small trucks are used to transport chips to the digester in plant building 2. Forklifts are used to transport separated fibers to the refining area. Finally, forklifts are used to transport rolls of paperboard to the labeling building.

   (c)   Wait time: Work-in-process inventory waits at several points in the production process until the next operation is ready to receive it. First, logs are stored in the woodyard. Second, chips are stored in bins near the chipping machines. Third, fibers are stored near the digester. Fourth, separated fibers are stored on pallets near the depressurized blow tank. Fifth, unlabeled rolls of paperboard are stored on pallets near the winding machines. As the problem states, the partially processed product sometimes waits for two to three days between production operations.

   (d)   Labor force: The labor force is probably larger than necessary. Much of this excess labor is involved in material-handling operations.

3.   Plan for revised production process:

   The plan for a new production process involves the following key changes:

   (a)   Direct transfer of harvested trees from railroad cars to the flume.

   (b)   Installation of an automated material-handling system (AMHS) to move all work in process after it enters plant building 1.

   (c)   No storage of work in process between production stages. Implementation of a pull method for production scheduling.

   (d)   New construction to house the AMHS between buildings.

   (e)   Movement of the labeling machines to the other end of the labeling building, closer to the winding machines.

   (f)   Reduction of finished-goods inventory.

PROBLEM 6-55 (CONTINUED)

A diagram of the new process is shown on the next page. The steps in the new process are as follows:

(1) Harvested trees arrive as needed for production by rail in the woodyard and are transferred to the flume.

(2) Logs are moved by a flume into the plant where they pass through a debarker and are cut up into chips.

(3) The chips are transported by the AMHS to the digester.

(4) The chips then are placed in a digester, a large pressure cooker where heat, steam, and chemicals convert the chips into moist fibers.

(5) The fibers are loaded onto the AMHS, which carries the fibers to a depressurized blow tank. This operation separates the fibers.

(6) The AMHS is used to carry the separated fibers to the refining area, where the fibers are washed, refined, and treated with chemicals and caustic substances until they become pulp.

(7) The wood pulp then enters the paper machines through a headbox, which distributes pulp evenly across a porous belt of forming fabric.

(8) Water is removed from the pulp by passing the pulp over a wire screen.

(9) Additional water is removed from the pulp in a series of presses.

(10) Driers then remove any remaining water from the pulp.

(11) The AMHS carries the sheets of pulp to the calenders. The thin, dry sheets of pulp are then smoothed and polished by the calendars.

(12) The paperboard is wound into large rolls and placed on the AMHS.

(13) The rolls are labeled and stored for shipment in the labeling building. Inventory is minimized.

(14) The rolls of paperboard are shipped to customers from the new loading dock in the labeling building.

PROBLEM 6-55 (CONTINUED)

Pickwick Paper Company: New production process.

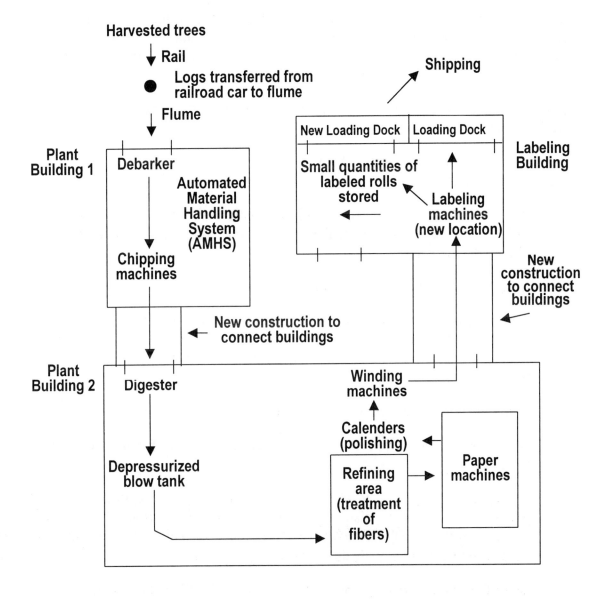

SOLUTIONS TO CASES

CASE 6-56 (45 MINUTES)

1. A proliferation of part numbers means that the company may be ordering and stocking many more types of unique parts than it needs to. Overordering and overstocking entail more costs in purchasing, receiving, inspecting, storing, and material handling than might otherwise be necessary.

2. Long production cycles may indicate that the production process is inefficient. Inefficiencies, in turn, imply non-value-added costs.

3. An ABC system can be used to help reduce costs by focusing attention on the problem of part number proliferation.

    a. The division's strategy is to be a product differentiator. It used to be a price leader, but now it must meet the market price, since new competitors have entered the market.

    b. Prices are currently being set by the market.

    c. Management's primary need is cost reduction so that the division can meet the market-driven price. More accurate product costs, while always desirable, are not the primary need here. The division will not be able to use cost-based pricing anyway.

    d. Cost reduction is the current goal of management.

    e. Part number proliferation is (at least partially) to blame for high production costs.

    f. The design engineers, who strive for "engineering elegance" in their product designs are largely to blame for part number proliferation. By designing products "from scratch," engineers often specify new parts—that is, parts that the division does not already use in its other products.

    g. An ABC system can help solve the problem of part number proliferation by focusing attention on it. One method of directing attention to this problem is to choose a cost driver that makes the design engineers aware of the implicit costs from specifying new unique parts in a product design.

CASE 6-56 (CONTINUED)

4. The objective is to find a cost driver that charges to a product the costs associated with purchasing, receiving, inspecting, storing, and handling the parts used in the product. Possible candidates for such a driver include (1) direct-material cost, (2) number of parts, and (3) number of part numbers.

   Driver number (3), the number of part numbers (i.e., the number of *different* parts in a product), would probably work the best. It focuses most directly on the problem at hand: part number proliferation. By charging a product for all the myriad support costs that go along with using many different types of parts, the design engineers will see more clearly the adverse cost effect of using new parts in a product design. They will be encouraged, when it is possible, to use parts that the division already stocks. The hope is that the design engineers will begin to make cost-effective trade-offs between engineering elegance and product cost.

5. The answer to this question is similar in spirit to the answer to requirement (4). The ABC system could use cycle time as a cost driver in assigning production-line costs to products. Thus, the longer a product's cycle time, the longer its assigned product cost. In this manner, the costing system focuses attention on a problem that management feels is unnecessarily inflating production costs.

6. In the Aerotech example used in Chapters 5 and 6, the fundamental role of the ABC system was to achieve more accurate product costs by eliminating (or minimizing) the problem of cost distortion that is so common in traditional, volume-based product-costing systems. The role of the ABC system here is fundamentally different. The objective of the ABC system is to *modify behavior.* By choosing cost drivers that focus attention on the implicit costs of part number proliferation and long production cycles, the system encourages employees to change the way they do their work. The design engineers, for example, are encouraged to use common parts in product designs whenever possible rather than always designing from scratch to achieve engineering elegance.

CASE 6-57 (30 MINUTES)

1. After the target price is established, in accordance with the new vehicle models' performance characteristics, the target profit for the vehicle model must be set.

2. The issues to be considered in setting a new vehicle model's target profit would include the following:

   • The target retail price and projected sales volume.

CASE 6-57 (CONTINUED)

- The profit achieved on the current vehicle model being redesigned.

- The profit achieved on other comparable vehicle models.

- The level of investment in the vehicle model.

3. After the target retail price and target profit have been set, the target cost is computed as the target price minus the target profit.

4. Value engineering accomplishes the really hard work of target costing: bringing the ultimate production cost of the new vehicle model into line with the target cost. Value engineering is a cost-reduction and process-improvement technique in which information is collected about a product's design and production process, and attributes of the design and process are then examined to identify candidates for improvement.

    The concept of value engineering can be related to all or most of the steps depicted in the diagram given in the problem. For example, the styling would be examined for ways to trim cost without diminishing the vehicle's attractiveness. The test model drawings would be carefully scrutinized for ways to cut costs, such as using common parts instead of unique parts. For example, an automobile manufacturer that has 50 different headlight housings will incur more cost overall than a manufacturer that uses 10 different housings. The facility and equipment used in the vehicle's production would be examined for potential improvements. The test model (prototype) would be carefully scrutinized for potential improvements and opportunities for cost savings. In short, every aspect of the new vehicle model's design and production process would be analyzed through value engineering for improvements and potential cost savings.

5. If the value-engineering team is unable to trim cost down to the target cost, the result will be one of the following:

- The target price will be reconsidered (and possibly raised).

- The target profit will be reduced.

- The basic development proposal for the new vehicle model will be revised.

- Another attempt to trim the cost using value engineering will be made.

CURRENT ISSUES IN MANAGERIAL ACCOUNTING

ISSUE 6-58

"MEXICO WEAVES MORE TIES--NO. 1 IN GARMENTS, IT MIGHT SOON BE TOP TEXTILE SOURCE," *THE WALL STREET JOURNAL*, AUGUST 21, 2000, JOEL MILLMAN.

1. A just-in-time inventory system keeps minimum inventory on site. Inventory arrives from vendors just in time to fill orders and make sales.

2. A just-in-time inventory system allows greater managerial control and quick turnaround on changes in orders.

ISSUE 6-59

"AS THE TELECOMS EMERGE AND CUT COSTS, SERVICE IS OFTEN A CASUALTY," *THE WALL STREET JOURNAL*, JANUARY 19, 2000, REBECCA BLUMENSTEIN AND STEPHANIE N. MEHTA.

1. Merging companies are cutting fat, automating functions that humans used to provide, and abandoning white glove services in order to please an increasingly fickle Wall Street. Communication problems often result. Sometimes personnel do not communicate with each other, and often their technology is not compatible. Blending company cultures, procedures and policies sometimes presents problems.

2. The cost-reduction methods discussed in the chapter are designed to cut costs without any loss in customer service or perceived value. However, implementing cost reduction programs is a challenge, and in many cases, unintended reductions in service or value do occur.

ISSUE 6-60

"BUILT FOR THE LONG HAUL," *BUSINESS WEEK*, JULY 3, 2000, MICHAEL ARNDT.

Paccar shuns many capital costs and keeps asset costs low. When orders slacken, Paccar can cut costs by furloughing employees at its union and nonunion plants, rather than idling expensive equipment. By using labor-intensive assembly plants, it holds down capital investments, and this lets Paccar cut costs with layoffs when orders slacken. The company does no size up for peaks, but takes care of peaks with extra shifts and some selective contracting. Paccar stays lean by purchasing 75 percent of every Peterbilt and Kenworth truck from outside vendors.

ISSUE 6-61

"ALIENATING CUSTOMERS ISN'T ALWAYS A BAD IDEA, MANY FIRMS DISCOVER," *THE WALL STREET JOURNAL*, JANUARY 7, 1999, RICK BROOKS.

First Union profiles its customers according to a formula, which determines a customer's profitability to the bank. Data for the formula is gathered from a myriad of computer systems with profitable customers flagged as green, unprofitable customers flagged as red, and in between customers as yellow. Green customers are given preferred treatment, while red customers incur additional charges for services provided free to green customers. Some customers are told they no longer are eligible for personal treatment. Although denied by management, these measures often encourage non-profitable customers to take their business elsewhere. When this happens, profits increase since the bottom 20 percent of customers account for a drain on profits by as much as 50 percent, while the top one fifth of the customer base account for a large share of the bank's profitability.

ISSUE 6-62

"THE GLOBAL SIX," *BUSINESS WEEK*, JANUARY 25, 1999, KEITH NAUGHTON AND KAREN LOWRY MILLER.

1. Designing auto models with computers instead of traditional drafting methods is called computer-aided design.

2. Computer-aided design allows auto manufacturers to develop vastly different models from one basic chassis. This new technology has cut time to market by one third. It now takes about 14 1/2 months to bring a new design to market as opposed to the previous time of about 21 months.

CHAPTER 7
Activity Analysis, Cost Behavior, and Cost Estimation

ANSWERS TO REVIEW QUESTIONS

7-1   Cost behavior patterns are important in the process of making cost predictions. Cost predictions are used in planning, control, and decision making. For example, cost budgets are based on predictions of costs at various levels of activity. Cost control is accomplished by comparing actual costs against budgeted costs, which are based on cost predictions. Cost predictions are also important in decision making, since the desirability of various alternatives often depends on the costs that will be incurred under those alternatives.

7-2   a. Cost estimation is the process of determining how a particular cost behaves.

   b. Cost behavior is the relationship between cost and activity.

   c. Cost prediction is the forecast of cost at a particular level of activity.

   Cost estimation determines the cost behavior pattern, which is used to make a cost prediction about the cost at a particular level of activity contemplated in the future.

7-3   a. Hotel: Percentage of rooms occupied or the number of occupancy-days, where an occupancy-day is defined as one room occupied for one day.

   b. Hospital: Patient-days, where a patient-day is defined as a one-day stay by one patient.

   c. Computer manufacturer: Number of computers manufactured, throughput, engineering specifications, engineering change orders, or number of parts in the finished product.

   d. Computer sales store: Sales revenue.

   e. Computer repair service: Repair calls or hours of repair service.

   f. Public accounting firm: Hours of auditing service provided by each classification of personnel (partner, manager, supervisor, senior accountant, and staff accountant).

7-4 Graphs of the cost behavior patterns are as follows:

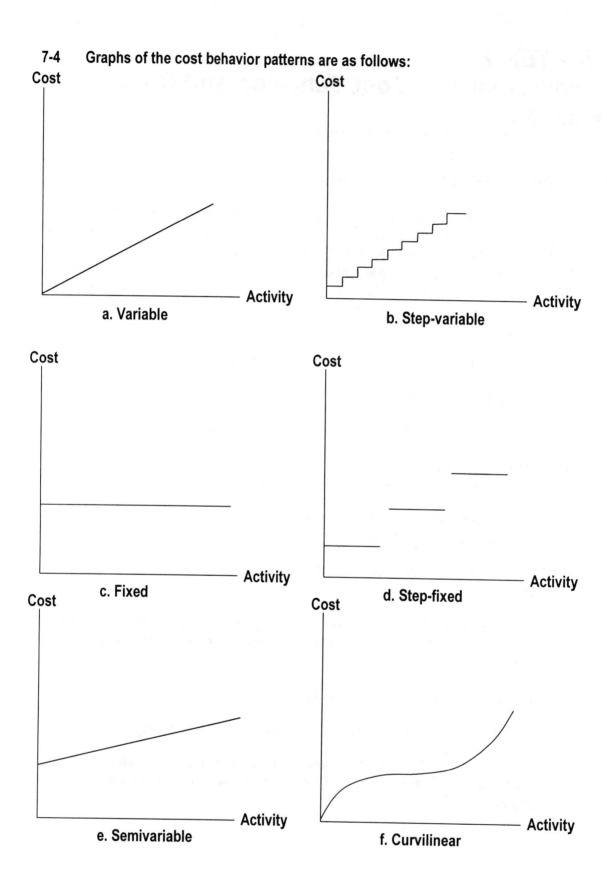

a. Variable

b. Step-variable

c. Fixed

d. Step-fixed

e. Semivariable

f. Curvilinear

7-5   As the level of activity (or cost driver) increases, total fixed cost remains constant. However, the fixed cost per unit of activity declines as activity increases.

7-6   A manufacturer's cost of supervising production might be a step-fixed cost, because one supervisor is needed for each shift. Each shift can accommodate a certain range of production activity; when activity exceeds that range, a new shift must be added. When the new shift is added, a new production supervisor must be employed. This new position results in a jump in the step-fixed cost to a higher level.

7-7   As the level of activity (or cost driver) increases, total variable cost increases proportionately and the variable cost per unit remains constant.

7-8   a.   A semivariable cost behavior pattern can be used to approximate a step-variable cost as shown in the following graph:

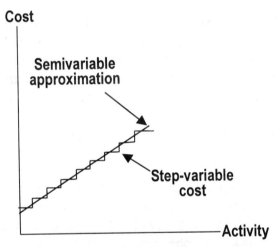

b. A semivariable cost behavior pattern can be used to approximate a curvilinear cost as shown in the following graph:

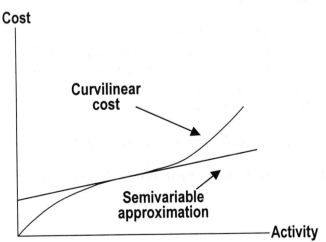

7-9   (a) Annual cost of maintaining an interstate highway: committed cost. (Once the highway has been built, it must be maintained. The transportation authorities are largely committed to spending the necessary funds to maintain the highway adequately.)

(b) Ingredients in a breakfast cereal: engineered cost.

(c) Advertising for a credit card company: discretionary cost.

(d) Depreciation on an insurance company's computer: committed cost.

(e) Charitable donations: discretionary cost.

(f) Research and development: discretionary cost.

7-10   The cost analyst should respond by pointing out that in most cases a cost behavior pattern should be limited to the relevant range of activity. When the firm's utility cost was shown as a semivariable cost, it is likely that only some portion in the middle of the graph would fall within the relevant range. Within the relevant range, the firm's utility cost can be approximated reasonably closely by a semivariable cost behavior pattern. However, outside that range (including an activity level of zero), the semivariable cost behavior pattern should not be used as an approximation of the utility cost.

7-11   A learning curve shows how average labor time per unit of production changes as cumulative output changes. In many production processes, as production activity increases and learning takes place, there is a significant reduction in the amount of labor time required per unit. The learning phenomenon is important in cost estimation, since estimates must often be made for the level of cost to be incurred after additional production experience is gained.

7-12   Work measurement is the systematic analysis of a task for the purpose of determining the inputs needed to perform the task. Work measurement is sometimes used to help in estimating the costs of various nonmanufacturing activities. The unit of analysis in work measurement often is called a control factor unit. Appropriate control factor units for several tasks are as follows:

a.   Handling materials at a loading dock: Weight of materials handled.

b.   Registering vehicles at a county motor vehicle office: Number of registrations processed.

c. Picking oranges: Volume or weight of oranges picked.

d. Inspecting computer components in an electronics firm: Number of components inspected.

7-13   An outlier is a data point that falls far away from the other points in the scatter diagram and is not representative of the data. One possible cause of an outlier is simply a mistake in recording the data. Another cause of an outlier is a random event that occurred, which caused the cost during a particular period to be unusually high or low. For example, a power outage may have resulted in unusually high costs of idle time for a particular time period. Outliers should be eliminated from a data set upon which cost estimates are based.

7-14   Fixed costs are often allocated on a per unit-of-activity basis. For example, fixed manufacturing-overhead costs, such as depreciation, may be allocated to units of production. As a result, such costs may appear to be variable in the cost records. Discretionary costs often are budgeted in a manner that makes them appear variable. A cost such as charitable donations, for example, may be fixed once management decides on the level of donations to be made. If management's policy is to budget charitable donations on the basis of sales dollars, however, the cost will appear to be variable to the cost analyst. An experienced analyst should be wary of allocated and discretionary costs and take steps to learn how the amounts are determined.

7-15   In the first step of the visual-fit method of cost estimation, data points are plotted on graph paper to form a scatter diagram. Then a line is drawn through the scatter diagram in an attempt to minimize the distance between the line and the plotted points. The scatter diagram and the visually-fitted cost line provide a valuable first approximation in the analysis of any cost suspected to be semivariable or curvilinear. The method is easy to use and to explain to others and provides a useful view of the overall cost behavior pattern. The visual-fit method also enables an experienced cost analyst to spot outliers in the data. The primary drawbacks of the visual-fit method are its lack of objectivity. Two cost analysts may draw two different visually-fitted cost lines.

7-16   The chief drawback of the high-low method of cost estimation is that it uses only two data points. The rest of the data are ignored by the method. An outlier can cause a significant problem when the high-low method is used if one of the two data points happens to be an outlier. In other words, if the high activity level happens to be associated with a cost that is not representative of the data, the resulting cost line may not be representative of the cost behavior pattern.

7-17 The term *least squares* in the least-squares regression method of cost estimation refers to the process of minimizing the sum of the squares of the distances between the data and the regression line.

7-18 A least-squares regression line may be expressed in equation form as follows:

$$Y = a + bX$$

In this equation, X is referred to as the independent variable, since it is the variable upon which the estimate is based. Y is called the dependent variable, since its estimate depends on the independent variable. The intercept of the line on the vertical axis is denoted by a, and the slope of the line is denoted by b. Within the relevant range, a is interpreted as an estimate of the fixed-cost component, and b is interpreted as an estimate of the variable cost per unit of activity.

7-19 In simple regression there is a single independent variable. In multiple regression there are two or more independent variables.

7-20 Advanced manufacturing technology, such as FMS and CIM systems, have resulted in a shift in the cost structure toward fixed costs. Moreover, many of these fixed costs are committed costs.

7-21 A particular least-squares regression line may be evaluated on the basis of economic plausibility or goodness of fit.

   The cost analyst should always evaluate a regression line from the perspective of economic plausibility. Does the regression line make economic sense? Is it intuitively plausible? An experienced cost analyst should have a good feel for whether the regression line looks reasonable.

   Statistical methods can also be used to determine how well a regression line fits the data upon which it is based. This method is referred to as assessing the goodness of fit of the regression. A commonly used measure of goodness of fit is the coefficient of determination, which is described in the appendix at the end of the chapter. The coefficient of determination is also denoted by R^2.

SOLUTIONS TO EXERCISES

EXERCISE 7-22 (40 MINUTES)

1. Cost of food:

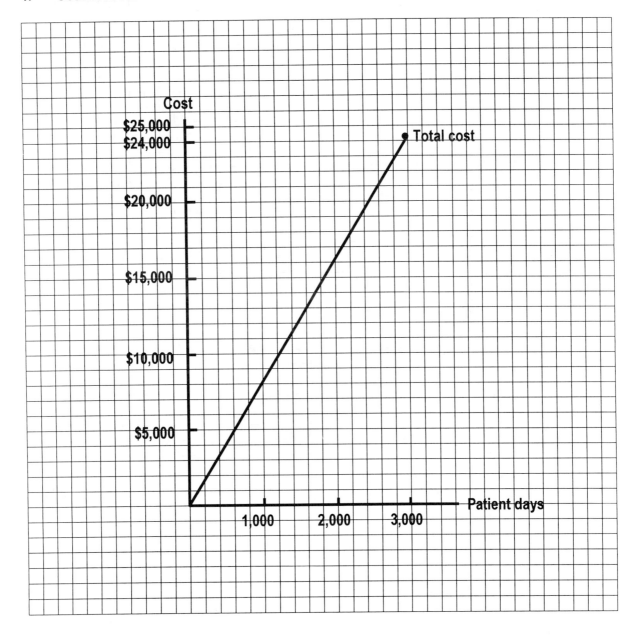

2.   Cost of salaries and fringe benefits for administrative staff:

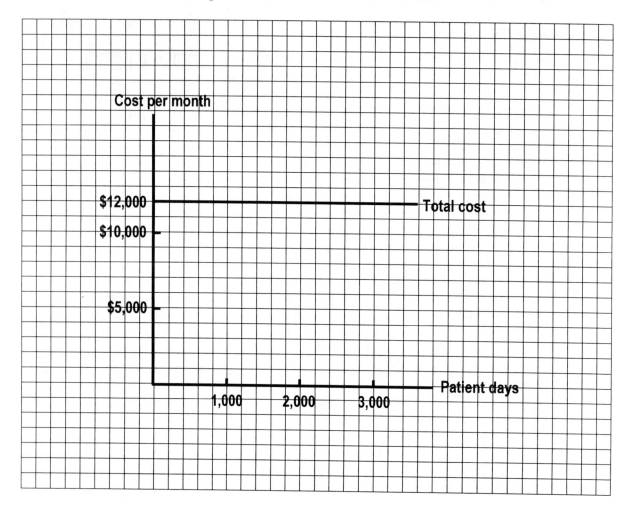

EXERCISE 7-22 (CONTINUED)

3.   Laboratory costs:

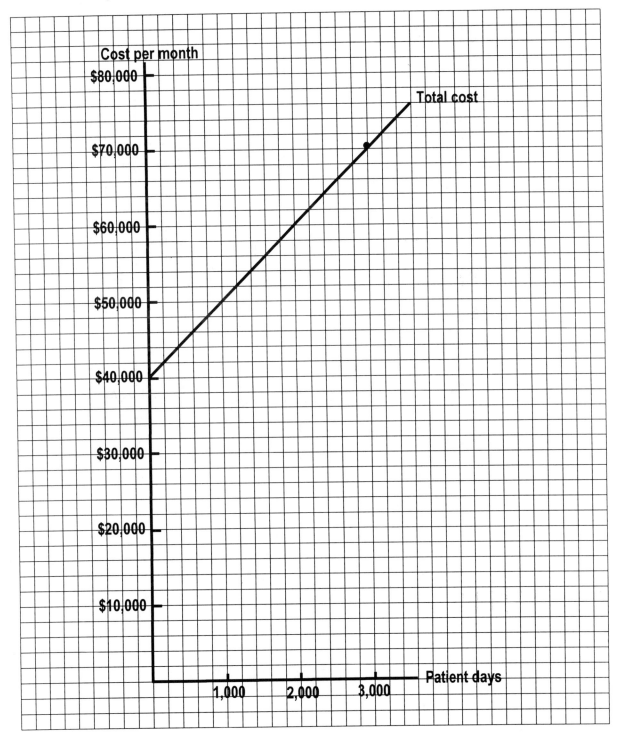

EXERCISE 7-22 (CONTINUED)

4.   **Cost of utilities:**

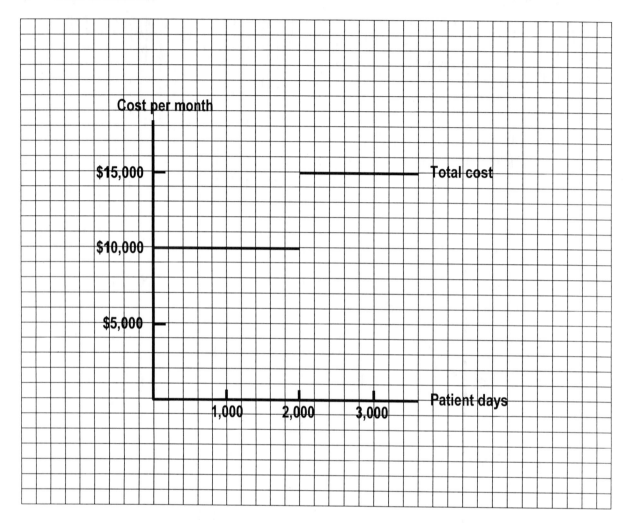

5.   Nursing costs:

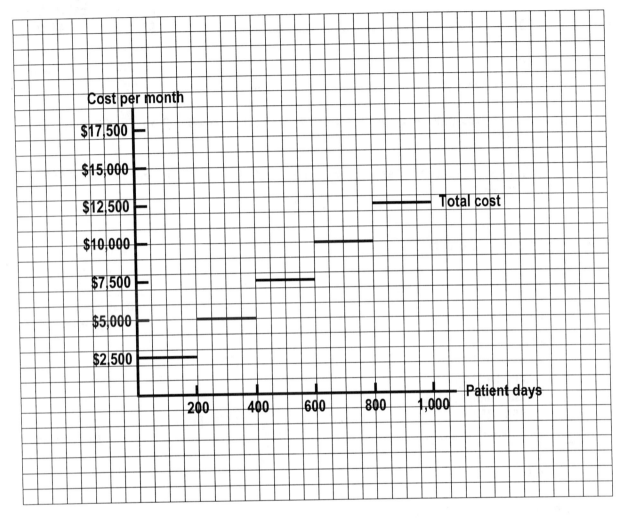

EXERCISE 7-23 (15 MINUTES)

1.

		Actual	Estimated
a.	20,000 miles	$3,900	$4,400
b.	40,000 miles	5,200	5,200
c.	60,000 miles	6,000	6,000
d.	90,000 miles	8,500	7,200

2. (a) The approximation is very accurate in the range 40,000 to 60,000 miles per month.

   (b) The approximation is less accurate in the extremes of the longer range, 20,000 to 90,000 miles.

EXERCISE 7-24 (15 MINUTES)

1.

	Cost per Broadcast Hour	
Cost Item	July	September
Production crew:		
$4,875/390 hr.	$12.50 per hr.	
$8,000/640 hr.		$12.50 per hr.
Supervisory employees:		
$5,000/390 hr.	12.82 per hr.*	
$5,000/640 hr.		7.81 per hr.*

*Rounded.

2. December cost predictions:

Production crew (420 × $12.50 per hr.)	$5,250
Supervisory employees	5,000

3.

Cost Item	Cost per Broadcast Hour in December
Production crew	$12.50 per hr.
Supervisory employees ($5,000/420 hr.)	11.90 per hr.*

*Rounded.

EXERCISE 7-25 (15 MINUTES)

1. Variable cost per pint of applesauce produced $= \dfrac{\$24,100 - \$22,100}{41,000 - 21,000} = \$.10$

Total cost at 41,000 pints..	$24,100
Variable cost at 41,000 pints	
(41,000 × $.10 per pint)...	4,100
Fixed cost	$20,000

Cost equation:

Total energy cost = $20,000 + $.10X, where X denotes pints of applesauce produced

2. Cost prediction when 26,000 pints of applesauce are produced

Energy cost = $20,000 + ($.10)(26,000) = $22,600

EXERCISE 7-26 (30 MINUTES)

1.   Scatter diagram and visually-fitted line:

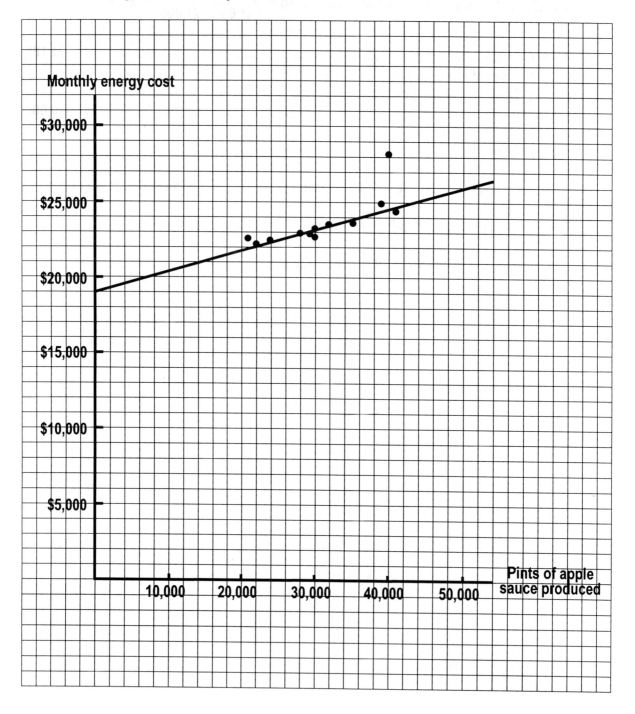

EXERCISE 7-26 (CONTINUED)

2. Answers will vary on this requirement because of variation in the visually-fitted lines.

    Based on the preceding plot, the cost prediction at 26,000 pounds is:

    Energy cost = $22,600

3. The July cost observation at the 40,000-pint activity level appears to be an outlier. The cost analyst should check the observation data for accuracy. If the data are accurate, the outlier should be ignored in making cost predictions.

EXERCISE 7-27 (30 MINUTES)

Answers will vary widely, depending on the company and costs selected. Some examples of typical manufacturing costs follow.

Direct material: variable

Electricity: variable

Depreciation on plant and equipment: fixed

Plant manager's salary: fixed

Property taxes: fixed

EXERCISE 7-28 (30 MINUTES)

1. Scatter diagram and visually-fitted line:

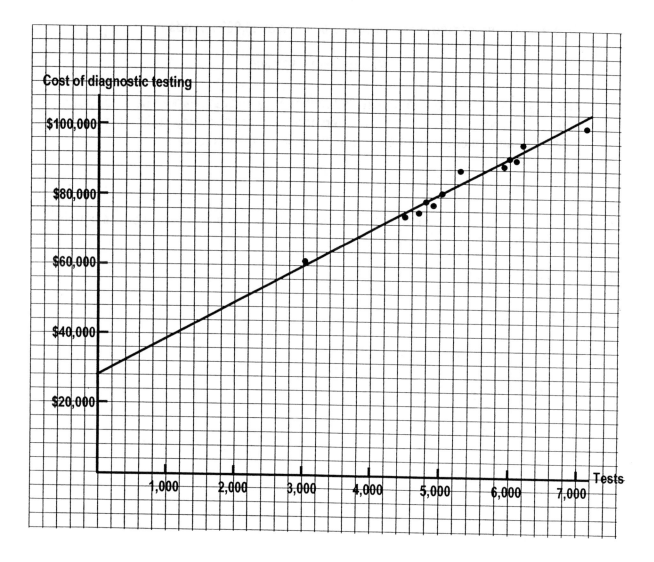

EXERCISE 7-28 (CONTINUED)

2. Answers will vary on this requirement because of variation in the visually-fitted lines.

Based on the preceding plot:

Monthly fixed cost...	$28,000
Variable cost per diagnostic test	$ 10.56*

*Calculation of variable cost:

Total cost at	7,200	tests...	$ 104,000
Total cost at	0	tests...	28,000
Difference:	7,200	tests...	$ 76,000

$$\text{Variable cost per diagnostic test} = \frac{\$76,000}{7,200}$$

$$= \$10.56†$$

†Rounded.

EXERCISE 7-29 (15 MINUTES)

1. a. Fixed

    b. Variable

    c. Variable

    d. Fixed

    e. Semivariable (or mixed)

2. Production cost per month = $33,000* + $2.00X†

    *33,000 = $19,000 + $10,000 + $4,000
    †$2.00 = $1.10 + $.70 + $.20

EXERCISE 7-30 (15 MINUTES)

1. Variable maintenance

    cost per tour mile   =   (12,500*r*-11,000*r*) / (20,000 miles – 8,000 miles)

                            =   .125*r*

    r denotes the *real*, Brazil's national currency.

Total maintenance cost at 8,000 miles	11,000*r*
Variable maintenance cost at 8,000 miles (.125*r* × 8,000)	1,000*r*
Fixed maintenance cost per month	10,000*r*

2. Cost formula:

    Total maintenance cost per month = 10,000*r* + .125*rX* , where *X* denotes tour miles traveled during the month.

3. Cost prediction at the 22,000-mile activity level:

    Maintenance cost   =   10,000*r* + (.125*r*)(22,000)

                            =   12,750*r*

EXERCISE 7-31 (15 MINUTES)

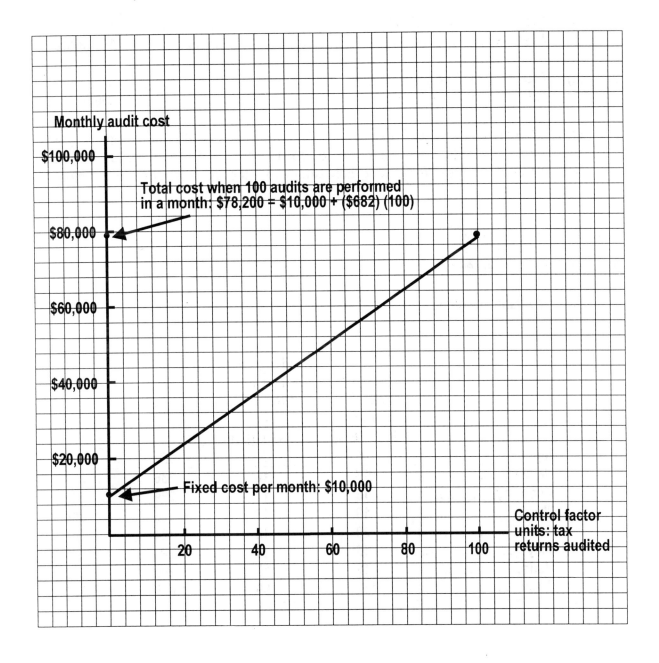

Monthly audit cost

$100,000

Total cost when 100 audits are performed
in a month: $78,200 = $10,000 + ($682) (100)

$80,000

$60,000

$40,000

$20,000

Fixed cost per month: $10,000

Control factor
units: tax
returns audited

20   40   60   80   100

EXERCISE 7-32 (10 MINUTES)

1. (a) Average time for 4 satellites .... 130 hours
    (b) Average time for 8 satellites .... 100 hours

2. (a) Total time for 4 satellites (130 hr. X 4).. 520 hours
    (b) Total time for 8 satellites (100 hr. X 8).. 800 hours

3. Learning curves indicate how labor costs will change as the company gains experience with the production process. Since labor time and costs must be predicted both for budgeting and for setting cost standards, the learning curve is a valuable tool.

EXERCISE 7-33 (45 MINUTES)

1. Least-square regression:

    (a) Tabulation of data:

Month	Dependent Variable (cost in thousands) Y	Independent Variable (thousands of passengers) X	X^2	XY
January.........................	18	16	256	288
February......................	18	17	289	306
March..........................	19	16	256	304
April	20	18	324	360
May	18	15	225	270
June.............................	19	17	289	323
Total............................	112	99	1,639	1,851

EXERCISE 7-33 (CONTINUED)

(b) Calculation of parameters:

$$a = \frac{(\sum Y)(\sum X^2) - (\sum X)(\sum XY)}{n(\sum X^2) - (\sum X)(\sum X)}$$

$$= \frac{(112)(1,639) - (99)(1,851)}{(6)(1,639) - (99)(99)} = 9.667 \text{ (rounded)}$$

$$b = \frac{n(\sum XY) - (\sum X)(\sum Y)}{n(\sum X^2) - (\sum X)(\sum X)}$$

$$= \frac{(6)(1,851) - (99)(112)}{(6)(1,639) - (99)(99)} = .545 \text{ (rounded)}$$

(c) Cost formula:

Monthly cost of flight service = $9,667 + $545X, where X denotes thousands of passengers.

2. Calculation and interpretation of R^2:

(a) Formula for calculation:

$$R^2 = 1 - \frac{\sum(Y - Y')^2}{\sum(Y - \bar{Y})^2}$$

where   Y   denotes the observed value of the dependent variable (cost) at a particular activity level.

           Y'   denotes the predicted value of the dependent variable (cost) based on the regression line, at a particular activity level.

           $\bar{Y}$ denotes the mean (average) observation of the dependent variable (cost).

EXERCISE 7-33 (CONTINUED)

(b)   Tabulation of data:*

Month	Y	X	Predicted Cost (in thousands) Based on Regression Line Y'	$[(Y - Y')^2]^\dagger$	$[(Y - \bar{Y})^2]^\dagger$
January..........	18	16	18.387	.150	.445
February........	18	17	18.932	.869	.445
March.............	19	16	18.387	.376	.111
April	20	18	19.477	.274	1.777
May	18	15	17.842	.025	.445
June...............	19	17	18.932	.005	.111
Total..............				1.699	3.334

*Y' = ($9,667 + $545X)/$1,000
$\bar{Y}$ = $\sum Y/6$ = 18.667 (rounded)
†Rounded.

(c)   Calculation of R^2:

$$R^2 = 1 - \frac{1.699}{3.334} = .49 \text{ (rounded)}$$

(d)   Interpretation of R^2:

The coefficient of determination, R^2, is a measure of the goodness of fit of the least-squares regression line. An R^2 of .49 means that 49% of the variability of the dependent variable about its mean is explained by the variability of the independent variable about its mean. The higher the R^2, the better the regression line fits the data. The interpretation of a high R^2 is that the independent variable is a good predictor of the behavior of the dependent variable. In cost estimation, a high R^2 means that the cost analyst can be relatively confident in the cost predictions based on the estimated-cost behavior pattern.

EXERCISE 7-34 (45 MINUTES)

1. Variable utility cost per hour $= \dfrac{\$1{,}900 - \$1{,}300}{700 - 400} = \$2.00$

Total utility cost at 700 hours.. $ 1,900
Variable utility cost at 700 hours ($2.00 × 700 hours)........................... 1,400
Fixed cost per month .... $ 500

Cost formula:

Monthly utility cost = $500 + $2.00 X , where X denotes hours of operation.

2. Variable-cost estimate based on the scatter diagram on the next page:

Cost at	600 hours	....	$1,700
Cost at	0 hours	....	450
Difference	600 hours	....	$1,250

Variable cost per hour = $1,250/600 hr. = $2.08 (rounded)

EXERCISE 7-34 (CONTINUED)

Scatter diagram and visually-fitted line:

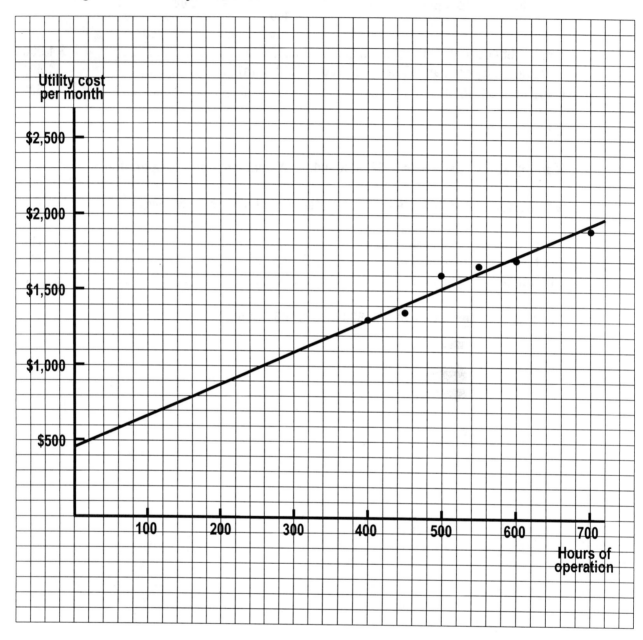

EXERCISE 7-34 (CONTINUED)

3. Least-square regression:

(a) Tabulation of data:

Month	Dependent Variable (cost) Y	Independent Variable (hours) X	X^2	XY
January........................	1,620	550	302,500	891,000
February......................	1,700	600	360,000	1,020,000
March..........................	1,900	700	490,000	1,330,000
April	1,600	500	250,000	800,000
May	1,350	450	202,500	607,500
June...........................	1,300	400	160,000	520,000
Total..........................	9,470	3,200	1,765,000	5,168,500

(b) Calculation of parameters:

$$a = \frac{(\Sigma Y)(\Sigma X^2) - (\Sigma X)(\Sigma XY)}{n(\Sigma X^2) - (\Sigma X)(\Sigma X)}$$

$$= \frac{(9,470)(1,765,000) - (3,200)(5,168,500)}{(6)(1,765,000) - (3,200)(3,200)} = 501$$

$$b = \frac{n(\Sigma XY) - (\Sigma X)(\Sigma Y)}{n(\Sigma X^2) - (\Sigma X)(\Sigma X)}$$

$$= \frac{(6)(5,168,500) - (3,200)(9,470)}{(6)(1,765,000) - (3,200)(3,200)} = 2.02$$

(c) Cost formula:

Monthly utility cost = $501 + $2.02X, where X denotes hours of operation.

Variable utility cost = $2.02 per hour of operation

EXERCISE 7-34 (CONTINUED)

4.   Cost predictions at 300 hours of operation:

   (a)   High-low method:

Utility cost   = $500 + ($2.00)(300) = $1,100

   (b)   Visually-fitted line:

Utility cost   = $1,095

This cost prediction was simply read directly from the visually-fitted cost line. This prediction will vary because of variations in the visually-fitted lines.

   (c)   Regression:

Utility cost   = $501 + ($2.02)(300) = $1,107

SOLUTIONS TO PROBLEMS

PROBLEM 7-35 (20 MINUTES)

1. e
2. a
3. g
4. c

5. b
6. h
7. i
8. f

9. d
10. k
11. l

Note that j was not used.

PROBLEM 7-36 (25 MINUTES)

1. Machine supplies: $102,000 \div 34,000$ direct-labor hours = $3 per hour
    January: 23,000 direct-labor hours x $3 = $69,000
    Depreciation: Fixed at $15,000

2. Plant maintenance cost:

	March (34,000 hours)	January (23,000 hours)
Total cost*............................	$ 586,000	$ 454,000
Less: Machine supplies........	(102,000)	(69,000)
Depreciation...............	(15,000)	(15,000)
Plant maintenance...............	$ 469,000	$ 370,000

* Excludes supervisory labor cost

Variable maintenance cost = difference in cost $\div$ difference in direct-labor hours
= ($469,000 − $370,000) $\div$ (34,000 − 23,000)
= $99,000 $\div$ 11,000 hours
= $9 per hour

PROBLEM 7-36 (CONTINUED)

Fixed maintenance cost:

	March (34,000 hours)	January (23,000 hours)
Total maintenance cost.................	$469,000	$370,000
Less: Variable cost at $9 per hour....	306,000	207,000
Fixed maintenance cost.................	$163,000	$163,000

3. Manufacturing overhead at 29,500 labor hours:

Machine supplies at $3 per hour.......	$ 88,500
Depreciation...................................	15,000
Plant maintenance cost:	
Variable at $9 per hour...............	265,500
Fixed.......................................	163,000
Supervisory labor...........................	90,000
Total...................................	$622,000

4. A fixed cost remains constant when a change occurs in the cost driver (or activity base). A step-fixed cost, on the other hand, remains constant within a range but will change (rise or fall) when activity falls outside that range.

5. Ideally, the company should operate on the right-most portion of a step, just prior to the jump in cost. In this manner, a firm receives maximum benefit (i.e., the maximum amount of activity) for the dollars invested.

PROBLEM 7-37 (25 MINUTES)

1. Straight-line depreciation—committed fixed
    Charitable contributions—discretionary fixed
    Mining labor/fringe benefits—variable
    Royalties—semivariable
    Trucking and hauling—step-fixed
    The per-ton mining labor/fringe benefit cost is constant at both volume levels presented, which is characteristic of a variable cost.

    $345,000 ÷ 1,500 tons = $230 per ton
    $598,000 ÷ 2,600 tons = $230 per ton

Royalties have both a variable and a fixed component, making it a semivariable (mixed) cost.

Variable royalty cost = difference in cost ÷ difference in tons
= ($201,000 − $135,000) ÷ (2,600 − 1,500)
= $66,000 ÷ 1,100 tons
= $60 per ton

Fixed royalty cost:

	June (2,600 tons)	December (1,500 tons)
Total royalty cost............................	$201,000	$135,000
Less: Variable cost at $60 per ton.....	156,000	90,000
Fixed royalty cost...........................	$ 45,000	$ 45,000

2. Total cost for 1,650 tons:

Depreciation...	$ 25,000
Charitable contributions......................................	----
Mining labor/fringe benefits at $230 per ton.......	379,500
Royalties:	
Variable at $60 per ton................................	99,000
Fixed..	45,000
Trucking and hauling..	275,000
Total...	$823,500

3. Hauling 1,500 tons is not very cost effective. Antioch will incur cost of $275,000 if it needs 1,500 tons hauled or, for that matter, 1,899 tons. The company would be better off if it had 1,499 tons hauled, saving outlays of $25,000. In general, with this type of cost function, effectiveness is maximized if a firm operates on the right-most portion of a step, just prior to a jump in cost.

2. A committed fixed cost results from an entity's ownership or use of facilities and its basic organizational structure. Examples of such costs include property taxes, depreciation, rent, and management salaries. Discretionary fixed costs, on the other hand, arise from a decision to spend a particular amount of money for a specific purpose. Outlays for research and development, advertising, and charitable contributions fall in this category.

PROBLEM 7-37 (CONTINUED)

In times of severe economic difficulties, management should try to cut discretionary fixed costs. Such costs are more easily altered in the short run and do not have significant long-term ramifications for a firm. The decision to close a manufacturing facility, for example, could reduce property taxes, rent, and/or depreciation. However, that decision may result in a significant long-run change in operations that may be difficult to overturn when economic conditions rebound.

5.   Antioch uses a calendar year for tax-reporting purposes. At year-end, it may have ample funds available and decide to make donations to charitable causes. Such contributions are deductible in computing the company's tax obligation to the government. Tax deductions reduce taxable income and, therefore, produce a tax savings for the firm.

PROBLEM 7-38 (25 MINUTES)

1.   Variable maintenance cost per hour of service $= \dfrac{\$4{,}470 - \$2{,}820}{520 - 300}$

$$= \$7.50$$

Total maintenance cost at 300 hours of service...	$2,820
Variable maintenance cost at 300 hours of service (300 hr. × $7.50).......	2,250
Fixed maintenance cost per month	$ 570

Cost formula:

Monthly maintenance cost = $570 + $7.50X, where X denotes hours of maintenance service.

2.   The variable component of the maintenance cost is $7.50 per hour of service.

3.   Cost prediction at 590 hours of activity:

Maintenance cost = $570 + ($7.50)(590) = $4,995

PROBLEM 7-38 (CONTINUED)

4. Variable cost per hour [from requirement (2)] $7.50
    Fixed cost per hour at 600 hours of activity ($570/600) .... $ .95

    The fixed cost per hour is a misleading amount, because it will change as the number of hours changes. For example, at 500 hours of maintenance service, the fixed cost per hour is $1.14 ($570/500 hours).

PROBLEM 7-39 (15 MINUTES)

An appropriate activity measure for the school would be hours of instruction. The costs are classified as follows:

1. Fixed
2. Fixed
3. Variable
4. Semivariable (or mixed)*
5. Fixed

6. Variable
7. Fixed
8. Fixed
9. Semivariable (or mixed)

*The fixed-cost component is the salary of the school's repair technician. As activity increases, one would expect more repairs beyond the technician's capability. This increase in repairs would result in a variable-cost component equal to the dealer's repair charges.

PROBLEM 7-40 (40 MINUTES)

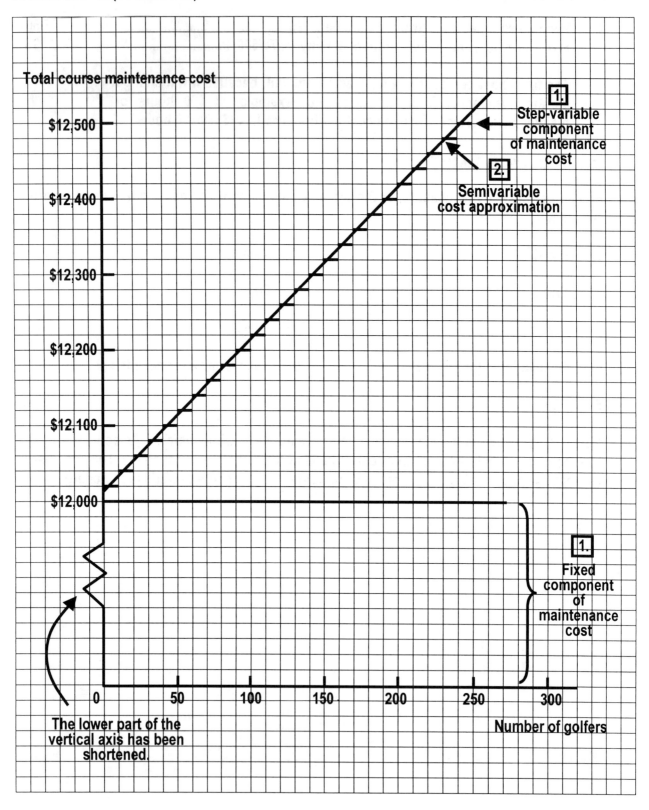

PROBLEM 7-40 (CONTINUED)

3. Fixed-cost component = $12,010

Variable-cost component:

$$\frac{\text{Variable cost}}{\text{per golfer}} = \frac{\$12,410 - \$12,010}{200 - 0}$$

$$= \$2$$

Cost equation:

Maintenance cost per month = $12,010 + $2X, where X denotes the number of golfers during the month.

4.   Predicted Course Maintenance Costs

	Using Fixed Cost Coupled with Step-Variable Cost Behavior Pattern	Using Semivariable Cost Approximation
150 people tee off.............................	$12,300	$12,310
158 people tee off.............................	12,320	12,326

PROBLEM 7-41 (40 MINUTES)

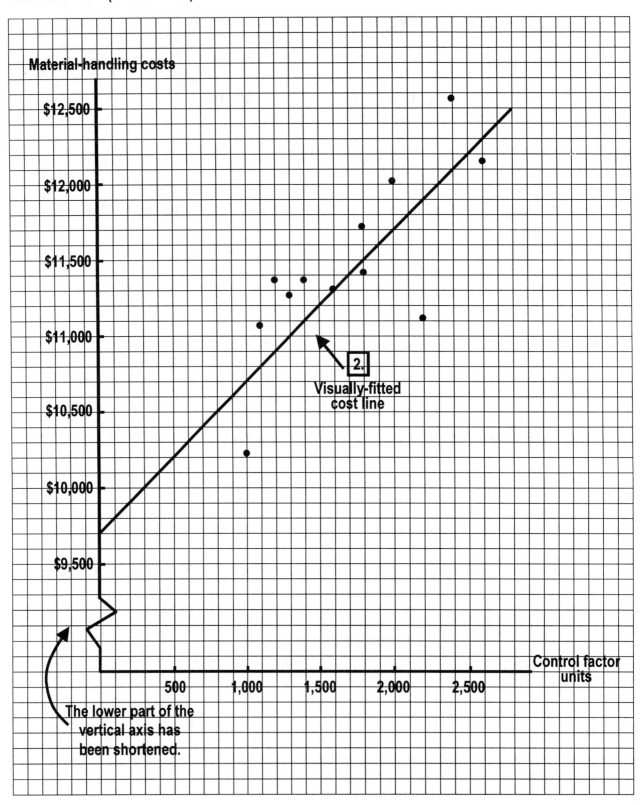

PROBLEM 7-41 (CONTINUED)

2. See graph for requirement (1).

3. The estimate of the fixed cost is the intercept on the vertical axis.

Fixed-cost component = $9,700

To estimate the variable-cost component, choose any two points on the visually-fitted cost line. For example, choose the following points:

Activity	Cost
0	$ 9,700
2,000	11,700

Then proceed as follows to estimate the variable-cost component:

$$\text{Variable cost per control factor unit} = \frac{\$11,700 - \$9,700}{2,000 - 0}$$

$$= \$1.00$$

4. Cost equation:

Total material-handling cost = $9,700 + $1.00X, where X denotes the number of control factor units of activity during the month.

5. High-low method:

$$\text{Variable cost per control factor unit} = \frac{\$12,120 - \$10,200}{2,600 - 1,000}$$

$$= \$1.20$$

Total cost at 2,600 control factor units	$12,120
Deduct: Variable cost at 2,600 control factor units (2,600 × $1.20)	3,120
Fixed cost	$ 9,000

Cost equation based on high-low method:

Material-handling cost per month = $9,000 + $1.20X, where X denotes the number of control factor units of activity during the month.

PROBLEM 7-41 (CONTINUED)

6.

Memorandum

Date: Today

To: President, Martha's Vineyard Marine Supply

From: I.M. Student

Subject: Material-handling cost estimates

On the basis of a scatter diagram and visually-fitted cost line, the Material-Handling Department's monthly cost behavior was estimated as follows:

> Material-handling cost per month = $9,700 + $1.00 per control factor unit

A control factor unit is defined in this department as 100 pounds of equipment loaded or unloaded at the loading dock.

Using the high-low method, the following cost estimate was obtained:

> Material-handling cost per month = $9,000 + $1.20 per control factor unit

The two methods yield different estimates because the high-low method uses only two data points, ignoring the rest of the information. The method of visually fitting a cost line, while subjective, uses all of the data available.

In this case, the two data points used by the high-low method do not appear to be representative of the entire set of data.

7.

Predicted Material-Handling Costs

Using Visually-Fitted Cost Line*	Using High-Low Method
$12,000 = $9,700 + ($1.00)(2,300)	$11,760 = $9,000 + ($1.20)(2,300)

*This method is preferable, because it uses all of the data.

PROBLEM 7-42 (45 MINUTES)

1. Least-squares regression:

    (a) Tabulation of data:

Month	Dependent Variable (cost in thousands) Y	Independent Variable (units of activity in thousands) X	X²	XY
January........................	11.35	1.4	1.96	15.890
February.....................	11.35	1.2	1.44	13.620
March.........................	11.05	1.1	1.21	12.155
April	12.12	2.6	6.76	31.512
May	11.40	1.8	3.24	20.520
June..........................	12.00	2.0	4.00	24.000
July	12.55	2.4	5.76	30.120
August.......................	11.10	2.2	4.84	24.420
September..................	10.20	1.0	1.00	10.200
October......................	11.25	1.3	1.69	14.625
November...................	11.30	1.6	2.56	18.080
December...................	11.70	1.8	3.24	21.060
Total..........................	137.37	20.4	37.70	236.202

    (b) Calculation of parameters:

$$a = \frac{(\sum Y)(\sum X^2) - (\sum X)(\sum XY)}{n(\sum X^2) - (\sum X)(\sum X)}$$

$$= \frac{(137.37)(37.7) - (20.4)(236.202)}{(12)(37.7) - (20.4)(20.4)} = 9.943 \text{ (rounded)}$$

$$b = \frac{n(\sum XY) - (\sum X)(\sum Y)}{n(\sum X^2) - (\sum X)(\sum X)}$$

$$= \frac{(12)(236.202) - (20.4)(137.37)}{(12)(37.7) - (20.4)(20.4)} = .885 \text{ (rounded)}$$

    (c)   Fixed- and variable-cost components:

        Monthly fixed cost = $9,943*

        Variable cost = $.89 per control factor unit (rounded)[†]

        *The intercept parameter (*a*) computed above is the cost per month *in thousands.*
        [†]The slope parameter (*b*) calculated above is the cost *in thousands* of dollars *per thousand* units of activity. Equivalently, it is the cost per unit of activity.

2.   Total monthly cost = $9,943 + $.89 per control factor unit

3.   Cost prediction for 2,300 control factor units of activity:

     Total monthly cost = $9,943 + ($.89)(2,300) = $11,990

4.   The cost predictions differ because the cost formulas differ under the three cost-estimation methods. The high-low method, while objective, uses only two data points. Ten observations are excluded.

     The visual-fit method, while it uses all of the data, is somewhat subjective. Different analysts may draw different cost lines.

     Least-squares regression is objective, uses all of the data, and is a statistically sound method of estimation.

     Therefore, least-squares regression is the preferred method of cost estimation.

PROBLEM 7-43 (25 MINUTES)

1.   Scatter diagrams:

   - Present, in graphic form, the relationship between costs and cost drivers via a plot of data points
   - Require that a straight line be fit through the data points, with approximately the same number of data points above and below the line
   - Easy to use
   - Provide a means to easily recognize outliers

   Least-squares regression:

   - Uses statistical formulas to fit a cost line through the data points
   - Is a very objective method of cost estimation that uses all the data points
   - Requires more computation than other cost-estimation methods; however, software programs are readily available

   High-low method:

   - Relies on only two data points (for the highest and lowest activity levels) in drawing conclusions about cost behavior
   - Is considered more objective than the scatter diagram; however, is weaker than the scatter diagram because it relies on only two data points

   The least-squares regression method will typically produce the most accurate results.

2.   Yes. The three methods produce equations by different means. Scatter diagrams and least-squares regression rely on an examination of all data points. The scatter diagram, however, requires an analyst to fit a line through the points by visual approximation, or "eyeballing." In contrast, least-squares regression involves the use of statistical formulas to derive the best possible fit of the line through the points. Finally, the high-low method is based on an analysis of only two data points: the highest and the lowest activity levels.

PROBLEM 7-43 (CONTINUED)

3.   These amounts represent the fixed and variable cost associated with the ticketing operation. Fixed cost totals $312,000 within the relevant range, and Global American incurs $2.30 of variable cost for each ticket issued.

4.   C = $320,000 + $2.15PT
     C = $320,000 + ($2.15 x 580,000)
     C = $1,567,000

5.   Yes, she did err by including November data. November is not representative because of the effects of the Delta Western strike. The month is an outlier and should be eliminated from the data set.

6.   Currently, most of the airline's tickets are written through reservations personnel, whose wages are likely variable in nature. Heavier reliance on the Internet means a greater investment in software, Web-site maintenance and development, and other similar expenditures. Outlays that fall in these latter categories are typically fixed costs, assuming that the cost driver is the number of tickets. The outcome would parallel the experiences of a manufacturing firm that automates its processes and reduces its reliance on direct-labor personnel.

PROBLEM 7-44 (35 MINUTES)

1. The regression equation's intercept on the vertical axis is $200. It represents the portion of indirect material cost that does not vary with machine hours when operating within the relevant range. The slope of the regression line is $4 per machine hour. For every machine hour, $4 of indirect material costs are expected to be incurred.

2. Estimated cost of indirect material at 900 machine hours of activity:

$$S = \$200 + (\$4 \times 900)$$
$$= \$3,800$$

3. Several questions should be asked:

    (a) Do the observations contain any outliers, or are they all representative of normal operations?

    (b) Are there any mismatched time periods in the data? Are all of the indirect material cost observations matched properly with the machine hour observations?

    (c) Are there any allocated costs included in the indirect material cost data?

    (d) Are the cost data affected by inflation?

4.

	April	August
Beginning inventory	$1,200	$ 950
+ Purchases	6,000	6,100
– Ending inventory	(1,550)	(2,900)
Indirect material used	$5,650	$4,150

5. High-low method:

   Variable cost per machine hour

$$= \frac{\text{difference in cost levels}}{\text{difference in activity levels}}$$

$$= \frac{\$5,650 - \$4,150}{1,100 - 800} = \frac{\$1,500}{300} = \$5 \text{ per machine hour}$$

PROBLEM 7-44 (CONTINUED)

Fixed cost per month:

Total cost at 1,100 hours	$5,650
Variable cost at 1,100 hours	
($5 × 1,100)...	5,500
Fixed cost	$ 150

Equation form:

Indirect material cost = $150 + ($5 × machine hours)

6. The regression estimate should be recommended because it uses all of the data, not just two pairs of observations.

PROBLEM 7-45 (40 MINUTES)

1. The original method was simply the average overhead per hour for the last 12 months and did not distinguish between fixed and variable costs. Rand divided total overhead by total labor hours, which effectively treated all overhead as variable. Regression analysis measures the behavior of the overhead costs in relation to labor hours and is a model that distinguishes between fixed and variable costs within the relevant range of 2,500 to 7,500 labor hours.

2. a. Based on the regression analysis, the variable cost per person for a cocktail party is $22, calculated as follows:

Food and beverages..	$15
Labor (.5 hr. @ $10/hr.)...	5
Variable overhead (.5 hr. @ $4/hr.)	2
Total..	$22

   b. Based on the regression analysis, the full absorption cost per person for a cocktail party is $27, calculated as follows:

Food and beverages..	$15
Labor (.5 hr. @ $10/hr.)...	5
Variable overhead (.5 hr. @ $4/hr.)	2
Fixed overhead (.5 hr. @ $10/hr.)*	5
Total..	$27

*$48,000 x 12 months = $576,000
$576,000/57,600 hr. = $10/hr.

3. The minimum bid for a 200-person cocktail party would be $4,400. The amount is calculated by multiplying the variable cost per person of $22 by 200 people. At any price above the variable cost, Dana Rand will be earning a contribution toward her fixed costs.

4. Other factors that Dana Rand should consider in developing a bid include the following:

- The assessment of the current capacity of her business. If the business is at capacity, other work would have to be sacrificed at some opportunity cost.

- Analyses of the competition. If competition is rigorous, she may not have much bargaining power.

- A determination of whether or not her bid will set a precedent for lower prices.

- The realization that regression analysis is based on historical data, and that any anticipated changes in the cost structure should be considered.

PROBLEM 7-46 (45 MINUTES)

Month	Applications Received (in thousands) X	Cost of Operating the Admissions Office (in thousands) Y	X²	XY
August........................	20	8.9	400	178.0
September.................	30	10.0	900	300.0
October......................	25	9.6	625	240.0
November..................	22	9.1	484	200.2
December..................	15	8.7	225	130.5
January.....................	10	8.0	100	80.0
Total.........................	122	54.3	2,734	1,128.7

a. Least-squares regression:

$$7.076^* = \frac{(54.3)(2{,}734) - (122)(1{,}128.7)}{(6)(2{,}734) - (122)(122)}$$

$$.097^* = \frac{(6)(1{,}128.7) - (122)(54.3)}{(6)(2{,}734) - (122)(122)}$$

Total monthly admissions department costs = $7,076 + $.097X, where X denotes the number of applications in thousands.

*Rounded.

PROBLEM 7-46 (CONTINUED)

b. High-low method:

$$\text{Variable cost per thousand applications} = \frac{10-8}{30-10} = \frac{2}{20}$$

$$= \$.10$$

Total cost at 30 thousand applications..	$10,000
Variable cost at 30 thousand applications (30,000 × $.10)...............	3,000
Fixed cost per month	$ 7,000

Total monthly admissions department costs   = $7,000 + $.10X

c. Visual-fit method:

Total monthly admissions department costs   = $7,100 + $.095X

PROBLEM 7-47 (45 MINUTES)

1.   Scatter diagram:

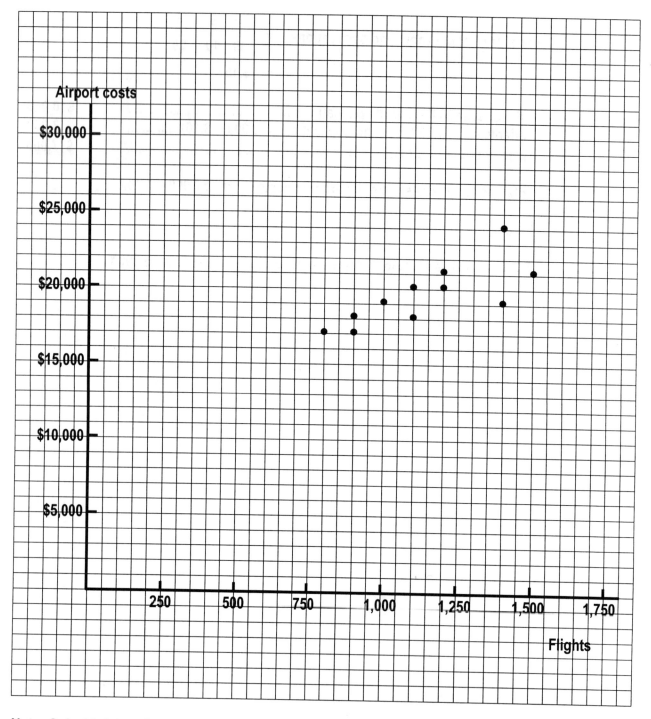

Note: Only 11 data points appear, because two monthly observations were identical (May and September).

PROBLEM 7-47 (CONTINUED)

2.   Least-squares regression:

(a)   Tabulation of data:

Month	Dependent Variable (cost in thousands) Y	Independent Variable (flights in hundreds) X	X^2	XY
January.......................	20	11	121	220
February.....................	17	8	64	136
March........................	19	14	196	266
April	18	9	81	162
May	19	10	100	190
June..........................	20	12	144	240
July	18	11	121	198
August.......................	24	14	196	336
September..................	19	10	100	190
October......................	21	12	144	252
November..................	17	9	81	153
December	21	15	225	315
Total.........................	233	135	1,573	2,658

(b)   Calculation of parameters:

$$a = \frac{(\Sigma Y)(\Sigma X^2) - (\Sigma X)(\Sigma XY)}{n(\Sigma X^2) - (\Sigma X)(\Sigma X)}$$

$$= \frac{(233)(1,573) - (135)(2,658)}{(12)(1,573) - (135)(135)} = 11.796 \text{ (rounded)}$$

$$b = \frac{n(\Sigma XY) - (\Sigma X)(\Sigma Y)}{n(\Sigma X^2) - (\Sigma X)(\Sigma X)}$$

$$= \frac{(12)(2,658) - (135)(233)}{(12)(1,573) - (135)(135)} = .677 \text{ (rounded)}$$

PROBLEM 7-47 (CONTINUED)

(c)   Fixed- and variable-cost components:

Monthly fixed cost = $11,796

Variable cost = $677 per hundred flights

3.   Cost equation:

Total monthly airport cost = $11,796 + $677X, where X denotes the number of flights in hundreds.

4.   Cost prediction for 1,600 flights:

Airport cost for the month = $11,796 + ($677)(16) = $22,628

5.   Calculation and interpretation of R^2:

(a)   Formula for calculation:

$$R^2 = 1 - \frac{\Sigma(Y - Y')^2}{\Sigma(Y - \bar{Y})^2}$$

where Y denotes the observed value of the dependent variable (cost) at a particular activity level.

Y' denotes the predicted value of the dependent variable (cost) based on the regression line, at a particular activity level.

$\bar{Y}$ denotes the mean (average) observation of the dependent variable (cost).

(b)   Tabulation of data:*

Month	Y	X	Predicted Cost (in thousands) Based on Regression Line Y'	$[(Y-Y')^2]^\dagger$	$[(Y-\bar{Y})^2]^\dagger$
January..........	20	11	19.243	.573	.340
February	17	8	17.212	.045	5.842
March.............	19	14	21.274	5.171	.174
April	18	9	17.889	.012	2.008
May	19	10	18.566	.188	.174
June	20	12	19.920	.006	.340
July	18	11	19.243	1.545	2.008
August	24	14	21.274	7.431	21.004
September.....	19	10	18.566	.188	.174
October..........	21	12	19.920	1.166	2.506
November......	17	9	17.889	.790	5.842
December	21	15	21.951	.904	2.506
Total..............				18.019	42.918

$*Y'$ = ($11,796 + $677X)/$1,000

$\bar{Y}$ = $\sum Y/12 = 233/12 = 19.417$ (rounded)

$\dagger$Rounded.

(c)   Calculation of R^2:

$$R^2 = 1 - \frac{18.019}{42.918} = .58 \text{ (rounded)}$$

PROBLEM 7-47 (CONTINUED)

(d) Interpretation of R^2:

The coefficient of determination, R^2, is a measure of the goodness of fit of the least-squares regression line. An R^2 of .58 means that 58% of the variability of the dependent variable about its mean is explained by the variability of the independent variable about its mean. The higher the R^2, the better the regression line fits the data. The interpretation of a high R^2 is that the independent variable is a good predictor of the behavior of the dependent variable. In the county's cost estimation, a high R^2 would mean that the county budget officer can be relatively confident in the cost predictions based on the estimated-cost behavior pattern. An R^2 of .58 is not particularly high.

SOLUTIONS TO CASES

CASE 7-48 (45 MINUTES)

1. Cairns' preliminary estimate for overhead of $18.00 per direct-labor hour does not distinguish between fixed and variable overhead. This preliminary rate is applicable only to the activity level at which it was computed (36,000 direct-labor hours per year) and may not be used to predict total overhead at other activity levels.

    The overhead rate developed from the least-squares regression recognizes the relationship between cost and volume in the data. The regression suggests that there is a component of the cost ($26,200 per month) that is unrelated to total direct-labor hours. This cost component is the intercept on the vertical axis and is often considered to be the fixed cost as long as the activity level is within the relevant range. Thus, the least-squares regression results in a cost function with two components: fixed cost per month and variable cost per direct-labor hour. This cost formula can be used to predict total overhead at any activity level.

2. | | |
    |---|---:|
    | Direct material .... | $400.00 |
    | Direct labor (5 DLH* × $10.00 per DLH) .... | 50.00 |
    | Variable overhead (5 DLH × $9.25 per DLH)................................. | 46.25 |
    | Total variable cost per 1,000 square feet .... | $496.25 |

    *DLH denotes direct-labor hour.

3. The minimum bid should include the following incremental costs of the project.:

Direct material ($400.00 × 60)..	$24,000
Direct labor ($50.00 × 60)...	3,000
Variable overhead ($9.25 per DLH × 5 DLH × 60)	2,775
Overtime premium ($5.00 per DLH × 5 DLH × 60 × .4)	600
Minimum bid..	$30,375

4. Yes, Cairns can rely on the formula as long as she recognizes that there are some shortcomings. The fact that least-squares regression estimates cost behavior increases the usefulness of rates computed from cost data. However, the regression is based on historical costs that may change in the future, and Cairns must assess whether the cost equation would need to be revised for future cost increases or decreases.

CASE 7-48 (CONTINUED)

5. a. Variable OH_1 (60 × 5 × $4.10)... $1,230
        Variable OH_2 (60 × $13.50) 810
        Variable OH_3 (80 × $6.60) 528
        Total incremental variable overhead...................................... $2,568

    b. Variable OH_1 (60 × 5 × $4.10)... $1,230
        Variable OH_2 (30 × $13.50) 405
        Variable OH_3 (250 × $6.60) 1,650
        Total incremental variable overhead...................................... $3,285

    c. The two scenarios in (a) and (b) differ in terms of the activities to be undertaken. Scenario (a) involves a large amount of seeding activity and relatively little planting activity. Scenario (b) involves considerably less seeding activity, but a great deal more planting activity. An activity-based costing system accounts for the different costs in projects involving different mixes of activity.

CASE 7-49 (45 MINUTES)

1. Scatter diagram:

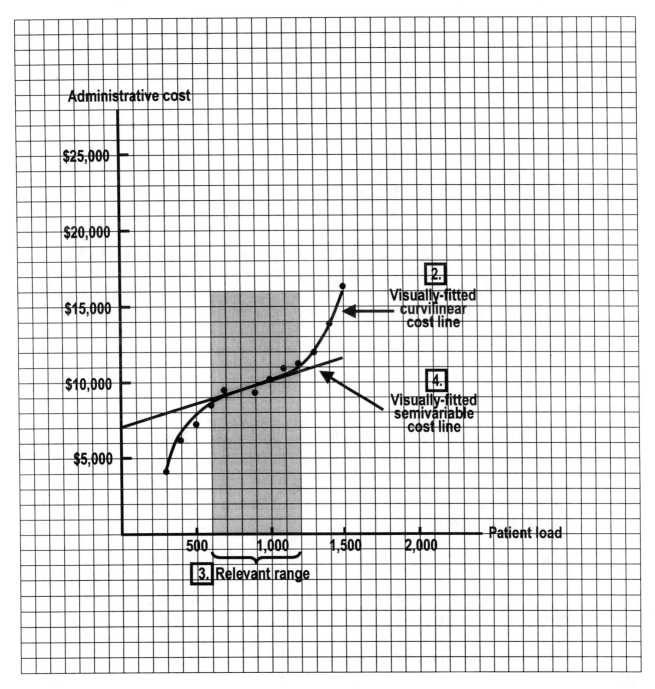

2. through 4.　See scatter diagram for requirement (1).

McGraw-Hill/Irwin

Managerial Accounting, 5/e

© 2002 The McGraw-Hill Companies, Inc.

7-53

CASE 7-49 (CONTINUED)

5. Fixed cost = $6,900

    $$\text{Variable cost per patient} = \frac{\$10,600 - \$6,900}{1,200 - 0} = \$3.08 \text{ (rounded)}$$

6. Administrative cost = $6,900 + $3.08X, where X denotes the number of patients.

7. Cost predictions:

Patient Load	Cost Prediction
800............................	$9,300
300............................	4,000

It makes no difference which cost line is used to make the cost prediction for 800 patients. The semivariable approximation is very accurate at this patient load, which is near the middle of the relevant range. However, for a patient load of 300 patients, the curvilinear cost line yields a much more accurate prediction.

CASE 7-50 (50 MINUTES)

1. High-low method:

    $$\text{Variable administrative cost per patient} = \frac{\$16,100 - \$4,100}{1,500 - 300} = \$10$$

Total cost at 1,500 patients..	$16,100
Variable cost at 1,500 patients	15,000
Fixed cost per month...	$ 1,100

Cost formula:

Total monthly administrative cost = $1,100 + $10X, where X denotes the number of patients for the month.

The variable cost per patient is $10.

CASE 7-50 (CONTINUED)

2. Least-squares regression:

(a) Tabulation of data:

Month	Dependent Variable (cost in hundreds) Y	Independent Variable (patients in hundreds) X	X^2	XY
January......................	139	14	196	1,946
February....................	70	5	25	350
March........................	60	4	16	240
April..........................	100	10	100	1,000
May	119	13	169	1,547
June..........................	92	9	81	828
July	102	11	121	1,122
August......................	41	3	9	123
September.................	94	7	49	658
October.....................	111	12	144	1,332
November..................	83	6	36	498
December..................	161	15	225	2,415
Total..........................	1,172	109	1,171	12,059

(b) Calculation of parameters:

$$a = \frac{(\sum Y)(\sum X^2) - (\sum X)(\sum XY)}{n(\sum X^2) - (\sum X)(\sum X)}$$

$$= \frac{(1,172)(1,171) - (109)(12,059)}{(12)(1,171) - (109)(109)} = 26.707 \text{ (rounded)}$$

$$b = \frac{n(\sum XY) - (\sum X)(\sum Y)}{n(\sum X^2) - (\sum X)(\sum X)}$$

$$= \frac{(12)(12,059) - (109)(1,172)}{(12)(1,171) - (109)(109)} = 7.812 \text{ (rounded)}$$

CASE 7-50 (CONTINUED)

(c) Cost behavior in formula form (with rounded parameters):*

Total monthly administrative cost = $2,671 + 7.81X$, where X denotes the number of patients for the month.

*When interpreting the regression parameters, remember that both the cost and patient data were transformed to hundreds. Thus, the 26.707 intercept parameter (*a*) is in terms of hundreds of dollars of cost, or $2,671 (rounded). The 7.812 slope parameter (*b*) is in terms of hundreds of dollars of cost per hundred patients, or $781 (rounded) per hundred patients. This amount is equivalent to $7.81 per patient.

(d) The variable cost per patient is $7.81, as explained above.

3.

Memorandum

Date: Today

To: Jeffrey Mahoney, Administrator

From: I.M. Student

Subject: Comparison of cost estimates for clinic administrative costs

Three alternative cost-estimation methods were used to estimate the pediatric clinic's administrative cost behavior. The results of these three approaches (in formula form) are shown below. In each formula, X denotes the number of patients in a month.

(a) Least-squares regression method:

Total monthly administrative cost = $2,671 + 7.81X$

(b) High-low method:

Total monthly administrative cost = $1,100 + 10X$

CASE 7-50 (CONTINUED)

(c) Visual-fit method:

Total monthly administrative cost = $6,900 + 3.08X$

These cost estimates differ very significantly. The activity level in the clinic during its first year of operation fluctuated greatly. This fluctuation is not expected in the future; patient loads in the range of 600 to 1,200 patients per month are anticipated.

The cost estimates differ so greatly because two of the methods (least-squares and high-low) used data from outside the relevant range of activity. The clinic's administrative cost behavior appears from the scatter diagram to be curvilinear over the entire range. The cost behavior pattern exhibits very low costs in the range of activity below the relevant range and very high costs in the activity range above the relevant range. Since the regression and high-low estimates are so heavily influenced by observations outside the relevant range, they do not provide the best estimate in this case of how administrative costs are likely to behave within the relevant range. In this instance, the visually-fitted cost line probably provides the best estimate. The visually-fitted cost line has a much flatter slope than the other two cost lines, indicating that total variable administrative costs will probably rise at about $3.25 per patient.

Another possible approach would be to use least-squares regression, but restrict the data to those observations within the relevant range. However, only a handful of observations would remain to include in the analysis.

My overall recommendation is to use the visually-fitted cost line as the best estimate until the clinic has operated for its second year. Then I would recommend a new cost analysis using least-squares regression on all of the data from the relevant range of activity.

CASE 7-50 (CONTINUED)

4.   It is very inappropriate for the hospital administrator to manipulate the cost information supplied by the controller in order to push his own agenda before the board of trustees. It is the board's legitimate role to decide whether or not to establish and continue operations in the clinic. In making decisions about the clinic, the board should have the best information possible, including the controller's best estimate as to how administrative costs will behave.

Megan McDonough, the hospital's Director of Cost Management, has a professional obligation to provide her best professional judgment to the board of trustees. The standards of ethical conduct for management accountants include the following requirements concerning objectivity:

(a)   Communicate information fairly and objectively.

(b)   Disclose fully all relevant information that could reasonably be expected to influence an intended user's understanding of the reports, comments, and recommendations presented.

McDonough should insist that the best and most appropriate estimate of the clinic's administrative cost behavior be presented to the board.

CURRENT ISSUES IN MANAGERIAL ACCOUNTING

ISSUE 7-51

"DRUG-PRICE PROGRAM NOTES," *THE WALL STREET JOURNAL*, AUGUST 10, 2000.

1. A fixed cost is a cost that will not change in total as production levels change within the relevant range. Common examples include straight-line depreciation, supervisory salaries, and rent. The pharmaceutical industry has high fixed costs and low variable costs. Its high fixed costs are "baked in the cake" because of the research and development necessary to yield a profitable drug. Therefore, research and development is a fixed cost of the drug industry. Variable costs are low because, after the discovery and approval process has been completed, it's not very expensive to manufacture the pills.

2. A variable cost is a cost that will change in total as production levels change. Direct material and electricity are often classified as variable costs. Many costs are semivariable (or mixed); they contain both variable and fixed cost components.

ISSUE 7-52

"DELTA, NORTHWEST POST STRONG NET DESPITE FUEL COSTS, HIGHER FARES," *THE WALL STREET JOURNAL*, JULY 21, 2000, MARTHA BRANNIGAN AND MICHAEL J. MCCARTHY.

1. Fuel costs are variable. The distance flown, as well as the weight of the cargo and/or passengers, determines how much fuel is used during a flight.

2. An airline would benefit from estimating costs since management needs cost information to schedule routes and determine the sales price of tickets.

ISSUE 7-53

"AIRBUS 'CRUISE SHIP IN THE SKY'," *THE WALL STREET JOURNAL*, AUGUST 30, 2000, JEFF COLE AND DANIEL MICHAELS.

1. Significantly different costs would be the variable costs per passenger such as fuel, food, and personnel costs for the flight attendants. Increased costs of hangar space due to the size of the plane would be considered fixed costs.

2. Maintenance costs for a new aircraft are always difficult to predict.

3. An airline would benefit from estimating costs. Management needs cost estimates to schedule routes and to determine the sales price of tickets.

ISSUE 7-54

"DELTA PILOTS' UNION PROPOSES PAY RAISES MAKING SALARIES HIGHER THAN UNITED'S," *THE WALL STREET JOURNAL*, OCTOBER 16, 2000, MARTHA BRANNIGAN.

1. Pilots' salaries are considered a fixed cost of a particular flight, in the sense that the cost would not vary with respect to the number of passengers. However, pilots' salaries do vary with the number of flights and their length.

2. An airline would benefit from estimating costs. Management needs cost estimates to schedule routes and to determine the sales price of tickets.

ISSUE 7-55

"HOSPITALS IN NH POST MORE LOSSES," *THE WALL STREET JOURNAL*, APRIL 26, 2000, JAMES BANDLER.

1. Fixed costs are costs that remain the same in total as the volume of activity changes.

2. Sharing laboratory expenses with other hospitals would be an example of a way to reduce fixed costs.

ISSUE 7-56

"HOLLYWOOD RUSHES TO BEAT A STRIKE," *BUSINESS WEEK*, JANUARY 8, 2001, RONALD GROVER.

1. Will Smith will receive $20 million and 20% of revenues. This is a semivariable cost.

2. Colin Farrell will receive $2.5 million for Tigerland. This is a fixed cost.

CHAPTER 8
Cost-Volume-Profit Analysis

ANSWERS TO REVIEW QUESTIONS

8-1   The term *unit contribution margin* refers to the contribution that each unit of sales makes toward covering fixed expenses and earning a profit. The unit contribution margin is defined as the sales price minus the unit variable expense.

8-2   In addition to the break-even point, a CVP graph shows the impact on total expenses, total revenue, and profit when sales volume changes. The graph shows the sales volume required to earn a particular target net profit. The firm's profit and loss areas are also indicated on a CVP graph.

8-3   a. In the contribution-margin approach, the break-even point in units is calculated using the following formula:

$$\text{Break-even point} = \frac{\text{fixed expenses}}{\text{unit contribution margin}}$$

   b. In the equation approach, the following profit equation is used:

$$\left(\begin{array}{c}\text{unit} \\ \text{sales price}\end{array} \times \begin{array}{c}\text{sales volume} \\ \text{in units}\end{array}\right) - \left(\begin{array}{c}\text{unit variable} \\ \text{expense}\end{array} \times \begin{array}{c}\text{sales volume} \\ \text{in units}\end{array}\right) - \begin{array}{c}\text{fixed} \\ \text{expenses}\end{array} = 0$$

   This equation is solved for the sales volume in units.

   c. In the graphical approach, sales revenue and total expenses are graphed. The break-even point occurs at the intersection of the total revenue and total expense lines.

8-4   The safety margin is the amount by which budgeted sales revenue exceeds break-even sales revenue.

8-5   An increase in the fixed expenses of any enterprise will increase its break-even point. In a travel agency, more clients must be served before the fixed expenses are covered by the agency's service fees.

8-6   A decrease in the variable expense per pound of oysters results in an increase in the contribution margin per pound. This will reduce the company's break-even sales volume.

8-7 The president is correct. A price increase results in a higher unit contribution margin. An increase in the unit contribution margin causes the break-even point to decline.

The financial vice president's reasoning is flawed. Even though the break-even point will be lower, the price increase will not necessarily reduce the likelihood of a loss. Customers will probably be less likely to buy the product at a higher price. Thus, the firm may be less likely to meet the lower break-even point (at a high price) than the higher break-even point (at a low price).

8-8 When the sales price and unit variable cost increase by the same amount, the unit contribution margin remains unchanged. Therefore, the firm's break-even point remains the same.

8-9 The fixed annual donation will offset some of the museum's fixed expenses. The reduction in net fixed expenses will reduce the museum's break-even point.

8-10 A profit-volume graph shows the profit to be earned at each level of sales volume.

8-11 The most important assumptions of a cost-volume-profit analysis are as follows:

(a) The behavior of total revenue is linear (straight line) over the relevant range. This behavior implies that the price of the product or service will not change as sales volume varies within the relevant range.

(b) The behavior of total expenses is linear (straight line) over the relevant range. This behavior implies the following more specific assumptions:

(1) Expenses can be categorized as fixed, variable, or semivariable.

(2) Efficiency and productivity are constant.

(c) In multiproduct organizations, the sales mix remains constant over the relevant range.

(d) In manufacturing firms, the inventory levels at the beginning and end of the period are the same.

8-12 Operating managers frequently prefer the contribution income statement because it separates fixed and variable costs. This format makes cost-volume-profit relationships more readily discernible.

8-13   The *gross margin* is defined as sales revenue minus all variable and fixed manufacturing expenses. The *total contribution margin* is defined as sales revenue minus all variable expenses, including manufacturing, selling, and administrative expenses.

8-14   East Company, which is highly automated, will have a cost structure dominated by fixed costs. West Company's cost structure will include a larger proportion of variable costs than East Company's cost structure.

A firm's operating leverage factor, at a particular sales volume, is defined as its total contribution margin divided by its net income. Since East Company has proportionately higher fixed costs, it will have a proportionately higher total contribution margin. Therefore, East Company's operating leverage factor will be higher.

8-15   When sales volume increases, Company X will have a higher percentage increase in profit than Company Y. Company X's higher proportion of fixed costs gives the firm a higher operating leverage factor. The company's percentage increase in profit can be found by multiplying the percentage increase in sales volume by the firm's operating leverage factor.

8-16   The sales mix of a multiproduct organization is the relative proportion of sales of its products.

The weighted-average unit contribution margin is the average of the unit contribution margins for a firm's several products, with each product's contribution margin weighted by the relative proportion of that product's sales.

8-17   The car rental agency's sales mix is the relative proportion of its rental business associated with each of the three types of automobiles: subcompact, compact, and full-size. In a multi-product CVP analysis, the sales mix is assumed to be constant over the relevant range of activity.

8-18   Cost-volume-profit analysis shows the effect on profit of changes in expenses, sales prices, and sales mix. A change in the hotel's room rate (price) will change the hotel's unit contribution margin. This contribution-margin change will alter the relationship between volume and profit.

8-19   Budgeting begins with a sales forecast. Cost-volume-profit analysis can be used to determine the profit that will be achieved at the budgeted sales volume. A CVP analysis also shows how profit will change if the sales volume deviates from budgeted sales.

Cost-volume-profit analysis can be used to show the effect on profit when variable or fixed expenses change. The effect on profit of changes in variable or fixed advertising expenses is one factor that management would consider in making a decision about advertising.

8-20   The low-price company must have a larger sales volume than the high-price company. By spreading its fixed expense across a larger sales volume, the low-price firm can afford to charge a lower price and still earn the same profit as the high-price company. Suppose, for example, that companies A and B have the following expenses, sales prices, sales volumes, and profits.

	Company A	Company B
Sales revenue:		
350 units at $10	$3,500	
100 units at $20		$2,000
Variable expenses:		
350 units at $6	2,100	
100 units at $6		600
Contribution margin	$1,400	$1,400
Fixed expenses	1,000	1,000
Profit	$ 400	$ 400

8-21   The statement makes three assertions, but only two of them are true. Thus the statement is *false*. A company with an advanced manufacturing environment typically will have a larger proportion of fixed costs in its cost structure. This will result in a higher break-even point and greater operating leverage. However, the firm's higher break-even point will result in a *reduced* safety margin.

8-22   Activity-based costing (ABC) results in a richer description of an organization's cost behavior and CVP relationships. Costs that are fixed with respect to sales volume may not be fixed with respect to other important cost drivers. An ABC system recognizes these nonvolume cost drivers, whereas a traditional costing system does not.

SOLUTIONS TO EXERCISES

EXERCISE 8-23 (25 MINUTES)

	Sales Revenue	Variable Expenses	Total Contribution Margin	Fixed Expenses	Net Income	Break-even Sales Revenue
1	$160,000[a]	$40,000	$120,000	$30,000	$90,000	$40,000
2	80,000	65,000	15,000	15,000[b]	-0-	80,000
3	120,000	40,000	80,000	30,000	50,000	45,000[c]
4	110,000	22,000	88,000	50,000	38,000	62,500[d]

Explanatory notes for selected items:

[a]Break-even sales revenue	$40,000
Fixed expenses	30,000
Variable expenses	$10,000

Therefore, variable expenses are 25 percent of sales revenue.

When variable expenses amount to $40,000, sales revenue is $160,000.

[b]$80,000 is the break-even sales revenue, so fixed expenses must be equal to the contribution margin of $15,000 and profit must be zero.

[c]$45,000 = $30,000 ÷ (2/3), where 2/3 is the contribution-margin ratio.

[d]$62,500 = $50,000/.80, where .80 is the contribution-margin ratio.

EXERCISE 8-24 (20 MINUTES)

1. $$\text{Break-even point (in units)} = \frac{\text{fixed expenses}}{\text{unit contribution margin}}$$

$$= \frac{\$40,000}{\$10 - \$5} = 8,000 \text{ pizzas}$$

2. $$\text{Contribution-margin ratio} = \frac{\text{unit contribution margin}}{\text{unit sales price}}$$

$$= \frac{\$10 - \$5}{\$10} = .5$$

3.   Break-even point (in sales dollars) $= \dfrac{\text{fixed expenses}}{\text{contribution-margin ratio}}$

$$= \dfrac{\$40,000}{.5} = \$80,000$$

4.   Let X denote the sales volume of pizzas required to earn a target net profit of $65,000.

$$\$10X - \$5X - \$40,000 = \$65,000$$

$$\$5X = \$105,000$$

$$X = 21,000 \text{ pizzas}$$

EXERCISE 8-25 (25 MINUTES)

1.   Break-even point (in units) $= \dfrac{\text{fixed costs}}{\text{unit contribution margin}}$

$$= \dfrac{4,000,000p}{3,000p - 2,000p} = 4,000 \text{ components}$$

p denotes Argentina's peso, worth 1.004 U.S. dollars on the day this exercise was written.

2.   New break-even point (in units) $= \dfrac{(4,000,000p)(1.10)}{3,000p - 2,000p}$

$$= \dfrac{4,400,000\,p}{1,000p} = 4,400 \text{ components}$$

3.

Sales revenue (5,000 × 3,000p)	15,000,000p
Variable costs (5,000 × 2,000p)	10,000,000p
Contribution margin	5,000,000p
Fixed costs	4,000,000p
Net income	1,000,000p

4. New break-even point (in units) = $\dfrac{4{,}000{,}000p}{2{,}500p - 2{,}000p}$

= 8,000 components

5. Analysis of price change decision:

	Price	
	3,000p	2,500p
Sales revenue: (5,000 × 3,000p)	15,000,000p	
(6,200 × 2,500p)		15,500,000p
Variable costs: (5,000 × 2,000p)	10,000,000p	
(6,200 × 2,000p)		12,400,000p
Contribution margin	5,000,000p	3,100,000p
Fixed expenses	4,000,000p	4,000,000p
Net income (loss)	1,000,000p	(900,000p)

The price cut should not be made, since projected net income will decline.

EXERCISE 8-26 (25 MINUTES)

1.   Cost-volume-profit graph:

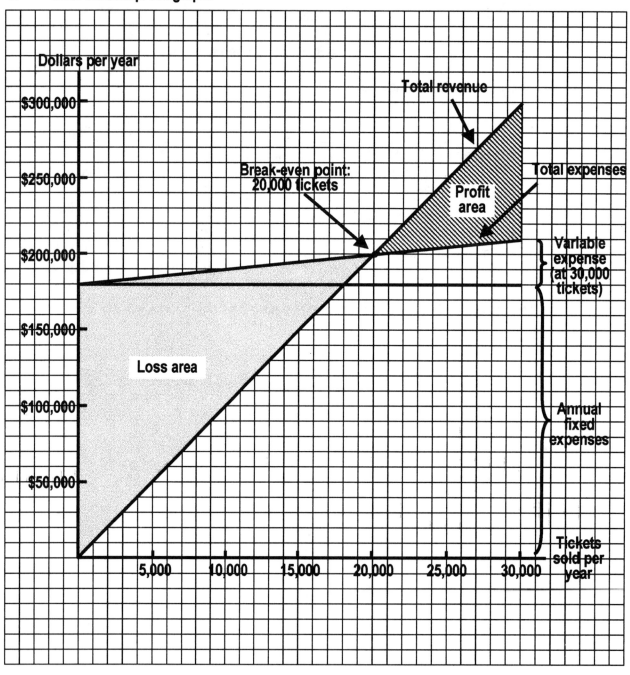

2. Stadium capacity 10,000
    Attendance rate.. × 50%
    Attendance per game 5,000

$$\frac{\text{Break-even point (tickets)}}{\text{Attendance per game}} = \frac{20,000}{5,000} = 4$$

The team must play 4 games to break even.

EXERCISE 8-27 (25 MINUTES)

1.   Profit-volume graph:

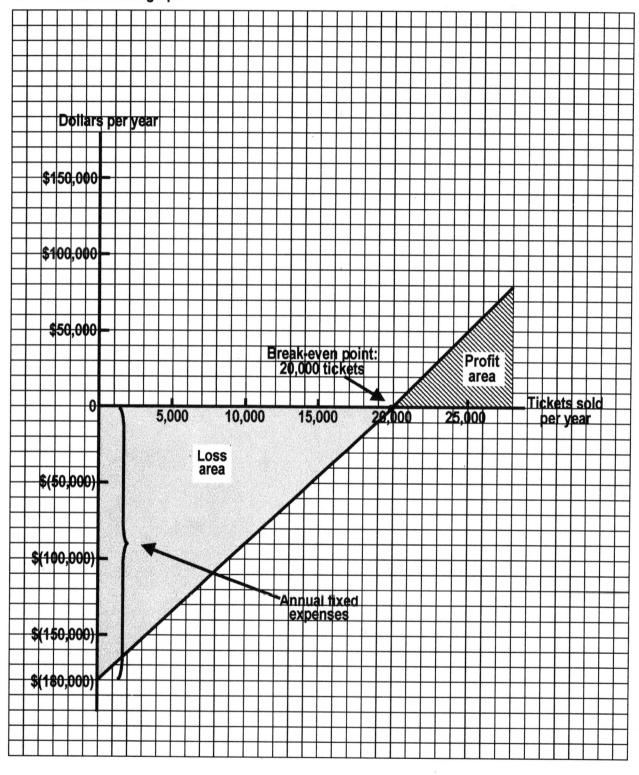

2. **Safety margin:**

Budgeted sales revenue	
(12 games × 10,000 seats × .30 full × $10)	$360,000
Break-even sales revenue	
(20,000 tickets × $10)	200,000
Safety margin	$160,000

3. Let *P* denote the break-even ticket price, assuming a 12-game season and 50 percent attendance:

$$(12)(10,000)(.50)P - (12)(10,000)(.50)(\$1) - \$180,000 = 0$$
$$60,000P = \$240,000$$
$$P = \$4 \text{ per ticket}$$

EXERCISE 8-28 (25 MINUTES)

1. (a) Traditional income statement:

EUROPA PUBLICATIONS, INC.
INCOME STATEMENT
FOR THE YEAR ENDED DECEMBER 31, 20XX

Sales		$2,000,000
Less: Cost of goods sold		1,500,000
Gross margin		$ 500,000
Less: Operating expenses:		
Selling expenses	$150,000	
Administrative expenses	150,000	300,000
Net income		$ 200,000

(b) Contribution income statement:

EUROPA PUBLICATIONS, INC.
INCOME STATEMENT
FOR THE YEAR ENDED DECEMBER 31, 20SXX

Sales		$2,000,000
Less: Variable expenses:		
Variable manufacturing	$1,000,000	
Variable selling	100,000	
Variable administrative	30,000	1,130,000
Contribution margin		$ 870,000
Less: Fixed expenses:		
Fixed manufacturing	$ 500,000	
Fixed selling	50,000	
Fixed administrative	120,000	670,000
Net income		$ 200,000

2. Operating leverage factor (at $2,000,000 sales level) $= \dfrac{\text{contribution margin}}{\text{net income}}$

$$= \frac{\$870,000}{\$200,000} = 4.35$$

EXERCISE 8-28 (CONTINUED)

3. Percentage increase in net income = $\begin{pmatrix} \text{percentage increase} \\ \text{in sales revenue} \end{pmatrix} \times \begin{pmatrix} \text{operating} \\ \text{leverage factor} \end{pmatrix}$

$$= 10\% \times 4.35$$

$$= 43.5\%$$

4. Most operating managers prefer the contribution income statement for answering this type of question. The contribution format highlights the contribution margin and separates fixed and variable expenses.

EXERCISE 8-29 (30 MINUTES)

1.

Bicycle Type	Sales Price	Unit Variable Cost	Unit Contribution Margin
High-quality	$500	$300 ($275 + $25)	$200
Medium-quality	300	150 ($135 + $15)	150

2. Sales mix:

High-quality bicycles 25%
Medium-quality bicycles 75%

3. Weighted-average unit contribution margin $= (\$200 \times 25\%) + (\$150 \times 75\%)$

$$= \$162.50$$

4. Break-even point (in units) $= \dfrac{\text{fixed expenses}}{\text{weighted-average unit contribution margin}}$

$$= \frac{\$65,000}{\$162.50} = 400 \text{ bicycles}$$

Bicycle Type	Break-Even Sales Volume	Sales Price	Sales Revenue
High-quality bicycles	100 (400 × .25)	$500	$ 50,000
Medium-quality bicycles	300 (400 × .75)	300	90,000
Total			$140,000

EXERCISE 8-29 (CONTINUED)

5. Target net income:

Sales volume required to earn target net income of $48,750 $= \dfrac{\$65,000 + \$48,750}{\$162.50}$

$= 700$ bicycles

This means that the shop will need to sell the following volume of each type of bicycle to earn the target net income:

High-quality .... 175 (700 × .25)
Medium-quality .... 525 (700 × .75)

EXERCISE 8-30 (30 MINUTES)

Answers will vary on this question, depending on the airline selected as well as the year of the inquiry. In a typical year, most airlines report a breakeven load factor of around 65 percent.

EXERCISE 8-31 (25 MINUTES)

1. The following income statement, often called a *common-size income statement*, provides a convenient way to show the cost structure.

	Amount	Percent
Revenue	$500,000	100
Variable expenses...	300,000	60
Contribution margin	$200,000	40
Fixed expenses	150,000	30
Net income...	$ 50,000	10

2.

Decrease in Revenue		Contribution Margin Percentage		Decrease in Net Income
$75,000*	×	40%†	=	$30,000

*$75,000 = $500,000 × 15%

†40% = $200,000/$500,000

EXERCISE 8-31 (CONTINUED)

3.   Operating leverage factor (at revenue of $500,000) $= \dfrac{\text{contribution margin}}{\text{net income}}$

$$= \dfrac{\$200,000}{\$50,000} = 4$$

4.   Percentage change in net income $= \left(\begin{array}{c} \text{percentage increase} \\ \text{in revenue} \end{array} \right) \times \left(\begin{array}{c} \text{operating leverage} \\ \text{factor} \end{array} \right)$

$$= 20\% \times 4$$

$$= 80\%$$

EXERCISE 8-32 (10 MINUTES)

	Requirement (1)	Requirement (2)
Revenue	$600,000	$ 500,000
Less: Variable expenses	360,000	600,000
Contribution margin	$240,000	$ (100,000)
Less: Fixed expenses	210,000	125,000
Net Income (loss)	$ 30,000	$ (225,000)

EXERCISE 8-33 (20 MINUTES)

1.   Break-even volume of service revenue $= \dfrac{\text{fixed expenses}}{\text{contribution margin ratio}}$

$$= \dfrac{\$120,000}{.20} = \$600,000$$

2.   Target before-tax income $= \dfrac{\text{target after-tax net income}}{1 - \text{tax rate}}$

$$= \dfrac{\$48,000}{1 - .40} = \$80,000$$

EXERCISE 8-33 (CONTINUED)

3. Service revenue required to earn target after-tax income of $48,000

$$= \frac{\text{fixed expenses} + \dfrac{\text{target after-tax net income}}{(1-t)}}{\text{contribution margin ratio}}$$

$$= \frac{\$120,000 + \dfrac{\$48,000}{1-.40}}{.20} = \$1,000,000$$

4. A change in the tax rate will have no effect on the firm's break-even point. At the break-even point, the firm has no profit and does not have to pay any income taxes.

SOLUTIONS TO PROBLEMS

PROBLEM 8-34 (30 MINUTES)

1. Break-even point in units, using the equation approach:

$$\$16X - (\$10 + \$2)X - \$600,000 = 0$$

$$\$4X = \$600,000$$

$$X = \frac{\$600,000}{\$4}$$

$$= 150,000 \text{ units}$$

2.

$$\text{New projected sales volume} = 200,000 \times 110\%$$

$$= 220,000 \text{ units}$$

$$\text{Net income} = (220,000)(\$16 - \$12) - \$600,000$$

$$= (220,000)(\$4) - \$600,000$$

$$= \$880,000 - \$600,000 = \$280,000$$

3. Target net income = $200,000 (from original problem data)

New disk purchase price = $10 × 130% = $13

Volume of sales dollars required:

$$\text{Volume of sales dollars required} = \frac{\text{fixed expenses} + \text{target net profit}}{\text{contribution-margin ratio}}$$

$$= \frac{\$600,000 + \$200,000}{\dfrac{\$16 - \$13 - \$2}{\$16}} = \frac{\$800,000}{.0625}$$

$$= \$12,800,000$$

PROBLEM 8-34 (CONTINUED)

4. Let *P* denote the selling price that will yield the same contribution-margin ratio:

$$\frac{\$16 - \$10 - \$2}{\$16} = \frac{P - \$13 - \$2}{P}$$

$$.25 = \frac{P - \$15}{P}$$

$$.25P = P - \$15$$

$$\$15 = .75P$$

$$P = \$15/.75$$

$$P = \$20$$

Check: New contribution-margin ratio is:

$$\frac{\$20 - \$15}{\$20} = .25$$

PROBLEM 8-35 (30 MINUTES)

1. Break-even point in sales dollars, using the contribution-margin ratio:

$$\text{Break-even point} = \frac{\text{fixed expenses}}{\text{contribution-margin ratio}}$$

$$= \frac{\$180,000 + \$72,000}{\dfrac{\$20 - \$8 - \$4}{\$20}} = \frac{\$252,000}{.4}$$

$$= \$630,000$$

2. Target net income, using contribution-margin approach:

$$\text{Sales units required to earn income of \$180,000} = \frac{\text{fixed expenses} + \text{target net income}}{\text{unit contribution margin}}$$

$$= \frac{\$252,000 + \$180,000}{\$20 - \$8 - \$4} = \frac{\$432,000}{\$8}$$

$$= 54,000 \text{ units}$$

PROBLEM 8-35 (CONTINUED)

3.   New unit variable manufacturing cost   = $8 × 110%

                                            = $8.80

Break-even point in sales dollars:

$$\text{Break - even point} = \frac{\$252,000}{\dfrac{\$20.00 - \$8.80 - \$4.00}{\$20}} = \frac{\$252,000}{.36}$$

$$= \$700,000$$

4.   Let *P* denote the selling price that will yield the same contribution-margin ratio:

$$\frac{\$20.00 - \$8.00 - \$4.00}{\$20.00} = \frac{P - \$8.80 - \$4.00}{P}$$

$$.4 = \frac{P - \$12.80}{P}$$

$$.4P = P - \$12.80$$

$$\$12.80 = .6P$$

$$P = \$12.80/.6$$

$$P = \$21.33 \text{ (rounded)}$$

Check: New contribution-margin ratio is:

$$\frac{\$21.33 - \$8.80 - \$4.00}{\$21.33} = .4 \text{ (rounded)}$$

PROBLEM 8-36 (30 MINUTES)

1. Unit contribution margin:

Sales price.....................................		$64.00
Less variable costs:		
Sales commissions ($64 x 5%)......	$ 3.20	
System variable costs..................	16.00	19.20
Unit contribution margin...................		$44.80

Break-even point = fixed costs ÷ unit contribution margin
= $985,600 ÷ $44.80
= 22,000 units

2. Model no. 4399 is more profitable when sales and production average 46,000 units.

	Model No. 6754	Model No. 4399
Sales revenue (46,000 units x $64.00).........	$2,944,000	$2,944,000
Less variable costs:		
Sales commissions ($2,944,000 x 5%)...	$ 147,200	$ 147,200
System variable costs:.........................		
46,000 units x $16.00......................	736,000	
46,000 units x $12.80......................		588,800
Total variable costs.............................	$ 883,200	$ 736,000
Contribution margin..............................	$2,060,800	$2,208,000
Less: Annual fixed costs.........................	985,600	1,113,600
Net income...	$1,075,200	$1,094,400

3. Annual fixed costs will increase by $90,000 ($450,000 ÷ 5 years) because of straight-line depreciation associated with the new equipment, to $1,203,600 ($1,113,600 + $90,000). The unit contribution margin is $48 ($2,208,000 ÷ 46,000 units). Thus:

Required sales = (fixed costs + target net profit) ÷ unit contribution margin
= ($1,203,600 + $956,400) ÷ $48
= 45,000 units

4. Let X = volume level at which annual total costs are equal
$16.00X + $985,600 = $12.80X + $1,113,600
$3.20X = $128,000
X = 40,000 units

PROBLEM 8-37 (35 MINUTES)

1.   Current income:

Sales revenue...............................		$3,360,000
Less: Variable costs.....................	$ 840,000	
Fixed costs.........................	2,280,000	3,120,000
Net income.................................		$ 240,000

Advanced Electronics has a contribution margin of $60 [($3,360,000 - $840,000) ÷ 42,000 sets] and desires to increase income to $480,000 ($240,000 x 2). In addition, the current selling price is $80 ($3,360,000 ÷ 42,000 sets). Thus:

   Required sales = (fixed costs + target net profit) ÷ unit contribution margin
                  = ($2,280,000 + $480,000) ÷ $60
                  = 46,000 sets, or $3,680,000 (46,000 sets x $80)

2.   If operations are shifted to Mexico, the new unit contribution margin will be $62 ($80 - $18). Thus:

   Break-even point = fixed costs ÷ unit contribution margin
                    = $1,984,000 ÷ $62
                    = 32,000 units

3.   (a)   Advanced Electronics desires to have a 32,000-unit break-even point with a $60 unit contribution margin. Fixed cost must therefore drop by $360,000 ($2,280,000 - $1,920,000), as follows:

   Let X = fixed costs
   X ÷ $60 = 32,000 units
   X = $1,920,000

   (b)   As the following calculations show, Advanced Electronics will have to generate a contribution margin of $71.25 to produce a 32,000-unit break-even point. Based on an $80.00 selling price, this means that the company can incur variable costs of only $8.75 per unit. Given the current variable cost of $20.00 ($80.00 - $60.00), a decrease of $11.25 per unit ($20.00 - $8.75) is needed.

   Let X = unit contribution margin
   $2,280,000 ÷ X = 32,000 units
   X = $71.25

PROBLEM 8-37 (CONTINUED

4. (a) Increase

    (b) No effect

    (c) Increase

    (d) No effect

PROBLEM 8-38 (40 MINUTES)

1. Sales mix refers to the relative proportion of each product sold when a company sells more than one product.

2. (a) Yes. Plan A sales are expected to total 65,000 units (45,500 + 19,500), which compares favorably against current sales of 60,000 units.

    (b) Yes. Sales personnel earn a commission based on gross dollar sales. As the following figures show, Deluxe sales will comprise a greater proportion of total sales under Plan A. This is not surprising in light of the fact that Deluxe has a higher selling price than Basic ($86 vs. $74).

	Current		Plan A	
	Units	Sales Mix	Units	Sales Mix
Deluxe.........	39,000	65%	45,500	70%
Basic..........	21,000	35%	19,500	30%
Total	60,000	100%	65,000	100%

    (c) Yes. Commissions will total $535,600 ($5,356,000 x 10%), which compares favorably against the current flat salaries of $400,000.

Deluxe sales: 45,500 units x $86...	$3,913,000
Basic sales: 19,500 units x $74.....	1,443,000
Total.....................................	$5,356,000

PROBLEM 8-38 (CONTINUED)

(d) No. The company would be less profitable under the new plan.

	Current	Plan A
Sales revenue:		
Deluxe: 39,000 units x $86; 45,500 units x $86...	$3,354,000	$3,913,000
Basic: 21,000 units x $74; 19,500 units x $74.....	1,554,000	1,443,000
Total revenue..	$4,908,000	$5,356,000
Less variable cost:		
Deluxe: 39,000 units x $65; 45,500 units x $65...	$2,535,000	$2,957,500
Basic: 21,000 units x $41; 19,500 units x $41.....	861,000	799,500
Sales commissions (10% of sales revenue).......		535,600
Total variable cost..................................	$3,396,000	$4,292,600
Contribution margin...	$1,512,000	$1,063,400
Less fixed cost (salaries).................................	400,000	----
Net income..	$1,112,000	$1,063,400

3. (a) The total units sold under both plans are the same; however, the sales mix has shifted under Plan B in favor of the more profitable product as judged by the contribution margin. Deluxe has a contribution margin of $21 ($86 - $65), and Basic has a contribution margin of $33 ($74 - $41).

	Plan A		Plan B	
	Units	Sales Mix	Units	Sales Mix
Deluxe.........	45,500	70%	26,000	40%
Basic..........	19,500	30%	39,000	60%
Total......	65,000	100%	65,000	100%

PROBLEM 8-38 (CONTINUED)

(b) Plan B is more attractive both to the sales force and to the company. Salespeople earn more money under this arrangement ($549,900 vs. $400,000) and the company is more profitable ($1,283,100 vs. $1,112,000).

	Current	Plan B
Sales revenue:		
Deluxe: 39,000 units x $86; 26,000 units x $86...	$3,354,000	$2,236,000
Basic: 21,000 units x $74; 39,000 units x $74.....	1,554,000	2,886,000
Total revenue......................................	$4,908,000	$5,122,000
Less variable cost:		
Deluxe: 39,000 units x $65; 26,000 units x $65...	$2,535,000	$1,690,000
Basic: 21,000 units x $41; 39,000 units x $41.....	861,000	1,599,000
Total variable cost.................................	$3,396,000	$3,289,000
Contribution margin...............................	$1,512,000	$1,833,000
Less: Sales force compensation:		
Flat salaries...	400,000	
Commissions ($1,833,000 x 30%)..................		549,900
Net income	$1,112,000	$1,283,100

PROBLEM 8-39 (35 MINUTES)

1. Plan A break-even point = fixed costs ÷ unit contribution margin
   = $22,000 ÷ $22*
   = 1,000 units

   Plan B break-even point = fixed costs ÷ unit contribution margin
   = $66,000 ÷ $30**
   = 2,200 units

   * $80 - [($80 x 10%) + $50]
   ** $80 - $50

2. Operating leverage refers to the use of fixed costs in an organization's overall cost structure. An organization that has a relatively high proportion of fixed costs and low proportion of variable costs has a high degree of operating leverage.

PROBLEM 8-39 (CONTINUED)

3. Calculation of contribution margin and profit at 6,000 units of sales:

	Plan A	Plan B
Sales revenue: 6,000 units x $80...............	$480,000	$480,000
Less variable costs:		
Cost of purchasing product:		
6,000 units x $50..........................	$300,000	$300,000
Sales commissions: $480,000 x 10%.........	48,000	----
Total variable cost............................	$348,000	$300,000
Contribution margin.....................................	$132,000	$180,000
Fixed costs...	22,000	66,000
Net income...	$110,000	$114,000

Operating leverage factor = contribution margin ÷ net income
Plan A: $132,000 ÷ $110,000 = 1.2
Plan B: $180,000 ÷ $114,000 = 1.58 (rounded)

Plan B has the higher degree of operating leverage.

4 & 5. Calculation of profit at 5,000 units:

	Plan A	Plan B
Sales revenue: 5,000 units x $80...............	$400,000	$400,000
Less variable costs:		
Cost of purchasing product:		
5,000 units x $50..........................	$250,000	$250,000
Sales commissions: $400,000 x 10%.........	40,000	----
Total variable cost............................	$290,000	$250,000
Contribution margin.....................................	$110,000	$150,000
Fixed costs...	22,000	66,000
Net income...	$ 88,000	$ 84,000

Plan A profitability decrease:
$110,000 - $88,000 = $22,000; $22,000 ÷ $110,000 = 20%

Plan B profitability decrease:
$114,000 - $84,000 = $30,000; $30,000 ÷ $114,000 = 26.3% (rounded)

PROBLEM 8-39 (CONTINUED)

Consolidated would experience a larger percentage decrease in income if it adopts Plan B. This situation arises because Plan B has a higher degree of operating leverage. Stated differently, Plan B's cost structure produces a greater percentage decline in profitability from the drop-off in sales revenue.

Note: The percentage decreases in profitability can be computed by multiplying the percentage decrease in sales revenue by the operating leverage factor. Sales dropped from 6,000 units to 5,000 units, or 16.67%. Thus:

Plan A: 16.67% x 1.2 = 20.0%
Plan B: 16.67% x 1.58 = 26.3% (rounded)

6. Heavily automated manufacturers have sizable investments in plant and equipment, along with a high percentage of fixed costs in their cost structures. As a result, there is a high degree of operating leverage.

In a severe economic downturn, these firms typically suffer a significant decrease in profitability. Such firms would be a more risky investment when compared with firms that have a low degree of operating leverage. Of course, when times are good, increases in sales would tend to have a very favorable effect on earnings in a company with high operating leverage.

PROBLEM 8-40 (30 MINUTES)

1. $\text{Break-even point (in units)} = \dfrac{\text{fixed costs}}{\text{unit contribution margin}}$

    $= \dfrac{\$468,000}{\$25.00 - \$19.80} = 90,000 \text{ units}$

2. $\text{Break-even point (in sales dollars)} = \dfrac{\text{fixed cost}}{\text{contribution-margin ratio}}$

    $= \dfrac{\$468,000}{\dfrac{\$25.00 - \$19.80}{\$25.00}} = \$2,250,000$

3. $\begin{aligned}\text{Number of sales units required to} \\ \text{earn target net profit}\end{aligned} = \dfrac{\text{fixed costs} + \text{target net profit}}{\text{unit contribution margin}}$

    $= \dfrac{\$468,000 + \$260,000}{\$25.00 - \$19.80} = 140,000 \text{ units}$

4. Margin of safety = budgeted sales revenue – break-even sales revenue

    = (120,000)($25) – $2,250,000 = $750,000

5. Break-even point if direct-labor costs increase by 8 percent:

    New unit contribution margin = $25.00 – $10.50 – ($5.00)(1.08) – $3.00 – $1.30

    = $4.80

    $\text{Break-even point} = \dfrac{\text{fixed costs}}{\text{new unit contribution margin}}$

    $= \dfrac{\$468,000}{\$4.80} = 97,500 \text{ units}$

PROBLEM 8-40 (CONTINUED)

6. Contribution margin ratio $= \dfrac{\text{unit contribution margin}}{\text{sales price}}$

Old contribution-margin ratio $= \dfrac{\$25.00 - \$19.80}{\$25.00}$

$= .208$

Let P denote sales price required to maintain a contribution-margin ratio of .208. Then P is determined as follows:

$$\frac{P - \$10.50 - (\$5.00)(1.08) - \$3.00 - \$1.30}{P} = .208$$

$$P - \$20.20 = .208P$$

$$.792P = \$20.20$$

$$P = \$25.51 \,(\text{rounded})$$

Check: New contribution-margin ratio $= \dfrac{\$25.51 - \$10.50 - (\$5.00)(1.08) - \$3.00 - \$1.30}{\$25.51}$

$= .208 \,(\text{rounded})$

PROBLEM 8-41 (40 MINUTES)

1. CVP graph:

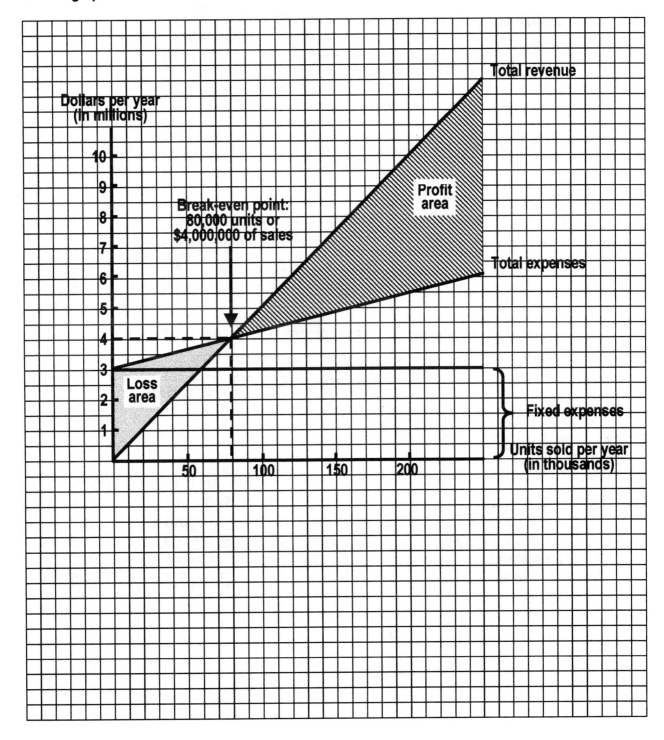

PROBLEM 8-41 (CONTINUED)

2. Break-even point:

$$\text{Contribution-margin ratio} = \frac{\text{contribution margin}}{\text{sales}} = \frac{\$6,000,000}{\$8,000,000} = .75$$

$$\text{Break-even point} = \frac{\text{fixed expenses}}{\text{contribution-margin ratio}} = \frac{\$3,000,000}{.75}$$

$$= \$4,000,000$$

3. Margin of safety = budgeted sales revenue – break-even sales revenue

= $8,000,000 – $4,000,000 = $4,000,000

4. Operating leverage factor
(at budgeted sales)

$$= \frac{\text{contribution margin (at budgeted sales)}}{\text{net income (at budgeted sales)}}$$

$$= \frac{\$6,000,000}{\$3,000,000} = 2$$

5. Dollar sales required to
earn target net profit

$$= \frac{\text{fixed expenses} + \text{target net profit}}{\text{contribution-margin ratio}}$$

$$= \frac{\$3,000,000 + \$4,500,000}{.75} = \$10,000,000$$

6. Cost structure:

	Amount	Percent
Sales revenue..	$8,000,000	100.0
Variable expenses..................................	2,000,000	25.0
Contribution margin	$6,000,000	75.0
Fixed expenses	3,000,000	37.5
Net income...	$3,000,000	37.5

PROBLEM 8-42 (35 MINUTES)

1. (a) $\text{Unit contribution margin} = \dfrac{\text{sales} - \text{variable costs}}{\text{units sold}}$

$$= \dfrac{\$1,000,000 - \$700,000}{100,000} = \$3\,\text{per unit}$$

$\text{Break-even point (in units)} = \dfrac{\text{fixed costs}}{\text{unit contribution margin}}$

$$= \dfrac{\$210,000}{\$3} = 70,000\,\text{units}$$

(b) $\text{Contribution-margin ratio} = \dfrac{\text{contribution margin}}{\text{sales revenue}}$

$$= \dfrac{\$1,000,000 - \$700,000}{\$1,000,000} = .3$$

$\text{Break-even point (in sales dollars)} = \dfrac{\text{fixed costs}}{\text{contribution-margin ratio}}$

$$= \dfrac{\$210,000}{.3} = \$700,000$$

2. $\begin{array}{l}\text{Number of units of sales required} \\ \text{to earn target after-tax net income}\end{array} = \dfrac{\text{fixed costs} + \dfrac{\text{target after-tax net income}}{(1-t)}}{\text{unit contribution margin}}$

$$= \dfrac{\$210,000 + \dfrac{\$90,000}{(1-.4)}}{\$3} = \dfrac{\$360,000}{\$3}$$

$$= 120,000\,\text{units}$$

3.   If fixed costs increase by $31,500:

$\text{Break-even point (in units)} = \dfrac{\$210,000 + \$31,500}{\$3} = 80,500\,\text{units}$

PROBLEM 8-42 (CONTINUED)

4. Profit-volume graph:

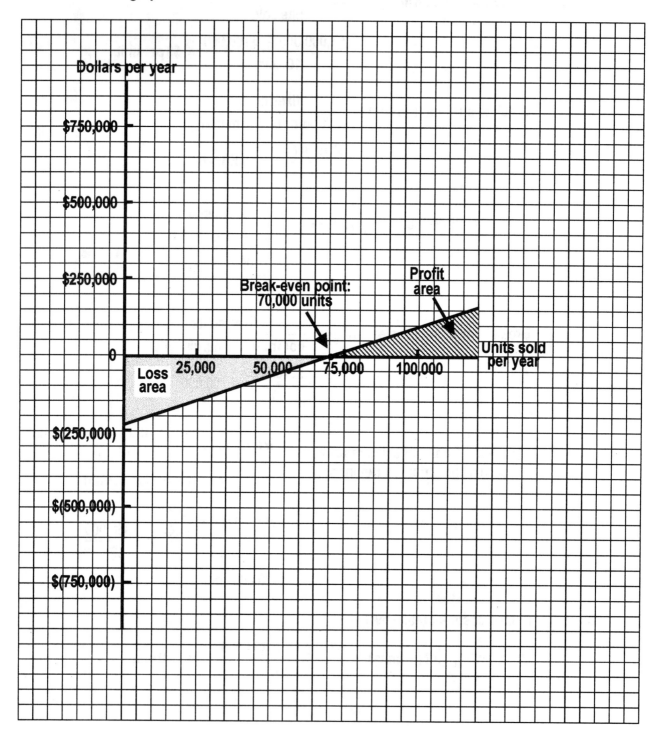

PROBLEM 8-42 (CONTINUED)

5.   Number of units of sales required to earn target after-tax net income

$$= \frac{\text{fixed costs} + \dfrac{\text{target after-tax net income}}{(1-t)}}{\text{unit contribution margin}}$$

$$= \frac{\$210,000 + \dfrac{\$90,000}{(1-.5)}}{\$3} = \frac{\$390,000}{\$3}$$

$$= \quad 130,000 \text{ units}$$

PROBLEM 8-43 (40 MINUTES)

1.   In order to break even, during the first year of operations, 10,220 clients must visit the law office being considered by Terry Smith and his colleagues, as the following calculations show.

Fixed expenses:

Advertising		$ 490,000
Rent (6,000 × $28)		168,000
Property insurance		27,000
Utilities		37,000
Malpractice insurance		180,000
Depreciation ($60,000/4)		15,000
Wages and fringe benefits:		
Regular wages		
($25 + $20 + $15 + $10) × 16 hours × 360 days	$403,200	
Overtime wages		
(200 × $15 × 1.5) + (200 × $10 × 1.5)	7,500	
Total wages	$410,700	
Fringe benefits at 40%	164,280	574,980
Total fixed expenses		$1,491,980

PROBLEM 8-43 (CONTINUED)

Break-even point:

$$0 = \text{revenue} - \text{variable cost} - \text{fixed cost}$$

$$0 = \$30X + (\$2,000 \times .2X \times .3)^* - \$4X - \$1,491,980$$

$$0 = \$30X + \$120X - \$4X - \$1,491,980$$

$$\$146X = \$1,491,980$$

$$X = 10,220 \text{ clients (rounded)}$$

*Revenue calculation:

$30X represents the $30 consultation fee per client. ($2,000 × .2X × .30) represents the predicted average settlement of $2,000, multiplied by the 20% of the clients whose judgments are expected to be favorable, multiplied by the 30% of the judgment that goes to the firm.

2.   Safety margin:

Safety margin = budgeted sales revenue − break-even sales revenue

Budgeted (expected) number of clients = 50 × 360 = 18,000

Break-even number of clients = 10,220 (rounded)

$$\text{Safety margin} = [(\$30 \times 18,000) + (\$2,000 \times 18,000 \times .20 \times .30)]$$
$$- [(\$30 \times 10,220) + (\$2,000 \times 10,220 \times .20 \times .30)]$$
$$= [\$30 + (\$2,000 \times .20 \times .30)] \times (18,000 - 10,220)$$
$$= \$150 \times 7,780$$
$$= \$1,167,000$$

PROBLEM 8-44 (45 MINUTES)

1. Break-even point in units:

$$\text{Break-even point} = \frac{\text{fixed costs}}{\text{unit contribution margin}}$$

Calculation of contribution margins:

	Computer-Assisted Manufacturing System		Labor-Intensive Production System	
Selling price................................		$30.00		$30.00
Variable costs:				
Direct material	$5.00		$5.60	
Direct labor	6.00		7.20	
Variable overhead	3.00		4.80	
Variable selling cost...................	2.00	16.00	2.00	19.60
Contribution margin per unit		$14.00		$10.40

(a) Computer-assisted manufacturing system:

$$\text{Break-even point in units} = \frac{\$2,440,000 + \$500,000}{\$14}$$

$$= \frac{\$2,940,000}{\$14}$$

$$= 210,000 \text{ units}$$

(b) Labor-intensive production system:

$$\text{Break-even point in units} = \frac{\$1,320,000 + \$500,000}{\$10.40}$$

$$= \frac{\$1,820,000}{\$10.40}$$

$$= 175,000 \text{ units}$$

PROBLEM 8-44 (CONTINUED)

2.   Celestial Products, Inc. would be indifferent between the two manufacturing methods at the volume (X) where total costs are equal.

$$\$16X + \$2,940,000 = \$19.60X + \$1,820,000$$

$$\$3.60X = \$1,120,000$$

$$X = 311{,}111 \text{ units (rounded)}$$

3.   Operating leverage is the extent to which a firm's operations employ fixed operating costs. The greater the proportion of fixed costs used to produce a product, the greater the degree of operating leverage. Thus, the computer-assisted manufacturing method utilizes a greater degree of operating leverage.

           The greater the degree of operating leverage, the greater the change in operating income (loss) relative to a small fluctuation in sales volume. Thus, there is a higher degree of variability in operating income if operating leverage is high.

4.   Management should employ the computer-assisted manufacturing method if annual sales are expected to exceed 311,111 units and the labor-intensive manufacturing method if annual sales are not expected to exceed 311,111 units.

5.   Celestial Products' management should consider many other business factors other than operating leverage before selecting a manufacturing method. Among these are:

- Variability or uncertainty with respect to demand quantity and selling price.

- The ability to produce and market the new product quickly.

- The ability to discontinue production and marketing of the new product while incurring the least amount of loss.

PROBLEM 8-45 (45 MINUTES)

1. Break-even sales volume for each model:

$$\text{Break-even volume} = \frac{\text{annual rental cost}}{\text{unit contribution margin}}$$

(a) Economy model:

$$\text{Break-even volume} = \frac{\$8,000}{\$1.75 - \$1.43} = 25,000 \text{ tubs}$$

(b) Regular model:

$$\text{Break-even volume} = \frac{\$11,000}{\$1.75 - \$1.35} = 27,500 \text{ tubs}$$

(c) Super model:

$$\text{Break-even volume} = \frac{\$20,000}{\$1.75 - \$1.26} = 40,816 \text{ tubs (rounded)}$$

PROBLEM 8-45 (CONTINUED)

2. Profit-volume graph:

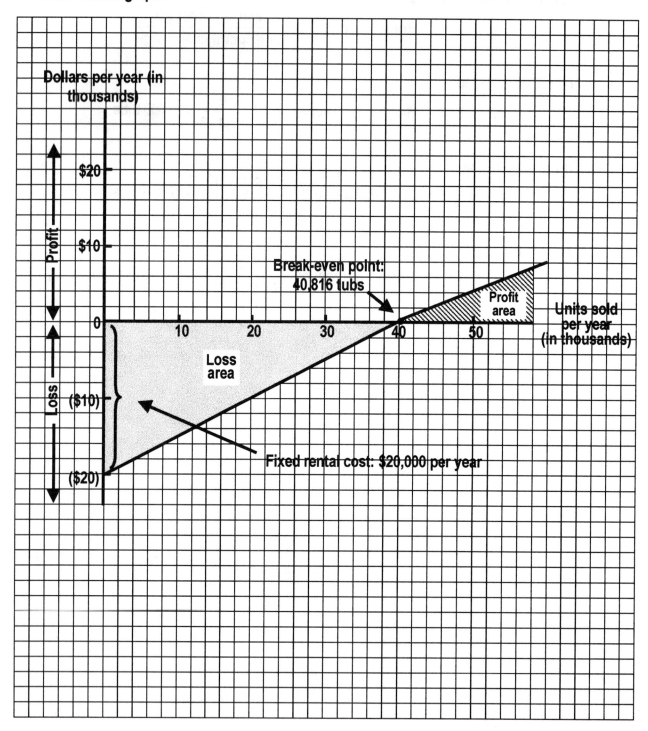

3. The sales price per tub is the same regardless of the type of machine selected. Therefore, the same profit (or loss) will be achieved with the Economy and Regular models at the sales volume, X, where the total costs are the same.

Model	Variable Cost per Tub	Total Fixed Cost
Economy..	$1.43	$ 8,000
Regular..	1.35	11,000

This reasoning leads to the following equation: $8,000 + 1.43X = 11,000 + 1.35X$

Rearranging terms yields the following:

$$(1.43 - 1.35)X = 11,000 - 8,000$$
$$.08X = 3,000$$
$$X = 3,000/.08$$
$$X = 37,500$$

Or, stated slightly differently:

$$\text{Volume at which both machines produce the same profit} = \frac{\text{fixed cost differential}}{\text{variable cost differential}}$$
$$= \frac{\$3,000}{\$.08}$$
$$= 37,500 \text{ tubs}$$

Check: the total cost is the same with either model if 37,500 tubs are sold.

	Economy	Regular
Variable cost:		
Economy, 37,500 × $1.43...........................	$53,625	
Regular, 37,500 × $1.35		$50,625
Fixed cost:		
Economy, $8,000.....................................	8,000	
Regular, $11,000......................................		11,000
Total cost..	$61,625	$61,625

Since the sales price for popcorn does not depend on the popper model, the sales revenue will be the same under either alternative.

PROBLEM 8-46 (35 MINUTES)

1. $\text{Unit contribution margin} = \dfrac{\$625,000 - \$375,000}{25,000 \text{ units}}$

$$= \$10 \text{ per unit}$$

$\text{Break-even point (in units)} = \dfrac{\text{fixed costs}}{\text{unit contribution margin}}$

$$= \dfrac{\$150,000}{\$10} = 15,000 \text{ units}$$

2.   Number of sales units required to earn target net profit $= \dfrac{\text{fixed costs} + \text{target net profit}}{\text{unit contribution margin}}$

$$= \dfrac{\$150,000 + \$140,000}{\$10} = 29,000 \text{ units}$$

3. $\text{New break-even point (in units)} = \dfrac{\text{new fixed costs}}{\text{new unit contribution margin}}$

$$= \dfrac{\$150,000 + (\$18,000/6)^{*}}{\$10 - \$2^{\dagger}} = 19,125 \text{ units}$$

*Annual straight-line depreciation on new machine

$\dagger$\$2.00 = \$4.50 − \$2.50 *increase* in the unit cost of the new part

4.   Number of sales units required to earn target net profit, given manufacturing changes $= \dfrac{\text{new fixed costs} + \text{target net profit}}{\text{new unit contribution margin}}$

$$= \dfrac{\$153,000 + \$100,000^{*}}{\$8}$$

$$= 31,625 \text{ units}$$

*Last year's profit: (\$25)(25,000) − \$525,000 = \$100,000

5. $$\text{Contribution-margin ratio} = \frac{\text{unit contribution margin}}{\text{sales price}}$$

$$\text{Old contribution-margin ratio} = \frac{\$10}{\$25^*} = .40$$

*Sales price = $25 = $625,000 ÷ 25,000 units.

Let *P* denote the price required to cover increased direct-material cost and maintain the same contribution margin ratio:

$$\frac{P - \$15^* - \$2^\dagger}{P} = .40$$

$$P - \$17 = .40P$$

$$.60P = \$17$$

$$P = \$28.33 \text{ (rounded)}$$

*Old unit variable cost = $15 = $375,000 ÷ 25,000 units

†Increase in direct-material cost = $2

Check:

$$\text{New contribution-margin ratio} = \frac{\$28.33 - \$15 - \$2}{\$28.33}$$

$$= .40 \text{ (rounded)}$$

PROBLEM 8-47 (40 MINUTES)

1.   **Memorandum**

Date: Today

To: Vice President for Manufacturing, Jupiter Game Company

From: I.M. Student, Controller

Subject: Activity-Based Costing

The $150,000 cost that has been characterized as fixed *is* fixed with respect to sales volume. This cost will not increase with increases in sales volume. However, as the activity-based costing analysis demonstrates, these costs are *not fixed* with respect to *other important cost drivers*. This is the difference between a traditional costing system and an ABC system. The latter recognizes that costs vary with respect to a variety of cost drivers, not just sales volume.

2.   New break-even point if automated manufacturing equipment is installed:

Sales price...	$26
Costs that are variable (with respect to sales volume):	
Unit variable cost (.8 × $375,000 ÷ 25,000)	12
Unit contribution margin..	$14
Costs that are fixed (with respect to sales volume):	
Setup (300 setups at $50 per setup)	$ 15,000
Engineering (800 hours at $28 per hour)	22,400
Inspection (100 inspections at $45 per inspection)	4,500
General factory overhead	166,100
Total	$208,000
Fixed selling and administrative costs..	30,000
Total costs that are fixed (with respect to sales volume)...........	$238,000

$$\text{Break-even point (in units)} = \frac{\text{fixed costs}}{\text{unit contribution margin}}$$

$$= \frac{\$238,000}{\$14}$$

$$= 17,000 \text{ units}$$

PROBLEM 8-47 (CONTINUED)

3.   Sales (in units) required to show a profit of $140,000:

$$\text{Number of sales units required to earn target net profit} = \frac{\text{fixed cost} + \text{target net profit}}{\text{unit contribution margin}}$$

$$= \frac{\$238,000 + \$140,000}{\$14}$$

$$= 27,000 \text{ units}$$

4. If management adopts the new manufacturing technology:

   (a) Its break-even point will be higher (17,000 units instead of 15,000 units).

   (b) The number of sales units required to show a profit of $140,000 will be lower (27,000 units instead of 29,000 units).

   (c) These results are typical of situations where firms adopt advanced manufacturing equipment and practices. The break-even point increases because of the increased fixed costs due to the large investment in equipment. However, at higher levels of sales after fixed costs have been covered, the larger unit contribution margin ($14 instead of $10) earns a profit at a faster rate. This results in the firm needing to sell fewer units to reach a given target profit level.

PROBLEM 8-47 (CONTINUED)

5.   The controller should include the break-even analysis in the report. The Board of Directors needs a complete picture of the financial implications of the proposed equipment acquisition. The break-even point is a relevant piece of information. The controller should accompany the break-even analysis with an explanation as to why the break-even point will increase. It would also be appropriate for the controller to point out in the report that the advanced manufacturing equipment would require fewer sales units at higher volumes in order to achieve a given target profit, as in requirement (3) of this problem.

    To withhold the break-even analysis from the controller's report would be a violation of the following ethical standards:

(a) Competence: Prepare complete and clear reports and recommendations after appropriate analysis of relevant and reliable information.

(b) Integrity: Communicate unfavorable as well as favorable information and professional judgments or opinions.

(c) Objectivity: Communicate information fairly and objectively. Disclose fully all relevant information that could reasonably be expected to influence an intended user's understanding of the reports, comments, and recommendations presented.

© 2002 The McGraw-Hill Companies, Inc.

Solutions Manual

PROBLEM 8-48 (25 MINUTES)

1. Closing of downtown store:

Loss of contribution margin at Downtown Store	$(36,000)
Savings of fixed cost at Downtown Store (75%)	30,000
Loss of contribution margin at Mall Store (10%)	(4,800)
Total decrease in operating income	$(10,800)

2. Promotional campaign:

Increase in contribution margin (10%)	$ 3,600
Increase in monthly promotional expenses ($60,000/12)	(5,000)
Decrease in operating income	$(1,400)

3. Elimination of items sold at their variable cost:

We can restate the November 20x1 data for the Downtown Store as follows:

	Downtown Store	
	Items Sold at Their Variable Cost	Other Items
Sales	$60,000*	$60,000*
Less: variable expenses	60,000	24,000
Contribution margin	$ -0-	$ 36,000

If the items sold at their variable cost are eliminated, we have:	
Decrease in contribution margin on other items (20%)	$(7,200)
Decrease in fixed expenses (15%)	6,000
Decrease in operating income	$(1,200)

*$60,000 is one half of the Downtown Store's dollar sales for November 20x1.

PROBLEM 8-49 (45 MINUTES)

1.

CINCINNATI TOOL COMPANY
BUDGETED INCOME STATEMENT
FOR THE YEAR ENDED DECEMBER 31, 20X2

	Weeders	Hedge Clippers	Leaf Blowers	Total
Unit selling price..............................	$28	$36	$48	
Variable manufacturing cost	$13	$12	$25	
Variable selling cost........................	5	4	6	
Total variable cost...........................	$18	$16	$31	
Contribution margin per unit.........	$10	$20	$17	
Unit sales..	× 50,000	× 50,000	× 100,000	
Total contribution margin	$500,000	$1,000,000	$1,700,000	$3,200,000
Fixed manufacturing overhead				$2,000,000
Fixed selling and administrative costs				600,000
Total fixed costs...........................				$2,600,000
Income before taxes.......................				$600,000
Income taxes (40%)				240,000
Budgeted net income....................				$ 360,000

2.

	(a) Unit Contribution	(b) Sales Proportion	(a) × (b)
Weeders..	$10	.25	$ 2.50
Hedge Clippers	20	.25	5.00
Leaf Blowers	17	.50	8.50
Weighted-average unit contribution margin...........................			$16.00

$$\text{Total unit sales to break even} = \frac{\text{total fixed costs}}{\text{weighted-average unit contribution margin}}$$

$$= \frac{\$2,600,000}{\$16} = 162,500 \text{ units}$$

PROBLEM 8-49 (CONTINUED)

Sales proportions:

	Sales Proportion	Total Unit Sales	Product Line Sales
Weeders...	.25	162,500	40,625
Hedge Clippers	.25	162,500	40,625
Leaf Blowers	.50	162,500	81,250
Total...			162,500

3.

	(a) Unit Contribution	(b) Sales Proportion	(a) × (b)
Weeders	$10	.20	$ 2.00
Hedge Clippers*	19	.20	3.80
Leaf Blowers†	12	.60	7.20
Weighted-average unit contribution margin ..			$13.00

*Variable selling cost increases. Thus, the unit contribution decreases to $19 [$36 – ($12 + $4 + $1)].

†The variable manufacturing cost increases 20 percent. Thus, the unit contribution decreases to $12 [$48 – (1.2 × $25) – $6].

$$\text{Total unit sales to break even} = \frac{\text{total fixed costs}}{\text{weighted-average unit contribution margin}}$$

$$= \frac{\$2,600,000}{\$13} = 200,000 \text{ units}$$

Sales proportions:

	Sales Proportions	Total Unit Sales	Product Line Sales
Weeders...	.20	200,000	40,000
Hedge Clippers	.20	200,000	40,000
Leaf Blowers	.60	200,000	120,000
Total...			200,000

PROBLEM 8-50 (45 MINUTES)

1.

$$\text{Unit contribution margin} = \frac{\$405,000}{1,800} = \$225 \text{ per ton}$$

$$\text{Break-even volume in tons} = \frac{\text{fixed costs}}{\text{unit contribution margin}}$$

$$= \frac{\$247,500}{\$225} = 1,100 \text{ tons}$$

2.   Projected net income for sales of 2,100 tons:

Projected contribution margin (2,100 × $225)	$472,500
Projected fixed costs	247,500
Projected net income	$225,000

3.   Projected net income including foreign order:

Variable cost per ton = $495,000/1,800 = $275 per ton

Sales price per ton for regular orders = $900,000/1,800 = $500 per ton

	Foreign Order	Regular Sales
Sales in tons..	1,500	1,500
Contribution margin per ton:		
Foreign order ($450 – $275)	× $175	
Regular sales ($500 – $275)		× $225
Total contribution margin	$262,500	$337,500

Contribution margin on foreign order	$262,500
Contribution margin on regular sales	337,500
Total contribution margin	$600,000
Fixed costs	247,500
Net income	$352,500

4. New sales territory:

To maintain its current net income, Ohio Limestone Company just needs to break even on sales in the new territory.

$$\text{Break-even point in tons} = \frac{\text{fixed costs in new territory}}{\text{unit contribution margin on sales in new territory}}$$

$$= \frac{\$61,500}{\$225 - \$25} = 307.5 \text{ tons}$$

5. Automated production process:

$$\text{Break-even point in tons} = \frac{\$247,500 + \$58,500}{\$225 + \$25}$$

$$= \frac{\$306,000}{\$250} = 1,224 \text{ tons}$$

$$\text{Break-even point in sales dollars} = 1,224 \text{ tons} \times \$500 \text{ per ton}$$

$$= \$612,000$$

6. Changes in selling price and unit variable cost:

$$\text{New unit contribution margin} = (\$500)(90\%) - (\$275 + \$40)$$

$$= \$135$$

$$\text{New contribution margin ratio} = \frac{\$135}{(\$500)(90\%)}$$

$$= .30$$

$$\text{Dollar sales required to earn target net profit} = \frac{\text{fixed costs} + \text{target net profit}}{\text{contribution margin ratio}}$$

$$= \frac{\$247,500 + \$94,500}{.30}$$

$$= \$1,140,000$$

PROBLEM 8-51 (35 MINUTES)

1. $$\text{Contribution margin ratio} = \frac{\$80.00 - \$52.80}{\$80.00} = .34$$

2. Number of units of sales required to earn target after-tax income

$$= \frac{\text{fixed expenses} + \dfrac{\text{target after-tax net income}}{(1-t)}}{\text{unit contribution margin}}$$

$$X = \frac{\$316,800 + \dfrac{\$22,080}{(1-.40)}}{\$80.00 - \$52.80} = \frac{\$353,600}{\$27.20}$$

$$X = 13,000 \text{ units}$$

3. Break-even point (in units) for the mountaineering model

$$= \frac{\$369,600}{\$88.00 - \$52.80} = 10,500 \text{ units}$$

Let Y denote the variable cost of the touring model such that the break-even point for the touring model is 10,500 units.

Then we have:

$$10,500 = \frac{\$316,800}{\$80.00 - Y}$$

$$(10,500) \times (\$80.00 - Y) = \$316,800$$

$$\$840,000 - 10,500Y = \$316,800$$

$$10,500Y = \$523,200$$

$$Y = \$49.83 \text{ (rounded)}$$

Thus, the variable cost per unit would have to decrease by $2.97 ($52.80 – $49.83).

4.
$$\text{New break-even point} = \frac{\$316,800 \times 110\%}{\$80.00 - (\$52.80)(90\%)}$$

$$= \frac{\$348,480}{\$32.48}$$

$$= 10,729 \text{ units (rounded)}$$

5.   Weighted-average unit contribution margin

$$= (50\% \times \$35.20) + (50\% \times \$27.20)$$

$$= \$31.20$$

$$\text{Break-even point} = \frac{\text{fixed costs}}{\text{weighted-average unit contribution margin}}$$

$$= \frac{\$343,200}{\$31.20} = 11,000 \text{ units (or 5,500 of each type)}$$

PROBLEM 8-52 (45 MINUTES)

1.   SUMMARY OF EXPENSES

	Expenses per Year (in thousands)	
	Variable	Fixed
Manufacturing..	$ 7,200	$2,340
Selling and administrative...	2,400	1,920
Interest...		540
Costs from budgeted income statement	$ 9,600	$4,800
If the company employs its own sales force:		
Additional sales force costs		2,400
Reduced commissions [(.15 – .10) × $16,000]............	(800)	
Costs with own sales force...	$ 8,800	$7,200
If the company sells through agents:		
Deduct cost of sales force		(2,400)
Increased commissions [(.225 – .10) × $16,000]........	2,000	
Costs with agents paid increased commissions	$10,800	$4,800

PROBLEM 8-52 (CONTINUED)

$$\text{Break-even sales dollars} = \frac{\text{total fixed expenses}}{\text{contribution margin ratio}}$$

$$\text{Contribution-margin ratio} = 1 - \frac{\text{total variable expenses}}{\text{sales revenue}}$$

(a) $\text{Contribution margin ratio} = 1 - \dfrac{\$9,600,000}{\$16,000,000}$

$= 1 - .60$

$= .40$

$\text{Break-even sales dollars} = \dfrac{\$4,800,000}{.40}$

$= \$12,000,000$

(b) $\text{Contribution margin ratio} = 1 - \dfrac{\$8,800,000}{\$16,000,000}$

$= 1 - .55$

$= .45$

$\text{Break-even sales dollars} = \dfrac{\$7,200,000}{.45}$

$= \$16,000,000$

2. $\text{Required sales dollars} = \dfrac{\text{total fixed costs} + \text{target income before income taxes}}{\text{contribution margin ratio}}$

$\text{Contribution margin ratio} = 1 - \dfrac{\$10,800}{\$16,000}$

$= 1 - .675$

$= .325$

$\text{Required sales dollars to break even} = \dfrac{\$4,800,000 + \$1,600,000}{.325}$

$= \dfrac{\$6,400,000}{.325}$

$= \$19,692,308$

PROBLEM 8-52 (CONTINUED)

3.   The volume in sales dollars (X) that would result in equal net income is the volume of sales dollars where total expenses are equal.

$$\text{Total expenses with agents paid increased commission} = \text{total expenses with own sales force}$$

$$\frac{\$10,800,000}{\$16,000,000}X + \$4,800,000 = \frac{\$8,800,000}{\$16,000,000}X + \$7,200,000$$

$$.675X + \$4,800,000 = .55X + \$7,200,000$$

$$.125X = \$2,400,000$$

$$X = \$19,200,000$$

Therefore, at a sales volume of $19,200,000, the company will earn equal before-tax income under either alternative. Since before-tax income is the same, so is after-tax net income.

SOLUTIONS TO CASES

CASE 8-53 (50 MINUTES)

1.   The break-even point is 16,900 patient-days calculated as follows:

COMPUTATION OF BREAK-EVEN POINT IN PATIENT-DAYS: PEDIATRICS FOR THE YEAR ENDED JUNE 30, 20x2

Total fixed costs:	
Medical center charges	$2,900,000
Supervising nurses ($25,000 × 4)......................................	100,000
Nurses ($20,000 × 10)......................................	200,000
Aids ($9,000 × 20).......................................	180,000
Total fixed costs	$3,380,000
Contribution margin per patient-day:	
Revenue per patient-day	$300
Variable cost per patient-day:	
($6,000,000 ÷ $300 = 20,000 patient-days)	
($2,000,000 ÷ 20,000 patient-days)..................................	100
Contribution margin per patient-day	$200

$$\text{Break-even point in patient-days} = \frac{\text{total fixed costs}}{\text{contribution margin per patient-day}} = \frac{\$3,380,000}{\$200}$$

$$= 16,900 \text{ patient days}$$

CASE 8-53 (CONTINUED)

2. Net earnings would decrease by $606,660, calculated as follows:

**COMPUTATION OF LOSS FROM RENTAL
OF ADDITIONAL 20 BEDS: PEDIATRICS
FOR THE YEAR ENDED JUNE 30, 20X2**

Increase in revenue	
(20 additional beds × 90 days × $300 charge per day)	$ 540,000
Increase in expenses:	
Variable charges by medical center	
(20 additional beds × 90 days × $100 per day)	$ 180,000
Fixed charges by medical center	
($2,900,000 ÷ 60 beds = $48,333 per bed, rounded)	
($48,333 × 20 beds)	966,660
Salaries	
(20,000 patient-days before additional 20 beds + 20 additional	
beds × 90 days = 21,800, which does not exceed 22,000 patient-days;	
therefore, no additional personnel are required)	-0-
Total increase in expenses	$1,146,660
Net change in earnings from rental of additional 20 beds...................................	$ (606,660)

CASE 8-54 (45 MINUTES)

1. a. In order to break even, Oakley must sell 500 units. This amount represents the point where revenue equals total costs.

   $\text{Revenue} = \text{variable costs} + \text{fixed costs}$

   $\$400X = \$200X + \$100,000$

   $\$200X = \$100,000$

   $X = 500 \text{ units}$

   b. In order to achieve its after-tax profit objective, Oakley must sell 2,500 units. This amount represents the point where revenue equals total costs plus the before-tax profit objective.

   $\text{Revenue} = \text{variable costs} + \text{fixed costs} + \text{before - tax profit}$

   $\$400X = \$200X + \$100,000 + [\$240,000 \div (1 - .4)]$

   $\$400X = \$200X + \$100,000 + \$400,000$

   $\$200X = \$500,000$

   $X = 2,500 \text{ units}$

2. To achieve its annual after-tax profit objective, Oakley should select the first alternative, where the sales price is reduced by $40 and 2,700 units are sold during the remainder of the year. This alternative results in the highest profit and is the only alternative that equals or exceeds the company's profit objective. Calculations for the three alternatives follow.

CASE 8-54 (CONTINUED)

Alternative (1):

$$Re \, venue = (\$400)(350) + (\$360)(2,700)$$
$$= \$1,112,000$$
$$Variable \, cost = \$200 \times 3,050$$
$$= \$610,000$$
$$Before \text{-} tax \, profit = \$1,112,000 - \$610,000 - \$100,000$$
$$= \$402,000$$
$$After \text{-} tax \, profit = \$402,000 \times (1 - .4)$$
$$= \$241,200$$

Alternative (2):

$$Re \, venue = (\$400)(350) + (\$370)(2,200)$$
$$= \$954,000$$
$$Variable \, cost = (\$200)(350) \times (\$175)(2,200)$$
$$= \$455,000$$
$$Before \text{-} tax \, profit = \$954,000 - \$455,000 - \$100,000$$
$$= \$399,000$$
$$After \text{-} tax \, profit = \$399,000 \times (1 - .4)$$
$$= \$239,400$$

Alternative (3):

$$Re \, venue = (\$400)(350) + (\$380)(2,000)$$
$$= \$900,000$$
$$Variable \, cost = \$200 \times 2,350$$
$$= \$470,000$$
$$Before \text{-} tax \, profit = \$900,000 - \$470,000 - \$90,000$$
$$= \$340,000$$
$$After \text{-} tax \, profit = \$340,000 \times (1 - .4)$$
$$= \$204,000$$

CASE 8-55 (50 MINUTES)

1. Break-even point for 20x2, based on current budget:

$$\text{Contribution-margin ratio} = \frac{\$10,000,000 - \$6,000,000 - \$2,000,000}{\$10,000,000} = .20$$

$$\text{Break-even point} = \frac{\text{fixed expenses}}{\text{contribution-margin ratio}}$$

$$= \frac{\$100,000}{.20} = \$500,000$$

2. Break-even point given employment of sales personnel:

New fixed expenses:

Previous fixed expenses...	$	100,000
Sales personnel salaries...		90,000
Sales manager's salary		160,000
Total	$	350,000

New contribution-margin ratio:

Sales...	$10,000,000
Cost of goods sold	6,000,000
Gross margin	$ 4,000,000
Commissions (at 5%)	500,000
Contribution margin	$ 3,500,000

$$\text{Contribution-margin ratio} = \frac{\$3,500,000}{\$10,000,000} = .35$$

$$\text{Estimated break-even point} = \frac{\text{fixed expenses}}{\text{contribution-margin ratio}}$$

$$= \frac{\$350,000}{.35} = \$1,000,000$$

CASE 8-55 (CONTINUED)

3. Assuming a 25% sales commission:

New contribution-margin ratio:

Sales..	$10,000,000
Cost of goods sold	6,000,000
Gross margin	$ 4,000,000
Commissions (at 25%)	2,500,000
Contribution margin	$ 1,500,000

$$\text{Contribution-margin ratio} = \frac{\$1,500,000}{\$10,000,000} = .15$$

$$
\begin{array}{l}
\text{Sales volume in dollars} \\
\text{required to earn after-tax} \\
\text{net income}
\end{array}
= \frac{\text{fixed expenses} + \dfrac{\text{target after-tax net income}}{(1-t)}}{\text{contribution-margin ratio}}
$$

$$
= \frac{\$100,000 + \dfrac{\$1,330,000}{(1-.3)}}{.15} = \frac{\$2,000,000}{.15}
$$

$$= \$13,333,333 \text{ (rounded)}$$

Check (all figures rounded to the nearest dollar):

Sales		$ 13,333,333
Cost of goods sold (60% of sales)		8,000,000
Gross margin		$ 5,333,333
Selling and administrative expenses:		
Commissions	$ 3,333,333	
All other expenses (fixed).............................	100,000	3,433,333
Income before taxes		$ 1,900,000
Income tax expense (30%).................................		570,000
Net income		$ 1,330,000

CASE 8-55 (CONTINUED)

4. Sales dollar volume at which Niagra Falls Sporting Goods Company is indifferent:

    Let X denote the desired volume of sales.

    Since the tax rate is the same regardless of which approach management chooses, we can find X so that the company's before-tax income is the same under the two alternatives. (In the following equations, the contribution-margin ratios of .35 and .15, respectively, were computed in the preceding two requirements.)

$$.35X - \$350,000 = .15X - \$100,000$$
$$.20X = \$250,000$$
$$X = \$250,000/.20$$
$$X = \$1,250,000$$

Thus, the company will have the same before-tax income under the two alternatives if the sales volume is $1,250,000.

Check:

	Alternatives	
	Employ Sales Personnel	Pay 25% Commission
Sales..	$1,250,000	$1,250,000
Cost of goods sold (60% of sales)	750,000	750,000
Gross margin..	$ 500,000	$ 500,000
Selling and administrative expenses:		
Commissions	62,500*	312,500†
All other expenses (fixed).................................	350,000	100,000
Income before taxes	$ 87,500	$ 87,500
Income tax expense (30%).....................................	26,250	26,250
Net income...	$ 61,250	$ 61,250

*$1,250,000 × 5% = $62,500
†$1,250,000 × 25% = $312,500

CURRENT ISSUES IN MANAGERIAL ACCOUNTING

ISSUE 8-56

"RELIANCE GROUP MAY SEE SHIELD FROM CREDITORS," *THE WALL STREET JOURNAL*, AUGUST 15, 2000, DEVON SPURGON, GREGORY ZUCKERMAN, AND FRANCINE L. POPE.

1. Managers apply operating leverage to convert small changes in sales into large changes in a firm's profitability. Fixed costs are the lever that managers use to take a small increase in sales and obtain a much larger increase in net income. Having a cost structure with relatively high fixed costs provides rewards and risks to a firm. With a high degree of operating leverage, each additional sale decreases the average cost per unit. Each dollar of revenue becomes pure profit once the fixed costs are covered. This is beneficial if sales are increasing; however, the reverse is true if sales are decreasing. With decreasing sales, the fixed costs do not decrease, and profit declines significantly more than revenue.

2. In the article, high operating leverage was not working to benefit Reliance Group Holdings, Inc. Consequently, its stock rating was downgraded.

ISSUE 8-57

"E-COMMERCE -- DEBATE -- TALKING TO THE PLAYERS: WILL THE INTERNET TAKE OVER COMMERCE? WE ASKED THREE PEOPLE WHO ASK THEMSELVES THAT QUESTION ALL THE TIME," *THE WALL STREET JOURNAL*, JULY 12, 1999, THOMAS E. WEBER.

According to Ken Seiff, Amazon is capturing such a huge amount of market share that it will eventually be able to build the most cost efficient distribution system, not only in the e-commerce field, but also in the traditional retail world. Once Amazon has developed this system and cemented its place as the online retailer of choice, price wars will not be as costly for Amazon as for its competitors.

ISSUE 8-58

"HAPPY SHOPPER," *MANAGEMENT ACCOUNTING*, JULY/AUGUST 2000, TONY BRABAZON.

The cost of losing a customer will vary across the customer life cycle. The loss can be estimated using discounted customer contribution margin, where the discounted customer contribution margin is calculated as the gross profit per customer less customer-related costs such as administration, distribution and financing.

ISSUE 8-59

"POSTAL SERVICE COULD FACE LOSS," *THE ASSOCIATED PRESS*, AUGUST 31, 2000, RANDOLPH E. SCHMID.

1. It is important for the U.S. Postal Service to forecast the volume and cost variables discussed in the article so its management can determine the revenue required to cover costs and determine cost of postage.

2. Unexpected costs will increase the break-even point in cost-volume-profit analysis. A decline in the volume of first-class mail will decrease the weighted-average contribution margin and increase the break-even point. An increase in advertising mail will increase revenue and decrease the breakeven point.

ISSUE 8-60

"START YOUR OWN FIRM," *JOURNAL OF ACCOUNTANCY*, MAY 2000, ROBERT B. SCOTT, JR.

1. The contribution margin is defined as sales revenue less all variable costs.

2. For a CPA firm, as described in the article, the contribution margin would be calculated as a client's total fees less all direct-service costs, such as staff time. According to the article, a client who generates total fees that are one and one half times the cost to service the engagement, especially a large client, may be worth keeping and developing. If the CPA is unable to recover at least one and one half times the direct-service cost, the CPA should consider ending the relationship.

ISSUE 8-61

"CHAIN REACTION," *CMA MANAGEMENT*, MARCH 1999, ANDREA SIGURDSON.

1. Cost-volume-profit analysis is a study of the relationships between sales volume, expenses, revenue, and profit.

2. CVP analysis can be applied to determine the effectiveness of an investment, for example, in seasonal price discounting or price specials. In price-sensitive categories, managers can use detailed studies of consumer price elasticity to better understand the ongoing relationship between pricing, volume and category profits. The principles of activity-based management applied to product categories can help management understand the actual costs of distribution and warehousing at the individual item level. A true picture of category and subcategory profitability can then be determined. Real estate and occupancy costs are also charged back to product categories within the store to develop a comprehensive picture of total profit or loss for each category. Using this information, retailers can assign strategic roles to each product category. High profile ones, although not always strong profit contributors, can help build overall customer traffic. Assigning clear category roles aids in the decision making process when allocating investment resources or scarce retail space among competing product categories.

CHAPTER 9
Profit Planning, Activity-Based Budgeting, and e-Budgeting

ANSWERS TO REVIEW QUESTIONS

9-1 A master budget, or profit plan, is a comprehensive set of budgets covering all phases of an organization's operations for a specified period of time. The master budget includes the following parts: sales budget, operational budgets (including a production budget, inventory budgets, a labor budget, an overhead budget, a selling and administrative expense budget, and a cash budget), and budgeted financial statements (including a budgeted income statement, budgeted balance sheet, and budgeted statement of cash flows).

9-2 A budget facilitates communication and coordination by making each manager throughout the organization aware of the plans made by other managers. The budgeting process pulls together the plans of each manager in the organization.

9-3 An example of using the budget to allocate resources in a university is found in the area of research funds and grants. Universities typically have a limited amount of research-support resources that must be allocated among the various colleges and divisions within the university. This allocation process often takes place within the context of the budgeting process.

9-4 The flowchart on the following page depicts the components of the master budget for a service station.

9-5 General economic trends are important in forecasting sales in the airline industry. The overall health of the economy is an important factor affecting the extent of business travel. In addition, the health of the economy, inflation, and income levels affect the extent to which the general public travels by air.

9-6 Operational budgets specify how an organization's operations will be carried out to meet the demand for its goods and services. The operational budgets prepared in a hospital would include a labor budget showing the number of professional personnel of various types required to carry out the hospital's mission, an overhead budget listing planned expenditures for such costs as utilities and maintenance, and a cash budget showing planned cash receipts and disbursements.

Flowchart for Review Question 9-4

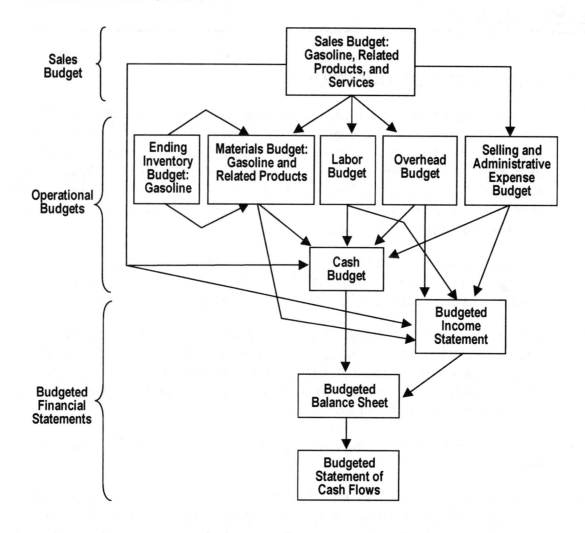

9-7   Application of activity-based costing to the budgeting process yields activity-based budgeting (ABB). Under ABB, the first step is to specify the products or services to be produced and the customers to be served. Then the activities necessary to produce these products and services are determined. Finally the resources needed to perform the specified activities are determined. ABB differs from traditional budgeting in the emphasis that it places on activities and its use of activity-based costing data in the budgeting process.

9-8   E-budgeting stands for an electronic and enterprise-wide budgeting process. Under this approach the information needed to construct a budget is gathered via the Internet from individuals and subunits located throughout the enterprise. The Internet also is used to disseminate the resulting budget schedules and information to authorized users throughout the enterprise.

9-9   The city of New York could use budgeting for planning purposes in many ways. For example, the city's personnel budget would be important in planning for required employees in the police and fire departments. The city's capital budget would be used in planning for the replacement of the city's vehicles, computers, administrative buildings, and traffic control equipment. The city's cash budget would be important in planning for cash receipts and disbursements. It is important for any organization, including a municipal government, to make sure that it has enough cash on hand to meet its cash needs at all times.

9-10   The budget director, or chief budget officer, specifies the process by which budget data will be gathered, collects the information, and prepares the master budget. To communicate budget procedures and deadlines to employees throughout the organization, the budget director often develops and disseminates a budget manual.

9-11   The budget manual says who is responsible for providing various types of information, when the information is required, and what form the information is to take. The budget manual also states who should receive each schedule when the master budget is complete.

9-12   A company's board of directors generally has final approval over the master budget. By exercising its authority to make changes in the budget and grant final approval, the board of directors can wield considerable influence on the overall direction the organization takes. Since the budget is used as a resource-allocation mechanism, the board of directors can emphasize some programs and curtail or eliminate others by allocating funds through the budgeting process.

9-13   Under zero-base budgeting, the budget for virtually every activity in the organization is initially set to zero. To receive funding during the budgeting process, each activity must be justified in terms of its continued usefulness. The zero-base budgeting approach forces management to rethink each phase of an organization's operations before allocating resources.

9-14   A master budget is based on many assumptions and predictions of unknown parameters. For example, the sales budget is built on an assumption about the nature of demand for goods or services. The direct-material budget requires an estimate of the direct-material price and the quantity of material required per unit of production. Many other assumptions are used throughout the rest of the budgeting process.

9-15   The difference between the revenue or cost projection that a person provides in the budgeting process and a realistic estimate of the revenue or cost is called budgetary slack. Building budgetary slack into the budget is called padding the budget. A significant problem caused by budgetary slack is that the budget ceases to be an accurate portrayal of likely future events. Cost estimates are often inflated, and revenue estimates are often understated. In this situation, the budget loses its effectiveness as a planning tool.

9-16   An organization can reduce the problem of budgetary slack in several ways. First, it can avoid relying on the budget as a negative, evaluative tool. Second, managers can be given incentives not only to achieve budgetary projections but also to provide accurate projections.

9-17   The idea of participative budgeting is to involve employees throughout an organization in the budgetary process. Such participation can give employees the feeling that "this is our budget," rather than the feeling that "this is the budget you imposed on us." When employees feel that they were part of the budgeting process, they are more likely to strive to achieve the budget.

9-18   This comment is occasionally heard from people who have started and run their own small business for a long period of time. These individuals have great knowledge in their minds about running their business. They feel that they do not need to spend a great deal of time on the budgeting process, because they can essentially run the business by feel. This approach can result in several problems. First, if the person who is running the business is sick or traveling, he or she is not available to make decisions and implement plans that could have been clarified by a budget. Second, the purposes of budgeting are important to the effective running of an organization. Budgets facilitate communication and coordination, are useful in resource allocation, and help in evaluating performance and providing incentives to employees. It is difficult to achieve these benefits without a budgeting process.

9-19 In developing a budget to meet your college expenses, the primary steps would be to project your cash receipts and your cash disbursements. Your cash receipts could come from such sources as summer jobs, jobs held during the academic year, college funds saved by relatives or friends for your benefit, scholarships, and financial aid from your college or university. You would also need to carefully project your college expenses. Your expenses would include tuition, room and board, books and other academic supplies, transportation, clothing and other personal needs, and money for entertainment and miscellaneous expenses.

9-20 Firms with international operations face a variety of additional challenges in preparing their budgets.

- A multinational firm's budget must reflect the translation of foreign currencies into U.S. dollars. Almost all the world's currencies fluctuate in their values relative to the dollar, and this fluctuation makes budgeting for those translations difficult.

- It is difficult to prepare budgets when inflation is high or unpredictable. Some foreign countries have experienced hyperinflation, sometimes with annual inflation rates well over 100 percent. Predicting such high inflation rates is difficult and complicates a multinational's budgeting process.

- The economies of all countries fluctuate in terms of consumer demand, availability of skilled labor, laws affecting commerce, and so forth. Companies with foreign operations face the task of anticipating such changing conditions in their budgeting processes.

9-21 The five phases in a product's life cycle are as follows:

(a) Product planning and concept design

(b) Preliminary design

(c) Detailed design and testing

(d) Production

(e) Distribution and customer service

It is important to budget these costs as early as possible in order to ensure that the revenue a product generates over its life cycle will cover all of the costs to be incurred. A large portion of a product's life-cycle costs will be committed well before they are actually incurred.

9-22　(a) Ordering costs: The cost of preparing, placing, and receiving a purchase order. (Examples include the clerical costs of preparing purchase orders, time spent finding suppliers and expediting orders, transportation, and receiving costs, such as unloading and inspection.)

(b) Holding costs: The cost incurred in keeping inventory on hand for some period of time. (Examples include the costs of storage space such as a warehouse, depreciation, security, insurance, forgone interest on working capital tied up in inventory, and the costs of deterioration and theft.)

(c) Shortage costs: The cost incurred by the organization when it does not have materials or finished goods on hand when needed. (Examples include the costs caused by disrupted production when raw materials are unavailable, lost sales, dissatisfied customers, and the loss of quantity discounts on purchases.)

9-23　The EOQ approach assumes that some inventory must be held. The objective of the model is to balance the cost of ordering against the cost of holding inventory. In contrast, the JIT philosophy is to reduce all inventories to the absolute minimum, eliminating them completely if possible. The JIT viewpoint asserts that inventory holding costs tend to be higher than may be apparent because of the inefficiency and waste involved in storing inventory. This view, coupled with the JIT goal of reducing ordering costs to very low amounts, results in the desirability of more frequent and smaller order quantities.

In addition, under JIT inventory management, order quantities typically will vary depending on requirements. In contrast, under the EOQ model, the order quantity remains constant.

SOLUTIONS TO EXERCISES

EXERCISE 9-24 (20 MINUTES)

1.

	April	May	June
Sales	$80,000	$60,000	$90,000[a]
Cash receipts:			
From cash sales..................................	$ 40,000[b]	$ 30,000[c]	$ 45,000
From sales on account.........................	36,000[d]	34,000	39,000[e]
Total cash receipts...................................	$ 76,000	$ 64,000	$ 84,000

[a]$90,000 = $45,000 × 2

[b]$40,000 = $80,000 × .5

[c]$30,000 = $60,000 × .5

[d]$36,000 = ($40,000 × .6) + ($30,000 × .4)

[e]$39,000 = ($45,000 × .6) + ($30,000 × .4)

2.

Accounts payable, 12/31/x0	300,000DM
Purchases of goods and services on account during 20x1	1,200,000DM
Payments of accounts payable during 20x1	(1,100,000DM)*
Accounts payable, 12/31/x1	400,000DM

*1,100,000DM = 300,000DM + 1,200,000DM – 400,000DM

3.

Accounts receivable, 12/31/x0	340,000y
Sales on account during 20x1	900,000y
Collections of accounts receivable during 20x1...................................	(780,000y)
Accounts receivable, 12/31/x1	460,000y

4.

Accumulated depreciation, 12/31/x0...	$ 810,000
Depreciation expense during 20x1..	150,000
Accumulated depreciation, 12/31/x1	$ 960,000

5.

Retained earnings, 12/31/x0...	$ 2,050,000
Net income for 20x1	400,000
Dividends paid in 20x1	-0-
Retained earnings, 12/31/x1	$ 2,450,000

EXERCISE 9-25 (30 MINUTES)

Answers will vary widely, depending on the governmental unit selected and the budgetary items on which the student focuses. In the past, students have expressed surprise at the proportion of the U.S. federal budget that goes to entitlement programs (e.g., Social Security and Medicare), interest expense, and the military.

EXERCISE 9-26 (15 MINUTES)

1. Production (in units) required for the year:

Sales for the year	480,000
Add: Desired ending finished-goods inventory on December 31	50,000
Deduct: Beginning finished-goods inventory on January 1......................	80,000
Required production during the year...	450,000

2. Purchases of raw material (in units), assuming production of 500,000 finished units:

Raw material required for production (500,000 × 2)...................................	1,000,000
Add: Desired ending inventory on December 31	45,000
Deduct: Beginning inventory on January 1..	35,000
Required raw-material purchases during the year	1,010,000

EXERCISE 9-27 (25 MINUTES)

1. Cash collections in October:

Month of Sale	Amount Collected in October	
July	$ 60,000 × 4%	$ 2,400
August..	70,000 × 10%	7,000
September...	80,000 × 15%	12,000
October...	90,000 × 70%	63,000
Total...		$84,400

Notice that the amount of sales on account in June, $49,000 was not needed to solve the exercise.

EXERCISE 9-27 (CONTINUED)

2.   Cash collections in fourth quarter from credit sales in fourth quarter.

		Amount Collected		
Month of Sale	Credit Sales	October	November	December
October...	$ 90,000	$ 63,000	$13,500	$ 9,000
November.......................................	100,000	–	70,000	15,000
December	85,000	–	–	59,500
Total..		$ 63,000	$83,500	$ 83,500
Total collections in fourth quarter from credit sales in fourth quarter...				$230,000

EXERCISE 9-28 (20 MINUTES)

1. The total required production is 655,720 units, computed as follows:

	Budgeted Sales (in units)	Planned Ending Inventory (in units)
June		160,000 (200,000 × 80%)
July	200,000 (given)	
August	210,000 (200,000 × 1.05)	
September	220,500 (210,000 × 1.05)	185,220 (231,525 × 80%)
October	231,525 (220,500 × 1.05)	

Sales in units:

July	200,000
August...	210,000
September..	220,500
Total for third quarter	630,500
Add: Desired ending inventory, September 30	185,220
Subtotal..	815,720
Deduct: Desired ending inventory, June 30............................	160,000
Total required production	655,720

2.
Assumed production during third quarter (in units)	600,000
Raw-material requirements per unit of product (in pounds)	× 4
Raw material required for production in third quarter (in pounds)	2,400,000
Add: Desired ending raw-material inventory, September 30 (2,400,000 × 25%)...	600,000
Subtotal..	3,000,000
Deduct: Ending raw-material inventory, June 30......................................	700,000
Raw material to be purchased during third quarter (in pounds)..............	2,300,000
Cost per pound of raw material	× $1.15
Total raw-material purchases during third quarter..................................	$2,645,000

EXERCISE 9-29 (20 MINUTES)

1.
BINGHAMTON FILM CORPORATION
EXPECTED CASH COLLECTIONS
AUGUST

Month	Sales	Percent	Expected Collections
June...	$60,000	9%	$ 5,400
July..	78,000	20%	15,600
August...	66,000	70%	46,200
Total			$67,200

2.
BINGHAMTON FILM CORPORATION
EXPECTED CASH DISBURSEMENTS
AUGUST

July purchases to be paid in August	$ 54,000
Less: 2% cash discount	1,080
Net	$ 52,920
Cash disbursements for expenses	14,400
Total	$ 67,320

3.
BINGHAMTON CORPORATION
EXPECTED CASH BALANCE
AUGUST 31

Balance, August 1	$ 22,000
Add: Expected collections	67,200
Less: Expected disbursements	67,320
Expected balance	$ 21,880

EXERCISE 9-30 (20 MINUTES)

Memorandum

Date: Today

To: President, East Bank of Mississippi

From: I.M. Student and Associates

Subject: Budgetary slack

Budgetary slack is the difference between a budget estimate that a person provides and a realistic estimate. The practice of creating budgetary slack is called padding the budget. The primary negative consequence of slack is that it undermines the credibility and usefulness of the budget as a planning and control tool. When a budget includes slack, the amounts in the budget no longer portray a realistic view of future operations.

The bank's bonus system for the new accounts manager tends to encourage budgetary slack. Since the manager's bonus is determined by the number of new accounts generated over the budgeted number, the manager has an incentive to understate her projection of the number of new accounts. The description of the new accounts manager's behavior shows evidence of such understatement. A 10 percent increase over the bank's current 10,000 accounts would mean 1,000 new accounts in 20x2. Yet the new accounts manager's projection is only 700 new accounts. This projection will make it more likely that the actual number of new accounts will exceed the budgeted number.

EXERCISE 9-31 (20 MINUTES)

1.

	Total Sales in January 20x2		
	$100,000	$130,000	$160,000
Cash receipts in January, 20x2			
From December sales on account...........	$ 7,125*	$ 7,125	$ 7,125
From January cash sales.........................	75,000†	97,500	120,000
From January sales on account...............	20,000**	26,000	32,000
Total cash receipts	$ 102,125	$130,625	$159,125

*$7,125 = $190,000 × .25 × .15
†$75,000 = $100,000 × .75
**$20,000 = $100,000 × .25 × .80

2. Operational plans depend on various assumptions. Usually there is uncertainty about these assumptions, such as sales demand or inflation rates. Financial planning helps management answer "what if" questions about how the budget will look under various sets of assumptions.

EXERCISE 9-32 (30 MINUTES)

1. Budgeted cash collections for December:

Month of Sale	Collections in December	
November..	$200,000 × 38%	$ 76,000
December..	220,000 × 60%	132,000
Total cash collections		$208,000

2. Budgeted income (loss) for December:

Sales revenue..		$220,000
Less: Cost of goods sold (75% of sales)..........................		165,000
Gross margin (25% of sales)...		$ 55,000
Less: Operating expenses:		
Bad debts expense (2% of sales)............................	$ 4,400	
Depreciation ($216,000/12)	18,000	
Other expenses...	22,600	
Total operating expenses		45,000
Income before taxes		$ 10,000

EXERCISE 9-32 (CONTINUED)

3. Projected balance in accounts payable on December 31:

The December 31 balance in accounts payable will be equal to December's purchases of merchandise. Since the store's gross margin is 25 percent of sales, its cost of goods sold must be 75 percent of sales.

Month	Sales	Cost of Goods Sold	Amount Purchased in December	
December....................	$220,000	$165,000	$165,000 × 20%	$ 33,000
January	200,000	150,000	150,000 × 80%	120,000
Total December purchases				$153,000

Therefore, the December 31 balance in accounts payable will be $153,000.

EXERCISE 9-33 (25 MINUTES)

1. Direct professional labor budget for the month of June:

Office visits per month = 48,000/12 = 4,000

Professional services in June:

One-hour visits (20% × 4,000 × 1 hr.).....................................	800	hours
Half-hour visits (80% × 4,000 × 1/2 hr.)..............................	1,600	hours
Total direct professional labor	2,400	hours
Hourly rate for dental associates	× $ 60	
Total direct professional labor cost.....................................	$144,000	

EXERCISE 9-33 (CONTINUED)

2. Cash collections during June:

	May	June
Half-hour visits (4,000 × 80%)...	3,200	3,200
Billing rate..	× $40	× $40
Total billings for half-hour visits	$128,000	$128,000
One-hour visits (4,000 × 20%)...	800	800
Billing rate..	× $70	× $70
Total billings for one-hour visits	$ 56,000	$ 56,000
Total billings during month..	$184,000	$184,000
Percentage of month's billings collected		
during June	× 10%	× 90%
Collections during June...	$ 18,400	$165,600
Total collections in June ($18,400 + $165,600)		$184,000

3. Overhead and administrative expense budget for June:

Patient registration and records (4,000 visits × $2.00 per visit) ...	$ 8,000
Other overhead and administrative expenses	
(2,400 hours × $5.00 per hour)	12,000
Total overhead and administrative expenses.........	$20,000

EXERCISE 9-34 (15 MINUTES)

$$EOQ = \sqrt{\frac{(2)(\text{annual requirement})(\text{cost per order})}{\text{annual holding cost per unit}}}$$

Case A : $EOQ = \sqrt{\dfrac{(2)(13,230)(\$250)}{\$6}} = \sqrt{1,102,500} = 1,050$

Case B : $EOQ = \sqrt{\dfrac{(2)(1,681)(\$40)}{\$20}} = \sqrt{6,724} = 82$

Case C : $EOQ = \sqrt{\dfrac{(2)(560)(\$10)}{\$7}} = \sqrt{1,600} = 40$

EXERCISE 9-35 (10 MINUTES)

1. Safety stock:

    The lead time is one month, so the safety stock is equal to the difference between average monthly usage and the maximum usage in a month. Average monthly usage is 65 tons (780/12), and the maximum usage is 80 tons. Therefore, the safety stock is 15 tons (80 – 65).

2. Reorder point:

    The reorder point is 80 tons. This is the maximum amount of the bonding agent that would be used in a month, which is the time required to receive an order after it is placed.

SOLUTIONS TO PROBLEMS

PROBLEM 9-36 (40 MINUTES)

1. Production and direct-labor budgets

SPIFFY SHADES CORPORATION
BUDGET FOR PRODUCTION AND DIRECT LABOR
FOR THE FIRST QUARTER OF 20X1

	Month			Quarter
	January	February	March	
Sales (units)...	10,000	12,000	8,000	30,000
Add: Ending inventory*..............................	16,000	12,500	13,500	13,500
Total needs..	26,000	24,500	21,500	43,500
Deduct: Beginning inventory........................	16,000	16,000	12,500	16,000
Units to be produced..................................	10,000	8,500	9,000	27,500
Direct-labor hours per unit...........................	× 1	× 1	× .75	
Total hours of direct labor time needed..	10,000	8,500	6,750	25,250
Direct-labor costs:				
Wages ($16.00 per DLH)†..........................	$160,000	$136,000	$108,000	$404,000
Pension contributions ($.50 per DLH)	5,000	4,250	3,375	12,625
Workers' compensation insurance ($.20 per DLH)	2,000	1,700	1,350	5,050
Employee medical insurance ($.80 per DLH)	8,000	6,800	5,400	20,200
Employer's social security (at 7%)	11,200	9,520	7,560	28,280
Total direct-labor cost.................................	$186,200	$158,270	$125,685	$470,155

*100 percent of the first following month's sales plus 50 percent of the second following month's sales.

†DLH denotes direct-labor hour.

PROBLEM 9-36 (CONTINUED)

2.   Use of data throughout the master budget:

Components of the master budget, other than the production budget and the direct-labor budget, that would also use the sales data include the following:

- Sales budget

- Cost-of-goods-sold budget

- Selling and administrative expense budget

Components of the master budget, other than the production budget and the direct-labor budget, that would also use the production data include the following:

- Direct-material budget

- Manufacturing-overhead budget

- Cost-of-goods-sold budget

Components of the master budget, other than the production budget and the direct-labor budget, that would also use the direct-labor-hour data include the following:

- Manufacturing-overhead budget (for determining the overhead application rate)

Components of the master budget, other than the production budget and the direct-labor budget, that would also use the direct-labor cost data include the following:

- Manufacturing-overhead budget (for determining the overhead application rate)

- Cost-of-goods-sold budget

- Cash budget

- Budgeted income statement

PROBLEM 9-36 (CONTINUED)

3. Manufacturing overhead budget:

SPIFFY SHADES CORPORATION
MANUFACTURING OVERHEAD BUDGET
FOR THE FIRST QUARTER OF 20X1

	Month			
	January	February	March	Quarter
Shipping and handling	$ 20,000	$ 24,000	$16,000	$ 60,000
Purchasing, material handling, and inspection............................	30,000	25,500	27,000	82,500
Other overhead	70,000	59,500	47,250	176,750
Total manufacturing overhead ..	$120,000	$109,000	$90,250	$319,250

PROBLEM 9-37 (25 MINUTES)

1. Tuition revenue budget:

Current student enrollment..........................	8,000
Add: 5% increase in student body...............	400
Total student body.....................................	8,400
Less: Tuition-free scholarships...................	120
Tuition-paying students...............................	8,280
Credit hours per student per year................	x 30
Total credit hours......................................	248,400
Tuition rate per hour..................................	x $75
Forecasted tuition revenue.........................	$18,630,000

2. Faculty needed to cover classes:

Total student body.......................................	8,400
Classes per student per year [(15 credit hours ÷ 3 credit hours) x 2 semesters]......................	x 10
Total student class enrollments to be covered....	84,000
Students per class...	÷ 25
Classes to be taught......................................	3,360
Classes taught per professor............................	÷ 5
Faculty needed..	672

PROBLEM 9-37 (CONTINUED)

3. Possible actions might include:
   - Hire part-time instructors
   - Use graduate teaching assistants
   - Increase the teaching load for each professor
   - Increase class size and reduce the number of sections to be offered
   - Have students take an Internet-based course offered by another university
   - Shift courses to a summer session

4. No. While the number of faculty may be a key driver, the number of faculty is highly dependent on the number of students. Students (and tuition revenue) are akin to sales—the starting point in the budgeting process.

PROBLEM 9-38 (30 MINUTES)

1. Schedule of cash collections:

	January	February	March
Collection of accounts receivable:			
$55,000 x 20%.....................................	$ 11,000		
Collection of January sales ($150,000):			
60% in January; 35% in February	90,000	$ 52,500	
Collection of February sales ($180,000):			
60% in February; 35% in March........		108,000	$ 63,000
Collection of March sales ($185,000):			
60% in March; 35% in April...............			111,000
Sale of equipment................................			5,000
Total cash collections......................	$101,000	$160,500	$179,000

2. Schedule of cash disbursements:

	January	February	March
Payment of accounts payable.....................	$ 22,000		
Payment of January purchases ($90,000):			
70% in January; 30% in February...........	63,000	$ 27,000	
Payment of February purchases ($100,000):			
70% in February; 30% in March..............		70,000	$ 30,000
Payment of March purchases ($140,000):			
70% in March; 30% in April....................			98,000
Cash operating costs................................	31,000	24,000	45,000
Total cash disbursements....................	$116,000	$121,000	$173,000

PROBLEM 9-38 (CONTINUED)

3.   Schedule of cash needs:

	January	February	March
Beginning cash balance............................	$ 20,000	$ 20,000	$ 44,300
Total receipts...	101,000	160,500	179,000
Subtotal...	$121,000	$180,500	$223,300
Less: Total disbursements........................	116,000	121,000	173,000
Cash excess (deficiency) before financing...	$ 5,000	$ 59,500	$ 50,300
Financing:			
Borrowing to maintain $20,000 balance..	15,000		
Loan principal repaid............................		(15,000)	
Loan interest paid.................................		(200)*	
Ending cash balance.................................	$ 20,000	$ 44,300	$ 50,300

* $15,000 x 8% x 2/12

PROBLEM 9-39 (45 MINUTES)

1.   Income statement for the two months ended March 31, 20x1:

Sales revenue ($250,000 + $260,000).............		$510,000
Cost of goods sold ($510,000 x 70%).............		357,000
Gross margin...		$153,000
Operating expenses:		
Cash operating expenses ($50,000 x 2)...	$100,000	
Depreciation ($12,000 x 2)......................	24,000	124,000
Net income...		$ 29,000

PROBLEM 9-39 (CONTINUED)

2. Balance sheet as of March 31, 20x1:

Assets:

Cash..	$114,000
Accounts receivable...........................	91,000
Merchandise inventory........................	14,000
Land..	62,000
Plant & equipment (net).......................	56,000
Total assets..................................	$337,000

Liabilities & stockholders' equity:

Accounts payable...............................	$180,000
Loan payable....................................	57,000
Common stock...................................	140,000
Retained earnings..............................	(40,000)
Total liabilities & stockholders' equity...	$337,000

Supporting calculations:

Cash: $22,000^a + $84,000^b + ($250,000 x 65\%)^c + ($250,000 x 35\%)^d + ($260,000 x 65\%)^e - $150,000^f - ($260,000 x 60\%)^g - $50,000^h - $50,000^h - $5,000^i = $114,000

[a]1/31/01 Cash balance
[b]1/31/01 Accounts Receivable balance
[c]65% of February sales
[d]35% of February sales
[e]65% of March sales
[f]1/31/01 Accounts Payable balance
[g]60% of March sales
[h]Monthly operating expenses
[i]Down payment on land purchase

Accounts receivable: 35% of March sales, or $260,000 x .35 = $91,000

Alternatively, a more detailed approach follows:
Accounts receivable: $84,000 - $84,000 + $250,000 – ($250,000 x 65%) + $260,000 – ($250,000 x 35%) – ($260,000 x 65%) = $91,000

Merchandise inventory: $35,000 + ($260,000 \times 60\%)^a$ – ($250,000 \times 70\%)^b$ + ($300,000 \times 60\%)^c$ – ($260,000 \times 70\%)^d$ = $14,000

[a]February purchases = 60% of March sales
[b]February cost of goods sold = 70% of February sales
[c]March purchases = 60% of April sales
[d]March cost of goods sold = 70% of March sales

Land: $0 + $62,000 = $62,000
Plant & equipment: $80,000 - $12,000 - $12,000 = $56,000
Accounts payable: $150,000 - $150,000 + ($260,000 \times 60\%)$ – ($260,000 \times 60\%)$ + ($300,000 \times 60\%)$ = $180,000
Loan payable: $0 + ($62,000 - $5,000) = $57,000
Common stock: $140,000
Retained earnings: $(69,000) + $250,000 + $260,000 – ($250,000 \times 70\%)$ – ($260,000 \times 70\%)$ - $50,000 - $50,000 - $12,000 - $12,000 = $(40,000)

3. Metroplex began February with a debit balance in Retained Earnings (i.e., a deficit), presumably because of cumulative losses. By the end of March, the deficit had been trimmed from $69,000 to $40,000 courtesy of profitable operations during the two-month period.

    Despite this turnaround, Metroplex may soon find itself in a cash bind. Cash and near-cash projected for 3/31/01 total $219,000 ($114,000 + $91,000 + $14,000), while short-term debt amounts to $237,000 ($180,000 + $57,000). The situation would be somewhat more favorable without the land acquisition, with cash and near-cash assets totaling $224,000 ($219,000 + $5,000) and Accounts Payable of $180,000 being the only liability outstanding. From a liquidity perspective, the acquisition will not help the firm.

PROBLEM 9-40 (30 MINUTES)

1. Sales are collected over a two-month period, 40% in the month of sale and 60% in the following month. December receivables of $216,000 equal 60% of December's sales; thus, December sales total $360,000 ($216,000 ÷ .6). Since the selling price is $40 per unit, Badlands sold 9,000 units ($360,000 ÷ $40).

2. Since the company expects to sell 10,000 units, sales revenue will total $400,000 (10,000 units x $40).

3. Badlands collected 40% of February's sales in February, or $156,800. Thus, February's sales total $392,000 ($156,800 ÷ .4). Combining January sales ($152,000 + $228,000), February sales ($392,000), and March sales ($400,000), the company will report revenue of $1,172,000.

4. Sixty percent of March's sales will be outstanding, or $240,000 ($400,000 x 60%).

5. Finished-goods inventories are maintained at 20% of the following month's sales. January sales total $380,000 ($152,000 + $228,000), or 9,500 units ($380,000 ÷ $40). Thus, the December 31 inventory is 1,900 units (9,500 x 20%).

6. February sales will total 9,800 units ($392,000 ÷ $40), giving rise to a January 31 inventory of 1,960 units (9,800 x 20%). Letting X denote production, then:

    12/31/x0 inventory + X – January 'x1 sales = 1/31/x1 inventory
    1,900 + X - 9,500 = 1,960
    X – 7,600 = 1,960
    X = 9,560

7. Financing required is $7,000 ($30,000 minimum balance - $23,000 ending balance):

Cash balance, January 1...............................	$ 45,000
Add: January receipts ($216,000 + $152,000)..	368,000
Subtotal...	$413,000
Less: January payments.............................	390,000
Cash balance before financing.....................	$ 23,000

PROBLEM 9-41 (25 MINUTES)

1. Sales budget

	April	May	June
Sales (in sets)	10,000	12,000	15,000
Sales price per set	× $50	× $50	× $50
Sales revenue	$500,000	$600,000	$750,000

2. Production budget (in sets)

	April	May	June
Sales	10,000	12,000	15,000
Add: Desired ending inventory	2,400	3,000	3,000
Total requirements	12,400	15,000	18,000
Less: Projected beginning inventory	2,000	2,400	3,000
Planned production	10,400	12,600	15,000

3. Raw-material purchases

	April	May	June
Planned production (sets)	10,400	12,600	15,000
Raw material required per set (board feet)	× 10	× 10	× 10
Raw material required for production (board feet)	104,000	126,000	150,000
Add: Desired ending inventory of raw material (board feet)	12,600	15,000	16,000
Total requirements	116,600	141,000	166,000
Less: Projected beginning inventory of raw material (board feet)	10,400	12,600	15,000
Planned purchases of raw material (board feet)	106,200	128,400	151,000
Cost per board foot	× $.50	× $.50	× $.50
Planned purchases of raw material (dollars)	$ 53,100	$ 64,200	$ 75,500

PROBLEM 9-41 (CONTINUED)

4. Direct-labor budget

	April	May	June
Planned production (sets)	10,400	12,600	15,000
Direct-labor hours per set	× 1.5	× 1.5	× 1.5
Direct-labor hours required	15,600	18,900	22,500
Cost per hour	× $20	× $20	× $20
Planned direct-labor cost	$312,000	$378,000	$450,000

PROBLEM 9-42 (40 MINUTES)

1. Empire Chemical Company's production budget (in gallons) for the three products for 20x2 is calculated as follows:

	Yarex	Darol	Norex
Inventory, 12/31/x2			
(.08 × 20x3 sales)	5,200	2,800	2,400
Add: Sales for 20x2	60,000	40,000	25,000
Total required	65,200	42,800	27,400
Deduct: Inventory, 12/31/x1			
(.08 × 20x2 sales)	4,800	3,200	2,000
Required production in 20x2	60,400	39,600	25,400

2. The company's conversion cost budget for 20x2 is shown in the following schedule:

Conversion hours required:	
Yarex (60,400 × .07)	4,228
Darol (39,600 × .10)	3,960
Norex (25,400 × .16)	4,064
Total hours	12,252
Conversion cost budget (12,252 × $20)	$245,040

PROBLEM 9-42 (CONTINUED)

3. Since the 20x1 usage of Islin is 100,000 gallons, the firm's raw-material purchases budget (in dollars) for Islin for 20x2 is as follows:

Quantity of Islin required for production in 20x2 (in gallons):

Yarex (60,400 × 1)	60,400
Darol (39,600 × .7)...	27,720
Norex (25,400 × .5)	12,700
Subtotal	100,820
Add: Required inventory, 12/31/x2 (100,820 × .10)	10,082
Subtotal	110,902
Deduct: Inventory, 1/1/x2 (100,000 × .10)...................................	10,000
Required purchases (gallons)	100,902
Purchases budget (100,902 gallons × $5 per gallon)	$504,510

4. The company should continue using Islin, because the cost of using Philin is $76,316 greater than using Islin, calculated as follows:

Change in material cost from substituting Philin for Islin:
20x2 production requirements:

Philin (100,820 × $5 × 1.2)	$604,920
Islin (100,820 × $5)...	504,100
Increase in cost of raw material	$100,820
Change in conversion cost from substituting Philin for Islin:	
Philin (12,252 × $20 × .9)	$220,536
Islin (12,252 × $20)...	245,040
Decrease in conversion cost...	$(24,504)
Net increase in production cost...	$ 76,316

PROBLEM 9-43 (60 MINUTES)

1. Sales budget for 20x0:

	Units	Price	Total
Light coils	60,000	$65	$3,900,000
Heavy coils	40,000	$95	3,800,000
Projected sales...			$7,700,000

PROBLEM 9-43 (CONTINUED)

2. Production budget (in units) for 20x0:

	Light Coils	Heavy Coils
Projected sales...	60,000	40,000
Add: Desired inventories,		
December 31, 20x0	25,000	9,000
Total requirements...	85,000	49,000
Deduct: Expected inventories, January 1, 20x0	20,000	8,000
Production required (units)...	65,000	41,000

3. Raw-material purchases budget (in quantities) for 20x0:

	Raw Material		
	Sheet Metal	Copper Wire	Platforms
Light coils (65,000 units projected			
to be produced)...	260,000	130,000	—
Heavy coils (41,000 units projected			
to be produced)...	205,000	123,000	41,000
Production requirements	465,000	253,000	41,000
Add: Desired inventories, December 31, 20x0......	36,000	32,000	7,000
Total requirements...	501,000	285,000	48,000
Deduct: Expected inventories,			
January 1, 20x0	32,000	29,000	6,000
Purchase requirements (units)...........................	469,000	256,000	42,000

4. Raw-material purchases budget for 20x0:

Raw Material	Raw Material Required (units)	Anticipated Purchase Price	Total
Sheet metal..	469,000	$8	$3,752,000
Copper wire	256,000	5	1,280,000
Platforms	42,000	3	126,000

PROBLEM 9-43 (CONTINUED)

5. Direct-labor budget for 20x0:

	Projected Production (units)	Hours per Unit	Total Hours	Rate	Total Cost
Light coils	65,000	2	130,000	$15	$1,950,000
Heavy coils	41,000	3	123,000	20	2,460,000
Total...					$4,410,000

6. Manufacturing overhead budget for 20x0:

	Cost Driver Quantity	Cost Driver Rate	Budgeted Cost
Purchasing and material handling	725,000 lb.[a]	$.25	$181,250
Depreciation, utilities, and inspection	106,000 coils [b]	$4.00	424,000
Shipping...	100,000[c]	$1.00	100,000
General manufacturing overhead.........................	253,000 hr. [d]	$3.00	759,000
Total manufacturing overhead			$1,464,250

[a]725,000 = 469,000 + 256,000 (from req. 4)
[b]106,000 = 65,000 + 41,000 (from req. 2)
[c]100,000 = 60,000 + 40,000 (total units sold, from problem)
[d]253,000 = 130,000 + 123,000 (from req. 5)

PROBLEM 9-44 (45 MINUTES)

1. The benefits that can be derived from implementing a budgeting system include the following:

    *   The preparation of budgets forces management to plan ahead and to establish goals and objectives that can be quantified.

    *   Budgeting compels departmental managers to make plans that are in congruence with the plans of other departments as well as the objectives of the entire firm.

    *   The budgeting process promotes internal communication and coordination.

    *   Budgets provide directions for day-to-day control of operations, clarify duties to be performed, and assign responsibility for these duties.

    *   Budgets help in measuring performance and providing incentives.

    *   Budgets provide a vehicle for resource allocation.

PROBLEM 9-44 (CONTINUED)

2.

a. Schedule	b. Subsequent Schedule
Sales Budget	Production Budget Selling Expense Budget Budgeted Income Statement
Ending Inventory Budget (units)	Production Budget
Production Budget (units)	Direct-Material Budget Direct-Labor Budget Manufacturing-Overhead Budget
Direct-Material Budget	Cost-of-Goods-Manufactured Budget
Direct-Labor Budget	Cost-of-Goods-Manufactured Budget
Manufacturing-Overhead Budget	Cost-of-Goods-Manufactured Budget
Cost-of-Goods-Manufactured Budget	Cost-of-Goods-Sold Budget
Cost-of-Goods-Sold Budget (includes ending inventory in dollars)	Budgeted Income Statement Budgeted Balance Sheet
Selling Expense Budget	Budgeted Income Statement
Research and Development Budget	Budgeted Income Statement
Administrative Expense Budget	Budgeted Income Statement
Budgeted Income Statement	Budgeted Balance Sheet Budgeted Statement of Cash Flows
Capital Expenditures Budget	Cash Receipts and Disbursements Budget Budgeted Balance Sheet Budgeted Statement of Cash Flows
Cash Receipts and Disbursements Budget	Budgeted Balance Sheet Budgeted Statement of Cash Flows
Budgeted Balance Sheet	Budgeted Statement of Cash Flows
Budgeted Statement of Cash Flows	

PROBLEM 9-45 (45 MINUTES)

1. The revised operating budget for Toronto Business Associates for the fourth quarter is presented below. Supporting calculations follow:

TORONTO BUSINESS ASSOCIATES
REVISED OPERATING BUDGET
FOR THE FOURTH QUARTER OF 20X1

Revenue:	
Consulting fees:	
Computer system consulting	$478,125
Management consulting	468,000
Total consulting fees	$946,125
Other revenue	10,000
Total revenue	$956,125
Expenses:	
Consultant salary expenses*	$510,650
Travel and related expenses	57,875
General and administrative expenses	93,000
Depreciation expense	40,000
Corporate expense allocation	75,000
Total expenses	$776,525
Operating income	$179,600

*$510,650 = $245,000 + $265,650. (See supporting calculations.)

PROBLEM 9-45 (CONTINUED)

Supporting calculations:

- Schedule of projected revenues for the fourth quarter of 20x1:

	Computer System Consulting	Management Consulting
Third Quarter:		
Revenue..	$421,875	$315,000
Hourly billing rate	÷ $75	÷ $90
Billable hours..	5,625	3,500
Number of consultants..	÷ 15	÷ 10
Hours per consultant...	375	350
Fourth-quarter planned increase...........................	50	50
Billable hours per consultant................................	425	400
Number of consultants	× 15	× 13
Billable hours	6,375	5,200
Billing rate..	× $75	× $90
Projected revenue	$478,125	$468,000

PROBLEM 9-45 (CONTINUED)

- Schedules of projected salaries, travel, general and administrative, and allocated corporate expenses:

	Computer System Consulting	Management Consulting
Compensation:		
Existing consultants:		
Annual salary	$ 46,000	$ 50,000
Quarterly salary	$ 11,500	$ 12,500
Planned increase (10%)	1,150	1,250
Total fourth-quarter salary per consultant	$ 12,650	$ 13,750
Number of consultants	× 15	× 10
Total	$ 189,750	$137,500
New consultants at old salary (3 × $12,500)	-0-	37,500
Total salary	$ 189,750	$175,000
Benefits (40%)	75,900	70,000
Total compensation	$ 265,650	$245,000
Travel expenses:		
Computer system consultants (425 hr × 15)		6,375
Management consultants (400 hr. × 13)		5,200
Total hours		11,575
Rate per hour*		× $5
Total travel expense		$ 57,875
General and administrative ($100,000 × 93%)		$ 93,000
Corporate expense allocation ($50,000 × 150%)		$ 75,000

*Third-quarter travel expense ÷ hours = rate

$45,625 ÷ 9,125[†] = $5.00

[†]9,125 = (350 × 10) + (375 × 15)

2. An organization would prepare a revised operating budget when the assumptions underlying the original budget are no longer valid. The assumptions may involve factors outside or inside the company. Changes in assumptions involving external factors may include changes in demand for the company's products or services, changes in the cost of various inputs to the company, or changes in the economic or political environment in which the company operates. Changes in assumptions involving internal factors may include changes in company goals or objectives.

PROBLEM 9-46 (60 MINUTES)

1. Sales budget:

	Box C	Box P	Total
Sales (in units)	500,000	500,000	
Sales price per unit	× $.90	× $1.30	
Sales revenue	$450,000	$650,000	$1,100,000

2. Production budget (in units):

	Box C	Box P
Sales	500,000	500,000
Add: Desired ending inventory	5,000	15,000
Total units needed	505,000	515,000
Deduct: Beginning Inventory	10,000	20,000
Production requirements	495,000	495,000

3. Raw-material budget:

PAPERBOARD

	Box C	Box P	Total
Production requirement (number of boxes)	495,000	495,000	
Raw material required per box (pounds)	× .3	× .7	
Raw material required for production (pounds)	148,500	346,500	495,000
Add: Desired ending raw-material inventory			5,000
Total raw-material needs			500,000
Deduct: Beginning raw-material inventory			15,000
Raw material to be purchased			485,000
Price (per pound)			× $.20
Cost of purchases (paperboard)			$ 97,000

PROBLEM 9-46 (CONTINUED)

CORRUGATING MEDIUM

	Box C	Box P	Total
Production requirements (number of boxes).........	495,000	495,000	
Raw material required per box (pounds)...............	× .2	× .3	
Raw material required for production (pounds)	99,000	148,500	247,500
Add: Desired ending raw-material inventory......................................			10,000
Total raw-material needs			257,500
Deduct: Beginning raw-material inventory			5,000
Raw material to be purchased................................			252,500
Price (per pound)...			× $.10
Cost of purchases (corrugating medium)			$ 25,250
Total cost of raw-material purchases ($97,000 + $25,250)..			$122,250

4. Direct-labor budget:

	Box C	Box P	Total
Production requirements (number of boxes)	495,000	495,000	
Direct labor required per box (hours).....................	× .0025	× .005	
Direct labor required for production (hours)	1,237.5	2,475	3,712.5
Direct-labor rate..			× $12
Total direct-labor cost..			$44,550

5. Manufacturing-overhead budget:

Indirect material	$ 10,500
Indirect labor	50,000
Utilities	25,000
Property taxes	18,000
Insurance	16,000
Depreciation	29,000
Total overhead..	$ 148,500

PROBLEM 9-46 (CONTINUED)

6. Selling and administrative expense budget:

Salaries and fringe benefits of sales personnel	$ 75,000
Advertising	15,000
Management salaries and fringe benefits	90,000
Clerical wages and fringe benefits	26,000
Miscellaneous administrative expenses	4,000
Total selling and administrative expenses	$ 210,000

7. Budgeted income statement:

Sales revenue [from sales budget, req. (1)]		$1,100,000
Less: Cost of goods sold:*		
Box C: 500,000 × $.21	$105,000	
Box P: 500,000 × $.43	215,000	320,000
Gross margin		$ 780,000
Selling and administrative expenses		210,000
Income before taxes		$ 570,000
Income tax expense (40%)		228,000
Net income		$ 342,000

*Calculation of cost of goods sold:

(a) Predetermined overhead rate

$$= \frac{\text{budgeted manufacturing overhead}}{\text{volume of direct-labor hours}}$$

$$= \frac{\$148,500}{(495,000)(.0025) + (495,000)(.005)}$$

$$= \frac{\$148,500}{3,712.5 \text{ hours}} = \$40 \text{ per hour}$$

PROBLEM 9-46 (CONTINUED)

(b) Calculation of manufacturing cost per unit:

	Box C	Box P
Direct material:		
Paperboard		
.3 lb. × $.20 per lb...................................	$.06	
.7 lb. × $.20 per lb...................................		$.14
Corrugating medium		
.2 lb. × $.10 per lb...................................	.02	
.3 lb. × $.10 per lb...................................		.03
Direct labor:		
.0025 hr. × $12 per hr.................................	.03	
.005 hr. × $12 per hr..................................		.06
Applied manufacturing overhead:		
.0025 hr. × $40 per hr.................................	.10	
.005 hr. × $40 per hr..................................		.20
Manufacturing cost per unit........................	$.21	$.43

PROBLEM 9-47 (40 MINUTES)

1. Strategic planning identifies the overall objective of an organization and generally considers the impact of external factors such as competitive forces, market demand, and technological changes when identifying overall objectives. Budgeting is the quantitative expression of plans evolving from strategic planning. The time horizon for budgeting is generally a year, or an operating cycle, and greater attention is focused on internal factors than on external factors.

PROBLEM 9-47 (CONTINUED)

2.   For each of the financial objectives established by the board of directors and president of Healthful Foods, Inc., the calculations to determine whether John Winslow's budget attains these objectives are presented in the following table.

CALCULATION OF FINANCIAL OBJECTIVES: HEALTHFUL FOODS, INC.

Objective	Attained/ Not Attained	Calculations
Increase sales by 12% ($850,000 × 1.12 = $952,000)	Not attained	($947,750–$850,000)/$850,000 = 11.5%
Increase before-tax income by 15% ($105,000 × 1.15 = $120,750)	Attained	($120,750–$105,000)/$105,000 = 15%
Maintain long-term debt at or below 16% of assets ($2,050,000 × .16 = $328,000)	Attained	$308,000/$2,050,000 = 15% (rounded)
Maintain cost of goods sold at or below 70% of sales ($947,750 × .70 = $663,425)	Attained	$574,725/$947,750 = 60.6% (rounded)

3.   The accounting adjustments contemplated by John Winslow are unethical because they will result in intentionally overstating income by understating the cost of goods sold. The specific standards of ethical conduct for management accountants violated by Winslow are as follows:

Competence. By making the accounting adjustments, Winslow violated the competency standard by not preparing financial statements in accordance with technical standards.

Integrity. Winslow violated the integrity standard by engaging in an activity that prejudiced his ability to carry out his duties ethically, by not communicating unfavorable as well as favorable information, and by engaging in an activity that appears to be a conflict of interest.

Objectivity. By overstating the inventory and reclassifying certain costs, Winslow has violated the objectivity standard. He has failed to communicate information fairly and objectively and has failed to disclose all relevant information that would influence the users' understanding of the report.

PROBLEM 9-48 (120 MINUTES)

1. Sales budget:

	20x0	20x1			
	December	January	February	March	First Quarter
Total sales........................	$400,000	$440,000	$484,000	$532,400	$1,456,400
Cash sales*......................	100,000	110,000	121,000	133,100	364,100
Sales on account†	300,000	330,000	363,000	399,300	1,092,300

*25% of total sales.
†75% of total sales.

2. Cash receipts budget:

	20x1			
	January	February	March	First Quarter
Cash sales..	$110,000	$121,000	$133,100	$ 364,100
Cash collections from credit sales made during current month*...	33,000	36,300	39,930	109,230
Cash collections from credit sales made during preceding month†...	270,000	297,000	326,700	893,700
Total cash receipts................................	$413,000	$454,300	$499,730	$1,367,030

*10% of current month's credit sales.
†90% of previous month's credit sales.

PROBLEM 9-48 (CONTINUED)

3. Purchases budget:

	20x0	20x1			
	December	January	February	March	First Quarter
Budgeted cost of goods sold..............	$280,000	$308,000	$338,800	$372,680	$1,019,480
Add: Desired ending inventory.....	154,000	169,400	186,340	186,340*	186,340†
Total goods needed	$434,000	$477,400	$525,140	$559,020	$1,205,820
Less: Expected beginning inventory.................	140,000	154,000	169,400	186,340	154,000**
Purchases	$294,000	$323,400	$355,740	$372,680	$1,051,820

*Since April's expected sales and cost of goods sold are the same as the projections for March, the desired ending inventory for March is the same as that for February.
†The desired ending inventory for the quarter is equal to the desired ending inventory on March 31, 20x1.
**The beginning inventory for the quarter is equal to the December ending inventory.

PROBLEM 9-48 (CONTINUED)

4. Cash disbursements budget:

	20x1			
	January	February	March	First Quarter
Inventory purchases:				
Cash payments for purchases during the current month*........	$129,360	$142,296	$149,072	$ 420,728
Cash payments for purchases during the preceding month†......................................	176,400	194,040	213,444	583,884
Total cash payments for inventory purchases.......................	$305,760	$336,336	$362,516	$1,004,612
Other expenses:				
Sales salaries...................................	$ 21,000	$ 21,000	$ 21,000	$ 63,000
Advertising and promotion.............	16,000	16,000	16,000	48,000
Administrative salaries	21,000	21,000	21,000	63,000
Interest on bonds**..........................	15,000	-0-	-0-	15,000
Property taxes**...............................	-0-	5,400	-0-	5,400
Sales commissions	4,400	4,840	5,324	14,564
Total cash payments for other expenses	$ 77,400	$ 68,240	$ 63,324	$ 208,964
Total cash disbursements....................	$383,160	$404,576	$425,840	$ 1,213,576

*40% of current months' purchases [see requirement (3)].
†60% of the prior month's purchases [see requirement (3)].
**Bond interest is paid every six months, on January 31 and July 31. Property taxes also are paid every six months, on February 28 and August 31.

PROBLEM 9-48 (CONTINUED)

5. Summary cash budget:

	20x1			
	January	February	March	First Quarter
Cash receipts [from req. (2)]	$ 413,000	$ 454,300	$ 499,730	$1,367,030
Cash disbursements [from req. (4)]	(383,160)	(404,576)	(425,840)	(1,213,576)
Change in cash balance during period due to operations	$ 29,840	$ 49,724	$ 73,890	$ 153,454
Sale of marketable securities (1/2/x1)	15,000			15,000
Proceeds from bank loan (1/2/x1)	100,000			100,000
Purchase of equipment	(125,000)			(125,000)
Repayment of bank loan (3/31/x1)			(100,000)	(100,000)
Interest on bank loan*			(2,500)	(2,500)
Payment of dividends			(50,000)	(50,000)
Change in cash balance during first quarter				$ (9,046)
Cash balance, 1/1/x1				35,000
Cash balance, 3/31/x1				$ 25,954

*$100,000 × 10% per year × 1/4 year = $2,500

6. Analysis of short-term financing needs:

Projected cash balance as of December 31, 20x0	$ 35,000
Less: Minimum cash balance	25,000
Cash available for equipment purchases	$ 10,000
Projected proceeds from sale of marketable securities	15,000
Cash available	$ 25,000
Less: Cost of investment in equipment	125,000
Required short-term borrowing	$(100,000)

PROBLEM 9-48 (CONTINUED)

7.

INTERCOASTAL ELECTRONICS COMPANY
BUDGETED INCOME STATEMENT
FOR THE FIRST QUARTER OF 20X1

Sales revenue		$1,456,400
Less: Cost of goods sold		1,019,480
Gross margin		$ 436,920
Selling and administrative expenses:		
Sales salaries	$63,000	
Sales commissions	14,564	
Advertising and promotion	48,000	
Administrative salaries	63,000	
Depreciation	75,000	
Interest on bonds	7,500	
Interest on short-term bank loan	2,500	
Property taxes	2,700	
Total selling and administrative expenses		276,264
Net income		$ 160,656

8.

INTERCOASTAL ELECTRONICS COMPANY
BUDGETED STATEMENT OF RETAINED EARNINGS
FOR THE FIRST QUARTER OF 20X1

Retained earnings, 12/31/x0	$ 107,500
Add: Net income	160,656
Deduct: Dividends	50,000
Retained earnings, 3/31/x1	$ 218,156

PROBLEM 9-48 (CONTINUED)

9.

INTERCOASTAL ELECTRONICS COMPANY
BUDGETED BALANCE SHEET
MARCH 31, 20x1

Cash..	$ 25,954
Accounts receivable*..	359,370
Inventory...	186,340
Buildings and equipment (net of accumulated depreciation)†	676,000
Total assets...	$1,247,664
Accounts payable**...	$ 223,608
Bond interest payable..	5,000
Property taxes payable...	900
Bonds payable (10%; due in 20x6)	300,000
Common Stock...	500,000
Retained earnings	218,156
Total liabilities and stockholders' equity...	$ 1,247,664
*Accounts receivable, 12/31/x0..	$ 270,000
Sales on account [see req. (1)]	1,092,300
Total cash collections from credit sales	
($109,230 + $893,700)...	(1,002,930)
Accounts receivable, 3/31/x1	$ 359,370
†Buildings and equipment (net), 12/31/x0..	$ 626,000
Cost of equipment acquired...	125,000
Depreciation expense for first quarter..	(75,000)
Buildings and equipment (net), 3/31/x1	$ 676,000
**Accounts payable, 12/31/x0...	$ 176,400
Purchases [req. (3)]...	1,051,820
Cash payments for purchases [req. (4)]	(1,004,612)
Accounts payable, 3/31/x1	$ 223,608

PROBLEM 9-49 (25 MINUTES)

1. Annual cost of ordering and storing XL-20 $= \left(\dfrac{\text{annual requirement}}{\text{order quanity}}\right)\left(\dfrac{\text{cost per order}}{}\right) + \left(\dfrac{\text{order quantity}}{2}\right)\left(\dfrac{\text{annual holding cost per unit}}{}\right)$

2. Economic order quantity

$$= \sqrt{\dfrac{(2)(\text{annual requirement})(\text{cost per order})}{\text{annual holding cost per unit}}}$$

$$= \sqrt{\dfrac{(2)(4,800)(\$150)}{\$4}}$$

$$= \sqrt{360,000} = 600$$

3. Using the formula given for requirement (1):

Total annual cost of ordering and storing XL-20 $= \left(\dfrac{4,800}{600}\right)(\$150) + \left(\dfrac{600}{2}\right)(\$4)$

$= \$2,400$

Note that this cost does *not* include the actual cost of XL-20 purchases (i.e., the quantity puchased multiplied by the price).

4. Orders per year:

Number of orders per year $= \dfrac{\text{annual requirement}}{\text{order quantity}} = \dfrac{4,800}{600} = 8$

5. Using the new cost data:

a. EOQ $= \sqrt{\dfrac{(2)(\text{annual requirement})(\text{cost per order})}{\text{annual holding cost per unit}}}$

$= \sqrt{\dfrac{(2)(4,800)(\$20)}{\$19.20}}$

$= \sqrt{10,000} = 100$

PROBLEM 9-49 (CONTINUED)

b. $\text{Number of orders per year} = \dfrac{\text{annual requirement}}{\text{order quantity}} = \dfrac{4,800}{100}$

$$= 48$$

PROBLEM 9-50 (20 MINUTES)

1. Tabulation of inventory ordering and holding costs:

	Order size		
	400	600	800
Number of orders (4,800 ÷ order size).............................	12	8	6
Ordering cost ($150 × number of orders).....................	$1,800	$1,200	$900
Average inventory (order size ÷ 2).....................................	200	300	400
Holding costs ($4 × average inventory)........................	$800	$1,200	$1,600
Total annual costs (ordering costs + holding costs)............................	$2,600	$2,400	$2,500

minimum (↑ under $2,400)

2. The tabular method is cumbersome and does not necessarily identify the optimal order quantity. If the optimal order quantity does not happen to be selected as one of the order quantities for the tabular analysis, an order quantity other than those included in the table will be the least-cost order quantity.

PROBLEM 9-51 (25 MINUTES)

Graphical analysis of economic order quantity:

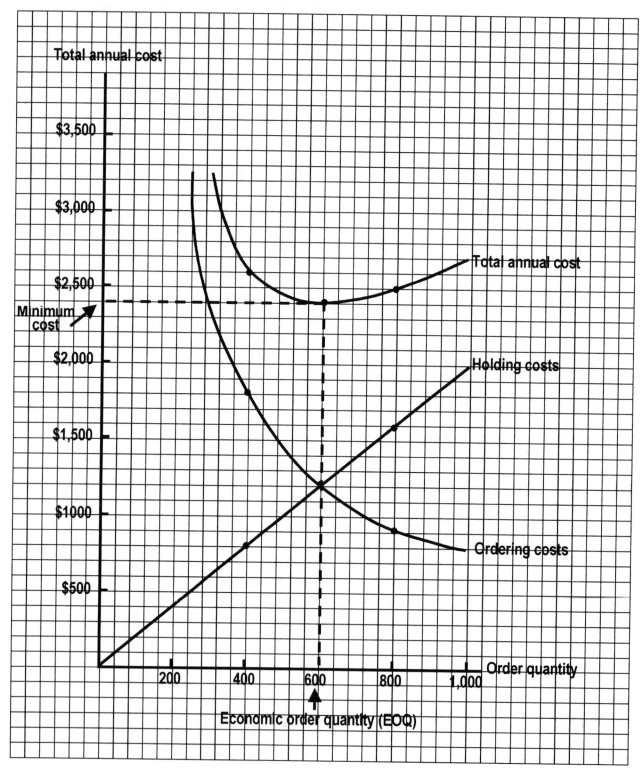

PROBLEM 9-52 (35 MINUTES)

1.   Reorder point:

$$\text{Monthly usage} = \frac{\text{annual usage}}{12}$$

$$= \frac{4,800}{12} = 400 \text{ canisters}$$

Usage during 1-month lead time = 400 canisters

Reorder point = 400 canisters

The chemical XL-20 should be ordered in the economic order quantity of 600 canisters when the inventory level falls to 400 canisters. In the one month it takes to receive the order, those 400 canisters will be used in production.

2.   Graph of usage, lead time and reorder point:

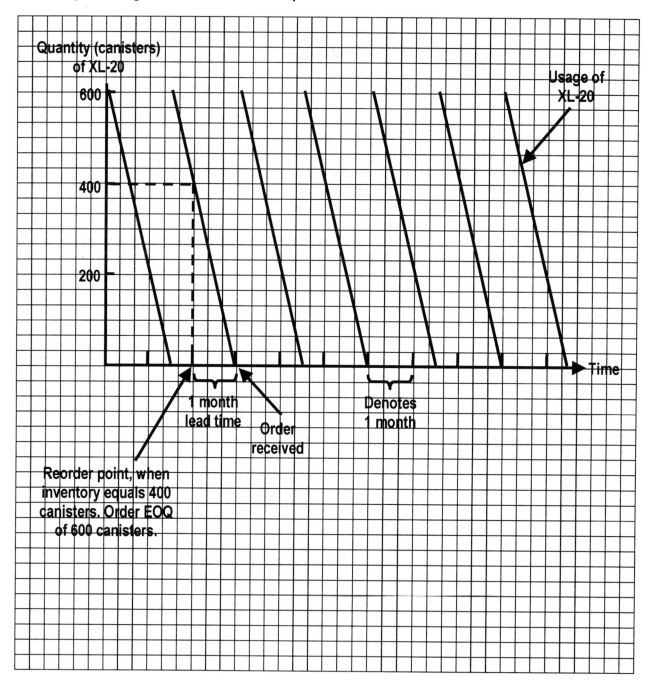

PROBLEM 9-52 (CONTINUED)

3. Safety stock and new reorder point:

    Monthly usage of XL-20 fluctuates between 300 and 500 canisters. Although average monthly usage still is 400 canisters, there is the potential for an excess range of 100 canisters in any particular month. The safety stock of XL-20 is equal to the potential excess monthly usage of 100 canisters. With a safety stock of 100 canisters, the reorder point is 500 canisters (400 + 100). The materials and parts manager should order the EOQ of 600 canisters when the inventory of XL-20 falls to 500 canisters. During the one-month lead time, another 300 to 500 canisters of XL-20 will be used in production.

PROBLEM 9-53 (45 MINUTES)

1. The ordering cost per order is composed of the following costs:

Inspection fee	$ 75.00
Direct labor: receiving clerk (8 hours × $9.00)	72.00
Variable overhead (8 hours × $2.50)	20.00
Processing cost*	5.80
Total ordering cost per order	$172.80

$$*\text{Processing cost per order} = \frac{\text{change in ordering cost}}{\text{change in number of orders}}$$

$$= \frac{\$12,300 - \$11,900}{95 - 15}$$

$$= \frac{\$400}{80}$$

$$= \$5.00$$

$$\text{Recognition of 16\% cost increase} = \$5.00 \times 1.16$$

$$= \$5.80$$

PROBLEM 9-53 (CONTINUED)

2. The storage cost per windshield is composed of the following costs:

Variable warehouse rent (fixed fee not relevant)	$ 5.35
Breakage cost	3.00
Taxes and fire insurance	1.15
Other storage costs	10.50
Total storage cost per windshield	$ 20.00

3. The economic order quantity (EOQ) is calculated as follows:

$$EOQ = \sqrt{\frac{(2)(10,800)(\$172.80)}{\$20.00}}$$

EOQ = 432 windshields per order

4. The minimum annual relevant cost at the economic order quantity is calculated as follows:

Minimum cost = ordering cost + storage cost

$$= \frac{10,800 \times \$172.80}{432} + \frac{432 \times \$20.00}{2}$$

= $4,320 + $4,320

= $8,640

5. The reorder point in units is calculated as follows:

Usage per day × lead time in days = 36* units × 6 days

= 216 windshields

*10,800 ÷ 50 weeks ÷ 6 days

PROBLEM 9-53 (CONTINUED)

6. Using the new cost estimates:

a.
$$EOQ = \sqrt{\frac{(2)(10,800)(\$32.40)}{\$60.00}}$$

$$= \sqrt{11,664} = 108 \text{ windshields per order}$$

b. Number of orders per year $= \dfrac{\text{annual requirement}}{\text{order quantity}} = \dfrac{10,800}{108}$

$$= 100 \text{ orders}$$

c. Minimum cost $=$ ordering cost + storage cost

$$= \frac{10,800 \times \$32.40}{108} + \frac{108 \times \$60.00}{2}$$

$$= \$3,240 + \$3,240$$

$$= \$6,480$$

SOLUTIONS TO CASES

CASE 9-54 (60 MINUTES)

1. Yes, City Raquetball Club (CRC) should be better able to plan its cash receipts with the new membership plan and fee structure. The cash flows should be more predictable and certain because the large, prepaid membership fee becomes the only factor affecting cash receipts. The hourly court fees, which were dependent upon a variable that could fluctuate daily, are eliminated.

2. a. Factors that CRC's management should consider before adopting the new membership plan and fee structure include:

    *   Costs associated with the plan changeover

    *   Public acceptance of the new proposal

    *   The expected number of memberships by classes that can be sold for each plan at the specified rates

    *   The anticipated rate of return for excess cash or cost of borrowing funds in periods of cash shortages

    b. Financial analyses conducted by CRC could include a forecast of projected cash inflows and outflows by months, an income statement including interest revenue and expense, a cost-volume-profit analysis, and a cash management plan for excess cash or cash shortages.

3. Because CRC's cash flows should be more predictable, management should be better able to plan for and control cash disbursements. In addition, management should be better able to plan for short-term investments when excess cash occurs or to arrange for short-term financing when there are cash shortages.

    The collection and billing function is also simplified with the new membership plan and fee structure. There would be only a one-time cash receipt rather than multiple transactions.

CASE 9-55 (35 MINUTES)

1. Some of the operational and behavioral benefits that are generally attributed to a participatory budgeting process are as follows:

- Utilization of the best knowledge of activities in a specific area, because the participants are close to daily operations.

- Goals that are more realistic and acceptable.

- Improved communication and group cohesiveness.

- A sense of commitment and willingness to be held accountable for the budget.

2. Four deficiencies in Patricia Eklund's participatory policy for planning and performance evaluation, along with recommendations of how the deficiencies can be corrected:

Deficiencies	Recommendations
The setting of constraints on fixed expenditures includes uncontrollable fixed costs, thereby mitigating the positive effects of participatory budgeting.	Rewards should be based on meeting budget and/or organizational goals or objectives.
The arbitrary revision of approved budgets defeats the participatory process.	The contingency budget should be separate, over and above each department's original submission.
The division manager holds back a percentage of each budget for discretionary use.	Managers should be involved in the revision of budgets. Managers could submit a budget with programs at different levels of funding.
Evaluation based on budget performance must be accompanied with intrinsic rewards.	Divisional constraints could be communicated at a budget "kick-off" meeting; however, individual limits of controllable expenses should be set by each manager.

CASE 9-56 (120 MINUTES)

1. Sales budget:

	20x0	20x1				
	4th Quarter	1st Quarter	2nd Quarter	3rd Quarter	4th Quarter	Entire Year
S frame unit sales....................	50,000	55,000	60,000	65,000	70,000	250,000
× S sales price.......	× $10	× $10	× $10	× $10	x $10	× $10
S frame sales revenue................	$ 500,000	$ 550,000	$ 600,000	$ 650,000	$ 700,000	$2,500,000
L frame unit sales....................	40,000	45,000	50,000	55,000	60,000	210,000
× L sales price.......	× $15	× $15	× $15	× $15	× $15	× $15
L frame sales revenue................	$ 600,000	$ 675,000	$ 750,000	$ 825,000	$ 900,000	$3,150,000
Total sales revenue................	$1,100,000	$1,225,000	$1,350,000	$1,475,000	$1,600,000	$5,650,000
Cash sales*...........	$ 440,000	$ 490,000	$ 540,000	$590,000	$640,000	$2,260,000
Sales on account†	660,000	735,000	810,000	885,000	960,000	3,390,000

*40% of total sales.
†60% of total sales.

CASE 9-56 (CONTINUED)

2. Cash receipts budget:

	20x1				
	1st Quarter	2nd Quarter	3rd Quarter	4th Quarter	Entire Year
Cash sales	$ 490,000	$ 540,000	$ 590,000	$ 640,000	$2,260,000
Cash collections from credit sales made during current quarter*	588,000	648,000	708,000	768,000	2,712,000
Cash collections from credit sales made during previous quarter†	132,000	147,000	162,000	177,000	618,000
Total cash receipts	$1,210,000	$1,335,000	$1,460,000	$1,585,000	$5,590,000

*80% of current quarter's credit sales.
†20% of previous quarter's credit sales.

CASE 9-56 (CONTINUED)

3. Production budget

	20x0	20x1				
	4th Quarter	1st Quarter	2nd Quarter	3rd Quarter	4th Quarter	Entire Year
S frames:						
Sales (in units)	50,000	55,000	60,000	65,000	70,000	250,000
Add: Desired ending inventory.........................	11,000	12,000	13,000	14,000	15,000	15,000
Total units needed	61,000	67,000	73,000	79,000	85,000	265,000
Less: Expected beginning inventory.........	10,000	11,000	12,000	13,000	14,000	11,000
Units to be produced	51,000	56,000	61,000	66,000	71,000	254,000
L frames:						
Sales (in units)	40,000	45,000	50,000	55,000	60,000	210,000
Add: Desired ending inventory.........................	9,000	10,000	11,000	12,000	13,000	13,000
Total units needed	49,000	55,000	61,000	67,000	73,000	223,000
Less: Expected beginning inventory.........	8,000	9,000	10,000	11,000	12,000	9,000
Units to be produced	41,000	46,000	51,000	56,000	61,000	214,000

4. Raw-material budget:*

	20x0 4th Quarter	20x1 1st Quarter	2nd Quarter	3rd Quarter	4th Quarter	Entire Year
Metal strips:						
S frames to be produced......................	51,000	56,000	61,000	66,000	71,000	254,000
× Metal quantity per unit (ft.).........................	× 2	× 2	× 2	× 2	× 2	× 2
Needed for S frame production	102,000	112,000	122,000	132,000	142,000	508,000
L frames to be produced......................	41,000	46,000	51,000	56,000	61,000	214,000
× Metal quantity per unit (ft.).........................	× 3	× 3	× 3	× 3	× 3	× 3
Needed for L frame production	123,000	138,000	153,000	168,000	183,000	642,000
Total metal needed for production; to be purchased (ft.)........	225,000	250,000	275,000	300,000	325,000	1,150,000
× Price per foot	× $1	× $1	× $1	× $1	× $1	× $1
Cost of metal strips to be purchased:	$225,000	$250,000	$275,000	$300,000	$325,000	$1,150,000

*Raw-material budget continued on next page.

Glass sheets:................						
S frames to be produced......................	51,000	56,000	61,000	66,000	71,000	254,000
× Glass quantity per unit (sheets)................	× .25	× .25	× .25	× .25	× .25	× .25
Needed for S frame production	12,750	14,000	15,250	16,500	17,750	63,500
L frames to be produced......................	41,000	46,000	51,000	56,000	61,000	214,000
× Glass quantity per unit (sheets)................	× .5	× .5	× .5	× .5	× .5	× .5
Needed for L frame production	20,500	23,000	25,500	28,000	30,500	107,000
Total glass needed for production (sheets)	33,250	37,000	40,750	44,500	48,250	170,500
Add: Desired ending inventory.....................	7,400	8,150	8,900	9,650	10,400	10,400
Total glass needs..........	40,650	45,150	49,650	54,150	58,650	180,900
Less: Expected beginning inventory....	6,650	7,400	8,150	8,900	9,650	7,400
Glass to be purchased...................	34,000	37,750	41,500	45,250	49,000	173,500
× Price per glass sheet...........................	× $8	× $8	× $8	× $8	× $8	× $8
Cost of glass to be purchased...................	$272,000	$302,000	$332,000	$362,000	$392,000	$1,388,000
Total raw-material purchases (metal and glass)	$497,000	$552,000	$607,000	$662,000	$717,000	$2,538,000

CASE 9-56 (CONTINUED)

5. Cash disbursements budget:*

	20×1				
	1st Quarter	2nd Quarter	3rd Quarter	4th Quarter	Entire Year
Raw-material purchases:					
Cash payments for purchases during the current quarter†	$441,600	$485,600	$529,600	$573,600	$2,030,400
Cash payments for purchases during the preceding quarter**	99,400	110,400	121,400	132,400	463,600
Total cash payments for raw-material purchases...	$541,000	$596,000	$651,000	$706,000	$2,494,000
Direct labor:					
Frames produced (S and L)............................	102,000	112,000	122,000	132,000	468,000
× Direct-labor hours per frame	× .1	× .1	× .1	× .1	× .1
Direct-labor hours to be used..................................	10,200	11,200	12,200	13,200	46,800
× Rate per direct-labor hour..................................	× $20	× $20	× $20	× $20	× $20
Total cash payments for direct labor	$204,000	$224,000	$244,000	$264,000	$936,000

*Cash disbursements budget continued on next page.
† 80% of current quarter's purchases
**20% of previous quarter's purchases

CASE 9-56 (CONTINUED)

Manufacturing overhead:					
Indirect material....................	$ 10,200	$ 11,200	$ 12,200	$ 13,200	$ 46,800
Indirect labor........................	40,800	44,800	48,800	52,800	187,200
Other.....................................	31,000	36,000	41,000	46,000	154,000
Total cash payments for manufacturing overhead..........................	$ 82,000	$ 92,000	$ 102,000	$ 112,000	$ 388,000
Cash payments for selling and administrative expenses...........................	$100,000	$ 100,000	$ 100,000	$ 100,000	$ 400,000
Total cash disbursements........	$927,000	$1,012,000	$1,097,000	$1,182,000	$4,218,000

CASE 9-56 (CONTINUED)

6. Summary cash budget:

	20x1				
	1st Quarter	2nd Quarter	3nd Quarter	4th Quarter	Entire Year
Cash receipts [from req. (2)]........	$1,210,000	$1,335,000	$1,460,000	$1,585,000	$5,590,000
Less: Cash disbursements [from req. (5)]........	927,000	1,012,000	1,097,000	1,182,000	4,218,000
Change in cash balance due to operations.....	$ 283,000	$ 323,000	$ 363,000	$ 403,000	$1,372,000
Payment of dividends........	(50,000)	(50,000)	(50,000)	(50,000)	(200,000)
Proceeds from bank loan (1/2/x1)..	1,000,000				1,000,000
Purchase of equipment.......	(1,000,000)				(1,000,000)
Quarterly installment on loan principal.....	(250,000)	(250,000)	(250,000)	(250,000)	(1,000,000)
Quarterly interest payment*.......	(25,000)	(18,750)	(12,500)	(6,250)	(62,500)
Change in cash balance during the period.....	$ (42,000)	$ 4,250	$ 50,500	$ 96,750	$ 109,500
Cash balance, beginning of period	95,000	53,000	57,250	107,750	95,000
Cash balance, end of period.......	$ 53,000	$ 57,250	$ 107,750	$ 204,500	$ 204,500

*$1,000,000 × 10% × 1/4 = $25,000
$750,000 × 10% × 1/4 = $18,750
$500,000 × 10% × 1/4 = $12,500
$250,000 × 10% × 1/4 = $6,250

7.
FRAME-IT COMPANY
BUDGETED SCHEDULE OF COST OF GOODS MANUFACTURED AND SOLD
FOR THE YEAR ENDED DECEMBER 31, 20X1

Direct material:		
Raw-material inventory, 1/1/x1		$ 59,200
Add: Purchases of raw material [req. (4)].............................		2,538,000
Raw material available for use		$2,597,200
Deduct: Raw-material inventory, 12/31/x1		
([req. (4)] 10,400 × $8)		83,200
Raw material used		$2,514,000
Direct labor [req. (5)]...		936,000
Manufacturing overhead:		
Indirect material	$ 46,800	
Indirect labor	187,200	
Other overhead	154,000	
Depreciation	80,000	
Total manufacturing overhead		468,000*
Cost of goods manufactured..		$3,918,000†
Add: Finished-goods inventory, 1/1/x1............................		167,000
Cost of goods available for sale....................................		$4,085,000
Deduct: Finished-goods inventory, 12/31/x1		235,000**
Cost of goods sold		$3,850,000††

In the budget, budgeted and applied manufacturing overhead are equal. The *applied* manufacturing overhead may be verified independently as follows:

Total number of frames produced	468,000
× Direct-labor hours per frame...	× .1
Total direct-labor hours	46,800
× Predetermined overhead rate per hour	× $10
Total manufacturing overhead applied.................................	$468,000

†See next page.
**See next page.
††See next page.

CASE 9-56 (CONTINUED)

†The cost of goods manufactured may be verified independently as follows:

	S Frames	L Frames
Frames produced	254,000	214,000
× Manufacturing cost per unit	× $7	× $10
Total manufacturing cost	$1,778,000	$2,140,000
Grand total	$3,918,000	

**The finished-goods inventory on 12/31/x1 may be verified independently as follows:

	S Frames	L Frames
Projected inventory on 12/31/x1	15,000	13,000
Manufacturing cost per unit	× $7	× $10
Cost of ending inventory	$ 105,000	$ 130,000
Total cost of ending inventory (S and L)	$235,000	

††The cost of goods sold may be verified independently as follows:

	S Frames	L Frames
Frames sold	250,000	210,000
Manufacturing cost per unit	× $7	× $10
Cost of goods sold	$1,750,000	$2,100,000
Total cost of goods sold (S and L)	$3,850,000	

8.
FRAME-IT COMPANY
BUDGETED INCOME STATEMENT
FOR THE YEAR ENDED DECEMBER 31, 20X1

Sales revenue		$5,650,000
Less: Cost of goods sold		3,850,000
Gross margin		$1,800,000
Selling and administrative expenses	$400,000	
Interest expense	62,500	462,500
Net income		$1,337,500

CASE 9-56 (CONTINUED)

9.

FRAME-IT COMPANY
BUDGETED STATEMENT OF RETAINED EARNINGS
FOR THE YEAR ENDED DECEMBER 31, 20x1

Retained earnings, 12/31/x0	$3,353,800
Add: Net income	1,337,500
Deduct: Dividends	200,000
Retained earnings, 12/31/x1	$4,491,300

10.

FRAME-IT COMPANY
BUDGETED BALANCE SHEET
DECEMBER 31, 20x1

Cash	$ 204,500
Accounts receivable*	192,000
Inventory:	
Raw material†	83,200
Finished goods	235,000
Plant and equipment (net of accumulated depreciation)**	8,920,000
Total assets	$9,634,700
Accounts payable††	$ 143,400
Common stock	5,000,000
Retained earnings	4,491,300
Total liabilities and stockholders' equity	$9,634,700

*Fourth-quarter sales on account × 20% = $960,000 × 20%
†10,400 units × $8
**$8,000,000 + $1,000,000 – $80,000
††Fourth-quarter purchases on account × 20% = $717,000 × 20%

CURRENT ISSUES IN MANAGERIAL ACCOUNTING

ISSUE 9-57

"U.S. AIRLINES CONSIDER IMPACT OF HIGHER FUEL BILL," *THE WALL STREET JOURNAL*, OCTOBER 13, 2000. "AMERICAN'S NET SOARS, BUT HIGH OIL PRICES STING U.S. AIRWAYS," *THE WALL STREET JOURNAL*, OCTOBER 19, 2000, MELANIE TRUTTMAN AND SUSAN CAREY.

1. Higher fuel costs mean that airlines may have to raise airfares so that costs are met.

2. Higher fuel costs result in many expenses increasing throughout society. Since airlines have to purchase many different kinds of supplies, many of which could be affected by rising prices, increased fuel prices could affect the airlines' budgets in many places in addition to their actual fuel costs.

ISSUE 9-58

"BUDGET PLANNING: THE NEXT GENERATION," *INFORMATIONWEEK.COM*, SEPTEMBER 25, 2000, RICK WHITING.

1. Budgeting has moved to a combination of top-down and bottom-up processes. The idea is that managers will be able to measure results more accurately. Strategic planning begins with the organization's objectives and then builds a budget designed to achieve those goals. Input from all levels is needed to make strategic planning successful.

2. New technology via computer software allows employees from different levels of an organization to provide integrated input into budget formation. This has allowed a faster and more accurate process on a national as well as an international scale that is updated on a continuous basis.

3. Amway Corporation incorporated Adaytum Software to project reducing travel expenses by 5% for its executives. Next year Amway will use the software to eventually link several hundred managers into the budgeting process.

ISSUE 9-59

"INEFFICIENT BUDGETING COSTS COMPANIES DEARLY," *MANAGEMENT ACCOUNTING*, FEBRUARY 2000, JOHN FANNING.

The traditional budget and associated processes, such as strategic planning, forecasting, monthly reviews and reward processes, consume an enormous amount of management time. If these processes are linked, rather than operating in isolation, the overall level of control over the business can be improved while eliminating, or substantially streamlining, redundant or superfluous activities.

ISSUE 9-60

"THE REVOLUTION IN PLANNING," *CFO*, AUGUST 1999, RUSS BANHAM.

There are fewer best practices that are directly transferable from company to company than exist with re-engineering. This article discusses re-engineering the planning process. Planning pervades every corner of an organization and is steeped in a tradition of negotiation. Planning is the most political of all processes. Success in this area requires patience, communication with employees, investment in new data-gathering tools and time. It also requires finance to evolve from being a reporter to being a facilitator of the process. Companies that succeed in revamping this process believe they can accurately assess strategic decisions based on metrics intrinsic to the business. Since this is a continuous process that starts when senior management defines business objectives and communicates them to the operating lines, benefits begin immediately.

ISSUE 9-61

"SELLING THE BUDGET," *STRATEGIC FINANCE*, SEPTEMBER 1999, CATHERINE M. STANKE.

Using too much detail can bog an audience down and make them miss the overall message. The author of the article suggests choosing the view of a picture that is best for the message the presenter is trying to convey. Use bar graphs, pie charts, line graphs, and/or scatter graphs for the purpose they were intended. Present high-level assumptions that don't give more detail than is needed to make an informed decision. The presenter can always give more detail when answering a specific question. Value an audience's time, and respect their intelligence level.

ISSUE 9-62

"MANAGEMENT ACCOUNTING IN CHINA CHANGES - PROBLEMS AND THE FUTURE," *MANAGEMENT ACCOUNTING*, JANUARY 1999, MIKE JONES AND JASON XIAO.

1. Economic Responsibility Contracts are designed to control and motivate enterprise management. Internal Responsibility Contracts are used by many enterprises to meet the ERC. While ERCs are becoming less popular, IRCs are still in operation in many companies. The IRC has four principal components. First, responsibility centers are established for appropriate internal departments, such as production, to facilitate income monitoring and cost control. Second, top management uses the company's overall financial targets to implement targets at the responsibility center level. Third, an internal bank is established which settles transactions between company divisions and lends funds raised from within or outside the company to internal divisions. Finally, performance by the IRC is evaluated periodically against pre-set targets.

2. ERCs involve management of a state-owned enterprise attaining an agreed level of sales and profit upon which it is then taxed. In return, the enterprise has autonomy to manage its business operations. A consequence of this system is that enterprises develop management accounting techniques, such as budgeting and standard costing, to help them meet targets.

CHAPTER 10
Standard Costing and Performance Measures for Today's Manufacturing Environment

ANSWERS TO REVIEW QUESTIONS

10-1 Management by exception is a managerial technique in which only significant deviations from expected performance are investigated.

10-2 Any control system has three basic parts: a predetermined or standard performance level, a measure of actual performance, and a comparison between standard and actual performance. The system works by making the comparison between actual and standard performance and then taking action to bring about a desired consequence.

10-3 One method of setting standards is the analysis of historical data. Historical cost data provide an indicator of future costs. The methods for analyzing cost behavior described in Chapter 7 are used to predict future costs on the basis of historical costs. These predictions then form the basis for setting standards. Another method for setting standards is task analysis, which is the analysis of a production process to determine what it should cost to produce a product or service. The emphasis shifts from what the product did cost in the past to what it should cost in the future. An example of task analysis is a time-and-motion study conducted to determine how long each step performed by direct laborers should require.

10-4 A perfection (or ideal) standard is the cost expected under perfect or ideal operating conditions. A practical (or attainable) standard is the cost expected under normal operating conditions. Many behavioral scientists question the effectiveness of perfection standards. They feel that employees are more likely to perform well when they strive to achieve an attainable standard than when they strive, often unsuccessfully, to achieve a perfection standard.

10-5 A bank could use standards to specify the required amount of time to process a loan application or process a bank transaction.

10-6 Standard material prices include the purchase price of the material and any transportation costs incurred to obtain the material. The standard quantity of material is the amount required to be included in the finished product plus an allowance for normal waste expected in the production process.

10-7 An unfavorable direct-material price variance means that a higher price was paid for the material than was expected when the standard was set. A favorable variance has the opposite interpretation.

10-8 The manager in the best position to influence the direct-material price variance is the purchasing manager.

10-9 An unfavorable direct-material quantity variance means that a larger amount of material was used in the production process than should have been used in accordance with the standard. A favorable variance has the opposite interpretation.

10-10 The manager in the best position to influence the direct-material quantity variance usually is the production manager.

10-11 The direct-material price variance is based on the quantity purchased (PQ). Deviations between the actual and standard price, which are highlighted by the price variance, relate to the purchasing function in the firm. Timely action to follow up a significant price variance is facilitated by calculating this variance as soon as possible after the material is purchased.

The direct-material quantity variance is based on the amount of material used in production (AQ). The quantity variance highlights deviations between the quantity of material actually used (AQ) and the standard quantity allowed (SQ). Therefore, it makes sense to compute this variance at the time the material is used in production.

10-12 An unfavorable direct-labor rate variance means that a higher labor rate was paid than was anticipated when the standard was set. One possible cause is that labor rate raises granted were above those anticipated in setting the standards. Another possible cause is that more highly skilled workers were used to perform tasks than were required or were anticipated at the time the standards were set. A favorable variance has the opposite interpretation.

10-13 In some cases, the manager in the best position to influence the direct-labor rate variance is the production manager. In other cases, the personnel manager or union negotiator would have greater influence.

10-14 The Interpretation of an unfavorable direct-labor efficiency variance is that more labor was used to accomplish a given task than was required in accordance with the standards. A favorable variance has the opposite interpretation.

10-15 The manager in the best position to influence the direct-labor efficiency variance usually is the production manager.

10-16 The issue of quantity purchased versus quantity used does not arise in the context of direct labor, because direct labor is purchased and used at the same time. Unlike direct material, direct labor cannot be purchased and inventoried for later use.

10-17 Several factors that managers often consider when determining the significance of a variance are as follows: size of variance, extent to which the variances are recurring, trends in the variances, controllability of the variances, and the perceived costs and benefits of investigating the variances.

10-18 Several ways in which standard-costing should be adapted in the new manufacturing environment are as follows:

(a) Reduced importance of labor standards and variances: As direct labor occupies a diminished role in the new manufacturing environment, the standards and variances used to control labor costs also decline in importance.

(b) Emphasis on material and overhead costs: As labor diminishes in its importance, material and overhead costs take on greater significance.

(c) Cost drivers: Identification of the factors that drive production costs takes on greater importance in the cost management system.

(d) Shifting cost structure: Advanced manufacturing systems require large outlays for production equipment, which entail a shift in the cost structure from variable costs toward fixed costs. Overhead cost control becomes especially critical.

(e) High quality and no defects: Total quality control programs that typically accompany a JIT approach strive for very high quality levels for both raw materials and finished products. One result should be very low material price and quantity variances and low costs of rework.

(f) Non-value-added costs: A key objective of a cost management system is the elimination of non-value-added costs. As these costs are reduced or eliminated, standards must be revised frequently to provide accurate benchmarks for cost control.

(g) New measures and standards: In the new manufacturing environment, new measures must be developed to control key aspects of the production process. As new measures are developed, standards should be established as benchmarks for performance. An example is the manufacturing cycle efficiency measure, which is defined as processing time divided by the sum of processing time, inspection time, waiting time, and move time.

(h) Real-time information systems: A computer-integrated manufacturing system enables the managerial accountant to collect operating data as production takes place and to report relevant performance measures to management on a real-time basis. This enables managers to eliminate the causes of unfavorable variances more quickly.

10-19 Under a standard-costing system, standard costs are used for product-costing purposes as well as for control purposes. The costs entered into Work-in-Process Inventory are standard costs. From that point forward, standard costs flow through all the manufacturing accounts. When goods are finished, the standard cost of the finished goods is removed from the Work-in-Process Inventory account and transferred to the Finished-Goods Inventory account. When goods are sold, the standard cost of the goods sold is transferred from the Finished-Goods Inventory account to Cost of Goods Sold.

10-20 Advantages of a standard-costing system include the following:

(a) Standard costs provide a basis for sensible cost comparisons. Standard costs enable the managerial accountant to compute the standard allowed cost, given actual output, which then serves as a sensible benchmark to compare with the actual cost incurred.

(b) Computation of standard costs and cost variances enables managers to employ management by exception.

(c) Variances provide a means of performance evaluation and rewards for employees.

(d) Since the variances are used in performance evaluation, they provide motivation for employees to adhere to standards.

(e) Use of standard costs in product costing results in more stable product costs than if actual production costs were used.

(f) A standard-costing system usually is less expensive than an actual- or normal-costing system.

10-21 Seven areas in which operational performance measures are being used are as follows:

(a) Raw material and scrap

(b) Inventory

(c) Machinery

(d) Product quality

(e) Production and delivery

(f) Productivity

(g) Innovation and learning

10-22 Manufacturing cycle efficiency (MCE) is defined as processing time divided by the sum of the following four items: processing time, inspection time, waiting time, and move time.

10-23 Examples of customer-acceptance measures include the number of customer complaints, the number of warranty claims, the number of products returned and the cost of repairing returned products.

10-24 An aggregate productivity measure is defined as total output divided by total input. Such a measure is limited because it is expressed in dollars, rather than in physical attributes of the production process, and it is too highly aggregated. A preferable approach to productivity measurement is to record multiple physical measures that capture the most important determinants of a company's productivity.

10-25 Eight criticisms of standard costing in an advanced manufacturing setting are the following:

(a) Variances are too aggregate and too late to be useful.

(b) Variances are not tied to specific product lines, production batches, or FMS cells.

(c) Standard-costing systems focus too much on direct labor.

(d) Frequent switching among products in an FMS cell makes cost standards less appropriate.

(e) Shorter product life cycles mean that individual standards are soon outmoded.

(f) Traditional standard costs are not defined broadly enough to include important costs, such as the total *cost of ownership.*

(g) Traditional standard-costing systems tend to focus too much on cost minimization, rather than increasing product quality or customer service.

(h) Automated manufacturing processes are highly reliable in meeting production specifications. As a result variances from standards tend to be very small or nonexistent.

10-26 Responses will vary widely on this question. Here are some possibilities for a bank:

- Financial: (a) profit; (b) cost of back-office (i.e., administrative) operations.

- Internal operations: (a) number of transaction errors; (b) employee retention and advancement.

- Customer: (a) local market share; (b) number of repeat customers.

- Innovation and learning: (a) new financial products; (b) employee suggestions received and implemented.

10-27 An airline could measure the frequency and cost of customer complaints about lost or damaged luggage. After reducing the number of such incidents, the cost savings could be shared with the relevant employees (e.g., front-counter ticket agents and baggage-handling personnel).

SOLUTIONS TO EXERCISES

EXERCISE 10-28 (15 MINUTES)

Direct-material price variance = $PQ(AP - SP)$

= 240,000($.81 - $.80)

= $2,400 Unfavorable

Direct-material quantity variance = $SP(AQ - SQ)$

= $.80(210,000 - 200,000*)

= $8,000 Unfavorable

*SQ = 200,000 kilograms = 50,000 units × 4 kilograms per unit

Direct-labor rate variance = $AH(AR - SR)$

= 13,000($16.30* - $16.00)

= $3,900 Unfavorable

*AR = $211,900 ÷ 13,000 hours

Direct-labor efficiency variance = $SR(AH - SH)$

= $16.00(13,000 - 12,500*)

= $8,000 Unfavorable

*SH = 12,500 hours = 50,000 units × .25 hours per unit

EXERCISE 10-29 (30 MINUTES)

DIRECT-MATERIAL PRICE AND QUANTITY VARIANCES

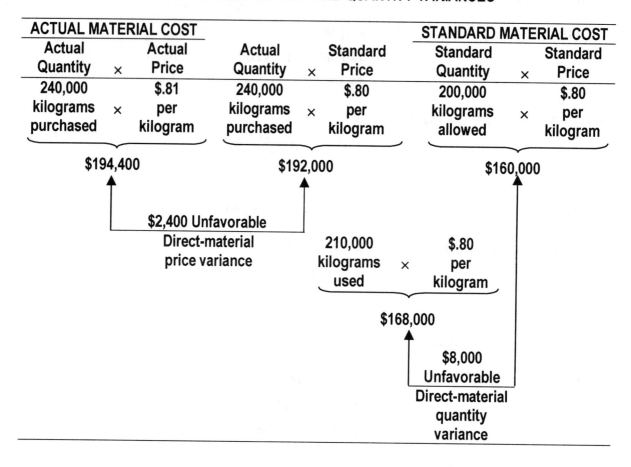

EXERCISE 10-29 (CONTINUED)

DIRECT-LABOR RATE AND EFFICIENCY VARIANCES

ACTUAL LABOR COST					STANDARD LABOR COST	
Actual Hours	×	Actual Rate	Actual Hours	×	Standard Rate	Standard Hours	×	Standard Rate
13,000 hours used	×	$16.30 per hour	13,000 hours used	×	$16.00 per hour	12,500 hours allowed	×	$16.00 per hour
$211,900			$208,000			$200,000		

$3,900 Unfavorable
Direct-labor rate variance

$8,000 Unfavorable
Direct-labor efficiency variance

$11,900 Unfavorable
Direct-labor variance

EXERCISE 10-30 (10 MINUTES)

Answers will vary widely, depending on the company and the product. Typically, new products present challenges in setting standards, particularly if they involve new production processes or materials. Managerial accountants and engineers often look to other similar products or other products manufactured using similar processes to get an idea as to what the standard cost of a new product should be.

EXERCISE 10-31 (10 MINUTES)

Standard quantity:

Hardwood in finished product	8	board feet
Allowance for normal scrap	2	board feet
Total standard quantity required per box	10	board feet

Standard price:

Purchase price per board foot of hardwood	$ 4.00	
Transportation cost per board foot	1.50	
Total standard price per board foot	$ 5.50	

EXERCISE 10-31 (CONTINUED)

Standard direct-material cost of a jewelry box:

Standard quantity	10	board feet
Price per board foot	× $ 5.50	
Standard direct-material cost	$55.00	

EXERCISE 10-32 (15 MINUTES)

Direct-material price variance = $PQ(AP - SP)$

= $6{,}000(\$7.30 - \$7.00)$

= $1,800 Unfavorable

Direct-material quantity variance = $SP(AQ - SQ)$

= $\$7.00(4{,}200^* - 4{,}000^\dagger)$

= $1,400 Unfavorable

*AQ = 4,200 pounds = $30,660 ÷ $7.30 per pound

†SQ = 4,000 pounds = 2,000 units × 2 pounds per unit

Direct-labor rate variance = $AH(AR - SR)$

= $6{,}450^*(\$18.10 - \$18.00)$

= $645 Unfavorable

*AH = 6,450 hours = $116,745 ÷ $18.10 per hour

Direct-labor efficiency variance = $SR(AH - SH)$

= $\$18(6{,}450 - 6{,}000)^*$

= $8,100 Unfavorable

*SH = 6,000 hours = 2,000 units × 3 hours per unit

EXERCISE 10-33 (30 MINUTES)

DIRECT-MATERIAL PRICE AND QUANTITY VARIANCES

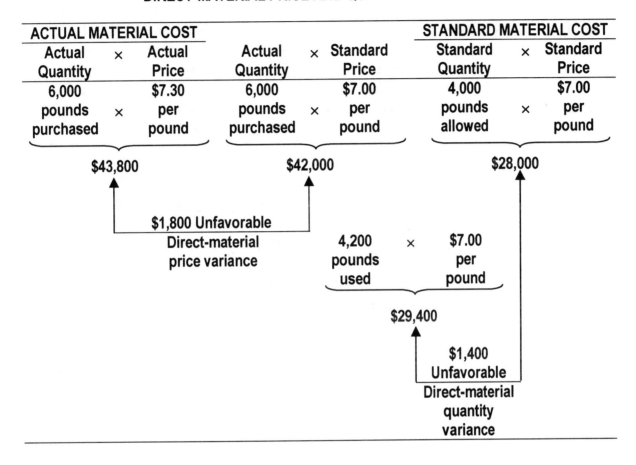

ACTUAL MATERIAL COST					STANDARD MATERIAL COST		
Actual Quantity	×	Actual Price	Actual Quantity	× Standard Price	Standard Quantity	×	Standard Price
6,000 pounds purchased	×	$7.30 per pound	6,000 pounds purchased	× $7.00 per pound	4,000 pounds allowed	×	$7.00 per pound

$43,800 $42,000 $28,000

$1,800 Unfavorable
Direct-material
price variance

4,200 pounds used × $7.00 per pound

$29,400

$1,400
Unfavorable
Direct-material
quantity
variance

EXERCISE 10-33 (CONTINUED)

DIRECT-LABOR RATE AND EFFICIENCY VARIANCES

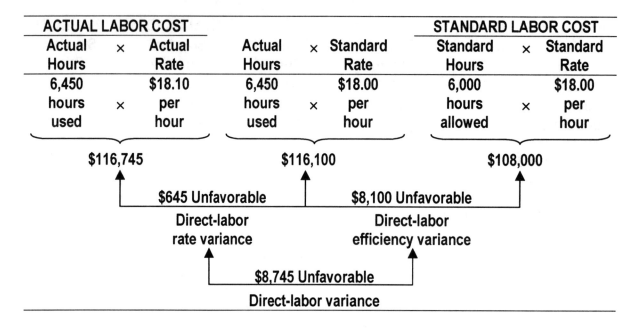

ACTUAL LABOR COST						STANDARD LABOR COST		
Actual Hours	×	Actual Rate	Actual Hours	×	Standard Rate	Standard Hours	×	Standard Rate
6,450 hours used	×	$18.10 per hour	6,450 hours used	×	$18.00 per hour	6,000 hours allowed	×	$18.00 per hour
$116,745			$116,100			$108,000		

$645 Unfavorable
Direct-labor rate variance

$8,100 Unfavorable
Direct-labor efficiency variance

$8,745 Unfavorable
Direct-labor variance

EXERCISE 10-34 (25 MINUTES)

1. (a)   Statistical control chart with variance data plotted:

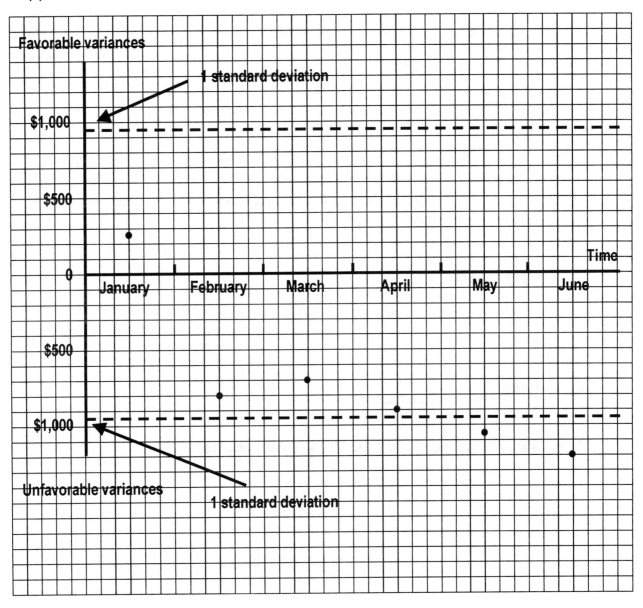

(b)   Only the variances in May and June would be investigated, since they are the only ones that exceed 1 standard deviation, $950.

EXERCISE 10-34 (CONTINUED)

2.   Rule of thumb:

Standard cost	$19,000
Cutoff percentage	× 6%
Cutoff value for investigation	$ 1,140

Only the June variance, $1,200 U, is equal to or greater than the cutoff value. Thus, only June's variance would be investigated. (U denotes unfavorable.)

3.   This is a judgment call, and there is no right or wrong answer. It would be reasonable to conclude that the consistent stream of relatively large unfavorable variances should be investigated before May. The three variances for February, March, and April would be cause for concern.

EXERCISE 10-35 (5 MINUTES)

Good output   =   (7/8) × input = .875 × input

$$\frac{\text{Good output}}{.875} = \text{standard allowed input}$$

$$\frac{4,200 \text{ pounds}}{.875} = 4,800 \text{ pounds of input}$$

The standard allowed input quantity in May was 4,800 pounds.

EXERCISE 10-36 (30 MINUTES)

	Direct Labor	Direct Material
Standard price or rate per unit of input............................	$20 per hr[e]	$8 per lb
Standard quantity per unit of output	4 hrs per unit[f]	2.75 lbs per unit[c]
Actual quantity used per unit of output...........................	3.5 hrs	3 lbs per unit[a]
Actual price or rate per unit of input...............................	$21 per hr	$7 per lb
Actual output..	10,000 units	10,000 units
Direct-material price variance...	—	$30,000 F
Direct-material quantity variance......................................	—	$20,000 U[b]
Total of direct-material variances.....................................	—	$10,000 F
Direct-labor rate variance...	$ 35,000 U[d]	—
Direct-labor efficiency variance..	$100,000 F	—
Total of direct-labor variances...	$ 65,000 F	—

Explanatory notes:

a.

$$\text{Direct-material price variance} = PQ(AP - SP)$$

$$\$30,000\text{ F} = PQ(\$7 - \$8)$$

$$PQ = 30,000\text{ lbs}$$

$$\text{Actual quantity used} = \text{quantity purchased}$$

$$AQ = PQ = 30,000\text{ lbs}$$

$$\text{Actual quantity per unit of output} = \frac{30,000\text{ lbs}}{10,000\text{ units}} = 3\text{ lbs per unit}$$

b.

$$\text{Total direct-material variance} = \text{price variance} + \text{quantity variance}$$

$$\$10,000\text{ F} = \$30,000\text{ F} + \text{quantity variance}$$

$$\text{Quantity variance} = \$20,000\text{ U}$$

c.

$$\text{Direct-material quantity variance} = SP(AQ - SQ)$$

$$\$20,000\text{ U} = \$8(30,000 - SQ)$$

$$SQ = 27,500\text{ lbs}$$

$$\text{Standard quantity per unit} = \frac{27,500\text{ lbs}}{10,000\text{ units}} = 2.75\text{ lbs per unit}$$

d.　　　　　Total direct-labor variance　=　rate variance + efficiency variance

$65,000 F　=　rate variance + $100,000 F

Rate variance　=　$35,000 U

e.　AH = 10,000 units × 3.5 hrs per unit　=　35,000 hrs

Direct-labor rate variance　=　$AH(AR - SR)$

$35,000 U　=　35,000($21 - SR)

SR　=　$20

f.　　　Direct-labor efficiency variance　=　$SR(AH - SH)$

$100,000 F　=　$20 (35,000 - SH)

SH　=　40,000 hrs

Standard hrs per unit　=　40,000 hrs/10,000 units

=　4 hrs per unit

EXERCISE 10-37 (10 MINUTES)

1.

$$\text{Manufacturing cycle efficiency} = \frac{\text{processing time}}{\text{processing time} + \text{inspection time} + \text{waiting time} + \text{move time}}$$

$$= \frac{8.5 \text{ hours}}{8.5 \text{ hours} + .5 \text{ hour} + .5 \text{ hour} + .5 \text{ hour}}$$

$$= 85\%$$

2.

$$\text{Manufacturing cycle time} = \frac{\text{total production time per batch}}{\text{units per batch}}$$

$$= \frac{10 \text{ hours}}{20 \text{ units per batch}}$$

$$= .5 \text{ hour (or 30 minutes) per unit}$$

3.

$$\text{Velocity} = \frac{\text{units per batch}}{\text{total production time per batch}}$$

$$= \frac{20 \text{ units}}{10 \text{ hours}} = 2 \text{ units per hour}$$

EXERCISE 10-38 (10 MINUTES)

1. Manufacturing cycle efficiency (MCE):

$$\text{MCE} = \frac{\text{processing time}}{\text{processing time} + \text{inspection time} + \text{waiting time} + \text{move time}}$$

$$= \frac{3 \text{ days}}{3 \text{ days} + 1.5 \text{ days} + 15 \text{ days} + 2.5 \text{ days}} = 3/22 = 13.6\% \text{ (rounded)}$$

2. Delivery cycle time is the average time between receipt of the customer's order until delivery of the goods. In this case the delivery cycle time is 22 days.

EXERCISE 10-39 (15 MINUTES)

1. Aggregate (or total) productivity $= \dfrac{\text{total output}}{\text{total input}}$

   $= \dfrac{\$10,000,000}{\$8,000,000} = 1.25$

2. This summary financial measure does not convey much information to management or other users of the data. A preferable approach would be to record multiple physical measures that capture the most important determinants of the bank's productivity. Examples include the following:

   a. Clerk time per bank window customer

   b. Errors per 1,000 transactions handled

   c. Checks miscoded per 1,000 checks processed

   d. Customers per day

   e. Customers per employee

   f. Square feet of space in bank per 1,000 customers

   g. Average time to process a loan application

EXERCISE 10-40 (15 MINUTES)

Raw-Material Inventory..	192,000	
Direct-Material Price Variance	2,400	
Accounts Payable		194,400
Work-in-Process Inventory	160,000	
Direct-Material Quantity Variance	8,000	
Raw-Material Inventory...		168,000
Work-in-Process Inventory	200,000	
Direct-Labor Rate Variance...	3,900	
Direct-Labor Efficiency Variance.......................................	8,000	
Wages Payable		211,900
Cost of Goods Sold	22,300	
Direct-Material Price Variance		2,400
Direct-Material Quantity Variance......................................		8,000
Direct-Labor Rate Variance...		3,900
Direct-Labor Efficiency Variance.......................................		8,000

EXERCISE 10-41 (15 MINUTES)

Raw-Material Inventory		Direct-Material Price Variance	
192,000	168,000	2,400	2,400

Work-in-Process Inventory		Direct-Material Quantity Variance	
160,000		8,000	8,000
200,000			

		Direct-Labor Rate Variance	
		3,900	3,900

Accounts Payable			
	194,400		

		Direct-Labor Efficiency Variance	
		8,000	8,000

Wages Payable			
	211,900		

		Cost of Goods Sold	
		22,300	

SOLUTIONS TO PROBLEMS

PROBLEM 10-42 (35 MINUTES)

1. Schedule of standard production costs:

NEW JERSEY VALVE COMPANY
CAMDEN PLANT
SCHEDULE OF STANDARD PRODUCTION COSTS
BASED ON 7,800 UNITS
FOR THE MONTH OF JANUARY

		Standard Costs
Direct material...	7,800 units × 3 lbs. × $2.50	$ 58,500
Direct labor...	7,800 units × 5 hrs. × $15.00	585,000
Total standard production costs.......................		$643,500

2. Variances:

    a.   Direct-material price variance = $(PQ \times AP) - (PQ \times SP)$

                                                    = $(25,000 \times \$2.60) - (25,000 \times \$2.50)$

                                                    = $2,500 Unfavorable

    b.   Direct-material quantity variance = $(AQ \times SP) - (SQ \times SP)$

                                                    = $(23,100 \times \$2.50) - (23,400^* \times \$2.50)$

                                                    = $750 Favorable

    *7,800 units × 3 lbs. per unit = 23,400 lb.

    c.   Direct-labor rate variance = $(AH \times AR) - (AH \times SR)$

                                                    = $(40,100 \times \$14.60) - (40,100 \times \$15.00)$

                                                    = $16,040 Favorable

    d.   Direct-labor efficiency variance = $(AH \times SR) - (SH \times SR)$

                                                    = $(40,100 \times \$15.00) - (39,000^* \times \$15.00)$

                                                    = $16,500 Unfavorable

    *7,800 units × 5 hours per unit = 39,000 hr.

PROBLEM 10-43 (15 MINUTES)

Direct Material	Initial Mix	Unit Cost	Standard Material Cost
Nyclyn	12 kg	1.45*real*	17.40*real*
Salex..	9.6 ltr	1.80*real*	17.28*real*
Protet...	5 kg	2.40*real*	12.00*real*
Standard material cost for each 10-liter container................................			46.68*real*

The *real* is Brazil's national currency.

PROBLEM 10-44 (25 MINUTES)

1. Direct-material price variance
    $= (PQ \times AP) - (PQ \times SP)$
    $= (18,000 \times \$1.38) - (18,000 \times \$1.35)$
    $= \$24,840 - \$24,300$
    $= \$540$ Unfavorable

2. Direct-material quantity variance
    $= (AQ \times SP) - (SQ \times SP)$
    $= (9,500 \times \$1.35) - (10,000^* \times \$1.35)$
    $= \$675$ Favorable

    *500 units $\times$ 20 yards per unit = 10,000 yards

3. Direct-labor rate variance
    $= (AH \times AR) - (AH \times SR)$
    $= (2,100 \times \$9.15) - (2,100 \times \$9.00)$
    $= \$19,215 - \$18,900$
    $= \$315$ Unfavorable

PROBLEM 10-44 (CONTINUED)

4. Direct-labor efficiency variance $= (AH \times SR) - (SH \times SR)$

    $= (2{,}100 \times \$9.00) - (2{,}000^* \times \$9.00)$

    $= \$18{,}900 - \$18{,}000$

    $= \$900$ Unfavorable

*500 units $\times$ 4 hours per unit = 2,000 hours

PROBLEM 10-45 (35 MINUTES)

1. Type I fertilizer:

    Price variance:

Actual quantity purchased x actual price	
5,000 pounds x $ .53..	$2,650
Actual quantity purchased x standard price	
5,000 pounds x $ .50..	2,500
Direct-material price variance...........................	$ 150 Unfavorable

Quantity variance:

Actual quantity used x standard price	
3,700 pounds x $ .50..	$1,850
Standard quantity allowed x standard price	
4,400 pounds* x $ .50..	2,200
Direct-material quantity variance.......................	$ 350 Favorable

* 40 pounds x 55 clients x 2 applications

Type II fertilizer:

Price variance:

Actual quantity purchased x actual price	
10,000 pounds x $ .40....................................	$4,000
Actual quantity purchased x standard price	
10,000 pounds x $ .42....................................	4,200
Direct-material price variance...........................	$ 200 Favorable

PROBLEM 10-45 (CONTINUED)

Quantity variance:

Actual quantity used x standard price

7,800 pounds x $ .42... $3,276

Standard quantity allowed x standard price

8,800 pounds* x $ .42...................................... 3,696

Direct-material quantity variance......................... $ 420 Favorable

* 40 pounds x 55 clients x 4 applications

2.   Direct-labor variances:

Rate variance:

Actual hours used x actual rate

165 hours x $11.50............................ $1,897.50

Actual hours used x standard rate

165 hours x $9.00............................. 1,485.00

Direct-labor rate variance..................... $ 412.50 Unfavorable

Efficiency variance:

Actual hours used x standard rate

165 hours x $9.00............................. $1,485.00

Standard hours allowed x standard rate

220 hours* x $9.00............................ 1,980.00

Direct-labor efficiency variance............. $ 495.00 Favorable

* 2/3 hours x 55 clients x 6 applications

3.   Actual cost of applications:

Type I fertilizer:

Actual quantity used x actual price (3,700 pounds x $ .53).... $1,961.00

Type II fertilizer:

Actual quantity used x actual price (7,800 pounds x $ .40).... 3,120.00

Direct labor:

Actual hours used x actual rate (165 hours x $11.50)............ 1,897.50

Total actual cost.. $6,978.50

Yes, the service was a financial success. Amato charged clients $40 per application, generating revenue of $13,200 (55 clients x 6 applications x $40). With costs of $6,978.50, the fertilization service produced a profit of $6,221.50.

PROBLEM 10-45 (CONTINUED)

4. (a)   Yes, the service was a success. Overall costs were controlled as indicated by a total favorable variance of $902.50. In addition, each of the three cost components (Type I fertilizer, Type II fertilizer, and direct labor) produced a net favorable variance. Amato did have a sizable unfavorable labor-rate variance as a result of his having to pay $11.50 per hour when a more typical wage rate would have been $9.00 per hour. This inflated rate is attributable to the tight labor market, which is beyond his control. Note: Part of the variance may have been caused by a standard rate that was set too low, especially given the fact that this is a new service.

Type I fertilizer:	
Price variance..	$150.00 Unfavorable
Quantity variance....................................	350.00 Favorable
Type II fertilizer:	
Price variance..	200.00 Favorable
Quantity variance....................................	420.00 Favorable
Direct labor:	
Rate variance..	412.50 Unfavorable
Efficiency variance..................................	495.00 Favorable
Total material and labor variances	$902.50 Favorable

   (b)   In this case, several of the favorable variances may have come back to haunt Amato. The favorable labor efficiency variance means that less time is being spent on the job than originally anticipated. This may indicate that the part-time employee is rushing and doing sloppy work. Also, less fertilizer used than budgeted (i.e., favorable quantity variances for both Type I and Type II) would likely give rise to an increased occurrence of weeds as well as a lack of greening in the lawn.

5. This is a management judgment for Amato to make. If the service is continued, Amato should consider hiring a full-time employee and insisting on the standard amount of fertilizer being applied to each lawn.

PROBLEM 10-46 (30 MINUTES)

1. No. The variances are favorable and small, with each being less than 2% of budgeted cost amounts ($350,000). However, by simply reporting total variances for material and labor, one cannot get a totally clear picture of performance. Price, quantity, rate, and efficiency variances should be calculated for further insight.

PROBLEM 10-46 (CONTINUED)

2. **Direct-material variances:**

Price variance:

Actual quantity purchased x actual price	
45,000 pounds x $7.70.................................	$346,500
Actual quantity purchased x standard price	
45,000 pounds x $8.80.................................	396,000
Direct-material price variance...........................	$ 49,500 Favorable

Quantity variance:

Actual quantity used x standard price	
45,000 pounds x $8.80.................................	$396,000
Standard quantity allowed x standard price	
39,900 pounds* x $8.80.............................	351,120
Direct-material quantity variance........................	$ 44,880 Unfavorable

* 9,500 units x 4.2 pounds

Total direct-material variance:
$49,500F + $44,880U = $4,620F

Direct-labor variances:

Rate variance:

Actual hours used x actual rate	
20,900 hours x $16.25......................	$339,625
Actual hours used x standard rate	
20,900 hours x $14.00......................	292,600
Direct-labor rate variance....................	$ 47,025 Unfavorable

Efficiency variance:

Actual hours used x standard rate	
20,900 hours x $14.00......................	$292,600
Standard hours allowed x standard rate	
24,700 hours* x $14.00.....................	345,800
Direct-labor efficiency variance.............	$ 53,200 Favorable

* 9,500 units x 2.6 hours

Total direct-labor variance:
$47,025U + $53,200F = $6,175F

PROBLEM 10-46 (CONTINUED)

3.   Yes.   Although the combined variances are small, a more detailed analysis reveals the presence of sizable, offsetting variances (all in excess of 12% of budgeted cost amounts).   A variance investigation should be undertaken if the likely benefits of the investigation appear to exceed the costs.

4.   No, things are not going as smoothly as the vice-president believes.   With regard to the new supplier, Santa Rosa is paying less than expected for direct materials. However, the quality may be poor, as indicated by the unfavorable quantity variance and increased usage.

   Turning to direct labor, the favorable efficiency variance means that the company is producing units by consuming fewer hours than expected.   This may be the result of the team-building/morale-boosting exercises, as a contented, well-trained work force tends to be more efficient.   However, another plausible explanation could be that Santa Rosa is paying premium wages (as indicated by the unfavorable rate variance) to hire laborers with above-average skill levels.

   As a side note, the favorable direct-labor efficiency variance may partially explain the unfavorable material quantity variance.   That is, laborers may be rushing through their jobs and using more material than the standards allow.

5.   Yes.   Schmidt is the production supervisor.   The prices paid for materials and the quality of material acquired are normally the responsibility of the purchasing manager.   The change to the new supplier may introduce problems of dealing with the unknown—the supplier's reliability, ability to deliver quality goods, etc.   Finally, direct-labor wage rates are often a function of market conditions, which would likely be uncontrollable from Schmidt's perspective.

PROBLEM 10-47 (35 MINUTES)

1. a. Machine hours x 4 = standard direct-labor hours
   165.5 x 4 = 662

   b. Direct-labor efficiency variance = (AH–SH)SR
   $$= (374-662)\$15.08$$
   $$= \$4,343 \text{ F}$$

2.

	a. Standard Direct-Labor Cost*	b. 20% of the Standard Direct-Labor Cost*
January	$ 9,983	$1,997
February	6,050	1,210
March	33,297	6,659
April	43,056	8,611
May	9,651	1,930
June	13,994	2,799
July	6,273	1,255
August	5,791	1,158
September	5,791	1,158
October	4,343	869

*Rounded.

3. The variances for all of the months except August and September exceed 20% of the standard direct-labor cost and would therefore be investigated.

4. **Statistical control chart for direct-labor efficiency variances:**

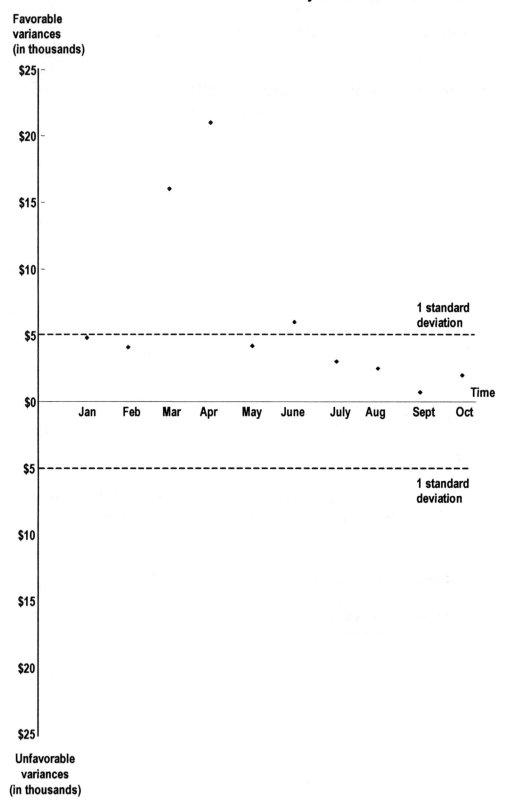

PROBLEM 10-47 (CONTINUED)

5. The variances for March, April, and June will be investigated, since they exceed one
    standard deviation.

6. The production volume was much greater in March, April, and June.

PROBLEM 10-48 (25 MINUTES)

1. Direct-material price variance   = $(PQ \times AP) - (PQ \times SP)$

                                     = $304,000 - (160,000 \times \$1.75)$

                                     = $304,000 - \$280,000$

                                     = $24,000 Unfavorable

2. Direct-material quantity variance = $SP(AQ - SQ)$

                                       = $1.75(142,500 - 152,000*)$

                                       = $16,625 Favorable

    *Standard quantity allowed = 19,000 units $\times$ 8 lbs. per unit = 152,000 lbs.

3. Direct-labor rate variance   = $(AH \times AR) - (AH \times SR)$

                                 = $37,800* - (5,000 \times \$8.00)$

                                 = $2,200 Favorable

    *90% $\times$ $42,000 = $37,800

4. Direct-labor efficiency variance = $SR(AH - SH)$

                                      = $8.00(5,000 - 4,750*)$

                                      = $2,000 Unfavorable

    *19,000 units $\times$ .25 hour per unit = 4,750 hours

PROBLEM 10-49 (30 MINUTES)

1. a. Responsibility for setting standards:

    Materials:

    The development of standard prices for material is primarily the responsibility of the materials manager.

    Operating departmental managers and engineers should be involved in setting standards for material quantities.

    Labor:

    The personnel manager or payroll manager would be involved in setting standard labor rates.

    Operating department managers with input from production supervisors and engineers would be involved in setting standards for labor usage.

    b. The factors that should be considered in establishing material standards include the following:

    -   Price studies, including expected general economic conditions, industry prospects, demand for the materials, and market conditions.

    -   Product specifications from descriptions, drawings, and blueprints.

    -   Past records on raw-material cost, usage, waste, and scrap.

    Factors in establishing labor standards:

    -   Engineering studies of the time required to complete various tasks.

    -   Learning.

    -   Expected wage rates.

    -   Expected labor mix (e.g., skilled versus unskilled).

PROBLEM 10-49 (CONTINUED)

2. The basis for assignment of responsibility under a standard-costing system is controllability. Judgments about whether departments or department managers are performing efficiently should not be affected by items over which they have no control.

    The responsibility for a variance should be assigned to the department or individual that has the greatest responsibility for deciding whether a specific cost should be incurred. Some variances, however, are interdependent and responsibility must be shared.

PROBLEM 10-50 (30 MINUTES)

1. Variances (U denotes unfavorable; F denotes favorable):

    a. Direct-labor rate variance for each labor class:

Labor Class	Actual Rate	Standard Rate	Difference in Rates	Actual Hours	Rate Variance
III	$17.20	$16.00	$1.20	550	$ 660 U
II	15.00	14.00	1.00	650	650 U
I	10.80	10.00	.80	375	300 U
Total					$1,610 U

    b. Direct-labor efficiency variance for each labor class:

Labor Class	Actual Hours	Standard Hours*	Difference in Hours	Standard Rate	Efficiency Variance
III	550	500	50	$16.00	$ 800 U
II	650	500	150	14.00	2,100 U
I	375	500	(125)	10.00	(1,250) F
Total					$1,650 U

*Given April's output of production.

PROBLEM 10-50 (CONTINUED)

2. The advantages of not changing the labor rate would include (1) comparison of actual operating results to a fixed base which was previously approved by management, and (2) the clerical or computer cost savings of not implementing the change. If labor standards are not changed during the year to incorporate significant changes in labor costs, a noncontrollable variance is created. This variance may mask actual operating variances. In addition, when reporting operating variances that contain a significant noncontrollable variance, a credibility gap may be created.

PROBLEM 10-51 (35 MINUTES)

1. Standard cost per cutting board:

Direct material:
Lumber (1.5 board ft.* × $3.00 per board ft.)	$4.50	
Footpads (4 pads × $.05 per pad)................................	.20	$4.70

Direct labor:
Prepare and cut (14.4†/60 hr. × $8.00 per hr.)..............	$1.92	
Assemble and finish (15/60 hr. × $8.00 per hr.)	2.00	3.92
Total standard unit cost		$8.62

$$*1.25 \text{ board ft.} \times \frac{(5+1)}{5} = 1.5 \text{ board ft.}$$

$$†12 \text{ min. per board} \times \frac{(5+1)}{5} = 14.4 \text{ min.}$$

PROBLEM 10-51 (CONTINUED)

2. a. The role of the purchasing manager in the development of standards includes establishing the standard cost for material required by the bill of materials, determining if the company should take advantage of price reductions available through economic order size, and obtaining data regarding the availability of materials.

    b. The role of the industrial engineer in the development of standards includes preparing the bill of materials that specifies the types and quantities of material required; establishing, in conjunction with the production supervisor, any allowances for scrap, shrinkage, and waste; and participating in time studies and test runs to facilitate the establishment of time standards.

    c. The role of the managerial accountant in the development of standards includes reviewing all information regarding material and labor standards received from other departments, establishing the labor rate standards based on the type of labor required, determining application rates for indirect costs such as material handling and manufacturing overhead, and converting physical standards such as hours and quantities to monetary equivalents.

PROBLEM 10-51 (CONTINUED)

3. Ethical issues:

    a. The purchasing manager, Smith, acted very unethically in purchasing off-standard material for the cutting boards. It was clear that the material was not well-suited for Ogwood's product. Smith placed his own annual bonus above the best interests of the company.

    b. When Rivkin, the controller, noticed the large, favorable price variance for the wood, he acted ethically and responsibly to check out the circumstances.

    c. When the controller failed to get a clear answer from the purchasing manager, he acted ethically and responsibly in raising the issue with another qualified individual. The production manager was a logical choice, since she would be familiar with the type of materials necessary for the production process.

    d. The controller should raise the entire issue with an individual in the company who is at a high enough level to take appropriate action. Preferably, this should be someone on a higher level in the organization than Smith, Rivkin, or Wilcox. Ogwood may be able to cancel its order with the new supplier, even if it means paying some sort of penalty.

    The managerial accountant's ethical standards for objectivity require that the controller, Rivkin, disclose what he knows about this unfortunate situation. These standards are as follows:

    *   Communicate information fairly and objectively.

    *   Disclose fully all relevant information that could reasonably be expected to influence an intended user's understanding of the reports, comments, and recommendations presented.

PROBLEM 10-52 (40 MINUTES)

1. The standard cost per 10-gallon batch of strawberry jam is determined as follows:

Strawberries (7.5 qts.* × $.80)...	$ 6.00
Other ingredients (10 gal. × $.45)	4.50
Sorting labor (3/60 hr. × 6 qt. × $9.00)	2.70
Blending labor (12/60 hr. × $9.00).....................................	1.80
Packaging (40 qt.† × $.38)..	15.20
Total standard cost per 10-gallon batch............................	$30.20

*6 quarts × 5/4 = 7.5 qt., needed to produce 6 good quarts.

†4 qt. per gal. × 10 gal. = 40 qt.

2. Joe Adams' behavior regarding the cost information is unethical because it violates the following ethical standards:

Competence. Prepare complete and clear reports and recommendations after appropriate analyses of relevant and reliable information.

Integrity. Avoid actual or apparent conflicts of interest and advise all appropriate parties of any potential conflicts. Refrain from either actively or passively subverting the attainment of the organization's legitimate and ethical objectives. Refrain from engaging in or supporting any activity that would discredit the profession.

Objectivity. Communicate information fairly and objectively.

3. a. In general, the purchasing manager is held responsible for unfavorable material price variances. Causes of these variances include the following:

   - Failure to forecast price increases correctly.

   - Purchasing nonstandard or uneconomical lots.

   - Purchasing from suppliers other than those offering the most favorable terms.

PROBLEM 10-52 (CONTINUED)

b. In general, the production manager is held responsible for unfavorable labor efficiency variances. Causes of these variances include the following:

- Poorly trained labor.

- Substandard or inefficient equipment.

- Substandard material.

PROBLEM 10-53 (40 MINUTES)

1. Variances to be investigated using rule of thumb:

Variance Type	Month	Amount	Percentage of Standard Cost
Efficiency...........................	August	38,000 U....................	7.60%
Efficiency...........................	September	37,000 U....................	7.40%
Efficiency...........................	October...............	42,000 U....................	8.40%
Efficiency...........................	November	60,000 U....................	12.00%
Efficiency...........................	December	52,000 U....................	10.40%

2. The company's direct-labor efficiency variances exhibit a consistent unfavorable trend throughout the year. Beginning in January with an unfavorable variance of $5,000, the variances gradually increase to unfavorable variances of $60,000 and $52,000 in November and December, respectively.

When to investigate the trend in the variances is a judgment call. A reasonable investigation point would be July, when the unfavorable trend has persisted for six months and the variance is just under the $30,000 threshold value.

It would also be reasonable to investigate the direct-labor rate variance. Although the variances are relatively small, they remain consistently favorable over the eight-month period from May through December. Once again, this is a judgment call.

3. It is important to follow up on favorable variances. A consistent pattern of favorable variances, a favorable trend, or a large favorable variance may indicate that employees have discovered a more efficient production method. Management should learn about such a development and may wish to implement the method elsewhere in the company.

4. Statistical control chart: investigate August and October variances.

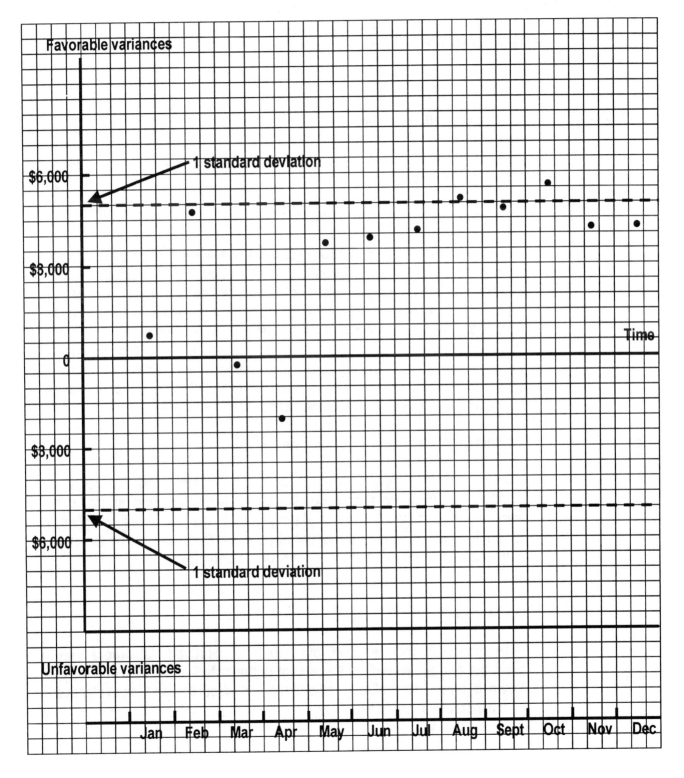

PROBLEM 10-54 (40 MINUTES)

Memorandum

Date: Today

To: President, Pittsburgh Plastics Corporation

From: I. M. Student

Subject: Performance of North Hills Plant

1.   The North Hills Plant's performance for the period January through June is summarized as follows:

    a.   Production processing and productivity:

    The plant's cycle time (or throughput time) has improved over the period from 20 hours to 17 hours (average of 18.8 hours). This indicates that the efficiency of the actual processing of products has improved. Consistent with this observation is the reduction in setup time from 70 to 62 hours (average of 65.5). However, the plant's manufacturing cycle efficiency has declined through the period, indicating that too much time is being spent on inspection time, waiting time, and move time, relative to actual processing time. Overtime hours have increased due to higher demand late in the period. Power consumption has remained stable.

    b.   Product quality and customer acceptance:

    The plant's quality control program appears to be paying off. The number of defective units in finished goods declined dramatically, and no products were returned. This is the result of the plant's inspectors more effectively identifying defective units while still in process. Effort should be devoted in the future to the reduction of the in-process defective rate.

    c.   Delivery performance:

    Delivery performance is good, but could be improved. All orders were filled, but only an average of 95 percent of the orders were filled on time in May and June. This probably reflects the increased demand, as evidenced by the increase in overtime hours.

    d.   Raw material, scrap and inventory:

The rate of defective raw materials has declined to zero. The purchasing team is doing a good job by ensuring delivery of high-quality raw materials. Inventory value has been steady through the period with an average of 4.8 percent of sales. This is probably as low as can reasonably be expected in this industry.

    e.   Machine maintenance:

Machine downtime improved during the period from 30 hours to 10 hours (average of 21.7 hours), but bottleneck machine downtime was too high, particularly in May. Also, unscheduled machine maintenance calls were up in May and June.

2.   Recommended actions:

    a.   Investigate the reasons behind the decline in manufacturing-cycle efficiency. Concentrate on the elimination of non-value-added activities, such as move time and wait time.

    b.   Maintain inspections in process. Try to reduce the in-process defective rate by emphasizing the importance of quality to the work force.

    c.   Investigate causes of bottleneck machine downtime and correct the situation.

PROBLEM 10-55 (45 MINUTES)

1. Categories of measures:

	Area of Manufacturing Performance
Cycle time (days)..	a
Number of defective finished products	b
Manufacturing-cycle efficiency....................................	a
Customer complaints	c
Unresolved complaints..	c
Products returned..	b,c
Warranty claims	b,c
In-process products rejected.......................................	d
Aggregate productivity..	a,e
Number of units produced per day per employee..........	a,e
Percentage of on-time deliveries.................................	f
Percentage of orders filled..	f
Inventory value/sales revenue	g,h
Machine downtime (minutes).......................................	i
Bottleneck machine downtime (minutes)	i
Overtime (minutes) per employee	a,e
Average setup time (minutes)......................................	a

PROBLEM 10-55 (CONTINUED)

2.   **Memorandum**

Date: Today

To: Management, MedTech, Inc.

From: I. M. Student

Subject: Performance of Harrisburg plant during 1st quarter

The performance of the Harrisburg plant is evaluated in nine key areas:

a. Production processing:

    Cycle time, manufacturing-cycle efficiency, and productivity measures all point to consistency and high-level performance throughout the measurement period. Both cycle time and manufacturing-cycle efficiency exhibit slight, favorable trends.

b. Product quality:

    The number of defective finished products, number of products returned, and warranty claims all show improvement over the period. All three measures suggest excellent performance in quality control.

c. Customer acceptance:

    Customer complaints are steady with an average of 6.5 complaints during a two-week period. The number of unresolved complaints improved during the period from 2 to 0. Performance in this area is very high, but there is a little room for improvement.

d. In-process quality control:

    The number of products rejected in process has increased. This speaks well for the in-process inspection effort. The cause of these defective in-process units should be investigated and corrected.

e. Productivity:

Both the aggregate productivity measure and the number of units produced per day per employee remained relatively steady throughout the period. The latter of these two measures exhibited a slight, favorable trend.

f. Delivery performance:

Both performance measures (percentages of on-time deliveries and orders filled) were very high through the period, finishing at 100 percent in period 6.

g. & h. Raw material and scrap; inventory:

Inventory value/sales revenue remained consistently low through the period (average of 1.83 percent).

i. Machine maintenance:

Machine downtime was low through the period (average of 84 minutes each two-week period). Bottleneck machine downtime was low except in period 5. The cause of that incident should be investigated.

Overall evaluation:

The Harrisburg plant has performed at a very high level of efficiency in virtually every phase of its operations during the 1st quarter.

PROBLEM 10-56 (45 MINUTES)

1. a. The semiannual installments and total bonus for the Charter Division are calculated as follows:

CHARTER DIVISION
GAIN-SHARING BONUS CALCULATION
FOR THE YEAR ENDED DECEMBER 31, 20X1

First installment, January–June:

Profitability (.02 × $462,000).................................	$ 9,240
Rework [(.02 × $462,000) – $11,500]	(2,260)
On-time delivery (no bonus—under 96%)............	-0-
Sales returns	
{[(.015 × $4,200,000) – $84,000] × 50%}........	(10,500)
Semiannual installment	$ (3,520)
First semiannual bonus awarded	$ 0

Second installment, July–December:

Profitability (.02 × $440,000).................................	$ 8,800
Rework [(.02 × $440,000) – $11,000]	(2,200)
On-time delivery (96%–98%).................................	2,000
Sales returns	
{[(.015 × $4,400,000) – $70,000] × 50%}........	(2,000)
Semiannual installment	$ 6,600
Second semiannual bonus awarded	6,600
Total bonus awarded for the year............................	$6,600

b. The employees of the Charter Division are likely to be frustrated by the new plan, since the division bonus is more than $20,000 less than that of the previous year, when sales and operating income were similar. However, both on-time deliveries and sales returns improved in the second half of the year, while rework costs were relatively even. If the division continues to improve at the same rate, the Charter Division bonus will approximate or exceed what it was under the old plan. The only open question is whether the employees have sufficient motivation to effect improvement.

PROBLEM 10-56 (CONTINUED)

2.   a.   The semiannual installments and total bonus for the Mesa Division are calculated as follows:

MESA DIVISION
GAIN-SHARING BONUS CALCULATION
FOR THE YEAR ENDED DECEMBER 31, 20X1

First installment, January–June:

Profitability (.02 × $342,000)	$6,840	
Rework [(.02 × $342,000) – $6,000]	-0-*	
On-time delivery (over 98%)	5,000	
Sales returns		
{[(.015 × $2,850,000] – $44,750] × 50%}	(1,000)	
Semiannual installment	$10,840	
First semiannual bonus awarded		$10,840

Second installment, July–December:

Profitability (.02 × $406,000)	$8,120	
Rework [(.02 × $406,000) – $8,000]	-0-*	
On-time delivery (no bonus—under 96%)	-0-	
Sales returns		
{[(.015 × $2,900,000] – $42,500] × 50%}	3,000†	
Semiannual installment	$11,120	
Second semiannual bonus awarded		11,120
Total bonus awarded for the year		$21,960

*Rework costs not in excess of 2 percent of operating income.
†$3,000, since sales returns are less than 1.5 percent of sales.

   b.   The employees of the Mesa Division should be as satisfied with the new plan as with the old plan, because the bonus was almost equivalent. However, there is no sign of improvements in this division; in fact, on-time deliveries declined considerably in the second half of the year. Therefore, the bonus situation may not be as favorable in the future. Decreased bonuses could motivate the employees to improve, or they could frustrate employees and undermine their motivation.

PROBLEM 10-56 (CONTINUED)

3. Harrington's revised bonus plan for the Charter Division fostered improvements including the following:

   - Increase of 1.9 percent in on-time deliveries

   - $500 reduction in rework costs

   - $14,000 reduction in sales returns

   However, operating income as a percentage of sales has decreased from 11 to 10 percent.

   The Mesa Division's bonus has remained at the status quo. The effects of the revised plan at MedLine Equipment Corporation have been offset by the following:

   - Increase of 2 percent in operating income as a percentage of sales (from 12 to 14 percent)

   - Decrease of 3.6 percent in on-time deliveries

   - $2,000 increase in rework costs

   - $2,250 decrease in sales returns

   These results suggest that the gain-sharing bonus plan needs revisions. Suggestions include the following:

   - Creating a reward structure for rework costs that are below 2 percent of operating income that would encourage employees to drive costs lower.

   - Reviewing the whole year in total. The bonus plan should carry forward the negative amounts for one six-month period into the next six-month period, incorporating the entire year when calculating a bonus.

   - Developing benchmarks, and then giving rewards for improvements over prior periods and encouraging continuous improvement.

PROBLEM 10-57 (50 MINUTES)

1. a.   Direct-labor rate variance = $(AH \times AR) - (AH \times SR)$

    = $(36,500 \times \$8.24^*) - (36,500 \times \$8.20)$

    = $\$1,460$ Unfavorable

    *$300,760 \div 36,500$ hours

    b.   Direct-labor efficiency variance = $(AH \times SR) - (SH \times SR)$

    = $(36,500 \times \$8.20) - (37,200^* \times \$8.20)$

    = $\$5,740$ Favorable

    *Standard allowed direct-labor hours:

Completed units	5,600 units × 6 hours per unit	33,600 hours
Partially completed units.............................	800 units × 75% × 6 hours per unit	3,600 hours
Total standard hours allowed...............		37,200 hours

    c.   Actual quantity of material used:

    Direct-material quantity variance = $(AQ \times SP) - (SQ \times SP)$

    = $(AQ \times \$5.00) - (51,200^* \times \$5.00)$

    = $\$1,500$ Unfavorable

    Therefore: $\$5(AQ - 51,200)$ = $\$1,500$

    $AQ - 51,200$ = 300

    AQ = $51,500$ kilograms

    *Standard quantity of material allowed:

Completed units	5,600 units × 8 kilograms	44,800 kilograms
Partially completed units.................................	800 units × 8 kilograms	6,400 kilograms
Total standard quantity allowed..............		51,200 kilograms

PROBLEM 10-57 (CONTINUED)

d.   Actual price paid per kilogram of direct material:

   Actual price = $249,250/50,000

   = $4.985 per kilogram

e.   Direct-material and direct-labor cost transferred to finished goods:

Direct-material cost transferred..	5,600 units × $40	$224,000
Direct-labor cost transferred..	5,600 units × $49.20	275,520
Total cost transferred		$499,520

f.   Direct-material and direct-labor cost in November 30 balance of Work-in-Process Inventory:

Direct material	800 units × $40 per unit	$32,000
Direct labor	800 units × 75% × $49.20	29,520
Total cost in ending Work-in-Process Inventory		$61,520

PROBLEM 10-57 (CONTINUED)

2. Raw-Material Inventory.. 250,000

        Direct-Material Price Variance.................................   750*

        Accounts Payable...   249,250

*Direct-material price variance = $PQ(AP - SP)$

                        =   50,000($4.985 – $5.00) = $750 Favorable

To record the purchase of raw material and the direct-material price variance.

Work-in-Process Inventory 256,000*

Direct-Material Quantity Variance.................................... 1,500

    Raw-Material Inventory ....   257,500†

*51,200 × $5.00 = $256,000

†51,500 × $5.00 = $257,500

To add the direct-material cost to work in process and record the direct-material quantity variance.

Work-in-Process Inventory 305,040*

Direct-Labor Rate Variance... 1,460

    Direct-Labor Efficiency Variance   5,740

    Wages Payable..   300,760

*37,200 × $8.20 = $305,040

To add the direct-labor cost to work-in-process, record the direct-labor rate and efficiency variances, and recognize the actual direct-labor cost.

PROBLEM 10-58 (25 MINUTES)

1. (a) Direct-material price variance = $PQ(AP - SP)$

Product	Calculation $PQ(AP - SP)$	Price Variance
Standard tent	2,100 ($6.40* − $6)	$840 U
Deluxe tent	800 ($7.90† − $8)	80 F
Direct-material price variance		$760 U

*$6.40 = $13,440 ÷ 2,100

†$7.90 = $6,320 ÷ 800

(b) Direct-material quantity variance = $SP(AQ - SQ)$

Product	Calculation $SP(AQ - SQ)$	Quantity Variance
Standard tent	$6 (1,250 − 1,200*)	$300 U
Deluxe tent	$8 (720 − 720†)	-0-
Direct-material quantity variance		$300 U

*1,200 = 100 tents × 12 lbs. per tent

†720 = 120 tents × 6 lbs. per tent

PROBLEM 10-58 (CONTINUED)

2.

Raw-Material Inventory...	19,000*	
Direct-Material Price Variance.................................	760	
Accounts Payable...		19,760

To record purchase of tent fabrics.

*$19,000 = (2,100 lbs. × $6 per lb.) + (800 lbs. × $8 per lb.)

Work-in-Process Inventory..	12,960*	
Direct-Material Quantity Variance.............................	300	
Raw-Material Inventory.....................................		13,260†

To record use of direct material.

*$12,960 = (1,200 lbs. × $6 per lb.) + (720 lbs. × $8 per lb.)

†$13,260 = (1,250 lbs. × $6 per lb.) + (720 lbs. × $8 per lb.)

PROBLEM 10-59 (60 MINUTES)

1. Standard cost schedule:

DIRECT MATERIAL

	Construction Department	Finishing Department
Standard quantity		
Direct material and parts in finished product:		
Veneered wood....................................	7 lbs	—
Bridge and strings...............................	—	1 set
Allowance for normal waste......................	1 lb	—
Total standard quantity per guitar................	8 lbs	1 set
Standard price:		
Direct material and parts:		
Veneered wood....................................	$12 per lb	—
Bridge and strings...............................	—	$15 per set
Standard direct-material cost:		
Standard quantity....................................	8 lbs	1 set
Standard price.......................................	× $12 per lb	× $15 per set
Standard cost per guitar..........................	$96 per guitar	$15 per guitar
Actual output in July...............................	× 500 guitars	× 500 guitars
Total standard cost of direct material in July..	$48,000	$7,500

DIRECT LABOR

	Construction Department	Finishing Department
Standard direct-labor cost:		
Standard quantity......................................	6 hrs	3 hrs
Standard rate...	× $ 20	× $15
Standard cost per guitar..........................	$120	$45
Actual output in July...............................	× 500 guitars	× 500 guitars
Total standard cost of direct labor in July..	$60,000	$22,500

PROBLEM 10-59 (CONTINUED)

2. (a) Construction Department:

DIRECT-MATERIAL PRICE AND QUANTITY VARIANCES

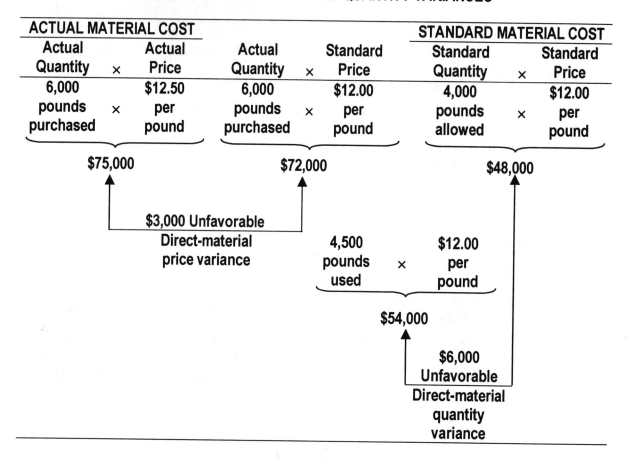

DIRECT-LABOR RATE AND EFFICIENCY VARIANCES

ACTUAL LABOR COST				STANDARD LABOR COST	
Actual Hours ×	Actual Rate	Actual Hours ×	Standard Rate	Standard Hours ×	Standard Rate
2,850 hours used ×	$19 per hour	2,850 hours used ×	$20 per hour	3,000 hours allowed ×	$20 per hour

$54,150 $57,000 $60,000

$2,850 Favorable $3,000 Favorable

Direct-labor rate variance   Direct-labor efficiency variance

$5,850 Favorable

Direct-labor variance

(b) Finishing Department:

DIRECT-LABOR RATE AND EFFICIENCY VARIANCES

ACTUAL LABOR COST				STANDARD LABOR COST	
Actual Hours ×	Actual Rate	Actual Hours ×	Standard Rate	Standard Hours ×	Standard Rate
1,570 hours used ×	$16 per hour	1,570 hours used ×	$15 per hour	1,500 hours allowed ×	$15 per hour

$25,120 $23,550 $22,500

$1,570 Unfavorable $1,050 Unfavorable

Direct-labor rate variance   Direct-labor efficiency variance

$2,620 Unfavorable

Direct-labor variance

PROBLEM 10-59 (CONTINUED)

3. Cost variance report:

SPRINGSTEEN COMPANY
COST VARIANCE REPORT
FOR THE MONTH OF JULY

	Construction Department		Finishing Department	
	Amount	Percentage of Standard Cost	Amount	Percentage of Standard Cost
Direct material:				
Standard cost, given actual output..............	$48,000	—	$ 7,500	—
Direct-material price variance......................	3,000 U	6.25%	-0-	-0-
Direct-material quantity variance......................	6,000 U	12.50%	-0-	-0-
Direct labor:				
Standard cost, given actual output..............	$60,000	—	$22,500	—
Direct-labor rate variance	2,850 F	4.75%	1,570 U	6.98%
Direct-labor efficiency variance......................	3,000 F	5.00%	1,050 U	4.67%

PROBLEM 10-60 (45 MINUTES)

1. Journal entries:

Raw-Material Inventory..	72,000	
Direct-Material Price Variance	3,000	
Accounts Payable..		75,000

To record purchase of veneered wood.

Raw-Material Inventory..	9,000	
Accounts Payable..		9,000

To record purchase of bridges and strings.

Work-in-Process Inventory	48,000	
Direct-Material Quantity Variance..	6,000	
Raw-material Inventory		54,000

To record usage of veneered wood.

Work-in-Process Inventory	7,500	
Raw-Material Inventory		7,500

To record usage of bridges and strings.

Work-in-Process Inventory	60,000	
Direct-Labor Rate Variance		2,850
Direct-Labor Efficiency Variance		3,000
Wages Payable..		54,150

To record Construction Department direct-labor costs and variances.

Work-in-Process Inventory	22,500	
Direct-Labor Rate Variance..	1,570	
Direct-Labor Efficiency Variance...	1,050	
Wages Payable..		25,120

To record Finishing Department direct-labor costs and variances.

PROBLEM 10-60 (CONTINUED)

Finished-Goods Inventory...	138,000	
Work-in-Process Inventory......................................		138,000

To record completion of 500 guitars at a standard cost of $276 each
($276 = $96 + $15 + $120 + $45).

Accounts Receivable	120,000	
Sales Revenue		120,000
Cost of Goods Sold	82,800	
Finished-Goods Inventory		82,800

To record sale of 300 guitars at a price of $400 each and a standard cost of $276 each.

Cost of Goods Sold..	5,770	
Direct-Labor Rate Variance..	1,280*	
Direct-Labor Efficiency Variance..	1,950†	
Direct-Material Price Variance...............................		3,000
Direct-Material Quantity Variance		6,000

To close variances into Cost of Goods Sold.

*Sum of direct-labor rate variances: $1,280 F = $2,850 F + $1,570 U

†Sum of direct-labor efficiency variances: $1,950 F = $3,000 F + $1,050 U

PROBLEM 10-60 (CONTINUED)

2.   Posting of journal entries:

Raw-Material Inventory	
72,000	54,000
9,000	7,500

Accounts Receivable	
120,000	

Work-in-Process Inventory	
48,000	138,000
7,500	
60,000	
22,500	

Accounts Payable	
	75,000
	9,000

Finished-Goods Inventory	
138,000	82,800

Wages Payable	
	54,150
	25,120

Cost of Goods Sold	
82,800	
5,770	

Sales Revenue	
	120,000

Direct-Material Price Variance	
3,000	3,000

Direct-Labor Rate Variance	
1,570	2,850
1,280	

Direct-Material Quantity Variance	
6,000	6,000

Direct-Labor Efficiency Variance	
1,050	3,000
1,950	

SOLUTIONS TO CASES

CASE 10-61 (60 MINUTES)

1. Standard cost of lots 22, 23, and 24:

EUROPEAN STYLES, INC.
STANDARD COST OF PRODUCTION
FOR NOVEMBER

Lot	Quantity (boxes)	Standard Cost per Box	Total Standard Cost
22	1,000	$106.50	$106,500
23	1,700	106.50	181,050
24	1,200	90.48*	108,576
Standard cost of production			$396,126

*Standard material cost plus 80 percent of standard cost of labor and overhead:

$26.40 + (80\%)(\$44.10 + \$36.00)$.

2. Variances (U denotes unfavorable; F denotes favorable):

EUROPEAN STYLES, INC.
DIRECT-MATERIAL PRICE VARIANCE
FOR NOVEMBER

Actual cost of materials purchased	$106,400
Standard cost of materials purchased	
(95,000 × $1.10)...	104,500
Direct-material price variance...	$ 1,900 U

CASE 10-61 (CONTINUED)

EUROPEAN STYLES, INC.
DIRECT-MATERIAL AND DIRECT-LABOR VARIANCES
FOR NOVEMBER

	Lot no.			
	22	23	24	Total
Direct-material quantity variance:				
Standard yards:				
Units in lot....................	1,000	1,700	1,200	3,900
Standard yards per lot............................	× 24	× 24	× 24	× 24
Total standard quantity..........................	24,000	40,800	28,800	93,600
Actual yards used	24,100	40,440	28,825	93,365
Variance in yards*........................	100	(360)	25	(235)
Standard price............................	×$1.10	× $1.10	×$1.10	× $1.10
Direct-material quantity variance..................	$ 110 U	$ (396) F	$27.50 U	$(258.50) F

*Parentheses denote favorable variance.

	Lot no.			
	22	23	24	Total
Direct-labor efficiency variance:				
Standard hours:				
Units in lot..............................	1,000	1,700	1,200	
Standard hours per lot............................	× 3	× 3	× 3	
Total	3,000	5,100	3,600	
Percentage of completion......	× 100%	× 100%	× 80%	
Total standard hours	3,000	5,100	2,880	10,980
Actual hours worked	2,980	5,130	2,890	11,000
Variance in hours*.......................	(20)	30	10	20
Standard rate	×$14.70	×$14.70	×$14.70	×$14.70
Direct-labor efficiency variance..............	$ (294) F	$441 U	$147 U	$294 U

*Parentheses denote favorable variance.

CASE 10-61 (CONTINUED)

	Lot no.			
	22	23	24	Total
Direct-labor rate variance:				
Actual hours worked	2,980	5,130	2,890	11,000
Rate paid in excess of standard ($15.00 – $14.70)................	×$ .30	×$ .30	×$ .30	×$ .30
Variance.....................................	$ 894 U	$1,539 U	$ 867 U	$ 3,300 U

3. Journal entries:

Raw-material Inventory...	104,500*	
Direct-Material Price Variance	1,900	
Accounts Payable...		106,400

*95,000 × $1.10 = $104,500

To record the purchase of raw material.

Work-in-Process Inventory	102,960*	
Direct-Material Quantity Variance............................		258.50
Raw-Material Inventory		102,701.50

*93,600 × $1.10 = $102,960

To add direct-material cost to work-in-process inventory and record the direct-material quantity variance.

Work-in-Process Inventory	161,406*	
Direct-Labor Rate Variance..	3,300	
Direct-Labor Efficiency Variance.......................................	294	
Wages Payable..		165,000

*10,980 × $14.70 = $161,406

To add direct-labor cost to work-in-process inventory, record the direct-labor variances, and record the incurrence of direct-labor cost.

CASE 10-62 (75 MINUTES)

The completed list is shown below. Begin by filling in the facts you know. The reasoning used to reduce the remaining data is explained after the list of answers.

1. Actual output (in drums)

$$= \frac{\text{standard quantity of direct material A allowed, given actual output}}{\text{standard quanity of direct material A per drum}}$$

$$= \frac{10,000\,\text{lb.}}{10\,\text{lb. per drum}} = 1,000\,\text{drums}$$

2. _____

Direct material		A	B
a.	Standard quantity per drum	10 lb.	5 gal.[a]
b.	Standard price	$5.00/lb.	$3.00/gal.[b]
c.	Standard cost per drum..	$50.00[c]	$15.00
d.	Standard quantity allowed, given actual output	10,000 lb.	5,000 gal.
e.	Actual quantity purchased	12,000 lb.	6,000 gal.
f.	Actual price..	$4.50/lb.	$3.20/gal.[d]
g.	Actual quantity used	10,500 lb.[e]	4,800 gal.
h.	Price variance..	$6,000 F[f]	$1,200 U
i.	Quantity variance	$2,500 U	$600 F[g]

[a]Standard quantity of direct material B per drum

$$= \frac{\text{standard quantity of direct material B allowed, given actual output}}{\text{actual output}}$$

$$= \frac{5,000\,\text{gal.}}{1,000\,\text{drums}} = 5\,\text{gal.}$$

[b]Standard price of direct material B $= \dfrac{\text{standard cost of material B per drum}}{\text{standard quantity allowed per drum}}$

$$= \frac{\$15.00\,\text{per drum}}{5\,\text{gal. per drum}} = \$3.00\,\text{per gal.}$$

CASE 10-62 (CONTINUED)

[c]Standard cost of direct material A per drum = 10 lbs. × $5.00 per lb. = $50.00.

[d]The reasoning for the actual price of direct material B is as follows, where the subscripts denote materials A and B:

$$\text{Increase in accounts payable} = \text{actual cost of material purchases} = (PQ_A \times AP_A) + (PQ_B \times AP_B)$$

$$\$73,200 = (12,000 \times \$4.50) + (6,000 \times AP_B)$$

$$AP_B = \$3.20 \text{ per gallon}$$

[e]This conclusion comes from the following formula for the quantity variance:

$$\text{Quantity variance (A)} = SP(AQ - SQ)$$

$$\$2,500 \text{ U} = (AQ - 10,000)\$5.00$$

$$AQ = 10,500 \text{ lb.}$$

[f]Direct material A price variance
$$= PQ(AP - SP)$$
$$= 12,000(\$4.50 - \$5.00)$$
$$= \$6,000 \text{ F}$$

[g]Direct material B quantity variance
$$= SP(AQ - SQ)$$
$$= \$3.00(s4,800 - 5,000)$$
$$= \$600 \text{ F}$$

CASE 10-62 (CONTINUED)

3.

Direct labor:	I (mixers)	II (packers)
a. Standard hours per drum	2 hr.[a]	4 hr.
b. Standard rate per hour	$15.00	$12.00[b]
c. Standard cost per drum	$30.00	$48.00
d. Standard quantity allowed, given actual output	2,000 hr.[c]	4,000 hr.[d]
e. Actual rate per hour	$15.30[e]	$11.90
f. Actual hours	2,000 hr[f]	4,100 hr.[g]
g. Rate variance	$600 U	$410 F[h]
h. Efficiency variance	-0-[i]	$1,200 U

[a]Standard hours of direct labor type I per drum

$$= \frac{\text{standard cost of direct labor I per drum}}{\text{standard rate per hour}}$$

$$= \frac{\$30.00 \text{ per drum}}{\$15.00 \text{ per hr.}} = 2 \text{ hr.}$$

[b]Direct labor type II, standard rate per hour

$$= \frac{\text{standard cost of direct labor type II per drum}}{\text{standard hours per drum}}$$

$$= \frac{\$48.00 \text{ per drum}}{4 \text{ hr. per drum}} = \$12.00$$

[c]Direct labor type I, standard quantity allowed, given actual output

= 1,000 drums × 2 hr. per drum

= 2,000 hr.

[d]Direct labor type II, standard quantity allowed given actual output

= 1,000 drums × 4 hr. per drum

= 4,000 hr.

CASE 10-62 (CONTINUED)

[e]Direct labor type I, actual rate per hour = $15.30. Use the formula for the direct-labor rate variance as follows:

$$\text{Direct-labor rate variance} = AH(AR - SR)$$
$$\$600\ U = 2{,}000\ (AR - \$15.00)$$
$$AR = \$15.30$$

[f]Direct labor type I, actual hours = 2,000 hr. Since there was no labor type I efficiency variance, actual hours and standard hours are equal.

[g]Direct labor type II, actual hours = 4,100 hr. Use the formula for the direct-labor efficiency variance, as follows:

$$\text{Direct-labor (II) efficiency variance} = SR\ (AH - SH)$$
$$\$1{,}200\ U = \$12.00\ (AH - 4{,}000)$$
$$AH = 4{,}100\ \text{hr.}$$

$$\text{[h]Direct-labor type II, rate variance} = AH\ (AR - SR)$$
$$= 4{,}100\ (\$11.90 - \$12.00)$$
$$= \$410\ F$$

CASE 10-62 (CONTINUED)

[i]Direct labor type I, efficiency variance = zero.

Just fill in the remaining variance in the following tabulation:

Direct-material variances:

A:	Price variance	$6,000	F
A:	Quantity variance	2,500	U
B:	Price variance	1,200	U
B:	Quantity variance	600	F

Direct-labor variances:

I:	Rate variance	600	U
I:	Efficiency variance	?	
II:	Rate variance	410	F
II:	Efficiency variance	1,200	U

Total (favorable variance because of credit to cost of Goods Sold) .... $1,510 F

Therefore, the direct-labor type I efficiency variance = $1,510 – $6,000 + $2,500 + $1,200 – $600 + $600 – $410 + $1,200 = 0

4. Total of all variances for the month: $1,510 F (favorable because of credit to Cost of Goods Sold).

CURRENT ISSUES IN MANAGERIAL ACCOUNTING

ISSUE 10-63

"U.S AUTO MAKERS TO REV UP OUTPUT OF 'HYBRID' VEHICLES," *THE WALL STREET JOURNAL*, OCTOBER 24, 2000, JEFFREY BALL.

1. Hybrids boost fuel economy by adding an electric motor to a traditional internal combustion engine.

2. Developing standards for a radically new product is difficult at best. Manufacturers generally try to find aspects of the new product (and the processes needed to produce it) that are similar to products and processes with which they have experience. Initial standards then can be inferred from these more familiar products and processes. Also, using a target price analysis would allow auto makers to determine what price consumers would pay for a hybrid vehicle. The auto makers could then work backwards toward reducing their costs in order to make an economically viable product.

ISSUE 10-64

"CAN YAHOO! THRIVE IN A HARSH CLIMATE," *THE WALL STREET JOURNAL*, OCTOBER 16, 2000.

1. Yahoo is an online business that provides many free services.

2. Yahoo offers search capabilities, an auction, classifieds, travel information, mail, photos, chat rooms, clubs and a myriad of other services.

3. The article questions whether Yahoo will be innovative enough to be competitive as the Internet business environment evolves over time. Innovation and learning is one of the four major areas covered by the balanced scorecard. Management could use the balanced scorecard to put a spotlight on this area of critical importance to the company.

CHAPTER 11
Flexible Budgeting and the Management of Overhead and Support Activity Costs

ANSWERS TO REVIEW QUESTIONS

11-1   The advantage of a flexible budget is that it is responsive to changes in the activity level. It enables a comparison between actual costs incurred at the actual level of activity and the standard allowed costs that should have been incurred at the actual level of activity.

11-2   A static budget is based on only one level of activity. A flexible budget allows for several different levels of activity.

11-3   Flexible overhead budgets are based on an input activity measure, such as process time, in order to provide a meaningful measure of production activity. An output measure, such as the number of units produced, could be used effectively only in a single-product enterprise. If multiple, heterogeneous products are produced, it would not be meaningful to base the flexible budget on an output measure aggregated across highly different types of products.

11-4   A columnar flexible budget has several columns listing the budgeted levels of cost at different levels of activity. Each column is based on a different activity level. A formula flexible budget is an equation expressed as follows: total cost equals fixed cost plus the product of the activity measure and the variable cost per unit of activity. The formula flexible budget allows for any level of activity, rather than only the activity levels for the various columns used in the columnar flexible budget.

11-5   Manufacturing overhead is added to Work-in-Process Inventory under standard costing as shown in the following T-accounts:

Work-in-Process Inventory	Manufacturing Overhead
X^*	X^*

*The amount of X is the following:

$$X = \begin{pmatrix} \text{predetermined} \\ \text{(standard)} \\ \text{overhead} \\ \text{rate} \end{pmatrix} \times \begin{pmatrix} \text{standard allowed} \\ \text{amount of} \\ \text{cost driver (e.g.,} \\ \text{direct-labor hours)} \end{pmatrix}$$

11-6 Computer-integrated manufacturing systems have resulted in a shift from variable toward fixed costs. In addition, as automation increases, more and more firms are switching to such measures of activity as machine hours or process time for their flexible overhead budgets. Machine hours and process time are linked more closely than direct-labor hours to the robotic technology and computer-integrated manufacturing systems becoming common in today's manufacturing environment.

11-7 The interpretation of the variable-overhead spending variance is that a different total amount was spent on variable overhead than should have been spent in accordance with the variable-overhead rate, given the actual level of the cost driver upon which the variable-overhead budget is based. For example, if direct labor hours are used to budget variable overhead, an unfavorable spending variance means that a greater total amount was spent on variable overhead than should have been spent, after adjusting for how much actual direct-labor time was used. The spending variance is the control variance for variable overhead.

11-8 An unfavorable variable-overhead spending variance does not imply that the company paid more than the anticipated rate per kilowatt-hour for electricity. An unfavorable spending variance could result from spending more per kilowatt-hour for electricity or from using more electricity than anticipated, or some combination of these two causes.

11-9 The interpretation of the variable-overhead efficiency variance is related to the efficiency in using the activity upon which variable overhead is budgeted. For example, if the basis for the variable-overhead budget is direct-labor hours, an unfavorable variable-overhead efficiency variance will result when the actual direct-labor hours exceed the standard allowed direct-labor hours. Thus, the variable-overhead efficiency variance will disclose no information about the efficiency with which variable-overhead items are used. Rather, it results from inefficiency or efficiency, relative to the standards, in the usage of the cost driver (such as direct-labor hours).

11-10 The interpretations of the direct-labor and variable-overhead efficiency variances are very different. The direct-labor efficiency variance does convey information about the efficiency with which direct labor was used, relative to the standards. In contrast, the variable-overhead efficiency variance conveys no information about the efficiency with which variable-overhead items were used.

11-11 The fixed overhead budget variance is defined as the difference between actual fixed overhead and budgeted fixed overhead. It is the control variance for fixed overhead.

11-12 The fixed-overhead volume variance is the difference between budgeted fixed overhead and applied fixed overhead. The best interpretation for this variance is a means of reconciling two disparate purposes of the standard-costing system: the control purpose and the product-costing purpose. For the control purpose, budgeted fixed overhead recognizes the fixed nature of this cost. Budgeted fixed overhead does not change as activity changes. For product-costing purposes, budgeted fixed overhead is divided by a denominator activity measure and applied to products on the basis of a fixed-overhead rate. The result of this dual purpose for the standard-costing system is that budgeted fixed overhead and applied fixed overhead will differ whenever the actual production activity differs from the budgeted production activity.

11-13 A common but misleading interpretation of the fixed-overhead volume variance is that it is a measure of the cost of underutilizing or overutilizing production capacity. For example, when budgeted fixed overhead exceeds applied fixed overhead, the fixed-overhead volume variance is positive. Some people interpret this positive variance to be unfavorable and claim that it is a measure of the cost of not having utilized production capacity to the level that was anticipated. However, this interpretation is misleading, because the real cost of underutilizing capacity lies in the forgone contribution margins from the products that were not produced and sold.

11-14 The following graph depicts budgeted and applied fixed overhead and displays a positive volume variance.

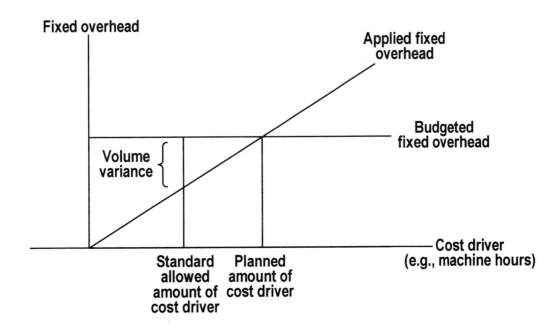

11-15 All kinds of organizations use flexible budgets, including manufacturing firms, retail firms, service-industry firms, and nonprofit organizations. For example, a hospital's flexible overhead budget might be based on different levels of activity expressed in terms of patient-days.

11-16 The conceptual problem in applying fixed manufacturing overhead as a product cost is that this procedure treats fixed overhead as though it were a variable cost. Fixed overhead is applied as a product cost by multiplying the fixed overhead rate by the standard allowed amount of the cost driver used to apply fixed overhead. For example, fixed overhead might be applied to Work-in-Process Inventory by multiplying the fixed-overhead rate by the standard allowed machine hours. As the number of standard allowed machine hours increases, the amount of fixed overhead applied increases proportionately. This situation is conceptually unappealing, because fixed overhead, although it is a fixed cost, appears variable in the way that it is applied to work in process.

11-17 The control purpose of a standard-costing system is to provide benchmarks against which to compare actual costs. Then management by exception is used to follow up on significant variances and take corrective action. The product-costing purpose of the standard-costing system is to determine the cost of producing goods and services. Product costs are needed for a variety of purposes in both managerial and financial accounting.

11-18 Fixed-overhead costs sometimes are called capacity-producing costs because they are the costs incurred in order to generate a place and environment in which production can take place. For example, a common fixed-overhead cost is depreciation, which is the cost of acquiring plant and equipment, allocated across time periods. Thus, depreciation is part of the cost of acquiring and maintaining a place in which production can occur.

11-19 The following graph depicts budgeted and applied variable overhead. Budgeted and applied variable overhead are represented by the same line because variable overhead is a variable cost. Both budgeted and applied variable overhead increase proportionately as production activity increases.

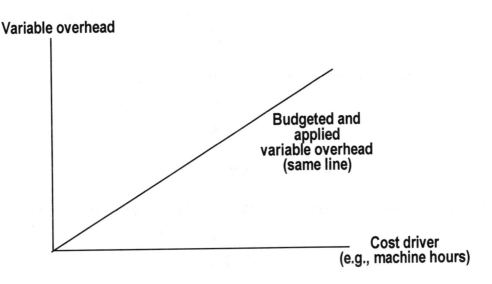

11-20 Plausible activity bases for a variety of organizations to use in flexible budgeting are as follows:

(a) Insurance company: Insurance policies processed or insurance claims processed.

(b) Express delivery service: Number of items of express mail or weight of express mail processed.

(c) Restaurant: Number of customers served.

(d) State tax-collection agency: Number of tax returns processed.

11-21 Conventional flexible budgets typically are based on a single cost driver, such as direct-labor hours or machine hours. Costs are categorized as variable or fixed. The fixed costs do not vary with respect to the single cost driver on which the flexible budget is based. An activity-based flexible budget is based on multiple cost drivers. Cost drivers are selected on the basis of how well they explain the behavior of the costs in the flexible budget. Costs that are treated as fixed in a conventional flexible budget may vary with respect to an appropriate cost driver in an activity-based flexible budget.

SOLUTIONS TO EXERCISES

EXERCISE 11-22 (20 MINUTES)

1. Variable-overhead spending variance $=$ actual variable overhead $- (AH \times SVR)$

    $=$ $320,000 - (50,000 \times \$6.00)$

    $=$ $20,000 U

2. Variable-overhead efficiency variance $=$ $SVR(AH - SH)$

    $=$ $6.00(50,000 - 40,000*)$

    $=$ $60,000 U

    *SH = 40,000 hrs. = 20,000 units $\times$ 2 hrs. per unit

3. Fixed-overhead budget variance $=$ actual fixed overhead $-$ budgeted fixed overhead

    $=$ $97,000 - \$100,000$

    $=$ $3,000 F

4. Fixed-overhead volume variance $=$ budgeted fixed overhead $-$ applied fixed overhead

    $=$ $100,000 - \$80,000$†

    $=$ $20,000 (positive sign**)

    †Applied fixed overhead $= \left(\begin{array}{c} \text{predetermined fixed} \\ \text{overhead rate} \end{array} \right) \times \left(\begin{array}{c} \text{standard allowed} \\ \text{hours} \end{array} \right)$

    $= \left(\dfrac{\$100,000}{25,000 \times 2} \right) \times (20,000 \times 2)$

    $=$ $80,000

**Consistent with the discussion in the text, we choose not to interpret the volume variance as either favorable or unfavorable. Some accountants would designate a positive volume variance as "unfavorable" and a negative volume variance as "favorable."

EXERCISE 11-23 (40 MINUTES)

1. Variable overhead variances:

VARIABLE-OVERHEAD SPENDING AND EFFICIENCY VARIANCES

(1) ACTUAL VARIABLE OVERHEAD			(2)			(3) FLEXIBLE BUDGET: VARIABLE OVERHEAD			(4)† VARIABLE OVERHEAD APPLIED TO WORK-IN-PROCESS		
Actual Hours (AH)	×	Actual Rate (AVR)	Actual Hours (AH)	×	Standard Rate (SVR)	Standard Allowed Hours (SH)	×	Standard Rate (SVR)	Standard Allowed Hours (SH)	×	Standard Rate (SVR)
50,000 hours	×	$6.40 per hour*	50,000 hours	×	$6.00 per hour	40,000 hours	×	$6.00 per hour	40,000 hours	×	$6.00 per hour
$320,000			$300,000			$240,000			$240,000		

$20,000 Unfavorable $60,000 Unfavorable   No difference

Variable-overhead spending variance   Variable-overhead efficiency variance

*Actual variable-overhead rate (AVR) = $\dfrac{\text{actual variable overhead cost}}{\text{actual hours}}$ = $\dfrac{\$320,000}{50,000}$ = $6.40 per hour

†Column (4) is not used to compute the variances. It is included to point out that the flexible-budget amount for variable overhead, $240,000, is the amount that will be applied to Work-in-Process inventory for product costing purposes.

EXERCISE 11-23 (CONTINUED)

2. Fixed-overhead variances:

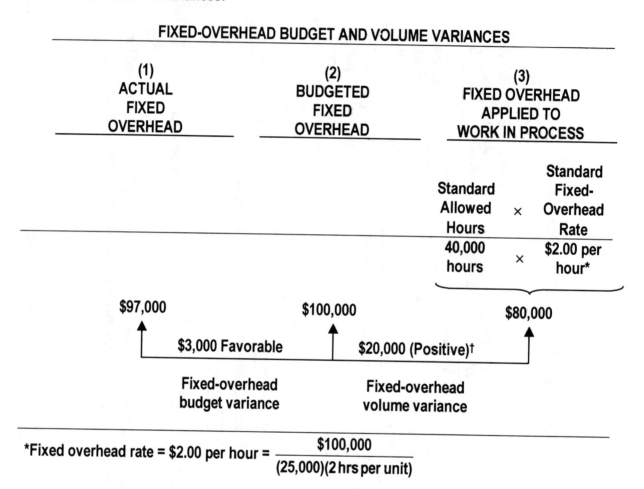

FIXED-OVERHEAD BUDGET AND VOLUME VARIANCES

(1) ACTUAL FIXED OVERHEAD	(2) BUDGETED FIXED OVERHEAD	(3) FIXED OVERHEAD APPLIED TO WORK IN PROCESS
		Standard Allowed Hours × Standard Fixed-Overhead Rate
		40,000 hours × $2.00 per hour*
$97,000	$100,000	$80,000
↑ $3,000 Favorable ↑		$20,000 (Positive)† ↑
Fixed-overhead budget variance	Fixed-overhead volume variance	

*Fixed overhead rate = $2.00 per hour = $\dfrac{\$100,000}{(25,000)(2\,\text{hrs per unit})}$

†Consistent with the discussion in the text, we choose not to interpret the volume variance as either favorable or unfavorable. Some accountants would designate a positive volume variance as "unfavorable" and a negative volume variance as "favorable."

EXERCISE 11-24 (35 MINUTES)

(a)   Graphical analysis of variable-overhead variances*:

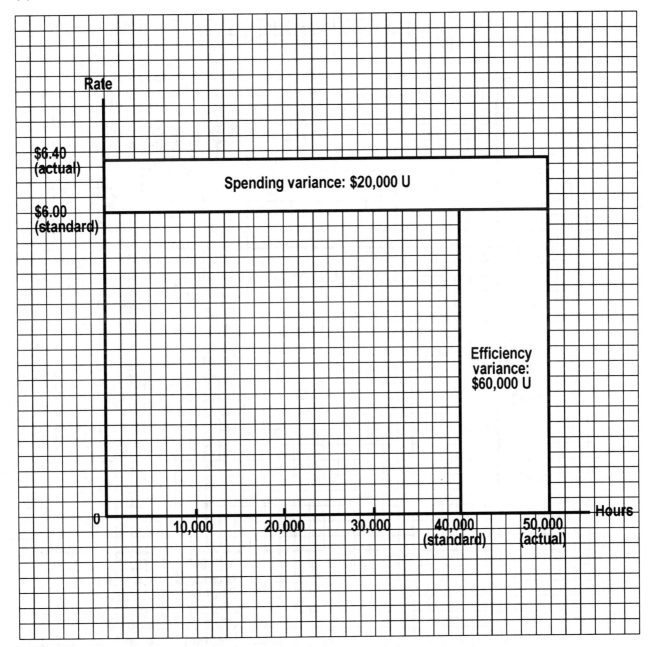

*The graph is not drawn to scale, in order to make it easier to visualize the overhead variances.

EXERCISE 11-24 (CONTINUED)

(b) Graphical analysis of budgeted versus applied fixed overhead:

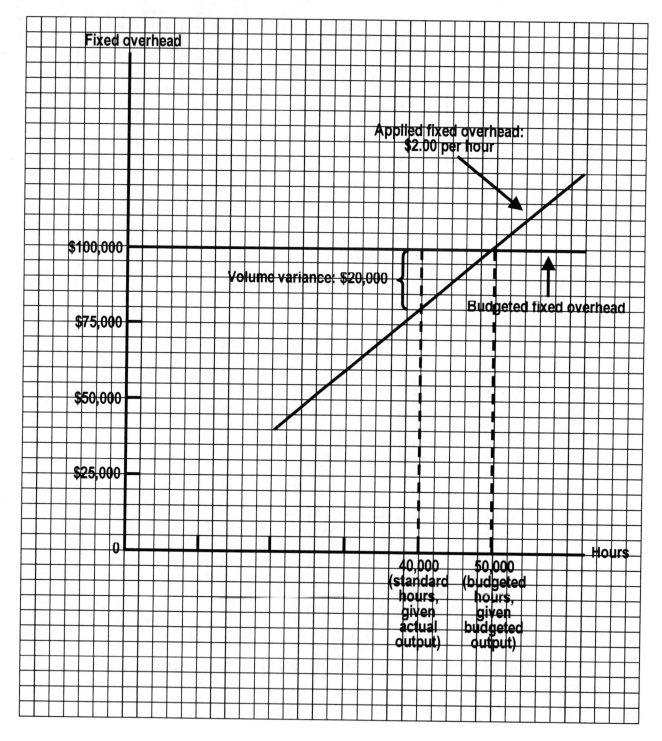

EXERCISE 11-25 (30 MINUTES)

1. Answers will vary widely, depending on the governmental unit selected and the budget items selected by the student. For example, fire fighting costs might be budgeted based on cost drivers such as the number of structure fires, severity of the structure fires (e.g., one or two alarm, etc.), the number of car fires, and so forth.

2. Again, the cost drivers would depend on the governmental unit and budget items selected.

EXERCISE 11-26 (20 MINUTES)

1. Variable-overhead spending variance   =   actual variable overhead – $(AH \times SVR)$

    = $405,000 – (40,500 × $9.00)

    = $40,500 U

2. Variable-overhead efficiency variance   = $SVR(AH - SH)$

    = $9.00(40,500 – 36,000*)

    = $40,500 U

SH = 36,000 hrs. = 9,000 cases × 4 hours per case

3. Fixed-overhead budget variance   =   actual fixed overhead – budgeted fixed overhead

    = $122,000 – $120,000

    = $2,000 U

4. Fixed-overhead volume variance   =   budgeted fixed overhead – applied fixed overhead

    = $120,000 – $108,000†

    = $12,000 (positive)**

†Applied fixed overhead   = $\left(\begin{array}{c} \text{predetermined fixed} \\ \text{overhead rate} \end{array} \right) \times \left(\begin{array}{c} \text{standard allowed} \\ \text{hours} \end{array} \right)$

= $\left(\dfrac{\$120,000}{10,000 \times 4} \right) \times (9,000 \times 4)$

= $108,000

**Consistent with the discussion in the text, we choose not to interpret the volume variance as either favorable or unfavorable. Some accountants would designate a positive volume variance as "unfavorable" and a negative volume variance as "favorable."

EXERCISE 11-27 (10 MINUTES)

1.

Product	Standard Hours per Unit	Number of Units	Total Standard Hours
Field	3	200	600
Professional	5	300	1,500
Total			2,100

The total standard allowed direct-labor hours in May is 2,100 hours.

2. Basing the flexible budget on the number of binoculars produced would not be meaningful. Production of 500 binoculars could mean 100 fields and 400 professionals, or 200 fields and 300 professionals, and so forth. Depending on the composition of the 500 units, in terms of production type, different amounts of direct labor would be expected. More to the point, different amounts of variable-overhead costs would be expected.

EXERCISE 11-28 (15 MINUTES)

1. Formula flexible budget:

Total budgeted monthly electricity cost = (3DM* × number of patient days) + 1,000DM

*3DM per patient day = 30 kwh per patient day × .10DM per kwh,
    where DM denotes deutsch mark, the German national currency.

2. Columnar flexible budget:

	Patient Days		
	30,000	40,000	50,000
Variable electricity cost............................	90,000DM	120,000DM	150,000DM
Fixed electricity cost	1,000DM	1,000DM	1,000DM
Total electricity cost.................................	91,000DM	121,000DM	151,000DM

EXERCISE 11-29 (15 MINUTES)

Memorandum

Date: Today

To: I. Makit, Production Supervisor

From: I. M. Student, Controller

Subject: Variable-overhead efficiency variance

The variable-overhead efficiency variance has a misleading name. This variance does not convey any information about the efficiency with which variable overhead items are used, such as electricity, manufacturing supplies, and indirect labor. An unfavorable variable-overhead efficiency variance occurs when there is inefficient usage of the cost driver (or activity base) upon which variable overhead is budgeted. For example, when direct-labor time is the cost driver, the variable-overhead efficiency variance is defined as $SR(AH - SH)$. Thus, the difference between actual direct-labor hours (AH) and standard allowed direct-labor hours (SH) causes the variance.

EXERCISE 11-30 (45 MINUTES)

Standard machine hours per unit of output	4 hours
Standard variable-overhead rate per machine hour	$8.00
Actual variable-overhead rate per machine hour	$9.00[b]
Actual machine hours per unit of output	3[d]
Budgeted fixed overhead	$50,000
Actual fixed overhead	$65,000[a]
Budgeted production in units	25,000
Actual production in units	24,000[c]
Variable-overhead spending variance	$72,000 U
Variable-overhead efficiency variance	$192,000 F
Fixed-overhead budget variance	$15,000 U
Fixed-overhead volume variance	$2,000[g] (positive)
Total actual overhead	$713,000
Total budgeted overhead (flexible budget)	$818,000[e]
Total budgeted overhead (static budget)	$850,000[f]
Total applied overhead	$816,000

EXERCISE 11-30 (CONTINUED)

Explanatory Notes:

a. Fixed-overhead budget variance = actual fixed overhead – budgeted fixed overhead

$$\$15,000 \text{ U} = X - \$50,000$$

$$X = \$65,000 = \text{actual fixed overhead}$$

b. Total actual overhead = actual variable overhead + actual fixed overhead

$$\$713,000 = X + \$65,000$$

$$X = \$648,000 = \text{actual variable overhead}$$

Variable-overhead spending variance = actual variable overhead – $(AH \times SR)$

$$\$72,000 \text{ U} = \$648,000 - (AH \times \$8)$$

$$\$8AH = \$576,000$$

$$AH = 72,000$$

$$\text{Actual variable-overhead rate per machine hour} = \frac{\text{actual variable overhead}}{\text{actual hours}}$$

$$= \frac{\$648,000}{72,000} = \$9 \text{ per hour}$$

EXERCISE 11-30 (CONTINUED)

c.   Fixed-overhead rate $= \dfrac{\text{budgeted fixed overhead}}{\text{budgeted machine hours}}$

$= \dfrac{\$50{,}000}{(25{,}000 \text{ units})(4 \text{ hrs. per unit})}$

$= \$.50$ per hr.

Total standard
overhead rate $=$ standard variable overhead rate + fixed-overhead rate

$\$8.50 = \$8.00 + \$.50$

Total applied overhead $=$ total standard hours $\times$ total standard overhead rate

$\$816{,}000 = X \times \$8.50$

$X = 96{,}000 =$ total standard hrs.

Actual production $= \dfrac{\text{total standard hrs.}}{\text{standard hrs. per unit}}$

$= \dfrac{96{,}000}{4} = 24{,}000$ units

d.   Actual machine hrs. per unit of output $= \dfrac{\text{total actual machine hrs.}}{\text{actual production}}$

$= \dfrac{72{,}000 \text{ hrs.}}{24{,}000 \text{ units}} = 3$ hrs. per unit

e.   Total budgeted overhead (flexible budget)

$=$ budgeted fixed overhead + *(SVR $\times$ SH)*

$= \$50{,}000 + (\$8.00 \times 24{,}000 \text{ units} \times 4 \text{ hrs. per unit})$

$= \$818{,}000$

EXERCISE 11-30 (CONTINUED)

f.   Total budgeted overhead (static budget)

$$= \begin{pmatrix} \text{total standard} \\ \text{overhead rate} \end{pmatrix} \begin{pmatrix} \text{budgeted} \\ \text{production} \end{pmatrix} \begin{pmatrix} \text{standard hrs.} \\ \text{per unit} \end{pmatrix}$$

$$= (\$8.50)(25,000)(4)$$

$$= \$850,000$$

g.   Fixed overhead volume variance

$$= \text{budgeted fixed overhead} - \text{applied fixed overhead}$$

$$= \$50,000 - (\$.50)(24,000 \times 4)$$

$$= \$2,000 \text{ (positive)}*$$

*Consistent with the discussion in the text, we choose not to interpret the volume variance as either favorable or unfavorable. Some accountants would designate a positive volume variance as "unfavorable" and a negative volume variance as "favorable."

EXERCISE 11-31 (10 MINUTES)

1.   Flexible budgeted amounts, using activity-based flexible budget:

a.   Indirect material: $27,500 ($15,000 + $2,500 + $2,500 + $7,500)

b.   Utilities: $5,000 ($3,750 + $1,250)

c.   Inspection: $4,400

d.   Engineering: $1,800

e.   Material handling: $4,000

f.   Total overhead cost: $60,300 ($37,500 + $10,400 + $1,800 + $4,000 + $6,600)

2.   Variance for setup cost:

a.   Using the activity-based flexible budget: $3,000 F (actual cost minus flexible budget = $3,000 – $6,000)

b.   Using the conventional flexible budget: zero (actual cost minus flexible budget = $3,000 – $3,000)

EXERCISE 11-32 (15 MINUTES)

Variable-overhead spending variance	=	actual variable overhead – *(AH × SVR)*
	=	$2,340,000 – (275,000 × $8.00)
	=	$140,000 U

Variable-overhead efficiency variance	=	*SVR (AH – SH)*
	=	$8.00 (275,000 – 280,000*)
	=	$40,000 F

*SH = 56,000 units × 5 hours per unit

Fixed-overhead budget variance	=	actual fixed overhead – budgeted fixed overhead
	=	$3,750,000 – $3,600,000*
	=	$150,000 U

*Budgeted fixed overhead = 300,000 hours × $12 per hour

Fixed-overhead volume variance	=	budgeted fixed overhead – applied fixed overhead
	=	$3,600,000 – $3,360,000*
	=	$240,000 (positive)†

*Applied fixed overhead = $12 per hour × 5 hours per unit × 56,000 units

†Consistent with the discussion in the text, we choose not to interpret the volume variance as either favorable or unfavorable. Some accountants would designate a positive volume variance as "unfavorable" and a negative volume variance as "favorable."

EXERCISE 11-33 (15 MINUTES)

Manufacturing Overhead..	417,000*	
Various Accounts..		417,000

To record actual overhead costs.

*$417,000 = $320,000 + $97,000

Work-in-Process Inventory	320,000†	
Manufacturing Overhead...		320,000

To record applied manufacturing overhead.

†$320,000 = $240,000 + $80,000

Cost of Goods Sold	97,000**	
Manufacturing Overhead...		97,000

To close underapplied overhead into Cost of Goods Sold:

**$97,000 = $417,000 – $320,000 (Also, $97,000 = sum of the four overhead variances.)

EXERCISE 11-34 (10 MINUTES)

$$\text{Sales-price variance} = \begin{pmatrix} \text{actual} & \text{expected} \\ \text{sales} & - & \text{sales} \\ \text{price} & \text{price} \end{pmatrix} \times \begin{array}{c} \text{actual sales} \\ \text{volume} \end{array}$$

($11.50* − $12.00†) × 9,000 = $4,500 Unfavorable

$$\text{Sales-volume variance} = \begin{pmatrix} \text{actual} & \text{budgeted} \\ \text{sales} & - & \text{sales} \\ \text{volume} & \text{volume} \end{pmatrix} \times \begin{array}{c} \text{budgeted unit} \\ \text{contribution margin} \end{array}$$

= (9,000 − 10,000) × $7.00** = $7,000 Unfavorable

*$11.50 = $103,500 ÷ 9,000

†$12.00 = $120,000 ÷ 10,000

**$7.00 = ($120,000 − $40,000 − $10,000) ÷ 10,000

SOLUTIONS TO PROBLEMS

PROBLEM 11-35 (45 MINUTES)

VARIABLE-OVERHEAD SPENDING AND EFFICIENCY VARIANCES

					FLEXIBLE BUDGET: VARIABLE OVERHEAD				
Actual Hours (AH)	×	Actual Rate (AVR)	Actual Hours (AH)	×	Standard Rate (SVR)	Standard Allowed Hours (SH)	×	Standard Rate (SVR)	Standard Allowed Hours (SH)	×	Standard Rate (SVR)
165,000 hours	×	$3.10 per hour*	165,000 hours	×	$3.00 per hour	160,000 hours	×	$3.00 per hour	160,000 hours	×	$3.00 per hour

$511,500 $495,000 $480,000 $480,000

$16,500 Unfavorable $15,000 Unfavorable   No difference

Variable-overhead   Variable-overhead
spending variance   efficiency variance

*Actual variable-overhead rate (AVR) = $\dfrac{\text{actual variable overhead cost}}{\text{actual hours}} = \dfrac{\$511,500}{165,000} = \$3.10$

†Column (4) is not used to compute the variances. It is included to point out that the flexible-budget amount for variable overhead, $480,000, is the amount that will be applied to Work-in-Process inventory for product costing purposes.

PROBLEM 11-35 (CONTINUED)

FIXED-OVERHEAD BUDGET AND VOLUME VARIANCES

(1) ACTUAL FIXED OVERHEAD	(2) BUDGETED FIXED OVERHEAD	(3) FIXED OVERHEAD APPLIED TO WORK IN PROCESS	
		Standard Allowed Hours	$\times$ Standard Fixed-Overhead Rate
		160,000 hours	$\times$ $5.00 per hour
$860,000	$900,000*		$800,000

$40,000 Favorable $100,000 (Positive)†

Fixed-overhead budget variance   Fixed-overhead volume variance

---

*Budgeted fixed overhead = 180,000 hrs. $\times$ $5 per hour.

†Consistent with the discussion in the text, we choose not to interpret the volume variance as either favorable or unfavorable. Some accountants would designate a positive volume variance as "unfavorable" and a negative volume variance as "favorable."

PROBLEM 11-36 (20 MINUTES)

1.

Policy Type	Standard Hours per Application	Actual Activity	Standard Hours Allowed
Automobile........................	1	250	250
Renter's	1	200	200
Homeowner's	2	100	200
Health...............................	2	400	800
Life....................................	5	200	1,000
Total.................................			2,450

2. The different types of applications require different amounts of clerical time, and variable overhead cost is related to the use of clerical time. Therefore, basing the flexible budget on the number of applications would give a misleading estimate of overhead costs. For example, processing 100 life insurance applications will entail much more overhead cost than processing 100 automobile insurance applications.

3. Formula flexible budget:

$$\text{Total budgeted monthly overhead cost} = \left(\begin{array}{c} \text{budgeted variable} \\ \text{overhead cost per} \\ \text{clerical hour} \end{array} \times \begin{array}{c} \text{total} \\ \text{clerical} \\ \text{hours} \end{array} \right) + \begin{array}{c} \text{budgeted fixed-} \\ \text{overhead cost} \\ \text{per month} \end{array}$$

Total budgeted monthly overhead cost = ($4.00 × X) + $2,000

where X denotes total clerical time in hours.

4. Budgeted overhead cost for July = ($4.00 × 2,450) + $2,000

  = $11,800

PROBLEM 11-37 (30 MINUTES)

1. The graphs are shown on the next page. On the variable overhead graph, the slope of the line is $4 per hour of production time ($4 = $40,000 ÷ 10,000 hours). On the fixed overhead graph, the slope of the applied fixed overhead line is $9 per hour of production time ($9 = $90,000 ÷ 10,000 hours).

2.   Memorandum

   Date: Today

   To: C. D. Tune, General Manager of Countrytime Studios

   From: I. M. Student

   Subject: Overhead graphs

The graphs of flexible budgeted variable overhead and applied variable overhead are the same line. Since this cost is truly variable, it is budgeted (for planning and control purposes) and applied (for product costing purposes) at the rate of $4 per hour of production time.

The graphs of flexible budgeted fixed overhead and applied fixed overhead are two different lines. The flexible budgeted overhead graph recognizes that fixed overhead does not vary across activity levels measured in production hours. Budgeted fixed overhead is used for planning and control purposes. The applied fixed overhead graph is used for product costing purposes. Each recording done in the studio is assigned production costs, including fixed overhead at the rate of $9 per hour of production time. The $9 rate is determined at the *budgeted* level of activity ($90,000 ÷ 10,000 hours).

The difference between the budgeted and applied fixed overhead line, at any level of production activity, is called the volume variance.

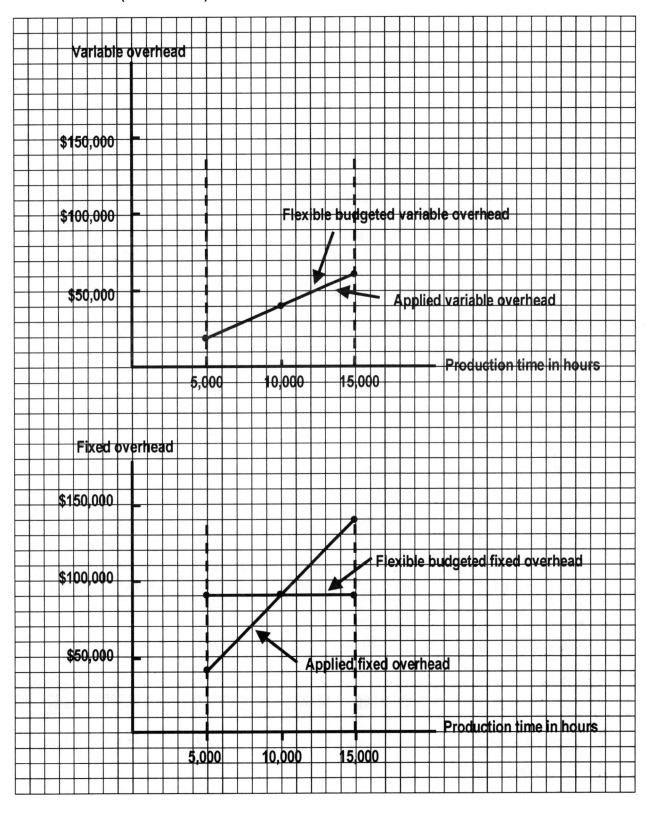

PROBLEM 11-38 (40 MINUTES)

1. a.
Units produced during May..	66,000
Overhead application rate per unit (budgeted overhead per unit at expected level of output)	× $6
Applied overhead costs...	$396,000

b.	Variable-overhead spending variance	$ 150	U*
c.	Fixed-overhead budget variance..	6,000	U
d.	Variable-overhead efficiency variance......................................	8,850	F
e.	Fixed-overhead volume variance..	18,300†	

*U denotes unfavorable; F denotes favorable.

†Negative sign. Consistent with the discussion in the chapter, we choose not to designate the volume variance as favorable or unfavorable. Some accountants would designate a negative volume variance as "favorable."

Supporting calculations are presented in the following schedule:

Variable Overhead	Actual Overhead	Spending Variance	Budgeted Overhead at Actual Hours	Efficiency Variance	Flexible Budget (Applied Overhead)
Indirect material	$111,000		$.34		$.34
Indirect labor	75,000		.25		.25
			$.59		$.59
Machine hours..............			× 315,000		× 330,000
	$186,000	$150 U	$185,850	$8,850 F	$194,700

Fixed Overhead	Actual Overhead	Budget Variance	Flexible Budget	Volume Variance	Applied Overhead
Supervision	$51,000		$54,000		$.18
Utilities..........................	54,000		45,000		.15
Depreciation	84,000		84,000		.28
					$.61
Machine hours*					× 330,000
	$189,000	$6,000 U	$183,000	$18,300**	$201,300

*3,600,000 machine hrs / 72,000 units = 5 hrs per unit, and 5 x 66,000 units = 330,000 hrs

**Negative sign

PROBLEM 11-38 (CONTINUED)

2. Graphical analysis of variable-overhead variances:*

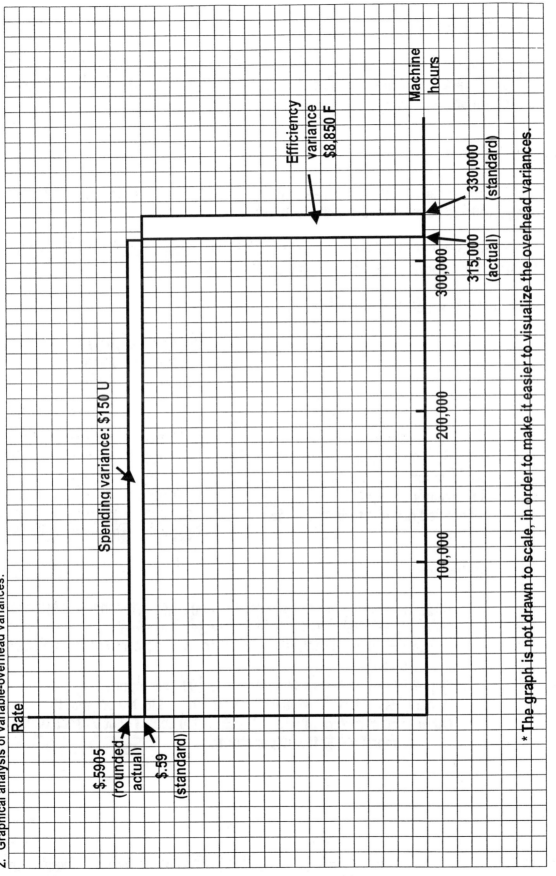

Rate

$.5905
(rounded
actual)

$.59
(standard)

Spending variance: $150 U

Efficiency
variance
$8,850 F

100,000   200,000   300,000

315,000
(actual)

330,000
(standard)

Machine
hours

* The graph is not drawn to scale, in order to make it easier to visualize the overhead variances.

PROBLEM 11-38 (CONTINUED)

3. The graph differs from the exhibit in the text, because in Newark Plastics' case, the efficiency variance is favorable. The example in the text included an unfavorable efficiency variance.

PROBLEM 11-39 (30 MINUTES)

1. A static budget is based on a single expected activity level. In contrast, a flexible budget reflects data for several activity levels.

2. Given the focus on a range of activity, a flexible budget would be more useful because it incorporates several different activity levels.

3. Static budget vs. actual experience:

	Static Budget: 24,000 Units	Actual: 20,000 Units	Variance
Direct material used ($20.00)...................	$ 480,000	$432,500	$47,500 F
Direct labor ($5.00).................................	120,000	110,600	9,400 F
Variable manufacturing overhead ($6.25)..	150,000	152,000	2,000 U
Depreciation..	24,000	24,000	----
Supervisory salaries..............................	36,000	37,800	1,800 U
Other fixed manufacturing overhead........	240,000	239,000	1,000 F
Total..	$1,050,000	$995,900	$54,100 F

Calculations:

Direct material used: $1,440,000 ÷ 72,000 units = $20.00 per unit
Direct labor: $360,000 ÷ 72,000 units = $5.00 per unit
Variable manufacturing overhead: $450,000 ÷ 72,000 units = $6.25 per unit
Depreciation: $72,000 ÷ 3 months = $24,000 per month
Supervisory salaries: $108,000 ÷ 3 months = $36,000 per month
Other fixed manufacturing overhead: ($900,000 - $72,000 - $108,000) ÷ 3 months = $240,000 per month

© *2002 The McGraw-Hill Companies, Inc.*

Solutions Manual

PROBLEM 11-39 (CONTINUED)

4. Flexible budget vs. actual experience:

	Flexible Budget: 20,000 Units	Actual: 20,000 Units	Variance
Direct material used ($20.00).....................	$400,000	$432,500	$32,500 U
Direct labor ($5.00).................................	100,000	110,600	10,600 U
Variable manufacturing overhead ($6.25)....	125,000	152,000	27,000 U
Depreciation...	24,000	24,000	----
Supervisory salaries.................................	36,000	37,800	1,800 U
Other fixed manufacturing overhead..........	240,000	239,000	1,000 F
Total...	$925,000	$995,900	$70,900 U

5. A performance report based on flexible budgeting is preferred. The report compares budgeted and actual performance at the same volume level, eliminating any variations in activity. In essence, everything is placed on a "level playing field."

The general manager's warning is appropriate because of the sizable variances that have arisen. With the static budget, performance appears favorable, especially with respect to variable costs. Bear in mind, though, that volume was below the original monthly expectation of 24,000 units, presumably because of the plant closure. A reduced volume will likely lead to lower variable costs than anticipated (and resulting favorable variances).

When the volume differential is removed, variable cost variances total $70,100U ($32,500U + $10,600U + $27,000U), or 11.2% of budgeted variable costs ($400,000 + $100,000 + $125,000). Variable cost incurrence appears excessive with respect to all of the total's components: direct material, direct labor, and variable manufacturing overhead.

PROBLEM 11-40 (30 MINUTES)

1.   Performance report:

	Budget: 1,580 Patients	Actual: 1,580 Patients	Variance
Medical assistants..............	$ 11,060	$ 13,020	$ 1,960 U
Clinic supplies...................	9,480	9,150	330 F
Lab tests..........................	308,100	318,054	9,954 U
Total	$328,640	$340,224	$11,584 U

Calculations:

Medical assistants:
  Budget: 1,580 patients x .5 hours x $14.00 = $11,060
  Actual: 840 hours x $15.50 = $13,020
Clinic supplies:
  Budget: 1,580 patients x .5 hours x $12.00 = $9,480
  Actual: $9,150 (given)
Lab tests:
  Budget: 1,580 patients x 3 tests x $65.00 = $308,100
  Actual: $318,054 (given)

2.   The variances do not reveal any significant problems. The $330 variance for clinic supplies is only 3.48% of the budgeted amount ($330 ÷ $9,480) and favorable. Similarly, the lab-test variance, while unfavorable, is only 3.23% of the budget ($9,954 ÷ $308,100).

PROBLEM 11-40 (CONTINUED)

3.   Variances for lab tests:

        Spending variance:

          Actual tests conducted x actual cost

            5,214 tests* x \$61**... \$318,054

          Actual tests conducted x standard cost

            5,214 tests x \$65... <u>338,910</u>

          Variable-overhead spending variance............................ <u>\$ 20,856</u> F

        * 1,580 patients x 3.3 tests

        ** \$318,054 ÷ 5,214 tests

        Efficiency variance:

          Actual tests conducted x standard cost

            5,214 tests x \$65... \$338,910

          Standard tests allowed x standard cost

            4,740 tests* x \$65... <u>308,100</u>

          Variable-overhead efficiency (quantity) variance.............. <u>\$ 30,810</u> U

        * 1,580 patients x 3 tests

Yes, Fall City does appear to have some problems. The two variances computed are fairly sizable in relation to the \$308,100 budget. The efficiency variance is of particular concern, given that it is 10% of budget (\$30,810 ÷ \$308,100) and unfavorable. This variance arises because the assistants are conducting an average of 3.3 tests per patient when the standard calls for only 3 tests. The standard may be set too low or perhaps the assistants are somewhat sloppy, having to re-do tests that were done improperly.

4.   The spending and efficiency variances add up to equal the flexible-budget variance (\$20,856F + \$30,810U = \$9,954U). The flexible-budget variance reflects the total of the individual standard-cost variances.

PROBLEM 11-41 (25 MINUTES)

1. Let X = budgeted fixed overhead

    X ÷ 20,000 machine hours = $4.00 per hour

    X = $80,000

2. Variable-overhead spending variance:

    Actual hours x actual rate

    23,100 hours x $2.40*........................ $55,440

    Actual hours x standard rate

    23,100 hours x $2.50........................ <u>57,750</u>

    Variable-overhead spending variance...... <u>$ 2,310</u> Favorable

    * $55,440 ÷ 23,100 hours

3. Fixed-overhead volume variance:

    Budgeted fixed overhead...................................... $80,000

    Standard hours allowed x standard rate

    5,350 hours* x $4.00... <u>21,400</u>

    Fixed-overhead volume variance............................ <u>$58,600</u>

    * 10,700 units x .5 hours per unit

    The fixed-overhead volume variance is positive;
    some managerial accountants would interpret it as
    an unfavorable variance.

4. Maxwell spent more than anticipated. Actual fixed overhead amounted to $100,460
    ($155,900 - $55,440) when the budget was set at $80,000. The fixed-overhead budget
    variance is $20,460 unfavorable ($100,460 - $80,000).

5. Variable overhead is underapplied by $42,065:

    Actual overhead: Actual hours x actual rate

    23,100 hours x $2.40... $55,440

    Applied overhead: Standard hours allowed x standard rate

    5,350 hours x $2.50... <u>13,375</u>

    Underapplied variable overhead..................................... <u>$42,065</u>

PROBLEM 11-41 (CONTINUED)

6.   Without having complete information, it is difficult to be 100% certain. However, by an analysis of data related to the volume variance, a lengthy strike appears to be a strong possibility. Maxwell had planned to work 20,000 machine hours during the period, giving the company the capability of producing 40,000 finished units (20,000 hours x 2 units per hour). Actual production amounted to only 10,700 units, leaving the firm far shy of its manufacturing goal. A strike is a plausible explanation.

PROBLEM 11-42 (40 MINUTES)

1.   Susan Porter recommended that SoftGro use flexible budgeting in this situation because a flexible budget would allow Mark Fletcher to compare SoftGro's actual selling expenses (based on current month's actual activity) with budgeted selling expenses. In general, flexible budgets:

   • Provide management with the tools to evaluate the effects of varying levels of activity on costs, revenues, and profits.

   • Enable management to improve planning and decision making.

   • Improve the analysis of actual results.

PROBLEM 11-42 (CONTINUED)

2.

SOFTGRO, INC.
REVISED MONTHLY SELLING EXPENSE REPORT FOR NOVEMBER

	Flexible Budget	Actual	Variance
Advertising	$1,650,000	$1,660,000	$10,000 (U)
Staff salaries....................................	125,000	125,000	
Sales salaries[a]..................................	115,200	115,400	200 (U)
Commissions[b]	496,000	496,000	
Per diem expense[c]	158,400	162,600	4,200 (U)
Office expenses[d]	366,000	358,400	7,600 (F)
Shipping expenses[e]	992,500	976,500	16,000 (F)
Total expenses	$3,903,100	$3,893,900	$ 9,200 (F)

Supporting calculations:

[a]Monthly salary for salesperson
$108,000 \div 90 = \$1,200$.

Budgeted amount
$\$1,200 \times 96 = \$115,200$.

[b]Commission rate
$\$448,000 \div \$11,200,000 = .04$.

Budgeted amount
$\$12,400,000 \times .04 = \$496,000$.

[c]$(\$148,500 \div 90) \div 15 \text{ days} = \$110 \text{ per day}$.
$(\$110 \times 15) \times 96 = \$158,400$.

[d]$(\$4,080,000 - 3,000,000) \div 54,000 = \$20 \text{ per order}$.
$(\$3,000,000 \div 12) + (\$20 \times 5,800) = \$366,000$.

[e]$[\$6,750,000 - (\$3 \times 2,000,000)] \div 12 = \$62,500$
monthly fixed expense.

$\$62,500 + (\$3 \times 310,000) = \$992,500$.

PROBLEM 11-43 (40 MINUTES)

1. The flexible budget for LawnMate Company for the month of May, based on 4,800 units, showing separate variable cost budgets is as follows:

LAWNMATE COMPANY
FLEXIBLE BUDGET
FOR THE MONTH OF MAY

Revenue [4,800 × ($1,200,000/5,000)]..............................		$ 1,152,000
Deduct: Variable costs:		
Direct material (4,800 × $60).......................................	$ 288,000	
Direct labor (4,800 × $44)...	211,200	
Variable overhead (4,800 × $36)..................................	172,800	
Variable selling (4,800 × $12)	57,600	
Total variable costs...		729,600
Contribution margin..		$ 422,400
Deduct: Fixed costs:		
Fixed overhead	$ 180,000	
Fixed general and administrative.................................	120,000	300,000
Operating income...		$ 122,400

2. For the month of May, the company's flexible/budget variances are as follows:

LAWNMATE COMPANY
FLEXIBLE-BUDGET VARIANCES
FOR THE MONTH OF MAY

	Actual	Flexible Budget	Flexible-Budget Variance
Units...	4,800	4,800	0
Revenue..	$1,152,000	$1,152,000	$ 0
Variable costs:			
Direct material..	$ 320,000	$ 288,000	$32,000 U
Direct labor..	192,000	211,200	19,200 F
Variable overhead..................................	176,000	172,800	3,200 U
Variable selling......................................	92,000	57,600	34,400 U
Deduct: Total variable costs............................	$ 780,000	$ 729,600	$50,400 U
Contribution margin	$ 372,000	$ 422,400	$50,400 U
Fixed costs:			
Fixed overhead..	$ 180,000	$ 180,000	$ 0
Fixed general and administrative...............	115,000	120,000	5,000 F
Deduct: Total fixed costs	$ 295,000	$ 300,000	$ 5,000 F
Operating income	$ 77,000	$ 122,400	$45,400 U

3. The revised budget and variance data are likely to have the following impact on Al Richmond's behavior:

- Richmond is likely to be encouraged by the revised data, since the major portion of the variable-cost variance (direct material and variable selling expense) is the responsibility of others.

- The detailed report of variable costs shows that the direct-labor variance is favorable. Richmond should be motivated by this report because it indicates that the cost-cutting measures that he implemented in the manufacturing area have been effective.

- The report shows unfavorable variances for direct material and variable selling expense. Richmond may be encouraged to work with those responsible for these areas to control costs.

PROBLEM 11-44 (45 MINUTES)

Missing amounts for case A:

2. $7.00[a] per hour

3. $9.50[b] per hour

6. $98,050[c]

9. $2,500 U[d]

10. $3,000 F[e]

11. $(42,000) (Negative)[f] (The negative sign means that applied fixed overhead exceeded budgeted fixed overhead.)

12. $8,050 underapplied[g]

13. $45,000 overapplied[h]

16. 6,000 units[i]

19. $90,000[j]

20. $252,000[k]

Explanatory notes for case A:

[a]Budgeted direct-labor hours

$$= \text{budgeted production} \times \text{standard direct-labor hours per unit}$$

$$= 5{,}000 \text{ units} \times 6 \text{ hrs.} = 30{,}000 \text{ hrs.}$$

$$\text{Fixed overhead rate} = \frac{\text{budgeted fixed overhead}}{\text{budgeted direct-labor hours}}$$

$$= \frac{\$210{,}000}{30{,}000 \text{ hrs.}} = \$7 \text{ per hr.}$$

[b]Total standard overhead rate

   = variable overhead rate + fixed overhead rate

   = $2.50 + $7.00 = $9.50

[c]Variable-overhead spending variance

   = actual variable overhead – (actual direct-labor hours × standard variable overhead rate)

   $5,550 U = actual variable overhead – (37,000 × $2.50)

   Actual variable overhead = $98,050

[d]Variable-overhead efficiency variance

   = SVR(AH – SH)

   = $2.50(37,000 – 36,000)

   = $2,500 U

[e]Fixed-overhead budget variance

   = actual fixed overhead – budgeted fixed overhead

   = $207,000 – $210,000

   = $3,000 F

[f]Fixed-overhead volume variance

   = budgeted fixed overhead – applied fixed overhead

   = $210,000 – (36,000 × $7)

   = $42,000 (negative sign)

[g]Underapplied variable overhead

   = actual variable overhead – applied variable overhead

   = $98,050 – (36,000 × $2.50)

   = $8,050 underapplied

PROBLEM 11-44 (CONTINUED)

[h]Overapplied fixed overhead

$$= \text{actual fixed overhead} - \text{applied fixed overhead}$$

$$= \$207,000 - (36,000 \times \$7)$$

$$= \$45,000 \text{ overapplied}$$

[i]Actual production $= \dfrac{\text{standard allowed direct-labor hours}}{\text{standard hrs. per unit}}$

$$= \dfrac{36,000}{6} = 6,000 \text{ units}$$

[j]Applied variable overhead

$$= SH \times SVR$$

$$= 36,000 \times \$2.50$$

$$= \$90,000$$

[k]Applied fixed overhead

$$= SH \times \text{fixed overhead rate}$$

$$= 36,000 \times \$7$$

$$= \$252,000$$

Missing amounts for case B:

1. $4.00[a] per hour

2. $9.00[b] per hour

4. $6,400[c]

5. $18,000[d]

6. $8,000[e]

7. $19,080[f]

12. $1,600 underapplied[g]

13. $4,680 underapplied[h]

14.   1,000 units[i]

16.   800 units[j]

19. $6,400[k]

20. $14,400[l]

PROBLEM 11-44 (CONTINUED)

Explanatory notes for case B:

[a]To find the standard variable overhead rate:

Variable-overhead efficiency variance

$$= SVR(AH - SH)$$
$$\$400\ F = SVR(1,500 - 1,600)$$
$$SVR = \$4$$

[b]Standard fixed-overhead rate

$$= \text{total standard overhead rate} - SVR$$
$$= \$13 - \$4 = \$9$$

[c]Flexible budget for variable overhead

$$= SH \times SVR$$
$$= 1,600 \times \$4 = \$6,400$$

[d]Flexible budget for fixed overhead

$$= \text{applied fixed overhead} + \text{volume variance}$$
$$= (1,600 \times \$9) + \$3,600$$
$$= \$18,000$$

[e]Actual variable overhead

$$= \text{applied variable overhead} + \text{spending variance} + \text{efficiency variance}$$
$$= (1,600 \times \$4) + \$2,000\ U - \$400\ F$$
$$= \$8,000$$

[f]Actual fixed overhead

$$= \text{budgeted fixed overhead} + \text{fixed-overhead budget variance}$$
$$= \$18,000 + \$1,080\ U$$
$$= \$19,080$$

PROBLEM 11-44 (CONTINUED)

[g]Underapplied variable overhead

= spending variance + efficiency variance

= $2,000 U* + $400 F*

= $1,600 underapplied

*Note that the signs cancel when adding variances of different signs.

[h]Underapplied fixed overhead

= fixed-overhead budget variance + volume variance

= $1,080 U + $3,600 (positive)

= $4,680 underapplied

[i]Budgeted direct-labor hours $= \dfrac{\text{budgeted fixed overhead}}{\text{fixed-overhead rate}}$

$= \dfrac{\$18,000}{\$9}$

= 2,000

Budgeted production $= \dfrac{\text{budgeted direct-labor hours}}{\text{standard hours per unit}}$

$= \dfrac{2,000}{2} = 1,000 \text{ units}$

[j]Actual production $= \dfrac{\text{standard allowed hours}}{\text{standard hours per unit}}$

$= \dfrac{1,600}{2} = 800 \text{ units}$

[k]Applied variable overhead

$= SH \times SVR = 1,600 \times \$4$

= $6,400

PROBLEM 11-44 (CONTINUED)

¹Applied fixed overhead

$$= SH \times \text{standard fixed-overhead rate}$$

$$= 1{,}600 \times \$9$$

$$= \$14{,}400$$

PROBLEM 11-45 (55 MINUTES)

1.

	Activity Level (Air Miles)		
	32,000	35,000	38,000
Variable expenses:			
Fuel	$ 16,000	$ 17,500	$ 19,000
Aircraft maintenance.........................	24,000	26,250	28,500
Flight crew salaries	12,800	14,000	15,200
Selling and administrative	25,600	28,000	30,400
Total variable expenses................	$ 78,400	$ 85,750	$ 93,100
Fixed expenses:			
Depreciation on aircraft	$ 2,900	$ 2,900	$ 2,900
Landing fees....................................	900	900	900
Supervisory salaries..........................	9,000	9,000	9,000
Selling and administrative	11,000	11,000	11,000
Total fixed expenses......................	$ 23,800	$ 23,800	$ 23,800
Total expenses	$102,200	$109,550	$116,900

2. First, there is a large unfavorable variance in passenger revenue, reflecting the fact that the company's actual activity level was considerably below the planned level. Second, there are unfavorable variances in fixed expenses. Finally, the favorable cost variances shown are misleading, as explained in requirement (3).

PROBLEM 11-45 (CONTINUED)

3.   Memorandum

Date: Today

To: Red Leif, Manager of Aircraft Operations

From: I. M. Student

Subject: Variance Report

The variance report is misleading because the expenses in the budget, which was prepared for an activity level of 35,000 air miles, are compared with actual expenses incurred at the actual activity level, which is considerably lower (32,000 air miles). Management should expect variable expenses to be lower at the lower activity level. The variance report should compare actual expenses with flexible budgeted expenses, given the actual activity level.

4.

	Formula Flexible Budget (per air mile)	Actual (32,000 air miles)	Flexible Budget (32,000 air miles)	Variance
Variable expenses:				
Fuel	$ .50	$ 17,000	$ 16,000	$1,000 U
Aircraft maintenance............	.75	23,500	24,000	500 F
Flight crew salaries	.40	13,100	12,800	300 U
Selling and administrative	.80	24,900	25,600	700 F
Total variable expenses ..	$ 2.45	$ 78,500	$ 78,400	$ 100 U
	Per Month			
Fixed expenses:				
Depreciation on aircraft	$ 2,900	$ 2,900	$ 2,900	$ -0-
Landing fees..........................	900	1,000	900	100 U
Supervisory salaries..............	9,000	8,600	9,000	400 F
Selling and administrative	11,000	12,400	11,000	1,400 U
Total fixed expenses	$23,800	$ 24,900	$ 23,800	$1,100 U
Total expenses		$103,400	$102,200	$1,200 U

© *2002 The McGraw-Hill Companies, Inc.*

Solutions Manual

5. Jacqueline Frost has acted properly in every way. She noticed a major conceptual error in the way Red Leif had prepared his performance report. She pointed this out to him, and she also provided him with a correct analysis of September's performance. Leif, however, insists on taking his original (and faulty) report to the company's owner. It sounds as though Leif resents the expertise that Frost has brought to the firm, and he is willing to mislead the owner.

    If Leif carries through with his stated intention to present his original report to the owner, Frost has an ethical obligation to make the owner aware that it is a faulty analysis. Frost should show the owner her memo to Leif as well as the revised expense variance report.

    Several ethical standards for managerial accountants apply in this situation. (See Chapter 1 for a listing of these standards.) Among the relevant standards are the following:

Competence

*   Prepare complete and clear reports and recommendations after appropriate analyses of relevant and reliable information.

Integrity

*   Communicate unfavorable as well as favorable information and professional judgments or opinions.

Objectivity

*   Communicate information fairly and objectivity.
*   Disclose fully all relevant information that could reasonably be expected to influence an intended user's understanding of the reports, comments, and recommendations presented.

PROBLEM 11-46 (20 MINUTES)

The purchase of the FMS could have caused the following variances:

(a) Favorable direct-material quantity variance, due to a decrease in material waste.

(b) Unfavorable direct-labor rate variance, due to the need for a more highly skilled labor force.

(c) Favorable direct-labor efficiency variance, due to increased automation and lower labor-time requirements.

(d) Unfavorable variable-overhead spending variance, due to additional production equipment requiring such support costs as electricity and maintenance.

(e) Favorable variable-overhead efficiency variance, due to the decreased usage of direct labor. (See point (c) in this list.)

(f) Unfavorable fixed-overhead budget variance, due to increased depreciation on the new production equipment.

(g) Fixed overhead volume variance:

The sign of the variance is negative, which means that applied fixed overhead exceeded the budgeted amount. It is likely that introduction of the new equipment enabled the company to operate at a higher level of production than was anticipated, due to the increased automation.

PROBLEM 11-47 (40 MINUTES)

1. a. Three weaknesses in WoodCrafts Inc.'s monthly Bookcase Production Performance Report are as follows:

    - The report is based on a static budget. WoodCrafts should use a flexible budget that compares the same level of activity, calculating variances between the actual results and the flexible budget. Also, WoodCrafts might consider implementing an activity-based costing system.

    - Costs over which the supervisors have no control, such as fixed production costs and allocated overhead costs, are included in the report.

    - The report uses a single plant-wide rate to allocate fixed production costs. Square footage may not drive the fixed production costs, and there may be a more appropriate base such as number of units produced. It may be more appropriate to use different cost drivers for each of the different product lines.

    b. Due to Sara McKinley's remarks Steve Clark is likely to:

    - Feel tense and apprehensive. The timing of McKinley's remarks, immediately before the meeting, without an opportunity for discussion and feedback, will leave Clark feeling tense and probably inattentive throughout the meeting.

    - Be frustrated and confused by the conflicting signals of the report and what is occurring in his department and in the market. This confusion about the department's results and, consequently, the uncertainty of his job will lead to stress which may negatively affect his performance.

2. a. To improve the monthly performance report, WoodCrafts Inc. should:

    - Use a flexible budget.

    - Hold supervisors responsible for only those costs over which they have control by using a contribution approach.

    - Include footnotes to make the report more understandable.

PROBLEM 11-47 (CONTINUED)

A revised monthly performance report based on a flexible budget is as follows:

WOODCRAFTS INC.
BOOKCASE PRODUCTION PERFORMANCE REPORT FOR NOVEMBER

	Actual	Flexible Budget	Variance
Units	3,000	3,000	
Revenue...	$161,000	$165,000[a]	$ 4,000 U
Variable production costs:.................................			
Direct material	$ 23,100	$ 24,000[b]	$ 900 F
Direct labor	18,300	18,000[c]	300 U
Machine time...	19,200	19,500[d]	300 F
Manufacturing overhead.............................	41,000	42,000[e]	1,000 F
Total variable costs....................................	$101,600	$103,500	$ 1,900 F
Contribution margin	$ 59,400	$ 61,500	$ 2,100 U

[a]($137,500 budget ÷ 2,500 budgeted units) × 3,000 actual units
[b]($ 20,000 budget ÷ 2,500 budgeted units) × 3,000 actual units
[c]($ 15,000 budget ÷ 2,500 budgeted units) × 3,000 actual units
[d]($ 16,250 budget ÷ 2,500 budgeted units) × 3,000 actual units
[e]($ 35,000 budget ÷ 2,500 budgeted units) × 3,000 actual units

b.   Steve Clark should be more motivated by the revised report since it clearly shows that the variable cost variances for his product line were better than Sara McKinley had thought, despite the fact that there is an unfavorable contribution margin variance. Clark is not responsible for the revenue variance which resulted from a decrease in the sales price.

In addition, the separation of costs into controllable and noncontrollable categories allows Clark to devote full effort to those costs which he can influence. Clark will probably exhibit a positive attitude and will continue looking for ways to improve his operation.

PROBLEM 11-48 (60 MINUTES)

1. Standard machine hours per unit $= \dfrac{\text{budgeted machine hours}}{\text{budgeted production}} = \dfrac{30,000}{6,000}$

    $= 5$ hours per unit

2. Actual cost of direct material per unit $= \dfrac{\$270,000 + \$83,000}{6,200 \text{ units}}$

    $= \$56.94$ per unit (rounded)

3. Standard direct-material cost per machine hour $= \dfrac{\$252,000 + \$78,000}{30,000}$

    $= \$11$ per machine hour

4. Standard direct-labor cost per unit $= \dfrac{\$273,000 + \$234,000}{6,000 \text{ units}} = \$84.50 \text{ per unit}$

5. Standard variable-overhead rate per machine hour $=$

    $\dfrac{\$647,200 - \$627,000}{32,000 - 30,000} = \dfrac{\$20,200}{2,000 \text{ hours}} = \$10.10$ per machine hour

6. First, continue using the high-low method to determine total budgeted fixed overhead as follows:

Total budgeted overhead at 30,000 hours...	$627,000
Total budgeted variable overhead at 30,000 hours (30,000 × $10.10)	303,000
Total budgeted fixed overhead...	$324,000

    The key here is to realize that fixed overhead includes not only insurance and depreciation but also the fixed component of the semivariable-overhead costs (including maintenance, supplies, supervision, and inspection).

    Now, we can compute the standard fixed-overhead rate per machine hour, as follows:

    Standard fixed-overhead rate per machine hour $= \dfrac{\$324,000}{30,000 \text{ hours}}$

    $= \$10.80$ per hour

PROBLEM 11-48 (CONTINUED)

7. First, compute actual variable overhead as follows:

Total actual overhead	$633,000
Total fixed overhead (given)	324,000
Total variable overhead..	$309,000

Variable-overhead spending variance = Actual variable overhead – $(AH \times SVR)$

$= \$309,000 - (32,000 \times \$10.10)$

$= \$14,200$ Favorable

8. Variable-overhead efficiency variance

$= (AH \times SVR) - (SH \times SVR)$

$= (32,000 \times \$10.10) - (31,000^* \times \$10.10) = \$10,100$ Unfavorable

*Standard allowed machine hours = 6,200 units $\times$ 5 hours per unit

9. Fixed-overhead budget variance

$=$ actual fixed overhead – budgeted fixed overhead

$= \$324,000 - \$324,000 = 0$

10. Fixed-overhead volume variance

$=$ budgeted fixed overhead – applied fixed overhead

$= \$324,000 - (31,000 \times \$10.80) = \$10,800$ (negative sign)*

*Consistent with the discussion in the text, we choose not to interpret the volume variance as either favorable or unfavorable. Some accountants would designate a positive volume variance as "unfavorable" and a negative volume variance as "favorable."

PROBLEM 11-48 (CONTINUED)

11. Flexible budget formula, using the high-low method of cost estimation:

Variable cost per machine hour = $\dfrac{\$1,540,000 - \$1,464,000}{32,000 - 30,000}$ = $38 per hour

Total budgeted cost at 30,000 hours..	$1,464,000
Total variable cost at 30,000 hours (30,000 × $38)	1,140,000
Fixed overhead cost	$ 324,000

Thus, the flexible budget formula is as follows:

Total production cost   = $38X + $324,000

where X = number of machine hours allowed.

Therefore, the total budgeted production cost for 6,050 units is:

($38 × 30,250*) + $324,000 = $1,473,500

*Standard allowed machine hours = 6,050 units × 5 hours per unit

PROBLEM 11-49 (35 MINUTES)

Direct-material price variance $= PQ(AP - SP)$

$= 30,000(\$2.20^* - \$2.00)$

$= \$6,000$ Unfavorable

*$2.20 = \$66,000 \div 30,000$

Direct-material quantity variance $= SP(AQ - SQ)$

$= \$2.00(30,000 - 29,000^*)$

$= \$2,000$ Unfavorable

*29,000 lbs. $= 1,450 \times 20$ lbs. per unit

Direct-labor rate variance $= AH(AR - SR)$

$= 8,000(\$18.90^* - \$18.00)$

$= \$7,200$ Unfavorable

*$18.90 = \$151,200 \div 8,000$

Direct-labor efficiency variance $= SR(AH - SH)$

$= \$18.00(8,000 - 7,250^*)$

$= \$13,500$ Unfavorable

*7,250 hours $= 1,450$ units $\times 5$ hours per unit

Variable-overhead spending variance

$=$ actual variable overhead $- (AH \times SVR)$

$= \$11,000 - (8,000)(\$1.50)$

$= \$1,000$ Favorable

Variable-overhead efficiency variance $= SVR(AH - SH)$

$= \$1.50(8,000 - 7,250)$

$= \$1,125$ Unfavorable

PROBLEM 11-49 (CONTINUED)

Fixed-overhead budget variance

= actual fixed overhead – budgeted fixed overhead

= $26,000 – $25,000*

= $1,000 Unfavorable

*$25,000 = $300,000 (annual) ÷ 12 months

Fixed-overhead volume variance   = budgeted fixed overhead – applied fixed overhead

= $25,000 – $21,750* = $3,250 (positive)†

*$21,750 = 1,450 units × $15.00 per unit

†Consistent with the discussion in the text, we choose not to interpret the volume variance as either favorable or unfavorable. Some accountants would designate a positive volume variance as "unfavorable" and a negative volume variance as "favorable."

PROBLEM 11-50 (30 MINUTES)

1. Variances:

    a. Variable-overhead spending variance

        = Actual variable overhead – (AH × SVR)

        = $1,701,000 – (764,000 × $2) = $173,000 Unfavorable

    b. Variable-overhead efficiency variance

        = (AH × SVR) – (SH × SVR)

        = (764,000 × $2) – (750,000* × $2) = $28,000 Unfavorable

    *Standard hours = 250,000 units × 3 hours per unit = 750,000 hours, where 3 hours per unit = $6 per unit ÷ $2 per hour

    c. Fixed-overhead budget variance

        = Actual fixed overhead – budgeted fixed overhead

        = $392,000 – $400,000* = $8,000 Favorable

    *Budgeted fixed overhead   = budgeted overhead – budgeted variable overhead

        = $2,000,000 – (800,000 × $2) = $400,000

    d. Fixed-overhead volume variance

        = budgeted fixed overhead – applied fixed overhead

        = $400,000 – (750,000* × $.50†) = $25,000 (positive)**

    *Standard allowed hours   = 250,000 units × 3 hours per unit

    †Predetermined fixed overhead rate   = $400,000 ÷ 800,000 budgeted machine hours

        = $.50 per machine hour

    **Consistent with the discussion in the text, we choose not to interpret the volume variance as either favorable or unfavorable. Some accountants would designate a positive volume variance as "unfavorable" and a negative volume variance as "favorable."

PROBLEM 11-50 (CONTINUED)

2.

| Manufacturing Overhead... | 2,093,000* | |
| Various Accounts.. | | 2,093,000 |

To record actual manufacturing overhead.

*$2,093,000 = $1,701,000 + $392,000

| Work-in-Process Inventory .... | 1,875,000† | |
| Manufacturing Overhead .... | | 1,875,000 |

To add manufacturing overhead to work in process.

†750,000 standard allowed hours $\times$ $2.50 per hour = $1,875,000, where $2.50 per hour is the sum of the variable and fixed predetermined overhead rates.

| Cost of Goods Sold .... | 218,000** | |
| Manufacturing Overhead .... | | 218,000 |

To close underapplied overhead into Cost of Goods Sold.

**$218,000 = $2,093,000 – $1,875,000 (Also, $218,000 = sum of the four overhead variances.)

PROBLEM 11-51 (60 MINUTES)

1. Formula flexible overhead budget:

$$\text{Total monthly overhead} = \$20,000 + \$9X^*$$

where X denotes activity measured in direct-labor hours

*The $9 standard variable-overhead rate is computed as follows: $9 = $13,500 ÷ 1,500 hours.

2. Variable-overhead spending and efficiency variances: See the diagram on the next page.

PROBLEM 11-51 (CONTINUED)

VARIABLE-OVERHEAD SPENDING AND EFFICIENCY VARIANCES

(1) ACTUAL VARIABLE OVERHEAD			(2)			(3) FLEXIBLE BUDGET: VARIABLE OVERHEAD			(4)† VARIABLE OVERHEAD APPLIED TO WORK-IN-PROCESS		
Actual Hours (AH)	x	Actual Rate (AVR)	Actual Hours (AH)	x	Standard Rate (SVR)	Standard Allowed Hours (SH)	x	Standard Rate (SVR)	Standard Allowed Hours (SH)	x	Standard Rate (SVR)
2,100 hours	x	$9.30 per hour*	2,100 hours	x	$9.00 per hour	2,000 hours	x	$9.00 per hour	2,000 hours	x	$9.00 per hour
$19,530			$18,900			$18,000			$18,000		

$630 Unfavorable
Variable-overhead spending variance

$900 Unfavorable
Variable-overhead efficiency variance

No difference

---

*Actual variable-overhead rate (AVR) = $\dfrac{\text{actual variable overhead cost}}{\text{actual hours}}$ = $\dfrac{\$19,530}{2,100}$ = $9.30

†Column (4) is not used to compute the variances. It is included to point out that the flexible-budget amount for variable overhead, $18,000, is the amount that will be applied to Work-in-Process inventory for product costing purposes.

PROBLEM 11-51 (CONTINUED)

3. Graphical analysis of variable-overhead variances:*

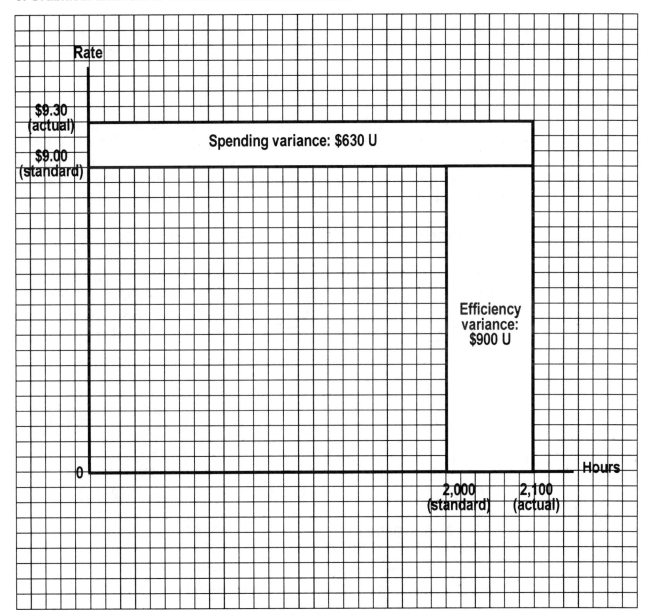

*The graph is not drawn to scale, in order to make it easier to visualize the overhead variances.

PROBLEM 11-51 (CONTINUED)

4. Interpretation of variable-overhead variances:

    (a) The $630 unfavorable spending variance means that the company spent more money on variable overhead in February than should have been spent, given that 2,100 direct-labor hours were used. This is the control variance for variable overhead.

    (b) The $900 unfavorable efficiency variance results from the fact that February's actual direct-labor usage exceeded the standard amount. Direct labor is the cost driver used to budget and apply variable overhead. The variance does not convey any information about the efficiency with which variable-overhead items, such as electricity, were used.

5.   FIXED-OVERHEAD BUDGET AND VOLUME VARIANCES

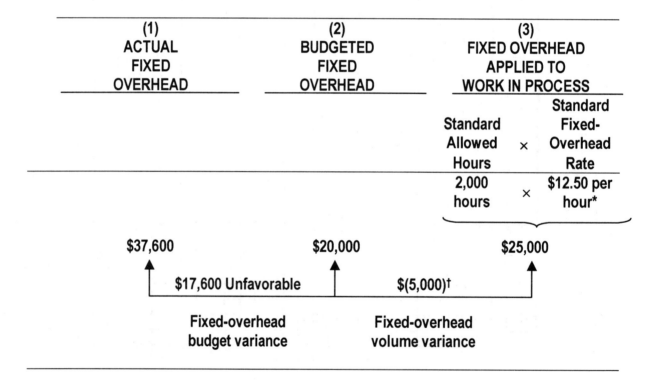

(1) ACTUAL FIXED OVERHEAD	(2) BUDGETED FIXED OVERHEAD	(3) FIXED OVERHEAD APPLIED TO WORK IN PROCESS
		Standard Allowed × Standard Fixed- Hours Overhead Rate
		2,000 hours × $12.50 per hour*
$37,600	$20,000	$25,000
$17,600 Unfavorable	$(5,000)†	
Fixed-overhead budget variance	Fixed-overhead volume variance	

$$* \text{ Standard fixed overhead rate} = \$12.50 = \frac{\$20,000}{(6,400)(.25)}$$

†Negative sign. Consistent with the discussion in the text, we choose not to designate the volume variance as favorable or unfavorable. Some accountants would designate a negative volume variance as "favorable."

PROBLEM 11-51 (CONTINUED)

6. Budgeted versus applied fixed overhead:

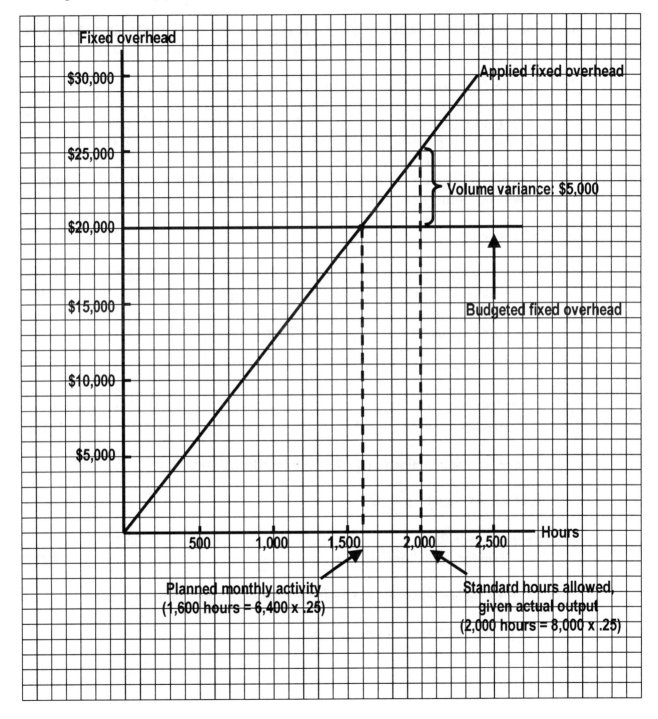

PROBLEM 11-51 (CONTINUED)

7. Interpretation of fixed-overhead variances:

    (a) The $17,600 unfavorable budget variance means that actual fixed overhead exceeded the budget by $17,600. This is the control variance for fixed overhead.

    (b) The ($5,000) negative volume variance is a means of reconciling the control purpose and the product costing purpose of the cost accounting system. The volume variance is the difference between budgeted monthly fixed overhead of $20,000, which is determined for control purposes, and the applied fixed overhead of $25,000, which is computed for product costing purposes. The negative sign of the volume variance results from the fact that the company's actual production activity in February exceeded planned activity.

8. Journal entries:

    (a)

Manufacturing Overhead	57,130*	
Various Accounts		57,130

    To record February's actual manufacturing overhead.

    *$57,130 = $19,530 + $37,600

    (b)

Work-in-Process Inventory	43,000†	
Manufacturing Overhead....................................		43,000

    To add applied manufacturing overhead to work in process.

    †$43,000 = $18,000 + $25,000

    (c)

Cost of Goods Sold	14,130**	
Manufacturing Overhead....................................		14,130

    To close underapplied manufacturing overhead into cost of goods sold:

    **$14,130 = $57,130 – $43,000

PROBLEM 11-51 (CONTINUED)

9. Posting of journal entries:

Manufacturing Overhead	
57,130	43,000
	14,130

Various Accounts	
	57,130

Work-in-Process Inventory	
43,000	

Cost of Goods Sold	
14,130	

PROBLEM 11-52 (20 MINUTES)

1. Sales price variance

   = (Actual sales price – expected sales price) × actual sales volume

   = ($48* – $50†) × 5,000 = $10,000 Unfavorable

   *Actual sales price = $240,000/5,000

   †Expected sales price = $300,000/6,000

2. Sales volume variance

   = (Actual sales volume – budgeted sales volume) × budgeted unit contribution margin

   = (5,000 – 6,000) × $20* = $20,000 Unfavorable

   *Budgeted unit contribution margin = $120,000/6,000

PROBLEM 11-53 (45 MINUTES)

1.   Sales-price variances and sales-volume variances:

Sales-Price Variance	Actual Sales Price	Budgeted Sales Price	Price Difference	Actual Sales Volume	Sales-Price Variance
Business......................	$115	$120	$5	74,000	$370,000 U
Residential..................	59	60	1	86,000	86,000 U
Total					$456,000 U

Sales-Volume Variance	Actual Sales Volume	Budgeted Sales Volume	Volume Difference	Budgeted Contribution Margin Per Unit*	Sales-Volume Variance
Business......................	74,000	80,000	6,000	$40	$240,000 U
Residential..................	86,000	120,000	34,000	10	340,000 U
Total					$580,000 U

*Since no other variable costs are associated directly with either product line, the
gross margin is equal to the contribution margin:

	Business	Residential
$\dfrac{\text{Budgeted contribution margin}}{\text{Budgted sales volume}}$	$\dfrac{\$3,200,000}{80,000}$	$\dfrac{\$1,200,000}{120,000}$
	= $40 per unit	= $10 per unit

PROBLEM 11-53 (CONTINUED)

2. The effectiveness of the marketing program is difficult to judge in the absence of actual industry-wide performance data. If the industry estimate of a 10% decline in the market for these products is used as a basis for comparison, then CCAC's gross margin should have fallen to $3,960,000 ($4,400,000 x .9) as follows (in thousands):

	Business	Residential	Total
Budgeted gross margin.....................................	$3,200	$1,200	$4,400
Budgeted adjusted for 10% industry decline...	$2,880	$1,080	$3,960
Actual gross margin	2,442	774	3,216
Variance (unfavorable)	$ 438	$ 306	$ 744

CCAC's gross margin actually fell to $3,216,000, which is $744,000 lower than might have been expected. To have been considered a success, the marketing program should have generated a gross margin above $4,020,000 (the original budget minus the projected industry decline plus the incremental cost of the special marketing program: $4,400,000 - $440,000 + $60,000). The $60,000 cost of the special marketing program is assumed equal to the unfavorable variance in the advertising cost shown in the performance report.

CCAC hoped to do better than the industry average by giving dealer discounts and increasing direct advertising. However, to be successful, the discounts and advertising must be offset by an increase in volume. The company was not successful in this regard; sales volume dropped 7.5 percent in the business line as compared to a 28.3 percent decline in residential volume. Note that the price of business-grade products was dropped by 4.2 percent, whereas residential-grade products declined in price by only 1.7 percent. Apparently the discounts and advertising did not generate enough sales volume to offset and compensate for the program.

SOLUTIONS TO CASES

CASE 11-54 (50 MINUTES)

1. Planned production = 5,000 units.

   The reasoning is as follows:

   (a) Fixed-overhead rate per direct-labor hour $= \dfrac{\text{budgeted fixed overhead}}{\text{planned direct-labor hours}}$

   $$\$4 \text{ per hr.} = \frac{\$40,000}{X}$$

   Therefore, planned direct-labor hours (X) equals 10,000 hours.

   (b) Planned direct-labor hours = planned production × standard hours per unit

   $$10,000 \text{ hr.} = X \times 2 \text{ hr. per unit}$$

   Therefore, planned production (X) equals 5,000 units.

2. Actual production = planned production – 500 units

   = 5,000 units – 500 units

   = 4,500 units

3. Actual fixed overhead = $43,250.

   Fixed overhead budget variance = actual fixed overhead – budgeted fixed overhead

   $$\$3,250 \text{ U} = X - \$40,000$$

   Therefore, actual fixed overhead (X) equals $43,250.

4. Total standard allowed direct-labor hours

   = 4,500 units produced × 2 hr. per unit

   = 9,000 hr.

CASE 11-54 (CONTINUED)

5. Actual direct-labor rate   = $15 per hour.

$$\text{Direct-labor rate variance} = AH(AR - SR)$$
$$\$8,800\ U = 8,800(AR - \$14)$$

   Therefore, $AR = \$15$.

6. Standard variable-overhead rate   = $6 per direct-labor hour.

$$\text{Variable-overhead efficiency variance} = SVR(AH - SH)$$
$$\$1,200\ F = SVR(8,800 - 9,000)$$

   Therefore, $SVR = \$6$ per hr.

7. Actual variable-overhead rate   = $6.30 per direct-labor hour.

$$\text{Variable-overhead spending variance} = AH(AVR - SVR)$$
$$\$2,640\ U = 8,800(AVR - \$6)$$

   Therefore, $AVR = \$6.30$ per hr.

8. $$\text{Standard direct-material quantity per unit} = \frac{\text{total standard direct-material quatity allowed}}{\text{actual production in units}}$$

$$= \frac{13,500\ \text{kg.}^*}{4,500\ \text{units}}$$

$$= 3\ \text{kg.}$$

$$^*\text{Direct-material quantity variance} = SP(AQ - SQ)$$
$$\$6,000\ U = \$12(14,000 - SQ)$$
$$SQ = 13,500\ \text{kg.}$$

9. $$\text{Direct-material price variance} = PQ(AP - SP)$$
$$= 14,000(\$13.50 - \$12.00)$$
$$= \$21,000\ U$$

CASE 11-54 (CONTINUED)

10. $\begin{array}{l}\text{Applied fixed}\\\text{overhead}\end{array}$ = standard fixed-overhead rate × standard allowed hours

= $4 per hr. × 9,000 hr.

= $36,000

11. $\begin{array}{l}\text{Fixed-overhead}\\\text{volume variance}\end{array}$ = budgeted fixed overhead – applied fixed overhead

= $40,000 – $36,000

= $4,000 (Positive)*

*Consistent with the discussion in the text, we choose not to interpret the volume variance as either favorable or unfavorable. Some managerial accountants would classify this as an unfavorable variance, because planned production exceeded actual production.

CASE 11-55 (50 MINUTES)

1. The $44,000 unfavorable variance between the budgeted and actual contribution margin for the chocolate nut supreme cookie product line during April is explained by the following variances:

   a. Direct-material price variance:

Type of Material	PQ*(AP⁺ – SP)	Variance
Cookie mix..........................	4,650,000($.02–$.02)............	$ 0
Milk chocolate....................	2,660,000($.20–$.15)............	133,000 U
Almonds	480,000($.50–$.50)...............	0
Total		$133,000 U

*PQ = AQ, because all materials were used during the month of purchase.
⁺AP = actual total cost (given) ÷ actual quantity

CASE 11-55 (CONTINUED)

b. Direct-material quantity variance:

Type of Material	SP(AQ – SQ*)	Variance
Cookie mix...........................	$.02(4,650,000–4,500,000) ...	$ 3,000 U
Milk chocolate....................	$.15(2,660,000–2,250,000) ...	61,500 U
Almonds	$.50(480,000–450,000).........	15,000 U
Total		$79,500 U

*SQ = standard ounces of input per pound of cookies × actual pounds of cookies produced.

c. Direct-labor rate variance = $AH(AR - SR) = 0$.

Dividing the total actual labor cost by the actual labor time used, for each type of labor, shows that the actual rate and the standard rate are the same (i.e., $AR = SR$). Thus, this variance is zero.

d. Direct-labor efficiency variance:

Type of Labor	SR*(AH – SH⁺)	Variance
Mixing	$.24(450,000–450,000).........	$ 0
Baking................................	$.30(800,000–900,000).........	30,000 F
Total		$30,000 F

*Standard rate per minute = standard rate per hour ÷ 60 minutes

⁺Standard minutes per unit (pound) × actual units (pounds) produced

e. Variable-overhead spending variance
    = actual variable overhead – (AH × SVR)
    = $750,000 – [(1,250,000*/60) × $32.40]
    = $75,000 U

*Total actual *minutes* of direct labor.

CASE 11-55 (CONTINUED)

f. Variable-overhead efficiency variance

$$= SVR(AH - SH^*)$$

$$= \$32.40 \left(\frac{1{,}250{,}00}{60} - \frac{3 \times 450{,}000}{60} \right)$$

$$= \$54{,}000 \text{ F}$$

*SH = (3 minutes per unit, or pound × 450,000 units, or pounds) ÷ 60 minutes

g. Sales-price variance = $\left(\begin{array}{c} \text{actual} \\ \text{sales price} \end{array} - \begin{array}{c} \text{expected} \\ \text{sales price} \end{array} \right) \times \begin{array}{c} \text{actual} \\ \text{sales volume} \end{array}$

$$= (\$7.90^* - \$8.00) \times 450{,}000$$
$$= \$45{,}000 \text{ U}$$

*Actual sales price = $3,555,000 ÷ 450,000 units sold

h. Sales-volume variance

$$= \left(\begin{array}{c} \text{actual} \\ \text{sales volume} \end{array} - \begin{array}{c} \text{budgeted} \\ \text{sales volume} \end{array} \right) \times \begin{array}{c} \text{budgeted unit} \\ \text{contribution margin} \end{array}$$

$$= (450{,}000 - 400{,}000) \times \$4.09^*$$
$$= \$204{,}500 \text{ F}$$

*Budgeted unit contribution margin = $1,636,000 ÷ 400,000 units

CASE 11-55 (CONTINUED)

Summary of variances:

Direct-material price variance..	$133,000 U
Direct-material quantity variance...	79,500 U
Direct-labor rate variance	0
Direct-labor efficiency variance...	30,000 F
Variable-overhead spending variance..	75,000 U
Variable-overhead efficiency variance...	54,000 F
Sales-price variance..	45,000 U
Sales-volume variance..	204,500 F
Total	$ 44,000 U

2.   a.   One problem may be that direct labor is not an appropriate cost driver for Aunt Molly's Old Fashioned Cookies because it may not be the activity that drives variable overhead. A good indication of this situation is shown in the variance analysis. The direct-labor efficiency variance is favorable, while the variable-overhead spending variable is unfavorable. Another problem is that baking requires considerably more power than mixing does; this difference could distort product costs.

        b.   Activity-based costing (ABC) may solve the problems described in requirement 2(a) and therefore is an alternative that Aunt Molly's should consider. Since direct labor does not seem to have a direct cause-and-effect relationship with variable overhead, the company should try to identify the activity or activities that drive variable overhead. If the same proportion of these activities is used in all of Aunt Molly's products, then ABC may not be beneficial. However, if the products require a different mix of these activities, then ABC could be beneficial.

CURRENT ISSUES IN MANAGERIAL ACCOUNTING

ISSUE 11-56

"XEROX PLEDGES TO CUT $1 BILLION IN COSTS, REPORTS A QUARTERLY LOSS OF $167 MILLION," *THE WALL STREET JOURNAL*, OCTOBER 25, 2000, JOHN HECHINGER AND LAURA JOHANNES. "GE SAYS EARNING ROSE 20% IN 3RD PERIOD: RESULTS REFLECT NET GROWTH IN EVERY MAJOR UNIT, THE FRUIT OF COST CUTS," *THE WALL STREET JOURNAL*, OCTOBER 12, 2000, MATT MURRAY.

1. Xerox plans to cut costs and raise capital by selling various assets such as its stake in Fuji Xerox, several business units, its China operations and its business equipment financing operations. Xerox gave scant details about how it would achieve projected savings or a timetable for asset sales. As many as 5000 layoffs could result.

2. Standard costing provides a benchmark against which management can judge the cost of producing a product or service. Large variances above the standard cost should be investigate, and can help management in cutting costs.

ISSUE 11-57

"USING ENHANCED COST MODELS IN VARIANCE ANALYSIS FOR BETTER CONTROL AND DECISION MAKING," *MANAGEMENT ACCOUNTING QUARTERLY*, WINTER 2000, KENNARD T. WING.

Student answers will vary. The instructor should point out that variance analysis is based on overly simplistic cost models in which every cost has to be treated as either fixed or variable. In the real world, many costs do not behave according to those idealized models, which means that managers can always legitimately point to shortcomings in the variance analysis. According to the article, variance reports may fail to help managers identify cost issues, and managers can use the limitations of the variance reports to reduce their own financial accountability.

ISSUE 11-58

"STANDARD COSTING IS ALIVE AND WELL AT PARKER BRASS," *MANAGEMENT ACCOUNTING QUARTERLY*, WINTER 2000, DAVID JOHNSEN AND PARVEZ SOPARIWALA.

If production variances exceed 5 percent of sales, the FBU managers are required to provide an explanation for the variances and to put together a plan of action to correct the detected problems. In the past, variances were reported only at month-end, but often a particular job already would have been off the shop floor for three or more weeks. When management questioned the variances, it was too late to review the job. Now, exception reports are generated the day after a job is closed. Any job with variances greater than $1,000 is displayed on this report. These reports are distributed to the managers, planners or schedulers, and plant accountants, which permits people to ask questions while the job is still fresh in everyone's mind.

ISSUE 11-59

"FORGET THE HUDDLED MASSES: SEND NERDS," *BUSINESS WEEK*, JULY 21, 1997, STEPHEN BAKER AND GARY MCWILLIAMS.

1. Failure to satisfy computer programming needs could lead to: (a) down-time; (b) production inefficiencies; (c) increased training costs; (d) high employee turnover; and (e) low employee satisfaction.

2. Similar to the flexible overhead budgets shown in the text.

ISSUE 11-60

"MANAGEMENT CONTROL SYSTEMS: HOW SPC ENHANCES BUDGETING AND STANDARD COSTING," *MANAGEMENT ACCOUNTING QUARTERLY*, FALL 2000, HARPER A. ROEHM, LARRY WEINSTEIN, AND JOSEPH F. CASTELLANO.

1. Organizations that use statistical process control (SPC) create processes and systems to achieve their mission and objectives. Control is about creating conditions that will improve the probability that desired outcomes will be achieved. A control system is comprised of a set of measures for defined entities, criteria for evaluating these measures, and processes for obtaining these measures and the criteria for evaluating them.

2. SPC adds value as a cost management technique in budgeting and standard costing systems by determining the ability of a system to achieved desired outcomes and determining if the system is accomplishing them.

ISSUE 11-61

"MANAGED CARE IS STILL A GOOD IDEA," *THE WALL STREET JOURNAL*, NOVEMBER 17, 1999, UWE REINHART.

Managed care simply means that those who pay for health care have some say over what services they will pay for and at what price. Periodic, statistical profiles of individual physicians' practices promise to be a more productive approach to cost and quality control. This is a common method of cost control in other countries. The method grants the physician clinical autonomy within some range of pre-established norms and intervenes only when physicians deviate substantially from them. In industry, this approach is known as management by exception. The development and updating of these practice norms is a perpetual search for the best clinical practices. To be effective, that search should be conducted in close cooperation with the practicing physicians to whom the norms apply.

ISSUE 11-62

"PERFORMANCE MEASUREMENT IN A TELEPHONE CALL CENTRE," *MANAGEMENT ACCOUNTING*, JANUARY 1999, GORDON BROWN, JOHN INNES, AND NOEL TAGOE.

The budgeting process includes predicting how many calls will be made and the duration of each call. The budgeted cost includes not only the cost of the telephone call but also the cost of the telephone operators and appropriate overhead costs. An important financial performance measure is the cost per call, which varies by country and by month.

The predicted level of telephone calls is very significant, because this anticipated level of usage determines the number of telephone operators at the call center. In addition to the actual number of telephone calls received, the following significant non-financial performance measures are reported via the system: call dropout rate, customer satisfaction measures, and average response time to answer calls. The call drop-out rate is the percentage of all callers who are put in a telephone queue and decide to hang up rather than wait in this queue for an operator to become free. These non-financial performance measures can provide information in terms of an international comparison of different call centers, which can lead to further investigation and resulting action.

ISSUE 11-63

"THE SATELLITE BIZ BLASTS OFF," *BUSINESS WEEK*, JANUARY 27, 1997, ERIC SCHINE AND PETER ELSTROM.

1. Overhead costs:

    Launch vehicle testing

    System setup

    Supervisors' salaries

    Insurance

    Launch costs

2. Increased volume could reduce prices. If a firm is able to cover its fixed costs and the marginal cost of providing an additional unit of service is low, it may be able to provide service at a much lower cost.

CHAPTER 12
Responsibility Accounting and Total Quality Management

ANSWERS TO REVIEW QUESTIONS

12-1   A responsibility-accounting system fosters goal congruence by establishing the performance criteria by which each manager will be evaluated. Development of performance measures and standards for those measures can help to ensure that managers are striving toward goals that support the organization's overall objectives.

12-2   Goal congruence results when the managers of subunits throughout an organization strive to achieve objectives that are consistent with the goals set by top management. In order for the organization to be successful, the managers and employees throughout the organization must be striving toward consistent goals.

12-3   Several benefits of decentralization are as follows:

(a) The managers of an organization's subunits have specialized information and skills that enable them to manage their departments most effectively.

(b) Allowing managers autonomy in decision making provides managerial training for future higher-level managers.

(c) Managers with some decision-making authority usually exhibit greater motivation than those who merely execute the decisions of others.

(d) Delegating some decisions to lower-level managers provides time relief to upper-level managers.

(e) Delegating decision making to the lowest level possible enables an organization to give a timely response to opportunities and problems.

Several costs of decentralization are as follows:

(a) Managers in a decentralized organization may have a narrow focus on their own units' performance.

(b) Managers may tend to ignore the consequences of their actions on the organization's other subunits.

(c) In a decentralized organization, some tasks or services may be duplicated unnecessarily.

12-4 (a) Cost center: A responsibility center, the manager of which is accountable for the subunit's costs. (An example is a production department in a manufacturing firm.)

(b) Revenue center: A responsibility center, the manager of which is accountable for the subunit's revenue. (An example is a sales district in a wholesaling firm.)

(c) Profit center: A responsibility center, the manager of which is accountable for the subunit's profit. (An example is a particular restaurant in a fast-food chain.)

(d) Investment center: A responsibility center, the manager of which is accountable for the subunit's profit and the capital invested to generate that profit. (An example is a commuter airline division of an airline company.)

12-5 It would be appropriate to change a particular hotel from a profit center to an investment center if the manager of the hotel is given the authority to make significant investment decisions affecting the hotel's resources.

12-6 Flexible budgeting allows a performance report to be constructed in a meaningful way. The performance report should compare actual expenses incurred with the expenses that should have been incurred, given the actual level of activity. The expenses that should have been incurred given the actual level of activity can be obtained from the flexible budget.

12-7 Under activity-based responsibility accounting, management's attention is directed toward activities, rather than being focused primarily on cost, revenue, and profit measures of subunit performance. Activity-based responsibility accounting uses the database generated by an activity-based costing system coupled with nonfinancial measures of operational performance for key activities. Such an approach can help management eliminate non-value-added activities and improve the cost effectiveness of activities that do add value to the organization's product or service.

12-8 Attention to the following two factors may yield positive behavioral effects from a responsibility-accounting system.

(a) When properly used, a responsibility-accounting system does not emphasize blame. The emphasis should be on providing the individual who is in the best position to explain a particular event or financial result with information to help in understanding reasons behind the event or financial result.

(b) Distinguishing between controllable and uncontrollable costs or revenues helps the individuals who are evaluated under a responsibility-accounting system to feel as though they are evaluated on the basis of events and results over which they have some control or influence.

12-9   Rarely does a single individual completely control a result in an organization. Most results are caused by the joint efforts of several people and the joint impact of several events. Nevertheless, there is usually a person who is in the best position to explain a result or who is in the best position to influence the result. In this sense, performance reports based on controllability really are based on a manager's ability to influence results.

12-10   (a) Cost pool: A collection of costs to be assigned to a set of cost objects. (An example of a cost pool is all costs related to material handling in a manufacturing firm.)

(b) Cost object: A responsibility center, product, or service to which a cost is assigned. (The various production departments in a manufacturing firm provide examples of cost objects. For example, the material-handling cost pool may be allocated across the various production departments that use material-handling services.)

12-11   Cost allocation (or distribution): The process of assigning costs in a cost pool to the appropriate cost objects. (An example of cost allocation would be the assignment of the costs in the material-handling cost pool to the production departments that use material-handling services. For example, the material-handling costs might be allocated to production departments on the basis of the weight of the materials handled for each department.)

12-12   An example of a common resource in an organization is a computer department. The resource includes the computer itself, the software, and the computer specialists who run the computer system and assist its users. The opportunity costs associated with one person using the computer resource include the possibility that another user will be precluded from or delayed in using the computer resource. Allocating the cost of the computer services department to the users makes the users aware of the opportunity cost of using the computer.

12-13   A computer system has a limited capacity at any one time. Allocating the cost of using the service to the user makes the user aware that his or her use of the system may preclude someone else from using it. Thus, the user is made aware of the potential opportunity cost associated with his or her use.

12-14 A cost allocation base is a measure of activity, physical characteristic, or economic characteristic associated with the responsibility centers, which are the cost objects in the allocation process. One sensible allocation base for assigning advertising costs to the various components of a large theme park is the number of people patronizing the park's various components. Presumably, the number of people attending a certain part of the theme park is an indication of how popular that part of the park is. Notice that in most cases the sales revenue generated by the various components of the theme park is not a viable allocation base, since most theme parks have a single admission fee for the entire park.

12-15 Marketing costs are distributed to the hotel's departments on the basis of budgeted sales dollars so that the behavior of one department does not affect the costs allocated to the other departments. If, on the other hand, the marketing costs had been budgeted on the basis of actual sales dollars, then the costs allocated to each department would have been affected when only one department's actual sales revenue changed.

12-16 A segmented income statement shows the segment margin for each major segment of the enterprise.

12-17 Many managerial accountants believe that it is misleading to allocate common costs to an organization's segments. Since these costs are not traceable to the activities of segments, they can be allocated to segments only on the basis of a highly arbitrary allocation base.

12-18 It is important in responsibility accounting to distinguish between segments and segment managers, because some costs that are traceable to a segment may be completely beyond the influence of the segment manager. Proper evaluation of the segment as an investment of the company's resources requires that these costs be included with costs associated with the segment. However, in evaluations of the manager's performance, these costs should be excluded, since the manager has no control over them.

12-19 Three key features of a segmented income statement are as follows: contribution format, identification of controllable versus uncontrollable expenses, and segmented reporting, which shows income statements for the company as a whole and for each of its major segments.

12-20 A common cost for one segment can be a traceable cost for another segment. For example, the salary of the general manager of a hotel is traceable to that segment of the entire hotel company. However, the salary of the hotel's general manager is a common cost for each of the departments in that hotel, such as the food and beverage department and the hospitality department.

12-21 Customer profitability analysis refers to using the concepts of activity-based costing to determine how serving particular customers causes activities to be performed and costs to be incurred. Examples of activities that can be differentially demanded by customers include order frequency, order size, special packaging or handling, customized parts or engineering, and special machine setups. Such activities can make some customers more profitable than others.

12-22 Four types of quality costs are as follows:

(a) Prevention costs: the costs of preventing defects.

(b) Appraisal costs: the costs of determining whether defects exist.

(c) Internal failure costs: the costs of repairing defects found prior to product sale.

(d) External failure costs: the costs incurred when defective products have been sold.

12-23 Observable quality costs can be measured and reported, often on the basis of information in the accounting records. For example, the cost of inspectors' salaries is an observable quality cost. Hidden quality costs cannot easily be measured, reported, or even estimated. For example, the opportunity cost associated with lost sales after a defective product is sold is a hidden quality cost to the company.

12-24 A product's quality of design is how well it is conceived or designed for its intended use. The product's quality of conformance refers to the extent to which a product meets the specifications of its design.

12-25 A product's grade is the extent of its capability in performing its intended purpose, viewed in relation to other products with the same functional use. An example in the service industry is airline travel. Airplane seats may be coach class or first class; the difference lies in seat size, comfort, and service. Either class will take you from Los Angeles to Chicago, but not with the same degree of comfort.

12-26 "An ounce of prevention is worth a pound of cure" can be interpreted in terms of resources expended on various categories of quality costs. A dollar spent on prevention may save many dollars of appraisal, internal failure, or external failure costs.

12-27 A cause and effect diagram shows by means of connected lines all the possible causes of a particular type of defect in a product or service.

SOLUTIONS TO EXERCISES

EXERCISE 12-28 (10 MINUTES)

The type of responsibility center most appropriate for each of the following organizational subunits is indicated below.

(1) Movie theater: Cost center or profit center.

(2) Radio station: Profit center.

(3) Claims department: Cost center.

(4) Ticket sales division of an airline: Revenue center.

(5) Bottling plant: Cost center.

(6) Orange juice factory: Profit center.

(7) College of engineering at a university: Profit center.

(By designating the college of engineering as a profit center, this subunit is encouraged to generate research grants and manage its operations most effectively. The term "profit center" is used in a slightly different way here. No subunit in a university really makes a profit. However, treating the college of engineering like a profit center means that this subunit's management will have considerable authority in managing the subunit's revenues and expenses.)

(8) European division of a multinational manufacturing company: Investment center.

(9) Outpatient clinic in a profit-oriented hospital: Profit center.

(10) Mayor's office of a city: Cost center.

EXERCISE 12-29 (10 MINUTES)

The appropriate responsibility-accounting treatment for each of the scenarios is the following:

(1) Since the cost of idle time incurred in Department B was due to the breakdown of improperly maintained machinery in Department A, the costs of the idle time should be charged to Department A.

(2) If the machinery had been properly maintained, it would be more appropriate not to charge the cost due to idle time in Department B back to Department A. This cost should be considered a normal cost of operating in a sequential production environment. The managers of Department B should anticipate such normal machine breakdowns and plan their production scheduling to accommodate such events.

EXERCISE 12-30 (10 MINUTES)

The Maintenance Department should not be charged for the excess wages of the skilled employees who are temporarily assigned to the Maintenance Department. Modifications should be made in the responsibility-accounting system as follows: (1) the Maintenance Department should be charged with only the normal wages for maintenance employees, $12 per hour. (2) The additional $10 per hour ($22 – $12) should be charged to a top management level account, since the decision to keep these employees on the payroll was made by top management.

EXERCISE 12-31 (10 MINUTES)

By designating this department as a profit center, the corporation has given the managers of the department an opportunity to manage their operation just like a full-fledged business. These managers have specialized knowledge and skills that make them experts in the area of logistics and distribution. They are in the best position to read the needs of other units to whom they provide logistics services, and are also in the best position to make cost-benefit trade-offs that arise in the provision of logistical services. By treating this service department as a profit center, the organization has given its managers an incentive to control costs and also provide a quality service that meets the needs of its customers.

A profit center such as this might not be free to sell its services outside the company. Moreover, the creation of this profit center suggests the need for an internal pricing structure for services supplied to other subunits.

EXERCISE 12-32 (50 MINUTES)

PERFORMANCE REPORTS FOR MARCH: SELECTED SUBUNITS OF ALOHA HOTELS AND RESORTS
(IN THOUSANDS)

	Flexible Budget*		Actual Results*		Variance†	
	March	Year to Date**	March	Year to Date**	March	Year to Date**
Food and Beverage Department						
Banquets & Catering..............	$ 650	$ 1,910	$ 658	$ 1,923	$ 8 F	$ 13 F
Restaurants...........................	1,800	5,550	1,794	5,534	6 U	16 U
Kitchen	(1,065)	(3,233)	(1,069)	(3,242)	4 U	9 U
Total profit............................	$ 1,385	$ 4,227	$ 1,383	$ 4,215	$2 U	$12 U
Kitchen						
Kitchen staff wages..............	$ (85)	$ (253)	$ (86)	$ (255)	$1 U	$ 2 U
Food.....................................	(690)	(2,110)	(690)	(2,111)	—	1 U
Paper products.....................	(125)	(375)	(122)	(370)	3 F	5 F
Variable overhead	(75)	(225)	(78)	(232)	3 U	7 U
Fixed overhead	(90)	(270)	(93)	(274)	3 U	4 U
Total expense	$ (1,065)	$ (3,233)	$(1,069)	$(3,242)	$4 U	$ 9 U

*Numbers without parentheses denote profit; numbers with parentheses denote expenses.

†F denotes favorable variance; U denotes unfavorable variance.

**Year-to-date column equals year-to-date column for February in Exhibit 12-4 in the text plus March amount. For example, $1,910 equals $1,260 plus $650.

EXERCISE 12-33 (30 MINUTES)

1. Allocation of costs:

Department and Allocation Base	Division			Total Cost Allocated
	Liberal Arts	Sciences	Business Administration	
Admissions (enrollment)	$36,000 (1,000/2,500)	$28,800 (800/2,500)	$25,200 (700/2,500)	$90,000
Registrar (credit hours)	$56,250 (30,000/80,000)	$52,500 (28,000/80,000)	$41,250 (22,000/80,000)	$150,000
Computer Services (courses requiring computer)	$64,000 (12/60)	$128,000 (24/60)	$128,000 (24/60)	$320,000

The Admissions Department costs are allocated on the basis of enrollment. The more students enrolled in a division, the more admissions there are to process.

The Registrar's costs are allocated on the basis of credit hours. The greater the number of credit hours, the more course registrations there are to process.

The Computer Services Department's costs are allocated on the basis of the number of courses requiring computer work. The greater the number of computer-intensive courses, the greater will be the demands placed on the Computer Services Department.

2. The number of courses would probably be a better allocation base for the Registrar's costs. Costs in this department are driven by processing course registrations, not credit hours. A four-credit course does not require any more registration effort than a three-credit course.

The estimated amount of computer time required would probably be a better allocation base for the Computer Services Department. Two different courses requiring computer work could place vastly different demands on the Computer Services Department.

EXERCISE 12-34 (40 MINUTES)

SEGMENTED INCOME STATEMENTS: COUNTYWIDE CABLE SERVICES, INC.

	Countywide Cable Services	Segments of Company		
		Metro	Suburban	Outlying
Service revenue	$2,200,000	$1,000,000	$ 800,000	$ 400,000
Variable expenses..................	450,000	200,000	150,000	100,000
Segment contribution margin	$1,750,000	$ 800,000	$ 650,000	$ 300,000
Less: Fixed expenses controllable by segment manager	870,000	400,000	320,000	150,000
Profit margin controllable by segment manager.................	$ 880,000	$ 400,000	$330,000	$ 150,000
Less: Fixed expenses, traceable to segment, but controllable by others..........	520,000	230,000	200,000	90,000
Profit margin traceable to segment	$ 360,000	$ 170,000	$130,000	$ 60,000
Less: Common fixed expenses	95,000			
Income before taxes	$ 265,000			
Less: Income tax expense......	145,000			
Net income.............................	$ 120,000			

EXERCISE 12-35 (5 MINUTES)

1. appraisal cost

2. external failure cost

3. internal failure cost

4. prevention cost

EXERCISE 12-36 (20 MINUTES)

SAN MATEO CIRCUITRY
QUALITY COST REPORT

	Current Month's Costs	Percentage of Total
Prevention costs:		
Training of quality-control inspectors......................................	$21,000	22.2
Total	$21,000	
Appraisal costs:		
Inspection of purchased electrical components......................	$12,000	12.7
Tests of instruments..	30,000	31.7
Total	$42,000	
Internal failure costs:		
Costs of rework..	$ 9,000	9.5
Costs of defective parts that cannot be salvaged...................	6,100	6.5
Total	$15,100	
External failure costs:		
Replacement of instruments already sold	$16,500	17.4
Total	$16,500	
Total quality costs	$94,600	100.00

EXERCISE 12-37 (10 MINUTES)

Observable quality costs in the airline industry:

- Cost of repairing damaged luggage.

- Cost of providing lodging for passengers stranded when a flight is cancelled due to equipment malfunction.

- Cost of cleaning a passenger's clothing when a flight attendant spills food or beverages on the passenger.

EXERCISE 12-37 (CONTINUED)

Hidden quality costs in the airline industry:

- Cost of lost flight bookings when passengers judge in-flight service to be substandard.

- Cost of lost flight bookings when potential passengers are unable to get through to the airline's reservations service.

- Cost of lost flight bookings when passengers react to cancelled or late flights.

EXERCISE 12-38 (30 MINUTES)

Answers will vary widely, depending on the company chosen. Some examples are as follows:

Marriott Hotels: Company-owned hotel, profit center

McDonald's Corporation: Company-owned resaurant, profit center

NationsBank: Regional division of company, investment center

Pizza Hut: Kitchen in an individual restaurant, cost center

Ramada Inn: National reservations center, revenue center

Xerox Corporation: Individual manufacturing department or work center, cost center

SOLUTIONS TO PROBLEMS

PROBLEM 12-39 (30 MINUTES)

A wide range of possible responses is possible for this problem. The organization chart and companion chart showing responsibility accounting designations should be similar to the charts given for Aloha Hotels and Resorts in Exhibits 12-1 and 12-2, respectively. The letter to stockholders should specify the responsibilities of the managers shown in the charts. Refer to the discussion of Exhibits 12-1 and 12-2 in the text. The charts in Exhibits 12-1 and 12-2 are repeated here for convenience.

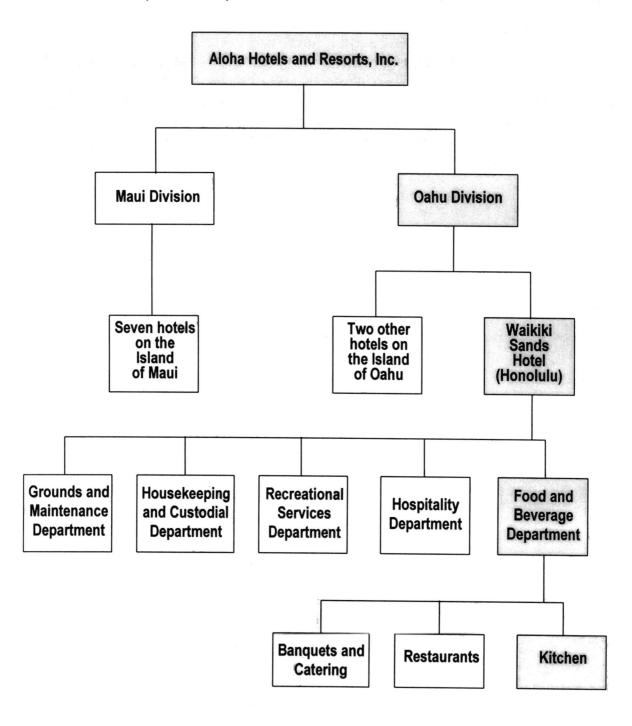

PROBLEM 12-39 (CONTINUED)

MANAGER

RESPONSIBILITY
CENTER

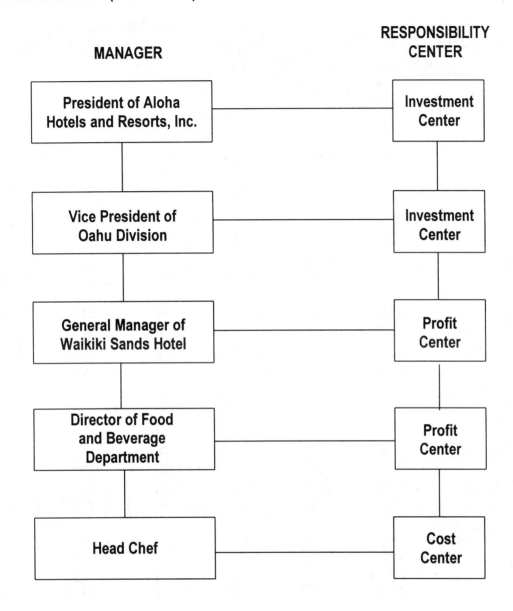

PROBLEM 12-40 (40 MINUTES)

Once again, a wide range of responses is possible, depending on the organization designed in the preceding problem. The format for the performance reports is given in Exhibit 12-4 for Aloha Hotels and Resorts. This exhibit is repeated here for convenience.

PERFORMANCE REPORTS FOR FEBRUARY: SELECTED SUBUNITS OF ALOHA HOTELS AND RESORTS (IN THOUSANDS)

	Flexible Budget*		Actual Results*		Variance†	
	February	Year to Date	February	Year to Date	February	Year to Date
Company	$30,660	$64,567	$30,716	$64,570	$ 56 F	$ 3 F
Maui Division..............	$18,400	$38,620	$18,470	$38,630	$ 70 F	$10 F
Oahu Division..............	12,260	25,947	12,246	25,940	14 U	7 U
Total Profit..................	$30,660	$64,567	$30,716	$64,570	$ 56 F	$ 3 F
Oahu Division						
Waimea Beach Resort	$ 6,050	$12,700	$ 6,060	$12,740	$ 10 F	$40 F
Diamond Head Lodge	2,100	4,500	2,050	4,430	50 U	70 U
Waikiki Sands Hotel...	4,110	8,747	4,136	8,770	26 F	23 F
Total Profit..................	$12,260	$25,947	$12,246	$25,940	$ 14 U	$ 7 U
Waikiki Sands Hotel						
Grounds & Maintenance	$ (45)	$ (90)	$ (44)	$ (90)	$ 1 F	--
Housekeeping & Custodial	(40)	(90)	(41)	(90)	1 U	--
Recreational Services	40	85	41	88	1 F	$ 3 F
Hospitality	2,800	6,000	2,840	6,030	40 F	30 F
Food and Beverage....	1,355	2,842	1,340	2,832	15 U	10 U
Total Profit..................	$ 4,110	$ 8,747	$ 4,136	$ 8,770	$ 26 F	$23 F
Food and Beverage Dept.						
Banquets & Catering	$ 600	$ 1,260	$ 605	$ 1,265	$ 5 F	$ 5 F
Restaurants	1,785	3,750	1,760	3,740	25 U	10 U
Kitchen.......................	(1,030)	(2,168)	(1,025)	(2,173)	5 F	5 U
Total profit..................	$ 1,355	$ 2,842	$ 1,340	$ 2,832	$ 15 U	$10 U
Kitchen						
Kitchen staff wages ...	$ (80)	$ (168)	$ (78)	$ (169)	$ 2 F	$ 1 U
Food..........................	(675)	(1,420)	(678)	(1,421)	3 U	1 U
Paper products	(120)	(250)	(115)	(248)	5 F	2 F
Variable overhead......	(70)	(150)	(71)	(154)	1 U	4 U
Fixed overhead	(85)	(180)	(83)	(181)	2 F	1 U
Total expenses..........	$(1,030)	$(2,168)	$(1,025)	$(2,173)	$ 5 F	$ 5 U

* Numbers without parentheses denote profit; numbers with parentheses denote expenses.
† F denotes favorable variance; U denotes unfavorable variance.

PROBLEM 12-41 (35 MINUTES)

Memorandum

Date: Today

To: Sandy Beach, General Manager of Waikiki Sands Hotel

From: I.M. Student

Subject: Responsibility Centers

The Waikiki Sands Hotel is a profit center as specified by the corporation's top management. The hotel's general manager does not have the authority to make significant investment decisions, so an investment-center designation would be inappropriate for the hotel. The Grounds and Maintenance Department and the Housekeeping and Custodial Department should be cost centers, since these departments do not generate revenue. The Food and Beverage Department should be a profit center, since the department's manager can influence both the costs incurred in the department and the revenue generated. The Food and Beverage Director can determine the menu, set meal prices, and make entertainment decisions, all of which significantly influence the department's revenue.

The Hospitality Department also should be a profit center. The Director of Hospitality has significant influence in setting room rates and making decorating decisions, which affect the department's revenue. The Director also makes hiring and salary decisions for the department's staff, which significantly affect departmental expenses. The Hospitality Department's three subunits (Front Desk, Bell Staff, and Guest Services) should be cost centers, since they do not generate revenue. The managers of these subunits can significantly influence the costs incurred in their units through hiring and salary recommendations, staff scheduling, and use of materials and equipment.

PROBLEM 12-42 (60 MINUTES)

1. Performance Report for August: Selected Subunits of Rocky Mountain General Hospital

	Flexible Budget		Actual Results		Variance*	
	August	Year to Date	August	Year to Date	August	Year to Date
Rocky Mountain General Hospital	$582,700	$4,661,600	$581,150	$4,658,300	$ 1,550 F	$ 3,300 F
General Medicine Division	$210,000	$1,680,000	$204,000	$1,670,900	$ 6,000 F	$ 9,100 F
Surgical Division...........	140,000	1,120,000	141,000	1,115,800	1,000 U	4,200 F
Medical Support Division	182,700	1,461,600	182,650	1,465,600	50 F	4,000 U
Administrative Division	50,000	400,000	53,500	406,000	3,500 U	6,000 U
Total cost......................	$582,700	$4,661,600	$581,150	$4,658,300	$ 1,550 F	$ 3,300 F
Medical Support Division						
Nursing Department	$ 70,000	$ 560,000	$ 75,000	580,000	$ 5,000 U	$20,000 U
Radiology and Laboratory Department	18,000	144,000	18,100	144,000	100 U	--
Nutrition Department....	71,700	573,600	71,950	578,600	250 U	5,000 U
Housekeeping Department	10,000	80,000	11,600	86,000	1,600 U	6,000 U
Maintenance Department	13,000	104,000	6,000	77,000	7,000 F	27,000 F
Total cost......................	$182,700	$1,461,600	$182,650	$1,465,600	$ 50 F	$ 4,000 U
Nutrition Department						
Regiestered Dieticians' Section.......................	$ 7,500	$ 60,000	$ 7,500	$ 60,000	--	--
Food Service Section ...	33,200	265,600	35,050	272,600	$1,850 U	$ 7,000 U
Kitchen.........................	31,000	248,000	29,400	246,000	1,600 F	2,000 F
Total cost......................	$71,700	$ 573,600	$71,950	$ 578,600	$ 250 U	$ 5,000 U
Food Service Section						
Patient Food Service	$17,000	$136,000	$18,500	$ 137,000	$1,500 U	$ 1,000 U
Cafeteria	16,200	129,600	16,550	135,600	350 U	6,000 U
Total cost......................	$33,200	$265,600	$35,050	$ 272,600	$1,850 U	$ 7,000 U
Cafeteria						
Food servers' wages	$ 8,000	$ 64,000	$ 9,000	$ 72,000	$1,000 U	$ 8,000 U
Paper products	4,500	36,000	4,400	36,200	100 F	200 U
Utilities.........................	1,000	8,000	1,050	8,100	50 U	100 U
Maintenance	400	3,200	100	1,100	300 F	2,100 F
Custodial	1,100	8,800	1,100	8,600	--	200 F
Supplies.......................	1,200	9,600	900	9,600	300 F	--
Total cost......................	$16,200	$129,600	$16,550	$ 135,600	$ 350 U	$ 6,000 U

*F denotes favorable variance; U denotes unfavorable variance.

2. Arrows are included on the performance report to show the cost relationships.

PROBLEM 12-42 (CONTINUED)

3. A variety of responses are reasonable for this question. Since the data given in the problem do not include the individual variances over several months, it is not possible to condition the investigation on trends. The largest variances in the performance report are the most likely to warrant an investigation. The following variances for August would likely catch the attention of the hospital administrator:

General Medicine Division	$6,000	F
Administrative Division	3,500	U
Nursing Department	5,000	U
Maintenance Department	7,000	F
Food servers' wages	1,000	U

The $1,000 variance for food servers' wages is smaller than some of the variances not listed above. However, it is a relatively large variance for only one cost item in the subunit. In contrast, the $1,600 variance for the kitchen is for an entire subunit of the hospital.

PROBLEM 12-43 (45 MINUTES)

1.

Cost Pool	Division	Allocation Base		Percentage of Total	Costs Distributed
Facilities	General Medicine........	15,000	sq. ft.	37.5%	$ 71,250
	Surgical	8,000	sq. ft.	20.0%	38,000
	Medical Support..........	9,000	sq. ft.	22.5%	42,750
	Administrative............	8,000	sq. ft.	20.0%	38,000
	Total.........................	40,000	sq. ft.	100.0%	$190,000
Utilities	General Medicine........	135,000	cu. ft.	33.75%	$ 8,100
	Surgical	100,000	cu. ft.	25.00%	6,000
	Medical Support..........	90,000	cu. ft.	22.50%	5,400
	Administrative............	75,000	cu. ft.	18.75%	4,500
	Total.........................	400,000	cu. ft.	100.00%	$ 24,000
General administration	General Medicine........	30	empl.	30.00%	$ 66,000
	Surgical	20	empl.	20.00%	44,000
	Medical Support..........	20	empl.	20.00%	44,000
	Administrative............	30	empl.	30.00%	66,000
	Total.........................	100	empl.	100.00%	$220,000
Community outreach	General Medicine........	$2,000,000		50.00%	$ 20,000
	Surgical	1,250,000		31.25%	12,500
	Medical Support..........	750,000		18.75%	7,500
	Administrative............	—		—	—
	Total.........................	$4,000,000		100.00%	$ 40,000

2. An alternative allocation base for community outreach costs is the number of hours spent by each division's personnel in community outreach activities. This base would be more reflective of the actual contribution of each division to the program.

3. The reason for allocating utility costs to the divisions is so that each division's cost reflects the total cost of running the division. Since none of the divisions can operate without electricity, heat, water, and so forth, these costs should be reflected in divisional cost reports. By allocating such costs, division managers are made aware of these costs and are able to reflect the costs when pricing services and seeking third-party reimbursements, such as those from insurance companies.

PROBLEM 12-44 (35 MINUTES)

1. Segmented income statement:

	Show-Off, Inc.	Las Vegas	Reno	Sacramento
Sales revenue..............................	$1,332,000	$444,000	$451,000	$437,000
Variable operating expenses:				
Cost of goods sold........................	$ 705,000	$203,500	$225,500	$276,000
Sales commissions........................	79,920	26,640	27,060	26,220
Total....................................	$ 784,920	$230,140	$252,560	$302,220
Segment contribution margin...............	$ 547,080	$213,860	$198,440	$134,780
Less: Fixed expenses controllable by				
segment manager:				
Local advertising...........................	$ 81,000	$ 11,000	$ 22,000	$ 48,000
Sales manager salary....................	32,000	----	----	32,000
Total.....................................	$ 113,000	$ 11,000	$ 22,000	$ 80,000
Profit margin controllable by segment				
manager....................................	$ 434,080	$202,860	$176,440	$ 54,780
Less: Fixed expenses traceable to				
segment, but controllable by				
others:				
Local property taxes......................	$ 12,500	$ 4,500	$ 2,000	$ 6,000
Store manager salaries..................	108,000	31,000	39,000	38,000
Other..	28,200	5,800	4,600	17,800
Total......................................	$ 148,700	$ 41,300	$ 45,600	$ 61,800
Segment profit margin.......................	$ 285,380	$161,560	$130,840	$ (7,020)
Less: Common fixed expenses.............	192,300			
Net income......................................	$ 93,080			

Calculations:

   Sales revenue: Las Vegas, 37,000 units x $12.00; Reno, 41,000 units x
      $11.00; Sacramento, 46,000 units x $9.50

   Cost of goods sold: Las Vegas, 37,000 units x $5.50; Reno, 41,000
      units x $5.50; Sacramento, 46,000 units x $6.00

   Sales commissions: Las Vegas, $444,000 x 6%; Reno, $451,000 x 6%;
      Sacramento, $437,000 x 6%

PROBLEM 12-44 (CONTINUED)

2. Sacramento is the weakest segment because of several factors:

    *   Las Vegas and Reno have much higher markups on cost [118%($6.50/$5.50) and 100% ($5.50/$5.50), respectively]. However, Sacramento's markup is only 58% ($3.50/ $6.00).
    *   Despite being the only store that has a sales manager, and spending considerably more on advertising than Las Vegas and Reno, Sacramento has the lowest gross dollar sales of the three stores. Sacramento's return on these outlays appears inadequate.
    *   Sacramento's "other" noncontrollable costs are much higher than those of Las Vegas and Reno.

3. Show-Off uses a responsibility accounting system, meaning that managers and centers are evaluated on the basis of items under their control. Since this is a personnel-type decision, the decision should be made by reviewing the profit margin controllable by the store (i.e., segment) manager. The segment contribution margin excludes fixed costs under a store manager's control; in contrast, a store's segment profit margin would reflect all traceable costs whether controllable or not.

PROBLEM 12-45 (35 MINUTES)

1. Warranty costs: External failure
   Reliability engineering: prevention
   Rework at AT's manufacturing plant: internal failure
   Manufacturing inspection: appraisal
   Transportation costs to customer sites: external failure
   Quality training for employees: prevention

2&3. Evaluation of quality costs:

	No. 165 $	No. 165 % of Sales	No. 172 $	No. 172 % of Sales
Sales revenue:				
$60,000 x 80; $55,000 x 100...	$4,800,000		$5,500,000	
Prevention:				
Reliability engineering				
1,600 hours x $150.........	$ 240,000			
2,000 hours x $150.........			$ 300,000	
Quality training..................	35,000		50,000	
Total.......................	$ 275,000	5.73%	$ 350,000	6.36%
Appraisal (inspection):				
300 hours x $50...................	$ 15,000	.31%		
500 hours x $50...................			$ 25,000	.45%
Internal failure (rework at AT):				
80 units x 35% x $1,900........	$ 53,200	1.11%		
100 units x 25% x $1,600......			$ 40,000	.73%
External failure:				
Warranty costs:				
80 units x 70% x $1,200...	$ 67,200			
100 units x 10% x $400....			$ 4,000	
Transportation to customers	29,500		15,000	
Total.......................	$ 96,700	2.01%	$ 19,000	.35%
Total quality costs...................	$ 439,900	9.16%	$ 434,000	7.89%

PROBLEM 12-45 (CONTINUED)

Individual quality costs as a % of total quality costs:

	No. 165		No. 172	
	$	% of Total	$	% of Total
Prevention...........	$275,000	62.51%	$350,000	80.65%
Appraisal	15,000	3.41%	25,000	5.76%
Internal failure	53,200	12.09%	40,000	9.22%
External failure....	96,700	21.98%	19,000	4.38%
Total	$439,900		$434,000	

4. Yes, the company is "investing" its quality expenditures differently for the two machines. Advanced is spending more up-front on no. 172 with respect to prevention and appraisal—over 86% of the total quality expenditures. (This figure is approximately 66% for no. 165.) The net result is lower internal and external failure costs and, perhaps more important, lower total quality costs as a percentage of sales (7.89% for no. 172 and 9.16% for no. 165).

This problem illustrates the essence of total quality management systems when compared with conventional quality control procedures. Overall costs are lower with TQM when compared against systems that focus on "after-the-fact" detection and rework.

5. Prevention, appraisal, internal failure, and external failure costs are observable in the sense that such amounts can be measured and reported. When inferior products make it to the marketplace, customer dissatisfaction will often increase, resulting in lost sales of the defective product and perhaps other goods as well. The "cost" of these lost sales is an opportunity cost—a "hidden" cost that is very difficult to measure.

PROBLEM 12-46 (75 MINUTES)

1. SEGMENTED INCOME STATEMENTS: BUCKEYE DEPARTMENT STORES, INC. (IN THOUSANDS)

	Buckeye Department Stores, Inc.	Segments of Company		Segments of Columbus Division			
		Cleveland Division	Columbus Division	Olentangy Store	Scioto Store	Downtown Store	Not Allocated
Sales revenue	$39,400	$21,000	$18,400	$5,000	$2,400	$11,000	
Variable operating expenses:							
Cost of merchandise sold	$23,000	$12,000	$11,000	$3,000	$2,000	$6,000	
Sales personnel—salaries	3,050	1,600	1,450	400	300	750	
Sales commissions	380	200	180	50	40	90	
Utilities	590	300	290	80	60	150	
Other	465	250	215	60	35	120	
Total variable expenses	$27,485	$14,350	$13,135	$3,590	$2,435	$7,110	
Segment contribution margin	$11,915	$6,650	$5,265	$1,410	$(35)	$3,890	
Less: Fixed expenses controllable by segment manager:							
Depreciation—furnishings	$ 560	$ 290	$ 270	$ 80	$ 50	$ 140	
Computing and billing	405	210*	195	40	30	75	50
Warehouse	780	450	330	70	60	200	
Insurance	355	200	155	40	25	90	
Security	350	210	140	30	30	80	
Total	$2,450	$1,360	$1,090	$ 260	$ 195	$ 585	$ 50
Profit margin controllable by segment manager	$9,465	$5,290	$4,175	$1,150	$ (230)	$3,305	(50)
Less: Fixed expenses, traceable to segment, but controllable by others:							
Depreciation—buildings	$ 930	$ 470	$ 460	$ 120	$ 90	$ 250	
Property taxes	305	170	135	35	20	80	
Supervisory salaries	1,750	1,000†	750	150	100	400	
Total	$2,985	$1,640	$1,345	$ 305	$ 210	$ 730	$ 100
Profit margin traceable to segment	$6,480	$3,650	$2,830	$ 845	$(440)	$2,575	$ 100
Less: Common fixed expenses	120						$ (150)
Income before taxes	$6,360						
Less: Income tax expense	1,950						
Net income	$4,410						

*$210 = $160 listed in table + $50 not allocated. †$1,000 = $900 listed in table + $100 not allocated.

PROBLEM 12-46 (CONTINUED)

2. The segmented income statement would help the president of Buckeye Department Stores gain insight into which division and which individual stores are performing well or having difficulty. Such information serves to direct management's attention to areas where its expertise is needed.

PROBLEM 12-47 (30 MINUTES)

Responsibility-accounting system:

1. At least two potential behavioral advantages if Building Services Co.'s (BSC's) managers accept and participate in the development of budgets are as follows:

    *   They would be motivated to plan ahead and promote goal congruence.
    *   They would be pleased to be responsible only for those items they can control.

2. At least two potential problems that could arise if the managers do not accept the change in philosophy are as follows:

    *   They could resent being measured on an individual basis, since they may be responsible for costs over which they have no control.

    *   The could focus too much on their own department's goals at the possible detriment to the organization as a whole (suboptimization).

3. If the managers support the new system, and most of the disadvantages pointed out above are avoided, the responsibility-center system will enhance the alignment of organizational and personal goals. Since Commercial Maintenance, Inc. (CMI) took the time to fully explain and communicate the system to BSC's managers, by pointing out the advantages and encouraging their participation, organizational and personal goals will likely become aligned.

PROBLEM 12-47 (CONTINUED)

Participatory budgeting system:

1. At least two potential behavioral benefits are the following:

    *   BSC's managers are likely to accept the system and be motivated to attain the budget targets, since they were actively involved in setting the goals and know what is expected of them.

    *   Communication and group cohesiveness would be improved, because the managers would feel part of a team.

2. At least two potential problems that could arise are as follows:

    *   The managers could be motivated to "pad" their budgets, putting slack in the plan to ensure meeting the goals.

    *   Overemphasis on departmental goals could hurt cross-departmental employee relations.

3. Participatory budgeting can contribute to an organization's goals by encouraging buy-in to the resulting budget and performance evaluation by the organization's employees. There is no reason to believe that such an approach would not be beneficial for BSC.

ROBLEM 12-48 (45 MINUTES)

Memorandum

Date: Today

To: Mathew Basler, President of Warriner Equipment Company

From: I. M. Student

Subject: Responsibility-Accounting System

Warriner Equipment Company's critical success factors are as follows:

1. Cost-efficient production: The firm must meet the market price, which implies producing in a cost-efficient manner.

2. High product quality: Stated by the company president as necessary for success.

3. On-time delivery: Also noted by the company president as critical to the firm's success.

Note that the product price is not a critical success factor, since it is largely beyond the company's control. The price is determined by the market.

A responsibility-accounting system in which the plants are profit centers is consistent with achieving high performance on the firm's critical success factors. The plant managers are in the best position to influence production cost control, product quality, and on-time delivery.

The sales districts should be revenue centers, in which the sales district managers are accountable for meeting sales projections.

Suppose the plants are cost centers and the sales districts are revenue centers. When a rush order comes in, the plant manager's incentive is to reject it because rush orders tend to increase production costs (due to increased setups, interrupted production, etc.). The sales district manager's incentive is to push rush orders, because accepting a rush order results in a satisfied customer and increased future business. Thus, there is a built-in conflict between the plant managers and the sales district managers.

PROBLEM 12-48 (CONTINUED)

If the plants are profit centers, then each plant manager is encouraged to consider both the costs and the benefits of a rush order. The cost is increased production cost, and the benefit is a satisfied customer. Since the plant manager is rewarded for achieving a profit, he or she has an incentive to weigh the cost-benefit trade-off inherent to the rush-order problem.

In conclusion, I recommend that the plants be designated as profit centers and the sales districts be designated as revenue centers.

PROBLEM 12-49 (40 MINUTES)

1. The factors that should be present for an organization's quality program to be successful include the following:

   - Evidence of top management support, including motivational leadership and resource commitments.

   - Training of those involved, including employees and suppliers.

   - A cultural change leading to a corporate culture committed to the customer and to continuous, dynamic improvement.

2. From an analysis of the cost-of-quality report, the program appears to have been successful, because of the following:

   - Total quality cost has declined from 23.4 to 13.1 percent of total production costs.

   - External failure costs, those costs signaling customer dissatisfaction, have declined from 8 percent of total production cost to 2.3 percent. These declines in warranty repairs and customer returns should translate into increased sales in the future.

   - Internal failure costs have been reduced from 4.6 to 2.3 percent of production costs, and the overall cost of scrap and rework has gone down by 45.7 percent ($188,000 – $102,000)/$188,000.

   - Appraisal costs have decreased by 43.4 percent [($205,000 – $116,000)/$205,000]. Higher quality is reducing the demand for final testing.

PROBLEM 12-49 (CONTINUED)

- Quality costs have shifted to the area of prevention, where problems are solved before the customer becomes involved. Maintenance, training, and design reviews have increased from 5.8 percent of total production cost to 6 percent and from 24.9 percent of total quality cost to 45.7 percent. The $30,000 increase is more than offset by decreases in other quality costs.

3. Tony Reese's current reaction to the quality improvement program is more favorable because he is seeing the benefits of having the quality problems investigated and solved before they reach the production floor. Because of improved designs, quality training, and additional preproduction inspections, scrap and rework costs have declined. Production personnel do not have to spend an inordinate amount of time on customer service, because they are now making the product right the first time. Throughput has increased and throughput time has decreased. Work is now moving much faster through the department.

4. To measure the opportunity cost of not implementing the quality program, management could do the following:

- Assume that sales and market share will continue to decline and then calculate the revenue and income lost.

- Assume that the company will have to compete on price rather than on quality and calculate the impact of having to lower product prices.

SOLUTIONS TO CASES

CASE 12-50 (45 MINUTES)

1.   Segmented income statement:

CATHY'S CLASSIC CLOTHES: NORTHEAST REGION
Segmented Income Statement
For May

	Coastal District	New Haven Store	Boston Store
Sales	$1,500,000	$600,000	$525,000
Less: Cost of goods sold	633,750	252,000	220,500
Gross margin................................	$ 866,250	$348,000	$304,500
Operating expenses:			
Variable selling........................	$ 90,000	$ 36,000	$ 31,500
Variable administrative	37,500	15,000	13,125
Other direct expenses:			
Store maintenance	12,600	7,500	600
Advertising	75,000	50,000	5,000
Rent and other costs..................	150,000	60,000	45,000
District general administrative expenses (allocated).................	180,000	72,000	63,000
Regional general and administrative expenses (allocated)	165,000	55,000	55,000
Total expenses	$ 710,100	$295,500	$213,225
Net Income................................	$ 156,150	$ 52,500	$ 91,275

CASE 12-50 (CONTINUED)

Supporting calculations:

	Coastal District	New Haven Store	Boston Store
Sales	Given	$1,500,000 x .40	$1,500,000 x .35
Cost of goods sold	Given	$600,000 x .42	$525,000 x .42
Variable selling	$1,500,000 x .06	$600,000 x .06	$525,000 x .06
Variable administrative	$1,500,000 x .025	$600,000 x .025	$525,000 x .025
Maintenance	$7,500 + $600 + $4,500	Given	Given
Advertising	Given	($75,000)(2/3)	$50,000 x .10 at New Haven
Rent	Given	$150,000 x .40	$150,000 x .30 for Coastal District
District expenses	Given	$180,000 x .40	$180,000 x .35

2. The Portland store's net income for May is $12,375 ($156,150 - $52,500 - $91,275).

3. The impact of the responsibility-accounting system and bonus structure on the managers' behavior and the effect of this behavior on the financial results for the two stores include the following:

    (a) New Haven Store:

*   Because the bonus is based on sales over $570,000, the manager has concentrated on maximizing sales and has paid little attention to controllable costs. As a result, the store's net income is less than 9 percent of sales and only 34 percent (rounded) of total net income.

*   In an effort to maximize sales, the New Haven store spent 10 times as much as the Boston store on advertising but generated only $75,000 more in sales. Thus the advertising must not have been very effective and should be better controlled.

CASE 12-50 (CONTINUED)

(b) Boston Store:

- Because the manager of the Boston store is motivated to maximize net income, there appears to be a tendency to cut back on discretionary expenses, such as store maintenance and advertising. While management is seeking cost control by implementing a bonus based on net income, the lack of spending on these discretionary items may have an adverse long-term effect.

- The manager of the Boston store will be unhappy with the inclusion of allocated district and regional expenses in the calculation of net income. These expenses are not likely to be controlled by the store manager and will reduce the bonus received by the manager of the Boston store.

4.   The assistant controller's actions violate several standards of ethical conduct for management accountants, including the following:

Competence

- Prepare complete and clear reports and recommendations after appropriate analysis of relevant and reliable information.

Integrity:

- Communicate unfavorable as well as favorable information and professional judgements of opinions.

- Refrain from engaging in any activity that would discredit the profession.

Objectivity:

- Communicate information fairly and objectively.

- Disclose fully all relevant information that could reasonably be expected to influence and intended user's understanding of the reports, comments, and recommendations presented.

CASE 12-51 (60 MINUTES)

1. Segmented income statement by geographic areas:

PACIFIC RIM INDUSTRIES

SEGMENTED INCOME STATEMENT BY GEOGRAPHIC AREAS
FOR THE FISCAL YEAR ENDED APRIL 30, 20x0

| | Geographic Areas | | | | |
	United States	Canada	Asia	Unallocated	Total
Sales in units[a]					
Furniture..................	64,000	16,000	80,000		160,000
Sports	72,000	72,000	36,000		180,000
Appliances................	32,000	32,000	96,000		160,000
Total unit sales.......	168,000	120,000	212,000		500,000
Revenue[b]					
Furniture..................	$ 512,000	$ 128,000	$ 640,000		$1,280,000
Sports	1,440,000	1,440,000	720,000		3,600,000
Appliances................	480,000	480,000	1,440,000		2,400,000
Total revenue	$2,432,000	$2,048,000	$2,800,000		$7,280,000
Variable costs[c]					
Furniture..................	$ 384,000	$ 96,000	$ 480,000		$ 960,000
Sports	864,000	864,000	432,000		2,160,000
Appliances................	336,000	336,000	1,008,000		1,680,000
Total variable costs	$1,584,000	$1,296,000	$1,920,000		$4,800,000
Contribution margin	$ 848,000	$ 752,000	$ 880,000		$2,480,000
Fixed costs					
Manufacturing overhead[d]	$ 165,000	$ 135,000	$ 200,000		$ 500,000
Depreciation[e]............	134,400	96,000	169,600		400,000
Administrative and selling expenses	60,000	100,000	250,000	$ 750,000	1,160,000
Total fixed costs.....	$ 359,400	$ 331,000	$ 619,600	$ 750,000	$2,060,000
Operating income (loss).........................	$ 488,600	$ 421,000	$ 260,400	$ (750,000)	$ 420,000

CASE 12-51 (CONTINUED)

SUPPORTING CALCULATIONS

[a]Sales in units

	Total Units	× % of Sales	= Units Sold
United States			
Furniture	160,000	.40	64,000
Sports..	180,000	.40	72,000
Appliances	160,000	.20	32,000
Canada			
Furniture	160,000	.10	16,000
Sports..	180,000	.40	72,000
Appliances	160,000	.20	32,000
Asia			
Furniture	160,000	.50	80,000
Sports..	180,000	.20	36,000
Appliances	160,000	.60	96,000

[b]Revenue

	Units Sold	Unit Price	Revenue
United States			
Furniture	64,000	$ 8.00	$ 512,000
Sports...	72,000	20.00	1,440,000
Appliances	32,000	15.00	480,000
Canada			
Furniture	16,000	8.00	128,000
Sports...	72,000	20.00	1,440,000
Appliances	32,000	15.00	480,000
Asia			
Furniture	80,000	8.00	640,000
Sports...	36,000	20.00	720,000
Appliances	96,000	15.00	1,440,000

CASE 12-51 (CONTINUED)

cVariable costs

	Units Sold (1)	Variable Mfg. Cost/Unit (2)	Variable Selling Cost/Unit (3)	Total Variable Cost (1) × [(2) + (3)]
United States				
Furniture	64,000	$4.00	$2.00	$ 384,000
Sports..............................	72,000	9.50	2.50	864,000
Appliances	32,000	8.25	2.25	336,000
Canada				
Furniture	16,000	4.00	2.00	96,000
Sports..............................	72,000	9.50	2.50	864,000
Appliances	32,000	8.25	2.25	336,000
Asia				
Furniture	80,000	4.00	2.00	480,000
Sports..............................	36,000	9.50	2.50	432,000
Appliances	96,000	8.25	2.25	1,008,000

dManufacturing overhead

	Total Manufacturing Overhead	Area Variable Costs	Proportion of total	Allocated Manufacturing Cost
United States	$500,000	$1,584,000	33%	$165,000
Canada	500,000	1,296,000	27%	135,000
Asia	500,000	1,920,000	40%	200,000
Total		$4,800,000		$500,000

CASE 12-51 (CONTINUED)

eDepreciation expense

	Total Depreciation	Area Units Sold	Proportion of Total	Allocated Depreciation
United States.....................	$400,000	168,000	33.6%	$134,400
Canada.............................	400,000	120,000	24.0%	96,000
Asia.................................	400,000	212,000	42.4%	169,600
Total...............................		500,000		$400,000

2. Areas where the company's management should focus its attention in order to improve corporate profitability include the following:

- The income statement by product line shows that the furniture product line may not be profitable. The furniture product line does have a positive contribution. However, the fixed costs assigned to the product line result in a loss. Management should investigate:

  —The possibility of increasing the selling price of these products.

  —The possibility of increasing volume by cutting prices or increasing advertising, resulting in a larger total contribution margin.

  —Cutting variable costs associated with this product line.

  —Discontinuing the manufacture of furniture and concentrating on the other product lines that are more profitable.

  —How much of the fixed costs allocated to furniture are separable (avoidable) if the product line is discontinued.

CASE 12-51 (CONTINUED)

- The income statement by geographic area shows that the Asian market is the least profitable sales area. In order to improve the profit margin in the Asian market, management should:

    — Investigate the selling and administrative expenses in this area as they are considerably higher than those in other areas.

    — Consider increasing the sales of product lines other than furniture as this product line makes the smallest contribution to profit.

- Management should review the unallocated expenses in an attempt to reduce these costs and improve overall profitability.

CURRENT ISSUES IN MANAGERIAL ACCOUNTING

ISSUE 12-52

"HOW FORD, FIRESTONE LET THE WARNINGS SLIDE BY AS DEBACLE DEVELOPED: THEIR SEPARATE GOALS, GAPS IN COMMUNICATION GAVE RISE TO RISKY SITUATION," *THE WALL STREET JOURNAL*, SEPTEMBER 6, 2000, TIMOTHY AEPPEL, CLARE ANSBERRY, MILO GEYELIN AND ROBERT I. SIMISON.

1. Firestone should have been more aggressive in keeping an eye out for defects since it previously had a major problem with tread peeling off its tires. Ford should have kept its own records of tire performance instead of depending on Firestone's reassurances.

2. The value chain is a set of business functions that add value to the products or services of an organization. The value chain includes functions such as the following: research and development: design of products, services, or processes; production; marketing; distribution; and customer service. In this scenario, Ford and Firestone are each part of the other's value chain.

ISSUE 12-53

"MANAGER'S JOURNAL: ANOTHER JACK WELCH ISN'T GOOD ENOUGH," *THE WALL STREET JOURNAL*, NOVEMBER 22, 1999, MICHAEL ALLEN.

The next leader of GE will need to have even bigger ideas and imagination than today's CEO. He or she must have the vision and foresight to anticipate what the enterprise will need to become over the next 20 years. He or she will need to lead leaders and have the political skills to deal with challenges from outside the company.

ISSUE 12-54

"HERB KELLEHER HAS ONE MAIN STRATEGY: TREAT EMPLOYEES WELL," *THE WALL STREET JOURNAL*, AUGUST 31, 1999, HAL LANCASTER.

1. Build a culture with an esprit de corps.

2. Structure training exercises so that everyone has to contribute to complete them successfully.

3. Give people the license to be themselves and motivate others in that way. Give each person the opportunity to be a maverick.

4. Allow and encourage people to take pride in what they're doing.

5. Fight bureaucracy and hierarchy.

6. Recognize that people are still the most important part of an organization. How management treats its employees determines how they treat people outside the company.

CHAPTER 13
Investment Centers and Transfer Pricing

ANSWERS TO REVIEW QUESTIONS

13-1　Goal congruence means a meshing of objectives, in which the managers throughout an organization strive to achieve goals that are consistent with the goals set by top management. Goal congruence is important for organizational success because managers often are unaware of the effects of their decisions on the organization's other subunits. Also, it is natural for people to be more concerned with the performance of their own subunit than with the effectiveness of the entire organization. In order for the organization to be effective, it is important that everyone in it be striving for the same ultimate objectives.

13-2　The managerial accountant's primary objective in designing a responsibility-accounting system is to provide incentives for the organization's subunit managers to strive toward achieving the organization's goals.

13-3　Under the management-by-objectives (MBO) philosophy, managers participate in setting goals that they then strive to achieve. These goals may be expressed in financial or other quantitative terms, and the responsibility-accounting system is used to evaluate performance in achieving them. The MBO approach is consistent with an emphasis on obtaining goal congruence throughout an organization.

13-4　An investment center is a responsibility-accounting center, the manager of which is held accountable not only for the investment center's profit but also for the capital invested to earn that profit. Examples of investment centers include a division of a manufacturing company, a large geographical territory of a hotel chain, and a geographical territory consisting of several stores in a retail company.

13-5　Return on investment (ROI) $= \dfrac{\text{income}}{\text{invested capital}} = \dfrac{\text{income}}{\text{sales revenue}} \times \dfrac{\text{sales revenue}}{\text{invested capital}}$

13-6　A division's ROI can be improved by improving the sales margin, by improving the capital turnover, or by some combination of the two. The manager of the automobile division of an insurance company could improve the sales margin by increasing the profit margin on each insurance policy sold. As a result, every sales dollar would generate more income. The capital turnover could be improved by increasing sales of insurance policies while keeping invested capital fixed, or by decreasing the invested assets required to generate the same sales revenue.

13-7   Example of the calculation of residual income: Suppose an investment center's profit is $100,000, invested capital is $800,000, and the imputed interest rate is 12 percent:

$$\text{Residual income} = \text{investment center's profit} - \left(\begin{array}{c}\text{investment center's}\\\text{invested capital}\end{array} \times \begin{array}{c}\text{imputed}\\\text{interest rate}\end{array}\right)$$

$$\text{Residual income} = \$100,000 - (\$800,000)(12\%) = \$4,000$$

The imputed interest rate is used in calculating residual income, but it is not used in computing ROI. The imputed interest rate reflects the firm's minimum required rate of return on invested capital.

13-8   The chief disadvantage of ROI is that for an investment that earns a rate of return greater than the company's cost of raising capital, the manager in charge of deciding about that investment may have an incentive to reject it if the investment would result in reducing the manager's ROI. The residual-income measure eliminates this disadvantage by including in the residual-income calculation the imputed interest rate, which reflects the firm's cost of capital. Any project that earns a return greater than the imputed interest rate will show a positive residual income.

13-9   The rise in ROI or residual income across time results from the fact that periodic depreciation charges reduce the book value of the asset, which is generally used in determining the investment base to use in the ROI or residual-income calculation. This phenomenon can have a serious effect on the incentives of investment-center managers. Investment centers with old assets will show higher ROIs than investment centers with relatively new assets. This result can discourage investment-center managers from investing in new equipment. If this behavioral tendency persists for a long time, a division's assets can become obsolete, making the division uncompetitive.

13-10   The economic value added (EVA) is defined as follows:

$$\begin{array}{c}\text{Economic}\\\text{value}\\\text{added}\end{array} = \begin{array}{c}\text{Investment center's}\\\text{after-tax}\\\text{operating income}\end{array} - \left[\left(\begin{array}{c}\text{Investment}\\\text{center's}\\\text{total assets}\end{array} - \begin{array}{c}\text{Investment}\\\text{center's}\\\text{current liabilities}\end{array}\right) \times \begin{array}{c}\text{Weighted-average}\\\text{cost of}\\\text{capital}\end{array}\right]$$

$$\text{Residual income} = \text{investment center's profit} - \left(\begin{array}{c}\text{investment center's}\\\text{invested capital}\end{array} \times \begin{array}{c}\text{imputed}\\\text{interest rate}\end{array}\right)$$

Economic value added differs from residual income in its subtraction of the investment center's current liabilities and its specific use of the weighted-average cost of capital.

13-11 a. Total assets: Includes all divisional assets. This measure of invested capital is appropriate if the division manager has considerable authority in making decisions about all of the division's assets, including nonproductive assets.

   b. Total productive assets: Excludes assets that are not in service, such as construction in progress. This measure is appropriate when a division manager is directed by top management to keep nonproductive assets, such as vacant land or construction in progress.

   c. Total assets less current liabilities: All divisional assets minus current liabilities. This measure is appropriate when the division manager is allowed to secure short-term bank loans and other short-term credit. This approach encourages investment-center managers to minimize resources tied up in assets and maximize the use of short-term credit to finance operations.

13-12 The use of gross book value instead of net book value to measure a division's invested capital eliminates the problem of an artificially increasing ROI or residual income across time. Also, the usual methods of computing depreciation, such as straight-line or declining-balance methods, are arbitrary. As a result, some managers prefer not to allow these depreciation charges to affect ROI or residual-income calculations.

13-13 It is important to make a distinction between an investment center and its manager, because in evaluating the manager's performance, only revenues and costs that the manager can control or significantly influence should be included in the profit measure. The objective of the manager's performance measure is to provide an incentive for that manager to adhere to goal-congruent behavior. In evaluating the investment center as a viable economic investment, all revenues and costs that are traceable to the investment center should be considered. Controllability is not an issue in this case.

13-14 Pay for performance is a one-time cash payment to an investment-center manager as a reward for meeting a predetermined criterion on a specified performance measure. The objective of pay for performance is to get the manager to strive to achieve the performance target that triggers the payment.

13-15 An alternative to using ROI or residual income to evaluate a division is to look at its income and invested capital separately. Actual divisional profit for a period of time is compared to a flexible budget, and variances are used to analyze performance. The division's major investments are evaluated through a postaudit of the investment decisions. This approach avoids the necessity of combining profit and invested capital in a single measure, such as ROI or residual income.

13-16 During periods of inflation, historical-cost asset values soon cease to reflect the cost of replacing those assets. Therefore, some accountants argue that investment-center performance measures based on historical-cost accounting are misleading. Most managers, however, believe that measures based on historical-cost accounting are adequate when used in conjunction with budgets and performance targets.

13-17 Examples of nonfinancial measures that could be used to evaluate a division of an insurance company include the following: (1) new policies issued and insurance claims settled in a specified period of time, (2) average time required to settle an insurance claim, and (3) number of insurance claims settled without litigation versus claims that require litigation.

13-18 Nonfinancial information is useful in measuring investment-center performance because it gives top management insight into the summary financial measures such as ROI or residual income. By keeping track of important nonfinancial data, top managers often can see a problem developing before it becomes a serious problem. For example, if a manufacturer's rate of defective products has been increasing over some period of time, management can observe this phenomenon and take steps to improve product quality before serious damage is done to customer relations.

13-19 The goal in setting transfer prices is to establish incentives for autonomous division managers to make decisions that support the overall goals of the organization. Transfer prices should be chosen so that each division manager, when striving to maximize his or her own division's profit, makes the decision that maximizes the company's profit.

13-20 Four methods by which transfer prices may be set are as follows:

(a) Transfer price = additional outlay costs incurred because goods are transferred + opportunity costs to the organization because of the transfer.

(b) Transfer price = external market price.

(c) Transfer prices may be set on the basis of negotiations among the division managers.

(d) Transfer prices may be based on the cost of producing the goods or services to be transferred.

13-21 When the transferring division has excess capacity, the opportunity cost of producing a unit for transfer is zero.

13-22 The management of a multinational company has an incentive to set transfer prices so as to minimize the income reported for divisions in countries with relatively high income-tax rates, and to shift this income to divisions with relatively low income-tax rates. Some countries' tax laws prohibit this practice, while other countries' laws permit it.

13-23 Multinational firms may be charged import duties, or tariffs, on goods transferred between divisions in different countries. These duties often are based on the reported value of the transferred goods. Such companies may have an incentive to set a low transfer price in order to minimize the duty charged on the transferred goods.

SOLUTIONS TO EXERCISES

EXERCISE 13-24 (10 MINUTES)

$$\text{Sales margin} = \frac{\text{income}}{\text{sales revenue}} = \frac{\$4,000,000}{\$50,000,000} = 8\%$$

$$\text{Capital turnover} = \frac{\text{sales revenue}}{\text{invested capital}} = \frac{\$50,000,000}{\$20,000,000} = 2.5$$

$$\text{Return on investment} = \frac{\text{income}}{\text{invested capital}} = \frac{\$4,000,000}{\$20,000,000} = 20\%$$

EXERCISE 13-25 (15 MINUTES)

There are an infinite number of ways to improve the division's ROI to 25 percent. Here are two of them:

1. Improve the sales margin to 10 percent by increasing income to $5,000,000:

    $$\text{ROI} = \text{sales margin} \times \text{capital turnover}$$

    $$= \frac{\$5,000,000}{\$50,000,000} \times \frac{\$50,000,000}{\$20,000,000}$$

    $$= 10\% \times 2.5 = 25\%$$

    Since sales revenue remains unchanged, this implies a cost reduction of $1,000,000 at the same volume.

2. Improve the turnover to 3.125 by decreasing average invested capital to $16,000,000:

    $$\text{ROI} = \text{sales margin} \times \text{capital turnover}$$

    $$= \frac{\$4,000,000}{\$50,000,000} \times \frac{\$50,000,000}{\$16,000,000}$$

    $$= 8\% \times 3.125 = 25\%$$

    Since sales revenue remains unchanged, this implies that the firm can divest itself of some productive assets without affecting sales volume.

EXERCISE 13-26 (5 MINUTES)

$$
\begin{array}{l}
\text{Residual} \\
\text{income}
\end{array}
= \text{investment center income} - \left(\begin{array}{c} \text{invested} \\ \text{capital} \end{array} \times \begin{array}{c} \text{imputed} \\ \text{interest rate} \end{array} \right)
$$

$$= \$4,000,000 - (\$20,000,000 \times 11\%)$$

$$= \$1,800,000$$

EXERCISE 13-27 (20 MINUTES)

The weighted-average cost of capital (WACC) is defined as follows:

$$
\begin{array}{c}
\text{Weighted - average} \\
\text{cost of} \\
\text{capital}
\end{array}
=
\dfrac{\left(\begin{array}{c} \text{After - tax cost} \\ \text{of debt} \\ \text{capital} \end{array} \right) \left(\begin{array}{c} \text{Market} \\ \text{value} \\ \text{of debt} \end{array} \right) + \left(\begin{array}{c} \text{Cost of} \\ \text{equity} \\ \text{capital} \end{array} \right) \left(\begin{array}{c} \text{Market} \\ \text{value} \\ \text{of equity} \end{array} \right)}{\begin{array}{c} \text{Market} \\ \text{value} \\ \text{of debt} \end{array} + \begin{array}{c} \text{Market} \\ \text{value} \\ \text{of equity} \end{array}}
$$

The interest rate on Golden Gate Construction Associates' $60 million of debt is 10 percent, and the company's tax rate is 40 percent. Therefore, Golden Gate's after-tax cost of debt is 6 percent [10% × (1–40%)]. The cost of Golden Gate's equity capital is 15 percent. Moreover, the market value of the company's equity is $90 million. The following calculation shows that Golden Gate's WACC is 11.4 percent.

$$
\begin{array}{c}
\text{Weighted - average} \\
\text{cost of capital}
\end{array}
=
\dfrac{(.06)(\$60,000,000) + (.15)(\$90,000,000)}{\$60,000,000 + \$90,000,000}
= .114
$$

EXERCISE 13-28 (20 MINUTES)

The economic value added (EVA) is defined as follows:

$$
\begin{array}{c}\text{Economic} \\ \text{value} \\ \text{added}\end{array} = \begin{array}{c}\text{Investment center's} \\ \text{after - tax} \\ \text{operating income}\end{array} - \left[\left(\begin{array}{c}\text{Investment} \\ \text{center's} \\ \text{total assets}\end{array} - \begin{array}{c}\text{Investment} \\ \text{center's} \\ \text{current liabilities}\end{array}\right) \times \begin{array}{c}\text{Weighted - average} \\ \text{cost of} \\ \text{capital}\end{array}\right]
$$

For Golden Gate Construction Associates, we have the following calculations of each division's EVA.

Division	After-Tax Operating Income (in millions)		Total Assets (in millions)		Current Liabilities (in millions)		WACC		Economic Value Added (in millions)
Real Estate	$20(1−.40)	−	[($100	−	$6)	×	.114]	=	$1.284
Construction	$18(1−.40)	−	[($ 60	−	$4)	×	.114]	=	$4.416

EXERCISE 13-29 (30 MINUTES)

1. Average investment in productive assets:

Balance on 12/31/x1	$12,600,000
Balance on 1/1/x1 ($12,600,000 ÷ 1.05).......................................	12,000,000
Beginning balance plus ending balance	$24,600,000
Average balance ($24,600,000 ÷ 2)...	$12,300,000

a. $$\text{ROI} = \frac{\text{income from operations before income taxes}}{\text{average productive assets}}$$

$$= \frac{\$2,460,000}{\$12,300,000}$$

$$= 20\%$$

b.
Income from operations before income taxes		$ 2,460,000
Less: imputed interest charge:		
Average productive assets......................................	$12,300,000	
Imputed interest rate...	× .15	
Imputed interest charge..		1,845,000
Residual income...		$ 615,000

EXERCISE 13-29 (CONTINUED)

2. Yes, Fairmont's management probably would have accepted the investment if residual income were used. The investment opportunity would have lowered Fairmont's 20x1 ROI because the project's expected return (18 percent) was lower than the division's historical returns (19.3 percent to 22.1 percent) as well as its actual 20x1 ROI (20 percent). Management may have rejected the investment because bonuses are based in part on the ROI performance measure. If residual income were used as a performance measure (and as a basis for bonuses), management would accept any and all investments that would increase residual income (i.e., a dollar amount rather than a percentage) including the investment opportunity it had in 20x1.

EXERCISE 13-30 (30 MINUTES)

1. Students' calculation of return on investment and residual income will depend on the company selected and the year when the internet search is conducted. Students will need to decide how to determine the income and the invested assets to use in both calculations. The discussion in the text will serve as a guide in this regard.

2. Some companies' annual reports include a calculation and discussion of ROI in the "management report and analysis" section or the "financial highlights" section. Students' calculation of ROI may differ from management's due to differing assumptions about the determination of income and invested capital.

EXERCISE 13-31 (15 MINUTES)

Memorandum

Date: Today

To: President, Sun Coast Food Centers

From: I. M. Student

Subject: Behavior of ROI over time

When ROI is calculated on the basis of net book value, it will typically increase over time. The net book value of the bundle of assets declines over time as depreciation is recorded. The income generated by the bundle of assets often will remain constant or increase over time. The result is a steady increase in the ROI, as income remains constant (or increases) and book value declines.

This effect will not exist (or at least will not be as pronounced) if the firm continues to invest in new assets at a roughly steady rate across time.

EXERCISE 13-32 (10 MINUTES)

1. The same employee is responsible for keeping the inventory records *and* taking the physical inventory count. In addition, when the records and the count do not agree, the employee changes the count, rather than investigating the reasons for the discrepancy. This leaves open the possibility that the employee would steal inventory and conceal the theft by altering both the records and the count. Even without any dishonesty by the employee, this system is not designed to control inventory since it does not encourage resolution of discrepancies between the records and the count.

2. The internal control system could be strengthened in two ways:

    (a) Assign two different employees the responsibilities for the inventory records and the physical count. With this arrangement, collusion would be required for theft to be concealed.

    (b) Require that discrepancies between the inventory records and the physical count be investigated and resolved when possible.

EXERCISE 13-33 (15 MINUTES)

1. $$\text{Sales margin} = \frac{\text{income}}{\text{sales revenue}} = \frac{£100,000*}{£2,000,000} = 5\%$$

    *Income = £100,000 = £2,000,000 – £1,100,000 – £800,000

    $$\text{Capital turnover} = \frac{\text{sales revenue}}{\text{invested capital}} = \frac{£2,000,000}{£1,000,000} = 2$$

    $$\text{ROI} = \frac{\text{income}}{\text{invested capital}} = \frac{£100,000}{£1,000,000} = 10\%$$

EXERCISE 13-33 (CONTINUED)

2. $\text{ROI} = 15\% = \dfrac{\text{income}}{\text{invested capital}} = \dfrac{\text{income}}{£\,1{,}000{,}000}$

Income $= 15\% \times £1{,}000{,}000 = £150{,}000$

Income $=$ sales revenue $-$ expenses $= £150{,}000$

Income $= £2{,}000{,}000 -$ expenses $= £150{,}000$

Expenses $= £1{,}850{,}000$

Therefore, expenses must be reduced to £1,850,000 in order to raise the firm's ROI to 15 percent.

3. Sales margin $= \dfrac{\text{income}}{\text{sales revenue}} = \dfrac{£\,150{,}000}{£\,2{,}000{,}000} = 7.5\%$

ROI $=$ sales margin $\times$ capital turnover

$= 7.5\% \times 2$

$= 15\%$

EXERCISE 13-34 (10 MINUTES)

1. Transfer price $= \dfrac{\text{outlay}}{\text{cost}} + \dfrac{\text{opportunity}}{\text{cost}}$

$= \$300^* + \$80^\dagger = \$380$

*Outlay cost $=$ unit variable production cost

†Opportunity cost $=$ forgone contribution margin

$= \$380 - \$300 = \$80$

2. If the Fabrication Division has excess capacity, there is no opportunity cost associated with a transfer. Therefore:

Transfer price $= \dfrac{\text{outlay}}{\text{cost}} + \dfrac{\text{opportunity}}{\text{cost}}$

$= \$300 + 0 = \$300$

EXERCISE 13-35 (25 MINUTES)

1. The Assembly Division's manager is likely to reject the special order because the Assembly Division's incremental cost on the special order exceeds the division's incremental revenue:

Incremental revenue per unit in special order......................		$465
Incremental cost to Assembly Division per unit		
in special order:		
Transfer price...	$374	
Additional variable cost..	100	
Total incremental cost..		474
Loss per unit in special order..		$ (9)

2. The Assembly Division manager's likely decision to reject the special order is not in the best interests of the company as a whole, since the *company's* incremental revenue on the special order exceeds the *company's* incremental cost:

Incremental revenue per unit in special order.....................		$465
Incremental cost to company per unit in special order:		
Unit variable cost incurred in Fabrication Division.........	$300	
Unit variable cost incurred in Assembly Division...........	100	
Total unit variable cost..		400
Profit per unit in special order...		$ 65

3. The transfer price could be set in accordance with the general rule, as follows:

    $$\text{Transfer price} = \frac{\text{outlay}}{\text{cost}} + \frac{\text{opportunity}}{\text{cost}}$$

    $$= \$300 + 0^*$$

    $$= \$300$$

    *Opportunity cost is zero, since the Fabrication Division has excess capacity.

    Now the Assembly Division manager will have an incentive to accept the special order since the Assembly Division's incremental revenue on the special order *exceeds* the incremental cost. The incremental revenue is still $465 per unit, but the incremental cost drops to $400 per unit ($300 transfer price + $100 variable cost incurred in the Assembly Division).

SOLUTIONS TO PROBLEMS

PROBLEM 13-36 (25 MINUTES)

The answer to the question as to which division is the most successful depends on the firm's cost of capital. To see this, compute the residual income for each division using various imputed interest rates.

(a) Imputed interest rate of 10%:

	Division I	Division II
Divisional profit	$900,000	$200,000
Less: Imputed interest charge:		
I: $6,000,000 × 10%...	600,000	
II: $1,000,000 × 10%..		100,000
Residual income..	$300,000	$100,000

(b) Imputed interest rate of 14%:

	Division I	Division II
Divisional profit	$900,000	$200,000
Less: Imputed interest charge:		
I: $6,000,000 × 14%...	840,000	
II: $1,000,000 × 14%..		140,000
Residual income..	$ 60,000	$ 60,000

(c) Imputed interest rate of 15%:

	Division I	Division II
Divisional profit	$900,000	$200,000
Less: Imputed interest charge:		
I: $6,000,000 × 15%...	900,000	
II: $1,000,000 × 15%..		150,000
Residual income..	$ 0	$ 50,000

If the firm's cost of capital is 10 percent, then Division I has a higher residual income than Division II. With a cost of capital of 15 percent Division II has a higher residual income. At a 14 percent cost of capital, both divisions have the same residual income. This scenario illustrates one of the advantages of residual income over ROI. Since the residual income calculation includes an imputed interest charge reflecting the firm's cost of capital, it gives a more complete picture of divisional performance.

PROBLEM 13-37 (45 MINUTES)

	Division A	Division B	Division C
Sales revenue	$2,000,000[e]	$10,000,000	$ 800,000[i]
Income	$ 400,000	$ 2,000,000	$ 200,000[k]
Average investment	$2,000,000[f]	$ 2,500,000	$1,000,000[j]
Sales margin	20%	20%[a]	25%
Capital turnover	1	4[b]	.8[i]
ROI	20%[g]	80%[c]	20%
Residual income	$ 240,000[h]	$ 1,800,000[d]	$ 120,000

Explanatory notes:

[a] $\text{Sales margin} = \dfrac{\text{income}}{\text{sales revenue}} = \dfrac{\$2,000,000}{\$10,000,000} = 20\%$

[b] $\text{Capital turnover} = \dfrac{\text{sales revenue}}{\text{invested capital}} = \dfrac{\$10,000,000}{\$2,500,000} = 4$

[c] ROI = sales margin × capital turnover = 20% × 4 = 80%

[d] Residual income = income – (imputed interest rate)(invested capital)

$= \$2,000,000 - (8\%)(\$2,500,000) = \$1,800,000$

[e] $\text{Sales margin} = \dfrac{\text{income}}{\text{sales revenue}}$

$20\% = \dfrac{\$400,000}{\text{sales revenue}}$

Therefore, sales revenue = $2,000,000

[f] $\text{Capital turnover} = \dfrac{\text{sales revenue}}{\text{invested capital}}$

$1 = \dfrac{\$2,000,000}{\text{invested capital}}$

Therefore, invested capital = $2,000,000

[g] ROI = sales margin × capital turnover

ROI = 20% × 1 = 20%

PROBLEM 13-37 (CONTINUED)

[h]Residual income = income – (imputed interest rate)(invested capital)

$$= \$400,000 - (8\%)(\$2,000,000)$$

$$= \$240,000$$

[i]ROI = sales margin × capital turnover

20% = 25% × capital trunover

Therefore, capital turnover = .8

[j]ROI $= \dfrac{\text{income}}{\text{invested capital}} = 20\%$

Therefore, income = (20%)(invested capital)

Residual income = income – (imputed interest rate)(invested capital)

$$= \$120,000$$

Substituting from above for income:

(20%)(invested capital) – (8%)(invested capital) = $120,000

Therefore, (12%)(invested capital) = $120,000

So, invested capital = $1,000,000

[k]ROI $= \dfrac{\text{income}}{\text{invested capital}}$

$20\% = \dfrac{\text{income}}{\$1,000,000}$

Therefore, income = $200,000

[l]Sales margin $= \dfrac{\text{income}}{\text{sales revenue}}$

$25\% = \dfrac{\$200,000}{\text{sales revenue}}$

Therefore, sales revenue = $800,000

PROBLEM 13-38 (20 MINUTES)

1. Three ways to increase Division B's ROI:

   (a) Increase income, while keeping invested capital the same. Suppose income increases to $2,250,000. The new ROI is:

   $$ROI = \frac{\text{income}}{\text{invested capital}} = \frac{\$2,250,000}{\$2,500,000} = 90\%$$

   (b) Decrease invested capital, while keeping income the same. Suppose invested capital decreases to $2,400,000. The new ROI is:

   $$ROI = \frac{\text{income}}{\text{invested capital}} = \frac{\$2,000,000}{\$2,400,000} = 83.3\% \text{ (rounded)}$$

   (c) Increase income and decrease invested capital. Suppose income increases to $2,100,000 and invested capital decreases to $2,400,000. The new ROI is:

   $$ROI = \frac{\text{income}}{\text{invested capital}} = \frac{\$2,100,000}{\$2,400,000} = 87.5\%$$

2. ROI = sales margin × capital turnover

       = 25% × 1

       = 25%

PROBLEM 13-39 (25 MINUTES)

This problem is similar to Problem 13-36, except that here students are given a hint in answering the question about which division is the most successful by requiring the calculation of residual income for three different imputed interest rates. If the firm's cost of capital is 12 percent, then Division I has a higher residual income than Division I. With a cost of capital of 15 percent or 18 percent, Division II has a higher residual income.

1. Imputed interest rate of 12%

	Division I	Division II
Divisional profit...	$900,000	$200,000
Less: Imputed interest charge:		
I: $6,000,000 × 12%......................................	720,000	
II: $1,000,000 × 12%....................................		120,000
Residual income...	$180,000	$ 80,000

2. Imputed interest rate of 15%

	Division I	Division II
Divisional profit...	$900,000	$200,000
Less: Imputed interest charge:		
I: $6,000,000 × 15%......................................	900,000	
II: $1,000,000 × 15%....................................		150,000
Residual income...	$ 0	$ 50,000

PROBLEM 13-39 (CONTINUED)

3   Imputed interest rate of 18%

	Division I	Division II
Divisional profit	$ 900,000	$200,000
Less: Imputed interest charge:		
I: $6,000,000 × 18%...	1,080,000	
II: $1,000,000 × 18%..		180,000
Residual income...	$(180,000)	$ 20,000

The imputed interest rate r, at which the two divisions' residual income is the same, is 14 percent, computed as follows:

Division II's residual income = Division I's residual income

$$\$200,000 - (r)(\$1,000,000) = \$900,000 - (r)(\$6,000,000)$$

$$(r)(\$5,000,000) = \$700,000$$

$$r = \$700,000/\$5,000,000$$

$$r = 14\%$$

For any imputed interest rate less than 14 percent, Division I will have a higher residual income. For any rate over 14 percent, Division II's residual income will be higher.

PROBLEM 13-40 (40 MINUTES)

Year	Income Before Depreciation	Annual Depreciation	Income Net of Depreciation	Average Net Book Value*	ROI Based on Net Book Value†	Average Gross Book Value	ROI Based on Gross Book Value
1	$150,000	$200,000	$(50,000)	$400,000	—	$500,000	—
2	150,000	120,000	30,000	240,000	12.5%	500,000	6.0%
3	150,000	72,000	78,000	144,000	54.2%	500,000	15.6%
4	150,000	54,000	96,000	81,000	118.5%	500,000	19.2%
5	150,000	54,000	96,000	27,000	355.6%	500,000	19.2%

*Average net book value is the average of the beginning and ending balances for the year in net book value. In Year 1, for example, the average net book value is:

$$\frac{\$500,000 + \$300,000}{2} = \$400,000$$

†ROI rounded to the nearest tenth of 1 percent.

1. This table differs from Exhibit 13-3 in that ROI rises even more steeply across time than it does in Exhibit 13-3. With straight-line depreciation, ROI rises from 11.1 percent in Year 1 to 100 percent in Year 5. Under the accelerated depreciation schedule used here, we have a loss in Year 1 and then ROI rises from 12.5 percent in Year 2 to 355.6 percent in Year 5.

2. One potential implication of such a ROI pattern is a disincentive for new investment. If a proposed capital project shows a loss or very low ROI in its early years, a manager may worry about the effect on his or her performance evaluation in the early years of the project. In an extreme case, a manager may worry that he or she will no longer have the job when the project begins to show a higher return in its later years.

PROBLEM 13-41 (40 MINUTES)

				Based on Net Book Value			Based on Gross Book Value		
Year	Income Before Depreciation	Annual Depreciation	Income Net of Depreciation	Average Net Book Value*	Imputed Interest Charge†	Residual Income	Average Gross Book Value	Imputed Interest Charge†	Residual Income
1	$150,000	$100,000	$50,000	$450,000	$45,000	$ 5,000	$500,000	$50,000	0
2	150,000	100,000	50,000	350,000	35,000	15,000	500,000	50,000	0
3	150,000	100,000	50,000	250,000	25,000	25,000	500,000	50,000	0
4	150,000	100,000	50,000	150,000	15,000	35,000	500,000	50,000	0
5	150,000	100,000	50,000	50,000	5,000	45,000	500,000	50,000	0

*Average net book value is the average of the beginning and ending balances for the year in net book value.

†Imputed interest charge is 10 percent of the average book value, either net or gross.

Notice in the table that residual income, computed on the basis of net book value, increases over the life of the asset. This effect is similar to the one demonstrated for ROI.

It is not very meaningful to compute residual income on the basis of gross book value. Notice that this asset shows a zero residual income for all five years when the calculation is based on gross book value.

PROBLEM 13-42 (35 MINUTES)

1. Current ROI of the Northeast Division:

Sales revenue...		$8,400,000
Less: Variable costs ($8,400,000 x 70%)......	$5,880,000	
Fixed costs.....................................	2,150,000	8,030,000
Income..		$ 370,000

ROI = Income ÷ invested capital
= $370,000 ÷ $1,850,000
= 20%

Northeast's ROI if competitor is acquired:

Sales revenue ($8,400,000 + $5,200,000).......		$13,600,000
Less: Variable costs [$5,880,000 +		
($5,200,000 x 65%)].....................	$9,260,000	
Fixed costs ($2,150,000 + $1,670,000)...	3,820,000	13,080,000
Income...		$ 520,000

ROI = Income ÷ invested capital
= $520,000 ÷ [$1,850,000 + ($625,000 +
$375,000)]
= 18.25%

2. Divisional management will likely be against the acquisition because ROI will be lowered from 20% to 18.25%. Since bonuses are awarded on the basis of ROI, the acquisition will result in less compensation.

3. An examination of the competitor's financial statistics reveals the following:

Sales revenue...		$5,200,000
Less: Variable costs ($5,200,000 x 65%)........	$3,380,000	
Fixed costs	1,670,000	5,050,000
Income...		$ 150,000

ROI = Income ÷ invested capital
= $150,000 ÷ $625,000
= 24%

PROBLEM 13-42 (CONTINUED)

Corporate management would probably favor the acquisition. Megatronoics has been earning a 13% return, and the competitor's ROI of 24% will help the organization as a whole. Even if the $375,000 upgrade is made, the competitor's ROI would be 15% if past earnings trends continue [$150,000 ÷ ($625,000 + $375,000) = 15%].

4. Yes, the divisional ROI would increase to 21.01%. However, the absence of the upgrade could lead to long-run problems, with customers being confused (and perhaps turned-off) by two different retail environments—the retail environment they have come to expect with other Megatronics outlets and that of the newly acquired, non-upgraded competitor.

Sales revenue ($8,400,000 + $5,200,000).......		$13,600,000
Less: Variable costs [$5,880,000 +		
($5,200,000 x 65%)]....................	$9,260,000	
Fixed costs ($2,150,000 + $1,670,000)...	3,820,000	13,080,000
Income..		$ 520,000

ROI = Income ÷ invested capital
= $520,000 ÷ ($1,850,000 + $625,000)
= 21.01%

5. Current residual income of the Northeast Division:

Divisional profit...	$370,000
Less: Imputed interest charge ($1,850,000 x 12%)......	222,000
Residual income...	$148,000

Residual income if competitor is acquired:

Divisional profit ($370,000 + $150,000)..................	$520,000
Less: Imputed interest charge [($1,850,000 +	
($625,000 + $375,000)) x 12%]...............	342,000
Residual income...	$178,000

Yes, management most likely will change its attitude. Residual income will increase by $30,000 ($178,000 - $148,000) as a result of the acquisition.

PROBLEM 13-43 (30 MINUTES)

1. Sales margin: income divided by sales revenue.

    Capital turnover: sales revenue divided by invested capital

    Return on investmenti: income divided by invested capital (or sales margin x capital turnover).

    Sales margin: $360,000 ÷ $4,800,000 = 7.5%
    Capital turnover: $4,800,000 ÷ $6,000,000 = 80%
    Return on investment: $360,000 ÷ $6,000,000 = 6%, or
                              7.5% x 80% = 6%

2. Strategy (a): Income will be reduced to $300,000 because of the loss, and invested capital will fall to $5,940,000 from the disposal. ROI = $300,000 ÷ $5,940,000, or 5.05%. This strategy should be rejected, since it further hurts Washburn's performance.

    Strategy (b): In terms of ROI, this strategy neither hurts nor helps. The acceleration of overdue receivables increases cash and decreases accounts receivable, producing no effect on invested capital. Of course, it is possible that the newly acquired cash could be invested in something that would provide a positive return for the firm.

3. Yes. A drastic cutback in advertising could lead to a loss of customers and a reduced market share. This could translate into reduced profits over the long term. With respect to repairs and maintenance, reduced outlays could prove costly by unintentional shortening of the useful lives of plant and equipment. Such action would likely result in an accelerated asset replacement program.

PROBLEM 13-43 (CONTINUED)

4. Anderson Manufacturing ROI: ($3,000,000 - $2,400,000) ÷ $5,000,000 = 12%
    Palm Beach Enterprises ROI: ($4,500,000 - $4,120,000) ÷ $4,750,000 = 8%

From the preceding calculations, both investments appear attractive given the current state of affairs (i.e.,Reliable's current 6% ROI). However, if Washburn desires to maximize ROI, he would be advised to acquire only Anderson Manufacturing.

	Current	Current + Anderson	Current + Anderson + Palm Beach
Income...................	$ 360,000	$ 960,000*	$ 1,340,000**
Invested capital......	6,000,000	11,000,000	15,750,000
ROI.......................	6%	8.73%	8.51%

* $360,000 + ($3,000,000 - $2,400,000)
** $360,000 + ($3,000,000 - $2,400,000) + ($4,500,000 - $4,120,000)

PROBLEM 13-44 (35 MINUTES)

1. The weighted-average cost of capital (WACC) is defined as follows:

$$\text{Weighted - average cost of capital} = \frac{\left(\begin{array}{c}\text{After - tax cost}\\\text{of debt}\\\text{capital}\end{array}\right)\left(\begin{array}{c}\text{Market}\\\text{value}\\\text{of debt}\end{array}\right) + \left(\begin{array}{c}\text{Cost of}\\\text{equity}\\\text{capital}\end{array}\right)\left(\begin{array}{c}\text{Market}\\\text{value}\\\text{of equity}\end{array}\right)}{\begin{array}{c}\text{Market}\\\text{value}\\\text{of debt}\end{array} + \begin{array}{c}\text{Market}\\\text{value}\\\text{of equity}\end{array}}$$

The interest rate on CCLS's $80 million of debt is 9 percent, and the company's tax rate is 40 percent. Therefore, the after-tax cost of debt is 5.4 percent [9% × (1–40%)]. The cost of CCLS's equity capital is 14 percent. Moreover, the market value of the company's equity is $120 million. The following calculation shows that Cape Cod Lobster Shacks' WACC is 10.56 percent.

$$\text{Weighted - average cost of capital} = \frac{(.054)(\$80,000,000) + (.14)(\$120,000,000)}{\$80,000,000 + \$120,000,000} = .1056$$

PROBLEM 13-44 (CONTINUED)

2. The economic value added (EVA) is defined as follows:

$$\begin{array}{c}\text{Economic}\\\text{value}\\\text{added}\end{array} = \begin{array}{c}\text{Investment center's}\\\text{after - tax}\\\text{operating income}\end{array} - \left[\left(\begin{array}{c}\text{Investment}\\\text{center's}\\\text{total assets}\end{array} - \begin{array}{c}\text{Investment}\\\text{center's}\\\text{current liabilities}\end{array}\right) \times \begin{array}{c}\text{Weighted - average}\\\text{cost of}\\\text{capital}\end{array}\right]$$

For Cape Cod Lobster Shacks, Inc., we have the following calculations of EVA for each of the company's divisions.

Division	After-Tax Operating Income (in millions)	Total Assets (in millions)	Current Liabilities (in millions)	WACC	Economic Value Added (in millions)
Properties	$29(1-.40)$	$-$ $\big[\big($ 145	$-$ $3\big]$	$\times$ $.1056\big]$ =	$2.4048
Food Service	$15(1-.40)$	$-$ $\big[\big($ 64	$-$ $6\big]$	$\times$ $.1056\big]$ =	$2.8752

PROBLEM 13-45 (35 MINUTES)

1. The weighted-average cost of capital (WACC) is defined as follows:

$$\begin{array}{c}\text{Weighted -}\\\text{average}\\\text{cost of}\\\text{capital}\end{array} = \dfrac{\left(\begin{array}{c}\text{After - tax}\\\text{cost of}\\\text{debt}\\\text{capital}\end{array}\right)\left(\begin{array}{c}\text{Market}\\\text{value}\\\text{of debt}\end{array}\right) + \left(\begin{array}{c}\text{Cost of}\\\text{equity}\\\text{capital}\end{array}\right)\left(\begin{array}{c}\text{Market}\\\text{value of}\\\text{equity}\end{array}\right)}{\begin{array}{c}\text{Market}\\\text{value}\\\text{of debt}\end{array} + \begin{array}{c}\text{Market}\\\text{value}\\\text{of equity}\end{array}}$$

The following calculation shows that All-Canadian's WACC is 9.72 percent.

$$\begin{array}{c}\text{Weighted - average}\\\text{cost of capital}\end{array} = \dfrac{(.063)(\$400,000,000) + (.12)(\$600,000,000)}{\$400,000,000 + \$600,000,000} = .0972$$

PROBLEM 13-45 (CONTINUED)

2. The three divisions' economic-value-added measures are calculated as follows:

Division	After-Tax Operating Income (in millions)		Total Assets (in millions)		Current Liabilities (in millions)		× WACC	=	Economic Value Added (in millions)
Pacific.....	$14 × (1–.30)	–	[($ 70	–	$6)		× .0972]	=	$ 3,579,200
Plains......	$45 × (1–.30)	–	[($300	–	$5)		× .0972]	=	$ 2,826,000
Atlantic....	$48 × (1–.30)	–	[($480	–	$9)		× .0972]	=	$(12,181,200)

3. The EVA analysis reveals that All-Canadian's Atlantic Division is in trouble. Its substantial negative EVA merits the immediate attention of the management team.

PROBLEM 13-46 (40 MINUTES)

1. a. Transfer price = outlay cost + opportunity cost

      = $65 + $15 = $80

   b. Transfer price = standard variable cost + (10%)(standard variable cost)

      = $65 + (10%) ($65) = $71.50

   Note that the Frame Division manager would refuse to transfer at this price.

2. a. Transfer price = outlay cost + opportunity cost

      = $65 + 0 = $65

   b. When there is no excess capacity, the opportunity cost is the forgone contribution margin on an external sale when a frame is transferred to the Glass Division. The contribution margin equals $15 ($80 – $65). When there is excess capacity in the Frame Division, there is no opportunity cost associated with a transfer.

PROBLEM 13-46 (CONTINUED)

c.   Fixed overhead per frame (125%)($20) = $25

Transfer price = variable cost + fixed overhead per frame

                   + (10%)(variable cost + fixed overhead per frame)

                = $65 + $25 + [(10%)($65 + $25)]

                = $99

d.   Incremental revenue per window $155
Incremental cost per window, for Clearview Window
Company:
   Direct material (Frame Division)............................... $15
   Direct labor (Frame Division)   20
   Variable overhead (Frame Division).........................   30
   Direct material (Glass Division)...............................   30
   Direct labor (Glass Division)   15
   Variable overhead (Glass Division)..........................   30
   Total variable (incremental) cost.............................   140

Incremental contribution per window in special order
   for Clearview Window Company .... $ 15

The special order should be accepted because the incremental revenue exceeds
the incremental cost, for Clearview Window Company as a whole.

e.   Incremental revenue per window .... $ 155
Incremental cost per window, for the Glass Division:
   Transfer price for frame [from requirement 2(c)]..... $99
   Direct material (Glass Division)...............................   30
   Direct labor (Glass Division)   15
   Variable overhead (Glass Division)..........................   30
   Total incremental cost   174

Incremental loss per window in special order
   for Glass Division .... $ (19)

The Glass Division manager has an incentive to reject the special order because
the Glass Division's reported net income would be reduced by $19 for every
window in the order.

PROBLEM 13-46 (CONTINUED)

f. One can raise an ethical issue here to the effect that a division manager should always strive to act in the best interests of the whole company, even if that action seemingly conflicts with the division's best interests. In complex transfer pricing situations, however, it is not always as clear what the company's optimal action is as it is in this rather simple scenario.

3. The use of a transfer price based on the Frame Division's full cost has caused a cost that is a fixed cost for the entire company to be viewed as a variable cost in the Glass Division. This distortion of the firm's true cost behavior has resulted in an incentive for a dysfunctional decision by the Glass Division manager.

PROBLEM 13-47 (25 MINUTES)

1. The Birmingham divisional manager will likely be opposed to the transfer. Currently, the division is selling all the units it produces at $775 each. With transfers taking place at $750, Birmingham will suffer a $25 drop in sales revenue and profit on each unit it sends to Tampa.

2. Although Tampa is receiving a $25 "price break" on each unit purchased from Birmingham, the $750 transfer price would probably be deemed too high. The reason: Tampa will lose $20 on each satellite positioning system produced and sold.

Sales revenue..		$1,400
Less: Variable manufacturing costs..........	$670	
Transfer price paid to Birmingham...	750	1,420
Income (loss)..		$ (20)

3. Although top management desires to introduce the positioning system, it should not lower the price to make the transfer attractive to Tampa. Cortez uses a responsibility accounting system, awarding bonuses based on divisional performance. Top management's intervention/price-lowering decision would undermine the authority and autonomy of Birmingham's and Tampa's divisional managers. Ideally, the two divisional managers (or their representatives) should negotiate a mutually agreeable price.

4. Cortez would benefit more if it sells the diode reducer externally. Observe that the transfer price is ignored in this evaluation—one that looks at the firm as a whole. Put simply, Birmingham would record the transfer price as revenue whereas Tampa would record the transfer price as a cost, thereby creating a "wash" on the part of the overall entity.

	Produce Diode; Sell Externally	Produce Diode; Transfer; Sell Positioning System
Sales revenue..................	$775	$1,400
Less: Variable cost::		
$500.....................	500	
$500 + $670.........		1,170
Contribution margin...........	$275	$ 230

PROBLEM 13-48 (30 MINUTES)

1. If the transfer price is set equal to the U.S. variable manufacturing cost, Alpha Communications will make $32.80 per circuit board:

   U.S. operation:

Sales revenue (transfer price).....................................	$130.00
Less: Variable manufacturing cost............................	130.00
Contribution margin..	$ --

   German operation:

Sales revenue...		$360.00
Less: Transfer price................................	$130.00	
Shipping fees...................................	20.00	
Additional processing costs..............	115.00	
Import duties ($130.00 x 10%)............	13.00	278.00
Income before tax......................................		$ 82.00
Less: Income tax expense ($82.00 x 60%)....		49.20
Income after tax.......................................		$ 32.80

2. If the transfer price is set equal to the U.S. market price, Alpha will make $39.20 per circuit board: $24.00 + $15.20 = $39.20. The U.S. market price is therefore more attractive as a transfer price than the U.S. variable manufacturing cost.

   U.S. operation:

Sales revenue...	$170.00
Less: Variable manufacturing cost............................	130.00
Income before tax...	$ 40.00
Less: Income tax expense ($40.00 x 40%)...................	16.00
Income after tax...	$ 24.00

   German operation:

Sales revenue...		$360.00
Less: Transfer price................................	$170.00	
Shipping fees...................................	20.00	
Additional processing costs..............	115.00	
Import duties ($170.00 x 10%)............	17.00	322.00
Income before tax......................................		$ 38.00
Less: Income tax expense ($38.00 x 60%)....		22.80
Income after tax.......................................		$ 15.20

3.   (a)   The head of the German division should be a team player; however, when the circuit board can be obtained locally for $155, it is difficult to get excited about doing business with the U.S. operation. Courtesy of the shipping fee and import duty, both of which can be avoided, it is advantageous to purchase in Germany. Even if the lower of the two transfer prices is adopted, the German division would be better off to acquire the circuit board at home ($155 vs. $130 + $20 + $13 = $163).

     (b)   Yes. Alpha will make $60.00 per circuit board ($24.00 + $36.00) if no transfer takes place and all circuit boards are sold in the U.S.

U.S. operation:

Sales revenue..		$170.00
Less: Variable manufacturing cost...........................		130.00
Income before tax...		$ 40.00
Less: Income tax expense ($40.00 x 40%).................		16.00
Income after tax...		$ 24.00

German operation:

Sales revenue..		$360.00
Less: Purchase price...............................	$155.00	
Additional processing costs............	115.00	270.00
Income before tax.....................................		$ 90.00
Less: Income tax expense ($90.00 x 60%)...		54.00
Income after tax.......................................		$ 36.00

4.   When tax rates differ, companies should strive to generate less income in high tax-rate countries, and vice versa. When alternatives are available, this can be accomplished by a careful determination of the transfer price.

PROBLEM 13-49 (40 MINUTES)

1. Among the reasons transfer prices based on total actual costs are not appropriate as a divisional performance measure are the following:

    *   They provide little incentive for the selling division to control manufacturing costs, because all costs incurred will be passed on to the buying division.

    *   They often lead to suboptimal decisions for the company as a whole, because they can obscure cost behavior. Costs that are fixed for the company as a whole can be made to appear variable to the division buying the transferred goods.

2. Using the market price as the transfer price, the contribution margin for both the Mining Division and the Metals Division is calculated as follows:

	Mining Division	Metals Division
Selling price	$90	$150
Less: Variable costs:		
Direct material	12	6
Direct labor	16	20
Manufacturing overhead	24*	10†
Transfer price	—	90
Unit contribution margin	$38	$ 24
Volume	x 400,000	x 400,000
Total contribution margin	$15,200,000	$9,600,000

*Variable overhead = $32 x 75% = $24
†Variable overhead = $25 x 40% = $10

Note: the $5 variable selling cost that the Mining Division would incur for sales on the open market should not be included, because this is an internal transfer.

3. If PCRC instituted the use of a negotiated transfer price that also permitted the divisions to buy and sell on the open market, the price range for toldine that would be acceptable to both divisions would be determined as follows.

    The Mining Division would like to sell to the Metals Division for the same price is can obtain on the outside market, $90 per unit. However, Mining would be willing to sell the toldine for $85 per unit, because the $5 variable selling cost would be avoided.

    The Metals Division would like to continue paying the bargain price of $66 per unit. However, if Mining does not sell to Metals, Metals would be forced to pay $90 on the open market. Therefore, Metals would be satisfied to receive a price concession from Mining equal to the costs that Mining would avoid by selling internally. Therefore, a negotiated transfer price for toldine between $85 and $90 would be acceptable to both divisions and benefits the company as a whole.

4. General transfer-pricing rule:

    Transfer price = outlay cost + opportunity cost
    = ($12 + $16 + $24)* + ($38 - $5) **
    = $52 + $33 = $85

    *Outlay cost = direct material + direct labor + variable overhead [see requirement (2)]
    **Opportunity cost = forgone contribution margin from outside sale on open market
    = $38 contribution margin from internal sale calculated in requirement (2), less the additional $5 variable selling cost incurred for an external sale

    Therefore, the general rule yields a minimum acceptable transfer price to the Mining Division of $85, which is consistent with the conclusion in requirement (3).

5. A negotiated transfer price is probably the most likely to elicit desirable management behavior, because it will do the following:

    • Encourage the management of the Mining Division to be more conscious of cost control.

    • Benefit the Metals Division by providing toldine at a lower cost than that of its competitors.

    • Provide the basis for a more realistic measure of divisional performance.

SOLUTIONS TO CASES

CASE 13-50 (40 MINUTES)

1. If New Age Industries continued to use return on investment as the sole measure of division performance, Holiday Entertainment Corporation (HEC) would be reluctant to acquire Recreational Leasing, Inc. (RLI), because the post-acquisition combined ROI would decrease.

	Return on Investment		
	HEC	RLI	Combined
Operating income	$2,000,000	$ 600,000	$ 2,600,000
Total assets	8,000,000	3,000,000	11,000,000
Return on investment (income/assets)	25%	20%	23.6%*

*Rounded.

The result would be that HEC's management would either lose their bonuses or have their bonuses limited to 50 percent of the eligible amounts. The assumption is that management could provide convincing explanations for the decline in return on investment.

2. Residual income is the profit earned that exceeds an amount charged for funds committed to a business unit. The amount charged for funds is equal to an imputed interest rate multiplied by the business unit's invested capital.

   If New Age Industries could be persuaded to use residual income to measure performance, HEC would be more willing to acquire RLI, because the residual income of the combined operations would increase.

	Residual Income		
	HEC	RLI	Combined
Total assets	$8,000,000	$3,200,000*	$11,200,000
Income	$2,000,000	$ 600,000	$ 2,600,000
Less: Imputed interest charge (assets × 15%)	1,200,000	480,000	1,680,000
Residual income	$ 800,000	$ 120,000	$ 920,000

*Cost to acquire RLI.

CASE 13-50 (CONTINUED)

3. a. The likely effect on the behavior of division managers whose performance is measured by return on investment includes incentives to do the following:

   - Put off capital improvements or modernization to avoid capital expenditures.

   - Shy away from profitable opportunities or investments that would yield more than the company's cost of capital but that could lower ROI.

   b. The likely effect on the behavior of division managers whose performance is measured by residual income includes incentives to do the following:

   - Seek any opportunity or investment that will increase overall residual income.

   - Seek to reduce the level of assets employed in the business.

CASE 13-51 (45 MINUTES)

1. Yes, Air Comfort Division should institute the 5% price reduction on its air conditioner units because net income would increase by $132,000. Supporting calculations follow:

	Before 5% Price Reduction		After 5% Price Reduction		Total Difference (in thousands)
	Per Unit	Total (in thousands)	Per Unit	Total (in thousands)	
Sales revenue	$400	$6,000	$380	$6,612.0	$612.0
Variable costs:					
Compressor	$70	$1,050	$70	$1,218.0	$168.0
Other direct material	37	555	37	643.8	88.8
Direct labor	30	450	30	522.0	72.0
Variable overhead	45	675	45	783.0	108.0
Variable selling	18	270	18	313.2	43.2
Total variable costs	$200	$3,000	$200	$3,480.0	$480.0
Contribution margin	$200	$3,000	$180	$3,132.0	$132.0

Summarized presentation:

Contribution margin of sales increase ($180 × 2,400)	$432,000
Loss in contribution margin on original volume arising from decrease in selling price ($20 × 15,000)	300,000
Increase in net income before taxes	$132,000

2. No, the Compressor Division should not sell all 17,400 units to the Air Comfort Division for $50 each. If the Compressor Division does sell all 17,400 units to Air Comfort, Compressor will only be able to sell 57,600 units to outside customers instead of 64,000 units due to the capacity restrictions. This would decrease the Compressor Division's net income before taxes by $35,500. Compressor Division would be willing to accept any orders from Air Comfort above the 64,000 unit level at $50 per unit because there would be a positive contribution margin of $21.50 per unit. Supporting calculations follow.

CASE 13-51 (CONTINUED)

	Outside Sales	Air Comfort Sales
Selling price	$100	$50.00
Variable costs:		
Direct material...	12	$10.50
Direct labor	8	8.00
Variable overhead	10	10.00
Variable selling expenses	6	—
Total variable costs	$ 36	$28.50
Contribution margin	$ 64	$21.50

Capacity calculation in units:

Total capacity	75,000
Sales to Air Comfort	17,400
Balance	57,600
Projected sales to outsiders	64,000
Lost sales to outsiders	6,400

Solution:

Contribution from sales to Air Comfort ($21.50 × 17,400)	$374,100
Loss in contribution from loss of sales to outsiders ($64 × 6,400)	409,600
Decrease in net income before taxes	$ 35,500

3.   Yes, it would be in the best interests of InterGlobal Industries for the Compressor Division to sell the units to the Air Comfort Division at $50 each. The net advantage to InterGlobal Industries is $312,500 as shown in the following analysis. The net advantage is the result of the cost savings from purchasing the compressor unit internally and the contribution margin lost from the 6,400 units that the Compressor Division otherwise would sell to outside customers.

CASE 13-51 (CONTINUED)

Cost savings by using compressor unit from Compressor Division:	
Compressor Division:	
Outside purchase price	$ 70.00
Compressor Division's variable cost to produce (see req. 2).	28.50
Savings per unit	$ 41.50
x Number of units	x 17,400
Total cost savings	$722,100
Compressor Division's loss in contribution from loss	
of sales to outsiders (see req. 2): $64 × 6,400	409,600
Increase in net income before taxes for InterGlobal Industries	$312,500

4. As the answers to requirements (2) and (3) show, $50 is not a goal-congruent transfer price. Although a transfer is in the best interests of InterGlobal Industries as a whole, a transfer of $50 will not be perceived by the Compressor Division's management as in that division's best interests.

CASE 13-52 (50 MINUTES)

1. Diagram of scenario:

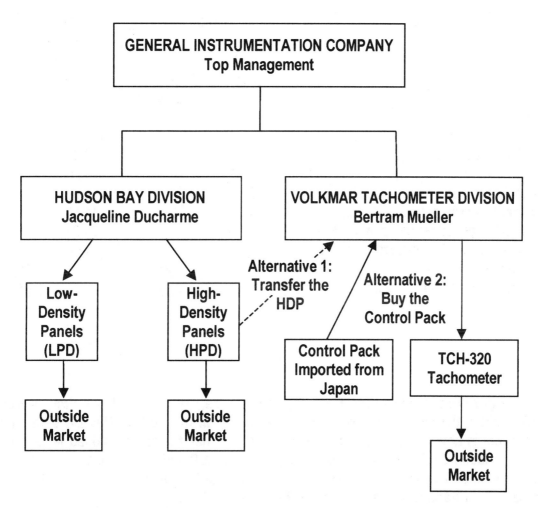

2. First, compute the unit contribution margin of an LDP and an HDP as follows:

	LDP		HDP	
Price		$28		$ 115
Less: Variable cost:				
Unskilled labor	$5		$ 5	
Skilled labor	5		30	
Raw material.................................	3		8	
Purchased components........................	4		12	
Variable overhead............................	5		15	
Total variable cost		22		70
Unit contribution margin........................		$ 6		$ 45

Second, compute the unit contribution margin of Volkmar's TCH-320 under each of its alternatives, as follows:

	TCH-320 Using Imported Control Pack		TCH-320 Using an HDP	
Price		$270.00		$270.00
Less: Variable cost:				
Unskilled labor..................................	$ 4.50		$ 4.50	
Skilled labor......................................	51.00		85.00	
Raw material	11.50		6.00	
Purchased components....................	150.00		5.00	
Variable overhead	11.00		11.00	
Variable cost of manufacturing HDP	-0-		70.00	
Variable cost of transporting HDP...	-0-		4.50	
Total variable cost............................		228.00		186.00
Unit contribution margin............................		$ 42.00		$ 84.00

Difference is $42.

From the perspective of the entire company, the scarce resource that will limit overall company profit is the limited skilled labor time available in the Hudson Bay Division. The question, then, is how can the company as a whole best use the limited skilled labor time available at Hudson Bay? The division has two products: LDP and HDP. One can view these as three products, though, in the sense that the HDP units can be produced either for outside sale or for transfer to the Volkmar Tachometer Division.

Hudson Bay's "Three" Products
HDP for external sale
HDP for transfer
LDP

CASE 13-52 (CONTINUED)

What is the unit contribution to covering the overall company's fixed cost and profit from each of these three products? The calculations above show that the unit contribution margin of an LDP is $6, and the unit contribution of an HDP sold externally is $45. Moreover, the unit contribution to the overall company of an HDP produced for transfer is $42, which is the *increase* in the unit contribution margin of the TCH-320 when it is manufactured with the HDP instead of the imported control pack. To summarize:

Hudson Bay's Product	Unit Contribution to Covering the Company's Fixed Cost and Profit
HDP sold externally	$45
HDP transferred internally	42
LDP	6

The analysis of these three products' contribution margins (to General Instrumentation as a whole) has not gone far enough, because the products do not require the same amount of the scarce resource, skilled labor time. The important question is how much one hour of limited skilled labor at Hudson Bay spent on each of the three products will contribute toward the overall firm's fixed cost and profit.

Hudson Bay's Product	Unit Contribution Margin	Skilled Labor per Unit Required at Hudson Bay	Contribution Margin per Hour
HDP sold externally	$45	1.50	$30
HDP transferred internally	42	1.50	28
LDP	6	.25	24

CASE 13-52 (CONTINUED)

This analysis shows that from the perspective of the entire company, Hudson Bay's best use of its limited skilled labor resource is to produce HDPs for external sale, up to the maximum demand of 6,000 units per year. The second best use of Hudson Bay's limited skilled labor is to produce HDPs for internal transfer, up to the maximum number of units needed by the Volkmar Tachometer Division. This number is 10,000 HDPs, since that is the demand for Volkmar's TCH-320. Hudson Bay's least profitable product is the LDP. Therefore, from the perspective of General Instrumentation as a whole, the Hudson Bay Division should use its limited skilled labor time as follows:

	Skilled labor time available at Hudson Bay.....................................	40,000	hours
(1)	Produce 6,000 HDPs for external sale		
	(6,000 units × 1.5 hours)	9,000	hours
	Hours remaining...	31,000	hours
(2)	Produce 10,000 HDPs for internal transfer		
	(10,000 units × 1.5 hours)	15,000	hours
	Hours remaining...	16,000	hours
(3)	Produce 64,000 LDPs (64,000 units × .25 hours).........................	16,000	hours
	Hours remaining...	-0-	

The final answer to requirement (2) is that all of the required 10,000 TCH-320 tachometers should be manufactured using the HDP unit from the Hudson Bay Division.

3. Given that 10,000 HDPs are transferred, there is no effect on General Instrumentation Company's overall income. The transfer price affects only the way the company's overall profit is divided between the two divisions.

4. Hudson Bay's minimum acceptable transfer price is given by the general transfer-pricing rule, as follows:

Minimum acceptable transfer price $=$ additional outlay costs incurred because goods are transferred $+$ opportunity cost to the organization because of the transfer

$$= \$70 + \$36$$

$$= \$106$$

CASE 13-52 (CONTINUED)

Explanatory notes:

(a)   The outlay cost is equal to the variable cost of manufacturing an HDP.

(b)   The opportunity cost is equal to the forgone contribution margins on the LDP units that Hudson Bay will be unable to produce because it is manufacturing an HDP for transfer. In the 1.5 hours of skilled labor time required to produce an HDP for transfer, Hudson Bay could manufacture six LDPs, since each LDP requires only .25 hours. Thus, the forgone contribution margin is $36 (6 units × $6 unit contribution margin).

5.   The maximum transfer price that the Volkmar Tachometer Division would find acceptable is $112, computed as follows:

Savings if TCH-320 is produced using an HDP:	
Imported control pack..	$145.00
Other raw material	5.50
Total savings...	$150.50
Less: Incremental costs if TCH-320 is produced using an HDP:	
Transportation cost..	(4.50)
Skilled labor	(34.00)
Net savings if HDP is used..	$112.00

If Volkmar's management must pay $112 for an HDP, it will be indifferent between using the HDP and the imported control pack. If the transfer price is lower than $112, the Volkmar Tachometer Division will be better off with the HDP. At a transfer price in excess of $112, Volkmar's management will prefer the control pack.

6.   The transfer is in the overall company's best interest. Thus, any transfer price in the interior of the range $106 to $112 will provide the proper incentives to the management of each division to agree to a transfer. For example, a transfer price of $109 would split the range evenly, and make each division better off by making the transfer.

CURRENT ISSUES IN MANAGERIAL ACCOUNTING

ISSUE 13-53

"WHAT'S A NEW ECONOMY WITHOUT RESEARCH," *FORTUNE*, MAY 15, 2000, STEWART ALSOP.

Money invested in R&D is tied up for the long term and cannot be turned over many times generating more profit in the short-run. With the current pressures on CEOs to add value to their companies, short-term investments look better on the balance sheet in the short-run.

ISSUE 13-54

"AT&T MEETS ANALYSTS, BOOSTS GOALS FOR REVENUE, BUT STOCK DOESN'T RESPOND," *THE WALL STREET JOURNAL*, DECEMBER 7, 1999, REBECCA BLUMENSTEIN AND NICOLE HARRIS.

AT&T intends to provide local phone service nationwide. The company will serve customers it cannot reach through its cable holdings or cable joint ventures.

ISSUE 13-55

"HARVARD UNIVERSITY -- SOROS SUIT BRINGS RUSSIAN BANKRUPTCY FIGHT TO U.S. COURT," *THE WALL STREET JOURNAL*, NOVEMBER 23, 1999, STEVE LIESMAN.

Tyumen Oil allegedly used transfer-pricing methods to divert oil revenue from the subsidiaries. The investors say oil was sold cheaply to buyers related to Tyumen Oil, which then sold the crude at world prices but failed to revert the profits to the Sidanco units.

ISSUE 13-56

"COOPERATION OR COMPETITION," *STRATEGIC FINANCE*, FEBRUARY 2000, DAN HILL.

Three core principles:

1. Focus:

   a. Employee rewards based on overall company results

   b. Employee rewards not based on local merits

2. Motivation that is fair:

   a. All employees share in the company's wealth creation

   b. Meaningful rewards for superior company performance

3. Ability to succeed:

   a. Comprehensive information feedback loop

   b. Information for improvement, not measurement

   c. Result is cooperation and unlocking of resources

ISSUE 13-57

"EXECUTIVE PAY," *BUSINESS WEEK*, APRIL 21, 1997, JENNIFER REINGOLD.

1. Management performance can be linked to financial and nonfinancial measures. Financial factors, such as earnings-per-share (EPS), profit, return on assets (ROA) and return on sales (ROS), could be used to assess management performance. Compensation packages could then be based on items other than share price.

2. Financial markets may decline due to general macroeconomic factors. This could unfairly penalize an executive.

3. No. Costs associated with issuing stock options include opportunity costs and administrative costs.

CHAPTER 14
Decision Making: Relevant Costs and Benefits

ANSWERS TO REVIEW QUESTIONS

14-1   The six steps in the decision-making process are as follows:

- Clarify the decision

- Specify the criterion

- Identify the alternatives

- Develop a decision model

- Collect the data

- Select an alternative

14-2   The managerial accountant's role in the decision-making process is to participate as a proactive member of the management team, and, in particular, to provide information relevant to the decision.

14-3   A decision model is a simplified representation of the choice problem. Unnecessary details are stripped away, and the most important elements of the problem are highlighted.

14-4   A quantitative analysis is expressed in numerical terms. A qualitative analysis focuses on the factors in a decision problem that cannot be expressed effectively in numerical terms.

14-5   The result of a quantitative analysis is that one alternative is preferred over the next-best alternative by some numerical amount, such as profit. The amount by which the best alternative dominates the second-best alternative establishes a "price" on the sum total of the qualitative characteristics that might favor the second-best alternative. Suppose, for example, that a hospital's board of directors is considering establishing an outpatient clinic in one of the two suburban communities. The quantitative analysis of the decision suggests that site A will be more cost effective for the clinic than site B. Assume that the annual cost of running the clinic at site A will be $50,000 less than the annual cost of running the clinic at site B. Now suppose that the board of directors feels that various qualitative considerations indicate that it would be preferable to locate the clinic at site B. For example, suburb B might be an economically depressed area, where it is important to bring better-quality health care to the community. Now the board of directors can put a price on these qualitative advantages to locating the clinic at site B. If the board of directors believes that the qualitative benefits at site B outweigh the $50,000 quantitative advantage at site A, then they should locate the clinic at site B.

14-6   Relevant information is pertinent to a decision problem. Accurate information is precise. Timely information is available to the decision maker in time to make the decision. Objective information need not be relevant or accurate. For example, several people may agree that the interest rate in the coming year in a local community will be 10 percent. However, this information may not be accurate, since that prediction may prove to be wrong. Moreover, information about the interest rate may not be pertinent to a decision about where to locate a new branch bank within the community.

14-7   Two important criteria that must be satisfied in order for information to be relevant are as follows:

(1) Relevant cost or benefit information must involve a future event. In other words, the information must have a bearing on the future.

(2) Relevant information must involve costs or benefits that differ among the alternatives. Costs or benefits that are the same across all of the available alternatives have no bearing on the decision.

14-8   The book value of an asset is its acquisition cost less its accumulated depreciation. The book value is not a relevant cost because it is a sunk cost. It occurred in the past and has no bearing on the future.

14-9   The book value of inventory, like the book value of any asset, is not a relevant cost. The inventory's book value is based on its acquisition cost or its production cost and is, therefore, a sunk cost. It has no bearing on any future course of action.

14-10 Managers sometimes exhibit a behavioral tendency to inappropriately consider a sunk cost in making a decision, because they believe that their original decision to incur the sunk cost, such as when an asset is acquired, will appear to have been a bad decision if the manager subsequently disposes of the asset. This perceived need by managers for their past decisions to appear to have been good ones may result in their inappropriate emphasis on sunk costs in making a decision.

14-11 An example of an irrelevant future cost is a cost that will occur in the future but does not differ among the alternatives. For example, a bank may be considering several sites for the location of a new branch office. If the cost of hiring an architect to design the new building will not differ among the alternatives, it is an irrelevant future cost.

14-12 An opportunity cost is the potential benefit given up when the choice of one action precludes a different action. For example, one opportunity cost associated with getting a college education is the student's forgone wages from a job that might have been held during the educational period.

14-13 People often exhibit a behavioral tendency to ignore or downplay the importance of opportunity costs in making a decision. Since an opportunity cost often is not a cash flow, people tend to think it is less important than costs that are represented by cash flows. This behavioral tendency can result in faulty decision making.

14-14 If a firm has excess production capacity, there is no opportunity cost to the acceptance of a special order. On the other hand, if the firm is already at capacity and there is no excess production capacity, the opportunity cost associated with accepting a special order involves the contribution margin from the products that would have been manufactured with the resources devoted to the special order.

14-15 In a differential-cost analysis, the decision maker determines the difference in each cost or revenue item that will occur under each of the alternatives under consideration. Then the decision maker focuses on the differences in the costs and revenues in making the decision.

14-16 In making a decision about adding or dropping a product line, the decision maker should consider the avoidable expenses if the product line is not carried as well as the impact of the decision to add or drop the product line on the firm's other operations.

14-17 A joint production process is one in which the processing of a common input results in two or more distinct products known as joint products. A special decision that commonly arises in the context of the joint production process is the decision whether or not to process further one of the joint products into a different product. The proper approach for making this type of decision is to compare the incremental benefits from further processing with the incremental costs.

14-18 The allocated joint processing costs are irrelevant when making a decision as to whether a joint product should be sold at the split-off point or processed further. The total joint cost will not change as a result of the decision to process further, and therefore it is irrelevant to the decision.

14-19 The proper approach to making a production decision when limited resources are involved is to maximize production of the product that has the highest contribution margin per unit of scarce resource. When two or more resources are limited, the technique of linear programming may be appropriate.

14-20 The contribution margin per unit of scarce resource is a product's unit contribution margin divided by the number of units of the scarce resource required to produce one unit of the product. For example, if a product's contribution margin per unit is $5 and it requires two hours of labor to produce one unit, the contribution margin per direct-labor hour is $2.50.

14-21 Sensitivity analysis may be used to cope with uncertainty in decision making by analyzing how sensitive a decision problem is to the estimates of certain parameters. One important question that can be answered is; How much can a particular parameter estimate change before the optimal decision changes?

14-22 There is an important link between decision making and managerial performance evaluation, because managers typically make decisions that maximize their perceived performance evaluations and rewards. If we want managers to make optimal decisions by properly evaluating the relevant cost and benefits, then the performance evaluation system and reward structure must be consistent with that goal.

14-23 Four potential pitfalls in decision making that represent common errors are the following:

(1) Paying too much attention to sunk costs.

(2) Basing the analysis on unitized fixed costs rather than total fixed costs. Using unitized fixed costs is dangerous because the fixed cost per unit changes as activity changes.

(3) Not identifying avoidable costs. In some kinds of decisions, it is important to identify the avoidable costs. It is critical that the decision maker make a distinction between the amount of the fixed costs that will be avoided and the amount that may have been arbitrarily allocated to a particular cost object.

(4) Overlooking opportunity costs or treating them as less important than out-of-pocket costs. In a decision analysis, it is important to pay special attention to identifying and including opportunity costs.

14-24 Unitized fixed costs can cause errors in decision making because the fixed cost per unit changes as the activity measure changes. For this reason, it is better to include fixed costs in the analysis in their total amounts.

14-25 Sunk costs are irrelevant in decision making because they have already occurred in the past and will not change under any future, alternative course of action. Two examples of sunk costs are the book value of equipment and the book value of inventory on hand.

14-26 This remark fails to recognize the fact that the identification of relevant information depends on the decision. Data that are relevant to one decision may be irrelevant to another one. Therefore, it would be impossible for the managerial-accounting system to produce only information that is relevant to all decisions.

14-27 The concepts underlying a relevant-cost analysis remain valid both in an advanced manufacturing environment and in a situation where activity-based costing is used. However, when an ABC system is used, the decision maker typically is able to more accurately determine the relevant costs than when a traditional, volume-based costing system is used.

14-28 Five ways to relax a bottleneck constraint are as follows:

- Working *overtime* at the bottleneck operation.

- *Retraining* employees and shifting them to the bottleneck.

- Eliminating any *non-value-added activities* at the bottleneck operation.

- *Outsourcing* (subcontracting) all or part of the bottleneck operation.

- Investing in additional production equipment and employing *parallel processing*, in which multiple product units undergo the same production operation simultaneously.

SOLUTIONS TO EXERCISES

EXERCISE 14-29 (25 MINUTES)

Students' answers to this exercise will vary widely. The following illustration is set in a small city in central New York. Residents of an outlying suburb of the city complained that it took too long for ambulances and fire engines to reach their area when emergencies occurred. They demanded that the city build a satellite fire and rescue station in their neighborhood. The steps in the city's decision-making process are summarized as follows:

QUANTITATIVE ANALYSIS

1. Clarify the decision problem: The first step was to clarify the problem. Was the perceived slow response time real or merely a perception by the residents of the neighborhood? What was the average response time for emergency vehicles to the area? Were proper procedures being followed? What was the condition of the roads, bridges, and traffic lights on the route to the neighborhood in question?

    The result of this inquiry was a realization that the emergency response time to the suburb was slower than that experienced by the rest of the city, although it was still within state guidelines. Moreover, procedures were being followed properly by emergency personnel, and the traffic system was adequate for emergency responses. The conclusion of the problem clarification stage was that the neighborhood was simply too far from the city's fire and rescue station to respond as quickly as the residents of the neighborhood would have liked.

2. Specify the criterion: The City Council decided that some type of action was warranted. They specified that the city engineer should find a way to cut response time to the neighborhood by five minutes without incurring unacceptable costs.

3. Identify the alternatives: The city engineer identified the following alternatives:

    a. Build a satellite fire and rescue station on the west end of the affected neighborhood.

    b. Station two fire trucks and an ambulance, along with the requisite personnel, in the parking lot of a shopping center in the suburb.

4. Develop a decision model: The decision model consisted of a computer program that would simulate emergency response times and costs under each of the two alternatives.

EXERCISE 14-29 (CONTINUED)

5.   Collect the data: The data needed for the decision model included employee compensation data, acquisition and maintenance costs for a satellite station, and the projected costs of operating the new station.

QUALITATIVE CONSIDERATIONS

The computer model indicated that either alternative would satisfy the criterion of reducing emergency response times by five minutes, and that the positioning of emergency vehicles at the shopping center would be less expensive. Nevertheless, the City Council felt that this solution would be perceived by the residents of the neighborhood as a temporary, stopgap measure that did not really address their needs.

6.   Make a decision: The City Council decided to build a satellite fire and rescue station. Although this alternative was somewhat more expensive, the Council felt that the qualitative considerations outweighed the cost advantage of the other alternative.

EXERCISE 14-30 (20 MINUTES)

FLIGHT ROUTE DECISION

	Revenues and Costs Under Two Alternatives		
	(a) Nonstop Route*	(b) With Stop In San Francisco*	(c) Differential Amount†
Passenger revenue	$240,000	$258,000	$(18,000)
Landing fee in San Francisco	-0-	(5,000)	5,000
Use of airport gate facilities	-0-	(3,000)	3,000
Flight crew cost	(2,000)	(2,500)	500
Fuel	(21,000)	(24,000)	3,000
Meals and services	(4,000)	(4,600)	600
Total revenue less costs	$213,000	$218,900	$ (5,900)

*In columns (a) and (b), parentheses denote costs, and numbers without parentheses are revenues.
†In column (c), parentheses denote differential items favoring option (b).

EXERCISE 14-31 (15 MINUTES)

1. The owner's reasoning probably reflects the following calculation:

Savings in annual operating expenses if old pizza oven is replaced	$2,600
Write-off of old oven's remaining book value ($9,000 ÷ 3)	(3,000)
"Loss" associated with replacement	$ (400)

2. The owner's analysis is flawed, because the book value of the old pizza oven is a sunk cost. It should not enter into the equipment replacement decision.

3. Correct analysis:

Savings in annual operating expenses if old pizza oven is replaced	$2,600
Acquisition cost of new oven, which will be operable for one year	(1,900)
Net benefit from replacing old pizza oven	$ 700

EXERCISE 14-32 (15 MINUTES)

Dear (president's name):

   We recommend against processing banolide into kitrocide. The incremental cost of further processing, $8,100, exceeds the incremental revenue, $7,500. This $7,500 incremental revenue is the difference between the sales value of the kitrocide, $10,000, and the sales value of the banolide, $2,500. We would also like to point out that the cost of the joint process, $19,000, and the allocation of that cost to the joint products is irrelevant to the decision.

   Sincerely,

   I.M. Student
   Partner, Student Consulting Associates

EXERCISE 14-33 (15 MINUTES)

The owner's analysis incorrectly includes the following allocated costs that will be incurred regardless of whether the ice cream counter is operated:

Utilities	$2,900
Depreciation of building	4,000
Deli manager's salary	3,000
Total	$9,900

It is possible that closing the ice cream counter might save a portion of the utility cost, but that is doubtful.

A better analysis follows:

Sales		$45,000
Less: Cost of food		20,000
Gross profit		25,000
Less: Operating expenses		
Wages of counter personnel	$12,000	
Paper products	4,000	
Depreciation of counter equipment and furnishings*	2,500	
Total		18,500
Profit on ice cream counter		$ 6,500

*Depreciation on the counter equipment and furnishings is included because it is traceable to the ice cream operation and is an expense in the determination of income. If a cash-flow analysis is desired, this noncash expense should be excluded.

EXERCISE 14-34 (30 MINUTES)

Answers will vary depending on the company and activity chosen. There are many trade-offs involved in outsourcing decisions, including the incremental savings or cost from outsourcing, quality of the service, reliability of the supplier, morale effects if outsourcing results in closing a department, and so forth.

EXERCISE 14-35 (15 MINUTES)

1. Relevant data:

Current sales value for unmodified parts	$ 9,000
Sales value for modified parts	22,300
Modification costs	12,000

    Irrelevant data:

Current book value of inventory	21,000

    This is a sunk cost. It will not affect any future course of action.

2. There are two alternatives for disposing of the obsolete parts: (a) sell in unmodified condition or (b) modify and then sell.

(a) Benefit if parts are sold without modification	<u>$ 9,000</u>

(b) Sales value for modified parts	$22,300
Cost of modification	<u>12,000</u>
Net benefit if parts are sold after being modified	<u>$10,300</u>

    Conclusion: Modify the parts and then sell them.

EXERCISE 14-36 (15 MINUTES)

1. The relevant cost of the theolite to be used in producing the special order is the 14,500p sales value that the company will forgo if it uses the chemical. This is an example of an opportunity cost.

    p denotes Argentina's peso.

2. (a) 14,500p sales value: Discussed in requirement (1).

    (b) 16,000p book value (8,000 kilograms $\times$ 2p per kilogram): Irrelevant, since the book value is a sunk cost.

    (c) 19,200p current purchase cost (8,000 kilograms $\times$ 2.40p per kilogram): Irrelevant, since the company will not be buying any theolite.

EXERCISE 14-37 (20 MINUTES)

1. The relevant cost of genatope is calculated as follows:

Cost of replacing the 1,000 kilograms to be used in the special order
(1,000 kilograms × 8.70p) 8,700p
*Additional cost incurred on the next order of genatope as a result of
having to place the order early [4,000 kilograms × (8.70p – 8.30p)] 1,600p
Total relevant cost 10,300p

p denotes Argentina's peso.

*This cost would not be incurred if the special order were not accepted.

2. (a) 64,800p book value (8,000 kilograms × 8.10p per kilogram): Irrelevant, since it is a sunk cost.

   (b) 1,000 kilograms to be used in the special order: Relevant, as shown in requirement (1).

   (c) 8.70p price if next order is placed early: Relevant, since this is the cost of replacing the used genatope.

   (d) 8.30p price if next order is placed on time: Relevant, because an additional 4,000 kilograms in the next order will be purchased at a .40p per kilogram premium. This .40p premium is the difference between the 8.70p price and the 8.30p price.

EXERCISE 14-38 (15 MINUTES)

1. (a) $9,100 allocation of rent on factory building: Irrelevant, since Fusion Metals Company will rent the entire factory building regardless of whether it continues to operate the Packaging Department. If the department is eliminated, the space will be converted to storage space.

   (b) $11,000 rental of storage space in warehouse: Relevant, since this cost will be incurred only if the Packaging Department is kept in operation. If the department is eliminated, this $11,000 rental cost will be avoided.

2. The $11,000 warehouse rental cost is the opportunity cost associated with using space in Fusion Metals Company's factory building for the Packaging Department.

EXERCISE 14-39 (15 MINUTES)

(a) $45,000 salary of Packaging Department manager: Irrelevant, since this manager will be employed by the company at $45,000 per year regardless of whether the Packaging Department is kept in operation.

(b) $60,000 salary of Cutting Department manager if a new person must be hired: Relevant, since this cost will be incurred only if the Packaging Department is kept in operation. If the Packaging Department is eliminated, then that department's current manager will move to the Cutting Department at $45,000 per year.

The following comparison may help to clarify the analysis:

ANNUAL SALARY COST INCURRED BY FUSION METALS COMPANY

	If Packaging Department is Kept		If Packaging Department is Eliminated
Salary of the person currently managing the Packaging Department	$ 45,000*		$45,000†
Salary of newly hired person to manage the Cutting Department	60,000		
Total	$105,000		$45,000
Difference		$60,000	

*Continues to manage Packaging Department.

†Moves to Cutting Department position.

Additional comment:

There are many possible reasons why it might cost Fusion Metals Company more to hire a new Cutting Department manager than to transfer a current employee to the position. One possible scenario is that the current Packaging Department manager is a relatively young and inexperienced manager, to whom top management is willing to give the Cutting Department opportunity if the Packaging Department is eliminated. However, if a new person must be hired, Fusion Metals Company will be forced to go into the job market for more senior and experienced managers. Other possible reasons include existing contractual agreements, union contracts, and so forth.

EXERCISE 14-40 (20 MINUTES)

Sales revenue for one jar of silver polish		$4.00
Sales revenue for 1/4 pound of grit 337		.50
Incremental revenue from further processing		$3.50
Incremental costs of further processing:		
Processing costs	$2.50	
Selling costs	.30	2.80
Incremental contribution margin from further		
processing into silver polish (per jar)		$ .70

$$\text{Indifference point in units} = \frac{\text{avoidable fixed costs of further processing}}{\text{incremental contribution margin}}$$

$$= \frac{\$5,600}{\$.70} = 8,000 \text{ jars}$$

If more than 8,000 jars of silver polish can be sold, Zytel Corporation should process the required amount of grit 337 further into the polish.

EXERCISE 14-41 (10 MINUTES)

The most profitable product is the one that yields the highest contribution margin per unit of the scarce resource, which is direct labor. We do not know the amount of direct-labor time required per unit of either product, but we do know that Dos requires six times as much direct labor per unit as Uno. Define an arbitrary time period for which direct laborers earn $1.00, and call this a "time unit." The two products' contribution margins per "time unit" are calculated as follows:

	Uno	Dos
Unit contribution margin	$3.00	$12.00
"Time units" required per unit of product	1	6
Contribution margin per "time unit"		
Uno: ($3.00 ÷ 1)	$3.00	
Dos: ($12.00 ÷ 6)		$ 2.00

Therefore, Uno is a more profitable product. Any arbitrary amount of direct labor time expended on Uno production will result in a greater contribution margin than an equivalent amount of labor time spent on Dos production.

EXERCISE 14-42 (15 MINUTES)

1.   Decision variables:

     X = number of units of Uno to be produced

     Y = number of units of Dos to be produced

2.   Objective function:

     Maximize 3X + 12Y

     The coefficients of X and Y are the unit contribution margins for Uno and Dos, respectively. Maximizing this objective function will result in the highest possible total contribution margin.

3.   Constraints:

     (a) Direct-labor time constraint: $(1/24)X + (1/4)Y \leq 10,000$

         The coefficients of X and Y are the number of hours of direct labor required to produce one unit of Uno and one unit of Dos, respectively. For example, the direct-labor cost per unit of Dos is $6.00, so it must require 1/4 direct-labor hour per unit of Dos.

     (b) Machine time constraint: $1X + 2Y \leq 8,000$

         The coefficients of X and Y are the numbers of hours of machine time required to produce one unit of Dos, respectively.

     (c) Nonnegative production quantities: $X, Y \geq 0$

     The complete linear program is the following

         Maximize 3X + 12Y

         Subject to: $(1/24)X + (1/4)Y \leq 10,000$

                      $1X + 2Y \leq 8,000$

                      $X, Y \geq 0$

EXERCISE 14-43 (30 MINUTES)

1.   (a) Notation: X   denotes the quantity of kreolite-red produced per day

Y   denotes the quantity of kreolite-blue produced per day

(b) Contribution margin:

	Kreolite-Red	Kreolite-Blue
Price	$36	$42
Unit variable cost	28	28
Unit contribution margin	$ 8	$14

(c) Linear program:

Maximize	8X + 14Y		
Subject to:	2X + 2Y	≤	24
	1X + 3Y	≤	24
	X, Y	≥	0

2.   Graphical solution: See next page.

Corner points in feasible region:		Objective function value:
X = 0	Y = 0	$ 0
X = 0	Y = 8	112
X = 6	Y = 6	132
X = 12	Y = 0	96

The maximum objective function value is achieved when X = 6 and Y = 6. Thus, the company should produce 6 drums of kreolite-red per day and 6 drums of kreolite-blue per day.

3.   The objective function value at the optimal solution is a $132 total contribution margin as shown in requirement (2).

EXERCISE 14-43 (CONTINUED)

Graphical solution:

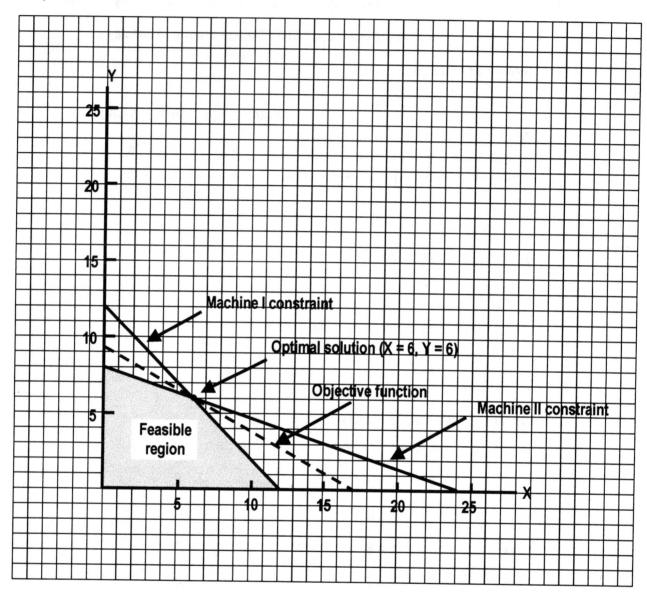

SOLUTIONS TO PROBLEMS

PROBLEM 14-44 (25 MINUTES)

1.

	Blender	Electric Mixer
Unit cost if purchased from an outside supplier	$20	$38
Incremental unit cost if manufactured:		
Direct material	$ 6	$11
Direct labor	4	9
Variable overhead		
$16 – $10 per hour fixed	6	
$32 – (2)($10 per hour fixed)		12
Total	$16	$32
Unit cost savings if manufactured	$ 4	$ 6
Machine hours required per unit	1	2
Cost savings per machine hour if manufactured		
$4 ÷ 1 hour	$4	
$6 ÷ 2 hours		$3

Therefore, each machine hour devoted to the production of blenders saves the company more than a machine hour devoted to mixer production.

Machine hours available	50,000
Machine hours needed to manufacture 20,000 blenders	20,000
Remaining machine hours	30,000
Number of mixers to be produced (30,000 ÷ 2)	15,000

Conclusion: Manufacture   20,000 blenders
                 Manufacture   15,000 mixers
                 Purchase   13,000 mixers

2.   If the company's management team is able to reduce the direct material cost per mixer to $6 ($5 less than previously assumed), then the cost savings from manufacturing a mixer are $11 per unit ($6 savings computed in requirement (1) plus $5 reduction in material cost):

PROBLEM 14-44 (CONTINUED)

	Blender	Electric Mixer
New unit cost savings if manufactured	$ 4.00	$11.00
Machine hours required per unit	1 MH	2 MH
Cost savings per machine hour if manufactured		
$4 ÷ 1 hour	$ 4.00	
$11 ÷ 2 hours		$ 5.50

Therefore, devote all 50,000 hours to the production of 25,000 mixers.

Conclusion: Manufacture: 25,000 mixers
Purchase: 3,000 mixers
Purchase: 20,000 blenders

PROBLEM 14-45 (25 MINUTES)

1.   Yes, the order should be accepted because it generates a profit of $34,050 for the firm. Note: The fixed administrative cost is irrelevant to the decision, because this cost will be incurred regardless of whether Jupiter accepts or rejects the order.

Selling price..		$15.75
Less: Direct material ($8.20 - $2.10).........................	$6.10	
Direct labor..	2.25	
Variable manufacturing overhead		
(.5 hours x $7.50*)....................................	3.75	12.10
Unit contribution margin...		$ 3.65
Total contribution margin (11,000 units x $3.65)........		$40,150
Less: Additional set-up costs..................................	$3,700	
Special device...	2,400	6,100
Net contribution to profit..		$34,050

* Fixed manufacturing overhead: $750,000 ÷ 60,000
        machine hours = $12.50 per hour
    Variable manufacturing overhead: $20.00 - $12.50 =
        $7.50

PROBLEM 14-45 (CONTINUED)

2. No, Jupiter lacks adequate machine capacity to manufacture the entire order.

Planned machine hours (5,000 hours x 3 months)......	15,000
Current usage (15,000 hours x 70%).........................	10,500
Available hours..	4,500
Required machine hours (11,000 units x .5 hours)......	5,500

3. Options include the following:

- Sacrificing some current business in the hope that a long-term relationship with Venus can be established and proves to be profitable
- Acquiring more machine capacity
- Outsourcing some units
- Working overtime

PROBLEM 14-46 (25 MINUTES)

1. Per-unit contribution margins:

	Basic	Enhanced
Selling price...	$250	$330
Less: Variable costs:		
Direct material.............................	$28	$45
Direct labor..................................	15	20
Variable manufacturing overhead ...	24	32
Sales commission		
$250 x 10%; $330 x 10%..........	25	33
Total unit variable cost..................	92	130
Unit contribution margin.............................	$158	$200

2. The following costs are not relevant to the decision:
- Development costs—sunk
- Fixed manufacturing overhead—will be incurred regardless of which product is selected
- Sales salaries—identical for both products
- Market study—sunk

PROBLEM 14-46 (CONTINUED)

3.   Johnson and Gomez, Inc. expects to sell 10,000 Basic units (40,000 units x 25%) or 8,000 Enhanced units (40,000 units x 20%). On the basis of this sales forecast, the company would be advised to select the Basic model.

	Basic	Enhanced
Total contribution margin:		
10,000 units x $158; 8,000 units x $200....	$1,580,000	$1,600,000
Less: Marketing and advertising..................	130,000	200,000
Income...	$1,450,000	$1,400,000

4.   The quantitative difference between the profitability of Basic and Enhanced is relatively small, which may prompt the firm to look at other factors before a final decision is made. These factors include:

- Competitive products in the marketplace
- Data validity
- Growth potential of the Basic and Enhanced models
- Production feasibility
- Effects, if any, on existing product sales
- Break-even points

PROBLEM 14-47 25 MINUTES)

1. Tipton will be worse off by $12,800 if it discontinues wallpaper sales.

	Paint and Supplies	Carpeting	Wallpaper
Sales.........................	$380,000	$460,000	$140,000
Less: Variable costs....	228,000	322,000	112,000
Contribution margin....	$152,000	$138,000	$ 28,000

If wallpaper is closed, then:

Loss of wallpaper contribution margin......	$(28,000)
Remodeling...	(12,400)
Added profitability from carpet sales*......	65,000
Fixed cost savings ($45,000 x 40%)..........	18,000
Decreased contribution margin from paint and supplies ($152,000 x 20%).................	(30,400)
Increased advertising.............................	(25,000)
Income (loss) from closure.....................	$(12,800)

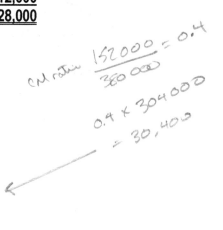

   * The current contribution margin ratio for carpeting is 30% ($138,000 ÷ $460,000). This ratio will increase to 35%, producing a new contribution for the line of $203,000 [($460,000 + $120,000) x 35%]. The end result is that carpeting's contribution margin will rise by $65,000 ($203,000 - $138,000), boosting firm profitability by the same amount.

2. This cost should be ignored. The inventory cost is sunk (i.e., a past cost that is not relevant to the decision). Regardless of whether the department is closed, Tipton will have a wallpaper inventory of $23,700.

3. The Internet- and magazine-based firms likely have several advantages:

    *   These companies probably carry little or no inventory. When a customer places an order, the firm simply calls its supplier and acquires the goods. The result may be lower expenditures for storage and warehousing.
    *   These firms do not need retail space for walk-in customers.
    *   Internet- and magazine-based firms can conduct business globally. Tipton, on the other hand, is confined to a single store in Des Moines.

PROBLEM 14-48 (20 MINUTES)

1. When there is no limit on production capacity the Pro model should be manufactured since it has the *highest contribution margin per unit*.

	Home Model	Deluxe Model	Pro Model
Selling price	$58	$65	$80
Direct material	16	20	19
Direct labor	10	15	20
Variable overhead	8	12	16
Total variable cost	$34	$47	$55
Contribution margin	$24	$18	$25

2. When labor is in short supply the Home model should be manufactured, since it has the *highest contribution margin per direct-labor hour*.

	Home Model	Deluxe Model	Pro Model
Contribution margin per unit	$24	$18	$25
Direct-labor hours required	1	1.5	2
Contribution margin per direct-labor hour	$24	$12	$12.50

PROBLEM 14-49 (20 MINUTES)

The analysis prepared by the engineering, manufacturing, and accounting departments of Casting Technology Resources (CTR) was not correct. However, their recommendation was correct, provided that potential labor-cost improvements are ignored. An incremental cost analysis similar to the following table should have been prepared to determine whether the pump should be purchased or manufactured. In the following analysis, fixed factory overhead costs and general and administrative overhead costs have not been included because they are not relevant; these costs would not increase, because no additional equipment, space, or supervision would be required if the pumps were manufactured. Therefore, if potential labor cost improvements are ignored, CTR should purchase the pumps because the purchase price of $68.00 is less than the $72.00 relevant cost to manufacture.

PROBLEM 14-49 (CONTINUED)

Incremental cost analysis:

	Cost of 10,000 Unit Assembly Run	Per Unit
Purchased components	$120,000	$12.00
Assembly labor	300,000	30.00
Variable manufacturing overhead	300,000	30.00
Total relevant cost..	$720,000	$72.00

PROBLEM 14-50 (40 MINUTES)

1.   a. An analysis of the relevant costs that shows whether the Midwest Division of Paibec Corporation should make MTR-2000 or purchase it from Marley Company is as follows:

	Amount Per Unit	Total for 32,000 Units
Cost to purchase MTR-2000 from Marley:		
Bid price from Marley	$17.30	$553,600
Equipment lease penalty ($36,000/12) × 2		6,000
Total cost to purchase		$559,600
Cost for Midwest to make MTR-2000:		
Direct material ($195,000/30,000) × 1.08	$ 7.02	$224,640
Direct labor ($120,000/30,000) × 1.05.............................	4.20	134,400
Variable manufacturing overhead		
($225,000 × .4)/30,000	3.00	96,000
Factory space rental		84,000
Equipment leasing costs		36,000
Total cost to make		$575,040
Savings if purchased from Marley		$ (15,440)

     b. Based solely on the financial results, the 32,000 units of MTR-2000 should be purchased from Marley. The total cost from Marley would be $559,600, or $15,440 less than if the units were made by the Midwest Division.

PROBLEM 14-50 (CONTINUED)

2.   The qualitative factors that the Midwest Division and Paibec Corporation should consider before agreeing to purchase MTR-2000 from Marley Company include the following:

*   The quality of the Marley component should be equal to, or better than, the quality of the internally made component, or else the quality of the final product might be comprised and Paibec's reputation adversely affected.

*   Marley's reliability as an on-time supplier is important, since late deliveries could hamper Paibec's production schedule and delivery dates for the final product.

*   Layoffs may result if the component is outsourced to Marley. This could impact Midwest's and Paibec's other employees and cause labor problems or affect the company's position in the community. In addition, there may be termination costs that have not been factored into the analysis.

3.   Lynn Hardt would consider the request of John Porter to be unethical for the following reasons, which are based on the Standards of Ethical Conduct for Management Accountants.

Competence

*   Prepare complete and clear reports and recommendations after appropriate analysis of relevant and reliable information. He has asked her to adjust and falsify her report and leave out some manufacturing overhead costs.

Integrity

*   Refrain from either actively or passively subverting the attainment of the organization's legitimate and ethical objectives. Paibec has a legitimate objective of trying to obtain the component at the lowest cost possible, regardless of whether it is manufactured by Midwest or outsourced to Marley.

*   Communicate unfavorable as well as favorable information and professional judgments or opinions. Hardt needs to communicate the proper and accurate results of the analysis, regardless of whether or not it is favorable to Midwest.

PROBLEM 14-50 (CONTINUED)

- Refrain from engaging in or supporting any activity that would discredit the profession. Falsifying the analysis would discredit Hardt and the profession.

Objectivity

- Communicate information fairly and objectively. Hardt needs to perform an objective make-versus-buy analysis and communicate the results fairly.

- Disclose fully all relevant information that could reasonably be expected to influence an intended user's understanding of the reports, comments, and recommendations presented. Hardt needs to fully disclose the analysis and the expected cost increases.

PROBLEM 14-51 (45 MINUTES)

RNA-1 is converted into Fastkil. RNA-2 can be sold as is or converted into two new products.

a. Management's analysis is incorrect because it incorporates allocated portions of the common costs of VDB. The weekly cost of VDB ($246,000) will be incurred whether or not RNA-2 is converted through further processing. Thus, any allocation of the common cost of VDB is strictly arbitrary and not relevant to the decision to market DMZ-3 and Pestrol.

   The decision not to process RNA-2 further is incorrect. This flawed decision resulted in the company failing to earn an incremental $20,000 in gross profit per week, as indicated by the following analysis.

b. Revenue from further processing of RNA-2:

DMZ-3 (400,000 × $57.50/100)	$230,000
Pestrol (400,000 × $57.50/100)	230,000
Total revenue from further processing	$460,000
Less revenue from sale of RNA-2	320,000
Incremental revenue	$140,000
Less incremental cost*	120,000
Incremental profit	$ 20,000

*The cost of VDB is not relevant and therefore is omitted from the solution.

PROBLEM 14-52 (50 MINUTES)

1. Sets result in a 20% increase, or 1,500 dresses (1,250 × 1.20 = 1,500).

	Percent of Total	Total Number of			
		Dresses	Capes	Handbags	Total
Complete sets	70%	1,050	1,050	1,050	
Dress and cape	6%	90	90		
Dress and handbag........................	15%	225		225	
Dress only......................................	9%	135	_____	_____	
Total units if accessories are introduced	100%	1,500	1,140	1,275	
Less: Unit sales if accessories are not introduced............................		1,250	—	—	
Incremental sales...........................		250	1,140	1,275	
Incremental contribution margin per unit (excluding material and cutting costs)		× $120	× $8	× $3	
Total incremental contribution margin		$30,000	$9,120	$3,825	$42,945

Additional costs:	
Additional cutting cost (1,500 × $9)	$13,500
Additional material cost (250 × $50)	12,500
Lost remnant sales (1,250 × $5)	6,250
Incremental cutting for extra dresses (250 × $20)............	5,000 37,250
Incremental profit...........................	$ 5,695

2. Qualitative factors that could influence the company's management team in its decision to manufacture matching capes and handbags include:

   • accuracy of forecasted increase in dress sales.

   • accuracy of forecasted product mix.

PROBLEM 14-52 (CONTINUED)

- company image of a dress manufacturer versus a more extensive supplier of women's apparel.

- competition from other manufacturers of women's apparel.

- whether there is adequate capacity (labor, facilities, storage, etc.).

PROBLEM 14-53 (40 MINUTES)

1. The costs that will be relevant in Peters' analysis of the special order being considered by Madeira Company are those expected future costs that are applicable to a particular decision (the costs that will differ between the alternatives of accepting or rejecting the offer). Only the variable costs of labor and material are relevant. Since the order was received directly by Madeira, variable marketing is not relevant, because additional marketing costs will not be incurred under this order. Also, the fixed costs are not relevant, because no additional capital investments are needed to meet the order. The firm is operating below full capacity and will be able to absorb this order.

2. Madeira Company should accept the offer. Although the *average* unit cost of $297.50 is higher than the price offered, the unit *incremental* cost is only $170.00. Accepting the special order will result in a contribution per unit of $30.00 ($200.00 less $170.00) and a total additional contribution margin of $18,750 (625 units × $30.00). The calculations follow.

	Current Monthly Production	Special Order	Combined Production
Units produced	1,875	625	2,500
Sales	$ 656,250[a]	$125,000[b]	$ 781,250
Variable costs:			
Direct labor	$ 187,500	$62,500[c]	$ 250,000
Direct material	131,250	43,750 [d]	175,000
Marketing	93,750	—	93,750
Total variable costs	$ 412,500	$106,250	$ 518,750
Fixed costs:			
Manufacturing	$ 137,500	—	$ 137,500
Marketing	87,500	—	87,500
Total fixed costs	$ 225,000	—	$ 225,000
Total costs	$ 637,500	$106,250	$ 743,750
Income before tax	$ 18,750	$ 18,750	$ 37,500
Cost per unit			
Variable[e]...	$220.00	$170.00	$ 207.50
Fixed[f]..	120.00	—	90.00
Average unit cost[g]........................	$340.00	$170.00	$297.50

[a]$350 × 1,875 units = $656,250

[b]$200 × 625 units = $125,000

[c]($187,500/1,875 units) × 625units = $62,500

[d]($131,250/1,875 units) × 625 units = $43,750

[e]Total variable cost/units produced = variable incremental cost per unit

[f]Total fixed cost/units produced = fixed cost per unit

[g]Total cost/units produced = average cost per unit

PROBLEM 14-53 (CONTINUED)

3. Other considerations that Samantha Peters should include in her analysis of the special order include the following:

    • Possible problems with other customers who pressure the company for similar treatment.

    • The future customer potential of the buyer of the special order, generating additional revenues.

4   Samantha Peters could try to resolve the ethical conflict arising out of the controller's insistence that the company avoid competitive bidding by taking the following steps:

    • She should follow the company's established policies on such matters.

    • If such policies do not exist, or if they do not resolve the conflict, she should discuss the situation with her manager unless, as in this case, the manager is involved in the conflict. Then, she should discuss the situation with the manager's supervisor.

    • If this approach does not help her resolve the matter, then she should continue going to the next-higher managerial level, including the audit committee of the board of directors, if necessary.

    • She should clarify relevant concepts by confidential discussions with an objective advisor to obtain an understanding of possible courses of action.

    • If the ethical conflict still exists after exhausting all of these avenues of internal review, she may have to resign from the company and submit an informative memorandum to the board of directors.

PROBLEM 14-54 (40 MINUTES)

1. The incremental cost of producing one unit of component B81 is computed as follows:

Direct material	$ 3.75
Direct labor	4.50
Variable overhead	2.25
Total variable cost per unit	$10.50

Purchase price quoted for component B81	$13.50
Incremental cost of production per unit	10.50
Net loss per unit if purchased	$ 3.00

Net loss per machine hour if component B81 is purchased = $3.00/3 machine hours = $1.00 per machine hour.

PROBLEM 14-54 (CONTINUED)

2.

	T79	B81
Purchase price quoted	$11.25	$13.5
Direct material	$ 2.25	$ 3.7
Direct labor	4.00	4.5
Variable overhead	2.00	2.2
Total variable cost	$ 8.25	$10.5
Net benefit per unit of making component	$ 3.00	$ 3.0
÷ Machine hours required per unit	÷ 2.5	÷
Net benefit per machine hour of making component	$ 1.20	$ 1.0
Machine hours available		41,000 hours
Best use of machine time: produce 8,000 units of component T79		
(8,000 × 2.5 hrs. per unit)		20,000 hours
Machine hours remaining for production of component B81		21,000 hours
Machine hours required per unit of component B81		3 hours per unit
Feasible production of component B81: (21,000/3)		7,000 units
Required quantity of component B81		11,000 units
Feasible production of component B81		7,000 units
Quantity of component B81 to be purchased		4,000 units

Conclusion: purchase 4,000 units of component B81 and manufacture the remaining bearings. Answer to requirement (2): d

3.	Variable cost per unit of component B81		$10.50
	Traceable, avoidable, fixed cost per unit of		
	component B81 ($44,000/11,000 units)		4.00
	Maximum price Upstate Mechanical should pay for component B81 ..		$14.50

PROBLEM 14-55 (60 MINUTES)

1.   Calculation of net revenue contributions:

Cost Items	Plain Paper Bulk	Colored Paper		Glossy Paper	
		Bulk	First Class	First Class	Late First Class
Design	$ 300	$ 1,000	$ 1,000	$ 3,000	$ 3,000
Word processing	100	800	800	2,000	2,000
Paper cost[a]	10,000	16,000	16,000	36,000	36,000
Printing cost[b]	6,000	20,000	20,000	80,000	80,000
Postage[c]	40,000	40,000	260,000	260,000	260,000
Handling[d]	20,000	20,000	20,000	40,000	40,000
Total cost	$ 76,400	$ 97,800	$ 317,800	$ 421,000	$ 421,000
Revenue potential	1,200,000	2,000,000	2,200,000	2,500,000	2,200,000
Net revenue contribution	$1,123,600	$1,902,200	$1,882,200	$2,079,000	$1,779,000

[a]Paper cost:

   Plain = $.005/unit $\times$ 2,000,000 units = $10,000
   Colored = $.008/unit $\times$ 2,000,000 units = $16,000
   Glossy = $.018/unit $\times$ 2,000,000 units = $36,000

[b]Printing cost:

   Plain = $.003/unit $\times$ 2,000,000 units = $6,000
   Colored = $.010unit $\times$ 2,000,000 units = $20,000
   Glossy = $.040/unit $\times$ 2,000,000 units = $80,000

[c]Postage:

   Bulk = $.02/unit $\times$ 2,000,000 units = $40,000
   First class = $.13/unit $\times$ 2,000,000 units = $260,000

[d]Handling:

   Plain & colored = $.01/unit $\times$ 2,000,000 units = $20,000
   Glossy = $.02/unit $\times$ 2,000,000 units = $40,000

2. *Net revenue realized:*

The glossy brochure provides the most net revenue as compared to the other alternatives if it can be mailed on time. However, there is a risk of earning only the fourth best net revenue if it is mailed late. The colored paper brochure, if it can be mailed at bulk mail rates, produces the second largest amount of net revenue. However, there is the risk of a lower amount if it must be mailed first class. The plain paper bulk mail brochure has a significantly lower net revenue than any of the other alternatives.

Image as a well-run organization:

The image would be based upon comparison of two things related to the mail campaign—the quality of the brochure (appearance) and the arrival of the brochure immediately following the radio and television coverage. The glossy brochure, if it arrives on time, would probably convey the best image; however, there is some risk that it would not arrive on a timely basis. The colored paper brochure would be the next best in terms of quality, but the bulk mail alternative raises some risk of a timely receipt of the brochures by the potential donors. The plain paper brochure would be the poorest quality, and because it is to be sent bulk mail, runs the additional risk of not being delivered on a timely basis.

Image as a fiscally responsible organization:

The image of fiscal responsibility will be based upon a comparison of potential donors' perceptions regarding the cost of the brochure and cost of the mailing. The glossy brochure mailed first class may be perceived as an extravagance by the potential donors. At the other extreme, the potential donors may conclude that the plain paper bulk mail alternative is an indication that the organization is unwilling to devote adequate financial resources to the fund-raising efforts.

Conclusions:

The foundation staff must weigh the consequences of each of the alternatives and the risks associated with them on the three criteria to select a specific alternative. The staff has good information on net revenue realized, but needs to obtain information on the effect of the quality of the brochure, the timeliness of mailing, and the type of mailing on potential donors' opinions as to what is a well-run and fiscally responsible organization.

PROBLEM 14-56 (25 MINUTES)

1. Incremental unit cost if purchased:

Purchase price	$15,000
Material handling	3,000
Total	$18,000

Incremental unit cost if manufactured:

Direct material	$ 1,000
Material handling	200
Direct labor	8,000
Variable manufacturing overhead ($12,000 × 1/3)	4,000
Total	$13,200
Increase in unit cost if purchased ($18,000 – $13,200)	$ 4,800

2.
Increase in monthly cost of acquiring part JR63 if purchased (10 × $4,800, as computed above)	$48,000
Less: rental revenue from idle space	25,000
Increase in monthly cost	$23,000

3.
Contribution forgone by not manufacturing alternative product	$52,000
Savings in the cost of acquiring JR63 (10 × $4,800 as computed in requirement 1)	48,000
Net cost of using limited capacity to produce part JR63	$ 4,000

PROBLEM 14-57 (45 MINUTES)

1.

	Sell to Kaytell as Special Order	Convert to Standard Model	Sell as Special Order as Is
Sales price	$68,400	$62,500	$52,000
Less cash discount	—	1,250	—
Net price	$68,400	$61,250	$52,000
Additional manufacturing costs			
Direct material	$ 6,200	$ 2,850	$ —
Direct labor	4,200	3,300	—
Variable manufacturing overhead	2,100	1,650	—
Total additional manufacturing costs	$12,500	$ 7,800	$ —
Commissions	2,052	1,250	1,560
Total costs and expenses	$14,552	9,050	1,560
Net contribution	$53,848	$52,200	$50,440

2.

Contribution from sale to Kaytell	$53,848
Contribution from next best alternative:	
sell as standard model	52,200
Difference in contribution	$ 1,648
Percentage of sales price received net of	
commission on special order: 100% – 3%	97%

$$\text{Acceptable reduction in sales price from Kaytell} = \frac{\$1,648}{.97} = \$1,699 \text{ (rounded)}$$

Original price quote to Kaytell	$68,400
Acceptable reduction	1,699
Minimum acceptable price from Kaytell	$66,701

Proof: Suppose Kaytell pays a price of $66,701:

Sales price	$66,701
Less: Sales commission (3%)	2,001 (rounded)
	$64,700
Less: Additional manufacturing costs	12,500
Contribution with reduced price to Kaytell	$52,200

PROBLEM 14-57 (CONTINUED)

Therefore, at a price of $66,701 to Kaytell, Miami Industries' management would be indifferent between selling the machine to Kaytell and converting it to a standard model. At any price quote from Kaytell below $66,701, Miami Industries' management would prefer to convert the machine to a standard model.

3. Fixed manufacturing overhead should have no influence on the sales price quoted by Miami Industries for special orders. Management should accept special orders whenever the firm is operating substantially below capacity, including below the breakeven point, whenever the marginal revenue from the order exceeds the marginal cost. Normally, this would mean that the order should be accepted as long as the sales price of the order exceeds the variable production costs. The special order will result in a positive contribution toward fixed costs. The fixed manufacturing overhead is not considered in pricing because it will be incurred whether the order is accepted or not.

PROBLEM 14-58 (40 MINUTES)

1. The costs that will be relevant in Senna's analysis of the special order being considered by Winner's Circle, Inc. are those expected future costs that are applicable to a particular decision (the costs that will differ between the alternatives of accepting or rejecting the offer). Only the variable costs of labor and material are relevant. Since the order was received directly by Winner's Circle, variable marketing is not relevant, because additional marketing costs will not be incurred under this order. Also, the fixed costs are not relevant, because no additional capital investments are needed to meet the order. The firm is operating below full capacity and will be able to absorb this order.

2. Winner's Circle, Inc. should accept the offer. Although the *average* unit cost of $148.75 is higher than the price offered, the unit *incremental* cost is only $85.00. Accepting the special order will result in a contribution per unit of $15.00 ($100.00 less $85.00) and a total additional contribution margin of $37,500 (2,500 units × $15.00). The calculations follow.

	Current Monthly Production	Special Order	Combined Production
Units produced	7,500	2,500	10,000
Sales	$1,312,500[a]	$250,000[b]	$1,562,500
Variable costs:			
Direct labor	$ 375,000	$125,000[c]	$ 500,000
Direct material	262,500	87,500[d]	350,000
Marketing	187,500	—	187,500
Total variable costs	$ 825,000	$212,500	$1,037,500
Fixed costs:			
Manufacturing	$ 275,000	—	$ 275,000
Marketing	175,000	—	175,000
Total fixed costs	$ 450,000	—	$ 450,000
Total costs	$1,275,000	$212,500	$1,487,500
Income before tax	$ 37,500	$ 37,500	$ 75,000
Cost per unit			
Variable[e]	$110.00	$85.00	$103.75
Fixed[f]	60.00	—	45.00
Average unit cost[g]	$170.00	$85.00	$148.75

[a]$175 × 7,500 units = $1,312,500

[b]$100 × 2,500 units = $250,000

[c]($375,000/7,500 units) × 2,500 units = $125,000

[d]($262,500/7,500 units) × 2,500 units = $87,500

[e]Total variable cost/units produced = variable incremental cost per unit

[f]Total fixed cost/units produced = fixed cost per unit

[g]Total cost/units produced = average cost per unit

PROBLEM 14-58 (CONTINUED)

3.   Other considerations that Cathy Senna should include in her analysis of the special order include the following:

  • Possible problems with other customers who pressure the company for similar treatment.

  • The future customer potential of the buyer of the special order, generating additional revenues.

4.   Cathy Senna could try to resolve the ethical conflict arising out of the controller's insistence that the company avoid competitive bidding by taking the following steps:

  • She should follow the company's established policies on such matters.

  • If such policies do not exist, or if they do not resolve the conflict, she should discuss the situation with her manager unless, as in this case, the manager is involved in the conflict. Then, she should discuss the situation with the manager's supervisor.

  • If this approach does not help her resolve the matter, then she should continue going to the next-higher managerial level, including the audit committee of the board of directors, if necessary.

  • Senna should clarify relevant concepts by confidential discussions with an objective advisor to obtain an understanding of possible courses of action.

  • If the ethical conflict still exists after exhausting all of these avenues of internal review, she may have to resign from the company and submit an informative memorandum to the board of directors.

PROBLEM 14-59 (45 MINUTES)

1. Machine hour requirements:

Product	Department			
	1	2	3	4
M07	500	500	1,000	1,000
T28............................	400	400	—	800
B19	2,000	2,000	1,000	1,000
Total required	2,900	2,900	2,000	2,800
Total available	3,000	3,100	2,700	3,300
Excess (deficiency)	100	200	700	500

Direct-labor hour requirements:

Product	Department			
	1	2	3	4
M07	1,000	1,500	1,500	500
T28..	400	800	—	800
B19	2,000	2,000	2,000	1,000
Total required	3,400	4,300	3,500	2,300
Total available	3,700	4,500	2,750	2,600
Excess (deficiency)	300	200	(750)	300

The monthly sales demand cannot be met for all three products as a result of the labor shortage in Department 3.

2. The goal is to maximize contribution margin. Fixed costs are not relevant. The scarce resource is direct-labor hours (DLH) in Department 3. Ozark should first produce the product that maximizes contribution margin per unit of the scarce resource (DLH). In this case two products, M07 and B19, require direct-labor hours in Department 3.

	Product		
	M07	T28	B19
Sales price	$196	$123	$167
Variable costs			
Direct material	$ 7	$ 13	$ 17
Direct labor	66	38	51
Variable overhead	27	20	25
Variable selling	3	2	4
Total variable costs	$103	$ 73	$ 97
Contribution margin	$ 93	$ 50	$ 70

Product	Contribution Margin	Department 3 DLH	Contribution Margin per DLH
M07	$93	3	$31
B19	70	2	35

	Units	Department 3 DLH Required	Balance (DLH)
Maximum DLH available in Department 3			2,750
Product B19 first	1,000	2,000	750
Product M07 second	250	750	-0-

RESULTING PRODUCTION SCHEDULE

Product	Units	Comments
M07	250	Produce as much as the constraint allows (750 ÷ 3 DLH per unit). Reduced production is based on its lower contribution margin per direct-labor hour.
T28	400	Produce up to monthly sales demand; unaffected by Department 3.
B19	1,000	Produce as much as possible to maximize contribution margin per DHL.

SCHEDULE OF CONTRIBUTION MARGIN BY PRODUCT

Product	Contribution Margin per Unit	Units Produced	Contribution to Profit
M07	$93	250	$ 23,250
T28	50	400	20,000
B19	70	1,000	70,000
Total contribution margin			$113,250

3. To supply the additional quantities of M07 that are required, Ozark should consider:

    • subcontracting the additional units.

    • operating on an overtime basis.

    • acquiring labor from outside the community.

PROBLEM 14-60 (30 MINUTES)

1. Costs to be avoided by purchasing (conventional analysis):

Direct material	$300,000
Direct labor	180,000
Variable overhead	120,000
Fixed overhead:	
Supervisory salaries	80,000
Machinery depreciation	28,000
Total	$708,000

2. Costs to be avoided by purchasing (ABC analysis):

Direct material		$300,000
Direct labor		180,000
Overhead:		
Product development	$600* × 10†	6,000
Supervisory salaries	$40 × 2,000	80,000
Material handling	$8 × 6,000	48,000
Purchasing	$250 × 55	13,750
Inspection	$300 × 30	9,000
Setup	$400 × 15	6,000
Electricity	$1.40 × 70,000	98,000
Oil and lubrication	$.24 × 70,000	16,800
Equipment maintenance	$.36 × 70,000	25,200
Machinery depreciation	$.40 × 70,000	28,000
Total		$810,750

*Pool rates for the Savannah plant from Exhibit 14-20.

†Levels of cost drivers associated with canister production (from the information given in the problem).

3.   Make-or-buy analysis using ABC data:

Cost savings if canisters are purchased (ABC analysis)	$810,750
Cost to purchase canisters	760,000
Net advantage to purchasing	$ 50,750

International Chocolate Company will save over $50,000 if it accepts Catawba's offer. The final decision, however, should take qualitative factors into account also. Issues such as supplier reliability, product quality, and employee morale should be considered.

The relevant costing approach remains valid when ABC data are used. The objective is to determine what costs will be avoided if the canisters are purchased. The ABC analysis is able to more accurately identify the avoidable costs. Costs that are assumed to be fixed and unavoidable under the conventional analysis are shown by the ABC analysis to vary with the appropriate cost drivers. In this light, many of these costs are seen to be avoidable if the canisters are purchased.

PROBLEM 14-61 (40 MINUTES)

1. In order to maximize contribution margin, the objective function and constraint functions would be formulated as follows:

    Notation:

    V = number of batches of Venus candy bars
    C = number of batches of Comet candy bars
    TCM = total contribution margin

    The contribution margin is the selling price less variable cost for each product. Thus, for the Comet candy bar, the contribution margin is $125 ($350 less $225), and for the Venus candy bar, it is $200 ($300 less $100). Therefore, the objective function is as follows:

    Maximize $TCM = 125C + 200V$

    Subject to the following constraints:

    Mixing Department: $1.5V + 1.5C \leq 525$
    Coating Department: $2.0V + 1.0C \leq 500$
    Materials: $C \leq 300$
    Nonnegativity: $V \geq 0$ and $C \geq 0$

2. The number of batches of each candy bar that should be produced to maximize contribution can be determined by graphing the linear program, as shown on the following page. The optimal solution is to produce 200 batches of Comet bars and 150 batches of Venus bars.

3. The total contribution margin, then, is $55,000 [(200 × $125) + (150 × $200)].

PROBLEM 14-61 (CONTINUED)

Graph of linear program:

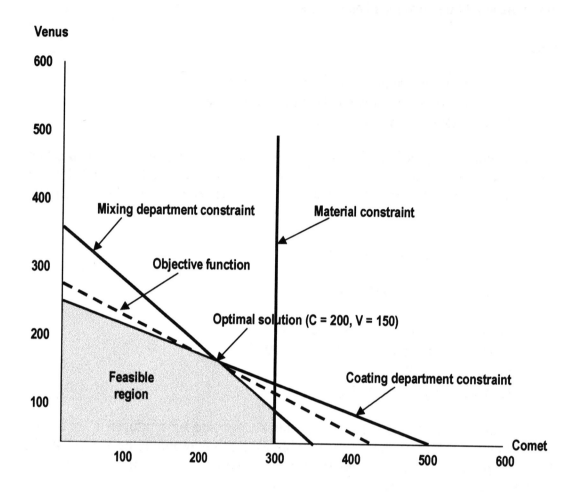

PROBLEM 14-62 (45 MINUTES)

1. The objective function and constraints that Meals for Professionals, Inc. should use to maximize profits are as follows:

Maximize	$120P + 90H$
Subject to:	$2P + H \leq 60$ (preparation)
	$2P + 3H \leq 120$ (cooking)
	$P \leq 45$ (freezing)
	$P \geq 0$
	$H \geq 0$

PROBLEM 14-62 (CONTINUED

2.   Graph of linear program:

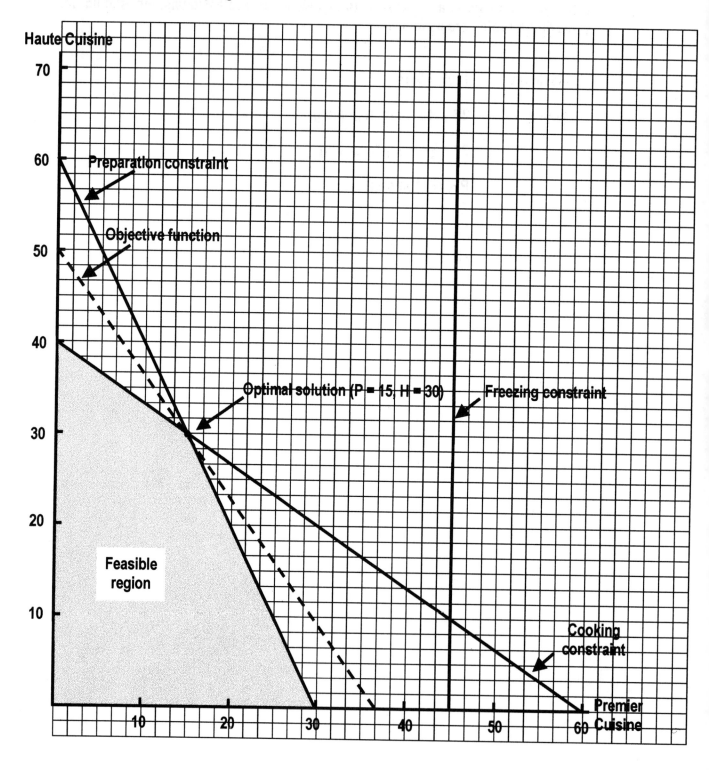

PROBLEM 14-62 (CONTINUED)

3. & 4.

Corner Points in Feasible Region		Objective Function Value
P = 0	H = 0	($120)(0) + ($90)(0) = 0
P = 0	H = 40	($120)(0) + ($90)(40) = $3,600
P = 15	H = 30	($120)(15) + ($90)(30) = $4,500
P = 30	H = 0	($120)(30) + ($90)(0) = $3,600

Contribution margin at the optimal solution = $4,500.

PROBLEM 14-62 (CONTINUED)

5.   Graph of linear program:

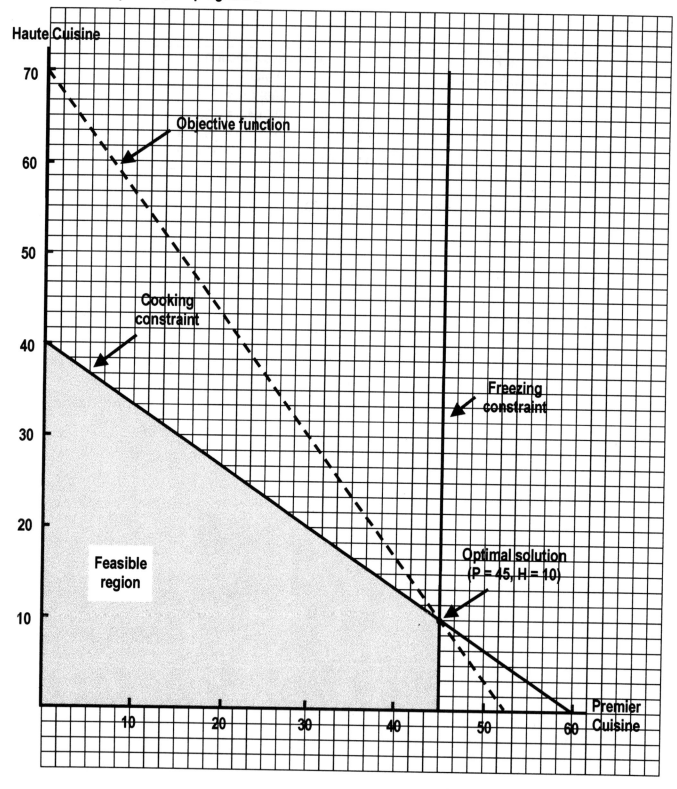

Corner Points in Feasible Region		Objective Function Value
P = 0	H = 0	($120)(0) + ($90)(0) = 0
P = 0	H = 40	($120)(0) + ($90)(40) = $3,600
P = 45	H = 10	($120)(45) + ($90)(10) = $6,300
P = 45	H = 0	($120)(45) + ($90)(0) = $5,400

Contribution margin at the optimal solution = $6,300.

PROBLEM 14-63 (50 MINUTES)

1. Linear programming (LP) is designed to determine the optimum mix when resources are limited and can be switched or allocated among products. LP would be appropriate for Colonial Corporation because the company has limited facilities (machine capacity), limited resources (labor), and contractual obligations (minimum quantities to be sold) that must be considered in order to maximize profit.

2. Notation:

R_L = Regular model in Labor Assembly
R_A = Regular model in Automated Assembly
D_L = Deluxe model in Labor Assembly
D_A = Deluxe model in Automated Assembly

a. Objective function: *

Maximize $10.30 R_L + $11.65 R_A + $18.55 D_L + $19.90 D_A

*Supporting calculations (per-unit basis):

	R_L	R_A	D_L	D_A
Selling price	$45.00	$45.00	$60.00	$60.00
Less: Variable costs:				
Raw material	$22.00	$22.00	$28.75	$28.75
Plating labor	2.00	2.00	2.00	2.00
Assembly labor	3.00	.60	3.00	.60
Plating supplies	1.25	1.25	1.25	1.25
Assembly supplies	1.50	1.50	1.50	1.50
Plating power	1.20	1.20	1.20	1.20
Assembly power	.75	1.80	.75	1.80
Selling	3.00	3.00	3.00	3.00
Total variable cost	$34.70	$33.35	$41.45	$40.10
Contribution margin	$10.30	$11.65	$18.55	$19.90

PROBLEM 14-63 (CONTINUED)

b. Constraints:

Direct labor (plating): $.2 R_L + .2 R_A + .2 D_L + .2 D_A \leq 30,000$ hours

Direct labor (assembly): $.25 R_L + .05 R_A + .25 D_L + .05 D_A \leq 40,000$ hours

Machine hours (plating): $.15 R_L + .15 R_A + .15 D_L + .15 D_A \leq 25,000$ hours

Machine hours (labor assembly): $.02 R_L + .02 D_L \leq 1,500$ hours

Machine hours (automated assembly): $.05 R_A + .05 D_A \leq 5,000$ hours

Sales contract (regular): $R_L + R_A \geq 35,000$ units

Sales contract (deluxe): $D_L + D_A \geq 35,000$ units

All variables nonnegative: $R_L, R_A, D_L, D_A \geq 0$

*Supporting calculations (direct-labor time requirements):

Plating...	$2.00/$10.00 = .20 hours
Assembly:	
Labor	$3.00/$12.00 = .25 hours
Automated...	$.60/$12.00 = .05 hours

SOLUTIONS TO CASES

CASE 14-64 (45 MINUTES)

In order to maximize the company's profitability, Sportway Corporation should purchase 9,000 tackle boxes from Maple Products, manufacture 17,500 skateboards, and manufacture 1,000 tackle boxes. This combination of purchased and manufactured goods maximizes the contribution per direct-labor hour available. The analysis supporting this conclusion follows:

1. Calculate unit contribution margins:

	Purchased	Manufactured	
	Tackle Boxes	Tackle Boxes	Skate-boards
Selling price	$86.00	$86.00	$45.00
Less:			
Material	(68.00)	(17.00)	(12.50)
Direct labor	—	(18.75)	(7.50)
Manufacturing overhead*	—	(6.25)	(2.50)
Selling and administrative cost[†]	(4.00)	(11.00)	(3.00)
Contribution margin	$14.00	$33.00	$19.50
Direct-labor hours per unit	—	1.25	.5
Contribution per hour	—	$26.40	$39.00

*Calculation of variable overhead per unit:

Tackle boxes:
Direct-labor hours	$18.75 ÷ $15.00 = 1.25 hours
Overhead per direct-labor hour	$12.50 ÷ 1.25 = $10.00
Capacity	8,000 boxes × 1.25 = 10,000 hours
Total overhead	10,000 hours × $10 per hour = $100,000
Total variable overhead	$100,000 – $50,000 = $50,000
Variable overhead per hour	$50,000 ÷ 10,000 = $5.00
Variable overhead per box	$5.00 × 1.25 = $6.25

Skateboards:
Direct-labor hours	$7.50 ÷ $15.00 = .5 hours
Variable overhead	$5.00 × .5 = $2.50

[†]In calculating the contribution margin, $6.00 of fixed overhead cost per unit for distribution must be deducted from the selling and administrative cost.

The optimal use of Sportway's scarce resource (direct labor) is to manufacture skateboards, up to the number of skateboards that the company can sell (17,500). With its remaining labor time, Sportway can produce 1,000 tackle boxes.

2. The following table shows the improvement in the company's total contribution margin if it manufactures 17,500 skateboards and 1,000 tackle boxes, rather than manufacturing 8,000 tackle boxes.

The optimal use of Sportway's available direct-labor hours (DLH):

Item	Quantity	DLH per Unit	Total DLH	Balance of DLH	Unit Contri- bution	Total Contri- bution
Total hours				10,000		
Skateboards	17,500	.50	8,750	1,250	$19.50	$341,250
Make boxes	1,000	1.25	1,250	—	33.00	33,000
Buy boxes	9,000	—	—	—	14.00	126,000
Total contribution						$500,250
Less:						
Contribution from manufacturing 8,000 boxes						
(8,000 × $33.00)						264,000
Improvement in contribution margin						$236,250

CASE 14-65 (60 MINUTES)

1.   **Memorandum**

   Date: Today

   To: Alice Carlo, President, Alberta Gauge Company, Ltd.

   From: I.M. Student

   Subject: Suggested revision of product-line income statement

   a. The product-line income statement is presented on an absorption-costing basis and, thus, is not suitable for analysis and decision making. The statement does not distinguish between variable and fixed costs, which hinders any analysis on the impact of volume changes on profit. In addition, the statement does not distinguish between costs that are directly related (traceable) to a product line from those that are shared among all products.

   b. An alternative income statement format that would be more suitable for analysis and decision making would incorporate the contribution approach. Expenses would be classified in terms of variability and controllability such as: variable manufacturing, variable selling and administrative, direct fixed controllable by segment, direct fixed controllable by others, and common fixed. The common fixed costs would not be assigned to the product lines because such an allocation would be arbitrary. The contribution approach is more suitable for analysis and decision making because there is a meaningful assignment of costs to product lines.

2.   a. The suggested discontinuance of the R-gauges would be cost effective, but the suggestions relating to E-gauges and Q-gauges would not be cost effective. These conclusions are based on the following quarterly analysis.

	E-Gauge	Q-Gauge	R-Gauge
Unit selling price	$90	$200	$180
Unit variable costs			
Raw material	$17	$31	$50
Direct labor	20	40	60
Variable manufacturing			
overhead	30	45	60
Shipping expenses	4	10	10
Total	71	126	180
Unit contribution margin	$19	$ 74	$ 0
Increase (decrease) in units*			
E-gauge: 10,000 × 50%	× (5,000)		
Q-gauge: 8,000 × 15%		× 1,200	
R-gauge: 5,000 × 100%			× (5,000)
Increase (decrease) in total			
contribution margin	$(95,000)	$ 88,800	$ 0
Decrease (increase) in fixed costs	80,000†	(100,000)	40,000
Increase (decrease) in segment			
contribution	$(15,000)	$(11,200)	$40,000

*Unit sales = sales dollars ÷ unit sales price

†$100,000 – $20,000

    b. Yes, the president was correct in eliminating the R-gauges. The R-gauge sales price covers only its variable cost and does not contribute anything to manufacturing overhead or promotion costs. Thus, the R-gauge has a zero contribution margin.

    c. Yes, the president was correct in promoting the Q-gauge line rather than the E-gauge line, because the unit contribution margin and contribution per labor dollar is greater for the Q-gauge line as follows:

	E-Gauge	Q-Gauge
Unit contribution	$19.00	$74.00
Contribution per direct-labor dollar	.95	1.85

CASE 14-65 (CONTINUED)

However, the president's decisions regarding promotion expense do not seem well conceived. The decreased promotion on the E-gauge line and the increased promotion on the Q-gauge line do not produce sufficient contribution to offset the promotional costs.

c. No. The proposed course of action does not make effective use of capacity. The 15 percent increase in production volume on the Q-gauge line will not require all of the capacity that has been released by discontinuing the R-gauge line or reducing the E-gauge line by 50 percent.

2. Yes. The qualitative factors that management should consider before it decides whether to drop the R-gauge line include:

   • *Customer relations.* The sale of E-gauges and Q-gauges may be related to the sale of R-gauges.

   • *Labor relations.* Reducing employment may create labor problems.

CURRENT ISSUES IN MANAGERIAL ACCOUNTING

ISSUE 14-66

"E-BOOKS HAVE A BIG FUTURE, BUT IT'S UNLIKELY TO COME ANYTIME SOON," *THE WALL STREET JOURNAL*, OCTOBER 2, 2000, MATTHEW ROSE.

1. Projected sales revenue, variable costs, contribution margin, and any additional fixed costs relating to a new product line would be useful managerial accounting information when making a decision regarding a new product line.

2. Pricing any new product is difficult, since management has little to go on from experience with similar products. Market research into likely consumer demand and prices that consumers would pay is important information for such a decision.

ISSUE 14-67

"PARTS SHORTAGES PLAGUE ELECTRONIC MAKERS," *THE WALL STREET JOURNAL*, OCTOBER 10, 2000, PUIWING TAM.

The advantage to outsourcing parts and services is the ability to contract with many different vendors and increase the available sources. The disadvantage is not directly controlling the source and having to rely on third party vendors.

ISSUE 14-68

"INTEGRATING ABC AND ABM AT DOW CHEMICAL," *MANAGEMENT ACCOUNTING QUARTERLY*, WINTER 2000, JAMES W. DAMITIO, GARY W. HAYES, AND PHILIP L. KINTZELE.

1. Activity-based costing focuses on the activities undertaken to design, produce, sell and deliver a company's products or services. ABC systems accumulate manufacturing overhead costs for each of the activities of an organization, and then assign the costs of activities to the products or services using activity cost drivers.

2. One challenge facing Dow Chemical was the coordination of ABC/ABM across a globally dispersed organization. Another challenge of ABC/ABM involved capturing cost driver metrics without adding work. Dow has learned that large companies like itself probably should not break activities down to task levels, but instead should stay at the activity level. Activities can be diced into component levels that are too small and too numerous to be useful for cost management and decision making.

ISSUE 14-69

"DON'T GET TRAPPED," *STRATEGIC FINANCE*, NOVEMBER 1999, DAPHNE MAIN AND CAROLYN L. LOUSTEAU.

Entrapment is the inability to eliminate an albatross project. There are four psychological reasons that can lead to entrapment. They are over-optimism/illusion of control, self-justification, framing, and sunk costs.

Over-optimism occurs when managers feel the need to sell their project. As a result, the projections are almost always rosy, which lead to inflated expectations for a project. Research has shown that people consistently overestimate revenue and under estimate costs. People also think they can control what happens to their decisions once they are in place. External factors, such as weather or changes in economic conditions, are beyond the control of project managers.

Managers tend to commit more resources to a losing project in order to justify their initial investment. They tend to search for evidence that suggests the project should be continued but disregard evidence to the contrary. This self-justification leads to entrapment.

How a decision is perceived or framed can lead to entrapment. When thinking in terms of saving jobs managers tend to be more conservative in decision making, while if a decision is framed in terms of losing jobs, managers tend to be more likely to make risky decisions.

When justifying the decision to continue a project, managers tend to argue that they should not waste money already sunk into a project. In fact, money already spent on a project should not influence decisions if entrapment is to be avoided.

The four psychological reasons leading to entrapment should be avoided when making sound business decisions concerning project continuance.

ISSUE 14-70

"WHAT A PEO CAN DO FOR YOU," *JOURNAL OF ACCOUNTANCY*, JULY 1999, BRUCE E. KATZ.

The IRS recognizes PEOs as employers. PEOs' responsibilities include the general aspects of the employer's role such as paying employee wages and associated withholding taxes. The PEO is responsible for paying these taxes whether or not the client actually pays the PEO. It also must provide employees with workers' compensation, federal and state unemployment benefits, and statutory disability coverage. A PEO administers any employee benefit programs, including retirement plans, cafeteria and health care plans, life, disability, accidental death and dismemberment insurance, credit unions, fitness club memberships, child care and tuition reimbursement programs. It assumes fiduciary responsibility for plan compliance with applicable federal and state laws when it sponsors employee benefit plans.

CHAPTER 15
Target Costing and Cost Analysis for Pricing Decisions

ANSWERS TO REVIEW QUESTIONS

15-1 Four major influences on pricing decisions are as follows:

(1) Customer demand: Management must consider customers' demand for their product, which reflects the price that customers are willing to pay for the product.

(2) Actions of competitors: When pricing its product, management must consider the likely pricing decisions and product design decisions of competing firms.

(3) Costs: No organization or industry can price its product below total production costs indefinitely.

(4) Political, legal, and image-related issues: Management must consider the way the public perceives the firm and must adhere to certain laws when setting prices.

15-2 The statement that prices are determined by production costs is too simplistic. Although firms must price their products and services above their total costs in the long run, management cannot ignore demand issues and the economic environment. Setting prices generally is a balance between cost-related issues and economic market forces.

15-3 In the long run, every organization must price its product or service above the total cost of production. While the market for the product also is critically important, costs cannot be ignored.

15-4 It is crucial to define the firm's product when considering the reaction of competitors, so that the competitors can be identified. For example, is a firm that produces glass bottles competing only with other firms that produce glass bottles, or is the firm competing with all companies that produce containers? Defining the product as glass bottles or containers is an important step in identifying who the firm's competitors are.

15-5 In most industries, both market forces and cost considerations heavily influence prices. No organization can price its products below their production costs in the long run. On the other hand, no company can set prices at cost plus a markup without keeping an eye on the market. The product or service must be sold at a price customers are willing to pay.

15-6 The profit-maximizing price is the price for which the associated quantity is determined by the intersection of the marginal cost and marginal revenue curves. This intersection is shown in Exhibit 15-3 in the text.

15-7 (a) Total revenue: Price multiplied by quantity sold.

(b) Marginal revenue: The amount by which total revenue increases when one additional unit is sold.

(c) Demand curve: A graphical or mathematical expression of the relationship between the price and the quantity sold.

(d) Price elasticity: The impact of price changes on sales volume.

(e) Cross-elasticity: The extent to which a change in a product's price affects the demand for substitute products.

15-8 (a) Total cost: Unit cost multiplied by quantity produced.

(b) Marginal cost: Additional cost when one more unit is produced.

15-9 Three limitations of the economic, profit-maximizing model of pricing are as follows:

(1) The firm's demand and marginal revenue curves are difficult to determine with precision.

(2) The marginal-cost, marginal-revenue paradigm, as described in the text, is not valid for all forms of market organization.

(3) Cost-accounting systems are not designed to measure the marginal changes in cost incurred as production and sales increase unit by unit. To measure marginal cost would entail a very costly information system.

15-10 Determining the best approach to pricing requires a cost-benefit trade-off. While the marginal-cost, marginal-revenue paradigm results in a profit-maximizing price, only a sophisticated and costly information system can collect marginal-cost data. Thus, the firm will incur greater cost in order to obtain better decisions.

15-11 The general formula for cost-plus pricing is as follows:

$$\text{Price} = \text{cost} + (\text{markup percentage} \times \text{cost})$$

The price is equal to cost plus a markup. Depending on how cost is defined, the markup percentage may differ. Several different definitions of cost, each combined with a different markup percentage, can result in the same price for a product or service.

15-12 The four cost bases commonly used in cost-plus pricing are the following: absorption manufacturing cost, total cost, variable manufacturing cost, and total variable cost. Each of these cost bases can result in the same price under cost-based pricing if the markup percentage used in the cost-plus pricing formula is changed. For example, a lower markup percentage would be applied to total cost than would be applied to total variable cost.

15-13 Four reasons often cited for the widespread use of absorption cost as the cost base in cost-plus formulas are as follows:

(1) In the long run, the price must cover all costs and a normal profit margin.

(2) Absorption-cost and total-cost pricing formulas provide a justifiable price that tends to be perceived as equitable by all parties.

(3) When a company's competitors have similar operations and cost structures, cost-plus pricing based on full costs gives management an idea of how competitors may set prices.

(4) Absorption-cost information is provided by a firm's cost-accounting system, because it is required for external financial reporting under generally accepted accounting principles. Since absorption-cost information already exists, it is cost-effective to use for pricing.

15-14 The primary disadvantage of absorption-cost or total-cost pricing formulas is that they obscure the cost behavior pattern of the firm. Since absorption-cost and total-cost data include allocated fixed costs, it is not clear from these data how the firm's total costs will change as volume changes.

15-15 Three advantages of pricing based on variable cost are as follows:

(1) Variable-cost data do not obscure the cost behavior pattern by unitizing fixed costs and making them appear variable.

(2) Variable-cost data do not require allocation of common fixed costs to individual product lines.

(3) Variable-cost data are exactly the type of information managers need when facing certain decisions, such as whether to accept a special order.

15-16 The behavioral problem that can result from the use of a variable-cost pricing formula is that managers may perceive the variable cost of a product or service as the floor for the price. They may tend to set the price too low for the firm to cover its fixed costs.

15-17 Return-on-investment pricing is an approach under which the price is set so that it will cover costs and also earn a profit that will provide a target return on the invested capital.

15-18 Price-led costing refers to the process under target costing of *first* determining the acceptable market price for a product or service and *then* determining the cost at which the product or service must be produced.

15-19 To be successful at target costing, management must listen to the company's customers. By doing so, management will learn the products, features, and quality that customers are willing to buy as well as the price they are willing to pay.

15-20 Value-engineering is a cost-reduction and process-improvement technique used to help bring the cost of manufacturing a product or providing a service into line with its target cost.

15-21 Tear-down methods can be used in a service-industry firm just as they are used in the manufacturing industry. The various steps in providing a service can be analyzed for cost improvements just as a product's materials and manufacturing operations can be analyzed for the same purpose.

15-22 Under time-and-material pricing, the price includes a cost-based charge for labor, a cost-based charge for material, and generally a markup on one or both of these production-cost factors.

15-23 When a firm has excess capacity, there is no opportunity cost in accepting an additional production job. Therefore, it is not necessary to reflect such an opportunity cost in setting a bid price. On the other hand, if the firm is already at full capacity, there is an opportunity cost to accepting another production job. In this case, it is appropriate to include in the price an estimate of the opportunity cost associated with the job for which the bid is being prepared.

15-24 The decision to accept or reject a special order and the selection of a price for a special order are similar decisions. If a price has been offered for a special order, management can base its acceptance or rejection decision on whether or not that price covers the incremental cost of producing the order. Another way of viewing the problem is to set the minimum price for the special order at a level sufficient to cover the incremental cost of producing the order.

15-25 (a) Skimming pricing: Setting a high initial price for a new product in order to reap short-run profits. Over time, the price is reduced gradually.

(b) Penetration pricing: Setting a low initial price for a new product in order to penetrate a market deeply and gain a large and broad market share.

(c) Target costing: Conducting market research to determine the price at which a new product will sell and then, given the likely sales price, computing the cost for which the product must be manufactured in order to provide the firm with an acceptable profit margin. Then engineers and cost analysts work together to design a product that can be manufactured for the allowable cost. This process is used widely in the development stages of new products.

15-26 (a) Unlawful price discrimination: Quoting different prices to different customers for the same product or service, even though the different prices cannot be justified by differences in the cost incurred to produce, sell, and deliver the product or service.

(b) Predatory pricing: Temporarily cutting a price to broaden demand for a product with the intention of later restricting the supply and raising the price again.

15-27 Traditional, volume-based product-costing systems often overcost high-volume and relatively simple products while undercosting low-volume and complex products. This practice can result in overpricing high-volume and relatively simple products and underpricing low-volume and complex products. Such strategic pricing errors can have a disastrous impact on a firm's competitive position.

SOLUTIONS TO EXERCISES

EXERCISE 15-28 (30 MINUTES)

1.   Tabulated price, quantity, and revenue data:

(1) Quantity Sold per Month		(2) Unit Sales Price		(3) Total Revenue per Month*		(4) Changes in Total Revenue†
20	....	$1,000	....	$20,000		
40	....	950	....	38,000	}	$18,000
60	....	900	....	54,000	}	16,000
80	....	850	....	68,000	}	14,000
100	....	800	....	80,000	}	12,000

*Column (1) times column (2).

†Differences between amounts in column (3).

EXERCISE 15-28 (CONTINUED)

2.   Total revenue curve:

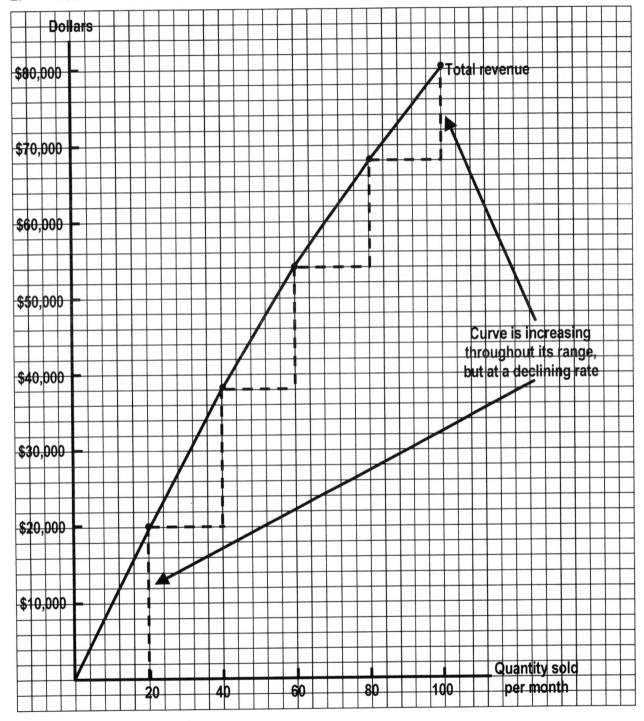

EXERCISE 15-29 (30 MINUTES)

1. Tabulated cost and quantity data:

(1) Quantity Produced and Sold per Month		(2) Average Cost per Unit		(3) Total Cost per Month*		(4) Changes in Total Cost†
20	....	$900	....	$18,000		
40	....	850	....	34,000	}	$16,000
60	....	820	....	49,200	}	15,200
80	....	860	....	68,800	}	19,600
100	....	890	....	89,000	}	20,200

*Column (1) times column (2).

†Differences between amounts in column (3).

EXERCISE 15-29 (CONTINUED)

2.   Total cost curve:

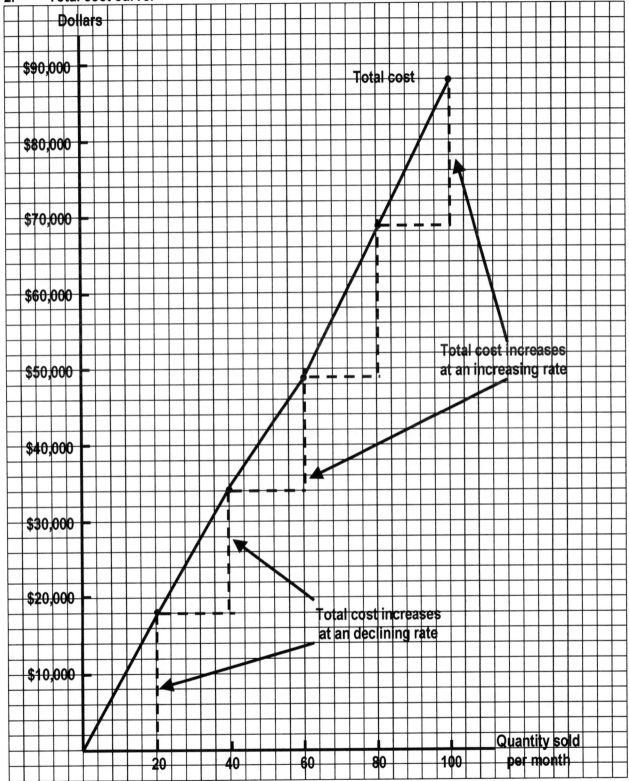

EXERCISE 15-30 (40 MINUTES)

1.   Tabulated revenue, cost, and profit data:

(1) Quantity Produced and Sold per Month		(2) Sales Price per Unit		(3) Total Revenue per Month*	(4) Total Cost per Month†		(5) Profit per Month**
20	....	$1,000	....	$20,000	$18,000	....	$2,000
40	....	950	....	38,000	34,000	....	4,000
60	....	900	....	54,000	49,200	....	4,800
80	....	850	....	68,000	68,800	....	(800)
100	....	800	....	80,000	89,000	....	(9,000)

*Column (1) times column (2).

†Column (1) times average cost per unit given in the preceding exercise.

**Column (3) minus column (4).

2.   Total revenue and cost curves: see next page.

3.   Of the five candidate prices listed, $900 is the optimal price. This price produces a monthly profit of $4,800, which is greater than the profit at the other four candidate prices.

2. Total revenue and cost curves:

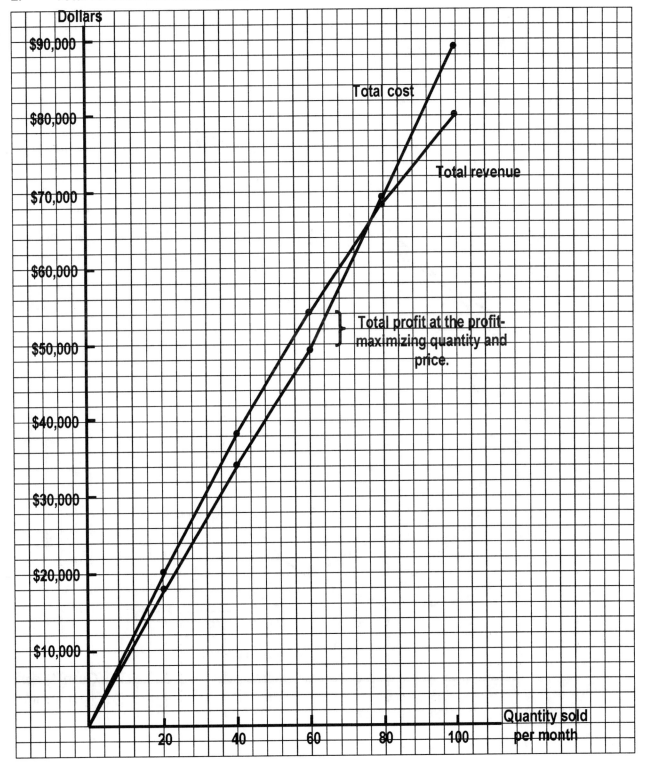

EXERCISE 15-31 (25 MINUTES)

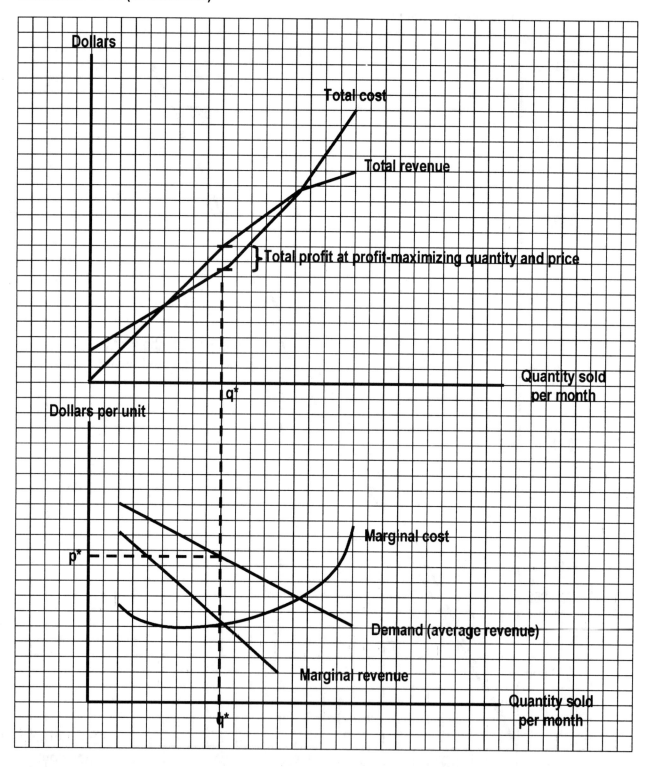

EXERCISE 15-32 (15 MINUTES)

1. Profit on sales of 60,000 units:

Sales revenue (60,000 × 6p)		360,000p
Less: Variable costs:		
Manufacturing and administrative (60,000 × 3p)	180,000p	
Sales commissions (60,000 × 6p × 10%)	36,000p	216,000p
Contribution margin		144,000p
Less: Fixed costs (60,000p + 5,000p)		65,000p
Profit		79,000p

p denotes Argentina's peso

2. Required price on special order:

$$\text{Unit contribution margin required on special order} = \frac{\text{target additional profit}}{\text{unit sales volume in special order}}$$

$$= \frac{20,000p}{10,000} = 2p \text{ per unit}$$

Sales price required   =   unit variable cost + required unit contribution margin

$$= 3p + 2p = 5p \text{ per unit}$$

As an alternative approach, let X denote the price required in order to earn additional profit of 20,000p on the special order:

$$10,000X - 10,000(3p) = 20,000p$$

$$10,000X = 50,000p$$

$$X = 5p \text{ per unit}$$

EXERCISE 15-33 (30 MINUTES)

Answers will vary widely, depending on the company and the product chosen. The answer should include a general discussion of the use of target costing in setting a price for a new product. The target-costing approach includes the following key features: price-led costing; focus on the customer; focus on product design; focus on process design; use of cross-functional teams; analysis of life-cycle costs; and a value-chain orientation. Target costing makes extensive use of value engineering to reduce production costs and bring them into line with the target cost.

EXERCISE 15-34 (30 MINUTES)

$$\text{Markup percentage applied to cost base in cost-plus pricing formula} = \frac{\text{profit required to achieve target ROI} + \text{total annual costs not included in cost base}}{\text{annual volume} \times \text{cost base per unit used in cost-plus pricing formula}}$$

1. Markup percentage

$$= \frac{\$60,000 + \text{total variable selling and administrative costs} + \text{total annual fixed costs}}{480 \times \$400}$$

$$= \frac{\$60,000 + (480 \times \$50) + [480 \times (\$250 + \$100)]}{480 \times \$400}$$

$$= \frac{\$60,000 + \$24,000 + \$168,000}{\$192,000}$$

$$= 131.25\%$$

Thus the Wave Darter's price would be set equal to $925, where
$925 = $400 + ($400 × 131.25%).

EXERCISE 15-34 (CONTINUED)

In the preceding formula:

$60,000 = target profit (given)
    480 = annual volume of Wave Darter production and sales (from Exhibit 15-5)
 $400 = variable manufacturing cost per unit (from Exhibit 15-5)
  $50 = variable selling and administrative cost per unit (from Exhibit 15-5)
 $250 = applied fixed manufacturing cost per unit (from Exhibit 15-5)
 $100 = allocated fixed selling and administrative cost per unit (from Exhibit 15-5)

2.

$$\text{Markup percentage} = \frac{\$60,000 + \begin{array}{c}\text{total selling and}\\ \text{administrative costs}\end{array}}{480 \times \$650^*}$$

$$= \frac{\$60,000 + [480 \times (\$50 + \$100)]}{480 \times \$650}$$

$$= \frac{\$60,000 + \$72,000}{\$312,000}$$

$$= 42.31\% \text{ (rounded)}$$

Thus the Wave Darter's price would be set equal to $925, where
$925 = $650 + ($650 × 42.31%) with rounding.

*$650 = absorption manufacturing cost (from Exhibit 15-5).

The other amounts used in this formula were defined in requirement (1).

EXERCISE 15-35 (30 MINUTES)

1. Price = total unit cost + (markup percentage × total unit cost)

    $450 = total unit cost + (12.5% × total unit cost)

    $450 = total unit cost × 1.125

    Total unit cost = $\dfrac{\$450}{1.125}$ = $400

Allocated fixed selling and administrative cost	=	total unit cost	–	all manufacturing costs	–	variable selling and administrative cost
	=	$400	–	($250 + $50)	–	$60
	=	$40				

				Cost-Plus Pricing Formula
2.	a.	Variable manufacturing cost $250		$450 = $250 + (80% × $250)*
		Applied fixed manufacturing cost .... __50__		
	b.	Absorption manufacturing cost $300		$450 = $300 + (50% × $300)†
		Variable manufacturing cost $250		
		Variable selling and administrative cost .... __60__		
	c.	Total variable cost $310		$450 = $310 + (45.16% × $310)**

*($450 – $250) ÷ $250 = 80%
†($450 – $300) ÷ $300 = 50%
**($450 – $310) ÷ $310 = 45.16% (rounded)

EXERCISE 15-36 (25 MINUTES)

			Cost-Plus Pricing Formula
(1)	Variable manufacturing cost	$200	$400 = $200 + (100% × $200)[a]
	Applied fixed manufacturing cost	70	
(2)	Absorption manufacturing cost	$270	$400 = $270 + (48.15% × $270)[b]
	Variable selling and administrative cost	30	
	Allocated fixed selling and		
	administrative cost	50	
(3)	Total cost	$350	$400 = $350 + (14.29% × $350)[c]
	Variable manufacturing cost	$200	
	Variable selling and administrative cost	30	
(4)	Total variable cost	$230	$400 = $230 + (73.91% × $230)[d]

Explanatory Notes:

[a]($400 – $200) ÷ $200 = 100%
[b]($400 – $270) ÷ $270 = 48.15% (rounded)
[c]($400 – $350) ÷ $350 = 14.29% (rounded)
[d]($400 – $230) ÷ $230 = 73.91% (rounded)

EXERCISE 15-37 (15 MINUTES)

1. Material component of time and material pricing formula:

$$\left[\begin{array}{c} \text{material} \\ \text{cost} \\ \text{incurred} \\ \text{on job} \end{array} + \left(\begin{array}{c} \text{material} \\ \text{cost} \\ \text{incurred} \\ \text{on job} \end{array} \times \frac{\text{material handling and storage costs}}{\text{annual cost of materials used in Repair Department}} \right) \right] \times 1.05$$

2. Material component of price, using formula developed in requirement (1):

[$8,000 + ($8,000 × .04)] × 1.05
    = $8,320 × 1.05
    = $8,736

EXERCISE 15-37 (CONTINUED)

New price to be quoted on yacht refurbishment:

Total price of job = time charges + material charges

$$= \$9,000^* + \$8,736^{**}$$

$$= \$17,736$$

*From Exhibit 15-7.

**From requirement (1).

SOLUTIONS TO PROBLEMS

PROBLEM 15-38 (25 MINUTES)

1. The manufacturing overhead rate is $18.00 per standard direct-labor hour, and the standard product cost includes $9.00 of manufacturing overhead per pressure valve. Accordingly, the standard direct-labor hours per finished valve is 1/2 hour ($9 ÷ $18). Therefore, 30,000 units per month would require 15,000 direct-labor hours.

2. The analysis of accepting the Glasgow Industries' order of 120,000 units is as follows:

	Per Unit	Totals for 120,000 Units
Incremental revenue	$19.00	$2,280,000
Incremental costs:		
Variable costs:		
Direct material	$ 5.00	$ 600,000
Direct labor	6.00	720,000
Variable overhead	3.00	360,000
Total variable costs	$14.00	$1,680,000
Fixed overhead:		
Supervisory and clerical costs		
(4 months @ $12,000)		48,000
Total incremental costs		$1,728,000
Total incremental profit		$ 552,000

The following costs are irrelevant to the analysis:

- Shipping

- Sales commission

- Fixed manufacturing overhead (both traceable and allocated)

PROBLEM 15-38 (CONTINUED)

3. The minimum unit price that Badger Valve and Fitting Company could accept without reducing net income must cover the variable unit cost plus the additional fixed costs.

Variable unit cost:		
Direct material	$ 5.00	
Direct labor	6.00	
Variable overhead	3.00	$14.00
Additional fixed cost ($48,000 ÷ 120,000)		.40
Minimum unit price		$14.40

4. Badger's management should consider the following factors before accepting the Glasgow Industries order:

- The effect of the special order on Badger's sales at regular prices.

- The possibility of future sales to Glasgow Industries and the effects of participating in the international marketplace.

- The company's relevant range of activity and whether or not the special order will cause volume to exceed this range.

- The effect on machinery or the scheduled maintenance of equipment.

- Other possible production orders that could come in and require the capacity allocated to the Glasgow job.

PROBLEM 15-39 (25 MINUTES)

1. $$\text{Direct-labor hours (DLH) required for job} = \frac{1,000,000 \text{ doses to be packaged}}{2,000 \text{ doses/DLH}}$$

$$= 500 \text{ DLH}$$

Traceable out-of-pocket costs:

Direct labor ($8.00 × 500)	$4,000
Variable overhead ($6.00 × 500)	3,000
Administrative cost	1,000
Total traceable out-of-pocket costs	$8,000

$$\text{Minimum price per dose} = \frac{\text{total traceable out-of-pocket costs}}{1,000,000 \text{ doses}}$$

$$= \frac{\$8,000}{1,000,000}$$

$$= \$.008$$

2. As in requirement (1), 500 direct-labor hours are required for the job.

Direct labor ($8.00 × 500)	$4,000
Variable overhead ($6.00 × 500)	3,000
Fixed overhead ($10.00 × 500)	5,000
Administrative cost	1,000
Total cost	$13,000
Maximum allowable return (15%)	1,950
Total bid price	$14,950

$$\text{Bid price per dose} = \frac{\text{total bid price}}{1,000,000 \text{ doses}}$$

$$= \frac{\$14,950}{1,000,000}$$

$$= \$.01495 \text{ per dose}$$

PROBLEM 15-39 (CONTINUED)

3.   Under the supposition that the price computed by North American Pharmaceuticals, Inc. using Wyant's criterion is greater than $.015, the factors that North American's management should consider before deciding whether or not to submit a bid at the maximum allowable price include whether North American has excess capacity, whether there are available jobs on which earnings might be greater, and whether the maximum bid of $.015 contributes toward covering fixed costs.

PROBLEM 15-40 (25 MINUTES)

1.   Target costing is more appropriate. MPE is limited in terms of what price it can charge due to market conditions. A cost-plus-markup approach will use the desired markup for the company; however, the resulting price may too high and not competitive. In such an environment it makes more sense to use target costing, which begins with the price to be charged and works backward to determine the allowable cost.

2.   Target profit = asset investment x rate of return
            = $18,000,000 x 12%
            = $2,160,000

3.   Revenue = target profit + variable cost + fixed cost
            = $2,160,000 + (25,000 hours x $22) + $1,900,000
            = $4,610,000

       Since total revenue must equal $4,610,000, the revenue per hour must be $184.40 ($4,610,000 ÷ 25,000 hours).

4.   Target profit = asset investment x rate of return
            = $18,000,000 x 14%
            = $2,520,000

       Revenue = target profit + variable cost + fixed cost
            = $2,520,000 + (25,000 hours x $22) + $1,900,000
            = $4,970,000

       No. A 14% return requires that MPE generate revenue per service hour of $198.80 ($4,970,000 ÷ 25,000 hours), which is clearly in excess of the $175 market price.

PROBLEM 15-40 (CONTINUED)

5.   To achieve a 14% return and a $175 revenue-per-hour figure, the company must trim
     its costs. MPE could use value engineering, a technique that utilizes information
     collected about a service's design and associated production process. The goal is
     to examine the design and process and then identify improvements that would
     produce cost savings.

PROBLEM 15-41 (30 MINUTES)

1.   Cost-plus pricing begins by computing an item's cost and then adds an appropriate
     markup. The result is the item's selling price. In contrast, target costing begins by
     determining an appropriate selling price. A target profit is next subtracted from that
     price to yield the cost (i.e., the "target cost") that must be achieved.

     Target costing could be labeled price-led costing because it begins by
     determining a target selling price. In contrast, cost-plus pricing methods begin with
     the cost and culminate in determination of the selling price.

2.   The current selling price is $225:

Direct material..	$ 30
Direct labor...	75
Manufacturing overhead...........................	50
Selling and administrative expenses....	25
Total cost..	$180
Markup ($180 x 25%).............................	45
Selling price..	$225

3.   Leno's markup is $45, which is 20% of the current $225 selling price ($45 ÷ $225). To
     achieve a 20% markup on a $195 selling price, the company must reduce its costs by
     $24.

Selling price..	$195
Less: 20% markup ($195 x 20%)..........	39
Target cost..	$156
Current cost...	$180
Less: Target cost.................................	156
Required cost reduction......................	$ 24

PROBLEM 15-41 (CONTINUED)

4. Yes. The company should focus its efforts on trimming non-value-added costs. These costs are associated with non-value-added activities (i.e., activities that are either (a) unnecessary and dispensable or (b) necessary, but inefficient and improvable).

5. If costs cannot be reduced below $180, Leno will have to reduce its markup to remain competitive. Assuming a desire to achieve the going market price of $195, the markup must equal $15 ($195 - $180), or 8.33 % of cost ($15 ÷ $180). Given that the current markup on cost is 25%, a reduction of 16.67% is needed (25.00% - 8.33%).

6. The statement means that selling prices are a function of market conditions; however, the selling prices must cover a company's costs in the long run. Also, in a number of industries, prices are based on costs. Yet, the prices are subject to the reaction of customers and competitors.

PROBLEM 15-42 (35 MINUTES)

1. Target costing is market driven, beginning with a determination of the selling price that customers are willing to pay. That price is dependent on the product they purchase and the product's features. It is only natural that a marketing team becomes heavily involved in this process, since customer feedback is crucial to the design process.

2. Add cabinet doors: [(10 x 1) + (20 x 2) + (30 x 3) + (60 x 4) + (80 x 5)] = 780; 780 ÷ 200 = 3.900

    Expand storage area: [(10 x 1) + (40 x 2) + (70 x 3) + (50 x 4) + (30 x 5)] = 650; 650 ÷ 200 = 3.250

    Add security lock: [(30 x 1) + (60 x 2) + (50 x 3) + (40 x 4) + (20 x 5)] = 560; 560 ÷ 200 = 2.800

    New appearance for table top: [(10 x 1) + (20 x 2) + (50 x 3) + (60 x 4) + (60 x 5)] = 740; 740 ÷ 200 = 3.700

    Extend warranty: [(40 x 1) + (70 x 2) + (30 x 3) + (35 x 4) + (25 x 5)] = 535; 535 ÷ 200 = 2.675

PROBLEM 15-42 (CONTINUED)

Ranking (from strongest to weakest):
1—Add cabinet doors (3.900)
2—New appearance for table top (3.700)
3—Expand storage area (3.250)
4—Add security lock (2.800)
5—Extend warranty (2.675)

3.　(a)　DF currently earns a $16 profit on each table sold ($80 - $64), which translates into a 20% markup on sales ($16 ÷ $80). The current competitive market price is $95, which means that if DF maintains the 20% markup, it will earn $19 ($95 x 20%) per unit. The maximum allowable cost is therefore $76 ($95 - $19).

　　(b)　Customers feel most strongly about adding cabinet doors and giving the table top a new appearance. Both of these features can be added, and DF will be able to earn its 20% markup. The third and fifth most desirable features (the expanded storage area and extended warranty) are too costly. If it desires, DF could also add a lock to the storage area. (Calculations follow.)

Maximum allowable cost...............	$76.00
Less: Current cost........................	64.00
Cost of additional features............	$12.00
1—Add cabinet doors...................	$ 6.00
2—New appearance for table top...	4.25
Subtotal................................	$10.25
4—Add security lock...................	1.65
Total...................................	$11.90

4.　An expanded storage area would be the most logical additional feature in view of its no. 3 ranking. DF might use value engineering to study the design and production process of both the table as currently manufactured as well as the proposed new features. The goal is to identify improvements and associated reductions in cost that may allow the company to add previously rejected options.

PROBLEM 15-43 (45 MINUTES)

1. The order will boost Graydon's net income by $27,900, as the following calculations show.

Sales revenue...	$165,000	
Less: Sales commissions (10%)	16,500	$148,500
Less manufacturing costs:		
Direct material..	$ 29,200	
Direct labor..	56,000	
Variable manufacturing overhead*	16,800	
Total manufacturing costs		102,000
Income before taxes		$ 46,500
Income taxes (40%)...		18,600
Net income		$ 27,900

*Based on an analysis of the year just ended, variable overhead is 30 percent of direct labor ($2,250 ÷ $7,500). For Premier's Foods' order:

Direct-labor cost x .30 = $56,000 x .30 = $16,800.

2. Yes. Although this amount is below the $165,000 full-cost price, the order is still profitable. Graydon can afford to pick up some additional business, because the company is operating at 75 percent of practical capacity.

Sales revenue...	$127,000	
Less: Sales commissions (10%)	12,700	$114,300
Less manufacturing costs:		
Direct material..	$ 29,200	
Direct labor..	56,000	
Variable manufacturing overhead..................	16,800	
Total manufacturing costs		102,000
Income before taxes		$ 12,300
Income taxes (40%)...		4,920
Net income		$ 7,380

Note that the fixed manufacturing overhead and fixed corporate administration costs are not relevant in this decision, because these amounts will remain the same regardless of what Graydon's management decides about the order.

PROBLEM 15-43 (CONTINUED)

3.   The break-even price is $113,333, computed as follows:

Let P = break-even bid price

$P - 0.1P - \$102,000 = 0$

$0.9P = \$102,000$

$P = \$113,333$

Income taxes can be ignored, because there is no tax at the break-even point.

4.   Profits will probably decline. Graydon originally used a full-cost pricing formula to derive a $165,000 bid price. A drop in the selling price to $127,000 signifies that the firm is now pricing its orders at less than full cost, which would decrease profitability.

Reduced prices could lead to an increase in income if the company is able to generate additional volume. This situation will not occur here, because the problem states that Graydon has operated and will continue to operate at 75 percent of practical capacity.

PROBLEM 15-44 (40 MINUTES)

1.   *Target costing* is the design of a product, and the processes used to produce it, so that ultimately the product can be manufactured at a cost that will enable a firm to make a profit when the product is sold at an estimated market-driven price. This estimated price is called the *target price,* the desired profit margin is called the *target profit,* and the cost at which the product must be manufactured is called the *target cost.*

2.   *Value engineering (or value analysis)* refers to a cost-reduction and process improvement technique that utilizes information collected about a product's design and production processes and then examines various attributes of the design and processes to identify candidates for improvement efforts.

      Value engineering focuses on improving those qualities that the customer desires, while reducing or eliminating unnecessary moves, queues, setups, and other such activities that the customer will not pay for. The process is reengineered to eliminate non-value-added work and thereby enhance the value of the process to the customer.

3. Pharsalia Electronics' current profit on sales is 10 percent [($350–$315)/$350]. Therefore, the target cost for the new product must be $300 less 10 percent, or $270 [$300 – ($300 × 10%)].

4. The proposed changes to the just-in-time cell manufacturing process at Pharsalia Electronics will bring costs down to $266 per unit, which is below the $270 target cost limit. Adjusted costs under the JIT cell manufacturing process are calculated as follows:

	Current	Increase/ (Decrease)	Revised
Material:			
Purchased components	$110		$110
All other	40		40
Labor:			
Manufacturing, direct	65	$ 15	80
Setups	9	(9)	0
Material handling	18	(18)	0
Inspection	23	(23)	0
Machining:			
All	35	(5)	30
Other:			
Finished-goods warehousing	5	(5)	0
Warranty*	10	(4)	6
Total JIT Cost	$315	$(49)	$266

*40% reduction

PROBLEM 15-45 (30 MINUTES)

1. (a) Time charges:

$$\text{Hourly labor cost} + \frac{\text{annual overhead (excluding material handling and storage)}}{\text{annual labor hours}} + \frac{\text{hourly charge to}}{\text{cover profit magin}}$$

$$= \$16 + \frac{\$108,000}{12,000} + \$4$$

$$= \$29 \text{ per labor hour}$$

(b) Material charges:

$$\frac{\text{Material cost}}{\text{incurred on job}} + \left(\frac{\text{material cost}}{\text{incurred on job}} \times \frac{\text{material handling and storage costs}}{\text{annual cost of materials used}} \right)$$

$$= \frac{\text{Material cost}}{\text{incurred on job}} + \left(\frac{\text{material cost}}{\text{incurred on job}} \times \frac{\$25,000}{\$250,000} \right)$$

2.   PRICE QUOTATION

Time charges:	Labor time	400	hours
	× Rate	× $29	per hour
	Total	$11,600	
Material changes:	Cost of materials for job	$60,000	
	+ Charge for material handling and storage ...	6,000*	
	Total	$66,000	
Total price of job:	Time	$11,600	
	Material	66,000	
	Total	$77,600	

*Charge for material handling and storage):
        10% = $25,000 ÷ $250,000; 10% × $60,000 = $6,000

PROBLEM 15-45 (CONTINUED)

3.	Price of job without markup on material costs (from requirement 2)	$77,600
	Markup on total material costs ($66,000 × 10%)	6,600
	Total price of job	$84,200

PROBLEM 15-46 (50 MINUTES)

1. Gargantuan Industries should price the standard compound at $22 per case and the commercial compound at $30 per case. The contribution margin is the highest at these prices as shown in the following calculations:

Standard Compound					
Selling price per case	$ 18	$ 20	$ 21	$ 22	$ 23
Variable cost per case	16	16	16	16	16
Contribution margin per case	$ 2	$ 4	$ 5	$ 6	$ 7
Volume in cases (in thousands)	×120	×100	× 90	× 80	× 50
Total contribution margin (in thousands)	$240	$400	$450	$480	$350

Commercial Compound					
Selling price per case	$ 25	$ 27	$ 30	$ 32	$ 35
Variable cost per case	21	21	21	21	21
Contribution margin per case	$ 4	$ 6	$ 9	$ 11	$ 14
Volume in cases (in thousands)	×175	×140	×100	× 55	× 35
Total contribution margin (in thousands)	$700	$840	$900	$605	$490

PROBLEM 15-46 (CONTINUED)

2. a. Gargantuan Industries should continue to operate during the final six months of the current year because any shutdown would be temporary. The company intends to remain in the business and expects a profitable operation during the next year. This is a short-run decision problem. Therefore, the fixed costs are irrelevant to the decision, because they cannot be avoided in the short run. The products do have a positive contribution margin so operations should continue.

GARGANTUAN INDUSTRIES
BOISE PLANT
PROJECTED CONTRIBUTION MARGIN
FOR THE SIX-MONTH PERIOD ENDING DECEMBER 31
(IN THOUSANDS)

	Standard	Commercial	Total
Sales	$1,150	$1,225	$2,375
Variable costs:			
Selling and administrative	$ 200	$ 245	$ 445
Manufacturing	600	490	1,090
Total variable costs	$ 800	$ 735	$1,535
Contribution margin	$ 350	$ 490	$ 840

b. Gargantuan Industries should consider the following qualitative factors when making the decision about the Boise Plant.

- The effect on employee morale.

- The effect on market share.

- The disruption of production and sales due to a shutdown.

- The effect on the local community.

PROBLEM 15-47 (30 MINUTES)

1. The minimum price per blanket that Omaha Synthetic Fibers, Inc. could bid without reducing the company's net income is $24 calculated as follows:

Raw material (6 lbs. @ $1.50 per lb.)	$ 9.00
Direct labor (.25 hrs. @ $7.00 per hr.)	1.75
Machine time ($10.00 per blanket)	10.00
Variable overhead (.25 hrs. @ $3.00 per hr.)	.75
Administrative costs ($2,500 ÷ 1,000)	2.50
Minimum bid price	$24.00

2. Using the full cost criteria and the maximum allowable return specified, Omaha Synthetic Fibers, Inc.'s bid price per blanket would be $29.90 calculated as follows:

Relevant costs from requirement (1)	$24.00
Fixed overhead (.25 hrs. @ $8.00 per hr.)	2.00
Subtotal	$26.00
Allowable return (.15 × $26)	3.90
Bid price	$29.90

3. Factors that management should consider before deciding whether to submit a bid at the maximum acceptable price of $25 per blanket include the following:

• The company should be sure there is sufficient excess capacity to fill the order and that no additional investment is necessary in facilities or equipment that would increase fixed costs.

• If the order is accepted at $25 per blanket, there will be a $1 contribution per blanket to fixed costs. However, the company should consider whether there are other jobs that would make a greater contribution.

• Acceptance of the order at a low price could cause problems with current customers who might demand a similar pricing arrangement.

© *2002 The McGraw-Hill Companies, Inc.*

Solutions Manual

PROBLEM 15-48 (50 MINUTES)

1. Budgeted overhead costs:

	Department I	Department II
Variable overhead		
Department I: 37,500 × $8	$300,000	
Department II: 37,500 × $4		$150,000
Fixed overhead	150,000	150,000
Total overhead	$450,000	$300,000
Total budgeted overhead for both		
departments ($450,000 + $300,000)		$750,000
Total expected direct-labor hours for		
both departments (37,500 + 37,500)		75,000

$$\text{Predetermined overhead rate} = \frac{\text{budgeted overhead}}{\text{budgeted direct-labor hours}}$$

$$= \frac{\$750,000}{75,000}$$

$$= \$10 \text{ per direct-labor hour}$$

2.

	Basic	Advanced
Total cost	$400	$500
Markup (15% of cost)		
Basic: $400 × .15	60	
Advanced: $500 × .15		75
Price	$460	$575

3.

	Department I	Department II
Budgeted overhead (from requirement 1)......................	$450,000	$300,000
Budgeted direct-labor hours	37,500	37,500
Calculation of predetermined overhead rate	$450,000	$300,000
	37,500	37,500
Predetermined overhead rate	$12	$8

4.

	Basic	Advanced
Direct material	$160	$260
Direct labor	140	140
Manufacturing overhead:		
Department I:		
Basic: 2 × $12	24	
Advanced: 8 × $12		96
Department II:		
Basic: 8 × $8	64	
Advanced: 2 × $8		16
Total cost	$388	$512

5.

	Basic	Advanced
Total cost (from requirement 4)	$388.00	$512.00
Markup (15% of cost)		
Basic: $388 × .15	58.20	
Advanced: $512 × .15		76.80
Price	$446.20	$588.80

6. The management of Sounds Fine, Inc. should use departmental overhead rates. The overhead cost structures in the two production departments are quite different, and departmental rates more accurately assign overhead costs to products. When the company used a plantwide overhead rate, the Basic speakers were overcosted and the Advanced speakers were undercosted. This in turn resulted in the Basic model being overpriced and the Advanced model being underpriced. The cost and price distortion resulted from the following facts: (1) the Basic speakers spend most of their production time in Department II, which is the least costly of the two departments; and (2) the Advanced speakers spend most of their production time in Department I, which is more costly than Department II.

PROBLEM 15-49 (40 MINUTES)

1. Bid based on standard pricing policy:

Direct material	$256,000
Direct labor (11,000 DLH @ $15)	165,000
Manufacturing overhead (11,000 DLH @ $9)	99,000
Full manufacturing costs	$520,000
Markup (50% of full cost)	260,000
Standard pricing policy bid	$780,000

2. Minimum bid acceptable to Zylar:

Direct material	$256,000
Direct labor (11,000 DLH @ $15)	165,000
Variable manufacturing overhead (11,000 @ $5.40[a])	59,400
Opportunity cost of lost sales[b]	35,200
Minimum bid	$515,600

[a]Proportion of variable overhead $= \dfrac{\text{budgeted variable overhead}}{\text{budgeted total overhead}}$

$$= \frac{\$972,000}{\$1,620,000}$$

$$= 60\%$$

Variable overhead rate $= \left(\begin{array}{c} \text{total overhead} \\ \text{rate} \end{array} \right) \times \left(\begin{array}{c} \text{variable} \\ \text{overhead proportion} \end{array} \right)$

$$= (\$9.00) \times (.6)$$

$$= \$5.40$$

[b]Selling price per unit of standard product		$12,000
Variable costs per unit		
Direct material	$2,500	
Direct labor (250 DLH @ $15)	3,750	
Variable overhead (250 DLH @ $5.40)	1,350	7,600
Net contribution per unit		$ 4,400
Standard product requirements (12,000 DLH × 3)	36,000 DLH	
Special order requirements	11,000 DLH	
Total hours required	47,000 DLH	
Plant capacity per quarter (15,000 DLH × 3)	45,000 DLH	
Shortage in hours	2,000 DLH	
Lost unit sales (2,000 DLH ÷ 250 DLH)		× 8
Lost contribution		$35,200

Lyan Company's assistant purchasing manager is not acting ethically. The details of the bid submitted by Zylar Industries are confidential between Zylar Industries and Lyan Company. It is unfair and unethical to give this information to Zylar's competitor. If Lyan Company had wanted competing bids on the specialized equipment, the bids should have been solicited at the same time from the relevant set of manufacturers. Each competing firm should receive the same specifications on the customized equipment and be given the same time frame in which to complete the bid. Moreover, the competing firms should be made aware that more than one bid is being solicited.

PROBLEM 15-50 (50 MINUTES)

1. The lowest price Biloxi Corporation would bid for a one-time special order of 25,000 pounds (25 lots) would be $34,750, which is equal to the variable costs of the order calculated as follows:

    (a) Direct material:

    On a one-time only special order, chemicals used in manufacturing the firm's main product have a relevant cost of their expected future cost, represented by the current market price per pound. Chemicals not used in current production have a relevant cost of their value to the firm.

    *   RH-3: (400 pounds per lot) × (25 lots) = 10,000 pounds.

Substitute CN-5 on a one-for-one basis to its total of 5,500 pounds. The relevant cost is the salvage value.	$ 500
The remaining 4,500 pounds would be RH-3 at a relevant cost of $.90 per pound, its expected future cost.	4,050

    *   JX-6: (300 pounds per lot) × (25 lots) = 7,500 pounds at

$.60 per pound.	4,500

    *   MZ-8: (200 pounds per lot) × (25 lots) = 5,000 pounds at

$1.60 per pound.	8,000

    *   BE-7: (100 pounds per lot) × (25 lots) = 2,500 pounds.

The relevant cost per pound is $.65 – $.10 (handling charge) = $.55. The amount the company could realize by selling BE-7. is 2,500 pounds at $.55 per pound	1,375
Total direct material cost	$18,425

PROBLEM 15-50 (CONTINUED)

(b) Direct labor:

(60 DLH per lot) × (25 lots) = 1,500 direct-labor hours (DLH)

Because only 800 hours can be scheduled during regular time this month, overtime would have to be used for the remaining 700 hours; therefore, overtime is a relevant cost of this order.

(1,500 DLH) × ($7.00 per DLH)	$10,500
(700 DLH) × ($3.50 per DLH)	2,450
Total direct-labor cost	$12,950

(c) Overhead:

This special order will not increase fixed overhead costs. Therefore, fixed overhead is not relevant, and the relevant overhead charge is the variable overhead rate:

(1,500 DLH) × ($2.25 per DLH) = ...	3,375
Total cost of special order	$34,750*

*$34,750 = $18,425 + $12,950 + $3,375

2.   Calculation of the price for recurring orders of 25,000 pounds (25 lots) is as follows.

(a) Direct material:

Because of the possibility of future orders, raw materials must all be charged at their expected future cost represented by the current market price per pound.

• RH-3: (10,000 pounds) × ($.90 per pound)	$ 9,000
• JX-6: (7,500 pounds) × ($.60 per pound)	4,500
• MZ-8: (5,000 pounds) × ($1.60 per pound)	8,000
• BE-7: (2,500 pounds) × ($.65 per pound)	1,625
Total direct-material cost	$23,125

© 2002 The McGraw-Hill Companies, Inc.

Solutions Manual

PROBLEM 15-50 (CONTINUED)

(b) Direct labor:

60% of the production of a batch (900 DLH) can be done on regular time; the remaining 600 DLH cause overtime to be incurred and are a relevant cost of this new product.

Regular time	
(1,500 DLH) × ($7.00 per DLH)	$10,500
Overtime premium	
(600 DLH) × ($3.50 per DLH)	2,100
Total direct-labor cost	$12,600

(c) Overhead:

All new products should contribute to fixed overhead as well as cover all variable costs and provide a markup. Therefore, the overhead charge would be:

(1,500 DLH) × ($6.00 per DLH)	$9,000

(d) Markup and price calculation:

Full manufacturing cost	$44,725 *
Markup (25%)	11,181 †
Full manufacturing cost plus 25% markup	$55,906

*$44,725 = $23,125 + $12,600 + $9,000

†Rounded.

3. The owner of Taylor Nursery is not acting ethically in this situation. It is inappropriate to allow Biloxi Corporation to revise its bid on the basis of confidential information included in the details of the Dalton Industries bid. All firms competing for the Taylor Nursery contract should be given the same product specifications, information, and time frame with which to prepare a bid.

SOLUTIONS TO CASES

CASE 15-51 (45 MINUTES)

1. The total sales price can be determined by the following formula:

Let S = $IC + T + NIAT$

Where S = total price

IC = incremental cost

T = taxes

T = $(S - IC)t$

t = tax rate

$NIAT$ = net income after taxes

$NIAT$ = $S \times$ desired return on total price

Substituting for the known items, the formula is revised to read:

$$S = IC + (S - IC).4 + .10S$$

The incremental costs for the three-year order are calculated as shown in the following schedule.

CASE 15-51 (CONTINUED)

Cost Item	Current Amounts (in thousands)	Contract Increase	Inflation Rate	Years	Details of Calculations	Amount (in thousands)
Direct material	$200	10%	5%	3	(200 × .10 × 1.05 × 3)	$ 63.0
Direct labor	400	10%	10%	3	(400 × .10 × 1.10 × 3)	132.0
Indirect labor	100	—	—	—	—	—
Supplies	40	10%	10%	3	(40 × .10 × 1.10 × 3)	13.2
Additional supplies	—	$4	10%	3	(4 × 1.10 × 3)	13.2
Power	120	10%	20%	3	(120 × .10 ×1.20 × 3)	43.2
Additional power	—	$10	20%	3	(10 × 1.20 × 3)	36.0
Factory administration	60	$15*	10%	3	(15 × 1.10 × 3)	49.5
Depreciation	70	—	—	—	—	—†
Sales commission	—	$10	—	—	—	10.0
Total incremental costs						$360.1

*The current amount of factory administration, $60,000, will be unchanged, but an additional part-time factory supervisor will be hired at an annual cost of $15,000.

†The company has idle capacity that will be fully utilized by this order. The capacity costs (i.e., depreciation) would be expensed whether management accepted the order or not. Therefore, the depreciation is a sunk cost and is not considered an incremental cost of the order.

CASE 15-51 (CONTINUED)

The total price needed by Polaski for the three-year order is $432,120 as shown in the calculations below:

$$S = IC + (S - IC).4 + .10S$$

$$S = \$360,100 + (S - \$360,100).4 + .10S$$

$$S = \$360,100 + .4S - \$144,040 + .10S$$

$$.5S = \$216,060$$

$$S = \$432,120$$

2. If the three-year order is to contribute nothing to net income after taxes, Polaski would set the total price at $360,100, an amount equal to the incremental costs to produce the order.

CASE 15-52 (60 MINUTES)

Memorandum

Date: Today

To: President, CPI

From: I.M. Student

Subject: Convention fee

CPI can maximize its contribution from its annual convention by charging a single, flat fee of $300. Using this fee structure, CPI's contribution will be $400,925 as shown by the detailed calculations for the separate pricing option and the three single, flat fee options that follow.

Pricing Option	Contribution
Separate pricing	$374,200
Flat fee options:	
$325	400,100
300	400,925
275	387,550

CASE 15-52 (CONTINUED)

(a) Contribution analysis for separate pricing
(estimated hotel registrations = 60% × 2,000 = 1,200):

Function	Estimated Attendance	Revenue	Expense	Contri- bution
Registration	100% × 2,000 = 2,000	$100,000	$ -0-	$100,000
Reception	100% × 2,000 = 2,000	-0-	50,000	(50,000)
Annual meeting*	100% × 2,000 = 2,000	-0-	-0-*	-0-
Keynote luncheon	90% × 2,000 = 1,800	72,000	45,000	27,000
Six concurrent sessions* ..	70% × 2,000 = 1,400	84,000	-0-*	84,000
Plenary session*	70% × 2,000 = 1,400	70,000	-0-*	70,000
Six workshops	50% × 2,000 = 1,000	100,000	-0-*	100,000
Banquet	90% × 2,000 = 1,800	90,000	54,000	36,000
Hotel credit for free rooms $\left(\dfrac{1,200}{50} \times \$125 \times .8^\dagger \times 3 \right)$			(7,200)	7,200
Total		$516,000	$141,800	$374,200

*Meeting rooms and halls are free when 1,000 members are expected to register at the hotel.

†Reflects 20% discount.

CASE 15-52 (CONTINUED)

(b) Contribution analysis for flat fee pricing.

	$325 Fee	$300 Fee	$275 Fee
Number of attendees (given)	1,600	1,750	1,900
Estimated hotel registrations (60%)	960	1,050	1,140
Number of free rooms (registration divided by 50, with no fractional credit)	19	21	22
Revenue (fee × attendees)	$520,000	$525,000	$522,500
Expenses			
Reception ($25 × 100% × attendees)	$ 40,000	$ 43,750	$ 47,500
Annual meeting*	2,000	-0-	-0-
Keynote luncheon ($25 × 90% × attendees)	36,000	39,375	42,750
Six concurrent sessions*	1,200	-0-	-0-
Plenary session*	2,000	-0-	-0-
Six workshops	1,200	-0-	-0-
Banquet ($30 × 90% × attendees)	43,200	47,250	51,300
Total expenses	$125,600	$130,375	$141,550
Revenue less expenses	$394,400	$394,625	$380,950
Room credit ($300† × free rooms)	5,700	6,300	6,600
Contribution	$400,100	$400,925	$387,550

*Meeting rooms and halls are free when 1,000 members are expected to register at the hotel.
†Reflects 20% discount.

CURRENT ISSUES IN MANAGERIAL ACCOUNTING

ISSUE 15-53

"HIGH FUEL PRICES MAY HURT STORES, NOT CONSUMERS," *THE WALL STREET JOURNAL*, SEPTEMBER 28, 2000, DANIEL MACHALABA AND REBECCA QUICK.

1. Retailers will absorb increased shipping costs instead of passing them along to customers for the holiday season discussed in this article. The highly competitive nature of the season determines that the cost of retail goods will be determined by market-based pricing.

2. Cost-based pricing is when sellers determine their costs and add a profit margin. Market-based pricing is when a competitive price is determined at which the product will sell. As mentioned above, market-based pricing is likely to prevail in this scenario.

ISSUE 15-54

"CAR MAKERS MAY TRY TO ALTER PRICING PRACTICES," *THE WALL STREET JOURNAL*, JANUARY 24, 2000, JOSEPH B. WHITE AND FARA WARNER.

U. S. auto dealers are changing their pricing policies as a result of the surge in online auto trading by adjusting their online prices on a daily basis. A growing number of dealers already are abandoning the practice of negotiating down from an MSRP, as more consumers come to showrooms armed with invoice price information downloaded from the internet.

ISSUE 15-55

"AUTO MAKERS BOOST CHARGES FOR SHIPPING NEW CARS BECAUSE OF HIGHER FUEL COSTS," THE WALL STREET JOURNAL, OCTOBER 25, 2000, SHOINN FREEMAN.

1. The issue involved in the decision to pass on to consumers the higher prices of fuel costs are increased pressure on profit margins as real prices for new cars actually decline.

2. As all auto makers feel the decline in profits, cost-based pricing takes priority across the industry. Without profits the auto industry cannot stay in business, and therefore all makers have to raise prices. The auto makers do not have to compete against each other on an unbalanced price-competitive field.

ISSUE 15-56

"VOLKSWAGEN AG PLANS ONLINE SUPPLY MARKET IN MOVE TO CUT COSTS," THE WALL STREET JOURNAL, APRIL 13, 2000.

In a competitive bidding situation, two or more companies submit sealed bids for a product, service, or project to a buyer. The buyer selects one of the companies for the job on the basis of the bid price and the design specifications for the job. Volkswagen hopes to take the lead in establishing a European Internet-supply network. Although the supply network could result in competitive bidding, its focus will be on the efficiency of the supply chain.

ISSUE 15-57

"CHANGING CODE: FOR POLICY MAKERS, MICROSOFT SUGGESTS NEED TO RECAST MODELS - AGENCIES SCRAMBLE AS WEB POSES GOOD MONOPOLIES, SKEWS CLASSIC ECONOMICS - AVALANCHE VS. THERMOSTAT, " THE WALL STREET JOURNAL, JUNE 9, 2000, ALAN MURRAY.

1. Several car manufacturers recently joined together to form a single linked exchange that big auto companies will use for purchasing parts. The combined purchasing platform is being done so the auto industry can have standards. The end result will be more competition.

2. In information businesses, the desire for everyone to be part of the same network is intense. This is the network effect.

ISSUE 15-58

"TARGET COSTING CAN BOOST YOUR BOTTOM LINE, " *STRATEGIC FINANCE*, JULY 1999, GERMAIN BOER AND JOHN ETTLIE.

Using the bottom-up approach engineers can add the estimated prices of purchased components and estimated production costs for each part that goes into a new product. Databases containing current component purchase prices, product routings, and bills of material for existing parts enable design engineers to estimate the cost of new parts. Another approach is to deduct the desired margin for a product from the predicted selling price. This approach is consistent with the Japanese concept of price-down, cost-down, which says production costs must decline as the price of a product declines. In other words, the market determines the acceptable cost for a product.

ISSUE 15-59

"MACHINE CIGARETTE VENDORS SUE PHILIP MORRIS ON PRICES," *THE WALL STREET JOURNAL*, FEBRUARY 4, 1999.

Price discrimination is when a vendor sells their products at different prices to various buyers, usually using such techniques as merchant rebates, buybacks and other promotional fees. Whether the case in question constitutes price discrimination will be determined by the courts.

ISSUE 15-60

"HOW SHOULD WE PRICE OUR PRODUCTS? " *CONVERTING*, AUGUST 2000, SKIP HEINTZELMAN.

The article discusses several methods of pricing products, including full-cost coverage, marking up material cost, marking up full factory cost, and marking up conversion cost.

According to the article, marking up material costs to price products will tend to encourage jobs using low-priced materials and penalize products requiring higher-priced materials.

CHAPTER 16
Capital Expenditure Decisions: An Introduction

ANSWERS TO REVIEW QUESTIONS

16-1 "Time is money" is an apt phrase for the evaluation of capital investment projects. A cash flow today is not economically equivalent to a cash flow in the future. Since cash received now can be invested for some rate of return, a dollar received now is more valuable than a dollar received in the future.

16-2 Acceptance-or-rejection decisions involve managers deciding whether they should undertake a particular capital investment project. In such a decision, the required funds are available or readily obtainable, and management must decide whether the project is worthwhile. In capital-rationing decisions, managers must decide which of several worthwhile projects makes the best use of limited investment funds.

16-3 Compound interest is interest earned not only on the principal invested but also on the interest earned in previous periods.

16-4 This formula says that the future value, F_n, is equal to the present value, P, multiplied by an accumulation factor equal to $(1 + r)^n$. The accumulation factor is included in the formula to reflect compound interest. (In the formula, r denotes the interest rate per year, and n denotes the number of years.)

16-5 The present value is the economic value now of a cash flow that will occur in the future.

16-6 This statement is false. As the discount rate increases, the present value of a future cash flow decreases. A higher discount rate means a higher return on funds that are invested now. If funds invested now can earn a greater return, it is even more important to have the funds now, instead of in the future, than it is if the rate of return is lower. Therefore, the greater the discount rate, or rate of return on invested funds, the lower will be the present value of any future cash flow.

16-7 These two cash flows are economically equivalent in the sense that a $100 cash flow now will be equal to a $161.10 cash flow at the end of five years. If the $100 received now is invested for five years at 10%, it will accumulate to $161.10 at the end of five years.

16-8 An annuity is a series of equally spaced, identical cash flows. For example, a five-year, $100 annuity is a series of $100 cash flows occurring at the end of each year for five years.

16-9   In a discounted-cash-flow (DCF) analysis, all cash flows over the life of an investment are discounted to their present value. The discounting process makes cash flows occurring at different points in time comparable in an economic sense. The two common methods of discounted-cash-flow analysis are the net-present-value method and the internal-rate-of-return method.

16-10   The four steps in using the net-present-value method are as follows:

   (1) Prepare a table showing the cash flows during each year of the proposed investment.

   (2) Compute the present value of each cash flow, using a discount rate called the hurdle rate or minimum desired rate of return.

   (3) Compute the net present value, which is the sum of the present values of the cash flows.

   (4) If the net present value (NPV) is positive, accept the investment proposal. Otherwise, reject it.

16-11   The internal rate of return on an investment is the discount rate that would be necessary to make the investment's net present value equal to zero.

16-12   (1) The decision rule used to accept or reject an investment proposal under the net-present-value method is stated as follows: Accept the proposal if the net present value is positive.

   (2) The decision rule used to accept or reject an investment proposal under the internal-rate-of-return method is as follows: Accept the investment proposal if its internal rate of return is greater than the hurdle rate.

16-13   The return on an investment is equal to the amount of the unrecovered investment multiplied by rate of return. The cash flow from the investment in a particular time period may be greater than the return on the investment. The excess of the cash flow over and above the return on the investment is called the recovery of the investment. This phenomenon reflects the fact that investments are undertaken in order to earn a return. Part of the cash flow from the investment each period provides that return, and part of the cash flow from the investment provides a partial recovery of the initial investment.

16-14   Two advantages of the net-present-value method over the internal-rate-of-return method are as follows:

   (1) If the investment analysis is done by hand, it is easier to compute a project's NPV than its IRR.

(2) Under the NPV method, the analyst can adjust for risk. This risk adjustment can be done by using a higher discount rate for later or more uncertain cash flows than for earlier or less uncertain cash flows.

16-15 Four assumptions underlying discounted-cash-flow analysis are as follows:

(1) In the present-value calculations, all cash flows are treated as though they occur at year end.

(2) Discounted-cash-flow analyses treat the cash flows associated with an investment project as though they were known with certainty.

(3) Both the NPV and IRR methods assume that each cash inflow is immediately reinvested in another project that earns a return for the organization. In the NPV method, each cash inflow is assumed to be reinvested at the same rate used to compute the project's NPV. In the IRR method, each cash inflow is assumed to be reinvested at the same rate as the project's internal rate of return.

(4) A discounted-cash-flow analysis assumes a perfect capital market. In a perfect capital market money can be borrowed or lent at an interest rate equal to the cost of capital (or hurdle rate) used in the analysis.

16-16 In a least-cost decision, the objective is to choose the project with the lowest present value of costs.

16-17 In the total cost approach, every cash flow for each project under consideration is included at its total amount. In the incremental cost approach, differences are calculated for each cash flow between the projects under consideration, and the net present value of these incremental amounts becomes the focus of the analysis.

16-18 Two techniques are used to analyze investment proposals for which the cash flow projections are very uncertain. First, the hurdle rate may be increased. The greater the uncertainty about a project's cash flows, the higher the hurdle rate. Second, the analyst may use sensitivity analysis. Under this approach, the analyst determines how much projections would have to change in order for a different decision to be indicated.

16-19 In a postaudit of an investment project, information is gathered about the actual cash flows generated by the project. Then the project's actual net present value or internal rate of return is computed. Finally, the projections made for the project are compared with the actual results.

16-20 An organization can be viewed as a collection of investment projects. The organization's performance in a particular time period comprises the combined results of several projects' performance during that period. The optimal method of evaluating individual projects is the discounted-cash-flow approach. However, the criterion used to evaluate an organization's overall performance in a particular period of time is the total income from all of the projects during that particular period. Under accrual accounting, the revenues and expenses associated with a particular time period, for the entire enterprise, may not reflect the timing of the cash flows and the associated present values for individual projects. For example, a project may have a positive net present value because of high cash inflows projected for the later years of the project's life. However, under accrual accounting, the income associated with the project in its early years may be very low, and the performance of the project may appear unfavorable. This potential conflict may result in a disincentive to invest in the project, even though its net present value is positive.

16-21 Several difficulties that are often encountered in justifying an investment in advanced manufacturing technology are as follows:

(1) High hurdle rates

(2) Short time horizons

(3) Bias toward incremental projects

(4) Greater uncertainty about operating cash flows

(5) Exclusion of benefits that are difficult to quantify

16-22 Benefits that are difficult to quantify include the following: (1) greater flexibility in the production process, (2) shorter cycle times and reduced lead times, (3) reduction of non-value-added costs, (4) reduced inventory levels, (5) lower floor-space requirements, and (6) greater and more consistent product quality.

SOLUTIONS TO EXERCISES

EXERCISE 16-23 (25 MINUTES)

1. Use formula (1):

$$F_n = P(1 + r)^n = \$2,500(1.14)^6$$

The accumulation factor, $(1.14)^6$, is given in Table I of the appendix. It is 2.195. Thus, the calculation is as follows:

$$F_n = \$2,500(2.195) = \$5,487.50$$

The future value of your investment will be $5,487.50.

2. Use formula (2):

$$P = F_n\left(\frac{1}{(1+r)^n}\right) = \$10,000\left(\frac{1}{(1.12)^5}\right)$$

The discount factor, $1/(1.12)^5$, is given in Table III. It is .567. Thus, the calculation is as follows:

$$P = \$10,000(.567) = \$5,670$$

The present value of the gift is $5,670.

3. You need to invest an amount, A, each year so that the following equation is satisfied:

$$A(4.375) = \$52,500$$

The number 4.375 is the annuity accumulation factor, from Table II, for $n = 4$ and $r = .06$. Rearranging the equation above, we solve for A as follows:

$$A = \frac{\$52,500}{4.375} = \$12,000$$

You need to invest $12,000 per year.

EXERCISE 16-23 (CONTINUED)

4. You need an amount, P, now so that the following equation is satisfied.

    $$P = (2.487)\$13,000$$

    The number 2.487 is the annuity discount factor, from Table IV, for $n = 3$ and $r = .10$. The solution is $P = \$32,331$. You need to invest $32,331 now in order to fund your educational expenses.

EXERCISE 16-24 (45 MINUTES)

1. Future value of investment:

Time 0	Amount at time 0	$2,500.00
Year 1	Interest, year 1 (.14 x $2,500.00)	350.00
Time 1	Amount at time 1	$2,850.00
Year 2	Interest, year 2 (.14 x $2,850.00)	399.00
Time 2	Amount at time 2	$3,249.00
Year 3	Interest, year 3 (.14 x $3,249.00)	454.86
Time 3	Amount at time 3	$3,703.86
Year 4	Interest, year 4 (.14 x $3,703.86)	518.54
Time 4	Amount at time 4	$4,222.40
Year 5	Interest, year 5 (.14 x $4,222.40)	591.14
Time 5	Amount at time 5	$4,813.54
Year 6	Interest, year 6 (.14 x $4,813.54)	673.90
Time 6	Amount at time 6	$5,487.44*

Time

* The discrepancy between $5,487.44 and $5,487.50 is due to rounding error.

EXERCISE 16-24 (CONTINUED)

2. Educational expense fund:

Time 0	Deposit $32,331	$32,331
Year 1	Earn interest ($32,331 x .10)..............................	3,233
Time 1	Accumulation at time 1.......................................	$35,564
	Withdrawal to cover educational expenses	(13,000)
	Amount remaining to earn interest in year 2 ...	$22,564
Year 2	Earn interest (22,564 x .10)................................	2,256
Time 2	Accumulation at time 2.......................................	$24,820
	Withdrawal to cover educational expenses	(13,000)
	Amount remaining to earn interest in year 3 ...	$11,820
Year 3	Earn interest ($11,820 x .10)..............................	1,182
Time 3	Accumulation at time 3.......................................	$13,002
	Withdrawal to cover educational expenses	(13,000)
Time	Amount remaining	$ 2*

* The $2 remainder is due to rounding error.

EXERCISE 16-25 (20 MINUTES)

1. To determine the amount you need to accumulate by the time you retire, calculate the present value of a 40-year annuity in the amount of $225,000. (Use Table IV in the Appendix.)

    Present value = (annuity discount factor for $n = 40$, $r = .12$)($225,000)
    = (8.244)($225,000) = $1,854,900

    Thus, you need to accumulate $1,854,900 in your account by the time you retire.

2. To determine the amount you need to deposit each year for 15 years, calculate the annuity amount that will accumulate to a future value of $1,854,900 in 15 years. (Use Table II in the Appendix.)

    Future value = (annuity accumulation factor for $n = 15$, $r = .12$)(annuity amount)
    $1,854,900 = (37.280)(annuity amount)

    Annuity amount = $\dfrac{\$1,854,900}{37.280}$ = $49,755.90

    Thus, you need to deposit $49,755.90 into your account each year from age 25 through age 39.

3. This is both a present-value and a future-value problem. The problem has two parts. Requirement (1) is a present-value problem; requirement (2) is a future-value problem.

EXERCISE 16-26 (15 MINUTES)

Cost of new well (time 0)	$(2,825)
Present value of annual savings: ($500 × 6.710*)	3,355
Net present value	$ 530

*From Table IV in the Appendix: $r = .08$ and $n = 10$.

The governing board should approve the new well, because the project's net present value is positive.

EXERCISE 16-27 (15 MINUTES)

$$\text{Annuity discount factor associated with the internal rate of return} = \frac{\text{initial cash outflow}}{\text{annual cost savings}}$$

$$= \frac{\$2,825}{\$500} = 5.650$$

Find 5.650 in the 10-year row of Table IV in the Appendix. This annuity discount factor falls in the 12 percent column. Thus, the project's internal rate of return is 12 percent. The governing board should approve the new well, because the project's internal rate of return is greater than the hurdle rate of 8 percent.

EXERCISE 16-28 (15 MINUTES)

Acquisition cost of site (time 0)	$(195,000)
Preparatory work (time 0)	(73,400)
Total cost at time 0	$(268,400)
Present value of annual savings in operating costs: ($40,000 × 7.360*)	294,400
Net present value	$ 26,000

*From Table IV in the Appendix: $r = .06$ and $n = 10$.

The board should approve a new landfill, because the project's net present value is positive.

EXERCISE 16-29 (15 MINUTES)

Acquisition cost of site (time 0)	$195,000
Preparatory work (time 0)	73,400
Total cash outflow at time 0	$268,400

$$\text{Annuity discount factor associated with the internal rate of return} = \frac{\text{initial cash outflow}}{\text{annual cost savings}}$$

$$= \frac{\$268,400}{\$40,000} = 6.710$$

Find 6.710 in the 10-year row of Table IV in the Appendix. This annuity discount factor falls in the 8 percent column. Thus, the project's internal rate of return is 8 percent. The board should approve the new landfill because the project's internal rate of return is higher than the hurdle rate of 6 percent.

EXERCISE 16-30 (45 MINUTES)

					Year					
	1	2	3	4	5	6	7	8	9	10
(1) Unrecovered investment at beginning of year	$268,400[a]	$249,872[b]	$229,862	$208,251	$184,911	$159,704	$132,480	$103,078	$71,324	$37,030
(2) Cost savings during year	40,000	40,000	40,000	40,000	40,000	40,000	40,000	40,000	40,000	40,000
(3) Return on unrecovered investment [8%[c] × amount in row (1)]	21,472	19,990	18,389	16,660	14,793	12,776	10,598	8,246	5,706	2,962
(4) Recovery of investment [row (2) amount minus row (3) amount]	18,528	20,010	21,611	23,340	25,207	27,224	29,402	31,754	34,294	37,038
(5) Unrecovered investment at end of year [row (1) amount minus row (4) amount]	249,872	229,862	208,251	184,911	159,704	132,480	103,078	71,324	37,030	(8)[d]

[a]Initial cash outflow: land cost of $195,000 plus preparation cost of $73,400.
[b]In years 2 through 10, the row (1) amount is from row (5) of the previous column.
[c]The project's internal rate of return is 8%, as calculated in the preceding exercise.
[d]The remainder is due to accumulated rounding errors.

EXERCISE 16-31 (25 MINUTES)

Acquisition cost of new computer	$65,500
Salvage of old computer	(11,500)
Net cash outflow at time 0	$54,000

Annuity discount factor associated with the internal rate of return

$$= \frac{\text{net cash outflow at time 0}}{\text{annual savings if new computer is purchased}}$$

$$= \frac{\$54,000}{\$14,000} = 3.857 \text{ (rounded)}$$

In row (5) of Table IV in the Appendix, 3.857 falls between the annuity discount factors in the 8 percent and 10 percent columns. Thus, the project's internal rate of return lies between 8 percent and 10 percent. We need to interpolate as follows:

		Annuity Discount Factor from Table IV	
Difference	8%	3.993	3.993
is	True IRR		3.857
2%	10%	3.791	
	Difference	.202	.136

$$\text{Internal rate of return} = 8\% + \left(\frac{.136}{.202}\right)(2\%) = 9.35\% \text{ (rounded)}$$

The project's internal rate of return is approximately 9.35 percent.

EXERCISE 16-32 (20 MINUTES)

Table III includes three discount rates between 8 and 16 percent. We could begin with 10, 12, or 14 percent. For completeness, the following solution computes the net present value of the overhaul using all three discount rates.

Year	Repair Costs Avoided by Overhaul	Present Value at 10%	12%	14%
1	3,000DM			
	3,000DM × .909[a]	2,727DM		
	3,000DM × .893		2,679DM	
	3,000DM × .877			2,631DM
2	5,000DM			
	5,000DM × .826[b]	4,130DM		
	5,000DM × .797		3,985DM	
	5,000DM × .769			3,845DM
Cost of overhaul (time 0)		(6,664DM)	(6,664DM)	(6,664DM)
Net present value		193DM	0	(188DM)

[a]Table III: r = 10%, n = 1.
[b]Table III: r = 10%, n = 2.

The internal rate of return of the overhaul is 12 percent, because the project's net present value is zero when a 12 percent discount rate is used.

EXERCISE 16-33 (30 MINUTES)

Answers will vary widely, depending on the organization and investment decision selected. For example, the American Red Cross might use discounted-cash-flow analysis to analyze the merits of building a new hurricane relief center in Dade County, Florida. Of course, in a decision such as this, significant qualitative , humanitarian issues bear on the decision in addition to the straight financial analysis.

EXERCISE 16-34 (25 MINUTES)

The net present value of the new utility truck is computed as follows:

Acquisition cost (time 0)	$(59,900)
Present value of operating-cost savings:	
Year 1: $11,000* × .943†	10,373
Year 2: $11,500 × .890	10,235
Year 3: $13,000 × .840	10,920
Year 4: $18,000 × .792	14,256
Year 5: $20,000 × .747	14,940
Net present value	$ 824

*Amounts in this column are the annual cash savings from reduced operating costs. Notice that no depreciation expense is included, since it is not a cash flow.

†The discount factors in this column are from Table III in the Appendix (r = .06)

    The supervisor did not make the economically optimal decision for the city. The net present value of the new utility truck is positive, so it should be purchased.

    The behavioral problem inherent in this situation is the conflict between (1) investment criteria based on discounted cash flow methods and (2) performance evaluation based on accrual accounting concepts. Specifically, the supervisor is concerned that the decision to buy the new utility truck will look bad because of the deduction of depreciation from the operating-cost savings. In making the acquisition decision, however, depreciation should be ignored, since it is not a cash flow.

EXERCISE 16-35 (15 MINUTES)

Discount Rate	Annuity Discount Factor*	Annual Savings	Present Value of Annual Savings	Acquisition Cost	Net Present Value†
8%	5.747	$18,000	$103,446	$86,500	$16,946
10%	5.335	18,000	96,030	86,500	9,530
12%	4.968	18,000	89,424	86,500	2,924
14%	4.639	18,000	83,502	86,500	(2,998)
16%	4.344	18,000	78,192	86,500	(8,308)

*Table IV: r = rate in left-hand column, n =8.
†Net present value = (annuity discount factor × annual savings) – acquisition cost.

Notice that the net present value in the right-hand column declines as the discount rate increases. A higher discount rate means greater urgency associated with having each cash flow earlier rather than later.

EXERCISE 16-36 (15 MINUTES)

The annuity discount factor in Table IV of the Appendix (for r = 12% and n = 8) is 4.968. The theater's board of directors will be indifferent about replacing the lighting system if its net present value is zero.

$$\text{Net present value} = \left(\begin{array}{c}\text{annuity}\\\text{discount factor}\end{array}\right)\left(\begin{array}{c}\text{annual}\\\text{savings}\end{array}\right) - \left(\begin{array}{c}\text{acquisition}\\\text{cost}\end{array}\right)$$

$$0 = (4.968)\text{ (annual savings when NPV is 0)} - \$86,500$$

$$\frac{\$86,500}{4.968} = \text{annual savings when NPV is 0} = \$17,411.43 \text{ (rounded)}$$

The annual savings associated with the new lighting system could be as low as $17,411.43 before the board would reject the proposal.

EXERCISE 16-36 (CONTINUED)

Check (not required):

Acquisition cost	$(86,500)
Present value of annual savings:	
(4.968* × $17,411.43)	86,500†
Net present value	$ 0

*Table IV: $r = .12$, $n = 8$.
†Rounded to the nearest dollar.

SOLUTIONS TO PROBLEMS

PROBLEM 16-37 (30 MINUTES)

1. Yes. This is a long-term decision, with cash flows that occur over a five-year period. Given that the cash flows have a "value" dependent on when they take place (e.g., cash inflows that occur in earlier years have a higher time value than cash inflows that take place in later years), discounting should be used to determine whether Community Challenges should outsource.

2. Community Challenges is better off to manufacture the igniters.

    Outsource:

Annual purchase (400,000 units x $62)......................	$(24,800,000)
Annuity discount factor (Table IV: r = .14, n = 5).......	x 3.433
Net present value	$(85,138,400)

    Manufacture in-house:

Annual variable manufacturing costs (400,000 units x $60)..	$(24,000,000)
Annual salary and fringe benefits...........................	(95,000)
Total annual cash flow.......................................	$(24,095,000)
Annuity discount factor (Table IV: r = .14, n = 5)......	x 3.433
Present value of annual cash flows........................	$(82,718,135)
New equipment (time 0)...	(60,000)
Repairs and maintenance: $4,500 x (3.433 – 1.647) (Table IV: r = .14, n = 3-5)	(8,037)
Equipment sale: $12,000 x .519 (Table III: r = .14, n = 5)..	6,228
Net present value..	$(82,779,944)

    Note: Depreciation is ignored because it is not a cash flow.

3. The company would be financially indifferent if the net present value of the *manufacture* alternative equals the net present value of the *outsource* alternative. Thus:

    Let X = purchase price
    3.433 x 400,000X = $82,779,944
    1,373,200X = $82,779,944
    X = $60.28 (rounded)

© 2002 The McGraw-Hill Companies, Inc.

Solutions Manual

PROBLEM 16-38 (30 MINUTES)

1. The team is better off financially if the trade does not occur.

    Keep Moran:

Salary, 20x1: $(600,000) x .893*............................	$ (535,800)
Salary, 20x2: $(650,000) x .797*............................	(518,050)
Salary, 20x3: $(750,000) x .712*............................	(534,000)
Free-agent inflow: $800,000 x .712*.....................	569,600
Net present value...	$(1,018,250)

    Acquire Mendoza:

Salary (annual)..	$(1,000,000)
Net cash inflows from attendance (annual)...........	570,000
Total annual cash flow..................................	$ (430,000)
Annuity discount factor (Table IV, r = .12, n = 3)....	x 2.402
Present value of annual cash flows......................	$(1,032,860)
Signing bonus (time 0).......................................	(1,230,000)
Free-agent inflow: $1,500,000 x .712*....................	1,068,000
Net present value...	$(1,194,860)

    * Table III, r = .12

    Note: With regard to Mendoza's signing bonus, the important point is when the cash flow occurs (time 0). How the Bullets treat the bonus for financial-reporting purposes (i.e., expensing the figure over a three-year period) is not relevant for purposes of computing discounted cash flows.

2. Mendoza would prefer the $1,230,000 bonus that he received. Although the cash flows are the same under both options (e.g., $410,000 x 3 years = $1,230,000), Mendoza has more cash up front, allowing him to invest a greater sum and receive added returns than if the money were spread over a three-year period. Mendoza's up-front bonus has a higher present value associated with it, because dollars received in early years have a greater time value than dollars received in the future.

3. The hurdle rate is the discount rate or the team's minimum desired rate of return. It is influenced by the investment opportunity rate—the rate that the team can earn on alternative investments of equivalent risk.

4. Events might include: player injury and/or suspension; other player trades; team morale; overall team performance; ability to make play-offs; changes in contracts for concessions, parking, and broadcasting rights; a significant change in the free-agent market; and so forth.

Generally speaking, an individual would have less faith in ten-year data than three-year data. The future is subject to change and as one goes further into the future, there is a greater degree of uncertainty.

PROBLEM 16-39 (60 MINUTES)

	Time 0	Year 1	Year 2	Year 3	Year 4	Year 5	Year 6	Year 7	Year 8	Year 9	Year 10
Contract with Diagnostic Testing Services											
Flat fee		$ (80,000)	$ (80,000)	$ (80,000)	$ (80,000)	$ (80,000)	$ (80,000)	$ (80,000)	$ (80,000)	$ (80,000)	$ (80,000)
Per-specimen charges ($20 × 20,000)		(400,000)	(400,000)	(400,000)	(400,000)	(400,000)	(400,000)	(400,000)	(400,000)	(400,000)	(400,000)
Lost contribution margin on referred cases		(100,000)	(100,000)	(100,000)	(100,000)	(100,000)	(100,000)	(100,000)	(100,000)	(100,000)	(100,000)
Total cash flow		$(580,000)	$(580,000)	$(580,000)	$(580,000)	$(580,000)	$(580,000)	$(580,000)	$(580,000)	$(580,000)	$(580,000)
Discount factor*		× .893	× .797	× .712	× .636	× .567	× .507	× .452	× .404	× .361	× .322
Present value		$(517,940)	$(462,260)	$(412,960)	$(368,880)	$(328,860)	$(294,060)	$(262,160)	$(234,320)	$(209,380)	$(186,760)

Net present value   Sum = $(3,277,580)

	Time 0	Year 1	Year 2	Year 3	Year 4	Year 5	Year 6	Year 7	Year 8	Year 9	Year 10
Establish in-house Diagnostic Testing Lab											
Rental of storage space	$(625,000)	$ (30,000)	$ (30,000)	$ (30,000)	$ (30,000)	$ (30,000)	$ (30,000)	$ (30,000)	$ (30,000)	$ (30,000)	$ (30,000)
Equipment					(300,000)						
Staff		(200,000)	(200,000)	(200,000)	(200,000)	(200,000)	(200,000)	(200,000)	(200,000)	(200,000)	(200,000)
Fixed operating costs		(50,000)	(50,000)	(50,000)	(50,000)	(50,000)	(50,000)	(50,000)	(50,000)	(50,000)	(50,000)
Variable operating costs ($10 × 25,000†)		(250,000)	(250,000)	(250,000)	(250,000)	(250,000)	(250,000)	(250,000)	(250,000)	(250,000)	(250,000)
Fees for lab services ($20 × 5,000**)		100,000	100,000	100,000	100,000	100,000	100,000	100,000	100,000	100,000	100,000
Total cash flow	$(625,000)	$(430,000)	$(430,000)	$(430,000)	$(730,000)	$(430,000)	$(430,000)	$(430,000)	$(430,000)	$(430,000)	$(430,000)
Discount factor*	× 1.000	× .893	× .797	× .712	× .636	× .567	× .507	× .452	× .404	× .361	× .322
Present value	$(625,000)	$(383,990)	$(342,710)	$(306,160)	$(464,280)	$(243,810)	$(218,010)	$(194,360)	$(173,720)	$(155,230)	$(138,460)

Net present value   Sum = $(3,245,730)

Difference in NPV $ (31,850)

(favors in-house lab)

*Table III: r = .12.

†The new lab will be operated at capacity, 25,000 tests per year.

**The excess capacity (5,000 tests annually) will be provided to private physicians for a fee.

PROBLEM 16-40 (45 MINUTES)

The only cash flows listed in the problem that are not annual cash flows are the purchases of equipment for the proposed lab at time 0 (now) and at the end of year 4. Therefore, the most efficient way to apply the incremental cost approach is to calculate the incremental annual cash flows with the proposed lab, and then use the annuity discount factor to compute the present value.

Incremental annual cash flows associated with proposed diagnostic testing lab:

Rental of storage space	$ (30,000)
Staff compensation	(200,000)
Fixed operating costs	(50,000)
Variable operating costs ($10 × 25,000)	(250,000)
Fees for lab services ($20 × 5,000)	100,000
Subtotal	$(430,000)
Deduct: Annual costs of contract:	
Flat fee	80,000
Per-specimen charges ($20 × 20,000)	400,000
Subtotal	$ 50,000
Add: Contribution margin on cases	
currently referred elsewhere	100,000
Incremental annual cash flow with proposed lab	$ 150,000
Annuity discount factor (Table IV: $r = .12$, $n = 10$)	× 5.650
Present value of incremental annual cash flows	$ 847,500
Deduct: Present value of equipment purchases:	
Time 0: $625,000 × 1.000	625,000
Year 4: $300,000 × .636 (Table III: $r = .12$, $n = 4$)	190,800
Net present value of incremental cash flows	
(favors in-house lab)	$ 31,700*

*The difference between $31,700 computed in this problem and $31,850 computed in the preceding problem is due to rounding error when the annuity discount factor is used.

A tabular presentation of the incremental cost approach, along the lines of Exhibit 16-10, would be more cumbersome than necessary given the equivalent annual cash flows (excluding the equipment purchases).

© *2002 The McGraw-Hill Companies, Inc.*

Solutions Manual

PROBLEM 16-41 (40 MINUTES)

1. Net present-value analysis:

Old machine:

Annual costs:		
Variable 300,000 × $.38		$114,000
Fixed		21,000
Total		$135,000
Annuity discount factor ($r = 16\%$; $n = 6$)		× 3.685
Present value of annual costs		$497,475
Salvage value, December 31, 20x6	$ 7,000	
Discount factor ($r = 16\%$; $n = 6$)	× .410	
Present value of salvage value		(2,870)
Net present value		$494,605

New machine:

Annual costs:		
Variable 300,000 × $.29		$87,000
Fixed		11,000
Total		98,000
Annuity discount factor ($r = 16\%$; $n = 6$)		× 3.685
Present value of annual costs		$361,130
Salvage value of new machine, December 31, 20x6	$20,000	
Discount factor ($r = 16\%$; $n = 6$)	× .410	
Present value of new machine's salvage value		(8,200)
Salvage value of old machine, December 31, 20x0		(40,000)
Acquisition cost of new machine		120,000
Net present value		$432,930

Conclusion: Purchase the new machine because the net present value of relevant costs is lower than with the old machine.

PROBLEM 16-41 (CONTINUED)

2.   Memorandum

    Date: Today

    To: President, Special People Industries

    From: I.M. Student

    Subject: Cookie machine replacement decision

    The nonquantitative factors that are important to the decision include the following:

- The lower operating costs (variable and fixed) of the new machine would enable Special People Industries to meet future competitive or inflationary pressures to a greater degree than the old machine.

    - If the increased efficiency of the new machine is due to labor or energy cost savings, then additional increases in these costs in the future will favor the new machinery even more.

    - Maintenance and servicing of both machines should be reviewed for reliability of the manufacturer and cost.

    - The potential technological advances for new machines over the next several years should be evaluated.

    - The space requirements for the new equipment should be reviewed and compared with the present equipment to determine if more or less space is required.

    - The retraining of personnel to use the new machine should be considered.

PROBLEM 16-42 (45 MINUTES)

1. Interior fire-control stations:

Staff compensation (annual)	$ (1,600,000)
Other operating costs (annual)	(800,000)
Total annual cash flow	$ (2,400,000)
Annuity discount factor (Table IV: r = .10, n = 10)	× 6.145
Net present value of costs	$(14,748,000)

Perimeter fire-control stations:

Staff compensation (annual)	$ (1,200,000)
Other operating costs (annual)	(440,000)
Total annual cash flow	$ (1,640,000)
Annuity discount factor (Table IV: r = .10, n = 10)	× 6.145
Present value of annual cash flows	$(10,077,800)
Construction costs (time 0)	(800,000)
Acquisition of equipment (time 0)	(2,000,000)
Salvage value of half of the old equipment (time 0)	480,000
Demolition of old stations	(80,000)
Net present value of costs	$(12,477,800)
Difference in NPV of costs	
(favors perimeter fire-control stations)	$ (2,270,200)

    A more elaborate, but also more cumbersome, tabular approach to this analysis is given on the next page. The slight differences in the NPV's shown in the table are due to rounding error when the annuity discount factor is used (as in the analysis above) instead of the individual discount factors (as in the table).

2.   Qualitative factors to be considered include such issues as public safety and aesthetics. For example, public safety might be greater with eight fire-control stations dispersed throughout the state forest. Aesthetic considerations, on the other hand, might favor the perimeter stations, which would not mar the beauty of the forest.

PROBLEM 16-42 (CONTINUED)

ALTERNATIVE FORMAT FOR ANALYSIS

	Time 0	Year 1	Year 2	Year 3	Year 4	Year 5	Year 6	Year 7	Year 8	Year 9	Year 10
Interior fire-control stations:											
Staff compensation		$(1,600,000)	$(1,600,000)	$(1,600,000)	$(1,600,000)	$(1,600,000)	$(1,600,000)	$(1,600,000)	$(1,600,000)	$(1,600,000)	$(1,600,000)
Other operating costs		(800,000)	(800,000)	(800,000)	(800,000)	(800,000)	(800,000)	(800,000)	(800,000)	(800,000)	(800,000)
Total cash flow		$(2,400,000)	$(2,400,000)	$(2,400,000)	$(2,400,000)	$(2,400,000)	$(2,400,000)	$(2,400,000)	$(2,400,000)	$(2,400,000)	$(2,400,000)
Discount factor*		× .909	× .826	× .751	× .683	× .621	× .564	× .513	× .467	× .424	× .386
Present value		$(2,181,600)	$(1,982,400)	$(1,802,400)	$(1,639,200)	$(1,490,400)	$(1,353,600)	$(1,231,200)	$(1,120,800)	$(1,017,600)	$(926,400)
Net present value of costs					Sum = $(14,745,600)						
Perimeter fire-control stations:											
Staff compensation		$(1,200,000)	$(1,200,000)	$(1,200,000)	$(1,200,000)	$(1,200,000)	$(1,200,000)	$(1,200,000)	$(1,200,000)	$(1,200,000)	$(1,200,000)
Other operating costs		(440,000)	(440,000)	(440,000)	(440,000)	(440,000)	(440,000)	(440,000)	(440,000)	(440,000)	(440,000)
Construction costs	$ (800,000)										
Acquisition of equipment	(2,000,000)										
Salvage value of old equipment	480,000										
Demolition of old stations	(80,000)										
Total cash flow	$(2,400,000)	$(1,640,000)	$(1,640,000)	$(1,640,000)	$(1,640,000)	$(1,640,000)	$(1,640,000)	$(1,640,000)	$(1,640,000)	$(1,640,000)	$(1,640,000)
Discount factor	× 1.000	× .909	× .826	× .751	× .683	× .621	× .564	× .513	× .467	× .424	× .386
Present value	$(2,400,000)	$(1,490,760)	$(1,354,640)	$(1,231,640)	$(1,120,120)	$(1,018,440)	$(924,960)	$(841,320)	$(765,880)	$(695,360)	$(633,040)
Net present value of costs					Sum = $12,476,160						
Difference in NPV of costs (favors perimeter fire-control stations)					$ (2,269,440)						

*Table III: r = .10.

PROBLEM 16-43 (30 MINUTES)

Incremental cost of interior fire-control stations over perimeter stations:

Staff compensation (annual)	$ (400,000)
Other operating costs (annual)	(360,000)
Excess annual cash outflows with interior stations	$ (760,000)
Annuity discount factor (Table IV: r = .10, n = 10)	× 6.145
Present value of excess cash outflows	$(4,670,200)
Construction costs (time 0)	800,000
Acquisition of equipment (time 0)	2,000,000
Salvage value of old equipment (time 0)	(480,000)
Demolition of old stations	80,000
Net present value of excess cash outflows with interior stations..	$(2,270,200)

The net present value of costs is $2,270,200 greater with the interior fire-control stations than with the perimeter stations. This amount is the same as that determined in requirement (1) of the preceding problem, which used the total cost approach (with annuity discount factors).

An alternative, but more cumbersome, approach would be to prepare a year-by-year table of cash flows similar to that given in Exhibit 16-10. This approach is not necessary in the fire-control station problem, because the annual cash flows are identical across all 10 years. The more elaborate, tabular approach is demonstrated for the total cost approach in the solution to the preceding problem.

PROBLEM 16-44 (25 MINUTES)

	Time 0	Time 1	Time 2	Time 3	Time 4
Acquisition cost	$(39,000)				
Investment in working capital	(3,000)				
Recovery of working capital					$ 3,000
Salvage value of old machinery	800				
Salvage value of new machinery					2,000
Annual operating cash savings	_____	$12,500	$12,500	$12,500	$12,500
Total cash flow	$(41,200)	$12,500	$12,500	$12,500	$17,500
Discount factor*	× 1.000	× .909	× .826	× .751	× .683
Present value	$(41,200)	$11,363	$10,325	$ 9,388	$11,953

Net present value   Sum = $1,829

*The discount factors are from Table III in the Appendix (r = .10)

Conclusion: The proposal to invest in new machinery has a positive net present value and should be accepted.

PROBLEM 16-45 (50 MINUTES)

1. See the following table.

2. See the following table.

3. See the following table.

4. The administrator should recommend that the clinic be built, because its net present value is positive.

PROBLEM 16-45 (CONTINUED)

Type of Cash Flow	20x0	20x1	20x2	20x3	20x4	20x5	20x6	20x7	20x8	20x9
(1) Construction of clinic	$(390,000)	$(390,000)								
(2) Equipment purchase		(150,000)								
(3) Staffing			$(800,000)	$(800,000)	$(800,000)	$(800,000)	$(800,000)	$(800,000)	$(800,000)	$(800,000)
(4) Other operating costs			(200,000)	(200,000)	(200,000)	(200,000)	(200,000)	(200,000)	(200,000)	(200,000)
(5) Increased charitable contributions			250,000	250,000	250,000	250,000	250,000	250,000	250,000	250,000
(6) Cost savings at hospital			1,000,000	1,000,000	1,000,000	1,000,000	1,000,000	1,000,000	1,000,000	1,000,000
(7) Cost of refurbishment						(180,000)				
(9) Salvage value										290,000
Incremental cash flow	$(390,000)	$(540,000)	$250,000	$250,000	$250,000	$70,000	$250,000	$250,000	$250,000	$540,000
Discount factor*	× 1.000	× .893	× .797	× .712	× .636	× .567	× .507	× .452	× .404	× .361
Present value	$(390,000)	$(482,220)	$199,250	$178,000	$159,000	$39,690	$126,750	$113,000	$101,000	$194,940

Sum=$239,410

Net present value

*Table III: r = .12.

PROBLEM 16-46 (45 MINUTES)

1. Research Proposal I has an NPV of $1,370 and Research Proposal II has an NPV of $(14,375). The calculations are shown in the table on the next page.

2. Marie Fenwar should approve Research Proposal I. It has a higher NPV than Research Proposal II. Moreover, the NPV of Proposal I is positive, while the NPV of Proposal II is negative.

PROBLEM 16-46 (CONTINUED)

	Time 0	Year 1	Year 2	Year 3	Year 4	Year 5
Research Proposal I:						
Equipment acquisition	$(40,000)					
Contract fee		$100,000	$100,000	$100,000	$100,000	$100,000
Operating costs		(150,000)	(120,000)	(75,000)	(40,000)	(40,000)
Total cash flow	$ (40,000)	$ (50,000)	$ (20,000)	$ 25,000	$ 60,000	$ 60,000
× Discount factor*	× 1.000	× .926	× .857	× .794	× .735	× .681
Present value	$ (40,000)	$ (46,300)	$ (17,140)	$ 19,850	$ 44,100	$ 40,860

Net present value   Sum = $1,370

	Time 0	Year 1	Year 2	Year 3	Year 4	Year 5
Research Proposal II:						
Equipment acquisition	$(70,000)					
Contract fee		$100,000	$100,000	$100,000	$100,000	$100,000
Operating costs		(75,000)	(75,000)	(95,000)	(95,000)	(95,000)
Total cash flow	$ (70,000)	$ 25,000	$ 25,000	$ 5,000	$ 5,000	$ 5,000
× Discount factor*	× 1.000	× .926	× .857	× .794	× .735	× .681
Present value	$ (70,000)	$ 23,150	$ 21,425	$ 3,970	$ 3,675	$ 3,405

Net present value   Sum = $(14,375)

*Table III: (r = .08).

3.   Marie Fenwar acted unethically in approving Research Proposal II. Proposal I has a positive NPV, and it is higher than the NPV for Proposal II, which is negative. Fenwar is placing her own perceived chances for a promotion ahead of the best interests of the IES. Moreover, if Fenwar explains the reason why Proposal I is preferable to Proposal II, in terms of discounted cash flows, it is likely that the board will understand why Proposal I is a better alternative.

PROBLEM 16-47 (25 MINUTES)

1. Initial cost of investment in a longer runway:

Land acquisition	$ (70,000)
Runway construction	(200,000)
Extension of perimeter fence	(29,840)
Runway lights	(39,600)
New snow plow	(100,000)
Salvage value of old snow plow	10,000
Initial cost of investment	$(429,440)

2. Annual net incremental benefit from runway:

Runway maintenance	$ (28,000)
Incremental revenue from landing fees	40,000
Incremental operating costs for new snow plow	(12,000)
Additional tax revenue	64,000
Annual incremental benefit	$ 64,000

3. Internal rate of return:

$$\text{Annuity discount factor associated with the internal rate of return} = \frac{\text{initial cost of investment}}{\text{annual incremental benefit}}$$

$$= \frac{\$429,440}{\$64,000} = 6.710$$

Find 6.710 in the 10-year row of Table IV of the Appendix. It falls in the 8 percent column, so the internal rate of return on the runway project is 8 percent.

Conclusion: From a purely economic perspective, the longer runway should not be approved, since its internal rate of return (8 percent) is lower than the hurdle rate (12 percent). Qualitative considerations, such as convenience for the county's residents, should also be considered.

PROBLEM 16-48 (45 MINUTES)

1. Net present-value analysis:

Runway maintenance	$ (28,000)
Incremental revenue from landing fees	40,000
Incremental operating costs for new snow plow	(12,000)
Additional tax revenue	64,000
Annual incremental benefit	$ 64,000
Annuity discount factor (Table IV: r = .12, n = 10)	× 5.650
Present value of annual benefits	$361,600
Less: Initial costs:	
Land acquisition	(70,000)
Runway construction	(200,000)
Extension of perimeter fence	(29,840)
Runway lights	(39,600)
New snow plow	(100,000)
Salvage value of old snow plow	10,000
Net present value	$ (67,840)

2. From a purely economic perspective, the board should not approve the runway, since its net present value is negative. Qualitative considerations, such as the convenience of the county's residents, should also be taken into consideration by the board.

3. (a) Data that are likely to be uncertain include the following:

   • Annual cost of maintaining new runway

   • Annual incremental revenue from landing fees

   • Annual additional tax revenue

   Each of these data covers a lengthy time horizon. Moreover, they depend on unpredictable factors, such as the level of economic activity in the county, the inflation rate, and the rate of deterioration of the runway (which depends on the weather).

PROBLEM 16-48 (CONTINUED)

(b) The least uncertain data would likely include the following:

- Cost of acquiring land

- Cost of runway lights

- Cost of new snow plow

- Salvage value of old snow plow

Almost as certain would be the following:

- Cost of runway construction

- Cost of extending perimeter fence

These data all refer to the present or near future. Acquisition costs can be determined by direct inquiry, and construction costs can be determined by obtaining estimates or bids from contractors.

PROBLEM 16-49 (30 MINUTES)

$$\text{Annuity discount factor associated with the internal rate of return} = \frac{\text{initial cost of investment}}{\text{annual incremental benefit}}$$

For the internal rate of return to be 12 percent, the annuity discount factor must be 5.650 (Table IV: $r = .12$, $n = 10$). Therefore:

$$5.650 = \frac{\text{initial cost of investment}}{\text{annual incremental benefit}}$$

$$5.650 = \frac{\$429,440*}{\text{annual incremental benefit}}$$

$$\text{Annual incremental benefit} = \frac{\$429,440}{5.650} = \$76,007 \text{ (rounded)}$$

*Initial cost = $70,000 + $200,000 + $29,840 + $39,600 + $100,000 – $10,000 [computed in Problem 16-47, req. (1)].

PROBLEM 16-49 (CONTINUED)

We calculate the required increase in annual tax revenue as follows:

Required incremental benefit		$ 76,007
Add: Annual costs to cover:		
Promotional campaign	$20,000	
Runway maintenance	28,000	
Incremental operating costs of new snow plow	12,000	
Total annual costs		60,000
Subtotal		$136,007
Deduct: Incremental revenue from landing fees		(40,000)
Required increase in tax revenue		$ 96,007

Conclusion: In order for the longer runway to be economically justifiable, the $20,000 annual promotional campaign must result in an increase in tax revenue of $96,007 per year.

PROBLEM 16-50 (50 MINUTES)

1. Incremental revenue from stadium expansion:

Revenue from exhibition game ticket sales:	
Bleachers: [(27,000* + 8,000) × $15] × 10 games	$5,250,000
Box seats: [(3,000[†] + 2,000) × $25] × 10 games	1,250,000
Total	$6,500,000
City' share	× .5
City's revenue from exhibition game ticket sales	$3,250,000
Less: Current spring revenue that will not continue	(500,000)
Incremental spring revenue to the city	$2,750,000
Incremental ticket revenue during summer, fall,	
and winter ($100,000 × 10%)	10,000
Total incremental revenue to the city	$2,760,000

*27,000 bleacher seats in current stadium (30,000 × 90%)
[†]3,000 box seats in current stadium (30,000 × 10%)

2. See the following table.

3. See the following table.

	Time 0	Year 1	Year 2	Year 3	Year 4	Year 5
Incremental revenue to city		$2,760,000	$2,760,000	$2,760,000	$2,760,000	$2,760,000
Incremental annual maintenance cost ...		(50,000)	(50,000)	(50,000)	(50,000)	(50,000)
Cost of stadium expansion	$(7,000,000)					
Total cash flows	$(7,000,000)	$2,710,000	$2,710,000	$2,710,000	$2,710,000	$2,710,000
Discount factor (Table III: r = .10)	× 1.000	× .909	× .826	× .751	× .683	× .621
Present value	$(7,000,000)	$2,463,390	$2,238,460	$2,035,210	$1,850,930	$1,682,910

Net present value   Sum = $3,270,900

The stadium expansion is economically justifiable, since its NPV is positive.

4.   Revised analysis:

City's revenue from exhibition games if stadium is filled [from requirement (1)]	$ 3,250,000
Percentage of tickets sold	× 60%
City's revenue from exhibition games if stadium is 60% full	$ 1,950,000
Less: Current spring revenue that will not continue	(500,000)
Add: Incremental revenue in summer, fall, and winter	10,000
Total incremental revenue to the city	$ 1,460,000
Less: Additional annual maintenance cost	(50,000)
Annual incremental cash flow	$ 1,410,000
Annuity discount factor (Table IV: r = .10, n = 5)	× 3.791
Present value of annual incremental cash flows	$ 5,345,310
Less: Cost of stadium expansion (time 0)	(7,000,000)
Net present value	$(1,654,690)

Conclusion: If only 60 percent of the exhibition game tickets can be sold, the stadium expansion is not economically justifiable, because its NPV is negative.

PROBLEM 16-51 (50 MINUTES)

1.   Net savings

	(1)	(2)	(3)	(4)	(5)	(6)
Year	Savings on Monitoring Activity	Current Cost of Replacing Stolen Books	Projected Cost of Replacing Stolen Books with New System	Savings on Book Replacement*	Cost of Installing Sensor Panels	Net Savings with New System†
1	$24,000	$27,000	$22,500	$ 4,500	$6,000	$22,500
2	24,000	27,000	13,500	13,500	6,000	31,500
3	24,000	27,000	4,500	22,500	6,000	40,500
4	24,000	27,000	-0-	27,000	-0-	51,000
5	24,000	27,000	-0-	27,000	-0-	51,000
6	24,000	27,000	-0-	27,000	-0-	51,000
7	24,000	27,000	-0-	27,000	-0-	51,000
8	24,000	27,000	-0-	27,000	-0-	51,000
9	24,000	27,000	-0-	27,000	-0-	51,000
10	24,000	27,000	-0-	27,000	-0-	51,000

*Column (2) amount – column (3) amount
†Column (1) amount + column (4) amount – column (5) amount

PROBLEM 16-51 (CONTINUED)

2. Internal rate of return: Using trial and error, try 14%, 16%, and 18%.

Net Savings with New Security System	14% Discount Factor	Present Value Using 14%	16% Discount Factor	Present Value Using 16%	18% Discount Factor	Present Value Using 18%
$22,500	.877	$ 19,732.50	.862	$ 19,395.00	.847	$ 19,057.50
31,500	.769	24,223.50	.743	23,404.50	.718	22,617.00
40,500	.675	27,337.50	.641	25,960.50	.609	24,664.50
51,000	.592	30,192.00	.552	28,152.00	.516	26,316.00
51,000	.519	26,469.00	.476	24,276.00	.437	22,287.00
51,000	.456	23,256.00	.410	20,910.00	.370	18,870.00
51,000	.400	20,400.00	.354	18,054.00	.314	16,014.00
51,000	.351	17,901.00	.305	15,555.00	.266	13,566.00
51,000	.308	15,708.00	.263	13,413.00	.225	11,475.00
51,000	.270	13,770.00	.227	11,577.00	.191	9,741.00
Cost of modifying exits (time 0)		(90,000.00)		(90,000.00)		(90,000.00)
Cost of equipment (time 0)		(110,697.00)		(110,697.00)		(110,697.00)
Net present value		$ 18,292.50		$ 0		$ (16,089.00)

The internal rate of return on the new security system is 16 percent, since the net present value is zero when the cash flows are discounted at 16 percent.

3. The board should approve the new security system, because its internal rate of return (16 percent) exceeds the hurdle rate (14 percent).

4. The most difficult data to estimate would be the cost of replacing stolen books if the new security system is installed. These estimates extend over 10 years, and the library has no experience with the system. The least difficult data to estimate would be the cost of modifying the library's exits and the cost of the new equipment. These amounts can be obtained from contractors' bids and price quotations.

PROBLEM 16-52 (30 MINUTES)

1. If the cost of installing new sensor plates is spread over the first six years instead of the first three, the net savings in the first three years will increase and the net savings in years 4, 5, and 6, will decline by an equivalent amount. Thus, the same total net savings will be obtained, but the savings will be realized earlier. Because of the time value of money, the new security system's internal rate of return will consequently increase.

2. Net present-value analysis:

Year	Schedule of Net Savings from Preceding Problem	Add Back $6,000 in Years 1-3	Subtract $3,000 in Years 1-6	Revised Schedule of Net Savings	Discount Factor (Table III: $r = .14$)	Present Value of Net Savings
1	$22,500	$6,000	$3,000	$25,500	.877	$ 22,363.50
2	31,500	6,000	3,000	34,500	.769	26,530.50
3	40,500	6,000	3,000	43,500	.675	29,362.50
4	51,000	—	3,000	48,000	.592	28,416.00
5	51,000	—	3,000	48,000	.519	24,912.00
6	51,000	—	3,000	48,000	.456	21,888.00
7	51,000	—	—	51,000	.400	20,400.00
8	51,000	—	—	51,000	.351	17,901.00
9	51,000	—	—	51,000	.308	15,708.00
10	51,000	—	—	51,000	.270	13,770.00
Present value of savings						$221,251.50
Cost of modifying exits (time 0)						(90,000.00)
Cost of equipment (time 0)						(110,697.00)
Net present value						$ 20,554.50

The net present value is positive, so the new security system should be installed.

SOLUTIONS TO CASES

CASE 16-53 (40 MINUTES)

1. Net present value, as projected in 20x0:

Predicted increase in annual tax revenue	$ 84,000
Annuity discount factor (Table IV: $r = .10$, $n = 5$)	× 3.791
Predicted present value of increased tax revenue	$318,444
Cost of channel dredging borne by city	
($576,800 × 50%)	(288,400)
Predicted net present value	$ 30,044

2. Internal rate of return, as projected in 20x0:

$$\text{Annuity discount factor associated with the internal rate of return} = \frac{\text{initial cash outflow}}{\text{predicted annual cash inflow}}$$

$$= \frac{\$288,400}{\$84,000} = 3.433$$

Find 3.433 in the five-year row of Table IV. It lies in the 14 percent column, so the city's predicted internal rate of return was 14 percent.

3. Net present value actually attained:

Actual increase in annual tax revenue	$ 80,000
Annuity discount factor (Table IV: $r = .10$, $n = 5$)	× 3.791
Actual present value in 20x0 of increased tax revenue	$303,280
Cost of channel dredging borne by city	
($576,800 × 50%)	(288,400)
Actual net present value in 20x0	$ 14,880

CASE 16-53 (CONTINUED)

4. Internal rate of return actually attained:

$$\frac{\text{Initial cash outflow}}{\text{Actual annual cash inflow}} = \frac{\$288,400}{\$80,000} = 3.605$$

Finding 3.605 in the five-year row of Table IV reveals that the project's actual internal rate of return was 12 percent.

5. Postaudit report:

Cost of 20x0 channel-dredging operation: $576,800
Cost to city (50% of total cost): $288,400

ANNUAL INCREASE IN TAX REVENUES

Projected	Actual	Variance
$84,000	$80,000	$4,000 Unfavorable

Net Present Value in 20x0		Internal Rate of Return	
Projected	Actual	Projected	Actual
$30,044	$14,880	14%	12%

CASE 16-54 (60 MINUTES)

1. The two main alternatives for the Board of Education are as follows:

   (a) Use full-size buses on regular routes

   (b) Use minibuses on regular routes

2. If the board decides to use minibuses, then there are two options for the full-size buses:

   (a) Sell them

   (b) Keep them in reserve

CASE 16-54 (CONTINUED)

3. Net-present-value analysis of options for full-size buses:

    (a) Sell five full-size buses:

Sales proceeds ($15,000 × 5)	<u>$75,000</u>*

    *No discounting necessary, since the buses would be sold now (time 0).

    (b)

Annual savings on bus charter fees ($30,000 – $5,000)	$25,000
Annuity discount factor (Table IV: r = .12, n = 5)	<u>× 3.605</u>
Present value of savings	<u>$90,125</u>

    The full-size buses should be kept in reserve, since the NPV of that option is greater.

4. Net present-value analysis of minibus purchase decision.

    In the following incremental cost analysis, parentheses denote cash flows favoring the *full-size* bus alternative.

Incremental annual cost of compensation for bus drivers if minibuses are used ($18,000 × 3 more buses required)	$ (54,000)
Incremental annual maintenance and operating costs if minibuses are used [($20,000 × 8) – ($50,000 × 5)]	<u>90,000</u>
Incremental annual cash flow (favors minibuses)	$ 36,000
Annuity discount factor (Table IV: r = .12, n = 5)	<u>× 3.605</u>
Present value of incremental annual cash flows	$129,780
Cost of redesigning bus routes, retraining drivers, etc. (time 0)	(15,250)
Acquisition cost of minibuses ($27,000 × 8)	(216,000)
Present value of savings on bus charter fees, if minibuses are purchased [from requirement (3)]	<u>90,125</u>
Net present value	<u>$ (11,345)</u>

    The minibuses should not be purchased.

CASE 16-54 (CONTINUED)

5. Internal rate of return on the minibuses:

   (a) First, calculate the annual cost savings if the minibuses are used. Remember that the full-size buses will be kept in reserve.

Annual savings on bus charter fees ($30,000 – $5,000)	$25,000
Annual incremental maintenance and operating costs [($20,000 × 8) – ($50,000 × 5)]	90,000
Annual incremental cost of compensation for bus drivers ($18,000 × 3 more buses required)	(54,000)
Total annual cost savings if minibuses are used	$61,000

   (b) Second, calculate the initial cost if the minibuses are purchased:

Cost of redesigning bus routes, retraining drivers, etc.	$ (15,250)
Acquisition cost of minibuses ($27,000 × 8)	(216,000)
Initial cost	$(231,250)

   (c) Third, find the internal rate of return:

   $$\text{Annuity discount factor associated with the internal rate of return} = \frac{\text{initial cost}}{\text{annual cost savings}}$$

   $$= \frac{\$231,250}{\$61,000} = 3.791 \text{ (rounded)}$$

   Find 3.791 in the five-year row of Table IV. It lies in the 10 percent column, so the IRR on the minibus alternative is 10 percent.

6. The cost of purchasing a full-size bus ($90,000) is irrelevant, because the board is not contemplating the purchase of any full-size buses. The depreciation method (straight-line) is also irrelevant, because depreciation is not a cash flow. The NPV and IRR methods focus on cash flows.

7. Peter Reynolds, the vice president for sales at the automobile dealership, is acting improperly. First, he should not try to pressure his friend into recommending that the minibuses be purchased. Second, he should not use the lure of a better job to try to persuade his friend to recommend in favor of the minibuses. Third, when the financial job becomes available at the dealership, there should be a search for the best qualified individual. It is not clear that Reynolds is in a position to offer the job to his friend.

CASE 16-54 (CONTINUED)

Ethical standards demand that Michael Jeffries refuse to alter his recommendation to the school board. The NPV analysis indicates that the full-size bus option is preferable, and he should recommend accordingly.

CURRENT ISSUES IN MANAGERIAL ACCOUNTING

ISSUE 16-55

"OIL COMPANIES SEEK TO DEVELOP ENERGY OPTIONS," *THE WALL STREET JOURNAL*, OCTOBER 4, 2000, THADDEUS HERRICK.

1. Oil companies such as BP Amoco, Texaco, and Shell would use discounted cash flow analysis or present value analysis in long-term capital investment analysis for energy-related research projects. These companies calculate the present value of the future cash inflows (revenues) from the research projects and the present value of the current and future cash outflows. If the net present value is positive and other variables are in favor of the research project, an investment will be made.

2. Future cash inflows (revenues) would be hard to predict for oil companies. The cost of developing renewable energy sources is very difficult to predict due to the newness of the technology. Moreover, as the technology for renewable energy sources becomes less expensive and the product(s) are mass marketed and distributed, the market price for the energy may fall. Predicting the price and volume will be challenging at best.

ISSUE 16-56

"THE FAP MODEL OF INVESTMENT APPRAISAL," *MANAGEMENT ACCOUNTING*, MARCH 2000, FRANK LEFLEY.

All major projects are considered by an appraisal team, which consists of an independent team facilitator and senior managers from the following departments: production, marketing and sales, environmental, personnel, and transport. This team is responsible for carrying out the FAP procedure for all major projects. Other advisors to the team are recruited as required.

The finance director has calculated the true cost of capital to be nine percent. This figure has been approved by the other corporate directors and is used in the FAP model to represent the discount rate applied in the NPV calculations. Besides the costs and financial benefits that are reasonably apparent from the investment, there are also risk and strategic implications. The production manager is concerned with the high level of complexity involved with an investment in new technology. The marketing and sales manager is mildly concerned that some of the inevitable product changes may not be readily acceptable by his customers. The sales department will be required to improve its customer order processing, while the manufacturing department will be required to move to a just-in-time philosophy. Accounting will be required to adopt an activity-based costing approach and supply more timely cost information to both the manufacturing and sales departments. Transport and logistics will have to be more flexible, yet work within a somewhat tight budget. Information processing will become more defined, structured, and interdepartmental.

ISSUE 16-57

"KELLOGG TO PAY $3.86 BILLION FOR KEEBLER," *THE WALL STREET JOURNAL*, OCTOBER 27, 2000, SCOTT KILMAN AND NIKHIL DEOGUN.

1. Companies calculate the present value of the future cash inflows (revenues) from the acquisition project and the present value of the current and future cash outflows of the project. If the net present value is positive and other variables are in favor of the acquisition project, an investment will be made.

2. Kellogg's objectives in the Keebler acquisition were to reduce its dependence on the breakfast cereal business, which has been flat for the past decade.

3. The main qualitative issue which enters into the decision is Kellogg tripling its debt load when acquiring the nation's second biggest maker of cookies and crackers. The largest acquisition in Kellogg's history would greatly expand the cereal giant's presence in snack sales, one of the fastest growing parts of the food industry, which is growing about 4 percent annually.

ISSUE 16-58

"CAPITAL BUDGETING FOR POLLUTION PREVENTION," *JOURNAL OF COST MANAGEMENT*, JULY/AUGUST 1999, D. JACQUE GRINNELL AND HERBERT G. HUNT III.

1. Businesses are increasingly moving away from a grudging compliance with environmental regulations and toward a new strategy of seeking ways to obtain competitive advantage through environmental leadership.

2. In competing with other projects for scarce resources, pollution prevention proposals should be considered on their own merits in terms of potential profitability. Companies view environmental impacts as opportunities to improve business performance and create environmental assets such as goodwill. They view efforts to reduce environmental impacts in the context of continuous improvement. Incorporating waste-reducing and recycling procedures into the manufacturing process can increase a company's profitability.

ISSUE 16-59

"KMART TO TAKE $230 MILLION CHARGE TO COVER GUARANTEES ON STORE LEASES," *THE WALL STREET JOURNAL*, JUNE 14, 1999, CALMETTA Y. COLEMAN AND JAMES R. HAGERTY.

1. Floyd Hall expects to convert or sublease most, if not all, of these properties within a reasonable time after they are returned to Kmart.

2. Fortunately, the cash outflows required by these leases should have no meaningful effect on the company's ongoing strategy or operations. On a pretax basis, the charge will be just over $350 million. The leases have a net present value of about $711 million.

CHAPTER 17
Further Aspects of Capital Expenditure Decisions

ANSWERS TO REVIEW QUESTIONS

17-1   Depreciation expense is an example of a noncash expense. A noncash expense has the effect of reducing income, and as a result it reduces the cash outflow for income taxes. The after-tax impact of a noncash expense is calculated by multiplying the expense by the tax rate.

17-2   The after-tax amount of a cash revenue or expense is calculated by multiplying the cash flow by one minus the tax rate.

17-3   A depreciation tax shield is the reduction in income taxes that results from the fact that depreciation expense reduces taxable income over the life of the asset being depreciated. The depreciation tax shield results in reduced cash outflows for income taxes in a capital-budgeting analysis.

17-4   An example of a cash flow that is not on the income statement is the acquisition cost of an asset purchased in cash. The after-tax amount of such a cash flow is simply the cash flow itself.

17-5   Under an accelerated depreciation method, the depreciation expense for an asset is higher in the earlier years and lower in the later years than it would be under the straight-line method. This method is advantageous to the business, because there are larger depreciation charges in the earlier years and these result in reduced cash outflows for taxes in the earlier years. Because of the time value of money, it is better to have the larger reductions in cash flows for taxes in the earlier years instead of the later years.

17-6   Under the Modified Accelerated Cost Recovery System (MACRS), each asset is placed in a property class (3-year, 5-year, 7-year, 10-year, etc.). The MACRS depreciation schedule specifies the amount of depreciation to be taken each year on an asset in a particular MACRS property class.

17-7   Office furniture with an estimated useful life of 15 years would be in the seven-year property class. Therefore, the depreciation schedule for the seven-year MACRS property class would be used to depreciate the asset. For example, 14.29% of the asset's cost would be depreciated in the first year, 24.49% of the asset's cost would be depreciated in the second year, and so forth.

17-8 Under the half-year convention, only a half year's depreciation is taken in the first year of the asset's depreciable life, and a half year's depreciation is taken in the last year of the asset's depreciable life.

17-9 A gain on disposal of an asset is the difference between the sales proceeds and the asset's book value, when the sales proceeds exceed the book value. A loss on disposal of an asset is the difference between the asset's book value and the sales proceeds, when the book value of the asset exceeds the sales proceeds.

17-10 A gain on disposal of an asset increases income. Therefore, it increases income tax and will increase the cash outflow for income tax. In a capital-budgeting analysis, the gain on disposal of the asset is multiplied by the tax rate to determine the increase in the cash outflow for tax purposes. Similarly, a loss on disposal of an asset is multiplied by the tax rate to determine the reduction in the cash outflow for tax purposes in a capital-budgeting analysis.

17-11 It is difficult to rank investment projects with positive net present values and different lives because it is unclear what the rate of return on the proceeds from the investment will be in the period after the end of one project's useful life but during the other project's useful life. The problem of ranking investment projects with positive net present values has not been solved in a satisfactory manner. From a discounted-cash-flow perspective, all projects with positive net present values are desirable and should be undertaken.

17-12 The net-present-value method and the internal-rate-of-return method may yield different rankings for investments with different lives because they make different implicit assumptions about the reinvestment of funds generated from the investment. Under the net-present-value method, cash flows are assumed to be reinvested at the rate used to discount the cash flows in the NPV analysis. In the internal-rate-of-return method, the cash flows are assumed to be reinvested at the internal rate of return.

17-13 The profitability index (PI) is defined as the present value of cash flows, exclusive of the initial investment, divided by the initial investment. Investment proposals sometimes are ranked by their profitability indexes, with a higher PI being ranked higher. Unfortunately, this method of ranking investment proposals suffers from some of the same drawbacks as other ranking methods.

17-14 A project's payback period is the number of years required for the cash inflows from the project to accumulate to an amount equal to the initial acquisition cost for the project. This criterion sometimes is used as a screening device in capital-budgeting decisions. Projects that have payback periods beyond a certain acceptable number are rejected under this criterion.

17-15 The payback method of evaluating investment proposals fails to consider the time value of money. Moreover, the method does not consider a project's cash flows beyond the payback period.

17-16 There are two ways to define an investment project's accounting rate of return:

- Accounting rate of return = (average incremental revenue – average incremental expenses, including depreciation and income taxes) ÷ initial investment.

- Accounting rate of return = (average incremental revenue – average incremental expenses, including depreciation and income taxes) ÷ average investment.

The accounting rate of return and the internal rate of return on a capital project generally differ because the accounting rate of return calculation does not take into account the time value of money.

17-17 The chief drawback of the accounting-rate-of-return method as an investment criterion is that it fails to account for the time value of money. Revenues and expenses in a project's later years are considered in the same way by the method as revenues and expenses in the project's earlier years. On the positive side, like the payback method, the accounting-rate-of-return method is a simple way of screening investment proposals. Some managers use this method because they believe it parallels financial-accounting statements.

17-18 Inflation is defined as a decline in the general purchasing power of a monetary unit, such as a dollar, across time. Inflation generally is measured by the percentage increase from year to year in the purchase price of an identical asset.

17-19 a. The real interest rate is the underlying interest rate in the economy, which includes compensation to an investor for the time value of money and the risk of the investment. The nominal interest rate is the real interest rate plus an additional premium to compensate investors for inflation.

b. A real dollar is a measure that reflects an adjustment for the purchasing power of the monetary unit. A nominal dollar is the measure used for an actual cash flow that is observed.

17-20 There are two correct methods of net-present-value analysis in an inflationary period. (1) The analyst can use real cash flows and discount them at a real discount rate based on the real interest rate. (2) The analyst can use nominal cash flows and discount them at a nominal discount rate based on the nominal interest rate. Both methods, if correctly applied, will yield the same conclusion.

SOLUTIONS TO EXERCISES

EXERCISE 17-21 (5 MINUTES)

(a)   Depreciation expense = $6,000

After-tax cash flow = ($6,000)(.30) = $1,800 savings in cash outflow for taxes

(b)   Salary expense = $32,000

After-tax cash outflow = ($32,000)(1 – .30) = $22,400

EXERCISE 17-22 (10 MINUTES)

1.   Microscope: 5-year class; double-declining balance

2.   Cattle barn: 20-year class; 150%-declining balance

3.   Industrial machine: 7-year class; double-declining balance

4.   Office desk: 7-year class; double-declining balance

5.   Delivery car: 5-year class; double-declining balance

EXERCISE 17-23 (30 MINUTES)

(1) Year	(2) MACRS Accelerated Depreciation	(3) Cash Flow: Tax Savings [Col. (2) × .30]	(4) Present Value of Cash Flow [Col. (3) × Col. (8)]	(5) MACRS Straight-Line Depreciation*	(6) Cash Flow: Tax Savings [Col. (5) × .30]	(7) Present Value of Cash Flow [Col. (6) × Col. (8)]	(8) Discount Factor (r = .12)†
1	$33,330 (33.33% × $100,000)	$ 9,999	$ 8,929**	$16,667**	$ 5,000**	$ 4,465	.893
2	44,450 (44.45% × $100,000)	13,335	10,628**	33,333**	10,000**	7,970	.797
3	14,810 (14.81% × $100,000)	4,443	3,163**	33,333**	10,000**	7,120	.712
4	7,410 (7.41% × $100,000)	2,223	1,414**	16,667**	5,000**	3,180	.636
Present value of depreciation tax shield			$24,134			$22,735	

*Straight-line depreciation with the half-year convention: Half the straight-line percentage of 33.33% in years 1 and 4.
†From Table III in the Appendix to Chapter 16.

**Rounded.

EXERCISE 17-24 (15 MINUTES)

1.   Book value   = acquisition cost – accumulated depreciation

                      = \$50,000 – \$38,845 = \$11,155

2.   Loss on sale = book value – sales proceeds

                      = \$11,155 – \$9,255 = \$1,900

3.   Reduced cash outflow for taxes (\$1,900 × .45) .... \$ 855
      Sales proceeds 9,255
      Total after-tax cash flow \$10,110

EXERCISE 17-25 (20 MINUTES)

1.   Payback period $= \dfrac{\text{initial investment}}{\text{annual after - tax cash flow}}$

                     $= \dfrac{\$124,200}{\$27,000} = 4.6$ years

2.   Net-present-value analysis:

	Discount Rate		
	10%	12%	14%
Present value of after-tax savings:			
$27,000 × 4.868*	\$131,436		
$27,000 × 4.564*		\$123,228	
$27,000 × 4.288*			\$115,776
Initial investment	(124,200)	(124,200)	(124,200)
Net present value	\$ 7,236	\$ (972)	\$ (8,424)

*From Table IV in the Appendix to Chapter 16 ($r = .10$; $r = .12$; $r = .14$)

EXERCISE 17-25 (CONTINUED)

3. Conclusion: The automatic teller machines are a sound economic investment if the after-tax hurdle rate is 10 percent, but not if it is 12 percent or 14 percent. The payback-period criterion fails to account for the time value of money. If management uses the payback method, the investment will be approved if the required payback period is 4.6 years or less. Otherwise the investment will be rejected. However, setting the cut-off value for the payback period has nothing to do with the bank's hurdle rate. In summary, the net-present-value method is preferable to the payback method.

EXERCISE 17-26 (15 MINUTES)

	Discount Rate		
	8%	10%	12%
Present value of after-tax savings:			
$4,000 × 6.710*	$26,840		
$4,000 × 6.145*		$24,580	
$4,000 × 5.650*			$22,600
Calculation of profitability index	$\dfrac{\$26,840}{\$25,000}$	$\dfrac{\$24,580}{\$25,000}$	$\dfrac{\$22,600}{\$25,000}$
Profitability index† (rounded)	1.07	.98	.90

*From Table IV in the Appendix to Chapter 16 ($n = 10$).

†Profitability index = $\dfrac{\text{present value of cash flows, exclusive of initial investment}}{\text{initial investment}}$

EXERCISE 17-27 (25 MINUTES)

1.

Year	Incremental Revenue	Incremental Operating Expenses	Incremental Depreciation	Incremental Before-Tax Profit	Incremental Income Tax	Incremental Net Income
1	$25,000	$10,000	$ 5,000	$10,000	$4,000	$6,000
2	25,000	10,000	10,000	5,000	2,000	3,000
3	25,000	10,000	10,000	5,000	2,000	3,000
4	25,000	10,000	10,000	5,000	2,000	3,000
5	25,000	10,000	10,000	5,000	2,000	3,000
6	25,000	10,000	5,000	10,000	4,000	6,000

EXERCISE 17-27 (CONTINUED)

2.   Accounting rate of return $=$ $$\frac{\left(\begin{array}{c}\text{average}\\\text{incremental}\\\text{revenue}\end{array}\right) - \left(\begin{array}{c}\text{average incremental expenses}\\\text{(including depreciation and}\\\text{income taxes)}\end{array}\right)}{\text{initial investment}}$$

$$= \frac{\text{average incremental net income}}{\text{initial investment}}$$

$$= \frac{\$4,000^*}{\$50,000} = 8\%$$

*Average incremental net income $= \left[\$6,000 + (\$3,000 \times 4) + \$6,000\right] \div 6$.

EXERCISE 17-28 (30 MINUTES)

1.   Payback period = 3 years

The accumulated after-tax incremental profit totals $99,300 in the first three years, as the following table shows ($30,000 + $33,000 + $36,300). The after-tax initial investment in advertising is also $99,300. (See the following table.)

2.   Net present value = $37,037

See the following table.

Year	Incremental Revenue	Incremental Expense	Incremental Profit	After-Tax Profit*	Discount Factor†	Present Value
1	$ 75,000	$25,000	$50,000	$30,000	.909	$ 27,270
2	82,500	27,500	55,000	33,000	.826	27,258
3	90,750	30,250	60,500	36,300	.751	27,261
4	99,825	33,275	66,550	39,930	.683	27,272
5	109,808	36,603	73,205	43,923	.621	27,276

Present value of after-tax incremental profit $136,337

Less: After-tax cash flow for initial expenditure on advertising (time 0)

        [$165,500 × (1 – .40)]   99,300

Net present value $ 37,037

*Incremental profit × (1 – .40).

†From Table III in the Appendix to Chapter 16 ($r = .10$)

EXERCISE 17-29 (25 MINUTES)

1. The project's payback period is 2.25 years, calculated as follows:

Year	After-Tax Cash Flows	
1	$ 50,000	
2	45,000	
3 (1st quarter)	10,000	(.25 × $40,000)
Total	$105,000	
Initial cost	$105,000	

2. The accounting rate of return is 18.1%, calculated as follows:

$$\text{Accounting rate of return} = \frac{\text{average net income}}{\text{initial investment}}$$

$$= \frac{\$19,000}{\$105,000} = 18.1\% \text{ (rounded)}$$

3. Net present value calculations:

Year	After-Tax Cash Flow	Discount Factor*	Present Value
0	$(105,000)	1.000	$(105,000)
1	50,000	.862	43,100
2	45,000	.743	33,435
3	40,000	.641	25,640
4	35,000	.552	19,320
5	30,000	.476	14,280
Net present value			$ 30,775

*From Table III in the Appendix to Chapter 16 (r = .16).

EXERCISE 17-30 (30 MINUTES)

Answers will vary widely, depending on the company chosen. The difficulties in assessing the benefits of advanced manufacturing equipment include issues such as the following: hurdle rates that are too high; time horizons that are too short; greater uncertainty about operating cash flows; and benefits that are difficult to quantify, such as greater production flexibility, shorter cycle times, reduced lead times, reduction of inventory levels and non-value-added costs, lower floor-space requirements, and increased product quality.

Taxes affect decisions to invest in advanced manufacturing equipment in significant ways. The huge investment results in a significant depreciation tax shield covering many years, and many of the related expenses, such as computer programmers' salaries, are deductible expenses for income-tax purposes.

EXERCISE 17-31 (20 MINUTES)

1.

Year	Cash Flow in Real Dollars	Discount Factor* (real interest rate = .20)	Present Value
0	$(100,000)	1.000	$(100,000)
1	30,000	.833	24,990
2	30,000	.694	20,820
3	30,000	.579	17,370
4	30,000	.482	14,460
5	30,000	.402	12,060
6	30,000	.335	10,050
7	30,000	.279	8,370
8	30,000	.233	6,990
Net present value			$ 15,110

*From Table III in the Appendix to Chapter 16 (r = .20).

2.   Net present value = $15,110 (See preceding table.)

A shorter method of calculating the net present value uses the annuity discount factor, since the savings, in real dollars, are identical for all eight years.

Net present value   =   ($30,000)(3.837[†]) – $100,000

   = $15,110

[†]From Table IV in the Appendix to Chapter 16 (r = .20, n = 8).

EXERCISE 17-32 (35 MINUTES)

1. Nominal interest rate:
    Real interest rate .... .20
    Inflation rate .... .10
    Combined effect (.20 × .10) .... .02
    Nominal interest rate .... .32

2.

(1) Year	(2) Cash Flow in Real Dollars*	(3) Price Index	(4) Cash Flow in Nominal Dollars [Col. (2) × Col. (3)]	(5) Discount Factor (nominal interest rate = .32)†	(6) Present Value [Col. (4) × Col. (5)]
0	$(100,000)	1.0000	$(100,000)	1.000	$(100,000)
1	30,000	$(1.10)^1 = 1.1000$	33,000	.758	25,014
2	30,000	$(1.10)^2 = 1.2100$	36,300	.574	20,836
3	30,000	$(1.10)^3 = 1.3310$	39,930	.435	17,370
4	30,000	$(1.10)^4 = 1.4641$	43,923	.329	14,451
5	30,000	$(1.10)^5 = 1.6105$	48,315	.250	12,079
6	30,000	$(1.10)^6 = 1.7716$	53,148	.189	10,045
7	30,000	$(1.10)^7 = 1.9487$	58,461	.143	8,360
8	30,000	$(1.10)^8 = 2.1436$	64,308	.108	6,945
Net present value					$ 15,100

*Expressed in terms of year 0 dollars.
†From Table III in the Appendix to Chapter 16 ($r = .32$).

3. Net present value = $15,100. See the preceding table. The $10 difference between the NPVs computed in this and the preceding exercise is due to the accumulated rounding errors in the price indexes and discount factors.

SOLUTIONS TO PROBLEMS

PROBLEM 17-33 (40 MINUTES)

1. MicroTest Technology, Inc. should not purchase the new pump because the net present value is a negative amount, $(70,547), as calculated in the following table:

	20x2	20x3	20x4	20x5	20x6
Equipment cost	$(608,000)				
Installation cost	(12,000)				
Sale of old pump [$50,000 × (1 − .4)]	30,000				
Depreciation tax shield*		$ 82,658	$110,236	$ 36,729	$ 18,377
Annual savings†		75,000	75,000	75,000	75,000
Incremental savings**		21,600	36,000	36,000	50,400
Salvage value of new pump [$80,000 × (1 − .4)]					48,000
After-tax cash flow	$(590,000)	$ 179,258	$221,236	$ 147,729	$191,777
Discount rate (Table III, Chapter 16)	× 1.000	× .862	× .743	× .641	× .552
Present value	$(590,000)	$ 154,520	$ 164,378	$ 94,694	$105,861

Net present value   Sum = $(70,547)

Explanatory Notes:s

*20x3: $620,000 × 33.33% × .4 = $82,658
 20x4: $620,000 × 44.45% × .4 = $110,236
 20x5: $620,000 × 14.81% × .4 = $36,729
 20x6: $620,000 × 7.41% × .4 = $18,377

†$125,000 each year × (1 − .4) = $75,000

** 20x3:   30 × [$3,500 − ($2,450 − $150)] × (1 − .4) = $21,600
   20x4, 20x5: 50 × [$3,500 − ($2,450 − $150)] × (1 − .4) = $36,000
   20x6:   70 × [$3,500 − ($2,450 − $150)] × (1 − .4) = $50,400

PROBLEM 17-33 (CONTINUED)

2.   Factors other than the net present value that management should consider before making the pump replacement decision include the following:

- availability of any necessary financing.

- likelihood of further technological changes for the vacuum pumps.

- reliability of the pumps.

PROBLEM 17-34 (20 MINUTES)

The net present value of the new equipment, as calculated in Exhibit 16-8, is $13,482. Let X denote the amount by which the annual after-tax increase in sales revenue must decline in order to drive the NPV to zero. The following defines X:

$$\text{(Annuity discount factor for } r = .10 \ n = 6) \ X \ = \ \$13,482$$

$$4.355 \ X \ = \ \$13,482$$

$$X \ = \ \frac{\$13,482}{4.355}$$

$$X \ = \ \$3,096 \text{ (rounded)}$$

Let Y denote the amount by which the *before-tax* increase in sales revenue must decline in order to drive the NPV to zero. Then Y is defined by:

$$(1 - \text{tax rate}) \ Y \ = \ \$3,096$$

$$(1 - .40) \ Y \ = \ \$3,096$$

$$Y \ = \ \frac{\$3,096}{.60}$$

$$Y \ = \ \$5,160$$

Conclusion: The increase in annual before-tax sales revenue could fall to $34,840 ($40,000 – $5,160) without driving the NPV on the new equipment below zero.

PROBLEM 17-35 (45 MINUTES)

(a) Computer-controlled printing press (MACRS 7-year property class):

(1) Year	(2) Straight-Line Depreciation for Book Purposes	(3) MACRS Depreciation	(4) Cash Flow: Tax Savings [Col. (3) × .40]	Discount Factor*	Present Value
1	$20,833	$250,000 × 14.29% = $35,725	$14,290	.909	$12,990
2	20,833	250,000 × 24.49% = 61,225	24,490	.826	20,229
3	20,833	250,000 × 17.49% = 43,725	17,490	.751	13,135
4	20,833	250,000 × 12.49% = 31,225	12,490	.683	8,531
5	20,833	250,000 × 8.93% = 22,325	8,930	.621	5,546
6	20,833	250,000 × 8.92% = 22,300	8,920	.564	5,031
7	20,833	250,000 × 8.93% = 22,325	8,930	.513	4,581
8	20,833	250,000 × 4.46% = 11,150	4,460	.467	2,083
9	20,833	—	—		
10	20,833	—	—	Present value	
11	20,833	—	—	of tax shield	$72,126
12	20,833	—	—		

*From Table III in the Appendix to Chapter 16 ($r = .10$).

(b) Duplicating equipment for the office (MACRS 5-year property class):

(1) Year	(2) Straight-Line Depreciation for Book Purposes	(3) MACRS Depreciation	(4) Cash Flow: Tax Savings [Col. (3) × .40]	Discount Factor[†]	Present Value
1	$10,000	$60,000 × 20.00% = $12,000	$4,800	.909	$ 4,363
2	10,000	60,000 × 32.00% = 19,200	7,680	.826	6,344
3	10,000	60,000 × 19.20% = 11,520	4,608	.751	3,461
4	10,000	60,000 × 11.52% = 6,912	2,765	.683	1,888
5	10,000	60,000 × 11.52% = 6,912	2,765	.621	1,717
6	10,000	60,000 × 5.76% = 3,456	1,382	.564	779

Present value of tax shield $18,552

[†]From Table III in the Appendix to Chapter 16 ($r = .10$).

PROBLEM 17-36 (50 MINUTES)

1. Calculation of incremental after-tax cash flows:

Purchase	Time 0
Purchase of new equipment	$(300,000)
One-time transfer expense net of tax ($30,000 × .6)	(18,000)
Sale of old equipment net of tax on gain ($10,000 × .6)	6,000
Total initial cash outflow	$(312,000)

PROBLEM 17-36 (CONTINUED)

	Annual Operation							
	Year 1	Year 2	Year 3	Year 4	Year 5	Year 6	Year 7	Year 8
Cash operating savings	$90,000*	$150,000	$150,000	$150,000	$150,000	$150,000	$150,000	$150,000
Less tax effect (40%)	36,000	60,000	60,000	60,000	60,000	60,000	60,000	60,000
Cash savings after tax	$54,000	$ 90,000	$ 90,000	$ 90,000	$ 90,000	$ 90,000	$ 90,000	$ 90,000
Depreciation tax shield								
(see following schedule)	17,148	29,388	20,988	14,988	10,716	10,704	10,716	5,352
After-tax operating cash flows	$71,148	$119,388	$110,988	$104,988	$100,716	$100,704	$100,716	$ 95,352

*$90,000 = $150,000 × 60%

PROBLEM 17-36 (CONTINUED)

		Depreciation Schedule		
Year	MACRS Percentage	Depreciation (MACRS Rate × $300,000)	Tax Rate	Depreciation Tax Shield
1	14.29%	$42,870	40%	$17,148
2	24.49%	73,470	40%	29,388
3	17.49%	52,470	40%	20,988
4	12.49%	37,470	40%	14,988
5	8.93%	26,790	40%	10,716
6	8.92%	26,760	40%	10,704
7	8.93%	26,790	40%	10,716
8	4.46%	13,380	40%	5,352

2. Net present value analysis:

Year	After-Tax Cash Flow	Discount Factor ($r = 12\%$; $n = 8$)	Present Value
0	$(312,000)	1.000	$(312,000)
1	71,148	.893	63,535
2	119,388	.797	95,152
3	110,988	.712	79,023
4	104,988	.636	66,772
5	100,716	.567	57,106
6	100,704	.507	51,057
7	100,716	.452	45,524
8	95,352	.404	38,522
Net present value			$184,691

Recommendation:

Management should purchase the new equipment because the proposal's net present value is positive.

PROBLEM 17-37 (45 MINUTES)

	Storage Racks			Forklift			
Year	MACRS Depreciation	Cash Flow: Tax Savings (Depr. × .35)	Present Value*	MACRS Depreciation	Cash Flow: Tax Savings (Depr. × .35)	Present Value*	Discount Factor
1	$200,000 × 10.00% = $20,000	$ 7,000	$ 6,139	$120,000 × 20.00% = $24,000	$ 8,400	$ 7,367	.877
2	200,000 × 18.00% = 36,000	12,600	9,689	120,000 × 32.00% = 38,400	13,440	10,335	.769
3	200,000 × 14.40% = 28,800	10,080	6,804	120,000 × 19.20% = 23,040	8,064	5,443	.675
4	200,000 × 11.52% = 23,040	8,064	4,774	120,000 × 11.52% = 13,824	4,838	2,864	.592
5	200,000 × 9.22% = 18,440	6,454	3,350	120,000 × 11.52% = 13,824	4,838	2,511	.519
6	200,000 × 7.37% = 14,740	5,159	2,353	120,000 × 5.76% = 6,912	2,419	1,103	.456
7	200,000 × 6.55% = 13,100	4,585	1,834				.400
8	200,000 × 6.55% = 13,100	4,585	1,609				.351
9	200,000 × 6.56% = 13,120	4,592	1,414				.308
10	200,000 × 6.55% = 13,100	4,585	1,238				.270
11	200,000 × 3.28% = 6,560	2,296	544				.237
Present value of depreciation tax shield			$39,748			$29,623	

*Cash flow × discount factor in right-hand column (from Table III in Appendix to Chapter 16, $r = .14$).

PROBLEM 17-38 (60 MINUTES)

Item Number	Type of Cash Flow	20x0	20x1	20x2	20x3	20x4	20x5	20x6	20x7	20x8
(1)	Acquisition cost and depreciation tax shield*	$(1,000,000)	$ 60,000	$ 96,000	$ 57,600	$ 34,560	$ 34,560	$ 17,280		
(2)	Software development [$25,000 × (1 – .30)]		(17,500)	(17,500)						
(3)	Computer expert's salary and fringe benefits [$80,000 × (1 – .30)]		(56,000)	(56,000)	(56,000)	(56,000)	(56,000)	(56,000)	$(56,000)	$(56,000)
(4)	Maintenance technicians' wages and fringe benefits [$150,000 × (1 – .30)]		(105,000)	(105,000)	(105,000)	(105,000)	(105,000)	(105,000)	(105,000)	(105,000)
(5)	Changeover of line [$90,000 × (1 – .30)]		(63,000)							
(6)	Employee training [20x1; $35,000 × (1 – .30)] [20x2; $25,000 × (1 – .30)] [20x3; $10,000 × (1 – .30)]		(24,500)	(17,500)	(7,000)					
(7)	Investment in working capital (spare parts)	(60,000)								60,000
(8)	Salvage value of equipment									50,000
	Tax effect of gain on sale [($50,000 – 0) × .30]									(15,000)
(9)	Savings on manufacturing costs [$480,000 × (1 – .30)]		336,000	336,000	336,000	336,000	336,000	336,000	336,000	336,000
(10)	Disposal of equipment: Sales proceeds		20,000	140,000						
	Tax effect of gain or loss [($50,000 – $20,000) × .30] [($90,000 – $140,000) × .30]		9,000	(15,000)						
	Total after-tax cash flow	**$(1,060,000)**	**$159,000**	**$361,000**	**$225,600**	**$209,560**	**$209,560**	**$192,280**	**$175,000**	**$270,000**

*Depreciation tax shield: MACRS percentage × .30 × $1,000,000.

PROBLEM 17-39 (15 MINUTES, ASSUMING THE PRECEDING PROBLEM HAS BEEN COMPLETED)

Year	After-Tax Cash Flow (from the preceding problem's solution)	Discount Factor*	Present Value
20x0	$(1,060,000)	1.000	$(1,060,000)
20x1	159,000	.893	141,987
20x2	361,000	.797	287,717
20x3	225,600	.712	160,627
20x4	209,560	.636	133,280
20x5	209,560	.567	118,821
20x6	192,280	.507	97,486
20x7	175,000	.452	79,100
20x8	270,000	.404	109,080
Net present value			$ 68,098

*From Table III in the Appendix to Chapter 16 ($r = .12$).

PROBLEM 17-40 (60 MINUTES)

1.   Net-present-value analysis:

	20x0	20x1	20x2	20x3	20x4	Net Present Value
Cost of equipment	$(1,500,000)					
MACRS tax shield*.......		$199,980	$266,700	$ 88,860	$ 44,460	
Labor savings net of tax[†].........................		240,900	240,900	251,850	251,850	
Maintenance costs net of tax effect: $6,000 × (1 − .40)		(3,600)	(3,600)	(3,600)	(3,600)	
Increased sales proceeds net of tax effect: ($1,000,000 − $800,000) × (1 − .40)					120,000	
Net cash flow before discounting	$(1,500,000)	$437,280	$504,000	$337,110	$412,710	
Discount factor (Table III, Chapter 16)	1.000	.862	.743	.641	.552	
Present value of cash flow	($1,500,000)	$376,935	$374,472	$216,088	$227,816	$(304,689)

*MACRS tax shield:

Year	Cost (1)	MACRS Rate (2)	MACRS Deduction [(1) × (2) = (3)]	Tax Shield [(3) × 40%]
20x1.............	$1,500,000	33.33%	$499,950	$199,980
20x2.............	1,500,000	44.45%	666,750	266,700
20x3.............	1,500,000	14.81%	222,150	88,860
20x4	1,500,000	7.41%	111,150	44,460

†Calculation of labor savings:

	20x1-20x2	20x3-20x4
Current wage rate	$ 10.00	$ 10.00
Increase at January 1, 20x1	1.00	1.00
Increase at January 1, 20x3		.50
Proposed wage rates	$ 11.00	$ 11.50
Employee benefits (40%)	4.40	4.60
Total hourly labor cost	$ 15.40	$ 16.10
Overtime premium rate (50% of proposed wage rates; no employee benefits on overtime)	$ 5.50	$ 5.75
Overtime hours saved	× 3,000	× 3,000
Overtime labor savings	$ 16,500	$ 17,250
Regular hours—current	40,000	40,000
Regular hours—proposed	15,000	15,000
Savings in hours	25,000	25,000
Total hourly labor cost	×$ 15.40	×$ 16.10
Labor savings—regular hours	$385,000	$402,500
Labor savings—overtime hours	16,500	17,250
Total before-tax labor savings	$401,500	$419,750
Tax effect (40%)	160,600	167,900
Labor savings net of tax	$240,900	$251,850

On the basis of the NPV analysis, the automated assembly equipment should not be purchased.

2. Some of the difficulties that management may face in using discounted-cash-flow analysis to make its decision regarding the high-tech assembly equipment are the following:

    (a) The hurdle rate may be too high. The key is to choose a discount rate that reflects the firm's investment opportunity rate for projects of equivalent risk.

    (b) The firm's management may be uncertain about some of the operating cost savings that could result if the equipment is purchased.

    (c) Intangible benefits may be ignored. For example, automated assembly equipment could result in greater flexibility in the production process, shorter manufacturing cycle times, reduced lead times, and a reduction of non-value-added costs.

3. The vice president for production acted improperly in asking the controller to alter the NPV analysis by overestimating the labor savings due to automation. If the VP believes there are intangible benefits, he should (1) try to quantify them, or (2) write a memo explaining such benefits and submit it to the board of directors along with the controller's NPV analysis.

   The controller should refuse to alter his NPV analysis as requested by the VP. The board has a right to know the facts when it makes the decision about automation. Several of the ethical standards for management accountants (listed in Chapter 1) are relevant, including the following:

   Competence:

   - Prepare complete and clear reports and recommendations after appropriate analysis of relevant and reliable information.

   Objectivity:

   - Communicate information fairly and objectively.

   - Disclose fully all relevant information that could reasonably be expected to influence an intended user's understanding of the reports, comments, and recommendations presented.

   The controller could offer to help the VP in assessing and quantifying the intangible benefits associated with automation.

4. The current NPV on the automation project is $(304,689). Thus, the present value of the annual, after-tax cash flows from any intangible benefits would have to be $304,689. Dividing by the four-year, 16% annuity discount factor (Table IV in Chapter 16), the annual, after-tax cash flow would have to be $108,895 ($304,689 ÷ 2.798). Let X denote the before-tax, annual cash flow required. Then:

$$X - .40X = \$108,895$$
$$.60X = \$108,895$$
$$X = \$181,492 \text{ (rounded)}$$

   Thus, the before-tax, annual cash flow from the intangible benefits would have to be $181,492 in order to bring the automation project's NPV up to zero.

PROBLEM 17-40 (CONTINUED)

Check:

Annual before-tax cash flow from intangible benefits	$181,492
× (1 – tax rate)	× (1 – .40)
Annual after-tax cash flow from intangible benefits	$108,895
× Annuity discount factor (4 years; r = .16)	× 2.798
Present value of intangible benefits	$304,688
NPV of project without intangible benefits	(304,689)
Revised NPV (differs from zero due to rounding error)	$ (1)

PROBLEM 17-41 (35 MINUTES)

Requirements 1 and 2:

Year	MACRS Depreciation	Cash Flow: Tax Savings [depreciation × .40]	Total After-Tax Cash Inflow
1	$100,000 × 20.00% = $20,000	$ 8,000	$ 8,000 + $25,000 = $33,000
2	100,000 × 32.00% = 32,000	12,800	12,800 + 25,000 = 37,800
3	100,000 × 19.20% = 19,200	7,680	7,680 + 25,000 = 32,680
4	100,000 × 11.52% = 11,520	4,608	4,608 + 25,000 = 29,608
5	100,000 × 11.52% = 11,520	4,608	4,608 + 25,000 = 29,608
6	100,000 × 5.76% = 5,760	2,304	2,304 = 2,304

3. Payback period:

The payback period is between two and three years. The after-tax cash inflows accumulate to only $70,800 after two years ($33,000 + $37,800). However, they accumulate to $103,480 after three years, which is more than enough to pay back the initial investment of $100,000.

4. The equipment does meet the company's criterion, since the payback period is less than three years.

PROBLEM 17-41 (CONTINUED)

5. Net present value:

Year	After-Tax Cash Flow	Discount Factor*	Present Value
0	$(100,000)	1.000	$(100,000)
1	33,000	.909	29,997
2	37,800	.826	31,223
3	32,680	.751	24,543
4	29,608	.683	20,222
5	29,608	.621	18,387
6	2,304	.564	1,299
Net present value			$ 25,671

*From Table III in the Appendix to Chapter 16 ($r = .10$).

PROBLEM 17-42 (45 MINUTES)

1.

Cash Flows	Timing	Before-Tax Amount	Tax Effect	After-Tax Cash Flow	After-Tax Net Income
Investment	Year 0	$(18,000)	—	$(18,000)	—
Cash savings	Years 1-5	$ 7,000	$(2,800)	$ 4,200	$ 4,200
Depreciation and related tax shield	Years 1-5	(3,600)	1,440	1,440	(2,160)
Totals				$ 5,640	$ 2,040

a. Payback period = $\dfrac{\text{investment}}{\text{after-tax cash flow}} = \dfrac{\$18,000}{\$5,640} = 3.19$ years

b. Accounting rate of return = $\dfrac{\text{annual after-tax net income}}{\text{investment (initial or average)}}$

Initial Investment

$\dfrac{\$2,040}{\$18,000} = 11.3\%$

Average Investment

$\dfrac{\$2,040}{\$9,000} = 22.7\%$

PROBLEM 17-42 (CONTINUED)

c. Net present value = (after-tax cash flows × annuity discount factor) – initial investment

   = ($5,640 × 3.433) – $18,000

   = $1,362 (rounded)

d. Profitability index (PI) = $\dfrac{\text{present value of after-tax cash flows}}{\text{initial investment}}$

   = $\dfrac{\$5,640 \times 3.433}{\$18,000} = \dfrac{\$19,362}{\$18,000} = 1.08$

e. Internal rate of return:

Present value at 16%	$5,640 × 3.274	$ 18,465
Present value at 18%	$5,640 × 3.127	17,636
Difference		$ 829
Present value (16%)		$ 18,465
Initial investment		18,000
Difference		$ 465

Estimated increment	465/829 × 2% = 1.12%
Internal rate of return	16% + 1.12% = 17.12%

PROBLEM 17-42 (CONTINUED)

2.   Memorandum

Date: Today

To: President, MedTech Company

From: I.M. Student

Subject: Decision models for proposed new equipment investment

The payback method is inferior because it ignores the time value of money and cash proceeds beyond the payback period. However, it is useful in that it tells management how long it will take to recoup its original investment.

The accounting rate of return method is inferior because it uses accounting income and investment instead of cash flows. In addition, it also ignores the time value of money.

The net present (NPV), profitability index (PI), and internal rate of return (IRR) methods are similar. These three discounted cash flow methods consider the time value of money and the timing of cash flows. Consequently, they are all superior to the first two methods.

PROBLEM 17-43 (45 MINUTES)

1.   Net-present-value analysis:

(a) Cost savings from manufacturing valve stems:

	Per Unit	Total
Cost to purchase pressure fittings from outside supplier	$20.00	$1,600,000
Incremental costs of manufacturing the pressure fittings*		
Direct material	$ 4.50	$ 360,000
Direct labor and variable overhead		
($3.70 + $1.70 − $1.60)	3.80	304,000
Total incremental costs	$ 8.30	$ 664,000
Cost savings from manufacturing pressure fittings	$11.70	$ 936,000
Taxes (40%)	4.68	374,400
After-tax cost savings of manufacturing pressure fittings	$ 7.02	$ 561,600

*No fixed overhead is included because it is not an incremental cost. The amount of fixed overhead would not be affected by this decision, and the breakdown of the fixed overhead between depreciation and cash expenditures is not relevant.

PROBLEM 17-43 (CONTINUED)

(b) Discounted-cash-flow analysis:

				Cash Flow	Discount Factor	Present Value
Annual cost savings				$561,600	3.605	$2,024,568
MACRS depreciation tax shield:						
Year	MACRS Percentage	MACRS Depreciation	Tax Rate	Tax Shield		
1	33.33%	$ 833,250	40%	$333,300	.893	297,637
2	44.45%	1,111,250	40%	444,500	.797	354,267
3	14.81%	370,250	40%	148,100	.712	105,447
4	7.41%	185,250	40%	74,100	.636	47,128
				Cash Flow		
Salvage Value of Tools						
Cash proceeds from sale				$100,000	.567	56,700
Gain on sale		$ 100,000	40%	40,000	.567	(22,680)
Initial investment						(2,500,000)
Net present value						$ 363,067

2. Factors that Life Line Corporation's management should consider in addition to the discounted-cash-flow analysis before a decision is made to replace the tools or purchase the pressure fittings from an outside supplier include:

- the possibility of negotiating a lower price for the pressure fittings.
- the capacity of the firm's manufacturing facilities.
- alternate uses of the manufacturing facilities.
- the reliability of the supplier to deliver quality parts on a timely basis.
- the ability of the supplier to meet an increased demand for the part.

PROBLEM 17-44 (45 MINUTES)

1. Net-present value analysis of the machine replacement:

	20x1	20x2	20x3	20x4	20x5
Acquisition cost	$(1,000,000)				
After-tax operating cost savings [$300,000 × (1 – .40)]		$180,000	$180,000	$180,000	$180,000

Depreciation tax shield:

Year	Acquisition Cost	MACRS Percentage	Tax Rate		20x1	20x2	20x3	20x4	20x5
20x2:	$1,000,000	× 33.33%	× .40			133,320			
20x3	$1,000,000	× 44.45%	× .40				177,800		
20x4	$1,000,000	× 14.81%	× .40					59,240	
20x5	$1,000,000	× 7.41%	× .40						29,640

Salvage value of old machine:

				20x1	20x2	20x3	20x4	20x5
Cash proceeds from sale				60,000				
Gain on sale	$60,000							
Tax rate	× .40							
Tax on gain	$24,000			(24,000)				
Total after-tax cash flow				$ (964,000)	$313,320	$357,800	$239,240	$209,640
Discount factor (Table III, Chapter 16)				× 1.000	× .893	× .797	× .712	× .636
Present value				$ (964,000)	$279,795*	$285,167*	$170,339*	$133,331*

Net present value .... Sum = $(95,368)

*Rounded.

PROBLEM 17-44 (CONTINUED)

2.   The machine replacement's internal rate of return is between 6% and 8%. The project's net present value is positive if a 6% discount rate is used, but it is negative if an 8% discount rate is used.

Year	Total After-Tax Cash Flow (from requirement 1)	6% Discount Factor	Present Value (using 6%)	8% Discount Factor	Present Value (using 8%)
20x1	$(964,000)	1.000	$(964,000)	1.000	$(964,000)
20x2	313,320	.943	295,461	.926	290,134
20x3	357,800	.890	318,442	.857	306,635
20x4	239,240	.840	200,962	.794	189,957
20x5	209,640	.792	166,035	.735	154,085
Net present value			$ 16,900		$ (23,189)

3.   The payback period on the machine replacement is between three and four years.

Year	Total After-Tax Cash Inflow (from requirement 1)
20x2	$ 313,320
20x3	357,800
20x4	239,240
Subtotal	$ 910,360< $964,000 = initial net cash outflow
20x5	209,640
Total	$1,120,000> $964,000 = initial net cash outflow

PROBLEM 17-44 (CONTINUED)

4. With a salvage value of zero on the new machine, the machine replacement's net present value is $(95,368). Thus, the after-tax discounted cash flow from the salvage of the new machine on December 31, 20x5 would have to exceed $95,368. Dividing by the year 4, 12% discount factor, the after-tax cash flow would have to exceed $149,950 ($95,368 ÷ .636, rounded). Let X denote the new machine's salvage value on December 31, 20x5. Then the gain on sale will also be X, since the new machine will be fully depreciated. The tax on this gain will be .40X. Therefore, the following equation must hold:

$$X - .40X \quad = \quad \$149,950$$
$$.60X \quad = \quad \$149,950$$
$$X \quad = \quad \$249,917 \text{ (rounded)}$$

Thus, the salvage value of the new machine must exceed $249,917 in order to turn the machine replacement into a positive net-present-value project.

Check:

Cash proceeds from sale of new machine		$249,917
Gain on sale	$249,917	
Tax rate	× .40	
Tax on gain	$ 99,967	(99,967)
After-tax cash flow from sale		$149,950
Discount factor (4 years, 12%)		× .636
Present value of cash flow from sale		$ 95,368

Adding the $95,368 to the negative net present value calculated in requirement (1) of $(95,368), the new net present value is zero.

PROBLEM 17-45 (40 MINUTES)

1. The net-present-value analysis of the after-tax cash flows that would result from purchasing the just-in-time system at Office Furnishings Company is presented in the following table.

	Year 0	Year 1	Year 2	Year 3	Year 4	Year 5
Purchase of equipment						
(a) Computer system	$(1,250,000)					
(b) Material handling	(450,000)					
Depreciation						
MACRS rates		.2000	.3200	.1920	.1152	.1152
Depreciation amounts:						
Computer system		$250,000	$400,000	$240,000	$144,000	$144,000
Material-handling equipment		90,000	144,000	86,400	51,840	51,840
Total depreciation		$340,000	$544,000	$326,400	$195,840	$195,840
(c) Tax savings at 40%		$136,000	$217,600	$130,560	$ 78,336	$ 78,336
(d) Total gain on disposal of equipment*						$129,168
Operating cash flows:						
Sales increase		$600,000	$660,000	$726,000	$798,600	$878,460
Contribution margin (at 60%)		$360,000	$396,000	$435,600	$479,160	$527,076
Material-ordering costs		(50,000)	(50,000)	(50,000)	(50,000)	(50,000)
Rent savings[†]		60,000	60,000	60,000	60,000	60,000
Taxable income		$370,000	$406,000	$445,600	$489,160	$537,076
Less: Taxes at 40%		148,000	162,400	178,240	195,664	214,830
(e) Cash flow from operations		$222,000	$243,600	$267,360	$293,496	$322,246
(f) Working capital savings		$150,000				
Net cash flow**	$(1,700,000)	$508,000	$461,200	$397,920	$371,832	$529,750
Discount factor[††]	1.000	.909	.826	.751	.683	.621
Present value	$(1,700,000)	$461,772	$380,951	$298,838	$253,961	$328,975
Net present value	$24,497					

	Computer Equipment	Material Handling	Total Cash Flow
*Gain on disposal:			
Proceeds	$100,000	$50,000	$150,000
Undepreciated tax basis	72,000	25,920	
Taxable gain	$ 28,000	$ 24,080	
Less: Taxes at 40%	11,200	9,632	20,832
Cash flow on disposal of equipment			$129,168

Undepreciated tax basis = purchase price minus accumulated MACRS depreciation deductions.

†Rent savings are 20 percent of current annual cost of $300,000, or $60,000 annually.

**Net cash flow = sum of amounts from rows (a), (b), (c), (d), (e), and (f).

††From Table III in the Appendix to Chapter 16 ($r = .10$).

2. The company should purchase the just-in-time (JIT) system because the net present value is $24,497. The positive net present value means the project will return more than the minimum required hurdle rate. Therefore, according to management's criteria, the JIT system will be cost beneficial to the organization. However, since the net present value is very small in relation to the $1,700,000 investment, management should investigate any other implications of the project or may wish to perform sensitivity analyses to gauge the likely success of the project.

PROBLEM 17-46 (50 MINUTES)

1. Office King Corporation should purchase the new equipment to manufacture waste containers. The net present value calculations are presented below.

	20x0	20x1	20x2	20x3	20x4	20x5
Equipment cost	$(945,000)					
Discount @ 2%	18,900					
Freight	(11,000)					
Installation cost	(22,900)					
Savage value—old equipment [$1,500 × (1 – .4)]	900					
Working capital reduction	2,500					
Manufacturing savings*...		$210,000	$210,000	$218,400	$231,000	$231,000
Supervision [$45,000 × (1 – .4)]		(27,000)	(27,000)	(27,000)	(27,000)	(27,000)
Depreciation tax shield[†]		127,987	170,688	56,870	28,454	—
Salvage value—new equipment [$12,000 × (1 – .4)]						7,200
After-tax cash flow	$(956,600)	$310,987	$353,688	$248,270	$232,454	$211,200
Discount rate (Table III, Chapter 16)	× 1.000	× .893	× .797	× .712	× .636	× .567
Present value	$(956,600)	$277,711	$281,889	$176,768	$147,841	$119,750
Net present value			Sum = $47,359			

PROBLEM 17-46 (CONTINUED)

Supporting calculations:

*Manufacturing unit cost savings versus unit purchase cost:

Unit purchase cost		$27.00

New unit variable manufacturing cost:

Material	$ 8.00 × 1.00 = $8.00	
Direct labor	10.00 × .75 = 7.50	
Variable overhead	6.00 × .75 = 4.50	20.00
Savings per unit		$ 7.00

Manufacturing savings:

Year	Unit Savings		Estimated Production		Estimated Cost		(1 – Tax Rate)		After-Tax Cost Savings
20x1	$7	×	50,000	=	$350,000	×	.6	=	$210,000
20x2	7	×	50,000	=	350,000	×	.6	=	210,000
20x3	7	×	52,000	=	364,000	×	.6	=	218,400
20x4	7	×	55,000	=	385,000	×	.6	=	231,000
20x5	7	×	55,000	=	385,000	×	.6	=	231,000

†MACRS depreciable base:

Installed cost for depreciation purposes:

Acquisition cost	$945,000
Discount (2%)	(18,900)
Freight	11,000
Installation	22,900
Net installed cost	$960,000

MACRS depreciation tax shield:

Year	Installed Cost		MACRS Rate		Depreciation		Tax Rate		Tax Benefit
20x1	$960,000	×	33.33%	=	$319,968	×	.4	=	$127,987
20x2	960,000	×	44.45%	=	426,720	×	.4	=	170,688
20x3	960,000	×	14.81%	=	142,176	×	.4	=	56,870
20x4	960,000	×	7.41%	=	71,136	×	.4	=	28,454

PROBLEM 17-46 (CONTINUED)

2. Many companies use the payback method, in addition to determining the net present value, because the payback method provides a preliminary screening of projects. It indicates how fast an original investment can be recovered from the cash flows, which is of particular interest when a project is considered risky.

3. The payback period is between 3 and 4 years:

Year	Total After-Tax Cash Flow (from requirement 1)
20x1	$ 310,987
20x2	353,688
20x3	248,270
Subtotal	$ 912,945 < $956,600* = initial net installed cost
20x4	232,454
Total	$1,145,399 > $956,600* = initial net installed cost

*See calculations in requirement (1).

PROBLEM 17-47 (35 MINUTES)

1. (a) Mall restaurant:

Net after-tax cash inflows	$ 50,000
× Annuity discount factor ($r = .10$, $n = 20$)	× 8.514
Present value of annual cash flows	$425,700
Cash outflow at time 0	400,000
Net present value	$ 25,700

(b) Downtown restaurant:

Net after-tax cash inflows	$ 35,800
× Annuity discount factor ($r = .10$, $n = 10$)	× 6.145
Present value of annual cash flows	$219,991
Cash outflow at time 0	200,000
Net present value	$ 19,991

2. Profitability index = $\dfrac{\text{present value of cash flows, exclusive of initial investment}}{\text{initial investment}}$

(a) Mall restaurant:

Profitability index = $\dfrac{\$425,700}{\$400,000}$ = 1.06 (rounded)

(b) Downtown restaurant:

Profitability index = $\dfrac{\$219,991}{\$200,000}$ = 1.10 (rounded)

3. The mall site ranks first on NPV, but the downtown site ranks first on the profitability index.

4. The two proposed restaurant projects have different lives, which makes it particularly difficult to rank them. It is not clear what will happen in years 11 through 20 if the downtown site is chosen.

PROBLEM 17-48 (30 MINUTES)

1. Payback period = $\dfrac{\text{initial investment}}{\text{annual after-tax cash inflow}}$

    (a) Mall restaurant:

    $$\text{Payback period} = \frac{\$400{,}000}{\$50{,}000} = 8 \text{ years}$$

    (b) Downtown restaurant:

    $$\text{Payback period} = \frac{\$200{,}000}{\$35{,}800} = 5.6 \text{ years (rounded)}$$

2. Accounting rate of return $= \dfrac{\left(\begin{array}{c}\text{average} \\ \text{incremental} \\ \text{revenue}\end{array}\right) - \left(\begin{array}{c}\text{average incremental expenses} \\ \text{(including depreciation and} \\ \text{income taxes)}\end{array}\right)}{\text{initial investment}}$

    (a) Mall restaurant:

    $$\text{Accounting rate of return} = \frac{\$50{,}000}{\$400{,}000} = 12.5\%$$

    (b) Downtown restaurant:

    $$\text{Accounting rate of return} = \frac{\$35{,}800}{\$200{,}000} = 17.9\%$$

3. The owner's criteria will lead to selection of the downtown site.

4. Neither the payback period nor the accounting-rate-of-return method considers the time value of money. Moreover, the payback method ignores cash flows beyond the payback period.

    On the positive side, both methods can provide a simple means of screening a large number of investment proposals.

PROBLEM 17-49 (35 MINUTES)

1. (a) Sacramento office:

Net after-tax cash flows	$ 80,000
× Annuity discount factor (r = .10, n = 20)	× 8.514
Present value of annual cash flows	$681,120
Cash outflow at time 0	597,520
Net present value	$ 83,600

(b) Bakersfield office:

Net after-tax cash flows	$110,000
× Annuity discount factor (r = .10, n = 10)	× 6.145
Present value of annual cash flows	$675,950
Cash outflow at time 0	596,860
Net present value	$ 79,090

2. Profitability index $= \dfrac{\text{present value of cash flows, exclusive of initial investment}}{\text{initial investment}}$

(a) Sacramento office:

Profitability index $= \dfrac{\$681,120}{\$597,520} = 1.14$ (rounded)

(b) Bakersfield office:

Profitability index $= \dfrac{\$675,950}{\$596,860} = 1.13$ (rounded)

3. The Bakersfield office ranks first on IRR, but the Sacramento office has a higher profitability index.

4. The two proposed offices have different lives, which makes it particularly difficult to rank them. It is not clear what will happen in years 11 through 20 if the Bakersfield office is chosen.

PROBLEM 17-50 (50 MINUTES)

1. Schedule of cash flows in nominal dollars:

(1) Year	(2) After-Tax Incremental Cash Flow in Real Dollars (not including depreciation shield)*†	(3) Price Index	(4) After-Tax Incremental Cash Flow in Nominal Dollars (not including depreciation shield)**	(5) MACRS Depreciation	(6) Cash Flow: Tax Savings (depreciation × .40)	(7) Total After-Tax Cash Flow in Nominal Dollars [Col. (4) + Col.(6)]
20x0	$(188,000)*†	1.0000	$(188,000)	—	—	$(188,000)
20x1	42,000	$(1.20)^1 = 1.2000$	50,400	$200,000 × 20.00% = $40,000	$16,000	66,400
20x2	42,000	$(1.20)^2 = 1.4400$	60,480	200,000 × 32.00% = 64,000	25,600	86,080
20x3	42,000	$(1.20)^3 = 1.7280$	72,576	200,000 × 19.20% = 38,400	15,360	87,936
20x4	42,000	$(1.20)^4 = 2.0736$	87,091	200,000 × 11.52% = 23,040	9,216	96,307
20x5	42,000	$(1.20)^5 = 2.4883$	104,509	200,000 × 11.52% = 23,040	9,216	113,725
20x6	42,000	$(1.20)^6 = 2.9860$	125,412	200,000 × 5.76% = 11,520	4,608	130,020
20x7	42,000	$(1.20)^7 = 3.5832$	150,494			150,494

*Acquisition cost of new satellite dish .... $(200,000)
Salvage value of old equipment 20,000
Incremental tax on gain on sale:
 [($20,000 – 0) × .40] .... (8,000)
Time 0 cash outflow .... $(188,000)

†Annual after-tax incremental cash inflow = [($80,000 – $10,000) × (1 – .40)]
= $42,000, expressed in real dollars

**Column (2) × column (3).

PROBLEM 17-50 (CONTINUED)

2. Nominal interest rate:

Real interest rate	.10
Inflation rate	.20
Combined effect (.10 × .20)	.02
Nominal interest rate	.32

3. Net present value analysis:

Year	After-Tax Cash Flow in Nominal Dollars	Discount Factor*	Present Value
20x0	$(188,000)	1.000	$(188,000)
20x1	66,400	.758	50,331
20x2	86,080	.574	49,410
20x3	87,936	.435	38,252
20x4	96,307	.329	31,685
20x5	113,725	.250	28,431
20x6	130,020	.189	24,574
20x7	150,494	.143	21,521
Net present value			$ 56,204

*From Table III in the Appendix to Chapter 16 ($r = .32$).

PROBLEM 17-51 (50 MINUTES)

1. Price indexes: See column (5) in the following table.

2. After-tax cash flows in real dollars: See the following table.

PROBLEM 17-51 (CONTINUED)

(1)	(2)	(3)	(4)	(5)	(6)	(7)
	After-Tax Incremental Cash Flow in Real Dollars (not including depreciation shield)*	MACRS Depreciation	Cash Flow: Tax Savings [depreciation × .40]	Price Index	Depreciation Tax Shield in Real Dollars [Col. (4) ÷ Col. (5)]	Total After-Tax Cash Flow in Real Dollars [Col. (2) + Col.(6)]
Year						
20x0	$(188,000)	—	—	1.0000	—	$(188,000)
20x1	42,000†	$200,000 × 20.00% = $40,000	$16,000	$(1.20)^1 = 1.2000$	$13,333	55,333
20x2	42,000	200,000 × 32.00% = 64,000	25,600	$(1.20)^2 = 1.4400$	17,778	59,778
20x3	42,000	200,000 × 19.20% = 38,400	15,360	$(1.20)^3 = 1.7280$	8,889	50,889
20x4	42,000	200,000 × 11.52% = 23,040	9,216	$(1.20)^4 = 2.0736$	4,444	46,444
20x5	42,000	200,000 × 11.52% = 23,040	9,216	$(1.20)^5 = 2.4883$	3,704	45,704
20x6	42,000	200,000 × 5.76% = 11,520	4,608	$(1.20)^6 = 2.9860$	1,543	43,543
20x7	42,000	—	—	$(1.20)^7 = 3.5832$	—	42,000

*Acquisition cost of new satellite dish .... $(200,000)
Salvage value of old equipment 20,000
Incremental tax on gain on sale:
    [($20,000 – 0) × .40] .... (8,000)
Time 0 cash outflow .... $(188,000)

†Annual after-tax incremental cash inflow = [($80,000 – $10,000) × (1 – .40)]
                                            = $42,000, expressed in real dollars

PROBLEM 17-51 (CONTINUED)

3.   Net present-value analysis:

Year	After-Tax Cash Flow in Real Dollars	Discount Factor*	Present Value
20x0	$(188,000)	1.000	$(188,000)
20x1	55,333	.909	50,298
20x2	59,778	.826	49,377
20x3	50,889	.751	38,218
20x4	46,444	.683	31,721
20x5	45,704	.621	28,382
20x6	43,543	.564	24,558
20x7	42,000	.513	21,546
Net present value			$ 56,100[†]

*From Table III in the Appendix to Chapter 16 ($r = .10$).

[†]The difference between the NPVs computed in this and the preceding problem is due to the cumulative rounding errors in the price indexes and discount factors.

PROBLEM 17-52 (50 MINUTES)

1.   Schedule of net after-tax, annual, real cash flows:

In the following schedule, the annual cost savings are already expressed in real dollars, since the data were given in the problem in terms of 20x0 prices. In contrast, the annual depreciation tax shield is in nominal dollars; it must be converted to real dollars by dividing by the price index. Finally, the acquisition cost of the machine is already stated in real dollars (20x0 prices).

	Year				
	20x0	20x1	20x2	20x3	20x4
Cost savings of wages and benefits ...		$50,000	$50,000	$50,000	$50,000
Cost of additional supplies		(3,000)	(3,000)	(3,000)	(3,000)
Cost of additional power		(10,000)	(10,000)	(10,000)	(10,000)
Net cost savings		$37,000	$37,000	$37,000	$37,000
Multiply by(1 – tax rate)		× .60	× .60	× .60	× .60
After-tax cost savings		$22,200	$22,200	$22,200	$22,200
Annual depreciation*		$15,000	$30,000	$30,000	$15,000
Multiply by tax rate		× .40	× .40	× .40	× .40
Depreciation tax shield (nominal dollars)		$ 6,000	$12,000	$12,000	$ 6,000
Divide by price index		÷ 1.08	÷ 1.17	÷ 1.26	÷ 1.36
Depreciation tax shield (real dollars)		$ 5,556[†]	$10,256[†]	$ 9,524[†]	$ 4,412[†]
Acquisition cost of machine	$(90,000)				
Total after-tax real cash flow	$(90,000)	$27,756	$32,456	$31,724	$26,612

*Incorporates half-year convention.
[†]Rounded.

2. Since the Communications Division bases its analysis on nominal cash flows, it should use the nominal discount rate, computed as follows:

Real discount rate	.1200
Inflation rate	.0800
Combined effect (.12 × .08)	.0096
Nominal discount rate	.2096

Equivalently, the nominal discount rate is given by $(1.12 \times 1.08) - 1.00$, which equals .2096.

3. Schedule of net after-tax annual nominal cash flows:

In the following schedule, the net after-tax cost savings are converted to nominal dollars by multiplying by the price index. The annual depreciation tax shield amounts are already in nominal dollars. Since the acquisition of the machine is at the end of 20x0, there is no difference between nominal and real dollars (as expressed in terms of 20x0 prices).

PROBLEM 17-52 (CONTINUED)

		Year			
	20x0	20x1	20x2	20x3	20x4
After-tax cost savings [real dollars, see schedule in req. (1)]		$22,200	$22,200	$22,200	$22,200
Multiply by price index		× 1.08	× 1.17	× 1.26	× 1.36
After-tax cost savings (nominal dollars)		$23,976	$25,974	$27,972	$30,192
Depreciation tax shield [nominal dollars; see schedule in req. (1)]		6,000	12,000	12,000	6,000
Acquisition cost of machine	$(90,000)				
Total after-tax nominal cash flow	$(90,000)	$29,976	$37,974	$39,972	$36,192

4.   Both of the methods used by the Communications Division and the Biotech Division are correct methods of incorporating inflation in a capital expenditure analysis. Choice between them is a matter of personal preference. As long as both methods are consistently applied, they will yield the same conclusion.

SOLUTIONS TO CASES

CASE 17-53 (60 MINUTES)

The net present value of the proposed investment is $(235,280), calculated as follows:

INSTANT DINNERS, INC.
NET-PRESENT-VALUE ANALYSIS

	Time 0	Year 1	Year 2	Year 3	Year 4	Year 5	Year 6	Year 7	Year 8
New equipment	$(4,500,000)								
Working capital	(1,000,000)								
Disposition of equipment									$1,000,000
Old forklift trucks	100,000								
New conveyor belt system									100,000
Operating revenue		$700,000	$700,000	$700,000	$700,000	$700,000	$700,000	$700,000	700,000
Operating savings[a]		600,000	600,000	600,000	600,000	(200,000)	600,000	600,000	600,000
Tax effect [b]	160,000	(335,000)	(335,000)	(335,000)	(335,000)	(15,000)	(295,000)	(295,000)	(335,000)
Total cash flows	$(5,240,000)	$965,000	$965,000	$965,000	$965,000	$485,000	$1,005,000	$1,005,000	$2,065,000
12% discount factor*	× 1.000	× .893	× .797	× .712	× .636	× .567	× .507	× .452	× .404
Present value	$(5,240,000)	$861,745	$769,105	$687,080	$613,740	$274,995	509,535	$ 454,260	$ 834,260
Net present value ...	$ (235,280)								

*From Table III in the Appendix to Chapter 16.

CASE 17-53 (CONTINUED)

[a]Operating savings for Years 1, 2, 3, 4, 6, 7, 8:

Manufacturing cost reduction	$ 500,000
Maintenance cost reduction	300,000
Less: Increased operating costs	(200,000)
Total	$ 600,000

Year 5:

Same as above	$ 600,000
Less: Equipment repairs	(800,000)
Total	$ (200,000)

[b]Tax effects:

At time 0; disposal of forklifts:

Book value	$ 500,000
Less: Salvage value...	(100,000)
Tax loss	$ 400,000
Tax rate..	$\times$ .40
Total cash inflow (tax savings)	$ 160,000

Years 1 through 4:

Revenue..	$ 700,000
Operating-cost savings	600,000
Loss of depreciation on forklifts	100,000*
Depreciation on new equipment	(562,500)[†]
Increase in taxable income	$ 837,500
Tax rate..	$\times$ .40
Total cash outflow (increased taxes)	$ (335,000)

*If the forklifts are sold, the loss of the depreciation deduction will increase taxes just as the increased revenue and operating cost savings will increase taxes.

[†]Ignoring the half-year convention, the annual straight-line depreciation is $562,500 ($4,500,000/8).

CASE 17-53 (CONTINUED)

Year 5:

Revenue..	$ 700,000
Operating-costs*...	(200,000)
Loss of depreciation on forklifts	100,000
Depreciation on new equipment	(562,500)
Increase in taxable income	$ 37,500
Tax rate..	× .40
Total cash outflow (increased taxes)	$ (15,000)

*$600,000 operating-cost savings less $800,000 equipment repairs to maintain production efficiency.

Years 6 and 7:

Revenue..	$ 700,000
Operating-cost savings...	600,000
Depreciation on new equipment	(562,500)
Increase in taxable income	$ 737,500
Tax rate..	× .40
Total cash outflow (increased taxes)	$ (295,000)

Year 8:

Revenue..	$ 700,000
Operating-cost savings...	600,000
Depreciation on new equipment	(562,500)
Salvage value of new equipment	100,000
Increase in taxable income	$ 837,500
Tax rate..	× .40
Total cash outflow (increased taxes)	$(335,000)

2. Referring to the specific ethical standards of competence, confidentiality, integrity, and objectivity, Leland Forrest should evaluate Bill Rolland's directives as follows:

Competence. Forrest has a responsibility to present complete and clear reports and recommendations after appropriate analyses of relevant and reliable information. Rolland does not wish the report to be complete or clear and has provided some information that is not reliable.

Confidentiality. Forrest should not disclose confidential information outside the organization. However, it also appears that Rolland wants to refrain from disclosing important information to the board.

Integrity. Rolland is engaging in activities that could prejudice him from carrying out his duties ethically. In evaluating Rolland's directive as it affects Forrest, Forrest has an obligation to communicate unfavorable as well as favorable information and professional judgments or opinions.

Objectivity. The responsibility to communicate information fairly and objectively, as well as to disclose fully all relevant information that could reasonably be expected to influence an intended user's understanding of the reports and recommendations presented, is being hampered. The board will not have the full scope of information they should have when they are presented with the analysis.

3. Leland Forrest should take the following steps to resolve this situation:

- Forrest should first investigate to see if Instant Dinners, Inc. (IDI) has an established policy for resolution of ethical conflicts and follow those procedures.

- If this policy does not resolve the ethical conflict, the next step is for Forrest to discuss the situation with his supervisor, Rolland, and see if he can obtain resolution. One possible solution is to present a "base case" and sensitivity analysis of the investment. Forrest should make it clear to Rolland that he has a problem and is seeking guidance.

- If Forrest cannot obtain a satisfactory resolution with Rolland, he should take the situation up to the next layer of management and inform Rolland that he is doing this. If this is not satisfactory, Forrest should progress to the next, and subsequent, higher levels of management (e.g., the president or board of directors) until the issue is resolved.

- Since Rolland has instructed him not to discuss the situation with anyone else at IDI, Forrest may want to have a confidential discussion with an objective advisor to clarify relevant concepts and obtain an understanding of possible courses of action. For example, he might want to talk to a close professional friend.

- If Forrest cannot satisfactorily resolve the situation within the organization, he may resign from the company and sub mit an informative memo to an appropriate person in IDI (e.g., the president or board of directors).

CASE 17-54 (120 MINUTES)

1. Liquid Chemical's four alternatives:

    - Manufacture containers and maintain them

    - Manufacture containers but contract the maintenance

    - Buy containers but continue to maintain them

    - Buy containers and contract the maintenance

2. Net-present-value analysis:

    The NPV analysis is presented in Tables A, B, and C, which follow. Table A details the recurring cash flows associated with each alternative. Table B lists the one-time, initial cash flows. Table C combines the amounts from Tables A and B and also discounts the amounts to determine their present values.

    As Table C shows, the net present values of the costs of Liquid Chemical's alternatives are as follows:

Alternative	Net Present Value
Manufacture; maintain	$1,418,687
Manufacture; contract maintenance	1,550,567
Buy; maintain	1,487,963
Contract both	1,466,307

Therefore, Liquid Chemical should continue to manufacture and maintain its own containers. This alternative has the lowest net present value of costs.

TABLE A: RECURRING CASH FLOWS

	Manufacture; Maintain	Manufacture; Contract Maintenance	Buy; Maintain	Contract Both
Purchase price for containers			$600,000	$600,000
Maintenance contract		$175,000		175,000
Container Department costs:				
Cash costs:				
Direct material other than GHL	$125,000	112,500[a]	12,500[a]	—
Direct labor	350,000	280,000[b]	70,000[b]	—
Severance pay	—	—	—	20,000
Manager's salary	80,000[c]	80,000[c]	60,000[d]	—
Maintenance of machinery	13,500	13,500	—	—
Rent	27,500[e]	27,500[e]	27,500[e]	—
Other overhead	63,000	37,000[f]	26,000[f]	—
Total cash expenses	$659,000	$725,500	$796,000	$795,000
After-tax cash costs:				
Cash expenses:				
$659,000 × (1 − .40)	$395,400			
$725,500 × (1 − .40)		$435,300		
$796,000 × (1 − .40)			$477,600	
$795,000 × (1 − .40)				$477,000
Noncash costs:				
Depreciation	60,000	60,000	—	—
GHL	75,000[g]	67,500[h]	7,500[h]	—
Tax effect from noncash costs (40%):				
Depreciation	24,000	24,000	—	—
GHL	30,000	27,000	3,000	—

Explanatory Notes for Table A:

[a]One-tenth of the required direct material is used in the maintenance operation.

[b]One-fifth of the direct labor is used in the maintenance operation.

CASE 17-54 (CONTINUED)

[c]Duffy will be retained regardless of the decision about the Container Department. However, if the Container Department is not shut down, someone else would need to be hired to fill the position that Duffy would fill if the department is shut down. Duffy's salary of $80,000 is used as an estimate for the new manager's salary.

[d]Under this alternative, Duffy moves to the new position, and the Container Department is managed by a department supervisor who earns $60,000 per year.

[e]The rental cost of $17,000 listed by Dyer is not a relevant cost for this decision. The space occupied by the Container Department, to which the $17,000 in rent is assigned, will be used regardless of which alternative is chosen. The rental cost that is relevant is the $27,500 cost of renting additional space in a warehouse. This cost will only be incurred if the Container Department is kept. Otherwise, the space currently occupied by the Container Department can be used for whatever operation currently takes place in the rental warehouse space. Thus the $27,500 is the opportunity cost of using space in Liquid Chemical's own facility for the Container Department.

[f]The other overhead costs associated with the maintenance operation amount to $26,000. Thus, $37,000 ($63,000 – $26,000) of the $63,000 in other overhead listed by Dyer must relate to the container manufacturing process.

[g]Since GHL will be consumed out of stock that is already on hand, it is a noncash expense, much like depreciation. In this case, both depreciation and the consumption of GHL will show up as an expense through Cost of Goods Sold expense.

[h]Only one-tenth of the direct material is used for the maintenance operation.

TABLE B: ONE-TIME INITIAL CASH FLOWS

	Manufacture; Maintain	Manufacture; Contract Maintenance	Buy; Maintain	Contract Both
Proceeds from sale of equipment			$ (80,000)*	$ (80,000)
Tax reduction from loss on sale of equipment ($240,000 − $80,000) × .40			(64,000)	(64,000)
Sale of GHL[i]				
150 × $1,200				(180,000)
150 × $1,200 × .9			(162,000)	
150 × $1,200 × .1		$(18,000)		
Tax reduction from loss on sale of GHL[j]				
($225,000 − $180,000) × .40				(18,000)
($225,000 − $180,000) × .40 × .9			(16,200)	
($225,000 − $180,000) × .40 × .1		(1,800)		
Total proceeds	-0-	$(19,800)	$(322,200)	$(342,000)

*Parentheses denote cash inflows.

Explanatory Notes for Table B:

[i]Since one-tenth of the GHL is needed for the maintenance operation, Liquid Chemical will sell 10 percent of its stock if it contracts the maintenance out. The firm will sell 90 percent of its stock if it purchases containers but continues to maintain them.

[j]Since Liquid Chemical will be selling its stock of GHL at a loss of $300 per ton ($1,500 − $1,200), there will be a tax benefit from the loss on the sale.

TABLE C: NET-PRESENT-VALUE ANALYSIS OF ALTERNATIVES

Manufacture; Maintain

Annual cash flows:

Cash costs (after taxes) ....$395,400 × 3.791		$1,498,961
Purchase GHL (years 4 & 5)[k] ....(50 × $1,800) × (.621 + .683) × (1 − .4)		70,416
Noncash costs:		
Depreciation (.4)($60,000) ....$24,000 × 3.170 (4 years)		(76,080)
GHL (.4)($75,000)[k] ....$30,000 × 2.487 (3 years)		(74,610)
Initial cash flow		-0-
Net present value		$1,418,687

Manufacture; Contract Maintenance

Annual cash flows:

Cash costs (after taxes) ....$435,300 × 3.791		$1,650,222
Purchase GHL (years 4 & 5) ....(45 × $1,800) × (.621 + .683) × (1 − .4)		63,374
Noncash costs:		
Depreciation (.4)($60,000) ....$24,000 × 3.170 (4 years)		(76,080)
GHL (.4)($75,000)(.9) ....$27,000 × 2.487 (3 years)		(67,149)
Initial cash flow		(19,800)
Net present value		$1,550,567

Buy; Maintain

Annual cash flows:

Cash costs (after taxes) ....$477,600 × 3.791		$1,810,582
Purchase GHL (years 4 & 5) ....(5 × $1,800) × (.621 + .683) × (1 − .4)		7,042
Noncash costs:		
GHL (.4)($75,000)(.1) ....$3,000 × 2.487 (3 years)		(7,461)
Initial cash flow		(322,200)
Net present value		$1,487,963

Table C continues on the next page.

CASE 17-54 (CONTINUED)

Contract Both

Annual cash flows:

Cash costs (after taxes) ....$477,000 × 3.791		$1,808,307
Initial cash flow		(342,000)
Net present value		$1,466,307

Explanatory Note for Table C:

[k]Liquid Chemical's stock of GHL will run out after three years. Thus, the firm must purchase more GHL (at $1,800 per ton) in years 4 and 5.

3.   Qualitative factors to be considered:

- Morale effect from department closing

- Effect of changes in demand

- Inflation (could be quantified in an inflation-adjusted net-present-value analysis)

- Flexibility considerations

- Quality considerations

CURRENT ISSUES IN MANAGERIAL ACCOUNTING

ISSUE 17-55

"BIG-BANK BUDGETS," *ABA BANKING JOURNAL*, AUGUST 2000, CHARLES M. WADE.

1. The accounting rate of return is a percentage formed by taking a project's average incremental revenue minus its average incremental expenses, including depreciation and income taxes, and dividing by the project's initial investment.

2. Reasons respondents stated that their banks are moving toward net-present-value analysis and the internal rate of return for capital budgeting techniques are:

   - More accuracy

   - Better long-term measurement

   - Best for true economic decisions

   - More reliable

   - New financial management team

ISSUE 17-56

"DEPRECIATION LIVES AND METHODS: CURRENT ISSUES IN THE U.S. CAPITAL COST RECOVERY SYSTEM," *NATIONAL TAX JOURNAL*, SEPTEMBER 2000, DAVID W. BRAZELL AND JAMES B. MACKIE III.

There are two ways to move toward a system based on economic depreciation.

- The first approach would require all assets to be revalued (marked-to-market) each year. This approach offers the possibility of measuring income correctly for each investment.

- A second approach to implementing economic depreciation would maintain scheduler deductions, but would base these deductions on empirical estimates of economic depreciation. This approach does not offer the possibility of getting depreciation exactly right for any particular individual investment. It does, however, represent a feasible approach to implementing tax depreciation deductions that might approximate economic depreciation on average.

ISSUE 17-57

"STRANGE CALCULATIONS," *THE WALL STREET JOURNAL*, MARCH 2, 1999, PAULA THROCKMORTON ZAKARIA.

Real dollars is the measure that reflects an adjustment for the purchasing power of a monetary unit. *Nominal dollars* is the actual cash flow observed.

ISSUE 17-58

"BACK-END FUNDS TAKE ON COSTLY PROBLEM," *THE WALL STREET JOURNAL*, MARCH 29, 1999, PUI-WING TAM.

1. The payback period is the time it will take to recoup, in the form of net cash inflows from operations, the initial dollars invested in a project. In this article, the payback period is the time it takes the fund to earn back the commission it pays to the broker.

2. A fund company prefers a front-end load because it reduces the payback period.

ISSUE 17-59

"CAPITAL BUDGETING PRACTICES IN THE ASIA-PACIFIC REGION: AUSTRALIA, HONG KONG, INDONESIA, MALAYSIA, PHILIPPINES, AND SINGAPORE," *FINANCIAL PRACTICE & EDUCATION*, SPRING/SUMMER 1999, GEORGE W. KESTER AND ROSITA P. CHANG.

1. Australia ranks the internal rate of return the highest as a quantitative technique used to rank proposed capital investments.

2. Malaysia ranks the accounting rate of return the lowest as a quantitative technique used to rank proposed capital investments.

ISSUE 17-60

"COMPARATIVE FINANCIAL PRACTICE IN THE U.S. AND CANADA: CAPITAL BUDGETING AND RISK ASSESSMENT TECHNIQUES," *FINANCIAL PRACTICE & EDUCATION*, SPRING/SUMMER 1999, JANET D. PAYNE AND WILL CARRINGTON HEATH.

There are some notable differences between capital budgeting practices in Canada and the U.S.

- In general, Canadian firms tend to formally evaluate all investment opportunities, while U.S. managers do a thorough analysis of only the large ones.

- Managers in Canadian firms are quite likely to use subjective adjustments of hurdle rates, based on previous experience. This is not true of the U.S., despite the fact that the length of time the respondent has been with the company is a little longer than for Canadian managers.

- It is useful for U.S. managers, who tend to prefer externally verifiable analysis, to understand that their Canadian counterparts are more reliant on their own judgment in decision-making. Yet, those same counterparts are likely to carefully examine all projects, not justs the very expensive ones.

ISSUE 17-61

"NET PRESENT VALUE," *COMPUTERWORLD*, JULY 26, 1999, JACQUELINE EMIGH.

1. NPV represents the relationship between a project's expected cash flows and the cost of capital, after adjusting for the timing of the cash flows. NPV can help an information technology department win internal investment dollars by showing the finance department that investing in a web server will yield a high return. Net present value is used for long-term investments in assets, for decisions about whether to invest in a new product line, and for decisions about whether to acquire an existing company.

2. In simplest terms, the cost of capital is the cost of acquiring resources for an organization, either through debt or through the issuance of stock.

CHAPTER 18
Allocation of Support Activity Costs and Joint Costs

ANSWERS TO REVIEW QUESTIONS

18-1 A service department is a unit in an organization that is not involved directly in producing the organization's goods or services. However, a service department does provide a service that enables the organization's production process to take place. Production departments, on the other hand, are units that are directly involved in producing the organization's goods and services. An example of a service department in a bank would be the computer department or the personnel department. An example of a "production" department in a bank would be the consumer loan department.

18-2 The term *reciprocal services* refers to the situation in which two or more service departments provide services to each other.

18-3 (a) Under the direct method of service department cost allocation, all service department costs are allocated directly to the production departments, and none of these costs are allocated to other service departments.

(b) Under the step-down method, a sequence is first established for allocation of service department costs. Then the costs incurred in the first service department in the sequence are allocated among all other departments that use that service department's services, including other service departments. The method proceeds in a similar fashion through the sequence of service departments.

(c) Under the reciprocal-services method, a system of simultaneous equations is established to reflect the reciprocal provision of services among service departments. Then all of the service departments' costs are allocated among all of the departments that use the various service departments' output of services. The reciprocal-services method of service department cost allocation is the only method that fully accounts for the reciprocal provision of services among departments.

18-4 The first department in the sequence under the step-down method is the service department that serves the largest number of other service departments. The second department in the sequence is the service department that serves the second-largest number of service departments, and so forth. The sequence among tied service departments usually is an arbitrary choice.

18-5 The dual-allocation approach improves the resulting cost allocations because variable costs are allocated in accordance with short-run usage, and fixed costs are allocated in accordance with long-run service requirements.

18-6 A potential behavioral problem that can result from the dual approach to service department cost allocation is that service department managers may have a disincentive to provide correct predictions for their departments' long-run service department needs.

18-7 Budgeted service department costs should be allocated rather than actual service department costs. Allocating actual costs would reduce the incentive for cost control in the service departments.

18-8 Under two-stage allocation with departmental overhead rates, costs first are distributed to *departments*; then they are allocated from service *departments* to production *departments*. Finally, they are assigned from production *departments* to products or services. *Departments* play a key role as intermediate cost objects under this approach. In an activity-based costing (ABC) system, on the other hand, the key role is played by *activities,* not departments. First, the costs of various *activities* are assigned to *activity*-cost pools; then these costs are assigned to products or services. The breakdown of costs by activity in an ABC system is much finer then a breakdown by departments. The ABC approach generally will provide a much more accurate cost for each of the organization's products or services.

18-9 (a) Joint-production process: A production process in which the processing of a common input results in two or more outputs called joint products.

(b) Joint cost: The cost incurred in a joint production process before the joint products become identifiable as separate products.

(c) Joint products: The output of a joint production process.

(d) Split-off point: The point in a joint production process at which the joint products become identifiable as separate products.

(e) Separable costs: Costs incurred to process joint products further after they pass the split-off point in a joint production process.

(f) By-product: A joint product with very little value relative to the other joint products.

18-10 Under the physical-units method of joint cost allocation, joint production costs are allocated among the joint products in proportion to a physical characteristic of those products, such as weight or volume.

18-11 Under the relative-sales-value method of joint cost allocation, joint production costs are allocated to the joint products in proportion to their sales value at the split-off point.

18-12 The net realizable value of a joint product is equal to its ultimate sales value minus the separable costs incurred between the split-off point and the product's final form. Under the net-realizable-value method of joint cost allocation, joint production costs are allocated among the joint products in proportion to their net realizable values.

18-13 Joint cost allocations are useful for product-costing purposes. Product costing is useful for income determination, for inventory valuation, for third-party reimbursement situations, and various other purposes.

18-14 The managerial accountant generally should be careful not to use joint cost allocations for making decisions.

SOLUTIONS TO EXERCISES

EXERCISE 18-15 (15 MINUTES)

| | | Academic Departments Using Services | | | |
| | | Liberal Arts | | Sciences | |
Provider of Service	Cost to Be Allocated	Proportion	Amount	Proportion	Amount
Library	$600,000	(3/5)	$360,000	(2/5)	$240,000
Computing Services	240,000	(3/8)	90,000	(5/8)	150,000
Total	$840,000		$450,000		$390,000
Grand total				$840,000	

EXERCISE 18-16 (15 MINUTES)

| | Service Departments | | Academic Departments Using Services | |
	Computing Services	Library	Liberal Arts	Sciences
Costs prior to allocation	$240,000	$600,000		
Allocation of Computing Service costs*	$240,000	48,000(2/10)	$ 72,000(3/10)	$120,000(5/10)
Allocation of Library costs		$648,000	388,800(3/5)	259,200(2/5)
Total costs allocated to each department			$460,800	$379,200
Total cost allocated to academic departments			$840,000	

*Allocated first because Computing Services provides service to the Library, but not vice versa.

EXERCISE 18-17 (15 MINUTES)

| | | Direct Customer Service Departments Using Services | | | |
| | | Deposit | | Loan | |
Provider of Service	Cost to Be Allocated	Proportion	Amount	Proportion	Amount
Personnel	$153,000	(6/9)	$102,000	(3/9)	$ 51,000
Computing	229,500	(50/85)	135,000	(35/85)	94,500
Total	$382,500		$237,000		$145,500
Grand total				$382,500	

EXERCISE 18-18 (15 MINUTES)

| | | | Direct Customer Service Departments Using Services | |
	Personnel	Computing	Deposit	Loan
Costs prior to allocation	$153,000	$229,500		
Allocation of Personnel Department costs	$153,000	15,300(1/10)	$ 91,800(6/10)	$ 45,900(3/10)
Allocation of Computing Department costs		$244,800	144,000(50/85)	100,800(35/85)
Total costs allocated to each department			$235,800	$146,700
Total cost allocated to direct customer service departments			$382,500	

EXERCISE 18-19 (30 MINUTES)

Answers will vary widely, depending on the organization chosen. Support departments at the Mayo Clinic, for example, include Admissions, Patient Records, and Housekeeping, among others. At Sheraton Hotels, support departments include Registration, Maintenance, and the Concierge, among others.

EXERCISE 18-20 (10 MINUTES)

Joint Cost	Joint Products	Quantity at Split-Off Point	Relative Proportion	Allocation of Joint Cost
	Yummies	12,000 kilograms	.60	$18,000*
$30,000				
	Crummies	8,000 kilograms	.40	12,000[†]
	Total	20,000 kilograms		$30,000

*$18,000 = $30,000 × .60
[†]$12,000 = $30,000 × .40

EXERCISE 18-21 (15 MINUTES)

Joint Cost	Joint Products	Quantity at Split-Off	Sales Price	Sales Value at Split-Off Point	Relative Proportion	Allocation of Joint Cost
	Yummies	12,000 kg	$2.00	$24,000	.545*	$16,350[†]
$30,000						
	Crummies	8,000 kg	2.50	20,000	.455*	13,650**
	Total			$44,000		$30,000

*Rounded.
[†]$16,350 = $30,000 × .545
**$13,650 = $30,000 × .455

EXERCISE 18-22 (25 MINUTES)

1. Decision analysis:

    Incremental revenue per kilogram:

Sales price of mulch	$3.50	
Sales price of Crummies	2.50	
Incremental revenue		$1.00
Incremental processing cost per kilogram		.50
Incremental revenue less incremental cost		$ .50

    The Crummies should be processed further into the mulch.

EXERCISE 18-22 (CONTINUED)

2. Joint cost allocation using net-realizable-value method:

Joint Cost	Joint Products	Sales Value of Final Product	Separable Cost of Processing	Net Realizable Value*	Relative Proportion	Allocation of Joint Cost
	Yummies	$24,000 (12,000 × $2.00)	-0-	$24,000	.50	$15,000[†]
$30,000						
	Mulch	28,000 (8,000 × $3.50)	$4,000 (8,000 × $.50)	24,000	.50	15,000[†]
				$48,000		$30,000

*Net realizable value = sales value of final product – separable cost of processing.
[†]$15,000 = $30,000 × .50

EXERCISE 18-23 (25 MINUTES)

(a) First, specify equations to express the relationships between the service departments.

Notation: P denotes the total cost of Personnel

C denotes the total cost of Computing

Equations: $P = 153,000 + .15C$ (1)

$C = 229,500 + .10P$ (2)

Solution of equations: Substitute from equation (2) into equation (1).

$$P = 153,000 + .15(229,500 + .10P)$$

$$.985P = 187,425$$

$$P = 190,279 \text{ (rounded)}$$

Substitute the value of P into equation (2).

$$C = 229,500 + .10(190,279)$$

$$C = 248,528 \text{ (rounded)}$$

EXERCISE 18-23 (CONTINUED)

(b)   Cost allocation using the reciprocal-services method:

	Service Departments		Direct Customer Service Departments	
	Personnel	Computing	Deposit	Loan
Traceable costs	$153,000	$229,500		
Allocation of Personnel				
Department costs	(190,279)	19,028*(.1)	$114,167*(.6)	$ 57,084*(.3)
Allocation of Computing				
Department costs	37,279*(.15)	(248,528)	124,264(.50)	86,985*(.35)
Total cost allocated to each direct customer service department			$238,431	$144,069
Total costs allocated			$382,500	

*Rounded.

© 2002 The McGraw-Hill Companies, Inc.

Solutions Manual

SOLUTIONS TO PROBLEMS

PROBLEM 18-24 (40 MINUTES)

1. Direct method:

| | | Production Departments | | | |
| | | Machining | | Assembly | |
Provider of Service	Cost to Be Allocated	Proportion	Amount	Proportion	Amount
Personnel	$250,000	(4/9)	$111,111*	(5/9)	$138,889*
Maintenance	230,000	(35/75)	107,333*	(40/75)	122,667*
CAD	350,000	(45/60)	262,500	(15/60)	87,500
Total	$830,000		$480,944		$349,056
Grand total				$830,000	

*Rounded

2. Sequence for step-down method:

1st: Personnel (serves 2 other service departments)
2nd: Maintenance (serves 1 other service department)
3rd: CAD (serves no other service departments)

PROBLEM 18-24 (CONTINUED)

3. Step-down method:

	Service Departments			Production Departments	
	Personnel	**Maintenance**	**CAD**	**Molding**	**Assembly**
Costs prior to allocation	$250,000	$230,000	$350,000		
Allocation of Personnel Department costs	$250,000	12,500(5/100)	12,500(5/100)	$100,000(40/100)	$125,000(50/100)
Allocation of Maintenance Department costs		$242,500	15,156*(5/80)	106,094*(35/80)	121,250(40/80)
Allocation of CAD Department costs			$377,656	283,242(45/60)	94,414(15/60)
Total cost allocated to each department				$489,336	$340,664

Total cost allocated to production departments $830,000

*Rounded.

PROBLEM 18-25 (70 MINUTES)

1. Direct method combined with dual allocation:

(a) Variable costs:

		Production Departments			
		Machining		Assembly	
Provider of Service	Cost to Be Allocated	Proportion*	Amount	Proportion*	Amount
Personnel	$ 50,000	(4/9)	$ 22,222[†]	(5/9)	$ 27,778[†]
Maintenance	80,000	(35/75)	37,333[†]	(40/75)	42,667[†]
CAD	50,000	(45/60)	37,500	(15/60)	12,500
Total variable cost	$180,000		$ 97,055		$ 82,945

*Short-run usage proportions (from preceding problem).
[†]Rounded.

(b) Fixed costs:

		Production Departments			
		Machining		Assembly	
Provider of Service	Cost to Be Allocated	Proportion*	Amount	Proportion*	Amount
Personnel	$200,000	(35/85)	$82,353[†]	(50/85)	$117,647[†]
Maintenance	150,000	(48/72)	100,000	(24/72)	50,000
CAD	300,000	(48/60)	240,000	(12/60)	60,000
Total fixed cost	$650,000		$422,353 **		$227,647**

*Long-run proportions (from this problem).
[†]Rounded.
**$422,353 + $227,647 = $650,000.

PROBLEM 18-25 (CONTINUED)

(c) Total costs allocated:

	Machining	Assembly
Variable costs	$ 97,055	$ 82,945
Fixed costs	422,353	227,647
Total costs	$519,408	$310,592
Grand total	$830,000	

2. **Step-down method combined with dual allocation:**

As in the preceding problem, the sequence of allocation is Personnel, Maintenance, and CAD, respectively.

PROBLEM 18-25 (CONTINUED)

(a) Variable costs:

	Service Departments			Production Departments	
	Personnel	Maintenance	CAD	Molding	Assembly
Costs prior to allocation	$50,000	$80,000	$50,000		
Allocation of Personnel					
Department costs	$50,000	2,500(5/100)*	2,500(5/100)	$20,000(40/100)	$25,000(50/100)
Allocation of Maintenance					
Department costs		$82,500	5,156†(5/80)	36,094†(35/80)	41,250(40/80)
Allocation of CAD					
Department costs			$57,656	43,242(45/60)	14,414(15/60)
Total variable cost allocated to each department				$99,336**	$80,664**

*Short-run usage proportions are used (from preceding problem).
†Rounded.
**$99,336 + $80,664 = $180,000

PROBLEM 18-25 (CONTINUED)

(b) Fixed costs:

	Service Departments			Production Departments	
	Personnel	Maintenance	CAD	Molding	Assembly
Costs prior to allocation	$200,000	$150,000	$300,000		
Allocation of Personnel Department costs	$200,000	10,000(5/100)*	20,000(10/100)	$70,000(35/100)	$100,000(50/100)
Allocation of Maintenance Department costs		$160,000	16,000(8/80)	96,000(48/80)	48,000(24/80)
Allocation of CAD Department costs			$336,000	268,800(48/60)	67,200(12/60)
Total fixed cost allocated to each department				$434,800†	$215,200†

*Long-run usage proportions are used (from this problem).
†$434,800 + $215,200 = $650,000

PROBLEM 18-25 (CONTINUED)

(c) Total costs allocated:

	Machining	Assembly
Variable costs	$ 99,336	$ 80,664
Fixed costs	434,800	215,200
Total costs	$534,136	$295,864
Grand total	$830,000	

PROBLEM 18-26 (40 MINUTES)

1. Direct method:

		Production Department			
		Etching		Finishing	
Provider of Service	Cost to Be Allocated	Proportion	Amount	Proportion	Amount
Maintenance	$ 48,000	(1/9)	$ 5,333	(8/9)	$ 42,667
Computing	250,000	(7/8)	218,750	(1/8)	31,250
Total service department costs allocated			$224,083		$ 73,917
Overhead costs traceable to production departments			200,000		320,000
Total overhead cost			$424,083		$393,917
Direct-labor hours (DLH)					
(20 × 2,000)			40,000		
(80 × 2,000)					160,000
Overhead rate per hour (total overhead ÷ DLH)			$10.602*		$2.462*
Check on allocation procedure:					
Service department costs allocated to Etching					$224,083
Service department costs allocated to Finishing					73,917
Total costs to be allocated ($48,000 + $250,000)					$298,000

*Rounded

PROBLEM 18-26 (CONTINUED)

2.   **Step-down method:**

	Service Departments		Production Departments	
	Computing	Maintenance	Etching	Finishing
Costs prior to allocation	$250,000	$48,000		
Allocation of Computing Department costs	250,000	50,000(2/10)	$175,000(7/10)	$ 25,000(1/10)
Allocation of Maintenance Department costs		98,000	10,889(1/9)	87,111(8/9)
Total service department cost allocated			$185,889	$112,111
Overhead costs traceable to production departments			200,000	320,000
Total overhead cost			$385,889	$432,111
Direct-labor hours (DLH)				
(20 × 2,000)			40,000	
(80 × 2,000)				160,000
Overhead rate per hour (total overhead ÷ DLH)			$9.647*	$2.70*
Check on allocation procedure:				
Service department costs allocated to Etching				$185,889
Service department costs allocated to Finishing				112,111
Total costs to be allocated ($48,000 + $250,000)				$298,000

*Rounded

PROBLEM 18-27 (30 MINUTES)

1.   Physical-units method of allocation:

Joint Cost	Joint Products	Quantity at Split-Off Point	Relative Proportion	Allocation of Joint Cost
$300,000	MSB	60,000	40%	$120,000
	CBL	90,000	60%	180,000
	Total	150,000		

The joint cost allocated to CBL is $180,000.

2.   Relative-sales-value method of allocation:

Joint Cost	Joint Products	Sales Value at Split-Off Point	Relative Proportion	Allocation of Joint Cost
$300,000	MSB	$120,000	25%	$ 75,000
	CBL	360,000	75%	225,000
	Total	$480,000		

The joint cost allocated to MSB is $75,000.

PROBLEM 18-27 (CONTINUED)

3.   Net-realizable-value method of allocation:

Joint Cost	Joint Products	Sales Value of Final Product	Additional Cost of Processing	Net Realizable Value	Relative Proportion	Allocation of Joint Cost
$300,000	MSB	$300,000*	$100,000	$200,000	25%	$ 75,000
	CBL	800,000†	200,000	600,000	75%	225,000
	Total ...			$800,000		

*$5 × 60,000
†$10 × (90,000 – 10,000)

The unit cost of CBL is computed as follows:

Joint cost allocation	$225,000
Additional processing costs	200,000
Total cost	$425,000
Quantity (good units)	80,000
Cost per unit ($425,000 ÷ 80,000)	$5.31 (rounded)

4.

Sales value if coated (60,000 × $5)	$300,000
Additional cost of coating	100,000
Incremental contribution if coated	$200,000
Sales value if uncoated (60,000 × $2)	120,000
Decline in contribution if uncoated	$ 80,000

The contribution would decrease by $80,000 if the mine support braces are not processed further.

5.   The allocation of joint costs is irrelevant to the decision about coating the mine support braces. The decision should be based entirely on information pertaining to events from the split-off point forward. Thus, the joint cost allocation results were not used in making this production decision.

PROBLEM 18-28 (50 MINUTES)

1. Plantwide overhead rates:

	Departments (numbers in thousands)			
	Molding	Component	Assembly	Total
Manufacturing departments:				
Variable overhead	$ 3,500	$10,000	$16,500	$30,000
Fixed overhead	17,500	6,200	6,100	29,800
Total manufacturing department overhead	$21,000	$16,200	$22,600	$59,800
Service departments:				
Power				18,400
Maintenance				4,000
Total estimated overhead				$82,200
Estimated direct-labor hours (DLH):				
Molding				500
Component				2,000
Assembly				1,500
Total estimated direct-labor hours				4,000

$$\text{Plantwide overhead rate} = \frac{\text{estimated overhead}}{\text{estimated DLH}}$$

$$= \frac{\$82,200}{4,000}$$

$$= \$20.55 \text{ per direct-labor hour}$$

PROBLEM 18-28 (CONTINUED)

2. Departmental overhead rates:

| | Departments (numbers in thousands) | | | | |
| | Service | | Manufacturing | | |
	Power	Maintenance	Molding	Component	Assembly
Departmental overhead costs	$18,400	$ 4,000	$21,000	$16,200	$22,600
a. Allocation of maintenance costs (direct method) Proportions: 90/125, 25/125, 10/125		(4,000)	2,880	800	320
b. Allocation of power costs (dual, direct method) Fixed costs ($12,000): Proportions: 500/1000, 350/1000, 150/1000	(12,000)		6,000	4,200	1,800
Variable costs ($6,400): Proportions: 360/800, 320/800, 120/800	(6,400)		2,880	2,560	960
Total allocated departmental overhead costs	$ 0	$ 0	$32,760	$23,760	$25,680
c. Cost driver			875 MH	2,000 DLH	1,500 DLH
Rate (departmental overhead ÷ units of cost driver)...			$37.44 per MH	$11.88 per DLH	$17.12 per DLH

PROBLEM 18-28 (CONTINUED)

3.   **Memorandum**

    Date: Today

    To: President, Travelcraft Company

    From: I.M. Student

    Subject: Use of departmental overhead rates

    Travelcraft should use departmental rates to assign overhead to its products. The criterion for choosing an allocation base is a close relationship between cost incurrence and use of the base. This relationship exists with different bases in different departments, necessitating the use of departmental rates. The company's production departments are dissimilar in that the Molding Department is machine-intensive while the other two departments are labor-intensive.

PROBLEM 18-29 (40 MINUTES)

1.   Net-realizable-value method of allocation:

Joint Cost per Run	Joint Products	Sales Value of Final Product*	Additional Cost of Processing	Net Realizable Value	Relative Proportion†	Allocation of Joint Cost
	HTP-3	$2,800,000	$874,000	$1,926,000	.....48.15%	$ 818,550
$1,700,000	PST-4	2,100,000	816,000	1,284,000	.....32.10%	545,700
	RJ-5	850,000	60,000	790,000	.....19.75%	335,750
	Total			$4,000,000		$1,700,000

*Sales price × quantity produced.

†Net realizable value ÷ $4,000,000, which is the sum of the net realizable values of the three joint products.

PROBLEM 18-29 (CONTINUED)

2. October production cost per gallon:

Product	HTP-3	PST-4	RJ-5
Joint cost allocation	$ 818,550	$ 545,700	$335,750
Additional processing costs	874,000	816,000	60,000
Total cost	$1,692,550	$1,361,700	$395,750
Quantity produced (gallons)	700,000	350,000	170,000
Cost per gallon (rounded)	$2.42	$3.89	$2.33

Inventory valuation:

Product	HTP-3	PST-4	RJ-5
October 1 inventory (gallons)	18,000	52,000	3,000
October production (gallons)	700,000	350,000	170,000
Quantity available (gallons)	718,000	402,000	173,000
October sales (gallons)	650,000	325,000	150,000
October 30 inventory (gallons)	68,000	77,000	23,000
× Cost per gallon	× $2.42	× $3.89	× $2.33
October 30 inventory (dollars)	$164,560	$299,530	$ 53,590

3. Biondi Industries should sell PST-4 at the split-off point. The incremental revenue of sales beyond the split-off point is less than the incremental cost of further processing.

Per gallon sales value beyond the split-off point	$6.00
Per gallon sales value at the split-off point	3.80
Incremental sales value	$2.20
Less: Additional processing costs per gallon	
($816,000 ÷ 350,000 gallons)	2.33 (rounded)
Per gallon gain (loss) of further processing	$ (.13)

PROBLEM 18-30 (35 MINUTES)

1. Joint cost allocations using the relative-sales-value method:

Omega: joint cost allocation $= \left(\dfrac{\text{Omega's sales value at split - off}}{\text{total sales value at split - off}} \right) \times \text{joint cost}$

$= \left(\dfrac{\$15,000}{\$100,000} \right) \times \$60,000 = \$9,000$

Kappa: joint cost allocation $=$ total joint cost – Delta's allocation
$\qquad$ – Omega's allocation

$= \$60,000 - \$36,000 - \$9,000 = \$15,000$

Summary of joint cost allocations:

Delta	$36,000(given)
Kappa	15,000
Omega	9,000
Total	$60,000

2. Delta's joint cost allocation $\left(\dfrac{\text{Delta's sales value at split - off}}{\text{total sales value at split - off}} \right) \times \text{joint cost}$

$\$36,000 \qquad \left(\dfrac{X}{\$100,000} \right) \times \$60,000$

$X \qquad \$36,000 \times \left(\dfrac{\$100,000}{\$60,000} \right)$

$X \qquad \$60,000$

Delta's sales value at split-off $\qquad \$60,000$

PROBLEM 18-30 (CONTINUED)

3. Joint cost allocation using the net-realizable-value method:

Joint Cost	Joint Products	Sales Value of Final Product	Separable Cost of Processing	Net Realizable Value	Relative Proportion	Allocation of Joint Cost
	Delta	$ 70,000	$ 7,000	$ 63,000	.63	$37,800
$60,000	Kappa	25,000	5,000	20,000	.20	12,000
	Omega	20,000	3,000	17,000	.17	10,200
	Total	$115,000	$15,000	$100,000		$60,000

PROBLEM 18-31 (40 MINUTES)

1. Joint costs arise from the simultaneous processing or manufacturing of two or more products made from the same process. These joint costs are not traceable to any single product.

    The split-off point is the stage in the manufacturing process at which joint products can be identified as individual units. Future costs are then accounted for separately.

2. The dollar value of the finished-goods inventories on November 30 for VX-4, HD-10, and FT-5 are calculated as follows:

Joint costs to be allocated:

Total joint costs incurred	$1,568,000
Less: Net realizable value (NRV) of FT-5*	68,000
Joint costs to be allocated..	$1,500,000

*NRV = 85,000 gal. $\times$ ($.90–$.10)

Allocation of joint costs:

	VX-4	HD-10
November production (in gallons)............................	600,000	320,000
Final sales value per gallon ....$\times$	$4.00	$\times$ $6.375
Total sales value...	$2,400,000	$2,040,000
Less: Separable-costs...	720,000	920,000
NRV at split-off..	$1,680,000	$1,120,000
Divided by total NRV at split-off ....$\div$	2,800,000	$\div$ 2,800,000*
Percentage allocation...	.60	.40
Joint cost to be allocated...	$\times$ $1,500,000	$\times$ $1,500,000
Joint cost allocation	$ 900,000	$ 600,000

*Total NRV at split-off equals $2,800,000 ($1,680,000 + $1,120,000).

PROBLEM 18-31 (CONTINUED)

Inventory values on November 30:

	VX-4	HD-10
Joint cost allocation	$ 900,000	$ 600,000
Additional processing costs	720,000	920,000
Total cost	$1,620,000	$1,520,000
Gallons produced	÷ 600,000	÷ 320,000
Cost per gallon	$ 2.70	$ 4.75
Finished-goods inventory (gallons)	× 9,000	× 26,000
Inventory value	$ 24,300	$ 123,500

3. Winchester Chemicals should continue to process HD-10 beyond the split-off point, since the incremental revenue is $.50 greater per gallon than the incremental cost. The joint cost is irrelevant to the decision because it will not change regardless of the decision to sell as is or process further. The analysis follows:

	Per Unit	Total
Per-gallon sales value after split-off	$6.375	
Per-gallon sales value at split-off	3.000	
Incremental sales value	$3.375	$1,080,000*
Additional processing cost	2.875†	920,000
Incremental revenue	$ .500	$ 160,000

*320,000 gal. × $3.375
†$920,000/320,000 gal.

PROBLEM 18-32 (45 MINUTES)

1. Physical-units method:

Joint Cost per Run	Joint Products	Quantity at Split-Off Point	Relative Proportion	Allocation of Joint Cost
$250,000	Compod .... 120,000 gallons.........		60%...........	$150,000
	Ultrasene .... 80,000 gallons.........		40%...........	100,000

The joint cost allocated to Compod is $150,000.

2. Relative-sales-value method:

Joint Cost per Run	Joint Products	Sales Value at Split-Off Point	Relative Proportion	Allocation of Joint Cost
$250,000	Compod	$240,000	48%	$120,000
	Ultrasene	260,000	52%	130,000

The joint cost allocated to Ultrasene is $130,000.

3. Now there are additional processing costs beyond the split-off point.

    a. Additional processing costs have no effect on the physical-units method of allocation. The joint cost allocated to Ultrasene is $100,000, as calculated in requirement (1).

    b. Net-realizable-value method:

Joint Cost per Run	Joint Products	Sales Value of Final Product	Separable Cost of Processing	Net Realizable Value	Relative Proportion	Allocation of Joint Cost
$250,000	Compod	$240,000......	$12,000	$228,000	57%.......	$142,500
	Ultrasene ...	260,000......	88,000	172,000	43%.......	107,500

The joint cost allocated to Compod is $142,500.

4.

Incremental revenue per gallon from further processing into Compodalene ($2.60 – $2.00)		$.60
Incremental cost per gallon from further processing:		
Processing cost	$.40	
Sales commission ($2.60 × 10%)	.26	.66
Incremental loss per gallon from further processing into Compodalene		$(.06)

Conclusion: Do not process Compod into Compodalene. The firm should sell Compod. (Note that the $.10 per gallon separable processing cost to *obtain* Compod is irrelevant. The question is what to do with the Compod *after* it has been obtained. The relevant data are the incremental costs and benefits associated with turning Compod into Compodalene.)

5. The director of research, Jack Turner, acted improperly in asking the assistant controller to alter her analysis in favor of producing Compodalene. If he believes the further processing of Compod is in Lafayette Company's best interests, he should try to back up his claim with some projected cost reductions and the potential impact on the company's market. He could present his own estimates to Christine Dalton, or directly to the managers responsible for making the final decision.

The assistant controller, Christine Dalton, should not alter her analysis to support the production of Compodalene. In the absence of any further information, she should recommend against the further processing of Compod. Several ethical standards for management accountants (listed in Chapter 1) are relevant, including the following:

Competence

- Prepare complete and clear reports and recommendations after appropriate analyses of relevant and reliable information.

Objectivity

- Communicate information fairly and objectively.

- Disclose fully all relevant information that could reasonably be expected to influence an intended user's understanding of the reports, comments, and recommendations presented.

PROBLEM 18-32 (CONTINUED)

6.   It is preferable to sell Compod than to sell Compodalene, as the solution to the preceding requirement showed. Nevertheless, it is preferable to sell Compodalene than to sell nothing, since each gallon of Compodalene makes a positive contribution toward covering the joint production cost, fixed costs, and profit.

Incremental revenue from sale of a gallon of
  Compodalene (if the alternative is no sale) $2.60
Incremental cost (if the alternative is to stop
  production at the split-off point):
    Separable processing to produce Compod after
      the split-off point .... $.10
    Further processing cost to turn Compod into Compodalene .... .40
    Sales commission .... .26
    Total .... .76
Contribution to the joint production cost, fixed costs,
  and profit $1.84

PROBLEM 18-33 (30 MINUTES)

1.   Reciprocal-services method:

Equations: $M = 48,000 + .2C$

$C = 250,000 + .1M$

Where M denotes the total cost of the Maintenance Department

C denotes the total cost of the Computing Department

PROBLEM 18-33 (CONTINUED)

Solution of equations:

$M = 48,000 + .2 (250,000 + .1M)$

$M = 48,000 + 50,000 + .02M$

$.98\ M = 98,000$

$M = 100,000$

$C = 250,000 + .1 (100,000)$

$C = 260,000$

Allocation:

	Service Departments		Production Departments	
	Maintenance	Computing	Etching	Finishing
Traceable costs	$ 48,000	$250,000		
Allocation of Maintenance				
Department costs	(100,000)	10,000(.1)	$ 10,000(.1)	$ 80,000(.8)
Allocation of Computing				
Department costs	52,000(.2)	(260,000)	182,000(.7)	26,000(.1)
Total service department costs allocated			$192,000	$106,000
Overhead costs traceable to production departments			200,000	320,000
Total overhead cost			$392,000	$426,000
Direct-labor hours (DLH)				
(20 × 2,000)			40,000	
(80 × 2,000)				160,000
Overhead rate per hour (total overhead ÷ DLH)			$9.80	$2.663
Check on allocation procedure:				
Service department costs allocated to Etching			$192,000	
Service department costs allocated to Finishing			106,000	
Total			$298,000	

2. The direct allocation method ignores any service rendered by one service department to another. Allocation of each service department's total cost is made directly to the production departments. The step-down method recognizes one service department's usage of services, but ignores the other's usage of services. The reciprocal services allocation method recognizes all service department support to other service departments through the use of simultaneous equations. This allocation procedure should lead to more accurate results that would be of greater value to management.

PROBLEM 18-34 (55 MINUTES)

1. Variable costs:

    Notation: *R* denotes the total variable cost of Patient Records
                P denotes the total variable cost of Personnel
                A denotes the total variable cost of Administration and Accounting

    Equations: $R = 24,000 + .05P$ (1)
                 $P = 15,000 + .05A$ (2)
                 $A = 47,500 + .20P$ (3)

    These equations are based on the *variable* costs and *short-run* usage proportions given in Exhibit 18-2.

    Solution of equations: Substitute from equation (3) into equation (2).

    $$P = 15,000 + .05(47,500 + .20P)$$
    $$.99P = 17,375$$
    $$P = 17,551 \text{ (rounded)}$$

    Substitute the value of P into equations (1) and (3).

    $$R = 24,000 + .05(17,551)$$
    $$R = 24,878 \text{ (rounded)}$$
    $$A = 47,500 + .20(17,551)$$
    $$A = 51,010 \text{ (rounded)}$$

PROBLEM 18-34 (CONTINUED)

Allocation of variable costs:

	Service Departments			Direct-Patient-Care Departments	
	Personnel	Administration and Accounting	Patient Records	Orthopedics	Internal Medicine
Traceable costs	$15,000	$47,500	$24,000		
Allocation of Personnel Department costs	(17,551)	3,510(.20)	878*(.05)	$ 4,388*(.25)	$ 8,776*(.50)
Allocation of Administration and Accounting Department costs	2,551*(.05)	(51,010)	-0-(0)	17,854*(.35)	30,606(.60)
Allocation of Patient Records Department costs	(0)	(0)	(24,878)	7,463*(.30)	17,415*(.70)
Total variable cost allocated to each direct-patient-care department				$29,705†	$56,797†

*Rounded.

†$29,705 + $56,797 = $86,502. Differs from the total variable cost ($86,500) because of cumulative rounding error.

PROBLEM 18-34 (CONTINUED)

2. **Fixed costs:**

Notation: R denotes the total fixed cost of Patient Records
P denotes the total fixed cost of Personnel
A denotes the total fixed cost of Administration and Accounting

Equations: $R = 76,000 + .10P$ (4)
$P = 45,000 + .10A$ (5)
$A = 142,500 + .10P$ (6)

These equations are based on the fixed costs given in Exhibit 18-2 and the *long-run* usage proportions given in Exhibit 18-5.

Solution of equations: Substitute from equation (6) into equation (5).

$$P = 45,000 + .10(142,500 + .10P)$$
$$.99P = 59,250$$
$$P = 59,848 \text{ (rounded)}$$

Substitute the value of P into equations (4) and (5).

$$R = 76,000 + .10(59,848)$$
$$R = 81,985 \text{ (rounded)}$$
$$A = 142,500 + .10(59,848)$$
$$A = 148,485 \text{ (rounded)}$$

PROBLEM 18-34 (CONTINUED)

Allocation of fixed costs:

	Service Departments			Direct-Patient-Care Departments	
	Personnel	Administration and Accounting	Patient Records	Orthopedics	Internal Medicine
Traceable costs	$45,000	$142,500	$76,000		
Allocation of Personnel Department costs	(59,848)	5,985*(.10)	5,985*(.10)	$11,970*(.20)	$35,909*(.60)
Allocation of Administration and Accounting Department costs	14,849*(.10)	(148,485)	-0-(0)	66,818*(.45)	66,818*(.45)
Allocation of Patient Records Department costs	-0-(0)	-0-(0)	(81,985)	32,794 (.40)	49,191(.60)
Total fixed cost allocated to each direct-patient-care department				$111,582†	$151,918†

*Rounded.

†$111,582 + $151,918 = $263,500.

Total costs allocated:

	Orthopedics	Internal Medicine
Variable costs	$ 29,705	$ 56,797
Fixed costs	111,582	151,918
Total costs	$141,287	$208,715
Grand total		$350,002*

*Differs from the total cost to be allocated ($350,000) due to cumulative rounding error in the allocation of the variable costs.

SOLUTIONS TO CASES

CASE 18-35 (40 MINUTES)

1.   Product output in pounds:

Product	Proportion	Total Pounds	Pounds Lost in Processing	Net Pounds
Slices	.35	94,500	—	94,500
Crushed	.28	75,600	—	75,600
Juice	.27	72,900	5,400*	67,500*
Animal feed	.10	27,000	—	27,000
Total		270,000	5,400	264,600

*Evaporation loss is 8% of the remaining good output. Let X denote the remaining quantity of juice:

$$72,900 - .08X = X$$
$$72,900 = 1.08\,X$$
$$67,500 = X$$

Check: evaporation loss = (8%)(67,500) = 5,400

2.   Net realizable value at the split-off point:

Product	Pounds of Production	Selling Price	Sales Revenue	Separable Cost	Net Realizable Value Amount	Percent
Slices	94,500	.60	$ 56,700	$ 4,700	$ 52,000	52%
Crushed	75,600	.55	41,580	10,580	31,000	31%
Juice	67,500	.30	20,250	3,250	17,000	17%
Total			$118,530	$18,530	$100,000	100%

3. Allocation of joint costs:

Cutting department costs			$60,000
Less net realizable value of by-product			
Sales value		$2,700	
Separable cost		(700)	
Net realizable value of animal feed			2,000
Balance of joint cost to be allocated to main products			
in proportion to net realizable value			$58,000

Allocation of joint cost:

Slices	52%	$30,160
Crushed	31%	17,980
Juice	17%	9,860
Total	....	$58,000

CASE 18-36 (50 MINUTES)

1. Diagram of joint production process:

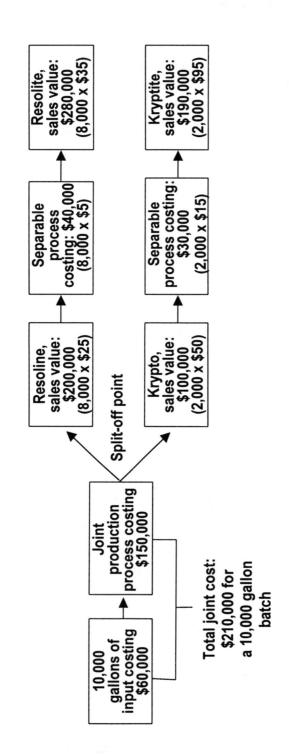

2. Allocation of joint costs:

a. Physical-units method:

Joint Cost	Joint Products	Quantity at Split-Off Point	Relative Proportion	Allocation of Joint Cost
$210,000	Resoline	8,000 pounds	8/10	$168,000
	Krypto	2,000 pounds	2/10	42,000
	Total	10,000 pounds		$210,000

b. Relative-sales-value method:

Joint Cost	Joint Products	Sales Value at Split-Off Point	Relative Proportion	Allocation of Joint Cost
$210,000	Resoline	$200,000	2/3	$140,000
	Krypto	100,000	1/3	70,000
	Total	$300,000		$210,000

c. Net-realizable-value method:

Joint Cost	Joint Products	Sales Value of Final Product	Separable Cost of Processing	Net Realizable Value	Relative Proportion	Allocation of Joint Cost
$210,000	Resolite	$280,000	$40,000	$240,000	.60	$126,000
	Kryptite	190,000	30,000	160,000	.40	84,000
	Total			$400,000		$210,000

CASE 18-36 (CONTINUED)

3. Decision analysis:

    Incremental revenue per pound:

Sales price of Omega	$130	
Sales price of Kryptite	95	
Incremental revenue		$ 35

    Incremental cost per pound:*

Separable processing	$40	
Packaging	6	
Incremental cost		46

Incremental loss per pound	$(11)

    Conclusion: The Kryptite should not be processed further into Omega.

    *Notice that these are the separable costs incurred after Kryptite has already been produced. The separable costs of processing Krypto into Kryptite are properly excluded.

4. The joint cost allocation should not be used in the decision analysis. The total joint cost will not be affected by the decision.

CURRENT ISSUES IN MANAGERIAL ACCOUNTING

ISSUE 18-37

"BENCHMARKING AND COST ACCOUNTING: THE NORTH CAROLINA APPROACH, " *JOURNAL OF PUBLIC BUDGETING, ACCOUNTING AND FINANCIAL MANAGEMENT*, SPRING 2000, WILLIAM C. RIVENBARK AND K. LEE CARTER.

Under the step-down method of service department cost allocation the managerial accountant first chooses a sequence in which to allocate the service departments' costs. A common way to select the first service department in the sequence is to choose the one that serves the largest number of other service departments. The service departments are ordered in this manner, with the last service department being the one that serves the smallest number of other service departments. Then the managerial accountant allocates each service department's costs among the production departments* and all of the other service departments that follow it in the sequence. The ultimate cost allocations assigned to the production departments will differ depending on the sequence chosen.

*The term production department refers to the departments that actually produce the goods or services which constitute the organization's primary mission or objective.

ISSUE 18-38

"THE GREAT DEBATE," *MANAGEMENT ACCOUNTING*, MAY 2000, TOM KENNEDY AND RICHARD BULL.

There are two differences between the absorption costing model and ABC. These lie in the structure and direction of the two models.

1. The traditional absorption-costing model starts with resources and seeks to allocate their costs to products. This gives a clue to the original force behind this approach: a financial accountant's desire to balance the books so that all costs can be fully accounted for.

2. In contrast, the ABC model starts with an enterprise's products and services. It then seeks to identify the activities required to produce or deliver the products and services and the resources required to carry out those activities.

   Thus, ABC uses a completely different starting point than absorption costing and reaches back to the organization's resources by a reverse route.

ISSUE 18-39

"LEARN THE ABC BASICS," *CREDIT UNION MANAGEMENT*, SEPTEMBER 2000, MICHAEL J. KOHL AND THOMAS G. PAGANO.

A few examples of the many kinds of costs credit unions encounter include:

- Absence of online Blue Book to figure loan values

- Check printer breaks down at least two to three times a week

- The phone system drops calls and angers members

- The copy machine is very slow and must be fed one sheet at a time

- High turnover in the teller position

ISSUE 18-40

"HOW KAISER'S COST-SLASHING NICKED ITS IMAGE", *BUSINESS WEEK*, APRIL 21, 1997, STEPHANIE ANDER FOREST AND ERIC SCHINE.

1. A hospital should strive to cut only non-value-added costs. Examples would include a reduction in excessive inventory levels, elimination of duplicate processes, and elimination of unnecessary treatments.

2. Service department cost allocation may help identify how service costs are driven by direct-patient-care activities.

3. Nonfinancial factors based on satisfaction could be used to compensate physicians.

4. Doctors that invest in for-profit hospitals in which they practice have a significant

"IS MEDICARE ABUSE AN EPIDEMIC?" *BUSINESS WEEK*, SEPTEMBER 22, 1997, JEANNE DUGAN.

1. Supply, equipment and labor costs could be allocated as well as a share of corporate overhead such as rent, salaries, and phone bills.

2. A healthcare provider could manipulate its Medicare expense reporting by seeking reimbursement for unrelated corporate overhead costs.

3. The government should allow all reasonable and necessary expenditures that ensure proper health treatment.

4. The costs of clearly unnecessary tests and treatments should, arguably, be disallowed. Of course, the identification of unnecessary procedures is seldom clear and is often subject to debate.

ISSUE 18-42

"GROUND CONTROL: COST CUTTING AT DELTA RAISES THE STOCK PRICE BUT LOWERS THE SERVICE," *THE WALL STREET JOURNAL*, JUNE 20, 1996, MARTHA BRANNIGAN AND ELEENA DE LISSER.

1. and 2. Airline service department costs and possible allocation methods:

Service	Possible Allocation Method
Maintenance	# of planes, # of parts replaced, # of flight hours, # of maintenance hours, # of employees
Reservations	# of reservations, # of employees
Food service	# of customers, # of seats
Training	# of employees, # of pilots

3. A good portion of these services could be outsourced. Training and maintenance expenditures could be reduced, but possibly at the expense of safety. Food service could be eliminated. However, this could create customer dissatisfaction.

CHAPTER 19
Absorption, Variable, and Throughput Costing

ANSWERS TO REVIEW QUESTIONS

19-1   Under absorption costing, fixed manufacturing-overhead costs are assigned to units of product as product costs. Under variable costing, fixed manufacturing-overhead costs are not assigned to units of product as product costs; rather they are treated as period costs and expensed during the period in which they are incurred.

19-2   Timing is the key in distinguishing between absorption and variable costing. All manufacturing costs will ultimately be expensed under either absorption costing or variable costing. The difference between the two methods lies in the time period during which fixed manufacturing-overhead costs are expensed. Under variable costing, the fixed manufacturing-overhead costs are expensed during the period in which they are incurred. Under absorption costing, fixed manufacturing-overhead costs are held in inventory as product costs until the period during which the units are sold. Then those costs flow into cost-of-goods-sold expense.

19-3   The term *direct costing* is a misnomer. Variable costing is a better term for this product-costing method. Under variable costing, the variable costs of direct material, direct labor, and variable overhead are treated as product costs. Fixed manufacturing-overhead costs are not treated as product costs. Thus, the important characteristic of a cost that determines whether it is treated as a product cost under variable costing is its cost behavior. Direct costing is a misnomer because variable-overhead costs are not direct costs, but they are treated as product costs under the variable-costing method.

19-4   When inventory increases, the income reported under absorption costing will be greater than the income reported under variable costing. This difference results from the fact that under absorption costing, some of the fixed manufacturing costs incurred during the period will not be expensed. In contrast, under variable costing all of the fixed manufacturing costs incurred during the period will be expensed during that period.

19-5   Many managers prefer variable costing over absorption costing because income statements prepared under variable costing more closely reflect operations. For example, when sales increase, other things being equal, income will also increase under variable costing. Under absorption costing, however, income will not necessarily increase when sales increase.

19-6 Under absorption costing, all manufacturing-overhead costs (including fixed costs) are assigned to units of product as product costs. Under variable costing, fixed manufacturing-overhead costs are not assigned to units of product as product costs; rather they are treated as period costs and expensed during the period in which they are incurred. Under throughput costing, only the unit-level spending for direct costs is assigned as a product cost.

19-7 Some managerial accountants believe that absorption costing may provide an incentive for managers to overproduce inventory so that the fixed manufacturing overhead costs may be spread over a larger number of product units, thereby lowering the reported product cost per unit. Throughput costing avoids this potential problem by not assigning fixed manufacturing overhead as a product cost.

19-8 Variable and absorption costing will not result in significantly different income measures in a JIT setting. Under JIT inventory and production management, inventories are minimal and as a result inventory changes are also minimal. Variable and absorption costing result in significantly different income measures only when inventory changes significantly from period to period.

19-9 Many managers prefer absorption-costing data for cost-based pricing decisions. They argue that fixed manufacturing overhead is a necessary cost of production. To exclude this fixed cost from the inventoried cost of a product, as is done under variable costing, is to understate the cost of the product. This, in turn, could lead to setting cost-based prices too low.

19-10 Proponents of variable costing argue that a product's variable cost provides a better basis for the pricing decision. They point out that any price above a product's variable cost makes a positive contribution toward covering fixed cost and profit.

19-11 Variable costing is consistent with cost-volume-profit analysis because it properly reflects the cost behavior of variable and fixed costs. Only variable manufacturing costs are treated as inventoriable product costs. Fixed manufacturing costs are recorded as a lump sum and expensed during the period incurred. CVP analysis also properly maintains the cost-behavior distinction between variable and fixed costs. In contrast, absorption costing is inconsistent with CVP analysis, because fixed overhead is applied to manufactured goods as a product cost on a per-unit basis.

19-12 An *asset* is a thing of value owned by the organization with future service potential. By accounting convention, assets are valued at their cost. Since fixed costs comprise part of the cost of production, advocates of absorption costing argue that inventory (an asset) should be valued at its full (absorption) cost of production. Moreover, they argue that these costs have future service potential since the inventory can be sold in the future to generate sales revenue.

Proponents of variable costing argue that the fixed-cost component of a product's absorption-costing value has no future service potential. Their reasoning is that the fixed manufacturing-overhead costs during the current period will not prevent these costs from having to be incurred again next period. Fixed-overhead costs will be incurred every period, regardless of production levels. In contrast, the incurrence of variable costs in manufacturing a product does allow the firm to avoid incurring these costs again.

SOLUTIONS TO EXERCISES

EXERCISE 19-13 (15 MINUTES)

1.   a. Inventory increases by 2,000 units, so income is greater under absorption costing.

   b. $\text{Fixed overhead rate per unit} = \dfrac{\$792,000}{110,000} = \$7.20$

   $\text{Difference in reported income} = \$7.20 \times 2,000 = \$14,400$

2.   a. Inventory decreases by 5,000 units, so income is greater under variable costing.

   b. $\text{Fixed overhead rate per unit} = \dfrac{\$792,000}{90,000} = \$8.80$

   $\text{Difference in reported income} = \$8.80 \times 5,000 = \$44,000$

3.   a. Inventory remains unchanged, so there is no difference in reported income under the two methods of product costing.

   b. No difference.

EXERCISE 19-14 (10 MINUTES)

1. Inventoriable costs under variable costing:

Direct material used	$290,000
Direct labor	100,000
Variable manufacturing overhead	50,000
Total	$440,000

2. Inventoriable costs under absorption costing:

Direct material used	$290,000
Direct labor	100,000
Variable manufacturing overhead	50,000
Fixed manufacturing overhead	80,000
Total	$520,000

3. Inventoriable costs under throughput costing:

Direct material used*	$290,000
Total	$290,000

*Under this scenario, direct material cost is the only throughput cost.

EXERCISE 19-15 (15 MINUTES)

Inventory calculations (units):

Finished-goods inventory, January 1	2,000	units
Add: Units produced	20,000	units
Less: Units sold	21,000	units
Finished-goods inventory, December 31	1,000	units

EXERCISE 19-15 (CONTINUED)

1. Variable costing:

Inventoriable costs under variable costing:

Direct material used	$ 600,000
Direct labor incurred	300,000
Variable manufacturing overhead	200,000
Total	$1,100,000

Cost per unit produced = $1,100,000/20,000 units = $55 per unit

Ending inventory: 1,000 units × $55 per unit $55,000

2. Absorption costing:

Predetermined fixed-overhead rate

$$= \frac{\text{fixed manufacturing overhead}}{\text{planned production}} = \frac{\$420,000}{20,000 \text{ units}}$$

$$= \$21 \text{ per unit}$$

$$\begin{pmatrix} \text{Difference in fixed} \\ \text{overhead expensed under} \\ \text{absorption and variable costing} \end{pmatrix} = \begin{pmatrix} \text{change in} \\ \text{inventory} \\ \text{in units} \end{pmatrix} \times \begin{pmatrix} \text{predetermined} \\ \text{fixed-overhead} \\ \text{rate} \end{pmatrix}$$

$$= (1,000 \text{ units}) \times (\$21 \text{ per unit})$$

$$= \$21,000$$

Difference in reported income:

Since *inventory decreased* during the year, income reported under absorption costing will be $21,000 lower than income reported under variable costing.

EXERCISE 19-16 (25 MINUTES)

Inventory calculations (units):

Finished-goods inventory, January 1	0	units
Add: Units produced	10,000	units
Less: Units sold	9,000	units
Finished-goods inventory, December 31	1,000	units

1. Variable costing:

   Inventoriable costs under variable costing:

Direct material used	$40,000
Direct labor incurred	20,000
Variable manufacturing overhead	12,000
Total	$72,000

   Cost per unit produced = $72,000/10,000 units = $7.20 per unit

   Ending inventory: 1,000 units $\times$ $7.20 per unit $7,200

2. Absorption costing:

   Predetermined fixed-overhead rate

   $$= \frac{\text{fixed manufacturing overhead}}{\text{planned production}} = \frac{\$25,000}{10,000 \text{ units}}$$

   = $2.50 per unit

   $$\begin{matrix} \text{Difference in fixed} \\ \text{overhead expensed under} \\ \text{absorption and variable costing} \end{matrix} = \begin{pmatrix} \text{change in} \\ \text{inventory} \\ \text{in units} \end{pmatrix} \times \begin{pmatrix} \text{predetermined} \\ \text{fixed-overhead} \\ \text{rate} \end{pmatrix}$$

   = (1,000 units) $\times$ ($2.50 per unit)

   = $2,500

   Difference in reported income:

   Since *inventory increased* during the year, income reported under absorption costing will be $2,500 higher than income reported under variable costing.

EXERCISE 19-16 (CONTINUED)

3. Throughput costing:

    Inventoriable costs under throughput costing:

Direct material used	**$40,000**
Total	**$40,000**

    Cost per unit produced = $40,000/10,000 units = $4.00 per unit

    Ending inventory: 1,000 units × $4.00 per unit $4,000

EXERCISE 19-17 (15 MINUTES)

1. a. Inventory decreases by 3,000 units, so income is greater under variable costing.

    b.
    $$\frac{\text{Fixed overhead}}{\text{rate per unit}} = \frac{\$2,200,000}{20,000} = \$110$$

    $$\frac{\text{Difference in}}{\text{reported income}} = \$110 \times 3,000 = \$330,000$$

2. a. Inventory remains unchanged, so there is no difference in reported income under the two methods of product costing.

    b. No difference.

3. a. Inventory increases by 2,000 units, so income is greater under absorption costing.

    b.
    $$\frac{\text{Fixed overhead}}{\text{rate per unit}} = \frac{\$2,200,000}{11,000} = \$200$$

    $$\frac{\text{Difference in}}{\text{reported income}} = \$200 \times 2,000 = \$400,000$$

EXERCISE 19-18 (20 MINUTES)

1.   Cost-volume profit graph:

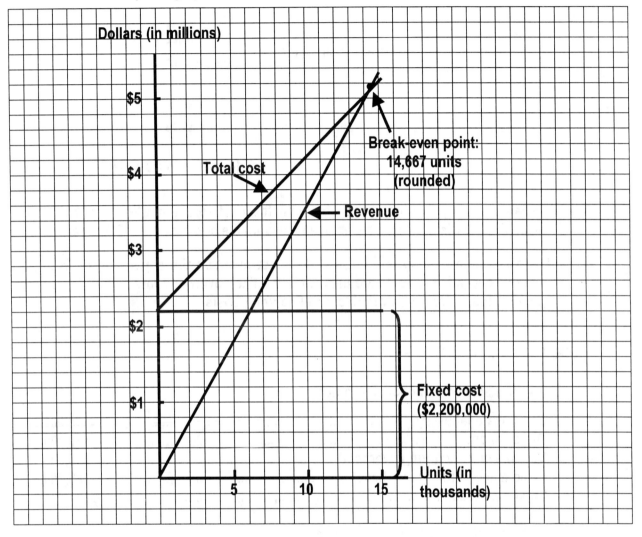

EXERCISE 19-18 (CONTINUED)

2. Calculation of break-even point:

$$\text{Break-even point} = \frac{\text{fixed cost}}{\text{unit contribution margin}}$$

$$= \frac{\$2,200,000}{\$350 - \$200}$$

$$= 14,667 \text{ units (rounded)}$$

3. Variable costing is more compatible with the cost-volume-profit chart, because it maintains the distinction between fixed and variable costs as does CVP analysis.

    Absorption costing, in contrast, does not maintain the separation of fixed and variable costs. Fixed costs are unitized in the fixed overhead rate and inventoried as product costs along with variable manufacturing costs.

EXERCISE 19-19 (10 MINUTES)

1. Inventoriable costs under absorption costing:

Direct material used	$340,000
Direct labor	160,000
Variable manufacturing overhead	75,000
Fixed manufacturing overhead	125,000
Total	$700,000

2. Inventoriable costs under variable costing:

Direct material used	$340,000
Direct labor	160,000
Variable manufacturing overhead	75,000
Total	$575,000

EXERCISE 19-20 (30 MINUTES)

The specifics of the answer will vary, depending on the company and product selected. However, the relative merits of absorption, variable and throughput costing as the basis for pricing decisions are generally the same, regardless of the company and product.

Many managers prefer absorption-costing data for cost-based pricing decisions. They argue that fixed manufacturing overhead is a necessary cost of production. To exclude this fixed cost from the inventoried cost of a product, as is done under variable costing, is to understate the cost of the product. This, in turn, could lead to setting cost-based prices too low.

Proponents of variable costing argue that a product's variable cost provides a better basis for the pricing decision. They point out that any price above a product's variable cost makes a positive contribution toward covering fixed cost and profit.

Proponents of throughput costing take the variable-costing argument a step further and argue that a product's throughput cost provides the best basis for a cost-based pricing decision. They argue that any price above a product's unit-level spending for direct costs (e.g., throughput costs) makes a positive contribution toward covering fixed cost and profit.

SOLUTIONS TO PROBLEMS

PROBLEM 19-21 (45 MINUTES)

1. Since there were no variances in 20x1, actual production and budgeted production must have been the same.

$$\text{Predetermined fixed overhead rate} = \frac{\text{budgeted fixed overhead}}{\text{budgeted production}}$$

$$= \frac{\$300,000}{150,000} = \$2 \text{ per unit}$$

Standard Cost per Unit

Direct material	$ 5
Direct labor	2
Variable overhead	3
a. Standard cost per unit under variable costing	$10
Fixed overhead per unit under absorption costing	2
b. Standard cost per unit under absorption costing	$12

2. a.

SKINNY DIPPERS, INC.
ABSORPTION-COSTING INCOME STATEMENT
FOR THE YEAR ENDED DECEMBER 31, 20X1

Sales revenue (125,000 units sold at $15 per unit)	$1,875,000
Less: Cost of goods sold (at standard absorption cost of $12 per unit)	1,500,000
Gross margin	$ 375,000
Less: Selling and administrative expenses:	
Variable (at $1 per unit)	125,000
Fixed	50,000
Net income	$ 200,000

PROBLEM 19-21 (CONTINUED)

b.

SKINNY DIPPERS, INC.
VARIABLE-COSTING INCOME STATEMENT
FOR THE YEAR ENDED DECEMBER 31, 20X1

Sales revenue (125,000 units sold at $15 per unit)	$1,875,000
Less: Variable expenses:	
Variable manufacturing costs	
(at standard variable cost of $10 per unit)	1,250,000
Variable selling and administrative costs	
(at $1 per unit)	125,000
Contribution margin	$ 500,000
Less: Fixed expenses:	
Fixed manufacturing overhead	300,000
Fixed selling and administrative expenses	50,000
Net income	$ 150,000

3.	Cost of goods sold under absorption costing	$1,500,000
	Less: Variable manufacturing costs under variable costing	1,250,000
	Subtotal	$ 250,000
	Less: Fixed manufacturing overhead as period expense	
	under variable costing	300,000
	Total	$ (50,000)
	Net income under variable costing	$ 150,000
	Less: Net income under absorption costing	200,000
	Difference in net income	$ (50,000)

4. $\begin{array}{c}\text{Difference in}\\\text{reported income}\end{array} = \begin{array}{c}\text{difference in fixed overhead expensed under}\\\text{absorption and variable costing}\end{array}$

$$= \left(\begin{array}{c}\text{change in inventory,}\\\text{in units}\end{array}\right) \times \left(\begin{array}{c}\text{predetermined fixed}\\\text{overhead rate per unit}\end{array}\right)$$

$$= (25,000 \text{ units}) \times (\$2 \text{ per unit})$$

$$= \$50,000$$

As shown in requirement (2), reported income is $50,000 lower under variable costing.

PROBLEM 19-22 (25 MINUTES)

1. Skinny Dippers produced 150,000 units (i.e., containers) and sold 125,000, which leaves an ending finished-goods inventory of 25,000 units. Because only direct material qualifies as a throughput cost, the cost of the ending inventory is $125,000 (25,000 containers x $5).

2.

SKINNY DIPPERS, INC.
THROUGHPUT-COSTING INCOME STATEMENT
FOR THE YEAR ENDED DECEMBER 31, 20X1

Sales revenue (125,000 units x $15)	$1,875,000
Less: Cost of goods sold (125,000 units x $5)	625,000
Gross margin	$1,250,000
Less: Operating costs:	
Direct labor (150,000 units x $2)	$ 300,000
Variable manufacturing overhead (150,000 units x $3)	450,000
Fixed manufacturing overhead	300,000
Variable selling and administrative costs	
(125,000 units x $1)	125,000
Fixed selling and administrative costs	50,000
Total operating costs	$1,225,000
Net income	$ 25,000

3. Gross margin is computed by subtracting cost of goods sold from sales revenue. The "cost" of a unit differs and depends on whether a firm uses absorption costing or throughput costing. With absorption costing, the product cost consists of four elements: direct material, direct labor, variable manufacturing overhead, and fixed manufacturing overhead. Throughput costing, on the other hand, assigns only the unit-level spending for direct costs (in this case, direct material) as the cost of a product.

PROBLEM 19-23 (45 MINUTES)

1. Since there were no variances, there was no volume variance. Therefore, since the planned production volume was 100,000 units, actual production must have been 100,000 units.

Beginning inventory	0	units
Production	100,000	units
Ending inventory	(20,000)	units
Sales	80,000	units

Since inventory increased during the year, reported income is higher under absorption costing.

$$\begin{matrix} \text{Difference in} \\ \text{reported income} \end{matrix} = \begin{matrix} \text{change in} \\ \text{inventory} \end{matrix} \times \begin{matrix} \text{fixed overhead} \\ \text{per unit} \end{matrix}$$

$$\$20,000 = 20,000 \text{ units} \times \frac{\text{fixed overhead}}{100,000 \text{ units}}$$

Solving this equation: fixed overhead = $100,000

Now we can compute the contribution margin:

Reported income under variable costing	$220,000
Fixed overhead	100,000
Total contribution margin	$320,000

PROBLEM 19-23 (CONTINUED)

$$\text{Contribution margin per unit} = \frac{\text{total contribution margin}}{\text{sales in units}}$$

$$= \frac{\$320,000}{80,000 \text{ units}} = \$4 \text{ per unit}$$

$$\text{Break-even point in units} = \frac{\text{fixed cost (overhead)}}{\text{unit contribution margin}}$$

$$= \frac{\$100,000}{\$4 \text{ per unit}} = 25,000 \text{ units}$$

PROBLEM 19-23 (CONTINUED)

2.   **Profit-volume graph:**

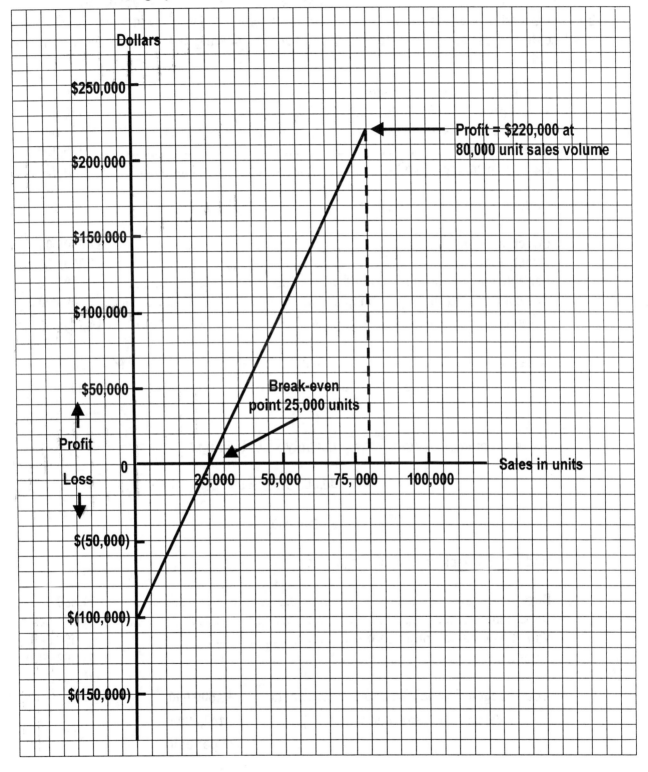

PROBLEM 19-24 (25 MINUTES)

Outback Corporation's reported 20x1 income will be higher under absorption costing because actual production exceeded actual sales. Therefore, inventory increased and some fixed costs will remain in inventory under absorption costing which would be expensed under variable costing.

1. Beginning inventory (in units) 35,000
    Actual production (in units) 130,000
    Available for sale (in units) 165,000
    Sales (in units) 125,000
    Ending inventory (in units) 40,000

    Budgeted manufacturing costs:

    Direct material $1,680,000
    Direct labor 1,260,000
    Variable manufacturing overhead 560,000
    Fixed manufacturing overhead 700,000
      Total $4,200,000

$$\frac{\text{Total budgeted manufacturing costs (variable and fixed)}}{\text{Total planned production (in units)}} = \frac{\$4,200,000}{140,000}$$

$$= \$30 \text{ per unit}$$

Value of ending inventory $=$ quantity $\times$ cost per unit

$=$ 40,000 units $\times$ \$30 per unit

$=$ \$1,200,000

2. Budgeted variable manufacturing costs:

    Direct material $1,680,000
    Direct labor 1,260,000
    Variable manufacturing overhead 560,000
    Total $3,500,000

$$\frac{\text{Total budgeted variable manufacturing costs}}{\text{Total planned production (in units)}} = \frac{\$3,500,000}{140,000}$$

$$= \$25 \text{ per unit}$$

PROBLEM 19-24 (CONTINUED)

Value of ending inventory   =   quantity $\times$ cost per unit

                 =   40,000 units $\times$ \$25 per unit

                 =   \$1,000,000

3.   Increase in inventory (in units)   =   production – sales

                              =   130,000 units – 125,000 units

                              =   5,000 units

Budgeted fixed manufacturing overhead per unit $= \dfrac{\$700,000}{140,000\ units}$

                                          = \$5 per unit

Difference in reported income

    = budgeted fixed overhead per unit $\times$ change in inventory (in units)

    = \$5 $\times$ 5,000 units = \$25,000

4.   If Outback Corporation had adopted a JIT program at the beginning of 20x1:

    a.   It is unlikely that the company would have manufactured 5,000 more units than it sold. Under JIT, production and sales would be nearly equal.

    b.   Reported income under variable and absorption costing would most likely be nearly the same. Differences in reported income are caused by changes in inventory levels. Under JIT, inventory levels would be minimal. Therefore, the change in these levels would be minimal.

PROBLEM 19-25 (40 MINUTES)

1. Standard cost per unit:

	(a) Absorption Costing	(b) Variable Costing
Direct material	$20	$20
Direct labor	11	11
Manufacturing overhead		
Variable	8	8
Fixed ($200,000 ÷ 20,000)	10	
Total standard absorption cost	$49	
Total standard variable cost		$39

2.

$$\begin{array}{ccccc}
\text{Fixed-overhead} \\ \text{volume variance} & = & \text{budgeted fixed} \\ \text{manufacturing overhead} & - & \text{applied fixed} \\ \text{manufacturing overhead}
\end{array}$$

$$\$(50,000)^* \quad = \quad \$200,000 \quad - \quad (25,000)(\$10)$$

*The volume variance is negative. Some accountants would designate it as favorable.

3. a.

GREAT OUTDOZE COMPANY
INCOME STATEMENT FOR THE YEAR ENDED DECEMBER 31, 20X1
ABSORPTION COSTING

Sales revenue (at $65 per unit)	$1,430,000
Less: Cost of goods sold (at standard absorption cost of $49 per unit)	1,078,000
Gross margin (at standard)	$ 352,000
Adjust for: Fixed-overhead volume variance	50,000
Gross margin (at actual)	$ 402,000
Less: Selling and administrative expenses:	
Variable (at $1 per unit)	22,000
Fixed	30,000
Net income	$ 350,000

PROBLEM 19-25 (CONTINUED)

b.
GREAT OUTDOZE COMPANY
INCOME STATEMENT FOR THE YEAR ENDED DECEMBER 31, 20X1
VARIABLE COSTING

Sales revenue (at $65 per unit)	$1,430,000
Less: Variable expenses:	
Variable manufacturing costs	
(at standard variable cost of $39 per unit)	858,000
Variable selling and administrative costs	
(at $1 per unit)	22,000
Contribution margin	$ 550,000
Less: Fixed expenses:	
Fixed manufacturing overhead	200,000
Fixed selling and administrative costs	30,000
Net income	$ 320,000

4.

Change in inventory (in units)		predetermined fixed overhead rate		absorption-costing income minus variable-costing income
	$\times$		$=$	
3,000 unit increase	$\times$	$10	$=$	$30,000

5. If Great Outdoze had implemented JIT and installed a flexible manufacturing system at the beginning of 20x1, it is unlikely that reported income would have differed by as great a magnitude. Under this scenario, production and sales would have been nearly the same. As a result reported income under variable and absorption costing would have been nearly equal. Differences in reported income are caused by significant changes in inventory levels, which do not occur under JIT because inventory is minimal.

PROBLEM 19-26 (40 MINUTES)

1. Standard throughput cost per unit:

    Direct material cost per unit* $20
    Total standard throughput
       cost per unit $20

    *Direct material is the only
    throughput cost.

2.

GREAT OUTDOZE COMPANY
INCOME STATEMENT FOR THE YEAR ENDED DECEMBER 31, 20X1
THROUGHPUT COSTING

Sales revenue (22,000 units at $65 per unit)	$1,430,000
Less: Cost of goods sold (at throughput standard cost, the standard direct-material cost, 22,000 x $20 per unit)	440,000
Gross margin	$ 990,000
Less: Operating costs:	
Direct labor[a]	275,000
Variable overhead[b]	200,000
Variable selling and administrative costs (at $1 per unit)[c]	22,000
Fixed manufacturing overhead	200,000
Fixed selling and administrative costs	30,000
Net income	$ 263,000

[a]Since the company manufactured more units than planned in the budget, we must assume that management has committed to direct labor sufficient to produce the actual production volume of 25,000 units; direct labor is *used* at the rate of $11 per unit produced.

[b]Since the company manufactured more units than planned in the budget, we must assume that management has committed to support resources sufficient to produce the actual production volume of 25,000 units; variable-overhead cost is *used* at the rate of $8 per unit produced.

[c]Variable selling and administrative costs amount to $1 per unit sold.

PROBLEM 19-26 (CONTINUED)

3.　*For throughput costing:*　Some managerial accountants believe that absorption costing may provide an incentive for managers to overproduce inventory so that the fixed manufacturing overhead costs may be spread over a larger number of product units, thereby lowering the reported product cost per unit.　Throughput costing avoids this potential problem by not assigning fixed manufacturing overhead as a product cost.

　　Against throughput costing:　Many managers prefer absorption-costing data for cost-based pricing decisions. They argue that fixed manufacturing overhead is a necessary cost of production. To exclude this fixed cost from the inventoried cost of a product, as is done under throughput (and variable) costing, is to understate the cost of the product. This, in turn, could lead to setting cost-based prices too low.

PROBLEM 19-27 (45 MINUTES)

1. Reported income will be higher under variable costing, because inventory is expected to decline by 2,000 units during the year. (Seventeen thousand units will be produced in the last two months, but 19,000 units will be sold.)

2. a. Variable costing: Total contribution during first 10 months is equal to the fixed costs plus profit for that period.

Fixed costs during first 10 months	$2,000,000
Profit during first 10 months	200,000
Total contribution margin	$2,200,000

   $$\text{Contribution margin per unit} = \frac{\$2,200,000}{100,000} = \$22 \text{ per unit}$$

   Projected total sales for the year are 119,000 units (100,000 in first 10 months plus 19,000 units in last 2 months). We can compute projected income for the year as follows:

Projected total contribution margin ($22 × 119,000)	$2,618,000
Projected fixed costs ($200,000 × 12)	2,400,000
Projected income	$ 218,000

   The net income projected for the year under variable costing is $218,000.

   Note: The problem states that the prior period's standard cost rates are the same as those of the current period. There are 10,000 units on hand at October 31, and production equals sales in the first 10 months. Thus, 10,000 units were on hand at January 1.

   b. Absorption costing: The gross margin for the first 10 months is $200,000. Notice that income and gross margin are the same, since there are no selling or administrative expenses. Therefore, during the first 10 months:

   $$\text{Gross margin per unit} = \frac{\$200,000}{100,000 \text{ units}} = \$2 \text{ per unit}$$

PROBLEM 19-27 (CONTINUED)

Projected sales for the year are 119,000 units, so we can compute projected income for the year as follows:

Projected gross margin ($2 × 119,000)	$238,000
Less: Projected volume variance ($20 × 3,000*)	60,000
Projected income	$178,000

*[(10,000 units per month, planned production) x 12] – 117,000 units produced = 3000

The volume variance is the difference between budgeted and applied fixed overhead for the year, computed as follows:

$$\text{Volume variance} = \text{budgeted fixed overhead} - \text{applied fixed overhead}$$

$$= \$2,400,000 - (\$20)(117,000) = \$60,000$$

$$\text{where } \$20 = \frac{\text{fixed overhead rate per unit}}{} = \frac{\$2,000,000 \text{ overhead in first 10 months}}{100,000 \text{ units in first 10 months}}$$

and 117,000 = current projected production for the year

Note that budgeted and actual production during the first 10 months were equal, because there was no volume variance. Therefore, budgeted production must be 10,000 units per month.

Projected net income for the year under absorption costing is $178,000.

Check: Our conclusions can be checked by noting the following relationship:

$$\text{Reported income under variable costing} - \text{reported income under absorption costing}$$

$$= \text{decline in inventory} \times \text{fixed-overhead rate}$$

$$= 2,000 \text{ units} \times \$20 \text{ per unit} = \$40,000$$

Therefore, reported income will be $40,000 higher under variable costing than under absorption costing.

PROBLEM 19-28 (35 MINUTES)

1. Total cost:

Direct material (10,000 units x $12).............	$120,000
Direct labor...	45,000
Variable manufacturing overhead................	65,000
Fixed manufacturing overhead....................	220,000
Variable selling and administrative costs	
(9,600 units x $8)....................................	76,800
Fixed selling and administrative costs.........	118,000
Total...	$644,800

2. The cost of the year-end inventory of 400 units (10,000 units produced – 9,600 units sold) is computed as follows:

	Absorption Costing	Variable Costing	Throughput Costing
Direct material................................	$120,000	$120,000	$120,000
Direct labor....................................	45,000	45,000	
Variable manufacturing overhead.....	65,000	65,000	
Fixed manufacturing overhead.........	220,000		
Total product cost....................	$450,000	$230,000	$120,000
Cost per unit (total ÷ 10,000 units)...	$45	$23	$12
Year-end inventory (400 units x cost per unit).....................................	$18,000	$9,200	$4,800

3. The total costs would be allocated between the current period's income statement and the year-end inventory on the balance sheet. Thus:

Absorption costing: $644,800 - $18,000 = $626,800
Variable costing: $644,800 - $9,200 = $635,600
Throughput costing: $644,800 - $4,800 = $640,000

© *2002 The McGraw-Hill Companies, Inc.*

Solutions Manual

Alternatively, these amounts can be derived as follows:

	Absorption Costing	Variable Costing	Throughput Costing
Cost of goods sold:			
9,600 units x $45............................	$432,000		
9,600 units x $23............................		$220,800	
9,600 units x $12............................			$115,200
Direct labor......................................			45,000
Variable manufacturing overhead........			65,000
Fixed manufacturing overhead............		220,000	220,000
Variable selling and administrative costs...	76,800	76,800	76,800
Fixed selling and administrative costs..	118,000	118,000	118,000
Total......................................	$626,800	$635,600	$640,000

4.   Throughput-costing income statement:

Sales revenue (9,600 units x $72).....................	$691,200
Less: Cost of goods sold	115,200
Gross margin..	$576,000
Less: Operating costs:	
Direct labor	$ 45,000
Variable manufacturing overhead	65,000
Fixed manufacturing overhead..................	220,000
Variable selling and administrative costs ...	76,800
Fixed selling and administrative costs.......	118,000
Total operating costs.........................	$524,800
Net income..	$ 51,200*

*As a check: Net income = sales revenue - all costs expensed
        = $691,200   - $640,000 (from req. 3)
        = $51,200

PROBLEM 19-29 (35 MINUTES)

1.   Absorption-costing income statements:

	Year 1	Year 2
Sales revenue	$125,000[a]	$125,000[d]
Less: Cost of goods sold:		
Beginning finished-goods inventory	$ 0	$ 10,500[e]
Cost of goods manufactured	63,000[b]	56,000[f]
Cost of goods available for sale	$ 63,000	$ 66,500
Ending finished-goods inventory	10,500[c]	0
Cost of goods sold	$ 52,500	$ 66,500
Gross margin	$ 72,500	$ 58,500
Selling and administrative expenses	45,000	45,000
Operating income	$ 27,500	$ 13,500

[a]2,500 units × $50 per unit
[b]$21,000 + $42,000 (i.e., *both* variable and fixed costs)
[c]500 units × ($63,000/3,000 units)
[d]2,500 units × $50 per unit
[e]Same as year 1 ending inventory
[f]$14,000 + $42,000 (i.e., *both* variable and fixed costs)

PROBLEM 19-29 (CONTINUED)

2. Variable-costing income statements:

	Year 1	Year 2
Sales revenue	$125,000[a]	$125,000[d]
Less: Cost of goods sold:		
Beginning finished-goods inventory	$ 0	$ 3,500[e]
Cost of goods manufactured	21,000[b]	14,000[f]
Cost of goods available for sale	$ 21,000	$ 17,500
Ending finished-goods inventory	3,500[c]	0
Cost of goods sold	$ 17,500	$ 17,500
Less: Variable selling and administrative costs	$ 25,000	$ 25,000
Total variable costs:	$ 42,500	$ 42,500
Contribution margin	$ 82,500	$ 82,500
Less: Fixed costs:		
Manufacturing	$ 42,000	$ 42,000
Selling and administrative	20,000	20,000
Total fixed costs	$ 62,000	$ 62,000
Operating income	$ 20,500	$ 20,500

[a]2,500 units $\times$ $50 per unit
[b]The variable manufacturing cost *only*, $21,000
[c]500 units $\times$ ($21,000/3,000 units)
[d]2,500 units $\times$ $50 per unit
[e]Same as year 1 ending inventory
[f]The variable manufacturing cost *only*, $14,000

3.   Reconciliation of reported income under absorption and variable costing:

Year	Change in Inventory (in units)		Actual Fixed-Overhead Rate	Difference in Fixed Overhead Expensed	Absorption-Costing Income Minus Variable-Costing Income
1	500 increase	×	$14	$ 7,000	$7,000
2	500 decrease	×	$14*	$(7,000)	(7,000)

*The 500 units which were sold in year 2, but which were *manufactured in year 1*, include an absorption-costing product cost of $14 per unit for fixed overhead. Since these 500 units were manufactured in year 1, it is the year 1 fixed-overhead rate that is relevant to this calculation, not the year 2 rate.

Explanation: At the end of year 1, under absorption costing, $7,000 of fixed overhead remained stored in finished-goods inventory as a product cost (year 1 fixed-overhead rate of $14 per unit × 500 units = $7,000). However, in year 1, under variable costing, that fixed overhead was expensed as a period cost.

In year 2, under absorption costing, that same $7,000 of fixed overhead was expensed when the units were sold. However, under variable costing, that $7,000 of fixed overhead cost had already been expensed in year 1 as a period cost.

PROBLEM 19-30 (30 MINUTES)

1.   Reconciliation of reported income:

Year 1	Absorption Costing Income Statement	Variable Costing Income Statement
Cost of goods sold	$52,500	$17,500
Fixed cost (expensed as period expense)	20,000*	62,000†
Total	$72,500	$79,500
Difference (cost greater on variable-costing income statement)		$7,000
Reported income	$27,500	$20,500
Difference in reported income (income greater on absorption-costing income statement)		$7,000

*Fixed selling and administrative cost *only*
†*Both* fixed selling and administrative cost *and* fixed manufacturing overhead

Year 2	Absorption Costing Income Statement	Variable Costing Income Statement
Cost of goods sold	$66,500	$17,500
Fixed cost (expensed as period expense)	20,000	62,000
Total	$86,500	$79,500
Difference (cost greater on absorption-costing income statement)		$7,000
Reported income	$13,500	$20,500
Difference in reported income (income greater on variable-costing income statement)		$7,000

PROBLEM 19-30 (CONTINUED)

2.   Total income across both years:

    a.   Absorption costing: $27,500 + $13,500 = $41,000

    b.   Variable costing: $20,500 + $20,500 = $41,000

3.   Total sales revenue across both years:

    a.   Absorption costing: $125,000 + $125,000 = $250,000

    b.   Variable costing: $125,000 + $125,000 = $250,000

4.   Total of all costs expensed across both years:

    a.   Absorption costing: $97,500 + $111,500 = $209,000

    b.   Variable costing: $104,500 + $104,500 = $209,000

5.   Total sales revenue minus total costs expensed across both years.

    a.   Absorption costing: $250,000 – $209,000 = $41,000

    b.   Variable costing: $250,000 – $209,000 = $41,000

PROBLEM 19-30 (CONTINUED)

6.   The total sales revenue across both of Lehighton's first two years of operation is the same under absorption and variable costing, $250,000, as shown in requirement (3). *Sales revenue has nothing to do with the costing method used.* Lehighton sold 5,000 units in years 1 and 2 combined, at a sales price of $50. This results in total sales revenue for the two years of $250,000.

The total of the costs expensed, across years 1 and 2, is the same under variable and absorption costing, $209,000, as shown in requirement (4). The reason for this result is that Lehighton produced the same number of units that the company sold, across the two-year period. Lehighton *produced and sold* 5,000 units during years 1 and 2 combined. Thus, the same amount of manufacturing cost is expensed, *during the two year period*, under absorption and variable costing.

Lehighton's combined income, across the two-year period, is $41,000 under both absorption and variable costing (requirement 2). This result must occur, of course, because total sales revenue and total expenses are the same under both costing methods.

As the analysis in requirement (1) shows, Lehighton's income is distributed differently across years 1 and 2 under absorption and variable costing. Both costing methods yield the same reported income across the two-year combined period, but the income is not the same *within each year*, under the two costing methods. Absorption costing yields a $7,000 higher income in year 1 and a $7,000 lower income in year 2. This result occurs because under absorption costing, Lehighton's expenses are $7,000 lower in year 1 and $7,000 greater in year 2.

Thus, the difference between absorption and variable costing is caused by the timing with which expenses are recognized. Under absorption costing, some of Lehighton's year 1 fixed manufacturing overhead is not expensed until year 2, when the units are sold. In contrast, under variable costing all of the year 1 fixed manufacturing overhead is expensed in year 1 as a period cost.

PROBLEM 19-31 (40 MINUTES)

1.   At the end of year 1, Lehighton has 500 units in its finished-goods inventory (production minus sales). The year-end balance in finished-goods inventory is higher under absorption costing because fixed manufacturing overhead cost is included in the inventory cost as a product cost. In contrast, under variable costing, fixed manufacturing overhead is not included in the inventory cost as a product cost.

2.   At the end of year 2, Lehighton has no finished-goods inventory on hand. The two-year total production of 5,000 units is equal to the two-year total sales. Since *there is no finished-goods inventory at the end of year 2*, the value of finished-goods inventory on the balance sheet is *zero*, no matter what product-costing system is used.

3.   Yes, this relationship will be true at any balance sheet date. For any balance sheet date when the company has nonzero finished-goods inventory, the cost of that inventory measured under absorption costing will be greater than the cost measured under variable costing. Under absorption costing, fixed manufacturing overhead is inventoried as a product cost. However, under variable costing, fixed manufacturing overhead is not inventoried as a product cost. It is treated as a period cost instead, and expensed during the period in which it is incurred.

4.

	Finished-Goods Inventory		Amount of Decline
	End of Year 1	End of Year 2	
Absorption costing	$10,500	$0	$10,500
Variable costing	3,500	0	3,500

5.

	Amount of Decline in Finished-Goods Inventory Balance During Year 2
Absorption costing	$10,500
Variable costing	3,500
Difference	$ 7,000

	Reported Income for Year 2
Absorption costing	$13,500
Variable costing	20,500
Difference	$ (7,000)

PROBLEM 19-31 (CONTINUED)

Reported income for year 2 is $7,000 lower under absorption costing. This amount matches the difference in the amount by which the year-end finished-goods inventory balance declined during year 2 under absorption versus variable costing. During year 2, the company sold more units than it produced. Under absorption costing, $7,000 of inventoried fixed manufacturing overhead was expensed during year 2. Under variable costing, this fixed manufacturing overhead had already been expensed during year 1. Therefore, the year-end balance in finished-goods inventory declined during year 2 by $7,000 more under absorption costing than under variable costing.

6. Yes, this relationship will always hold true at any balance sheet date. There are two ways to think about this issue.

    (a) As explained in the text, during any time period during which inventory increases (i.e., production exceeds sales), income reported under absorption costing will exceed income reported under variable costing. This result occurs because under absorption costing, some fixed manufacturing overhead costs will be stored as product costs and inventoried under absorption costing, but these fixed manufacturing overhead costs would be expensed as period costs under variable costing.

    Retained earnings, at any given balance sheet date, is the sum total of all income reported for the firm across its entire life since its inception (less the sum total of dividends declared). During the entire life of the enterprise, the company cannot have sold more units in total than it ever produced. Therefore, over the entire life of the enterprise, inventory cannot possibly have decreased. It will either have remained at zero or it will have increased. Thus, if we think of the entire life of the enterprise as its one and only accounting period, inventory has either increased or remained at zero, and income reported under absorption costing will be at least as great as income reported under variable costing *for that life-time accounting period*.

The following diagram may help in understanding the foregoing explanation.

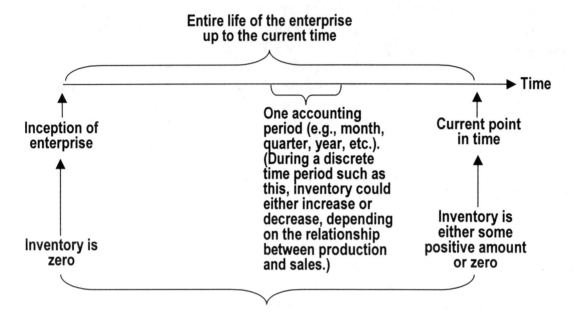

- During this life-time accounting period, inventory has either increased, or returned to zero, but it cannot have decreased.

- For this life-time accounting period, income reported under absorption costing is greater than or equal to income reported under variable costing.

- Thus, at the end of this life-time accounting period, retained earnings reported under absorption costing will be greater than or equal to retained earnings reported under variable costing.

(b) Another way to explain the answer to this question involves the basic accounting equation

Assets = Liabilities + Owners' Equity

Inventory (I) is included in assets

Retained earnings (RE) is included in owners' equity.

$I_a \geq I_v$ *Therefore* $RE_a \geq RE_v$

where a denotes absorption costing and v denotes variable costing.

PROBLEM 19-31 (CONTINUED)

The only elements in the accounting equation that are affected by the choice of absorption or variable costing are inventory (I) and retained earnings (RE). To maintain the accounting equation, if I (and therefore assets) are greater under absorption costing, then liabilities and equities must be greater under absorption costing. Therefore, RE is greater under absorption costing.

PROBLEM 19-32 (45 MINUTES)

1.   a. Absorption-costing income statements:

	Year 1	Year 2	Year 3
Sales revenue (at $50 per case)	$4,000,000	$3,000,000	$4,500,000
Less: Cost of goods sold (at standard			
absorption cost of $42 per case) *.........................	3,360,000	2,520,000	3,780,000
Gross margin	$ 640,000	$ 480,000	$ 720,000
Less: Selling and administrative expenses:			
Variable (at $1 per case)	80,000	60,000	90,000
Fixed	75,000	75,000	75,000
Operating income	$ 485,000	$ 345,000	$ 555,000

*Standard absorption cost per case is $42, calculated as follows:

$$\frac{\text{Budgeted fixed manufacturing overhead}}{\text{Planned production}} + \begin{array}{c}\text{variable manufacturing}\\ \text{cost per case}\end{array}$$

$$\frac{\$800,000}{80,000} + \$32$$

PROBLEM 19-32 (CONTINUED)

b. Variable-costing income statements:

	Year 1	Year 2	Year 3
Sales revenue (at $50 per case)	$4,000,000	$3,000,000	$4,500,000
Less: Variable expenses:			
Variable manufacturing costs (at standard variable cost of $32 per case)	2,560,000	1,920,000	2,880,000
Variable selling and administrative costs (at $1 per case)	80,000	60,000	90,000
Contribution margin	$1,360,000	$1,020,000	$1,530,000
Less Fixed expenses:			
Fixed manufacturing overhead	800,000	800,000	800,000
Fixed selling and administrative expenses	75,000	75,000	75,000
Operating income	$ 485,000	$ 145,000	$ 655,000

2. Reconciliation:

	Reported Income		Difference in Reported Income	Change in Inventory (in units)	Predetermined Fixed Overhead Rate*	Difference In Fixed Overhead Expensed Under Absorption and Variable Costing
Year	Absorption Costing	Variable Costing				
1	$485,000	$485,000	-0-	-0-	$10	0
2	345,000	145,000	$200,000	20,000	10	$200,000
3	555,000	655,000	(100,000)	(10,000)	10	(100,000)

*Predetermined fixed manufacturing overhead rate = $\dfrac{\$800,000}{80,000}$

PROBLEM 19-32 (CONTINUED)

3. a. In year 4, the difference in reported operating income will be $100,000, calculated as follows:

Change in inventory (in units)		Predetermined fixed overhead rate		
(10,000)	×	$10	=	$(100,000)

Income reported under absorption costing will be lower, because inventory will decline during year 4.

b. Over the four-year period, the total of all reported operating income will be the same under absorption and variable costing. This result will occur because inventory does not change over the four-year period. It starts out at zero on January 1 of year 1, and it ends up at zero on December 31 of year 4.

PROBLEM 19-33 (40 MINUTES)

Throughput-costing income statements:

	Year 1	Year 2	Year 3
Sales revenue (at $50 per case)	$4,000,000	$3,000,000	$4,500,000
Less: Cost of goods sold (at standard throughput cost, equal to direct-material cost of $15 per case)	1,200,000	900,000	1,350,000
Gross margin	$2,800,000	$2,100,000	$3,150,000
Less: Operating costs:			
Direct labor[a]...	400,000	400,000	400,000
Variable overhead[b].................................	960,000	960,000	960,000
Variable selling and administrative cost at $1 per unit[c]...........................	80,000	60,000	90,000
Fixed manufacturing overhead..............	800,000	800,000	800,000
Fixed selling and administrative costs	75,000	75,000	75,000
Net income	$ 485,000	$(195,000)	$ 825,000

[a] Assumes that management has committed to direct labor sufficient to produce the planned production volume of 80,000 units; direct labor is *used* at the rate of $5 per unit produced.

[b] Assumes that management has committed to support resources sufficient to produce the planned production volume of 80,000 units; variable-overhead cost is *used* at the rate of $12 per unit produced.

[c]Variable selling and administrative costs amount to $1 per unit sold.

SOLUTION TO CASE

CASE 19-34 (45 MINUTES)

1. The advantages and disadvantages of variable and absorption costing are summarized as follows:

    (a) *Pricing decisions*: Many managers prefer to use absorption-costing data in cost-based pricing decisions. They argue that fixed manufacturing overhead is a necessary cost incurred in the production process. To exclude this fixed cost from the inventoried cost of a product, as is done under variable costing, is to understate the cost of the product. For this reason, most companies that use cost-based pricing base their prices on absorption-costing data.

    Proponents of variable costing argue that a product's variable cost provides a better basis for the pricing decision. They point out that any price above a product's variable cost makes a positive contribution to covering fixed cost and profit.

    (b) *Definition of an asset*: Another controversy about absorption and variable costing hinges on the definition of an asset. An asset is a thing of value owned by the organization with future service potential. By accounting convention, assets are valued at their cost. Since fixed costs comprise part of the cost of production, advocates of absorption costing argue that inventory (an asset) should be valued at its full (absorption) cost of production. Moreover, they argue that these costs have future service potential since the inventory can be sold in the future to generate sales revenue.

    Proponents of variable costing argue that the fixed-cost component of a product's absorption-costing value has no future service potential. Their reasoning is that the fixed manufacturing-overhead costs during the current period will not prevent these costs from having to be incurred again next period. Fixed-overhead costs will be incurred every period, regardless of production levels. In contrast, the incurrence of variable costs in manufacturing a product does allow the firm to avoid incurring these costs again.

CASE 19-34 (CONTINUED)

(c) *Cost-volume-profit analysis*: Some managers find the inconsistency between absorption costing and CVP analysis troubling enough to warrant using variable costing for internal income reporting. Variable costing dovetails much more closely than absorption costing with any operational analyses that require a separation between fixed and variable costs.

(d) *External reporting*: For external reporting purposes, generally accepted accounting principles require that income reporting be based on absorption costing. Federal tax laws also require the use of absorption costing in reporting income for tax purposes.

2. To reconcile the reported fourth-quarter income under variable and absorption costing, simply examine the variable-costing and absorption-costing income statements in the three key places where they differ.

	4th Quarter Absorption-Costing Income Statement	4th Quarter Variable-Costing Income Statement	Difference
Cost of goods sold	$7,425,000		$2,475,000 [a]
Variable manufacturing cost		$4,950,000	
Volume variance	450,000	—	450,000 [b]
Fixed manufacturing cost (as period cost)	—	2,250,000	(2,250,000) [c]
Total			$ 675,000

4th quarter income under variable costing	$1,500,000
4th quarter income under absorption costing	825,000
Difference in reported income	$ 675,000

3. For any balance sheet date, when the company has nonzero inventory, the cost of that inventory measured under absorption costing will be greater than the cost measured under variable costing. Under absorption costing, fixed manufacturing overhead is inventoried as a product cost. However, under variable costing, fixed manufacturing overhead is not inventoried as a product cost. It is treated as a period cost instead, and expensed during the period in which it is incurred.

	Balance in Inventory Account		Amount of
	9/30/x0	12/31/x0	Decline
Absorption costing	$3,375,000	$1,350,000	$2,025,000
Variable costing	2,250,000	900,000	1,350,000

	Amount of Decline in Finished-Goods Inventory Balance During 4th Quarter
Absorption costing	$2,025,000
Variable costing	1,350,000
Difference	$ 675,000

	Reported Income for 4th Quarter
Absorption costing	$ 825,000
Variable costing	1,500,000
Difference	$ (675,000)

Reported income for the 4th quarter is $675,000 lower under absorption costing. This amount matches the difference in the amount by which the inventory balance declined during the 4th quarter under absorption versus variable costing. During the 4th quarter, the company sold more units than it produced. Under absorption costing, $675,000 of inventoried fixed manufacturing overhead was expensed during the 4th quarter. Under variable costing, this fixed manufacturing overhead had already been expensed previously. Therefore, the year-end balance in inventory declined during the 4th quarter by $675,000 more under absorption costing than under variable costing.

Retained earnings is also higher on the absorption-costing balance sheet than on the variable-costing balance sheet. Retained earnings, at any given balance sheet date, is the sum total of all income reported for the firm across its entire life since its inception (less the sum total of dividends declared). During the entire life of the enterprise, inventory cannot possibly have decreased. It will either have remained at zero or it will have increased. Thus, if we think of the entire life of the enterprise as its one and only accounting period, inventory has either increased or remained at zero, and income reported under absorption costing will be at least as great as income reported under variable costing, *for that life-time accounting period.*

The following diagram may help in understanding the foregoing explanation.

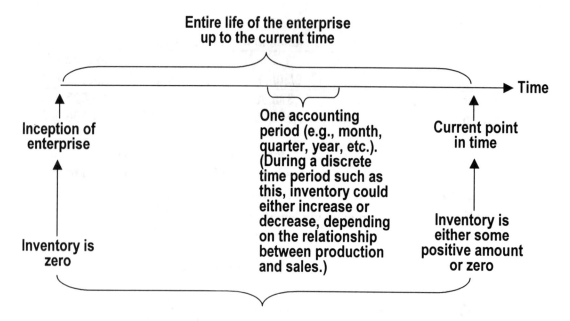

- During this life-time accounting period, inventory has either increased, or returned to zero, but it cannot have decreased.

- For this life-time accounting period, income reported under absorption costing is greater than or equal to income reported under variable costing.

- Thus, at the end of this life-time accounting period, retained earnings reported under absorption costing will be greater than or equal to retained earnings reported under variable costing.

Another way to explain the answer to this question involves the basic accounting equation:

Assets = Liabilities + Owners' Equity
↑   ↑
Inventory (I) is   Retained earnings
included in assets   (RE) is included in
                                           owners' equity.

$I_a \geq I_v$ Therefore $RE_a \geq RE_v$

where a denotes absorption costing and v denotes variable costing.

The only elements in the accounting equation that are affected by the choice of absorption or variable costing are inventory (I) and retained earnings (RE). To maintain the accounting equation, if I (and therefore assets) are greater under absorption costing, then liabilities and equities must be greater under absorption costing. Therefore, RE is greater under absorption costing.

4. Yes, during any accounting period when sales and production differ, income reported under variable and absorption costing will be different.

5. During the 4th quarter of 20x0, Screen Technology was approximately 80% as busy in its production activity as had been expected. This conclusion results from the following calculations.

First, note the following (FOH denotes fixed overhead):

$$\text{Predetermined FOH rate} = \frac{\text{budgeted FOH}}{\text{budgeted quantity of cost driver}}$$

Therefore:

Budgeted FOH = (predetermined FOH rate) (budgeted quantity of cost driver)

Second, note the following:

FOH volume variance = budgeted FOH – applied FOH variance

Therefore:

Applied FOH = budgeted FOH – FOH volume variance

Third, note the following:

$$\frac{\text{Applied FOH}}{\text{Budgeted FOH}} = \frac{\text{(predetermined FOH rate)(actual quantity of cost driver)}}{\text{(predetermined FOH rate)(budgeted quantity of cost driver)}}$$

Therefore:

$$\frac{\text{Applied FOH}}{\text{Budgeted FOH}} = \frac{\text{actual quantity of cost driver}}{\text{budgeted quantity of cost driver}}$$

CASE 19-34 (CONTINUED)

So, for Screen Technology, in the 4th quarter of 20x0:

Applied FOH = budgeted FOH − FOH volume variance

$1,800,000 = $2,250,000* − $450,000†

*From variable costing income statement. There were no variances, so budgeted and actual FOH are the same.

†From absorption costing income statement.

Therefore:

$$\frac{\text{Applied FOH}}{\text{Budgeted FOH}} = \frac{\$1,800,000}{\$2,250,000} = 80\%$$

6. If West were to follow Duval's suggestion, she would be violating several ethical standards for managerial accountants. Among the standards violated would be the following:

Competence

- Prepare complete and clear reports and recommendations after appropriate analysis of relevant and reliable information.

Integrity

- Avoid actual or apparent conflicts of interest and advise all relevant parties of any potential conflict.

- Communicate unfavorable as well as favorable information and professional judgments or opinions.

CURRENT ISSUES IN MANAGERIAL ACCOUNTING

ISSUE 19-35

"THE REALITY OF PRODUCT COSTING," *MANAGEMENT ACCOUNTING*, FEBRUARY 2000, MIKE LUCAS.

Some accountants defend the continued use of absorption costing on two grounds. First, in many situations the cost of implementing and maintaining a system such as ABC would exceed the benefits to be obtained from improved accuracy. Second, there is often a reasonably strong correlation between overhead costs and production volume measures, even if there is not a direct cause and effect relationship. Production volume measures can thus serve as a reasonably accurate proxy for activity cost drivers. Consequently, product costs will not be seriously distorted by using simpler absorption costing systems.

ISSUE 19-36

"BOOM IN AUTO INDUSTRY MAY END," *USA TODAY*, NOVEMBER 24, 2000, EARLE ELDRIDGE.

Absorption costing divides fixed manufacturing overhead between the balance sheet and the income statement. Variable costing and throughput costing charge all fixed manufacturing overhead against the income statement in the period incurred. Therefore, absorption costing will report a lower cost of goods sold and higher profit when production exceeds sales. Some accountants argue that this phenomenon provides an incentive for management to increase inventory levels even when sales are declining. Since the article reports that the auto manufacturer is idling several plants, the dysfunctional incentive noted above does not seem to be present in this instance.

ISSUE 19-37

"THROUGHPUT ACCOUNTING EXPLODING AN URBAN MYTH," *MANAGEMENT ACCOUNTING*, OCTOBER 1999, STEVEN BALDERSTONE AND STEPHEN P. KEEF.

Goldratt's three principles

- Throughput : How much money is captured by our company?

- Inventory: How much money is captured by our company?

- Operating expenses: How much money do we spend operating our company?

ISSUE 19-38

"UNDERSTANDING CAPACITY UTILIZATION AT ROCKETDYNE," *MANAGEMENT ACCOUNTING QUARTERLY*, WINTER 2000, THOMAS E. BUTTROSS, HAL BUDDENBOHM, AND DAN SWENSON.

Nonproductive capacity is capacity that does not add value to the product or service but is not classified as idle. Nonproductive capacity includes activities that often are absolutely necessary given current processes and operating conditions but that is desirable to curtail. Typical nonproductive uses of capacity include standby, waste, maintenance, and setups. They can be further subdivided into scheduled versus unscheduled maintenance.

ISSUE 19-39

"OLDER AND WISER," *MANAGEMENT ACCOUNTING*, JULY/AUGUST 2000, NORWOOD WHITTLE.

Perhaps one of the reasons why changes to the bases of overhead recovery are not made is an attempt to mirror Japanese companies. Japanese companies allocate fixed production costs based on labor hours to help direct the design engineers' attention to identifying opportunities for reducing the product's labor content and thus encouraging a move from labor to greater use of AMT.

ISSUE 19-40

"STANDARD COSTING: A TECHNIQUE AT VARIANCE WITH MODERN MANAGEMENT?" *MANAGEMENT ACCOUNTING*, NOVEMBER 1999, COLIN DRURY.

Under absorption costing, fixed factory overhead is treated as a product cost. Under variable costing, fixed factory overhead is treated as a period cost.

Proponents of variable costing argue that the fixed cost component of a product's absorption-costing value has no future service potential. Their reasoning is that the fixed manufacturing overhead costs during the current period will not prevent these costs from having to be incurred again next period. Fixed overhead costs will be incurred every period, regardless of production levels. In contrast, when variable costs are incurred in manufacturing a product, this does allow the firm to avoid incurring these costs again.